ISBN 978-1-331-92350-3
PIBN 10254491

TEN THOUSAND MILES IN PERSIA OR EIGHT YEARS IN IRÁN

BY MAJOR PERCY MOLESWORTH SYKES

(QUEEN'S BAYS)

H.M. CONSUL, KERMÁN AND PERSIAN BALUCHISTÁN;
AWARDED SILVER MEDAL BY THE SOCIETY OF ARTS, 1897; THE BACK GRANT IN 1899; AND THE GOLD MEDAL IN 1902 BY THE ROYAL GEOGRAPHICAL SOCIETY

DESIGN FROM A LEAD PLAQUE

WITH NUMEROUS ILLUSTRATIONS

NEW YORK
CHARLES SCRIBNER'S SONS
153-157 FIFTH AVENUE
1902

Printed in Great Britain.

HAWKING SCENE (FROM A VASE).

PREFACE

MY first literary effort is the outcome of many years of travel and study, not only in Persia itself, where some eight years have been spent, but also in adjacent countries, India, Russia, and Turkey having all been visited more than once.

I can claim, without fear of contradiction, that in the present generation no Englishman, and indeed no European, has travelled more extensively in Eastern and Southern Persia than myself, while my official position has given me exceptional opportunities, such as are rarely if ever enjoyed by unofficial travellers, of meeting the better classes of natives, and thereby of obtaining accurate information.

I have taken the deepest interest in the geography and history of this little known country, and have made a special study of the famous journeys of Alexander the Great and Marco Polo. Commercial questions, including the opening up of trade routes, have also been fully dealt with, from every point of view.

PREFACE

In the vexed question of spelling, I have practically followed the rules laid down by the Royal Geographical Society, as being most generally useful. I regret not to have seen my way to accepting Mr E. G. Browne's views on this subject.

Writing little more than a decade after the publication of the monumental work on Persia by Lord Curzon of Kedleston, I have touched but lightly on the provinces and cities exhaustively dealt with therein, and as far as possible, I have given information which is new and supplementary.

I would acknowledge my great indebtedness to many friends, but especially to Mr E. G. Browne, Major F. Younghusband, C.I.E., Mr H. B. Walters, and Miss Sykes, who have read through the whole of my proofs. Mr H. F. B. Lynch, Mr A. G. Ellis, and Mr M. Longworth Dames have also criticised the chapters relating to subjects on which they are authorities. Miss E. R. Sykes has drawn the headings to chapters from objects in my collection, and numerous friends have aided in providing the illustrations. Finally, the publishers have taken the greatest interest in the book, and have spared no expense to make it a success.

In conclusion, if this work, however deficient in literary merit, induces even a few of my fellow-countrymen to take an interest in Persia and the great problems connected with it, or furnishes any data which may be of value to those whose high mission it is to form or lead public opinion, that increasingly important influence in the Empire, my labours will be richly rewarded.

LONDON, *30th April* 1902.

DEDICATED

BY SPECIAL PERMISSION

TO THE RIGHT HONOURABLE

LORD CURZON OF KEDLESTON, G.M.S.I., G.M.I.E.

VICEROY AND GOVERNOR-GENERAL OF

INDIA

CONTENTS

CHAP.		PAGE
I.	FROM ENGLAND TO ASTRABÁD	1
II.	AMONG THE TURKOMAN	10
III.	ACROSS THE LUT TO KERMÁN	27
IV.	THE PROVINCE OF KERMÁN	43
V.	THE PROVINCE OF KERMÁN—(*continued*)	55
VI.	FROM KERMÁN TO BUSHIRE	72
VII.	THE PERSIAN GULF	82
VIII.	BALUCHISTÁN	89
IX.	BALUCHISTÁN—(*continued*)	98
X.	ACROSS MAKRÁN	109
XI.	SARHAD	125
XII.	FROM BAZMÁN TO KERMÁN	138
XIII.	THROUGH CENTRAL PERSIA	151
XIV.	THE MARCH OF ALEXANDER THE GREAT FROM THE INDUS TO THE KÁRUN	166
XV.	THE FOUNDING OF THE KERMÁN CONSULATE	176
XVI.	THE CITY OF KERMÁN	187
XVII.	LIFE AT KERMÁN	202
XVIII.	FROM KERMÁN TO KUHAK	213
XIX.	THE PERSO-BALUCH BOUNDARY COMMISSION	224
XX.	ACROSS BRITISH BALUCHISTÁN TO QUETTA	232
XXI.	A MISSION TO THE KÁRUN VALLEY	239
XXII.	A MISSION TO THE KÁRUN VALLEY—(*continued*)	250
XXIII.	MARCO POLO'S TRAVELS IN PERSIA	260
XXIV.	THE KARWÁN EXPEDITION	274

H.I.M. MUZAFFAR-U-DIN, SHÁH OF PERSIA.

[*Frontispiece.*

PLAN OF KERMÁN	*To face page*	188
THE ANCIENT FORTS OF KERMÁN	"	190
THE FOUNDER OF THE SHEIKHI SECT		196
ÁGHÁ MOHAMED KHÁN (CHIEF OF THE SHEIKHI SECT)	"	196
THE STONE OF THE ÁTÁBEG, KERMÁN		198
THE FORT AT BAM		218
THE PERSIAN COMMISSIONERS	"	222
NO. I. BOUNDARY CAIRN		226
TOMBS OF KEIANIAN MALIKS, JÁLK		230
KUHAK	"	234
THE KHÁN OF KALÁT AND COURT	"	236
MAP OF THE KÁRUN VALLEY	"	240
BASRA	"	244
SHUSTER FORT AND VALERIAN'S BRIDGE		252
SHUSTER	"	254
KUDUM ON THE RESHT ROAD		258
KUBA-I-SABZ, KERMÁN	"	264
THE KARWÁN EXPEDITION. THE START		276
THE KARWÁN EXPEDITION—A COUNCIL OF WAR		280
THE FUNERAL OF MR GRAVES		284
THE SULTÁN OF MASKAT		292
BANDAR ABBÁS		300
MAKRÁN SCENERY		310
DALIKI		316
THE PORCH OF XERXES		324
THE HALL OF XERXES		326
THE GOD ORMUZD HANDS THE KIDARIS TO SHÁPUR	"	328
SHÁPUR AND THE SUPPLIANT EMPEROR VALERIAN	"	328
YEZDIKHÁST		330
MASJID-I-SHÁH, ISFAHÁN (SHOWING ANCIENT GOAL-POSTS ON POLO GROUND)		332

SIAWUSH PLAYS POLO BEFORE AFRASIÁB . . . *To face page* 336
"O PRINCE OF RIDERS! HÁFIZ WELCOME CALLS
"SO RIDE APACE AND SHREWDLY SMITE THE BALLS" . . 340
GARDEN OF H.H. THE FARMÁN FARMÁ, MÁHUN . . 350
THE HELMAND DELTA—SKETCH NO. 1 364
" " SKETCH NO. 2 364
" " SKETCH NO. 3 364
" " SKETCH NO. 4 364
SKETCH MAP OF SISTÁN 372
KUH-I-KHOJA SISTÁN 378
THE HELMAND LAGOON 388
BIRJAND 398
BANA PASS (LOOKING NORTH) 408
THE PILLAR OF NÁDIR 418
YEZD 420
A PARSI FAMILY 422
GYPSIES OF SOUTH-EAST PERSIA . . . . . " 438
BRONZE AXE-HEAD FOUND AT KHINAMÁN (RIGHT) COMPARED
WITH AXE-HEAD FOUND IN ARMENIA . . . " 442
GREEK ALABASTER VASE FROM JÍRUFT 444
COPPER BOWLS FROM VICINITY OF KERMÁN, AND BRONZE
IMPLEMENTS FROM KHINAMÁN . . . 448

BRASS WITH NAME AND DATE OF HULÂKU KHÂN.

TEN THOUSAND MILES IN PERSIA

CHAPTER I

FROM ENGLAND TO ASTRABÁD

"Non semper imbres nubibus hispidos
Manant in agros; aut mare Caspium
Vexant inaequales procellae
Usque." —HORACE, Book II., *Ode* 9.

THE land of Persia has always exercised a strong fascination on my mind, but while serving in India I could gain little or no information about it, nor did there seem any likelihood of my ever visiting romantic Irán.[1] I therefore applied for permission to travel home across the Pamirs, which was not refused; but in the summer of 1891 events occurred which temporarily closed that region to private travellers, and left me but a small prospect of bagging an *Ovis Poli*, when I proceeded on leave to England in the autumn of that year.

During 1892 a few months were spent in Eastern Europe in an

[1] The word Irán is the classic Ariána, the land of the Arii, the capital of which is still Herát. Aryan is also the same word. *Cf.* Zand *airya*, Sans. *árya*, and Lat. *aráre*.

attempt to gain some insight into the various problems that will, within the next thirty years, call for solution; and, after spending Christmas at home, permission was granted me to rejoin the "Bays" *via* Persia. Consequently, I left London in January 1893, on what proved to be the first of many journeys.

A day was spent in Vienna, where the traffic was being carried on between high barriers of snow, and Odessa was reached very late, the line being much blocked by an unusually heavy fall. There I called on Colonel C. E. Stewart, Her Majesty's Consul-General, who is a noted Persian traveller, and explained to him my wish to commence my journey from the south-east corner of the Caspian. This plan he highly approved, and gave me some letters of introduction, which, as will appear later on, were invaluable.

The cold at Odessa was intense, and, in consequence, all rooms were so much heated that stuffiness reigned supreme; indeed, I always associate Russia in winter with headaches. Another result of the exceptional weather was that the ice brought down by the Bug and Dnieper had collected in the harbour to such an extent that the sea was frozen over for some twenty miles, and the sporting banker on whom I had a letter of credit offered to lay me long odds against the steamer being able to reach open water.

In spite of this discouraging outlook I went on board, and a tug was sent on to break the ice by reversing its engines for a few lengths and then charging with full steam ahead. This continued for twenty-four hours, when, rather to my regret, we were free, only to encounter a very heavy gale, during the course of which six ships foundered in the Black Sea alone.

It was extremely pleasant to reach the land-locked harbour of Sevastopol, where the climate felt quite mild, although cold enough for our ill-equipped troops forty years before; but apparently the sea never freezes, as at Odessa. I was shown over the dockyard, where a large ship was on the stocks, and I also visited the cemetery and strolled about the town, which has not, as yet, recovered from the bombardment. There is a most uninteresting and badly-arranged museum, where the only thing that I recollect is Todleben's coat.

Quitting Sevastopol, which is now considered to be a stronger fortress than it was at the time of the Crimean War, we steamed past Balaclava harbour, where, we were told, diving for the gold lost during the great storm was under consideration. Yalta, where the cliffs protect the famous monastery from the cold, seemed close enough for a stone to be thrown on shore, and at night we reached Feodosia, where there were numerous buildings and forts of Genoese and Armenian architecture still in a good state of preservation. It was founded as a Greek colony in the seventh century B.C.

Kertch being frozen up, we steamed straight to Novorosisk, where a fellow-countryman, with whom I had travelled from Austria, disembarked to visit some nitrate mines in the vicinity, in which he was interested.

The following day was actually fine, and as we steamed southwards, the temperature rose hourly until at Batum, the Land of the Golden Fleece, we found oranges growing on the trees.

Several days had already been spent by me at this maritime key to the Caucasus a few months previously. As I had arrived in a rowing-boat from Trebizond, no steamers then touching at that port owing to an outbreak of cholera, I was quarantined in a soldier's tent on the beach. Subsequently I was considered rather a suspicious character, at least, I was shadowed, until I demonstrated my harmlessness and the absurdity of their suspicion by asking the shadower to carry my waterproof. This, as I afterwards heard, elicited the remark of "Only a mad Englishman," and I was left in peace! It would appear that the Russian police had information that two Nihilists disguised as Englishmen were coming to Batum, so that my being suspected was quite natural.

At Batum there is a very hospitable and feverishly busy English community, but, as it rains practically every day, I was not sorry when all my impedimenta were safely collected and I found myself starting for Tiflis. The day train should always be selected, as otherwise the most beautiful scenery conceivable will be missed. Leaving the malarial swamps of Batum, where vegetation is tropically exuberant, the train runs north until it strikes the valley of the Rion, the ancient Phasis, up which sped the heroes of the Argo. Now, however, oil is the coveted source of wealth, supporting both Batum and Báku, while English is one of the languages of the former port, which has often six or more British vessels awaiting a cargo of petroleum.

The train ran through a thickly wooded country, said to be full of game, but there were few signs of any habitations, although each station produced its knot of officials and peasants. The latter in their Cossack dress are very handsome, and the beauty of the women is certainly no myth, but there is a noticeable absence of intellect in their faces, which are consequently somewhat lacking in expression. A recently completed tunnel was passed through at the watershed, and when we emerged from it, the valley of the Kur was entered.

As seems to be the unpleasant habit in Russia, the railway-station at Tiflis, which is a monumental edifice, was miles away from the town, and the roads were deep in mud. Russia is indeed the land of goloshes, the value of which the traveller learns to appreciate in the muddy streets, while at Tehrán they are also a necessity. It is curious in England to note the invincible prejudice of which they are the object, and I remember hearing some young fellows discussing a comrade whose good and evil points seemed fairly evenly balanced, until some one said that he had seen him wearing goloshes, after which not a voice was raised in his favour!

Sir Mortimer Durand afterwards told me that Tiflis reminded him of Kábul. It lies on both banks of the Kur, in a deep basin, the hills on two sides being particularly steep. The Hôtel de Londres is one of the most famous of hostelries, for, further east, there is neither comfort nor cleanliness, and, apart from the attractions of Tiflis, its polyglot population, its Georgian castle, and its museum, all travellers bound Eastward-Ho like to spend a few days at Madame Richter's before plunging into the known and unknown discomforts beyond.

For the rest of the journey to Báku the country was quite open and swarmed with small game: the snow-clad ranges too were superb. Indeed, although my Greek had become rusty, vague thoughts of Aeschylus's great tragedy came back to my mind:

> χθονὸς μὲν ἐς τηλουρὸν ἥκομεν πέδον,
> Σκύθην ἐς οἶμον, ἄβατον εἰς ἐρημίαν.—*Prom. Vinct.* 1.

and again:

> ὑψίκρημνον οἳ πόλισμα
> Καυκάσου πέλας νέμονται
> δαΐος στρατὸς, ὀξυπρῴροισι βρέμων ἐν αἰχμαῖς.—*Ibid.*, 421.

TURKOMAN AT BAKU.

[*To face p.* 4.

As the Caspian Sea is approached, there is a gradual change from fertility to sterility, while the country round Báku is as treeless as any part of Persia. I reached the terminus early in the morning, and drove to the dirty Hôtel d'Europe, where finding that there was a day or two to spare, I duly visited the lions.

The oil-wells a few miles inland are interesting, but far stranger is the sight of flames springing out of the ground at Sela Khána. We arrived at sunset, when the ground was covered with snow, the effect being intensely weird. There is a little courtyard with legible Hindi inscriptions, where an Indian fakir used to tend the Eternal Fire, but we were told that, being suspected of wealth, he was murdered by the Tatárs, and his post is still vacant. The "Black Town," a suburb of Báku, is also of interest, Messrs Nobel having enormous refineries,[1] and even devoting one section to ship-building.

Báku itself possesses some fine specimens of Persian architecture, and its wharves are a scene of great and increasing activity. On still nights one of the popular amusements is to set fire to the sea, the effect of which is said to be very fine.

The usual approach to Persia is *via* Enzeli and Resht, but, wishing to make for Bandar Gaz,[2] I took passage on board a steamer which, in the first place, crossed to Uzun Ada, or Long Island, the starting-point of the famous Transcaspian Railway.

After a rough crossing, which occupied a day, we slowly steamed up the narrow channel, where a stranded ship warned us of the penalty of carelessness, and, although we were drawing but nine feet, we were continually requested to rush aft to prevent the steamer grounding. The shallow sea had a skin of ice, and altogether Uzun Ada struck me as a most unsuitable base. A year later I was glad to hear that Krasnovodsk, which is much nearer the open sea, and possesses a harbour of greater depth, had finally been selected in supersession of Uzun Ada, which is simply a group of sand-hills, without even a good supply of water.

Returning on board, after an inspection of the line which was, at the time, so carefully closed to the outer world, we again painfully

[1] The crude oil produces (1) petroleum, 30 per cent.; (2) machine-oil, 26 per cent.; (3) benzine, 5 per cent. The refuse, known as *Astatki*, is used as fuel both for steamers and railway.

[2] *Bandar* means "port," and *Gaz* "tamarisk."

groped our way out, and then steamed south, reaching the Russian frontier roadstead of Chikishliár after a run of fifteen hours. Owing to the shallowness of the sea, the steamer lay to almost out of sight of the town, and there was no time to visit it; but there is not much to see, as Chikishliár bears an evil reputation both for climate and soil. Indeed, the horses in Lomakin's expeditions were decimated before starting from want of suitable grazing. It is now connected with the Persian telegraphic system, by a line running to Astrabád, but the Transcaspian Railway has robbed it of its former importance as a military base. As may be supposed, the garrison is small and is frequently relieved, a squadron of Cossacks from Astrakhan and a company of infantry occupying this dismal and unhealthy cantonment.

As we steamed south the climate again changed most rapidly, and, after luncheon, we lay to off the Russian Naval Station of Ashuráda, having in front of us the land of Irán, covered with thick mist.

The Islands of Ashuráda are, in reality, portions of a sand-bank which has been formed by the prevalent north wind, while beyond them lies a vast lagoon, locally termed a *Murdáb* or Dead Water, which the rivers, heavily freighted with alluvial matter, have formed. There are several of these lagoons along the coast, that of Enzeli being the best known; but Astrabád Bay, to use the term which appears on the map, is the deepest, steamers being able to run in close to the shore, and not being forced to discharge outside the bar, as at Enzeli.

Ashuráda, which must be a terribly unhealthy cantonment, was, in 1838, occupied by Russia, which power, in the interests of humanity, determined to crush Turkoman piracy as a preliminary to the final subjugation of those despicable man-stealers. The Government of the Tsar has been invited to retire from what is strictly speaking Persian soil, but were it to do so piracy, if only on a petty scale, would again raise its head. As the Persian flag, by the Treaty of Gulistán, may not fly on the Caspian, the result is that all police work is done by the great Northern Power. Three hulks were anchored off the island, which is so narrow that spray sweeps across it in bad weather, and our ship was boarded by the officials of the garrison, to whom even a fortnightly mail must be a great boon.

After a search for deserters, conducted by the naval police, the steamer slowly moved across the still lagoon, to a hulk anchored about a mile off Bandar Gaz. Here we collected our belongings, and were rowed to a pier in the last stages of decay, and at nightfall found ourselves on Persian soil, which was muddy, deep, and adhesive.

I should have been puzzled what to do and where to go, but Yusuf Abbás, an educated Persian, whom I had engaged at Odessa, and who must have travelled more than almost any man of his age, said that probably the Persian telegraph officer would put us up. This he most kindly agreed to do, and I was soon introduced to a Persian *pilo*, or boiled rice with various sorts of meat. Almost every traveller justly praises the cooking of *chilo* or boiled rice, but as no one, so far as I know, gives the secret of its preparation, I hasten to supply the omission, and trust that the recipe may find its way especially to India, where it would certainly improve curries; in fact, it would pay clubs to engage a Persian cook.[1]

By daylight Bandar Gaz is a melancholy spot, the mud being so deep, that a pair of waders were most useful. The log huts looked squalid and miserable, and the only touch of colour was a stack of gaudy tin-covered boxes containing crockery. The Russian merchants sell the boxes as well as their contents, and thereby make a profit on their packing-cases, which is a distinctly ingenious practice.

Mazanderán which, with Gilán, occupies the southern coast of the Caspian Sea, is a province of great interest, were it only for the startling contrast it affords to other parts of Persia, or, indeed, to the other districts bordering the inland sea. Leaving the

[1] The rice, which ought to be long and thin, must be sifted until the broken grains be extracted; it should then be thrown into lukewarm water and covered with a porous cloth, on which a lump of salt is placed. This soaking lasts about five or six hours. The rice is then strained and thrown into a pot of boiling water; it is stirred with a flat spoon with holes, and left in for about half an hour, or until it be soft all through, various rices taking shorter or longer periods; more salt is added during this stage. The rice is next turned out into a basin with holes, and strained, being washed with warm and then colder water to extract the salt. The empty pot is again set on the fire with a little butter, say four ounces for three pounds of rice: the rice is thrown in and made into a pile, and more butter melted in water is poured on top and all round. The pot is covered with fire above and below, and is baked for an hour, when it i ready.

lagoons, overgrown with rank vegetation, a belt of jungle of varying width is passed through, which is very dense and infested by all sorts of vermin, including mosquitoes, which make life intolerable in the summer. Tigers are said to abound, but are seldom if ever shot. When once the hills are reached there is a complete change, and the traveller can fancy himself in Kashmir, as there are the same trees and lawns, while above is the bare open hillside. This country is also the habitat of a magnificent stag, said to be larger than the *Bára Sing*[1] of the Happy Valley.

The Mazanderánis are rather sallow looking individuals, but by no means stunted, as might be expected from their surroundings. Dressed in wool, and living on rice, of which they consume enormous quantities, they are a contented race, and never wish to leave their country, in fact, they do not thrive in other parts of Persia.

Our first difficulty was transport, which was only to be engaged at fabulous rates, and as I objected to be cheated, I telegraphed to the British agent at Astrabád, who replied that six ponies would reach me on the following day.

The swamp was said to be full of pheasants, but as no dog was forthcoming, I preferred duck-shooting in the lagoon. In the morning I waded, but, the water being deep, a dug-out was engaged, from which a dozen or more duck were shot, comprising seven separate species.

At night, and indeed at all odd times, I studied Persian, and finally congratulated myself on having only begun the language in India, the Persian of Hindustan being less akin to the real tongue than the French of Stratford-atte-Bowe to that of Paris, as, in the latter case, the words used are the same, whereas the Persian of India is a corruption of the tongue as spoken in the days of Nádir Sháh.[2]

After spending many hours in tying up and assorting loads[3]—

[1] Or Twelve Horns.

[2] Upon my recommendation, a Persian translation of *Háji Baba* and the *Vazir-i-Khán-i-Lenkorán* have, I believe, been adopted as text-books by the Government of India. Both are full of the best modern colloquial Persian.

[3] I may here state that 450 lbs. is a fair weight for a camel, and 300 lbs. for a mule or pony. Bales make loads heavier than this, but a traveller's luggage is not as compact as a bale. Mules march at three and a half miles, and camels at two miles per hour.

an operation that must never be hurried—a start was made towards Astrabád, Yusuf and myself riding such diminutive steeds that much difficulty was experienced in keeping our feet out of the mud. The track was a morass, with dense jungle on either side, but no fine trees, while every half mile or so we crossed a black, evil-smelling stream which was almost stagnant. What with breakdowns and the vileness of the road, which was accentuated when we struck the famous *Sang-i-Farsh*, or Stone Carpet, constructed by Sháh Abbás, which, in decay, is but a series of pitfalls, five hours were occupied in accomplishing a very few miles, and at nightfall we stopped at the village of Kurd Mahálla, where, as at the port, the houses were raised some feet off the ground.

The Headman entertained us, as pitching the tent was out of the question, and he considerably astonished me after dinner, by saying that he knew that all Europeans worshipped engines, but that he wished to know whether the English worshipped a steamer or a locomotive!

Kurd Mahálla appeared to be a huge village, each house being surrounded by a garden. Riding through it on the following morning, we saw corn being thrashed by means of a see-saw—a girl sitting on one end of a plank and pulling herself up by a rope. The day was fine, and the country had become quite park-like; consequently our wretched ponies had easier work. We observed little or no bird life, only the crow appearing to flourish.

It was sunset when we drew near to broken-down, decayed Astrabád, and, passing into the town by a gateway, innocent alike of door or guard, the first object we espied was a jackal. Being ahead of our caravan, we rode on for some distance, until we actually saw a man in the deserted streets, who kindly guided us to the house of *Mírza*[1] Taki, the British agent, where it was a great comfort to be able to change into dry clothes. A combination of damp and cold is extremely unpleasant, not to say dangerous to health in the East, and I was thankful to have passed through the fever zone without feeling any the worse, and to have reached one of the famous cities of Persia.

[1] *Mírza*, a contraction of *Amirzáda* or Son of an Amir, strictly signifies "Secretary" when written before a name. Nowadays, however, it has much the same meaning as the English "Esquire." On the contrary, when it follows the name, it retains its original meaning of "Prince."

DESIGN FROM LUSTRED POTTERY.

CHAPTER II

AMONG THE TURKOMAN

"Wee found them to bee very badde and brutish people, for they ceased not dayly to molest us, either by fighting, stealing, or begging: and they forced us to buy the water that wee did drinke."—JENKINSON on the Turkoman.[1]

ASTRABÁD, known in Oriental hyperbole as *Dár-ul-Muminin* or Abode of the Faithful, is, so far as is known, not an ancient town, although legend maintains that it was founded by Noshirwán, with money supplied by Ázad Mahán, Governor of Kermán. Its interest for Englishmen may be said to originate with the attempt to open up an Anglo-Persian trade in the eighteenth century, which was even less successful than the venture two hundred years before.

Hanway, in connection with this scheme, was living at Astrabád, when a chief of the Kájár tribe seized the town and revolted against Nádir Sháh.

The rebellion was crushed with terrible severity, of which our fellow-countryman was an eye-witness. He wrote: "Upon my arrival I was informed that the executions of that day consisted in cutting out the left eyes of thirty men, beheading four, and burning one alive. . . . Two hundred women were also sent out of the city, of which one hundred and fifty were ordered to be sold as slaves to the soldiers."[2] Upon the assassination of Nádir Sháh

[1] *Early Voyages and Travels to Russia and Persia*, p. 65 (Hakluyt Soc.).

[2] *Travels in Persia*, vol. i., chap. xliv., p. 202.

a struggle for supreme power began, finally terminating in the advancement of the Kájár chief to the throne of Persia.

At the beginning of the nineteenth century, the strategical importance of Astrabád was much exaggerated, Napoleon and Tsar Paul of Russia drawing up a plan for the invasion of India by this route, which, on a map, seems feasible. During the Crimean War the scheme was revived, but it is certain that at either period the plan involved almost certain disaster, while to-day the Transcaspian Railway has taken away any importance that Astrabád may have had, although, for an attack on Persia from the north, the seizure of Shahrud through Astrabád would sever Meshed from the capital.

The town fills perhaps one half of its original area, and its population does not exceed ten thousand, I was told. Most of its streets are paved, probably by Sháh Abbás, and the buildings are of brick or stone, with roofs of red tiles or thatch, which look cheerful even in winter, while, as the tops of the walls are planted with flowers, the effect in spring must be very pleasing. Soap is largely produced, the potash being extracted from a curious-looking plant which grows on the river-banks, and gunpowder is also locally manufactured. These, with felt—all three products being of equally indifferent quality—complete the list of local industries.

From enquiries which I made, it appeared that the Persian Deputy-Governor would not favour my going alone among the Turkoman, and, as I could not afford the expense of a large escort, it seemed best to keep my plans to myself until all arrangements were completed, and then march off without applying to the authorities for assistance.

I called upon the Russian Consul, M. Piper, hoping to gain some information about the big game shooting, and perhaps secure a companion. However, he confessed that he detested shooting, and told me that he had had a very trying time during the past summer, as a terrible epidemic of cholera had broken out. Not only did the Consulate overlook a burying-ground, but the towns-people, growing fanatical from fear, had assumed such a threatening attitude that he had telegraphed for a guard of Cossacks, many of whom died on the way up from the coast; altogether, the out-look must have been thoroughly depressing.

A heavy fall of snow made the oranges on the trees look rather out of place, and as I hoped that it would bring the stags down from the higher country, I started off to shoot. We walked, or rather floundered about for a few days, and saw countless sounder of boar, one of which I shot to test a new rifle, but it seemed a waste to kill any more, although I could have secured almost any number, as they moved leisurely off within easy range. A few hinds were also seen, but my hopes of a stag were doomed to disappointment, although I worked hard for a week. In the meanwhile, my slender preparations being completed, I returned to Astrabád, and early the next morning marched north towards the land of the Turkoman.

The forest almost touches the southern side of the town, but the country to the north is perfectly level and open, with plenty of cultivation. A few small hamlets were passed, and some five miles after starting, we reached the Kara Su or Blackwater, which, like the stream of that name so familiar to officers who have been educated at Sandhurst, has a slow-flowing, muddy appearance. Approached by a causeway, it is spanned by a fine bridge, and having crossed it I was at last in the Turkoman country. A few miles of beautifully fertile plain brought us to the banks of the Gurgán, a name which contains the same root as Hyrcania,[1] signifying a wolf. A second solid bridge is commanded by Akkala or White Fort, one of the old Kájár strongholds which is still garrisoned, and presents an imposing appearance. We, however, did not cross the river, but swung east up its left bank, and, passing group after group of *áláchuk*,[2] halted at the camp of Musa Khán, chief of the Ak Átabai, for whom I had a letter from Colonel Stewart.

Here I was ushered into an *áláchuk*, and as I was destined to live in one of these superior nomad dwellings for some time, it may be worth while to give some description of them. Imagine, first of all, a framework of bent rods resembling a bee-hive and some twenty feet in diameter: over this thick black felt is stretched, and the result is a movable house, which, in cold weather at any rate, is superior to a tent, as the members of the Afghán Boundary Commission soon found out in 1885. Inside are collected the *lares*

[1] Ancient Hyrcania, apparently included Astrabád and Mazanderán. Mr E. G. Browne informs me that the word used in the *Zend-Avesta* is Vehrkáno.

[2] *Áláchik* is, I understand, the more correct form.

THE LUNCHEON PONY.

[*To face p.* 12.

et penates packed up in huge trunks, while the rifles of the owner hang within easy reach. Strips of carpet are stretched round wherever there are joinings in the felt, and, in short, when the fire is lit on the open hearth, there is a feeling of real comfort, even if the effect is somewhat marred by the prevalence of smoke. Each camp was occupied by from ten to thirty families, who spend five months south of the Gurgán, reap their crops, and then graze their flocks near the Atrek.

I now propose briefly to discuss the Turkoman question. The home of these nomads may be considered to be a belt of country running from Astrabád Bay on the west to the vicinity of Balkh on the east; consequently, according to the present territorial divisions of Asia, they mainly inhabit the frontiers of Russia, Persia, and Afghánistán. Their first prominent appearance on the stage of history was the overthrow given by them to Sultán Sanjar in the twelfth century. In the sixteenth century, Jenkinson was attacked by members of the race on his heroic journey to Bokhára, but, thanks to his "hand gunnes," the intrepid Englishman saved his party.

Sháh Abbás, when he came to the throne, settled large colonies of Kurds at Bujnurd, Kuchán, and Deregez, which act must have been a great blow to the man-stealers, but until their final overthrow, they were a veritable curse to Persia, raiding down almost to Baluchistán, although, generally speaking, the holding of a few passes would have paralysed their baleful activity.

In 1860 an attempt was made to cope with this terror, under which no Persian's life was safe for an hour, and a big force was despatched to attack Merv, but the Turkoman defeated the Persians, of whom so many were captured that slaves became a drug in the market of Khiva. After this, as might be expected, the number of raids increased, the road guards acting as informers and joining in the pillaging, and in 1871 a famine weakened Persia still more. However, the end was near, the capture of Khiva, when Kauffmann waged a war of extermination against the Yomuts, and the campaigns of Lomakin and Lazareff—the latter an Armenian General—paving the way for the victories of Skobeleff, who, like many successful commanders, learned from the reverses suffered by his predecessors how to organise victory. It is impossible not to be struck with the similarity of the steps he took with those recently adopted in the Soudan. In both cases a desert had to be crossed, and the main difficulty was the supply question, and, in both cases, it was a railway that overcame them.

After patiently waiting until overwhelming forces were ready, the Tekke Turkoman, who had insanely decided to hold the fort, generally known as Geok Tapa or Blue Mound,[1] were besieged. Finally a mine was exploded, the Russians stormed the enclosure, and the Turkoman terror was stamped out in a river of blood, their losses being enormous.

What it meant to Central Asia in general and to Persia in particular, can only be gauged by those who, like myself, have seen released captives and heard what they had to endure, especially as the hatred of Sunni for Shia was superadded: indeed Professor Vambéry has told me that, although treated most kindly himself on the Atrek, the sights that he saw caused him to loathe his hosts.

But to return to my adventures, I found to my chagrin that Musa Khán had gone into Astrabád for the night, and in consequence I was obliged to wait a day for his return, which I occupied in visiting the ruins of a town now known as Kizil Alan. There are also mounds dotted along the Gurgán valley, which have puzzled travellers. Some have imagined them to be a series of signalling stations, but the simplest solution is that they are ruined villages or towns. Further than this we cannot go until systematic excavations are undertaken, when a rich harvest will surely reward the investigator in Hyrcania.

Musa Khán, upon his return, told me through Yusuf that he could not accept the responsibility of allowing me to travel in the Turkoman country. I was sure to be killed or robbed, in which case he would be held responsible by the Persian Government. This objection was defeated by my giving him a letter to the effect that he had warned me of the risk, and that I absolved him of all responsibility. However, matters remained at a deadlock, as Musa did not see why I wished to run risks instead of keeping to the main road, and, when I tried to explain that I was anxious to explore for the Royal Geographical Society, his contempt for a body which existed for such a purpose was not

[1] *Vide* Skrine and Ross's *Heart of Asia*, p. 291 *et seqq.*

concealed! A present of a revolver had also but little effect, as Musa had originally been a Russian subject, and had visited Moscow, where he had seen shops full of weapons, but when I played my last card, and said that his reputation in Europe for hospitality would suffer, he yielded to this dire threat, and agreed to send three of his relatives with me as far as the Atrek, who would arrange for my journey onward.

This concession took me three days to obtain, so, fearing a change of purpose, I felt very happy when my host said good-bye at the ford of the Gurgán, and we struck north across the snowy steppe. At first there was level monotony, and we saw many flocks of sheep, but, upon approaching the Atrek, we passed through a range of low hills known as Kara Tapa, or Black Hill, where I bagged a dozen pigeons, which were a valuable addition to the larder in the absence of meat, as the sheep, besides being miserably thin, were dying by scores of some disease. We skirted two salt lakes, and at night reached a camp of Átabai at Tengli, in a heavy snowstorm.

The following morning my troubles began, as I was informed that I must carry forage for five stages, and a camel was offered for sale at £40—about eight times its value. Seeing that I was in for it, I asked that the barley should first be produced, but only a small supply was forthcoming, and we finally started about noon, my guides of the previous day expressing dissatisfaction with what I gave them, and saying that they had hoped for a revolver a-piece!

Our route ran parallel to the Atrek, across the lifeless steppe, the snow lying in great patches, and, after a weary march, we halted at an encampment of the Gán Yokmáz, a sub-tribe under the protection of the Átabai.[1] They told me many stories of their

[1] Note on the Yomut Turkoman—

(*a*) Jáfar Bai. This tribe inhabits the district round the mouths of the Atrek, and, as regards wealth and civilisation, may be considered the most important division. Their fisheries are valuable, and they have engaged in commerce since the Russians crushed piracy; they have two divisions, known as Yáráli and Nuráli, with an aggregate of 2000 families to the south, and 1000 families to the north of the Atrek, which, as far as Chát, is the Russo-Persian frontier. They are generally on bad terms with the Átabai.

(*b*) The Átabai include 2000 families in Persian and 1000 families in Russian territory. Lying between the Jáfar Bai and the smaller tribes, they have suc-

ancient prowess—in fact, a Turkoman is a greater braggart than an Afghán—and said that when they rose against the Persians, whole regiments would bolt if a dozen of them appeared in sight. I asked, if this were the case, where had the Persian general obtained the heads he had sent in. "Oh, he attacked and massacred a section that had joined him, and it was *their* heads which gained the Persian his promotion!" *Se non è vero, è ben trovato.*

A *mullá*, called Hak Nafas, was our guide for some stages, and the following day we passed by Yagli Olum, a little fortified post and telegraph office on the Russian side of the river. What especially struck the Turkoman was the fact that the sentry never went to sleep! We halted a day at a second camp of the Gán Yokmáz, and we then passed the old Persian fort at Chát,[1] where the Sambur river unites its stream with the Atrek. Further east, the frontier line runs up the watershed of the Sonar Dágh, which divides the two rivers.

We spent the night at a small encampment of the Dovoji, and, on continuing our journey, we struck the Atrek, which was flowing through a deep gorge with lofty cliffs. Skirting the river, we passed under a natural arch, and crossed it with difficulty, as the current was swift; the water was tawny and unpleasant to drink, owing to a strong taste of gypsum. The country was much cut

ceeded in controlling many of the latter; their subdivision is Ak-Átabai, under Musa Khán.

(*c*) Under the protection of the Átabai are the following, running from west to east:—

Bolgai	300 families.
Gán Yokmáz	400 "
Dáz	1000 "
Dovoji	1000 "
Bádragh	200 "

These divisions are generally on terms of feud with:—

Amir	100 families.
Kuchik	300 "
Tatár	100 "
Salák	100 "
Kujak	1000 "

To summarise, of the Yomut tribe, there are 8500 families subject to Persia, and 2000 families under Russian rule. Until quite recently, the tribes used to cross the Atrek to change their pasturage, but this is being stopped, from fear of taxation, which is not, however, heavy.

[1] *Chát* is the local word for the junction of two rivers, while *Dágh* signifies a range in Turki.

up, and we came quite suddenly upon a second and larger camp of the Dovoji after a wearisome march, which fatigued me the more from the lack of animal food.

Yusuf had previously warned me that *Mullá* Hak Nafas was an outlaw who was "wanted" both by Astrabád and Bujnurd, and the following morning he showed up in his true colours. He first intimated that he was not going any further, and when I sent him a present of a watch and money, he replied that he wanted my rifle. The muleteers, too, on being told that their animals would be seized, began to weep, which proceeding I interrupted, and made them load up. While superintending this operation a stormy debate was going on in the *áláchuk*, and Yusuf's voice rose shrill and loud; so, preparing for the worst, I went in, and was received with: "They mean to kill us, Sar, so let us shoot first." This being out of the question, I told Yusuf to inform the *mullá* that I loved him as a son, and so forth, and while this was being translated, I slapped him violently on the back, both to show my affection and to prevent him replying, and finally ran him out of the *áláchuk*, amid the delighted laughter of the Turkoman, and he rode off like a lamb.

I forgot to mention that early in the morning I had been asked to give a letter declaring my satisfaction with him, but, scenting trouble, I had written that I believed he meant to rob me. To ensure his producing this in the future, when our relations were strained, I asked for it back, and offered to write a second letter; but the *mullá* assured me that the one he had would suffice, feeling convinced that it was couched in laudatory terms!

The road was for some miles a regular labyrinth, after which we reached the open valley, and, as it was late, we crossed the river, and camped at a group of five tents. The *mullá*, before leaving us, which he did a few miles after starting, had held a whispered conference with our guides, and as, for the first time, we were not invited into the *áláchuk*, we felt sure that mischief was intended. The want of proper food, together with the great cold[1] and bad water, having caused a raging toothache, I barricaded our tent and tied the valance up in parts, keeping watch without any difficulty, as I could not sleep. About midnight out sneaked the Turkoman

[1] Even four pairs of stockings and loose Russian boots could not keep out the cold.

with their rifles, and I quietly awoke Yusuf, who, when they were some fifty yards from the tent, enquired after their health most politely, whereupon, without a word, they all went back. Before sunrise, the mules were loaded up, and Yusuf, who was splendidly plucky throughout, harangued our would-be robbers on their breach of hospitality, and threatened them with all sorts of punishment. They finally slunk off, and we were left in peace.

A short stage took us to yet another camp of the Dovoji, where, as we afterwards heard, our quondam guides again tried to get us robbed, having followed us along the other bank of the river, but the reply was that the *Sáhib* must have powerful protectors or else he would never have ventured among the Turkoman, while Bujnurd, into which district we had crossed, was too close to make the game worth the candle.

At Akchánim, above which the Atrek runs for some distance in a gorge, I experienced my first friendly reception, having reached the district of the Goklán Turkoman,[1] where I was greeted by Mustafa Kuli, who in 1874 had been attached to the present Colonel the Hon. G. Napier's mission to the Gurgán, and had received a carefully cherished pair of pistols and a character. He told me that Hak Nafas had murdered his two sons, and we were generally considered to have had a narrow escape; indeed, until I fell asleep, I heard Yusuf giving highly-coloured accounts of our adventures.

Continuing our journey, we rose over the side of the valley by a very stiff pass, known as the Kotal-i-Hanaki.[2] From its crest, at an

[1] Note on the Goklán Turkoman. The following divisions inhabit Russian territory:—

Soráli	Kal Gazl
Toktámash	Ak Kal
Kek	
	Total, 1500 families.

The following divisions inhabit Persian territory:—

Kal Gazl	Ark Kali
Toktámash	Kárnás
Kai	Dúdi
Tamak	Kar Abáli Khán
Eilyángi	Ján Shur Bálghi
	Total, 2500 families.
	Grand total, 4000 families.

[2] Kotal signifies a pass.

elevation of 3400 feet, the valley up which we had come looked just like the raised plans of country so popular for purposes of military instruction, while behind rose the Sonar Dágh. To the south there was snow everywhere, with a prospect of more to fall; we therefore hastened on, but it was not until sunset that we reached the ruined fort of Ament, round which were a few tents of the Toktámash. They stated that they were refugees from the Russian side, and had been compelled to start road-making, to which they strongly objected.

A long weary march up the valley of the Inchá led across a second pass, just below which we halted, near some shepherds' huts. The next morning we reached a cultivated district and the main Astrabád-Bujnurd road at Semalgán—probably the Samangán of the *Sháh Náma*—one of many villages belonging to the Kurds, and, needless to stay, I was delighted to have seen the last of the Turkoman, although I had gained an insight into their habits and ideas that would have been impossible had I travelled with an escort. At any rate, the risks I ran were nothing in comparison to those that threatened the intrepid Conolly,[1] who might have been sold for a slave, in the very district I had passed through.

I found the Goklán Turkoman, on the contrary, quite friendly, and they all complained of Yomut aggressiveness, not without reason. Throughout, I never saw a good horse, and, except a few owned by Persian grandees, there are few valuable Turkoman[2] horses left in Persia.

The Headman of the village of Kirik had also accompanied Colonel Napier, and was, in consequence, friendly. In fact, all the Kurds were, but I felt the want of presents greatly, the above-mentioned officer having been generous in distributing them, which made it unpleasant to go empty-handed where he had passed.

A high range still lay between us and Bujnurd, as we continued our march parallel to the mighty Ála Dágh which runs from east to west for many miles. We spent a night at Badránli, above which snow made the Halimu pass difficult, and, descending

[1] *Vide Journey to the North of India*, a charming record of travel.

[2] A Turkoman horse stands high, but is leggy, and has no barrel. The only good one I ever rode belonged to Sir Mortimer Durand. When pressed it was faint-hearted.

it, we were met by six Persian Cossacks, who looked delightfully smart. They had been sent out as an *istikbál* or reception-party, so, riding across a level plain under their escort, we entered the little town of Bujnurd, where the Governor insisted upon my being his guest, and where it was pleasant to rest for a day or two.

I was warmly congratulated upon having safely accomplished such a hazardous journey. I had not fully realised the risks I had run, but that they were considerable is proved by a reference to the recently published book, *Khorasán and Sistán*. Colonel Yate, who had a party of seventy and an escort, writes about his tour in the autumn of the following year: "We were now to leave the Goklans and to launch ourselves among the Yomuts, into a *terra incognita* in fact. No one that I knew of had ever entered their territory from the eastern side. . . . We were going plump into the wildest and most lawless portion of all, where no Persian dared set foot."[1]

Khorasán, which we had now entered, occupies the north-east corner of Persia, and forms its most important province, the name signifying "Land of the Sun." Its area was formerly enormous, stretching from the Caspian Sea to Samarkand and southwards to the confines of Sind. This historic fact was curiously illustrated by the delight of the Parsis at our occupation of Quetta, which they had always regarded as a portion of Irán, and in consequence had settled there in considerable numbers. To-day the province runs from Transcaspia on the north to Sistán on the south,[2] and from Afghánistán on the east to Astrabád on the west. Further south, its boundaries are the withering expanses of the Lut. Cultivation is carried on as in the province of Kermán,[3] and the rivers are few in number, and of little importance.

The area which Lord Curzon estimates at from 150,000 to 200,000 square miles, includes the most extreme varieties of physical conformation, from snowy ranges to low-lying deserts, and from the green sward of the Elburz to the parched monotony of the plains. Successive waves of conquest have left a medley of tribes, most of which will be mentioned as I come across them. To conclude this brief account, the population of the province is fully a million.

[1] *Khorasán and Sistán*, p. 237.

[2] Sistán and Káin are fully dealt with in this book.

[3] *Vide* chap. iv.

To resume, on the evening of my arrival I visited the *Sahám-u-Dola*,[1] who for many years had been Warden of the Marches, and enjoyed a great reputation. Head of the Shahdillu Kurds, who were planted on this frontier by Sháh Abbás, as mentioned in the previous chapter, the Governor of Bujnurd has been essentially a fighting man all his life, until Skobeleff's victory gave him comparative peace.

We conversed together on a variety of topics, the *Ilkháni*[2] being remarkably well-informed, especially about India. Among other things, he referred to the prowess of Colonel Napier as a sportsman; that officer had also justly praised the beautiful long amber-coloured grapes for which Bujnurd is celebrated. At first I did not mention that I was an officer travelling for my own amusement, but when I found that I was considered to be employed on some wonderful mission, I revealed the fact, and was not believed, no Oriental ever travelling except for gain or as a pilgrim.

Bujnurd is a small town of perhaps 10,000 inhabitants, with one long street, and is connected with Meshed by a telegraph line and a weekly post. Although I had heard much about Turkoman carpets, I had hitherto seen none; accordingly I told Yusuf as we walked up the *bázár* to ask whether there were any for sale. This he objected to do, and quite rightly, as I afterwards learned, it not being respectable in Persia to make one's own purchases. Half-way up the street, which was lined with shops full of Russian samovars and crockery and Manchester calico, a lounger, sitting in what I thought was a tea-house, asked me for money in good Russian. He was the only prisoner, I was told! Upon my return four Turkoman carpets were produced, one of which was full of holes, but the other three were in a perfect state of preservation, and I bought them for the equivalent of £7. Fortune favoured my ignorance, as they were worth four or five times that sum in England, and I bought them especially cheap, as they were not new!

In this deal I was initiated into what was to me a curious custom, as the following day, when my purchases were all packed up, the vendors came to take them back, saying that they had

[1] *Douleh* is the more usual spelling, and *Dawla* the more correct, but, as far as possible, I conform to the R. G. S. rules.

[2] *Ilkháni* signifies Head of Tribes.

changed their minds. However, I declined to pay any attention to them, and, no doubt, it was only a made-up case to get more money, as I had foolishly mentioned how pleased I was at the bargain I had struck.

After three or four days, having exhausted the sights of Bujnurd, we engaged fresh mules, and started for Kuchán. Shortly after passing through the Meshed gate, we skirted the ancient town, now in ruins,[1] and marched down towards the Atrek, Bujnurd occupying a little plain, and lying at an elevation of 3390 feet, considerably above the river. Some of the numerous villages possessed square towers quite like English churches in the distance, and there was a general air of prosperity that was absent from the naturally richer district of Astrabád. The track, upon reaching the valley of the Atrek, known as the Sámur in this particular section, swung up it, and we halted at the little village of Bagdamál, which has a fort perched on a high steep hill. The following morning we crossed the river by a bridge in good repair, and passing Sisáb, entered Kuchán territory. The valley widened out, and we rode through a most fertile district, in which the villages were almost as thick as in parts of the Panjáb.

During the march I witnessed an interesting survival of that most ancient custom, marriage by capture. We first overtook the bride's party, the lady dressed in a gorgeous white and red costume and riding on horseback. A little further on were scouts, and upon her approach a sort of running skirmish was organised, until apparently the fair maiden was surrendered. During this performance there were three spills, which, however, only increased the general hilarity.

At Shirwán, close to which is the almost equally important village of Ziárat, I again reached explored country, and struck the main Kuchán road at a point where there was evidently much intercourse with Geok Tapa, the nearest point on the Transcaspian Railway. Shirwán, which is the second town in the district, and was originally the capital, has a large artificial mound, which was formerly a great artillery position, as our guide informed us. The town appeared to be prosperous, but as we arrived at nightfall and left before dawn, I cannot speak from personal observation; the population is said to include 1200 families of Jeraili Turks.

[1] It is known as *Kala* or Fort.

The Atrek had now shrunk to the dimensions of a large brook; after crossing it we rode up one of the most fertile valleys in Persia, and a thirty-mile march brought us to Kuchán. This district, inhabited mainly by the Zafaranlu division, is the most important of the three Kurdish communities, and was, until quite recently, semi-independent, Nádir Sháh having been murdered in 1747, when besieging his intractable feudatory. The present *Ilkháni*, of whom Lord Curzon gives a delightful picture,[1] is almost always in such a state of intoxication from opium or spirits, that it is usual to give him three days' notice before a visit. This I did not do, as I was anxious to push on without delay. Riding past the dilapidated town which an earthquake in November of the same year levelled to the ground,[2] I crossed the recently constructed *chaussée*, and entered the *Mehmán Khána*, a somewhat glorified *caravanserai*, where all was life and animation, the clumsy waggons stacked in rows outside giving quite an idea of progress.

Beggars were for the first time troublesome, bringing in a piece of bread or something similar in hopes of receiving a present, but, finding that my heart was adamant, they gave up this game. A visitor of a different class was the post-master, who, after a somewhat lengthy call, said that he had a letter for me, and that the British Consul-General of Meshed had asked him to keep it for me. I politely asked for this long-delayed missive, but no, it had not been brought by my visitor, who sent me a message later on that it could not be found. However, at bedtime, it arrived, and Yusuf told me that the post-master expected a handsome present for his trouble.

Upon reading the letter I found that Mr Elias had very kindly sent a *sowár* and two horses to meet me a stage out of Meshed. I was therefore anxious to move as fast as possible, as I yearned for the sight of an English face after such a spell of loneliness. Only waggons were to be procured, and we engaged one to carry us and our property to Meshed in three days, the distance being some ninety miles. The cold false dawn saw us well on the road, but the fates were adverse, as a few miles out of Kuchán one of the two horses was attacked with colic, which necessitated halting for the rest of the day. I recommended the ordinary cures, but

[1] *Vide Persia*, vol. i., p. 94 *et seqq.* He died in 1898.

[2] *Vide* Colonel Yate's *Khorasán and Sistán*, p. 174.

they were too radically different from those in vogue in Persia, of which next morning I had an account. The horse was cut in the tongue and at the root of the tail, and a quantity of hot grease was then poured down its throat. In this particular case, a *Seiid*[1] had offered to effect a cure by weeping into the animal's eye, but the waggoner informed me that his fees were too high!

The country was monotonously level and fertile, the watershed dividing the basin of the Atrek from that of the Hari Rud being scarcely perceptible. The *chaussée*, owing to the hard frost, was hard and even, and on the afternoon of the third day I saw a man on the top of a *caravanserai*. This proved to be the *sowár*, and in less than five minutes I was cantering towards Meshed, leaving Yusuf to follow with the waggon. We covered mile after mile, the beautiful golden dome shining like a flame in the rays of the setting sun, and hardly drew rein until we reached the city gate. We rode along the *Khiábán* or Avenue, the "Unter den Linden" of Meshed, and then threaded our way through intricate streets, finally pulling up at the temporary Consulate-General, where a warm welcome and the general air of comfort, with my first news of the outer world for nearly two months, made me feel inexpressibly content, especially when I recollected the discomfort and lack of food of the previous nights.

Meshed,[2] which signifies a tomb of a martyr, is so termed as being the resting-place of the holy Reza, the eighth *Imám*. The shrine is among the richest in Asia, its treasury not only absorbing large annual contributions in money and jewellery, but also receiving lands and gardens from all classes. It is not open to Christian sightseers, a rule almost universal in Persia, which, generally speaking, it is a pity to ignore, as any infraction of it may entail serious consequences on the Europeans scattered about the country. Some three years later, at a time when there was a strong anti-Christian feeling in Bághdád, a fellow-countryman—I regret to own it—had the execrable taste to enter a mosque in disguise. Had he been discovered, not only his own, but perhaps hundreds of other lives would have been sacrificed.

At the same time, that this feeling is comparatively modern is

[1] A *Seiid* claims descent from the Prophet. In Persia he may be distinguished by a blue turban and a green waistcloth.

[2] The correct spelling would be *Mash-had*. Its altitude is about 3000 feet.

SHRINE OF THE IMÁM REZA AT MESHED.

[To face p. 24.

clearly proved by the following extract from the pen of the worthy Ruy Gonzalez de Clavijo, who headed an embassy from Spain to the court of Timur: "On the same day, the ambassadors reached the great city of Meshed, where the grandson of the Prophet Mohamed lies interred. He lies buried in a great mosque, in a large tomb, which is covered with silver gilt. . . . The ambassadors went to see the mosque; and afterwards, when, in other lands, people heard them say that they had been to this tomb, they kissed their clothes."[1] The actual shrine is, I learned, the centre of three very fine courts, its tile-work, jewelled lamps, and silver railings forming a blaze of beauty well calculated to impress the worshippers; and throughout my sojourn in Persia I have often been struck by the sublimity of the feeling inspired. Some wounded pilgrims, of whom I took charge at Kermán, declined to stay until they were healed, saying that they could not die better than on such a journey; and this, I fear, actually happened.

Nowadays, the political and commercial importance of Meshed is considerable. From our point of view, the west of Afghanistán can be watched to provide against any infraction of the frontier, and the large Anglo-Indian trade is another consideration. But for Russia the post is of still greater importance, Meshed being the capital of Khorasán, on which province Askabád depends for its daily bread. As may be supposed, Russian wares almost fill the *bázárs*, but British goods maintain a highly creditable position.

At the time of my visit the late Mr Ney Elias, the *doyen* of a

[1] Hakluyt Soc., *Embassy to the Court of Timur*, pp. 109-110. Of course the *Imám* Reza was not the grandson of the Prophet. I append his pedigree.

MOHAMED.
1. Fatima-Ali.
2. Hasan. 3. Husein.
4. Ali-Zein-ul-Abidin.
5. Mohamed Bákir.
6. Jafar.
7. Musa.
8. Reza.

series of great travellers in Central Asia, was holding the post of Consul-General, while the interests of Russia were in the hands of M. Vlassof, who has since been transferred to a wider sphere of labour in Abyssinia. As so often seems to be the case, both he and his secretary had married English ladies, which greatly added to the pleasures of social intercourse, and I have never been made more welcome than by that tiny European colony. The British Consulate-General was just completed but not occupied, and consisted of a spacious bungalow in a fine garden, but Mr Elias still inhabited an inconvenient Persian house.

Although I arrived the last day in February, there was a heavy fall of snow a day or two later, but this was the last effort of the winter, and, fearing to experience excessive heat on my onward journey, I was anxious not to delay too long at Meshed. Mr Elias, whose kindness is proverbial, gave me the benefit of his advice, which was to cross the Lut and visit Kermán, much of the intervening country being a blank on the map; he further insisted on my taking some stores, my own supply, which had consisted of a few jars of Bovril, being exhausted. I also had the great advantage of being allowed to borrow many books of Persian travel, which gave me much help, although neither for accuracy nor for recent information did they compare with the monumental work of the present Viceroy of India, whose account of Meshed is so complete that I would refer my readers to it.

Seven mules and two horses were engaged from *Seiid* Bai, who was the contractor for a section of the Quetta-Kandahár-Herát-Meshed post, which is maintained by the Indian Government, and I rode out of Meshed, feeling it quite a wrench to leave the few Europeans, none of whom I had known a week previously.

FROM AN ANCIENT BRASS PIPE.

CHAPTER III

ACROSS THE LUT TO KERMÁN

"Through a land of deserts and of pits, through a land of drought, and of the shadow of death, through a land that no man passed through, and where no man dwelt."—JEREMIAH ii. 6.

AFTER quitting Meshed, where the golden dome and the numerous graveyards are the two things that have most impressed themselves on my memory, the Tehrán road was followed for the first stage to Sharifabád. The track enters undulating country, and winds up to a point where the pilgrim from the south first views the sacred dome. Without this interest the stage would be a monotonous one.

Sharifabád has two fine *caravanserais*, but, although so near Meshed, is one of the most unsafe stages on the road. Indeed, the noted traveller, Dr Wolff, was nearly killed there by a band of Hazára, in the first half of the nineteenth century.

Next morning I started early in order to make a long march, and, when a few miles on the road, met Captain Duke of the Indian Medical Staff, who had travelled up from Bushire in thirty-two days, which must have been something like a record for a caravan journey, as he reached Meshed the same day. The country continued to be undulating, and at Káfir Kala or Infidel Fort, there was a stretch of turf and a stream, on which I bagged a duck; in fact, with the promise of spring, the country looked most attractive.

To reach Asadabád a hilly belt had to be crossed, there being a narrow defile with black perpendicular rocks about half way. We found the village to possess a remarkable door in the shape of a huge round stone. As it required ten men at least to roll it into position, it seemed somewhat unpractical, the Turkoman not being in the habit of giving warning; moreover, the walls were low and weak.

A carpet caravan was on its way from the province of Káin, and I bought a specimen of this work, which had a rather pretty blue and red pattern; its size was 17 feet 4 inches by 11 feet 10 inches, and I paid £11 at the current rate, 37 kráns being equivalent to £1, whereas, nowadays, 50 is an average rate of exchange. This fact has greatly injured the Imperial Bank of Persia, but is a boon to those whose incomes are in pounds sterling.

I rather foolishly decided to reach Turbat in one stage, the distance being perhaps thirty miles, or somewhat less, but I had forgotten to reckon with the pass. After a few miles of plain, we passed the hamlet of Shur Serai, which I chiefly recollect from the fact that it was shown as Shur Hissár on the map; we then entered a steep valley, and were soon in deep snow, somewhat to my surprise. The *crux* of the pass was a very narrow ledge, with a cliff on one side and a snow-drift on the other. I told the muleteer to let the animals go one by one, but he thought he knew better, and, as the leader was sniffing at the bad place before crossing it, the next mule, as I anticipated, shoved it, with the result that both fell into the deep snow below. I was just in time to prevent the others following, and the useless Turkoman, who was the worst muleteer I have had to endure, released the buried mules from their boxes, which were hauled up by ropes on to the ledge. A way out was finally found for the mules themselves, which at one time were lost to sight in the snow.

This accident occasioned a delay of four hours, and when we reached the crest of the Bidár pass, which rises to an altitude of 6500 feet, a heavy storm of sleet came on, to cool us after our labours. Descending the southern slope, I met an Armenian, who said that he was on his way back from Sistán, where he had been sent to investigate an outbreak of cholera, which, as a matter of fact, had never occurred. This he acknowledged, stating at the same time that he and a companion had travelled in a cart almost throughout. As the Kumári pass a few miles to the west is open to wheeled traffic, I imagine that he had adopted that route.

After exchanging the news, we parted, and I descended into the valley of a river which is known in its lower reaches as the Kal-i-Salá, running east through a rocky gorge. It was spanned by a newly-constructed bridge, a *rara avis* in Persia, and, after traversing a second belt of hilly country, we reached the open plain of Turbat. It was, however, night before we got in, and I weakly agreed to put up at the crowded *caravanserai*. This is a great mistake for a European, as, to secure any privacy at all, the only opening must be curtained across, while every loafer thinks that a *Farangi*[1] is a curious kind of beast to be carefully watched and followed.

Turbat-i-Haideri, as the maps have it, is nowadays an obsolete term, although there is still the large red-brick tomb of the saint whose full title was Kutb-u-Din[2] Haider. So great is his reputation that not only the boys, but even the men of Persian towns, divide into two parties, Haideri and Namati—the latter term being derived from *Sháh* Namat Ulla of Máhun—when they wish to have a stone-throwing contest, which often terminates in loss of life. The town is generally spoken of as *Turbat*, signifying grave, and I made a point of asking at least four different people whose was the *Turbat*, the invariable reply being Turbat-i-Ishák-Khán; Haider must therefore yield up the place on the map which he has so long occupied.

Isházk Khán was a chief of the Kárai or Karait, which was the tribe formerly ruled by the famous Prester John, and finally subdued by Chengiz Khán. He was apparently a genius, as, in a few years, he raised the district under his rule to a pitch of prosperity that excited the admiration and envy of his neighbours. He was finally put to death after having tried to capture Meshed by a combination of tribes.

Turbat, which may have a population of 15,000 inhabitants, is surrounded by many gardens, and is now, in 1901, a considerable Russian centre, a doctor being established under the protection of Cossacks, to watch the plague, or perhaps the cholera. Silk used to be the staple product, and its culture is once again a reviving industry, but, in common with other districts, the

[1] *Farangi* is the Oriental form of Frank.
[2] Kutb-u-Din signifies Pillar of the Faith.

famine dealt it a blow that is still felt, following, as it did, the silk-worm disease.

Being, as ever, anxious to avoid routes which were known, I made enquiries from various sources, with the result that I heard of a track to Jumein, which lay to the east of the one usually followed, and, feeling the immense change in temperature, which made travelling all day rather trying, we crossed the low hills of Turbat, and struck almost due south. From Hendabád we ought to have continued on in the same direction, but on learning from our guide that there was no road, we kept south-east through a fertile, level district, and re-crossing the Kal-i-Salá, which was running red with mud, we camped at Buzbar. As soon as the village elders had collected, we were informed of our mistake, and the next morning we followed down the left bank of the river. It was interesting to note that every village shown on the map was a ruin, other hamlets having sprung up, while, still greater surprise, the river which bends to the west was shown on the map as trending south-east. A long march of thirty miles, during which we crossed and re-crossed the river, brought us to Jangal, a walled village with so many towers that the effect was grotesque, and from there we traversed a bare level desert of what is known as *pat* in India, where the mirage was superb. This was succeeded by a belt of sandhills, and beyond these lay Bimurgh which, with Jangal, and indeed many other villages in this district, is the property of the Meshed shrine.

Our route now lay almost due west, and, crossing a belt of sand dunes, we gained an excellent view of the Gunabád plain, the first village of which we reached at sixteen miles from Bimurgh. A little further on we passed Beidukht, which is noted as being the home of one of the few great *Murshid* of Persia. This "teacher," who has immense influence, especially with the merchants of Tehrán, is called *Háji*[1] *Mullá* Sultán Ali, and has built a fine *madresa* or college, where he daily teaches and preaches; he is said to be about sixty.

Jumein, the little town of the district, which is under the Governor of Tabas, has a population of perhaps 8000 and a small

[1] *Háji* is a man who has performed the pilgrimage to Mecca. It is also given as a name to boys born in the sacred month of *Zi Hijja*. The Greeks use the same term for pilgrims to Jerusalem.

bázár. Its speciality is a very rude manufacture of pottery, which was so ugly that I refrained from making any purchases.

The plain of Gunabád lies at the foot of an important range which runs from south-east to north-west, and, in this particular part of Persia, separates the comparatively elevated tract, across which I had been travelling, from the funereal waste of the Lut which I was so soon to enter. Further west it sinks into the northerly portion of the same desert.

We were but three stages from Tun, and, following in the steps of the late Sir Charles MacGregor, who was among the first to demonstrate the necessity of exploring the states contiguous to the Indian Empire, ascended the skirt of the mountain to the pleasant village of Kalát, which is built in terraces up the hillside. Rather more than five years later I again looked down upon this village, and thus connected the systematic exploration of Káin with what was of necessity but a narrow line running through the country, my observations being practically limited to what I could see from the road.

A sullen gorge of a most lifeless aspect led up to the watershed at 6600 feet, and a march of sixteen miles brought us right across the range, which rapidly dwindles to the west. After camping near a hamlet, we rode leisurely downhill towards Tun, passing a splendid stretch of gardens on the way. The town, with a population of 4000 inhabitants, is walled, but most of its interior is cultivated, and altogether its appearance was not unpleasing. Indeed, with an altitude of 4300 feet, it should not be very hot; and yet "Go to Tun and Tabas" is a strong expression in a Persian's mouth, and the equivalent of "Go to Jericho."

I had now reached the northern edge of the great desert which, before crossing for the first of many times, I propose to describe, the question of its origin being also discussed in chap. viii. And firstly, I would urge that geographers have, without sufficient grounds, divided the great desert of Persia into two regions, that to the north being termed the Dasht-i-Kavir and that further south the Dasht-i-Lut. Lord Curzon,[1] quoting from General Schindler three possible derivations of the word *Kavir*, rightly selects the Arabic *Kafr* or saline swamp. This is, without

[1] *Persia*, vol. ii., p. 247.

doubt, the origin of *Kavir*, and remains in common use even to the present day in Southern Persia. As regards the term Lut, in the great desert the guides point out one or more *Shahr-i-Lut* or Cities of Lot, which are in reality freaks of nature! They explain that The Almighty destroyed them by fire from heaven, as was the case with the cities above which now roll the waters of the Dead Sea. Furthermore, *Luti*, which to-day signifies a buffoon, originally meant a Sodomite. I am convinced that in this way, the name of Lut or Lot[1] has become associated, and, I would maintain, most appropriately, with perhaps the greatest waste in Asia.

The striking effect produced by these Cities of Lot can be best illustrated by a reference to Pierre Loti's romantic account of the desert of Sinai: "Devant nous vient de s'ouvrir un lugubre dédale de vallées faites de ces pierres-là, jaunâtres ou blanches; leurs parois, stratifiées horizontalement, donnent l'illusion de murailles aux assises régulières, bâties de main d'homme. On croit circuler au milieu de cités détruites, passer dans des rues, dans des rues de géants, entre des ruines de palais et de citadelles. Les constructions, par couches superposées, sont toujours plus hautes, toujours plus surhumaines, affectent des formes de temples, de pyramides, de colonnades, ou de grandes tours solitaires. Et la mort est là partout, la mort souveraine, avec son effroi et son silence. . . ."[2]

After having made constant enquiries, I have come to the conclusion that the whole desert bears but the one name of Lut, and that not only is there a considerable amount of *Kavir* in each, but that their general features are identical. I freely admit, however, that owing to the larger volume of water flowing in on the north, there is a greater area impregnated with salt in that division. A Persian educated in England has told me that he saw the Yezd-Tabas road indicated on the map as the line where the two deserts met. All his attempts, however, to gain local corroboration of the existence of a desert known as the Dasht-i-Kavir were a failure, and he continued his journey with a diminished respect for European cartography.

Having, as I would fain hope, convinced my readers that Lut

[1] The Persian spelling is the same for Lot as well as for the desert, while for a Sodomite the root is also similar.

[2] *Le Désert*, p. 85.

is the one name for the whole desert, Dasht-i-Lut[1] being almost a redundancy, and that *Kavir* is applied to every saline swamp in the whole blighted expanse, I will now continue my description.

This great desert stretches from a few miles out of Tehrán practically to the British frontier, a distance exceeding 700 miles, while from Tun to Bampur is about 500 miles. The easterly edge appears to be the highest, the village of Basirán, which I visited in 1899, lying at an altitude of 4800 feet. Tun is 4300 feet, and elsewhere the average elevation may be perhaps 2000 feet. Near Khabis the lowest levels appear to be about 1000 feet. The worst portion of the Lut is that lying between Eastern Persia and Khabis, which was crossed by M. Khanikoff in the middle of the nineteenth century, and was twice traversed by Captain Galindo in the eighties. The former traveller writes: "Our delight at finding ourselves safe and sound can easily be imagined after crossing a desert unequalled in aridity on the whole of the Asiatic continent, for the Gobi and Kizil-Kum are fertile prairies compared to the Lut. I have seen the dreary aspect of the Isthmus of Suez. Many parts of that arid region seem struck with the same sterility as the Lut, but it never retains that character over such a vast surface."[2] As M. Khanikoff possessed such a wide field for comparison, I think that his views may be accepted as final.

As to the origin of the Lut, it is considered to have been originally an inland sea, which theory is supported by the presence of the active volcano of Sarhad,[3] the extinct volcano of Bazmán, and many legends.

I am also of opinion that, owing to the exterminating wars from which Persia has suffered, its limits have been extended. My journeys show that Persia is, generally speaking, a desert with villages every few miles, laboriously kept in existence by means of irrigation. Should the supply of water cease, the villagers are forced to leave, and again, if the villagers be killed off, the *kanáts*[4] become choked up, causing a stoppage of the water-supply, and an enlargement of the desert. Apart from the Lut, there are many

[1] The term *Dasht-i-Lut* is rarely heard, and almost every one of whom I enquired denied its correctness.

[2] *Mémoire*, p. 120.

[3] *Vide* chaps. viii. and x.

[4] For a description of a *kanát*, *vide* the beginning of chap. iv.

parts of Persia where for three or more stages there are no villages, and all these minor deserts reproduce the features of the great waste which, near Sistán, for instance, could easily be inhabited. I would also add that everything points to the fact that the rainfall has diminished, while both as a cause and a consequence of this, the country is practically treeless. I would therefore urge that for the material regeneration of Persia the two great necessities are, a provision of water and re-afforestation.

I believe that I may claim to be the first European who has crossed this section of the Lut, although, until I studied the question, I believed myself to be following in the footsteps of Marco Polo. At the same time, given proper arrangements, there should be no great difficulty in making the journey, at any rate during seven months in the year. This is, in fact, the main Kermán-Meshed route, and is consequently used by thousands of travellers, mostly pilgrims.

Upon quitting Tun, whence the Tabas and Yezd road ran nearly west, we kept south, and, after clearing the cultivated zone, entered a district of low, black, sun-scorched hills. Every four miles were water-tanks, known as *hauz*, which consist of underground vaults entered by steps; these receive the drainage from every point, and the water is generally polluted, as may be supposed. The whole is covered by a domed roof, and, seeing that they depend upon the rainfall, these *hauz* remain empty in dry years, which was emphatically the case in 1893.

We camped near a well of brackish water termed Khusháb,[1] and the following morning I found that I had only half a bottle of sweet water left with which to face the heat of the day. However, as we were promised a good supply at the end of the stage, it did not appear to signify.

After the first mile, we crawled over a dead level plain, and, to my joy, a range of snow-clad mountains appeared which had no existence on the map. About 2 P.M. I began to feel the heat, the contents of my bottle having been exhausted, and, had it not been for a puddle of dirty water left at the bottom of a *hauz*, I should perhaps have got sunstroke; but the moisture applied externally pulled me through, and I finally reached Chahár Gumbaz,[2] where, to my dismay, the water was as green as the sea.

[1] *I.e.* Sweet Water.

[2] *I.e.* Four Domes.

THE LUT.

[*To face p.* 34.

Washing was some relief, but I could not sleep from thirst, and when the mules were rested, we rode on to the hills, reaching the important village of Duhuk the following morning. Personally I had taken all precautions, but my servants, who had drunk the salt water, were, to a man, violently ill for six or eight hours.

Duhuk contains a most picturesque old fort, below which cluster some two hundred houses, and there is much cultivated land, the village occupying a break in the hills, which are in reality a continuation of the Tabas range. Our camp was pitched at an altitude of 4500 feet, and as the hilltops were covered with snow—it was late March—I estimated their approximate elevation to be at least 9000 feet. To the east of the gap, through which runs the road to Tabas, the Mur Kuh, as it is termed, bends round from the almost west and east trend of the Tabas range to a south-south-east direction.

The inhabitants showed intense and not unnatural curiosity to see the first European who had come their way, which they frankly explained had been increased by hearing from pilgrims of the wonders that were done by *Farangis*, especially at Bombay.

After a much needed day's halt, we continued our journey, and were delighted to hear that at the next stage too there was a village, proving that this section of the Lut is really quite thickly populated. The track, as hitherto, ran across hard gravel, so that when we reached Arababád at twenty-one miles, we decided to continue on to Zenagun, where there was a small date-grove, showing that we had reached a hotter climate; to the west is the village of Isfandiár, near which there is a lead mine.

Profiting by former experience, we hired three donkeys to carry water, and upon leaving Zenagun and the hamlets round it, we felt no fears for the fifty miles on to Naiband. After crossing what appeared to be an off-shoot of the Mur Kuh, we halted to rest the mules at Ab-i-Garm, which was a genuine *Kavir*, although not of the normal type. The surrounding district drained into the swamp, in which were pools of brine. Tamarisks were in abundance, and some cattle were grazing on the coarse green grass, while we also roused a few duck. The ground struck me as exactly resembling a ploughed field frozen and covered with hoar frost; at the same time, walking in it meant sinking up to the knees. So far as I could judge this *Kavir* runs east and west for some miles, its width being inconsiderable.

After enduring the burning heat of the day, we continued our march, till a storm[1] prevented us from seeing the track, when we lay down until dawn. Again, owing to leakage, there was no water left, and, not knowing how far distant Naiband might be, I rode on ahead, in order to send back water for the party. Fortunately, the track was fairly distinct, but as hour after hour passed and my pony began to give in, I feared that I had lost my way, especially as at one place there were two tracks. The one I followed hugged what I afterwards knew to be the Naiband range, and the track crossed several deep *nalas*, up and down which the pony could hardly struggle. Finally, however, I turned a corner and came upon a vision of fairyland, as I beheld the opposite hillside covered with waving palms, against which the bright green crops formed a most exquisite contrast, the hill being topped by a picturesque old red fort. Upon entering the grove, there were streams running in every direction, while huge grottoes completed the picture. My first care was to despatch two donkey-loads of water, which met our exhausted party five miles out. Not knowing the road, they had halted at the bifurcation.

The camp was pitched on the top of the hill, and across the dull green of the palms the burning yellow Lut stretched far away to the horizon; although, no doubt, the desert rendered me appreciative, I have never seen a fairer view than Naiband as entered from the north.

The village, I learned, was founded some two centuries ago as an outpost against the Baluchis, whose sphere of evil activity we had now entered. Situated in the centre of the desert, at a considerable distance from any other village, and at the point where the Meshed road joins that from Birjand, Naiband occupies an important position.

As the mules required rest, I determined to spend a couple of days in exploring the hills, which rise to an elevation of perhaps 9000 feet. I scaled what I conceived to be the highest peak, but

[1] This was also the case when Nádir Sháh was passing this very spot. He ordered his guns to be fired to assist the stragglers, but "heaven's artillery" was louder. Thanks to lyddite, this is no longer the case.

found another yet higher; want of water, however, forced me to return. Yet I obtained a good idea of the range, which is practically waterless, and a still better one of the surrounding Lut, and of the tracks branching off to Káin, Sistán, Sarhad, Khabis, and Yezd, about all of which I collected details. They are, of course, only used during the winter months, when Yezd imports a proportion of its wheat from Sistán, and a considerable percentage of the English goods sold in Birjand reach it by this roundabout way.

Owing to the drought, we had to make a 40-mile march, and the mules, which had picked up a bit, met me at *Chashma*[1] Mokik, a few miles from Naiband, where there is a spring of fair water. It is the point at which the Yezd road branches off. Before coming to Persia the only desert I had seen was that of Suez, which is apparently an unlimited expanse of yellow sand. Here, however, I was in a distinctly mountainous country, and just as my childhood's idea of the East always included a palm-tree, so a desert had hitherto conveyed the vision of a level expanse of sand; but experience has certainly tended to modify both these ideas. The track rose through low hills to a pass at an elevation of 3950 feet, after which we passed two empty reservoirs, the second of which is a very fine structure, known as the Hauz-i-Khán. According to a Persian historian, it was built by Ganj Ali Khán, Zík, who was the second great ruler of Kermán.[2]

About half-way we passed between hills with scarped sides, where we had visions of towers, houses, and figures of men under the bright moonlight: these indeed are the fantastic rocks which gave rise to the legend of the Cities of Lot. We then appeared to be approaching a range without any opening, but there proved to be a *nala* with the same scarped cliffs, and at length we reached Chehel Pái or the Forty Steps. It is just off the river-bed, and owes its name to the number of steps by which the water is approached. It used to be a favourite spot for a Baluchi ambuscade, the *hauz* being commanded by the surrounding cliffs.

After a long sleep we continued our journey, reaching the open plain an hour after starting. The lowest point on it constitutes the boundary between Khorasán and Kermán, a dry bed being crossed at an elevation of 2130 feet. Every two miles there were pillars,

[1] *Chashma* signifies a spring. [2] *Vide* chap. v.

a great boon to the traveller, while to the south of the track is another City of Lot, of which, however, I saw nothing, as it was already night. We finally entered low hills, and following up a salt-stream, reached the *caravanserai* of Darband, kept by a solitary soldier, who made his living by selling supplies at famine rates.

The Darband range, which I explored, runs up to over 8000 feet. It is full of game, but I had no luck; and it also possesses a mine of asbestos. In fact, the hills all round are stated to be full of minerals, and as water is not wanting, Darband should be re-peopled, now that the Baluchis have been reduced to peace. The soldier, who was an excellent guide, pointed out a ridge running across the narrow valley on which were two towers, termed Burj-i-Dárghá[1] and Burj-i-Dukhtar, which closed the road, and thus gave the place the name of Stop Gate, a title which appears in the shape of "Derbent," in the case of the famous city of the Caucasus. According to legend, Kakkár was the king of the Shahr-i-Lut, and his daughter fled with a lover styled Dárghá to this spot, where they levied blackmail on all passers-by. There were little watch-towers in the hills to prevent escape, and, if the story be true, the lovers must have soon waxed rich.

To the west is the district of Gujar, which has since been explored by Captain Wyatt, enabling us to define the limit of the Lut in this particular direction. Thenceforward we skirted it, which was a pleasanter experience than crossing. With our mules refreshed, we prepared to continue the journey, and after thirteen miles in the hills, reached Cháh Kuru, where I saw a *caravanserai* and a well which had recently been constructed. The route to Tabas, *via* Gujar, branches off up the valley, and every year there were many deaths from thirst, until a true public benefactor sunk the well.

Steadily rising through clay hills, we reached a pass, from which the great range behind Rawár reared its snow-tipped peaks, and below us lay the sandy plain. Rawár is a little town of 8000 inhabitants, including sixty families belonging to the Il Nakhái nomads, and was reached by us after a weary march of thirty-four miles. It is famous for figs and pomegranates, and is also a principal

[1] *Burj* signifies a tower, and *Dárghá* is probably a corruption of *Dárúghá*, the nearest approach to our magistrate.

centre of the carpet industry, for which it is second only to Kermán, the coarser qualities being woven almost entirely in this district. The gardens looked very bright, but the situation is bad, a heavy fall of snow frequently resulting in floods and causing the destruction of houses and walls, when a thaw comes.

Laying in a stock of tea, sugar, and other provisions, we started late in the afternoon, clearing the cultivated area some two miles from Rawár. We then made for a conspicuous flat-topped hill, which appeared to block up the end of the valley, and spent the night at a *haus* of evil-smelling water. We were, however, informed that a new tank, then in course of construction, would ensure a good supply.

The following morning we passed the flat-topped hill which we had sighted on the previous day, and halted for lunch at Abid, where a tiny stream trickles out from under a fine old willow, Abid[1] signifying Water of the Willow. While enjoying the cool air—we were now at an elevation of 6000 feet—a gang of Arabs appeared on the scene. At first some children arrived clad in filthy rags, to whom we gave a few coppers, and then a gang of twenty men, across whose foreheads scoundrel was stamped in large type. They surrounded us, and begged incessantly, saying that as men they wanted money more than children, while as pilgrims they had a claim on our sympathy. After an hour of persistent begging an offer of £5 was made for Yusuf's revolver, and this being declined, the demand for coppers was renewed, almost with menaces. However, failing to bleed us, they went into the *caravanserai*, whence we soon heard howling and weeping as they were robbing its keeper. On the top of this, two men came running up, and said that their camp had been looted, and would we help them to recover their property. "Gladly," was the reply, and it was a real treat to make the ruffians disgorge. At first they drew their knives, but the sight of two revolvers proving too much for them, they grovelled, and said that they would beat the children, who were the real thieves. They finally gave up everything, and I then made them move on, knowing that if I left them at Abid they would again steal all they could find.

So far, from Naiband I had kept to the Kermán road, on which my solitary predecessor was Colonel St G. Gore, now Surveyor-

[1] It is a contraction of Áb-i-Bid.

General of India. I had, however, learned that there was an elevated fertile district between Abid and Khabis, to which I determined to give an existence on the map, which was quite blank in that direction.

Our mules having overtaken us, we ascended to the watershed, and, two miles further on, we quitted the main road and followed a track to the south-east. Passing some extraordinary strawberry-and-cream coloured hills, we finally struck a fine brook at Hur, and there encamped. Colonel Gore, who crossed this same stream higher up, said that it was the first he had seen since he entered Persia from Herát; this fact speaks for itself.

Hur is a little hamlet originally occupied by a few families of soldiers, who were posted as a guard against the Baluchis, one of whose favourite raiding roads ran from the Lut up the valley of this stream; its water, sad to say, is mostly wasted. Upon leaving camp, we followed down the brook to a point where a tributary joined in, and ascended the latter for some miles. We then marched between high rugged hills, which we crossed at an altitude of 7300 feet. To the south, the Kuhpaia range which bounds the Kermán plain on the north raised its even snow-clad line, and we descended into an elevated valley, which was guarded to the east by a tower. Passing Hanni and other hamlets, we camped at Gwárk, which had a population of some thirty families. The district is a very hilly one, and above Gwárk we crossed another pass, where there are two ancient forts which I was told were used as landmarks by caravans from Sistán.

The following day we descended into the main valley of Kuhpaia, and rather suddenly came upon Gaz, which is hidden in a fold of the ground; it is equidistant from Kermán and Khabis. Following down the valley, we crossed a second brook, which is lost in the *Kavir* to the east. Yet another stream, a salt one, and we finally camped at the hamlet of Tejen. Almost throughout the march, the valleys had been carpeted with hyacinths, and I heard a cuckoo, which is a comparatively rare bird in Persia.

I now determined to ride down to within a few miles of Khabis,[1] in order to complete my exploration in this direction,

[1] The nomads in the district consist of fifty families of the Musáfiri, who, wintering in Khabis and Kashit, spend the summer in Sirch and Ráin.

and therefore had my camp pitched a few miles further on, as otherwise the distance for a day's work would have been too great. Just above Tejen was the watershed of the Khabis drainage. It was crossed at an altitude of 7300 feet, and as the town was twenty-five miles distant, and lies at an elevation of 1800 feet, the descent is rapid, being accomplished in less than twenty miles. It appears probable that the mountains, which are some eight miles from Khabis, formed the western shore of the prehistoric sea of Irán.

The valley rapidly narrowed until at length the river-bed completely filled it, and passing a mill, we reached the famous Khar-i-Shikan or Donkey Destroying defile, a huge rock barring up the valley to such an extent, that all loads have to be taken off and carried by hand. At the same time, a little dynamite would speedily remedy the evil, and in other respects the track, although rugged, offers no special difficulties. A small *caravanserai* with a guard is situated below the Donkey Destroyer, from which it derives its name, and lower down are two hamlets constituting the furthest point we visited, for from them we could look down on to the palm-groves of Khabis.

This little town with a population of 8000 inhabitants produces excellent dates, oranges, and henna, and is a favourite winter resort. It was held, off and on, by the Afghâns, until the Kájár dynasty was firmly established, and to-day some of the choked-up *kanáts* are being repaired. Khabis, so a learned Persian informed me, is Arabic for a cake covered with lard and dates, and rolled up—a great dainty!

The Rev. A. R. Blackett of the Church Missionary Society, who visited the little town in 1900, told me that he had seen the ruins of what was probably a Christian church, in a group of buildings a mile to the east of the town, known as *Ákus*. He described the ruins as being of unequal antiquity, the newer portion consisting of the remains of a shrine, and the more ancient of a pre-Mohamedan building. The shrine occupies a dismantled tower constructed of brick and beams, the roof of which has disappeared. At the base of the tower, a room contains a brick grave bearing the date A.H. 173 (789), and round the wall is a dado of blue, yellow, and black mosaic. Behind this is a second chamber of meaner appearance, and opening out of it is the vestibule of the older structure, of which only portions of the walls remain, but what was once vestry, apse, and sedilia, can be traced. The local name of *Ákus* may be a corruption of *Nákus*, the wooden gong used by Christians in Mohamedan countries. Another possible derivation is the Greek *Hagios* or Holy, but this seems far-fetched.

From Deh Rud, which was held by an Afghán chief[1] well into the ninteenth century, we retraced our steps, preparatory to crossing the Kuhpaia range. The track was very steep, and the summit of the Gudár-i-Khusháb, as the pass was termed, rose to an elevation of 7800 feet, the average height of the hills being at least 2000 feet higher. Descending, we reached an extensive plain, across which runs the main Khabis-Kermán road, which is, however, almost impassable for camels. We camped at the small village of Anaristán, and in the morning rose for five miles to the Gudár-i-Galgazut, whence we gradually descended on to the Kermán plain.

At the point where the hills are quitted is a fine old plane-tree, and the weary traveller looks down upon one of the great cities of Persia, which does not, however, present an imposing appearance, houses and soil alike being of kháki hue. Near the outskirts of the town the Zoroastrian quarter, which was destroyed by the Afgháns, showed every sign of melancholy decay, while to the left front ruined forts covered the limestone hills. After passing a belt of gardens and houses the town wall was reached, and for the first time I entered Kermán, little thinking that in the future I was to be so closely connected with it.

[1] His name was Taki Khán, and he was imprisoned and finally killed at Tehrán.

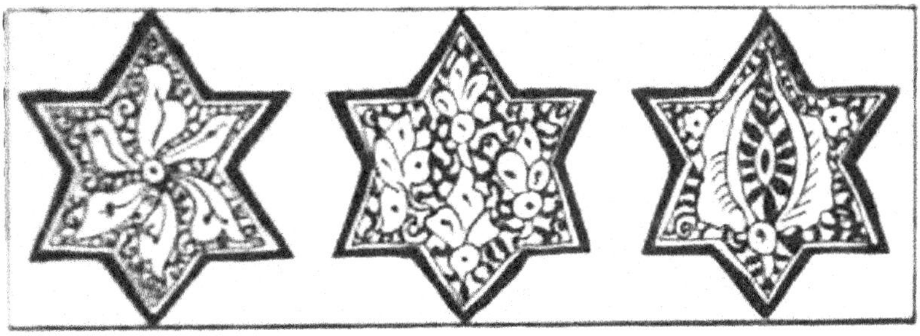

FROM LUSTRED POTTERY.

CHAPTER IV

THE PROVINCE OF KERMÁN

"The poet, wandering on, through Arabie,
And Persia, and the wild Carmanian waste,
And o'er the aërial mountains which pour down
Indus and Oxus from their icy caves,
In joy and exultation held his way."—SHELLEY'S *Alastor*.

THE province of Kermán has, from its earliest appearance on the stage of history, been of considerable, if never of first-rate, importance. Perhaps, owing to its physical surroundings, its extent to-day is approximately what it was more than two thousand years ago, while the difference between the classic "Karmania" and the modern "Kermán" is slight.

Geographically speaking, the province, which is almost as large as France, is of great interest if only for the various climates, products, and peoples that it contains. For a considerable distance inland the country is low, the palm flourishes, and the inhabitants are almost as dark as those of the Panjáb, while wheat and barley are grown as winter crops, reaped in the early spring. In some parts, Jíruft for instance, this *Garmsír*, as it is termed, runs up to the mighty mountain barrier which separates it from the uplands known as Sárdu. This district, with fine plateaux rising to 9000 feet, is the most southern portion of the main orographic system of Persia, in which the ranges trend approximately north-west, and to the south of Kermán there are peaks which attain the great altitude of nearly 14,000 feet. To the north and east of the province there is a gradual decrease in elevation, although round the capital the mountains are high, but beyond them are the low-lying wastes of the Lut.

The whole province, indeed, can be best described as partly desert pure and simple, and partly desert tempered by oases. For instance, to the west, south, and east of Kermán there is desert, while at distances of a few miles tiny hamlets, or in some cases villages, are kept alive by springs tapped in the hills, the water of which is laboriously conveyed for many miles to the level plain by the underground channels termed *kanáts*; in some cases the original well may be 400 feet deep, and as every few yards other wells must be dug, it is impossible not to admire the patient industry of the peasant, who gains a living in spite of great difficulties, a heavy shower or a sandstorm frequently choking up the *kanát*.

As may be supposed, the rivers are unimportant, the Hali or Halil alone meriting notice. Rising to the south of the great barrier mentioned above, it flows through Jíruft, and commingles with the Bampur river, no attempt being made to husband its priceless water.

As yet there is no record of the rainfall, but as at Tehrán it is about ten inches, perhaps seven inches, or even less, for Kermán would be a fair average. At the same time districts vary, Jíruft being the most favoured in this respect.

In the uplands spring is ushered in by almost incessant gales and dust-storms, mainly from the south-west, while showers are frequent in good years. In the middle of the summer at Kermán the days are hot [1] but the nights are pleasant, while there is almost always an afternoon breeze. The heat is over by the middle of September, and after the autumnal equinox, there are a few days of what is best described as a dense dry fog. This was undoubtedly the haze referred to by Marco Polo, when he wrote:—
"And you must know that when these Caraonas wish to make a plundering incursion, they have certain devilish enchantments whereby they do bring darkness over the face of the day, insomuch that you can scarcely discern your comrade riding beside

[1] Average maximum temperatures in 1900 were as follows:—June, 90°; July, 88°; August, 89°; September, 79°.

you; and this darkness they will cause to extend over a space of seven days' journey."[1]

With this exception the autumn is most delightful, although the Persians deem it feverish, which is accounted for in their case by the fact that they eat too much fruit. In the winter there is sharp frost with beautifully still bright days. There is generally a day's rain towards the end of November, and a slight fall of snow in December. In January, if the year be favourable, there are three or four heavy falls of snow, which soon melts in the plains, as Omar Khayyám sings:

> "The Worldly Hope men set their Hearts upon
> Turns Ashes—or it prospers; and anon,
> Like Snow upon the Desert's dusty Face,
> Lighting a little hour or so—is gone."

At the same time, but for the mountains, in which are the "treasures of the snow reserved against the time of trouble,"[2] South-Eastern Persia would, so far as I can judge, be almost uninhabitable. In the *Garmsír* the winter months are pleasant enough, but even in March a tent becomes unpleasantly hot, and the summer is both trying and unhealthy, although in many cases there are cool hills within easy reach.

The inhabitants of this huge province number perhaps 750,000, and may be divided into dwellers in houses and nomads, the latter forming a large percentage of the population. The townspeople and villagers are mostly Iránians, the successive hordes[3] of invaders having in almost every case kept to a wandering life, which is much the same as that depicted in the book of Job.

Coming from Europe, the sterility strikes the traveller as appalling, and, sad to say, is on the increase. As the country becomes more settled, the supply of timber is gradually exhausted, mainly by the charcoal-burner—there is no coal[4]—and there are few ranges with anything approaching to a forest. To prove that this

[1] *Vide* Yule's *Marco Polo*[2], vol. i., p. 99.

[2] Job xxxviii. 23.

[3] Horde is a corruption of Urdú, which was the Mongol word for army; it is now applied to the language generally termed Hindustáni.

[4] The scanty supply of mineral products are all referred to in the various chapters. They consist of copper, asbestos, and sulphate of zinc.

is nothing new, I cannot do better than quote from Josafa Barbaro, who wrote: "In those parties are no woodes nor yet trees, no not so much as one, except it be fruite trees, which they plante, whereas they may water them; for otherwise they wolde not take."[1] As a matter of fact, sparse bushes are generally all that can be found, from one mountain species of which the valuable tragacanth gum is extracted. Malodorous asafoetida is also collected in the same fashion, and, as a correspondent once pointed out to me, the mountains are the home of every sort of alpine plant.

Travelling in South-East Persia generally implies marching in a pitiless glare between ranges of stony hills, while the dusty plains are practically bare and naked; the weary wayfarer hails with enthusiasm any little spring, and even a stunted willow seems to be a thing of beauty in such a treeless expanse.

The products of the country are wheat, barley, and opium, with millet, cotton, and beetroot as autumn crops in the uplands, while in the high plateaux and valleys peas are much grown. In the *Garmsír* rice and maize are the summer crops; the valuable henna is also a great source of wealth, especially to Bam and Khabis. Melons, water-melons, grapes, broad beans, lucerne, castor-oil, cucumbers, cabbages, lettuces, onions, egg-plants, pumpkins, turnips, and lentils, complete the crops, although potatoes are gaining in popularity. Apples, pears, apricots, mulberries, quinces, nectarines, peaches, plums, cherries, figs, pomegranates, almonds, filberts, walnuts, and pistachio-nuts grow most readily, but, as no care is taken, the fruit is, as a rule, poor, albeit the oranges and limes of Khabis and Bam are excellent, and the pistachio[2] of the province is famous.

The trees, almost all of which depend on irrigation, as mentioned above, are few in number, the plane ranking first, then the poplar, the ordinary and the weeping willow, the wych-elm, the Bohemian olive, the cypress, the fir, the acacia, and the deliciously-scented sweetbriar, while roses, almost wild, and jessamine, represent the flowers. But seeds from Europe are highly appreciated, Persians being passionately fond of floriculture. Rose-water is much used, even for drinking purposes.

[1] *Travels of Venetians in Persia*, p. 71 (Hakluyt Soc.).

[2] The average output of pistachios is 120,000 lbs. per annum, with a value of £2500.

As to big game, the leopard frequents the hills, but is rarely seen or shot, and the same may be said of the bear. Wild sheep and ibex have given me many a day's sport, while the gazelle[1] is to be found on every plain. Wolves, hyenas, jackals, foxes, wild cats, the wild ass and the boar are occasionally seen, and red-legged, sand, and black partridge,[2] sand-grouse and pigeons, are the commonest small game. Quails are rare, and so are duck and snipe.

At the present day, as from earliest times in Persia, the province is bestowed on a Governor-General, who makes himself responsible for its revenue; in addition he has to pay the Sháh a *pishkash* or official present, and the ministers also receive "fees." In 1900 the revenue was 315,000 tomans, or £63,000, while the amount collected may have been £90,000, the Sháh's *pishkash* of £10,000, other presents and the Governor-General's own profit being drawn from the balance. Owing to the custom of giving salaries to the descendants of almost every official, or indeed to every *Khán*—one official is said to draw 172 salaries for himself and relations—practically the whole of this sum is spent locally, with the result that the exchequer of the Sháh does not receive its due, His Majesty drawing but little profit from the Crown property.

To preserve order in this desert province[3] there are two regiments of infantry, some four companies of which are always on duty, while the remainder of the force is disbanded. There is also a handful of artillerymen and a few light field-guns. Bam and Narmáshir maintain a regiment, half of which garrisons Baluchistán, and attached to it are a few antique cannon. In addition, there are several levies of foot and horse which generally do police work, and are stationed along the main roads. The soldiers, as a rule, have good physique and are very hardy, but at present they

[1] The Jabal Báriz range separates the habitat of the *Gazella Benetii* from that of the *Gazella fuscifrons* of the plateau of Irán.

[2] The black partridge, *francolinus vulgaris*, is practically confined to the *Garmsír*.

[3] There are eighteen districts in the Kermán province. Commencing from the north, there is Kuhpaia, Rawár, Zarand, and Kubenán. Continuing westwards, Khinamán lies due west of Kermán, and then Rafsinján and Anár, south of which are Páriz and Sirján. Due south of Kermán lies Bardsír, and more towards the coast Akta (with Urzu), Rahbur, Jíruft, and Rudbár (with Bashákird). To the east Bam (with Narmáshir), Ráin, Sárdu, and Khabis. These, with the district round the city, complete the total.

have scarcely advanced beyond the stage of raw material, and are armed with a very obsolete weapon, whereas brigands generally possess sporting Martini rifles.

After this brief description of the province I now propose to discuss its history. Herodotus mentions the Germanii as forming one of the twelve tribes of Persia, while the 14th satrapy of Darius, as he describes it, includes the province of Kermán as it is to-day.[1]

The next full account of Karmania is contained in Strabo's great work:[2] "Karmania . . . is of considerable extent, situated in the interior, and lying between Gedrosia and Persia, but extending more to the north than Gedrosia. This is indicated by its fertility, for it not only produces everything, but the trees are of a large size, excepting, however, the olive; it is also watered by rivers." . . . Again: "Onesikratos states that there is a river in Karmania which brings down gold dust; that there are mines of silver, copper, and red ochre (μίλτος), and that there are two mountains, one of which contains arsenic and the other salt.[3] It includes also a desert tract, which is contiguous to Parthia and Paraetakene. . . . On account of the scarcity of horses, asses are generally made use of even in war;[4] they sacrifice an ass to Ares, who is the only deity worshipped by them, and are a warlike people. No one marries until he has cut off the head of an enemy and presented it to the king. . . . According to Nearchos, most of the customs and the language of the inhabitants of Karmania resemble those of the Persians and Medes."[5]

In the *Sháh Náma*, it is mentioned that when Kei Khusru collected a force to fight against Turán, the kings of Khuzistán and Kermán had the honour of fighting near him in battle. Again, in the same great epic, the scene of the meeting between

[1] *Vide* Rawlinson's *Herodotus*, vol. ii., p. 483.

[2] See also Ptolemy, *Geogr.*, vi. 8, Ammianus Marcellinus, xxiii. 6, 48, and Pomponius Mela, 375.

[3] The report about gold dust is corroborated by Afzal Kermáni, who, writing in A.D. 1188, mentions that "there is a spot in Jíruft called Fadwand, its soil is gold, and gold was formerly seen in its dust." Silver I have never heard of, but copper is still smelted in the Bahr Asman range. About arsenic I know nothing, but salt is extensively mined at Hormuz, and also at a point on the mainland behind Kishm.

[4] This is equally true to-day.

[5] Strabo, xv. 2, 14.

the dying Dara[1] and Alexander the Great is laid in this province, but this is erroneous, as it was a few stages to the east of Rei that Bessus carried out his fell purpose. However, as recounted in chap. xiv., Karmania was traversed from east to west by the mighty Greek, while Krateros also entered it from Sistán, and rejoined his royal master in the Halíl valley. Finally, it was in the same district that the admiral Nearchos reported to Alexander the safety of his fleet.

During the period of what is now termed the Parthian dynasty, I have found no reference to Kermán, but it became famous when, after the conquest of Fárs, it was seized by Ardeshir, the son of Pápak, who finally defeated Artabanus or Ardavan in a desperately contested battle near Ram Hormuz,[2] with the result that, after enduring a foreign yoke for five centuries, a national dynasty was re-established in the house of Sásán, which lasted until the Arab conquest. Ardeshir's exploits are mentioned in chap. xviii.

While the house of Sásán reigned, Kermán, probably owing to its remoteness from the western and northern frontiers, enjoyed a state of general peace, and was selected by Shápur, known as Lord of the Shoulder, as the place of abode of 5000 families of Arabs, whom, following well-known precedents, he transported from Nejd and Bahrein.

Under the illustrious Noshirwán, we gain a glimpse of the prosperity of the province, its governor Ázad Mahán having accumulated enormous wealth. Noshirwán was then engaged in constructing the Gate of Gates,[3] but found his treasury empty. Nothing daunted, he paid a surprise visit to Ázad Mahán, who provided a sum of money sufficient not only to complete the great work, but also to found the city of Astrabád, as narrated in chap. ii.

When the Nestorian sect[4] spread over Persia, Kermán became a see under the metropolitan of Fárs. Indeed, so far was Persia once identified with Christianity, that, in China, churches are referred to in a decree of the Emperor Hiwentsung as "Persian

[1] Darius II. of Greek History.

[2] *Circ.* 218 A.D.

[3] The Báb-ul-Ábáb—the modern Derbent.

[4] Nestorius, patriarch of Constantinople from 428 to 431, was excommunicated for his opposition to the term Θεοτόκος or Mother of God, being applied to the Virgin Mary.

Temples." However, the Sasánian dynasty was effete, and the hapless Yezdijird, ever retreating from the terrible legions of Omar, halted for a while in Kermán, before fleeing to the trackless wilds.

It is mentioned in the *Tárikh-i-Gusida*, that at the time of the Arab invasion the Baluch were implored to come to the rescue, but in vain; and Kermán, like other provinces of Persia, apparently offered little resistance, the stricken field of Nahávand[1] having crushed the national spirit, as indeed it was calculated to do, following on one long series of disasters.

Upon the death of Omar, in A.H. 23 (644), a general rising took place in Persia, but the only result was to rivet the chain of conquest more firmly, at any rate in the case of the less remote provinces, of which Kermán was one. Forts were constructed and Arab colonies planted, especially in the Hot Country, as the Zoroastrians held the highlands, which were too cold for the Arabs. A few years later an entire army was lost in the snow, probably in Sárdu, two men only escaping to tell the tale.

During the reign of Ali, Khárijite[2] risings brought about renewed disturbances, both Fárs and Kermán throwing off their allegiance, until the diplomatic talents of Ziád induced the various rebel chiefs to attack each other.

In A.H. 67-9 (687-8), the Khárijites again overran Kermán, but were dispersed by Musab, brother of Ibn Zobeir, yet, nothing daunted, a few years later a section of them, known as Azrakites, held the province for a year and a half, until internal dissensions brought about their fall. In A.H. 83 (702), Abdur Rahman ibn Áshath was superseded when engaged in a campaign in Afghanistán against the King of Kábul. He promptly rebelled, and, being defeated, fled to the wastes of Kermán, but finally retired even further east, and joined his late enemies. In connection with the operations against him, the notorious Hajjáj-bin-Yusuf despatched a certain Abdulla to visit the province. Upon his return, he reported that it was too poor to feed a large army, and so turbulent, that a small force could not hold it.

[1] Fought in A.H. 21 (642).

[2] The Khárijite or Separatist party had as a creed "No arbitration but that of the Lord alone." They objected to the appointment of umpires to decide between the claims of Ali and of Muávia. Their frequent risings were a terrible scourge to Islam.

At the close of the first century of Mohamedanism, until which date the Zoroastrians were not entirely crushed, a certain Ghinán was appointed to rule Kermán. He governed for seven years, and, during this period, destroyed many fire-temples, and forced thousands to embrace Mohamedanism.

In A.H. 101 (720) Yezid, the son of Mohallab, rose against his namesake, the *Caliph*, and was for a while so successful as to be able to appoint Governors to Fárs, Kermán, and other provinces. Upon his defeat and death, his brothers took ship to the Kermán province, hoping that the Governor of a certain fort, who owed his position to them, would be faithful, but they were put to death, and their families were sold into slavery, which was contrary to Mohamedan custom.

In A.H. 126 (744) Ibn Muávia, great-grandson of Jafar, brother of Ali, claimed the throne upon the succession of Merwan, and his cause was warmly espoused by the unstable Kufans. As usual, they failed to support their choice, and he withdrew across the Tigris. During the next two years, with the support of the Khárijites, he established his court at Istakhr,[1] and was acknowledged throughout Persia. In A.H. 129 (747), the Khárijites having been subdued, he was forced to fly, and, entering into negotiations with Abú Muslim, who had raised the black banner of the house of Abbás, was smothered under a mattress by that unscrupulous agent's orders, his claims being dangerously strong.

His defeat was, however, the last success of the Omeyyad family, and Nahávand was already being besieged by Kahtaba, the famous general of Abu Muslim. The *Caliph's* army, 100,000 strong, was now free on the termination of the campaign against Ibn Muávia, and, advancing from Kermán, where thousands of recruits had been enrolled, received a crushing defeat at the hands of Kahtaba, which was one of a series of overthrows, culminating in the battle of the Záb,[2] whereby the *Caliphate* was secured to the Abbáside branch of the Koreish tribe. The atrocious massacres and excesses perpetrated by Abul Abbás, known as Es-saffa or the Shedder of Blood, almost swept the rival section of the family from the face of the earth, but it also rang the knell of Moslem unity, and the dismemberment of the *Caliphate*. The seed thus sown soon germinated, and at the beginning of the third century of

[1] Or Persepolis.

[2] A.H. 132 (750).

the *Hijra*, Khorasán became, for all practical purposes, independent of Baghdád. To quote Mr Ross, "the falling away of this essentially Persian province was but the first step towards the final separation of the Arabs and the Persians which was shortly to follow, after two hundred years of involuntary and unnatural association."[1]

On more than one occasion the national hero of Persia has started life as a robber, which profession, when carried on openly, is still considered by no means disreputable. Yákub-bin-Lais, known as Saffár, the Arabic for a coppersmith, was emphatically a man of this class, and soon became a leader of armies in Sistán, his birthplace; in A.H. 253 (867) he made himself master of Herát, Kermán, and Fárs.

It is stated by Afzal Kermáni, who quotes from an earlier history, that Yákub was opposed in Jíruft by the Kufij tribe, whose headquarters were in the Kuh-i-Bárjan,[2] but that their chief was seized, thrown into chains, and sent to Bam, where he died. This brilliant career of conquest was only terminated by Yákub's death, after which his brother Amr was altogether unsuccessful, and the only possessions left to the family seem to have been Sistán and Baluchistán, the former for a few generations, the latter for many centuries.

In the meanwhile the house of Sámán, whose founder, a Zoroastrian of Balkh, had become a Mohamedan from gratitude for assistance rendered him by a Governor-General of Khorasán, rose to supreme power in the north. Ismáíl,[3] its greatest member, who embarked on a holy war against the Christians of Central Asia, became ruler of Khorasán and Turkestán, with his capital at Bokhára, which, from that reign onwards, grew to be a great centre of Mohamedan learning.

His descendants were, however, incapable, and Persia being in a state of chronic anarchy, Mohamed, son of Iliás or Eliás, known as Abu Ali, a glorified robber, heard when at Nishapúr in A.H. 315 (928) that Kermán was at the mercy of any adventurer. He crossed the

[1] *Heart of Asia*, p. 102.

[2] It is now termed the Kuh-i-Bárchi, and is a mountain to the west of Sárdu, the summer quarters of the Jíruft nomads.

[3] He died in A.H. 295 (907). Mr E. G. Browne informs me that the Samán dynasty professed descent from Bahrám Chubín, the general who rebelled against Khusru Parvíz.

Lut and seized the province, but the *Muiz-u-Dola*, the most famous member of the rival Deilami dynasty, attacked and captured Sirján. At Kermán,[1] however, Abu Ali adopted the curious plan of fighting by day and sending gifts by night, with the result that the *Muiz-u-Dola* accepted him as his tributary, and continued his triumphant career, which culminated in the capture of Baghdád in A.H. 334 (945), and the blinding of the miserable *Caliph*[2] Mustakfi, the Deilami dynasty ruling until Toghrul Beg entered Baghdád in A.H. 447 (1055).

Abu Ali in his old age was driven out by his son Yási, and returned to Khorasán, the rebel being so proud at having defeated his father that he invaded Fárs. But this led to his ruin, as he was speedily defeated, and Kermán was then actually occupied by the Deilami family. They resisted an invasion by Amr, the great-grandson of Yákub-bin-Lais, who, when he failed, was put to death by his father Khalaf Ibn Ahmad.

This cruel monster, feeling anxious about his position in Baluchistán (Kermán having been placed under the Deilami Governor of Hormuz), desired to seize Kermán, but, as the Sistánis would not support him, he hit on the device of sending one of their leaders on an embassy to the province, where he was poisoned by his master's orders! His subjects, not suspecting Khalaf's treachery, agreed to again invade Kermán, which they took on this occasion, but only held for a short period. Another son, however, growing suspicious of his father, rebelled and defeated him. Khalaf rose to the occasion, and sent a message to the effect that he was dying, and forgave his son, who would, he hoped, visit him, in order to prevent the family treasure being looted. When he unsuspectingly obeyed the summons, Khalaf leaped up

[1] According to Mokaddasi, whose work was brought out in A.H. 375 (985), Kermán was divided into five districts, with one sub-district.

- *a.* Bardsír, pronounced Guwashir locally (with capital of same name). Sub-district Khabis.
- *b.* Narmásyn, with capital of same name (this is evidently Narmáshir).
- *c.* Sirján, with capital of same name: was formerly the capital of the province.
- *d.* Bam.
- *e.* Jíruft.

[2] *Khalifa* is the most correct form of this word, but *Caliph* is more familiar; Longfellow uses the form Kalif.

and stabbed him to the heart! Not long after the brutal murderer's return to Sistán, he was besieged and taken prisoner by Mahmud of Ghazni, who, flattered by being addressed as *Sultán*, spared his life, and made him his Master of Horse.

For some years there is a record of family feuds among the Deilami, Abu Nasr fighting Abu Jafar, the representative of the Hormuz branch. In A.H. 403 (1013) the *Sultán-u-Dola* sent his younger brother, Abul Favăris, to rule Kermán. Having collected troops from Baluchistán he revolted, but being defeated, fled to Mahmud of Ghazni. That monarch helped Abul Faváris to seize both Kermán and Shiráz, whereupon the latter promptly threw off his suzerainty also. Being again defeated by his brother, he fled to Hamadán, but a few years later he was Governor of Kermán under the *Sultán-u-Dola*, until that long-suffering prince died, and was succeeded by the ill-fated Abu Kálinjár.

Abul Faváris again chanced the fortunes of war, and finally died from the hardships, consequent on his march at Shahr-i-Bábek, when he was leading Kermán and Baluch troops against Shiráz for the last of many times. This occurred in A.H. 419 (A.D. 1028). But enough of this uninteresting dynasty, which was soon destined to disappear before the onset of a more vigorous stock.

FROM AN IRÁK CARPET.

CHAPTER V

THE PROVINCE OF KERMÁN—(*continued*)

"Amir Timur, considering the situation, saw that victory could not be with his side, if the sword of valour were not brightened with the polish of good counsel, and he understood that if the arrow of courage were not let fly from the thumb-stall of deliberation, its whistling would not sound to them as news of triumph."—*Tárikh-i-Rashídi*, p. 25.

A MIGHTY wave of conquest rolled across Asia when the Seljuks, a shepherd tribe of Turkestán driven west by scarcity of pasture, captured Merv and Nishápur eight years after the death of Mahmúd of Ghazni.[1] *Malik*[2] Káward, a son of Chakar Beg, hewed out a kingdom for himself in Kermán, which was held by his descendants for a century and a half; and as this period has produced two historians, whose works have not been translated into a European language, I propose to treat it somewhat more fully.

Malik Káward was evidently a man of immense energy, and the first great ruler of Kermán of whom there is any record. He experienced little difficulty in seizing the province, and when Abu Kálinjár came to attack him, he arranged to have him poisoned,

[1] He died in A.H. 421 (1030).
[2] *Malik* signifies a chief. The members of the Saffár dynasty in Baluchistán were all apparently known as *Malik*.

after which he was left in undisputed possession of the Cold Country, and was able to re-organise it. A quaint law of his was that of forbidding lambs to be killed, on the theory that, if allowed to graze, they would become food for twenty men!

The Cold Country then drew its supplies from the Hot Country, which was in the hands of the Kufij and Kufus (the former opponents of Yákub-bin-Lais), who, owing to the weakness of the Deilami, had seized all the country from Jíruft to the sea, and raided into Fárs and Khorasán. Káward, finding that the difficult passes rendered an open attack out of the question, wove an elaborate plot. He expelled with every appearance of ignominy one of his chief officers, who succeeded in entirely gaining the confidence of the simple nomad chief. Finally when a marriage feast was held, Káward, being informed of it, was able to surprise and almost annihilate the tribe after a forced march culminating in a sudden attack.

On hearing that Omán was undefended and full of riches, he ordered the *Amir* of Hormuz to transport his army across the straits, and seized the country without any resistance being offered, its Governor, Shahriár-bin-Táfil, taking refuge in an oven! His hiding-place was discovered, but his life was spared, and he surrendered all his jewels. Omán, until the reign of Arslán Sháh, remained subject to Kermán.

Káward next turned his attention to Sistán, building a fort to close the only road leading to Kermán, and constructing other public works, the ruins of which I saw in 1899.[1] Hearing once when in Jíruft that the price of bread had risen, he rode back to the capital, assembled the bakers, and demanded the reason; as they had no excuse, he baked them alive! He also captured Fárs, but gave it up to his elder brother, Alp Arslán, who besieged him in Kermán. After his brother's death the ambitious Káward contested the throne with *Malik* Sháh, the son of Alp Arslán, and, after a three days' engagement, was defeated and captured. He had a strong party in his nephew's camp, but just as matters came to a crisis he was secretly strangled. This occurred in A.H. 466 (1073).

His son, Kermán Shah, only reigned for a year, dying just as Sultán Sháh, who had been partially blinded, escaped from his

[1] *Vide* chap. xxxv.

cousin and succeeded to the throne. *Malik* Sháh determined to root out the whole family, but, when besieging Kermán, he was induced by pity for the forty daughters of Káward to forego his resolve. Turán Sháh, the builder of the Masjid-i-Malik, succeeded his brother, and died in A.H. 490 (1096), five years after the great *Malik* Sháh and his greater minister *Nizám-ul-Mulk*. His son, Irán Sháh, was such a "monster,"[1] that the *mullás* contrived his death, and it was not until after a search that a member of the Seljuk family was found in the Zoroastrian quarter. This was Arslán Sháh, who, during a prosperous reign of forty years, so improved Kermán that it compared favourably with Khorasán and Irák, caravans from every direction passing through the province, while Fárs was also subdued.

Sultán Sanjar, the head of the family, remarked to his envoy: "I hear that in Kermán there is a district where the narcissus blooms." "True, O King," was the reply, "but there are sharp thorns also." Apparently the hint was taken, as no attack was made on the province. When Arslán Sháh grew old and feeble, his son *Malik* Mohamed seized the throne, and after killing or blinding his relations, ruled very justly, and encouraged education by granting scholarships for a certain standard of proficiency. He founded many colleges and mosques, and the *caravanserai* he built at Sarbizan is still in use, although in rather a dilapidated condition.

Tabas became a district of Kermán, which was now at the zenith of its prosperity, and Isfahán was also to have been handed over, but its Governor died just before the final arrangements were concluded. This occurred a year previous to the death of the ill-starred Sultán Sanjar,[2] whose glorious capital of Merv was sacked by the hitherto insignificant Ghazz, a tribe which, a few years later, was destined to convert Kermán into a desert.

Toghrul Sháh succeeded his father, but upon his death, his four sons[3] reduced the province to a condition of anarchy, during which Komádin, Marco Polo's "Camadi," was sacked for the first time. So terrible was the state of affairs that a Kermán wit wrote that every ear of corn brought a new pennon, and death became the one punishment for all offences.

[1] Probably this only signified that he favoured the Ismáíli heresy.

[2] He died broken-hearted in A.H. 552 (1157).

[3] *Malik* Arslán, Turán Sháh, Bahrám Sháh, and Turkán Sháh.

To add to the general misery, a few years later Sultán Sháh, brother of Tekish, overthrew the last of the great Seljuks, and expelled the Ghazz from Sarakhs, 5000 families travelling to Kermán, and a similar number to Fárs. At first they pretended that they wished to serve the king, but finding him weak, they marched to Bághin, then some thirty miles[1] to the west of Kermán, where they defeated the force sent against them, after which they raided Jíruft, killing, harrying, and destroying. This district having been swept clean, they proceeded to Narmáshir, where they tortured the wretched inhabitants, by pouring hot ashes down their throats. This mixture was grimly termed "Ghazz coffee," the *modus operandi* being to fill the throat with the ashes and then ram them down with a stick! This was no short-lived invention, as the following lines written in memory of a victim done to death by the Mongols shows: "Among Mohamed's followers there has not been a more highly gifted man than Mohamed Yahya, killed by dust."

Turán Sháh was finally murdered, and his son Mohamed succeeded him, but Kermán was practically deserted, and as the chronicler writes, only hope was left. *Malik* Dinár of the Ghazz tribe arrived from Khorasán at this juncture,[2] and finally seized the whole province, but not without much difficulty, owing to the strength of the capital.

Following wise advice, he then proceeded to Hormuz, where the Governor paid him a large sum and gave him a stud of horses. Not content with this, he accepted presents from the Governor of Keis, at that time also a great emporium, and recently visited by Benjamin of Tudela (1160 to 1173 A.D.), who wrote: "The traders of Mesopotamia, Yemen, and Persia import all sorts of silk and purple cloths, flax, cotton, hemp, mash (a kind of pea), etc., and the inhabitants of the island live by what they gain in the capacity of brokers to both parties."[3]

The Governor of Keis, a most deluded man, hoped to oust the Governor of Hormuz, but *Malik* Dinár only wished for money from both parties, and having acquired all he could, returned to the capital, escaping a plot of the faithless Ghazz, who tried to waylay

[1] Ancient Bághin was on the site of the modern Robát, between the modern Bághin and Kabútar Khán.

[2] In A.H. 581 (1185).

[3] *Itinerary of Rabbi Benjamin of Tudela*, p. 137.

him. Upon his death, in A.H. 591 (1195), anarchy again desolated this hapless province, Ferrukh Sháh, who only reigned for a year, squandering his father's treasure. An appeal was made to the Court of Khiva, but for various reasons it was not responded to, and Kermán tasted the dregs of misery at the hands of the Ghazz.

A new power now appeared on the scene, in the shape of the Ik or Shabankára, whose headquarters were near Daráb, and who were so powerful that Soncara[1] is mentioned by Marco Polo not long afterwards as one of the divisions of Persia. Led by two chiefs, who were brothers, the newcomers crushed the Ghazz and occupied the capital amid universal joy. However, owing to anxiety about their property in Fárs, they left but a small force to garrison the province, and the *Amir* of Hormuz, the Ghazz and the "Kuj and Baluch" formed a confederacy against the Ik, but received a crushing defeat in the district of Mazraán, somewhere near the coast.

Peace being thus established, the Ik ruler, *Nizám-u-Din*, began to tyrannise, and, as the chronicler writes, "even levied a poll-tax on Zoroastrians and Jews." A rising ensued which brought back Ajam Sháh, a son of *Malik* Dinár, who captured *Nizám-u-Din*, but could not seize the forts. The Ghazz, who were his allies for the nonce, insisted that the only way to gain possession of the forts, which were practically impregnable, was to dishearten the defenders by killing *Nizám-u-Din*. Ajam Sháh, however, counted the cost, and having substituted a man who had a striking likeness to his prisoner, executed him in public, but at night. A few days later Ik envoys arrived, who were prepared to treat on the condition that *Nizám-u-Din* should be released and the garrisons withdrawn with the honours of war. The prisoner was thereupon produced from a well, and the Ik now disappear from the Kermán stage as a power. Their example was almost immediately followed by the Ghazz, as an army from Fárs, sent by Sadi's patron, *Atábeg* Sad-bin-Zangi, finally crushed this accursed tribe, which never again raised its head; it is now said to be represented by the Ráis, a nomad tribe of no importance.

Kermán, however, still had no rest, the Ik raiding and the Ghazz stealing, until an army came from Khiva, which destroyed what little was left, and its leader, *Razi-u-Din*, finally captured the city.

[1] An obvious corruption of Shabankára.

He ruled for a few years, and was succeeded by his son, *Malik Shujá-u-Din* of Zuzan, who apparently might have founded a new dynasty but for events happening elsewhere that brought about his fall.

The irruption of Mongol tribes under the mighty Chengiz Khán has perhaps produced a more baneful effect on the history of the world than any other conquest for, if Bismarck was able to say that Germany had not recovered from the Thirty Years' War, it is yet more probable that Central Asia, Persia, and Russia are still suffering from the Tatár cataclysm, which, in many cases, included the annihilation of the inhabitants. For instance, Herát and Nishápur were stormed, and the entire population massacred, while, in the case of the former city, a body of troops was despatched two years later to glean up any inhabitants who had escaped, and the miserable total of forty was added to the number of victims murdered.

Kermán was fortunately saved from these horrors, thanks again, in part, to its remoteness, but at the same time its history was closely affected by the changes on the chessboard of Central Asia, albeit in a somewhat indirect fashion.

A certain Borák *Hájib*,[1] an official of the Kara Khitei *Gúr Khán*,[2] was sent to collect tribute from the Court of Khiva, to which he finally transferred his services, and, upon the approach of the Mongol terror, he was despatched on an embassy to India to fetch *Jalál-u-Din*, son of Sultán Mohamed, the last Khwárizm[3] Sháh. Passing through the province of Kermán, he was treacherously attacked by *Shujá-u-Din*, who, knowing that he had only a small party, hoped to seize his treasure and women. However, his calculations failed, as the ladies all fought, and, by their aid, *Shujá-u-Din* was captured and promptly put to death.

Borák felt that it would be tempting Providence not to occupy a province without a master, and thereupon decided to abandon his journey and become ruler of Kermán. When *Jalál-u-Din* finally marched from India *via* Makrán, he was treated somewhat cavalierly, and later on his younger brother, *Ghiás-u-Din*, was strangled by

[1] *Hájib* at that time signified Chief Guardian; nowadays, a *farráshbáshi* or chief carpet-spreader would be its equivalent.

[2] *Gúr Khán* means Universal Lord.

[3] Khwárizm is the ancient name for Khiva.

the disloyal servant, who despatched his head as a gift to Chengiz Khán. For this service he received the title of *Kutluk Sultán*, and was formally invested with the Governorship, which he enjoyed until his death in A.H. 632 (1234).

His son-in-law and cousin, *Sultán Kutb-u-Din*, who was married to Turkán Khátun, ruled for a year, but Ogotei Kaán[1] finally appointed *Rukn-u-Din*, Borák's son, who remained in power for fifteen years; he was then handed over by Mangku Kaán to the tender mercies of his brother-in-law, who killed him, and again became Governor of Kermán. *Kutb-u-Din* finally died from the effects of a wound inflicted by an ibex on the Jupár range in A.H. 656 (1258), the same year that the *Caliph* Mostasim Billa was done to death by Huláku Khán, this great historic event being described by Longfellow in the following stirring lines:

> "I said to the Kalif: Thou art old;
> Thou hast no need of so much gold.
> Thou should'st not have heaped and hidden it here
> Till the breath of Battle was hot and near,
> But have sown through the land these useless hoards,
> To spring into shining blades of swords,
> And keep thine honour sweet and clear.
>
> . . . .
>
> "Then into his dungeon I locked the drone,
> And left him there to feed all alone
> In the honey-cells of his golden hive:
> Never a prayer nor a cry nor a groan
> Was heard from those massive walls of stone,
> Nor again was the Kalif seen alive."

Kutb-u-Din's widow succeeded him, and under her rule villages were founded, two of which, Sar Asiáb and Chátrud, are still flourishing, while *kanáts* were dug in every direction: in fact, I have seen *kanát* pipes stamped with her name in more than one part of the province. She occupied the throne when Marco Polo passed through on his outward journey, and died about A.H. 681 (1282), being heart-broken by the news that her son, Surkatmush *Jalál-u-Din*, had been appointed to Kermán.

In A.H. 690 (1291) he was dismissed, and succeeded by his sister

[1] Kaán is used in the sense of Great Khán or Khán of Kháns.

Pádsháh Khátun, wife of Kei Khátu, whose nephew married the Lady Kokachin. The nephew in question was the son of Arghun Khán, who despatched ambassadors to his kinsman, the *Kaán*, Kublei, to ask for a princess in marriage. It is also of great interest to note that it was he who sent embassies to the Pope and the kings of France and England. Edward I., in 1290, accredited Geoffrey de Langley to the Mongol, whom he presented with "some gerfalcons and other jewels of our land." Upon the death of Arghun Khán, in A.H. 690 (1291), Kei Khátu seized the throne, which he, however, only held for a few years, when his uncle succeeded him, but was speedily defeated in A.H. 695 (1295), by Gházán Khán, who continued his intercourse with the sovereigns of Europe, and was a great ruler. Pádsháh Khátun was capable, and, among her other accomplishments, was a poetess, but family affection was not her strong point, for she strangled her brother. However, his blood cried for vengeance, and his widow and sister brought about a rising, Pádsháh Khátun in her turn being duly strangled and laid to rest in the Kuba-i-Sabz in A.H. 694 (1294).

She was succeeded by her nephew, Mohamed Sháh, *Musaffar-u-Din*, who was little else but a drunkard. He died in A.H. 702 (1302), and *Sháh Jahán*, son of Surkatmush, ruled until the death of Gházán Khán,[1] when he foolishly ceased to pay the tribute of 600,000 dinárs, or 300,000 napoleons,[2] to his successor, Mohamed Khuda Banda, who summoned him to Sultánia. There, although forgiven, he was not sent back to Kermán, and was, in consequence, the last ruler of the Kara Khitei family.

It is interesting to note that during this period Hormuz was under Kermán, as is shown by Marco Polo: "And when the Melic[3] of Hormos, who is Melic of Calatu[4] also, and is vassal to the Soldan of Kermán, fears anything at the hand of the latter, he gets on board his ships, and comes from Hormos to Calatu. And then he prevents any ship from entering the Gulf."[5] It was probably owing to this state of affairs that Hormuz was transferred, a few years later, to the island of Jerun. To

[1] In A.H. 703 (1303).

[2] Compare this with the £50,000 now paid as revenue.

[3] *Melic* is a corruption of *Malik*.

[4] Calatu is Kalhat, the chief port of Omán, which has now been superseded by Maskat.

[5] Yule's *Marco Polo*, vol. ii. p. 448.

resume, in A.H. 707 (1307), a certain *Amir Násir-u-Din* Mohamed-bin-Burhán was appointed to Kermán, and was succeeded by his son, Nikruz, who ruled in a somewhat precarious fashion until A.H. 741 (1340),[1] when *Mobáriz-u-Din* Mohamed Muzaffar of Meibud, now Meibut, near Yezd, who was married to Kotluk Turkán, Sháh Jahán's only daughter, raided and seized Kermán, thus founding the Muzaffar dynasty. After constant fighting and intriguing to hold his own, he became extremely powerful, capturing Shiráz in A.H. 755 (1354). Isfahán and Tabríz also fell into his power, but when it appeared to be at its zenith, his sons conspired against him and blinded him. He lingered for a few years, finally dying in A.H. 765 (1363).

His son, Sháh Shujá, succeeded him, Kermán being temporarily bestowed on his uncle, *Imád-u-Din*, Sultán Ahmad, who founded the Pá Minár mosque, which is still standing at Kermán, and it is his name which is carved on the great stone pulpit I saw at the Kala-i-Sang of Sirján.[2] In A.H. 769 (1367), Sháh Shujá proceeded to Bam and thence to Jíruft, in order to take vengeance on the Jermán and Afghán troops,[3] who sought refuge in the Manuján fort, but submitted after the plundering of their flocks and other property. Sháh Shujá having quarrelled with his brother, Dolat Sháh and *Malik* Mohamed were appointed to Kermán, where they imprisoned his son, Sháh Shiblí, and transferred their allegiance to Sháh Mohamed. *Sultán* Oweis, a second son, was despatched against Kermán, but accepted presents, and returned without accomplishing anything; Sháh Shujá thereupon proceeded in person against the rebels, and, defeating them at Deh Shuturán, a few miles to the south of Shahr-i-Bábek, regained possession of the province, leaving his sons as governors of the capital and Sirján. In fact, until the death of Sháh Shujá in A.H. 786 (1384), the *Imád-u-Dín* was only occasionally in power, being superseded for a while by a certain Asad *Pahlawán*,[4] who rebelled, but was eventually assassinated.

[1] Nikruz, with the help of the Governor of Herát, recovered Kermán after this date, but only temporarily.

[2] *Vide* chap. xxxvi.

[3] These soldiers had been originally sent at the request of *Sultán Jalál-u-Din* of the Kara Khitei dynasty, and had been a thorn in the side of most subsequent rulers. *Vide* p. 48.

[4] *Pahlawán* signifies a professional wrestler.

The star of Tímúr "The Lame," had already risen on the horizon, and, commencing from A.H. 782 (1380), his armies overran Persia. The Muzaffar dynasty at first submitted to his rule, but finally rebelled, and Sháh Mansúr, a son of Sháh Shujá, having attacked the victorious warrior and nearly killed him, it was deemed politic to extirpate the Muzaffar family: this execution took place in A.H. 796 (1393), *Imád-u-Din* being sent for to Meiár. Perhaps the chief claim of the Muzaffar dynasty to fame is, that it is celebrated by the immortal Háfiz, who flourished under its patronage.

Kermán was bestowed on *Amir* Adugui, nephew of *Amir* Jargui, Barlás,[1] who died in A.H. 806 (1403), a year before the mighty Tímúr. His son, *Sultán* Oweis, who succeeded him, took advantage of the struggle for the succession to the world-wide empire to cease paying tribute. However, he was attacked and twice defeated by *Mírza* Abubekr, a grandson of Tímúr, who held the eastern division of the province, until finally slain in Jíruft in A.H. 811 (1408). Thirteen years later, Sháh Rúkh, after seizing Azerbaiján, marched to Kermán. He was met in Sirján by *Sultán* Oweis, whom he determined to flay alive, but a *Seiid* interceded, so he changed his sentence to one of imprisonment at Herát. Tímúr's great son then proceeded to Kermán, where he was visited by the famous *Sháh* Namat Ulla of Mahún.[2]

In A.H. 845 (1442), Abdur Razzák, having been sent by Sháh Rúkh on an embassy to the Samuri, passed through Kermán on his way to India, and met *Amir* Borhán-u-Din, *Sháh* Khalil Ulla, son of the saint who had died in A.H. 834 (1430). The ambassador mentions that the Governor was Kaiaschirin, which is possibly *Ghiás-u-Din*; the native chronicler only speaks of a certain Baiis Sangar as ruling in A.H. 855 (1451).

It was about this time that Jahán Sháh, son of Kara Yusuf, and the most famous member of the Kara Koinlu or Black Sheep dynasty of Turkoman, overran Irák, and seizing Isfahán, ordered a massacre. He sent his son Abul Kásim to Kermán, which capitulated without resistance, and so firmly was his rule established, that he was able to join his father, who finally captured

[1] This was the Great Conqueror's own tribe.
[2] *Sháh* is here used as a spiritual title.

Herát. However, his day of reckoning was at hand, for he in his turn was defeated and slain by Hassan Beg, Baiendari of the Ak-koinlu or White Sheep dynasty, who also killed Abu Seiid, the last sovereign of the house of Tímúr.

Meanwhile, *Amir* Abul Kásim had returned to Kermán and ruled there until his father's death, when he quarrelled with his brother and was murdered by him, during the progress of peace negotiations! Kermán was then bestowed on the son of the victorious Uzún Hasan, who was, however, in A.H. 874 (1469) ordered to Khorasán, and the following year, at the request of its chiefs, the Káin province was added to Kermán.

In A.H. 878 (1473) Kermán was united to Fárs under the rule of Sháh Khalíl, his brother, this arrangement holding good until A.H. 882 (1477), when Sháh Khalíl succeeded to the throne, and Alvand Beg, son of Rustam Beg, was appointed to Fárs and Kermán. He apparently held the post until A.H. 906 (1500), when he made peace with his brother Sultán Murád, who was given Irák, Fárs, and Kermán.

It was during this period that Athanasius Nikitín of Twer (A.D. 1468-74) passed through Yezd and Sirján on his way to Hormuz; and it should also be noted that Hasan Beg is the Ussun Cassano, *i.e.* Uzún or "Long" Hasan, who married Despina, daughter of Calo Johannes, one of the last of the Comneni Emperors of Trebizond. Persuaded by Caterino Zeno, a nephew of Despina and ambassador from Venice, which state was viewing the advance of the Turkish hosts with dismay, in A.H. 877 (1472), he invaded Asia Minor, but was finally defeated by Sultán Mohamed II., and wisely declined a second campaign, although strongly urged to undertake it by his European allies. After his death a few years later, family rivalries speedily ruined the Ak-koinlu, and made the way easy for the rise of a national dynasty.

Sheikh Heider, who married a daughter of Uzún Hasan and Despina, failed and paid the death penalty, but his son Sháh Ismáíl succeeded, and founded the great Sefavi dynasty. After conquering Fárs, he sent a small force of cavalry to take Kermán, which offered no resistance. In A.H. 915 (1509) the Uzbegs raided the province, crossing the desert from Káin, but they were finally

[1] Cf. Uzún Ada.

beaten off. In A.H. 916 (1510) Sheibáni Khán, their chief, was defeated and killed by Sháh Ismáíl at a battle near Merv.

Kermán, being remote from the western and northern frontiers, once again had no history, and I will merely give a list of its rulers, so far as the chronicler records them.[1]

In A.H. 1005 (1596) Ganj Ali Khán, Zík, the second great ruler of Kermán, reached the capital, and at once began to improve the province, building numerous *caravanserais*, *bázárs*, and tanks: one of the latter was so large that its fittings furnished 1800 lbs. of lead to Lutf Ali Khán, nearly two hundred years later, while a square still bears his name. In addition to this, a Kermán contingent assisted Sháh Abbás in all his wars, especially distinguishing itself at the capture of Shimakhi, which was the famous port on the Caspian, where Jenkinson landed; Baluchistán also was successfully invaded. In A.H. 1031 (1621) Ganj Ali Khán was appointed to the Governorship of Kandahár, where he died. He was succeeded by his son Ali Mardán, who however upon the accession of Sháh Safi, resenting the death of his brother-in-law, *Mírza* Talik Khán, the Prime Minister, proceeded to Agra, to the Court of Sháh Jahán.

Again nothing of interest occurs,[2] the Kermán contingent, as usual, fighting away from home, and being cut up at Baghdád. However, the general immunity which the province had enjoyed was soon destined to be rudely disturbed, when the despised Afgháns killed their ruler, a Georgian, and having learned the weak condi-

[1] Khán Mohamed governed Kermán until A.H. 920 (1514). Ahmad Sultán, Sufi, Oghalán, was Governor at the beginning of the reign of Sháh Tahmásp.

About A.H. 933 (1526) Sháh Kuli Sultán, Afshár, was appointed Governor, and led a contingent which took part in the capture of Kuchán. He was succeeded by Sadr-u-Din Khán, Sefavi, who ruled through a deputy: in A.H. 975 (1567) the Kermán contingent took part in the Gilán campaign.

In A.H. 985 (1577) Sultán Mahmud was appointed Governor.

In A.H. 996 (1587) Baktash Khán, son of Vali Khán, ruled Kermán as his father's deputy.

[2] The Governors are—

A.H. 1035 (1625) Tahmásp Kuli Khán.
A.H. 1038 (1628) Amír Khán, Keeper of the Seal.
A.H. 1046 (1636) Jáni Khán, Shámlu.
A.H. 1052 (1642) Murtazá Kuli Khán.
A.H. 1077 (1666) *Gurchibáshi* of the Sháh.
A.H. 1105 (1693) Mohamed Ali Khán, *Gurchibáshi*.

Gurchibáshi signifies chief scout.

tion of Persia, invaded it by way of Narmáshir. After ravaging the district, their leader Mahmud found Kermán too strong to be stormed, and while he was besieging it, an army from Fárs came to the rescue, but was defeated, mainly owing to the drunken condition of the soldiers, who did not expect an attack at Bághin.[1] Hearing of trouble at Kandahár, Mahmud returned home, but in A.H. 1133 (1720) again invaded the province, and this time the city of Kermán capitulated, though the fort was not captured. Using it as a base, the following year he marched on Isfahán; he defeated the Persian troops near Gulnábád, a stage on the Yezd road, and finally seized the capital, murdering hundreds of thousands of its cowardly inhabitants.

A deliverer finally arose in the person of Nádir Kuli, a robber chief, who practically exterminated the invaders, their Baluch allies taking care to murder all refugees, in order to obtain possession of their effects. In A.H. 1148 (1735), when Nádir Sháh invaded Afghánistán, Imám Verdi Beg accompanied him with a Kermán detachment, in which, according to the Zoroastrians, their co-religionists were represented. In A.H. 1160 (1747) the last great Asiatic conqueror, who was now more or less insane, visited Kermán, and, after humorously remarking that the Governor Kuli Beg had grown fat, ordered him to be pulled through a hole in the wall, the unhappy man's head being screwed off during the operation! He also strangled the mayor, *Ághá* Fath Ali, and seven hundred citizens, whose skulls he built up into a pillar.

Upon the murder of Nádir Sháh in A.H. 1160 (1747), anarchy again ensued, during which it appears that the Afgháns raided Kermán and destroyed the Zoroastrian quarter, imperfectly protected as it was by a half-built wall, which Nádir Sháh had allowed to be constructed as a recognition of their valour at Kandahár.[2]

Seizing his opportunity, Sháhrukh Khán, Afshár, obtained possession of Kermán, beat off an invasion by Sistánis and Baluchis, and in his turn raided Sistán, where he was mollified by

[1] According to Malcolm's *History of Persia* (vol. i. p. 416), Lutf Ali Khán, brother of Fath Ali Khán the Grand Vizier, defeated the Afgháns, who fled back home.

[2] The local historian writes that this quarter was destroyed during the first Afghán raid in Sefavi times, but the Zoroastrians are positive as to the truth of the version given above.

presents of money and feathers. The times were, however, unsettled, as shortly after Kermán was invaded by Násir Khán of Tárum; but he too was finally repulsed.

By A.H. 1172 (1758) Kerim Khán, Zand, had beaten off Mohamed Hasan, Kájár, and being free to consolidate his power, sent a force under Khudá Murád Khán to attack Kermán. Sháhrukh Khán was killed, and his conqueror ruled the province for four years, when he too was put to death under circumstances which throw an interesting light on the internal administration.

A certain Takí Derráni, a noted shot of Kuhpaia, brought in a moufflon as a present to the Governor, hoping for a present. Not only was he disappointed in this, but the servants seized his gun until he should give them something. Next morning he appealed to the Governor, but only received a beating for his pains; accordingly he returned home, collected three hundred of his friends, and seized the city, murdering Murád Khán. Hearing of this, Kerim Khán sent Mohamed Amin, Garrús and an Afshár chief to expel him. The latter deserted and returned to Shiráz, where he was duly "sticked," but the former, aided by the citizens, expelled Takí, who was finally killed.

During the reign of Kerim Khán, *Seiid* Abul Hasan, Mahallati, the descendant of the chief of the Assassins, was Governor of Kermán for some years, and built the house which was afterwards used as the Consulate, but upon the death of the great *Vakil*, Kermán, for the last time it is to be hoped, acquired a melancholy fame, at the price of the number of beggars who throng its *básárs* to-day.

Kerim Khán's relatives were generally as cruel as he himself was kindly in disposition, but in A.H. 1204 (1789) Lutf Ali Khán succeeded to the throne, and created a reputation for heroism which has never since been equalled in Persia. According to the native chronicler, he had invaded the province in A.H. 1196 (1781), but owing to lack of supplies was forced to abandon the enterprise. A few years later, when betrayed by *Háji* Ibráhim and in difficulties, he was invited to Kermán by *Mullá* Abdulla, the *Imám Juma*.[1] The city thus became the scene of the last act of the struggle for power, which resulted in seating the Kájár dynasty on the throne;

[1] The *Imám Juma* is the official *mullá* who prays for the Sháh's health in each city.

indeed Kermán was by no means entirely in favour of Lutf Ali Khán, Murtaza Kuli Khán of Zarand, a partisan of Ághá Mohamed, having been appointed Governor by the latter in A.H. 1208 (1793).

The Kájár Eunuch marched towards his prey by Shahr-i-Bábek and Máshiz, and constructed a fortified camp, which is still standing some three miles to the west of the city. At first Lutf Ali Khán fought in the open, but he was finally besieged, and his position becoming desperate, he threw a plank across the ditch, and escaped to Bam. There he was betrayed by his host, who ham-strung his horse as he was mounting. This scene, which would form a grand theme for a painter, terminated the career of the hero, who, after being blinded, was finally put to death. Kermán suffered horrors from which it will not recover for at least another century, 20,000 women and children being sold into slavery, while 70,000 eyes were counted by the brutal conqueror, who, turning to his minister, said: "Had one been wanting, yours would have been taken."

Fath Ali Khán, the heir of Ághá Mohamed, expelled the Afgháns from Khabis and Narmáshir, Fahraj being their last stronghold in the latter district, and for many years Kermán lay practically desolate, with a population of blind men, its Governor being Mohamed Takí. In A.H. 1216 (1801), it was blessed with yet another great Governor in the shape of Ibráhim Khán, *Záhir-u-Dola*, a member of the Kájár tribe,[1] who during the next twenty-four years, restored some measure of prosperity to the war-worn province, not only rebuilding the town mainly to the west of its original site, but also digging *kanáts* and founding villages. Upon his death in A.H. 1240 (1824) his son Abbás Kuli *Mírza* collected a force to attack Yezd, but was deserted by his soldiers at Shims, and fled to Mazanderán. Kermán was then given to Hasan Ali *Mírza*, *Shuja-u-Sultana*, brother of Husein Ali *Mírza*, Governor-General of Fárs, and remained in his family for some years. A few years later Abbás *Mírza*, the heir-apparent of Fath Ali Sháh, marched from Kashán to Yezd and Kermán, both of which cities seem to have been in rebellion, but to have speedily submitted.

In A.H. 1255 (1839) Ághá Khán, grandson of *Seiid* Abul Hasan, was appointed Governor of Kermán, but almost immedi-

[1] His daughter was the mother of H.I.M. Muzaffar-u-Din.

ately revolted and seized Bam. Firuz *Mírza* started to besiege this formidable fortress, but, probably from lack of supplies, no defence was attempted, Ághá Khán flying to Tehrán, where he was pardoned. Retiring to his family estates at Mahallát to the west of Kashán, under pretence of a pilgrimage he collected a large force, and in A.H. 1256 (1840) again started for Kermán. He hoodwinked the Governor of Yezd by producing forged letters, and when the latter was undeceived and pursued him, it was only to suffer defeat near Shahr-i-Bábek, where Ághá Khán was re-inforced by the Khorasáni and Ata Illáhi nomads. In spite of this Fazl Ali Khán, the Governor of Kermán, a Karabághi, attacked and expelled Ághá Khán, who retired to Lár and Bandar Abbás, where he spent the winter.

In the spring he again advanced on Kermán and fortified a position at Máshiz, hoping that his party would rise. However, it failed him, and being surrounded by Persian troops, he again marched to Bam, which he held for nearly a year; but on breaking out, he was overtaken and defeated at Rigán in the Narmáshir district. He then fled across Baluchistán to Kandahár, whence he proceeded to Sind; shortly afterwards his brother, Abul Hasan Khán, known as the *Sardár*, invaded Baluchistán from Karachi, as mentioned in chap. ix.

Three Governors of no note succeeded Fazl Ali Khán,[1] and in A.H. 1276 (1859) Mohamed Ismáíl Khán, Núri, came to Kermán as the minister of Keiúmars *Mírza*. The following year he became Governor with the title of *Vakil-ul-Mulk*, and although he only lived for nine years, he did so much for the province as to earn the right of being considered one of its great rulers, almost every *caravanserai* now in repair, the *bázárs* of Kermán, and many villages being constructed by him.

Sistán was also visited by the *Vakil-ul-Mulk*, who, indeed, died from the effects of a summer spent there. He was succeeded by *Háji* Husein Khán, father of the present *Ásaf-u-Dola*, who, after being Governor for a short period, was replaced by Murtaza Kuli Khán, the second *Vakil-ul-Mulk*, who, according to the native chronicler, had the honour of seizing Kuhak![2]

[1] Tahmásp *Mírza*, Governor A.H. 1262-68 (1845-51).
Mohamed Hasan Ali, *Sardár*, Eriváni, 1268-72 (1851-55).
Gholám Husein Khán, Sipahdár, 1272-76 (1855-59).

[2] *Vide* chap. xix.

After an equally wise government of nine years, he was dismissed, and *Háji* Gholám Riza Khán, now the *Ásaf-u-Dola*, ruled for a short period, being replaced by Firuz *Mírza*, who a year later, was succeeded by his son, Sultán Hamid *Mírza*. This prince governed for eleven years and died in A.H. 1309 (1891), leaving behind him the reputation of having been a great sportsman. His brother, Abdul Husein *Mírza*, *Farmán Farmá*, was then appointed to the post, but was dismissed in A.H. 1312 (1894), and the octogenarian, Sáhib Diván, a grandson of the notorious *Háji* Ibráhim, held the post for about a year. The *Farmán Farmá* was then re-appointed and remained in office for some months after the Sháh's murder in May 1896.

The *Ásaf-u-Dola* was then again sent to Kermán, being succeeded in the spring of A.H. 1317 (1899) by the nonagenarian Hasan Ali Khán, Garrus, *Amir Nizám*. In 1317 (January, 1900) he died, and was, after some months' delay, succeeded by Zein-ul-Abidin Khán, *Hissam-ul-Mulk*, a nobleman of Hamadán, and one of the wealthiest men in Persia. The present ruler of Kermán is *Mírza* Mahmud Khán, *Ala-ul-Mulk*, who, from the fact that he has held the post of Ambassador at Constantinople, must feel that Kermán is somewhat out of the world.

FROM LUSTRED POTTERY.

CHAPTER VI

FROM KERMÁN TO BUSHIRE

"They say the Lion and the Lizard keep
The Courts where Jamshýd gloried and drank deep:
And Bahrám, that great Hunter—the wild Ass
Stamps o'er his Head, but cannot break his Sleep."
—FITZGERALD'S *Omar Khayyám*.

BESIDES what I have been able to glean anent the history of the province, I am devoting a separate chapter to the city of Kermán, which I explored very imperfectly during my first visit. After resting for nearly a week, during which period I visited the lions, I attempted to engage fresh mules; but as the caravans are almost entirely composed of camels or donkeys in South-east Persia, there were few mules to be had, and I was obliged to resign myself to the unsatisfactory Turkoman, who, so far as he could, made my life a burden.

From Kermán, one road appeared on the map as running to Shiráz and a second to Yezd, but, as I was anxious to visit Persepolis, I was delighted to see the map full of blanks in that direction, which I determined to fill in to the best of my ability.

Leaving a small garden which I had rented in the Zoroastrian quarter, the first stage was to Bághin, which was shown on the old maps of Persia, on both the Yezd and also the Shiráz road! It is a prosperous village, with a house in a pleasant garden. Thence, quitting the Tehrán road, we struck south-west, entering a broad belt of hills covered with rhubarb, in which we found a filthy little *caravanserai*, known as Khán-i-Kuh. Just below it the direct route from Kermán *via* Kheirabád joined in, which had been explored by Captain Gill in 1880, and was traversed by myself in 1900. It is not generally known that Professor Palmer's companion was also a Persian traveller, but, as a matter of fact, his explorations in the "Land of the Lion and the Sun" were most extensive. At the *caravanserai* I met a mild-looking old gentleman, who informed me that he was the General of the Kermán regiment, and on his way home. He had quitted the *Farmán Farmá* at Sirján after several months' pursuit of Husein Khán, Bahárlu.[1]

Our mules having passed us, we followed them across the hills, which are very rugged, there being two passes, known as the Gudár-i-Dukhtar, both of which have an elevation of 7200 feet above the sea. On the western side the hills gradually opened out, and we emerged on to the fertile plain of Bardsír,[2] which is watered by the Lalazár River. A mile short of Máshiz are extensive ruins of the ancient town,[3] among which is a shrine known as Pir-i-Jásus or the Old Spy, referring to a servant of Ali. The building is octagonal and domed, but is rapidly falling into decay. Inside, the walls

[1] This very powerful chief rose not against the Sháh, but against the Governor-General of Fárs, and finally gained the day, his enemy being dismissed from office.

[2] The district of Bardsír abounds in nomads, as follows :—

Kotlu	650	families
Surkhi Arab Khán . .	250	,,
Noshádi	250	,,
Badúi	250	,,
Badúi Háji Káka . .	200	,,
Ghurabba	100	,,
Sia Jul	80	,,
Sar-i-Gudári . . .	20	,,
Pusht-i-Gudári . . .	10	,,
Izája	7	,,
Yúnusi	10	,,
Yakúbi	10	,,
Askar Sirjáni . . .	20	,,
Ghiási	10	,,
Háfizi	20	,,
Zulala	20	,,
Carry forward	1907	

Brought forward	1907	families
Mazzang	50	,,
Baluch	300	,,
Pusht Kuhi	80	,,
Komachái	10	,,
Ahmad Nazzari . . .	20	,,
Mastafái	10	,,
Badavi Kuh-i-Panj . .	100	,,
Gudri	60	,,
Afshár Amui . . .	250	,,
Afshár Mir Habíbi . .	25	,,
Ilághi	50	,,
Luri of Kuh-i-Panj . .	200	,,
Masúmi of Kuh-i-Panj . .	100	,,
Sheikh Kuh Sufídi . .	70	,,
Total	3232	families

[3] This must have been the town which was once held by the Azrakites.

have a conventional Kufic pattern, while the dome shows remains of stencil. The style of the decoration resembles that of the Vukt-i-Sáat at Yezd, but the oldest tomb, which was evidently not contemporary with the original structure, only dates back some three hundred years.

Máshiz, a village of perhaps a thousand inhabitants, is the capital of Bardsír, and the headquarters of the Kermán regiment, much of the property being owned by the Government. In the centre is a modern fort in ruins; it was seized by Ághá Khán, and apparently destroyed after his retreat to India. The name of Mashish, which appears on all maps, is erroneous.

I was anxious to make for Páriz, but no guide being procurable, we kept to the main Sirján road as far as a tributary of the Lalazár River, which we forded, camping at Tajabád. About half-way across the fertile level plain, we crossed the main route from Bahramabád to Bandar Abbás, along which we heard that there was a great export of cotton in the winter.

Leaving Tajabád we marched for ten miles across a plain, and thence rose into the hills, said to abound in copper, which are crossed by a pass known as Mazár at an elevation of 8200 feet. This was my first experience of the high rolling uplands of Southern Persia, which are never hot, and are inhabited by nomads for the few summer months. In this particular section we found Arabs, whose *patois* none of the party could understand, and, having no guide, and there being no main road to follow, we travelled more or less by the compass.

The next surprise was to see a fine river running north and termed the Givi Dur, which further down joins the Lalazár River, and where we crossed it, divides Bardsír from Páriz. As there were no supplies to be had, we continued the march always due west, and late at night, after crossing yet another watershed, stopped at a little hamlet, all tired out and hungry. We were, however, but four miles from Gaud Ahmar or Red Hollow, so termed from the pink colour of the soil. In the vicinity are turquoise mines, some of which are close to the Páriz road, and others twenty miles to the north of Shahr-i-Bábek, but the pits dug in the hillside have been filled up by silt. It would appear that the industry was by no means a paying one, the quality of the stones being poor.

After a few hours' rest at Gaud Ahmar, we marched south along

NOMADS OF ARAB EXTRACTION.

[*To face p.* 74.

the skirt of the lofty Mamsár range, which was covered with snow; two passes, or rather high spurs, one of which rose to 8600 feet, had to be crossed, and late at night we reached Páriz,[1] where a small house was obtained for our party.

Páriz lies at an elevation of 7550 feet, and is surrounded by a mass of gardens. With a population of perhaps 3000 inhabitants, and being the capital of a small district, it would be prosperous were it not one of the first points struck by Fárs raiders. Apparently this game has been carried on from time immemorial, the local authorities not uniting to crush it, and in 1900 *chapau* is still as profitable an occupation as ever, though to put an end to it would require a very small amount of combination.

The following morning our muleteers deserted, saying that the district ahead was full of robbers. We secured the mules, and Yusuf interviewed the Governor, who finally forced the men to return to duty. They were, however, a whole day making up their mind to continue the journey.

At nightfall there was a thundering at the door of the house, which proved to be a message from the Governor-General, who wrote that he had only just heard of my being at Páriz, which he had quitted early in the morning, and that he was staying for a couple of days at Gaud Ahmar, where he hoped that I would visit him. At first I was somewhat loath to retrace my footsteps, but thinking that it would be discourteous not to accept the invitation, I ordered my mules to follow, and rode back to Gaud Ahmar, where all was now life and bustle. Passing through the camp, I was ushered into a large tent, where I was greeted in French by His Highness the *Farmán Farmá*. I was first of all put through a full examination as to my status, which struck me as curious, but Persians are so often taken in, that precautions are necessary. At the same time, I was made to feel thoroughly at home, His Highness's doctor, *Mirza* Mahmud Khán, having spent many years in Europe.

[1] The nomads of Páriz consist of the following tribes:—

Luri	200 families.
Arab Háji Huseini	200 ,,
Rudkhána Feriduni	10 ,,
Badui	60 ,,
Laku	10? ,,
Total	480 families.

presents of money and feathers. The times were, however, unsettled, as shortly after Kermán was invaded by Násir Khán of Tárum; but he too was finally repulsed.

By A.H. 1172 (1758) Kerim Khán, Zand, had beaten off Mohamed Hasan, Kájár, and being free to consolidate his power, sent a force under Khudá Murád Khán to attack Kermán. Sháhrukh Khán was killed, and his conqueror ruled the province for four years, when he too was put to death under circumstances which throw an interesting light on the internal administration.

A certain Takí Derráni, a noted shot of Kuhpaia, brought in a moufflon as a present to the Governor, hoping for a present. Not only was he disappointed in this, but the servants seized his gun until he should give them something. Next morning he appealed to the Governor, but only received a beating for his pains; accordingly he returned home, collected three hundred of his friends, and seized the city, murdering Murád Khán. Hearing of this, Kerim Khán sent Mohamed Amin, Garrús and an Afshár chief to expel him. The latter deserted and returned to Shiráz, where he was duly "sticked," but the former, aided by the citizens, expelled Takí, who was finally killed.

During the reign of Kerim Khán, *Seiid* Abul Hasan, Mahallati, the descendant of the chief of the Assassins, was Governor of Kermán for some years, and built the house which was afterwards used as the Consulate, but upon the death of the great *Vakil*, Kermán, for the last time it is to be hoped, acquired a melancholy fame, at the price of the number of beggars who throng its *básárs* to-day.

Kerim Khán's relatives were generally as cruel as he himself was kindly in disposition, but in A.H. 1204 (1789) Lutf Ali Khán succeeded to the throne, and created a reputation for heroism which has never since been equalled in Persia. According to the native chronicler, he had invaded the province in A.H. 1196 (1781), but owing to lack of supplies was forced to abandon the enterprise. A few years later, when betrayed by *Háji* Ibráhim and in difficulties, he was invited to Kermán by *Mullá* Abdulla, the *Imám Juma*.[1] The city thus became the scene of the last act of the struggle for power, which resulted in seating the Kájár dynasty on the throne;

[1] The *Imám Juma* is the official *mullá* who prays for the Sháh's health in each city.

indeed Kermán was by no means entirely in favour of Lutf Ali Khán, Murtaza Kuli Khán of Zarand, a partisan of Ághá Mohamed, having been appointed Governor by the latter in A.H. 1208 (1793).

The Kájár Eunuch marched towards his prey by Shahr-i-Bábek and Máshiz, and constructed a fortified camp, which is still standing some three miles to the west of the city. At first Lutf Ali Khán fought in the open, but he was finally besieged, and his position becoming desperate, he threw a plank across the ditch, and escaped to Bam. There he was betrayed by his host, who ham-strung his horse as he was mounting. This scene, which would form a grand theme for a painter, terminated the career of the hero, who, after being blinded, was finally put to death. Kermán suffered horrors from which it will not recover for at least another century, 20,000 women and children being sold into slavery, while 70,000 eyes were counted by the brutal conqueror, who, turning to his minister, said: "Had one been wanting, yours would have been taken."

Fath Ali Khán, the heir of Ághá Mohamed, expelled the Afgháns from Khabis and Narmáshir, Fahraj being their last stronghold in the latter district, and for many years Kermán lay practically desolate, with a population of blind men, its Governor being Mohamed Takí. In A.H. 1216 (1801), it was blessed with yet another great Governor in the shape of Ibráhim Khán, *Záhir-u-Dola*, a member of the Kájár tribe,[1] who during the next twenty-four years, restored some measure of prosperity to the war-worn province, not only rebuilding the town mainly to the west of its original site, but also digging *kanáts* and founding villages. Upon his death in A.H. 1240 (1824) his son Abbás Kuli *Mírza* collected a force to attack Yezd, but was deserted by his soldiers at Shims, and fled to Mazanderán. Kermán was then given to Hasan Ali *Mírza*, *Shuja-u-Sultana*, brother of Husein Ali *Mírza*, Governor-General of Fárs, and remained in his family for some years. A few years later Abbás *Mírza*, the heir-apparent of Fath Ali Sháh, marched from Kashán to Yezd and Kermán, both of which cities seem to have been in rebellion, but to have speedily submitted.

In A.H. 1255 (1839) Ághá Khán, grandson of *Seiid* Abul Hasan, was appointed Governor of Kermán, but almost immedi-

[1] His daughter was the mother of H.I.M. Muzaffar-u-Din.

I heard about some ancient copper mines to the south, and on visiting them, found that they consisted of a tunnel run into the cliff side, and appeared very extensive; the name given was Gohar,[1] perhaps a corruption of *Gabr* or Infidel, from the title generally given by the Persians to the men of yore. Everywhere we had heard that brigands were about, but hitherto we had escaped their attentions, mainly owing to the rate at which we marched. Upon leaving the copper mines, however, we saw a band of seven horsemen, who rode for the next three days about half a mile off us.

At Mazián we struck the river which flows to Marvás, the chief town to the north of Arávirjun; it was a large village, but its inhabitants said that they were sure to be robbed if they left home. Next morning we again sighted the same band, and as I felt rather anxious, I determined to march as far and as fast as possible, hoping thereby to get off their beat. Both my gun and my rifle were useless, the stocks being broken, but we carried them ostentatiously, and this no doubt saved us. At night I pitched my tent, but watched some distance from it, hoping thereby to surprise any raiders.

We appeared to be passing across very high country, which sloped down south to Arsinján. This is described as a hot country, and I much regretted not being able to devote more time to exploration, but under the circumstances it would have been inadvisable. In the late evening we reached the village of Bágh-i-Siá, situated on the bank of a river draining south, and were glad to hear that we were only a stage from the main road.

Again the next day our seven companions appeared, but only once, and with the growing openness of the country, we felt that their power for harm had ceased. A steep descent brought us into the fertile plain of the Polvár, where we crossed two of its tributaries, and were delighted to strike the main road and the British telegraph line at Mashad-i-Murgháb.

Hastening on towards Shiráz, I met a line inspector on tour, Mr Jefferies, who informed me that there was a riot taking place in the capital of Fárs. Accordingly, with very brief visits to the stupendous monuments of Persepolis, which I fortunately was able to examine carefully five years later, marched rapidly on, and being warned to avoid the town, proceeded to the beautiful

[1] *Gohar* also means a pearl or jewel, so this may be its origin.

THE SHIRÁZ ROAD—PASS OF THE DAUGHTER.

[*To face p.* 80.

Telegraph Garden, where I was most hospitably received by Dr Scully, the entertainer of almost every European traveller in Persia.

Matters were distinctly interesting, as the Shirázis were taking sanctuary in the British Telegraph Office—they had forcibly closed their own—and were clamouring for the dismissal of the *Kawám-ul-Mulk*, the hereditary mayor. This, however, was not acceded to, the Sháh telegraphing to the Governor-General that he expected him to keep order. The people ultimately lost faith in the British, and began to utter threats; and all the staff were glad to leave the town office, their lives being undoubtedly in danger. Rumours were impending of an attack on the garden, which lies about a thousand yards from the city walls, and the whole night we listened to the dull roar of the mob.

At sunrise firing began, and by the aid of field-glasses we saw the *Kawám-ul-Mulk* and his servants ride out of the city gate, firing on all sides. A party of Bahárlu tribesmen came to his support, and we watched the skirmish, in which two or three men were wounded. One unfortunate, who had been hit, and had fallen off his horse when riding behind the *Kawám-ul-Mulk* out of the town, was hacked to bits. In the afternoon a telegram came, ordering the Kawám to Tehrán, and he started with the pleasant wish of the Shirázis, that he should meet the fate of his great-grandfather, *Háji* Ibráhim, who had been boiled[1] to death by Fath Ali Sháh.

Turning night into day, I rode down to Bushire in five days, and just caught the mail, on board which I thoroughly enjoyed a rest, with the satisfactory feeling that I had ridden some 1300 miles across Persia, without loss of health or unpleasant experiences.

[1] In this connection, I heard a good story of a member of the family who insulted a Frenchman and called him "son of a burnt father," the most usual term of abuse, to which the ready repartee was, "son of a *boiled* father!"

FROM A LUSTRED TILE.

CHAPTER VII

THE PERSIAN GULF

"Soon as the sun shone forth from the height of heaven,
The heart of stone grew hot beneath its orb;
The bodies of the fishes, at the bottom of the fish-ponds,
Burned like the silk which is exposed to the fire;
Both the water and the air gave out so burning a heat,
That the fish went away to seek refuge in the fire.
In the plains the chase became a matter of perfect ease,
For the desert was filled with roasted gazelles."—ABDUR RAZZÁK.

IN the present chapter I propose to give some account of the Persian Gulf, up and down which I have steamed many times, having also enjoyed the opportunity of visiting some of the ports which are not touched at by the mail steamers.

The Persian Gulf, known in common with the Indian Ocean and the Red Sea as Erythrean by the ancients, is one of the most interesting bodies of water in the world from the historic point of view, and perhaps in the near future the eyes of Europe may be directed to it as forming the shortest route to the East. Although constituting a waterway between the ancient civilisations of the world, yet few coasts are more forbidding, and even nowadays sailors always complain that there is either too much or too little wind in "the Gulf," as it is termed. Serrated ranges running parallel to the coast, an absence of sheltered harbours, sunken reefs and dangerous currents, added to the storms so prevalent, must have constituted terrible dangers to mariners attempting voyages, and the inhospitable shores have ever been the abode of a low class of Ichthyophagi, who would have had no mercy on a shipwrecked crew. On the other hand, the climate is never cold, while the extreme heat, which is so trying to Europeans, is agreeable to the native of its shores; and heat was undoubtedly favourable to civilisation at its inception, as the inhabitants of harsh climates were almost compelled to be hunters to keep themselves clothed, and consequently remained longer in a savage state.

Chaldaea, according to the tradition preserved by Berosus, was civilised by a creature half man and half fish, which came from the Erythrean Sea and taught men the arts of life. Its name was Oannes, no doubt derived from the name of the Chaldaean god of the primeval waters, Ea. This legend undoubtedly points to some higher race arriving by sea, but further than this the mists have not been rolled away.

There is, perhaps, no recorded expedition by sea so ancient as that of Sargon I. of Chaldaea, who navigated the Mediterranean about B.C. 3800. His son Naramsin[1] led an army against Magan,[2] which may be identified with the mainland opposite the Bahrein Islands. It is here, indeed, that, in my opinion, excavations should be made, which might possibly establish records of still earlier voyages. For instance, we learn that in the third millennium B.C. timber and diorite were procured for a priest king of Lagash (Shirpurla) in Shumer, from Magan and Melukhkha, Nituk[3] and Gubi, and this points to an established trade.

The oldest legends of the Phoenicians place the cradle of the race in the marshes on either side of the Tigris and Euphrates, or in the Bahrein Islands, the largest of which, Tylos and Arados, bore names that were still more famous on the Mediterranean as Tyre and Arvad. It was, indeed, only on account of violent earthquakes that this interesting race migrated across Syria to the Mediterranean Sea—at least, that was their own belief.

[1] *The Dawn of Civilisation*, by Prof. Maspero, p. 600.

[2] *Ibid.*, p. 564, note 3.

[3] *R. A. S. Journal*, April 1898, p. 241 *et seqq.*, *The Early Commerce of Babylon with India*, by J. Kennedy. Nituk is considered to be Bahrein.

But the known history of navigation in the Persian Gulf hardly begins before the end of the eighth century B.C., when Sennacherib crushed the refugees who had fled to the islands in the Gulf by means of ships built by Phoenicians and Cypriote Greeks, whom he brought across from the Mediterranean Sea. On the Taylor cylinder the campaign is described as follows: "The remnant of the men of Bit-Yakin . . . took all the gods of the country and crossed the Great Sea of the Sunrising, and took up their abode in Elam. On ships of Hatti-land I traversed the sea. . . ."[1]

The story of Sennacherib then informs us that navigation was known in the Persian Gulf at least as early as the eighth century B.C., and it is unlikely that it was ever entirely suspended, as the land routes lay across the deserts of Central Asia, ever the haunt of predatory tribes, which routes are not, even in the twentieth century, opened up to commerce.

We next come to the period when Babylon was at her zenith, and trade was so flourishing that peacocks and rice were known even in distant Athens at the time of Sophocles and Aristophanes, and that by their Tamil names.[2] Under Persian rule Babylon declined, and with her fall direct intercourse with India may have gradually ceased; thus when Nearchos appeared on the scene in 326 B.C., he practically re-discovered what was already a very ancient trade route. I cannot dwell on his famous voyage from the mouth of the Indus to the Kárun, although I shall incidentally refer to it, and as Persia throughout the period of her history never was a sea-faring nation, we come to the times when, in the fifth century after Christ, Chinese ships were seen in the Euphrates.[3] This adventurous commerce is first mentioned by Masudi in the following passage: "The principal branch of the Euphrates ran past Hira. . . . To this port arrived ships from China and from India."[4] The Chinese annals of the Thang dynasty of the seventh and eighth centuries describe in detail the course followed by the junks.

[1] *Light from the East*, by C. J. Ball, p. 197.

[2] Ταώς and ὄρυζα are words of Indian origin. Cf. Kennedy in *R. A. S. Journal*, *loc. cit.*

Vide Yule's *Cathay and the Way Thither*, vol i. p. lxxvii. In the ninth century the Chinese only came up the Persian Gulf as far as Siráf, the modern Táhiri, and later on Hormuz was their furthest point west.

[4] *Les Praires d'Or*, vol. i. p. 216.

This extraordinary activity was eclipsed by the teeming prosperity of the Arabs in the ninth century, when the trade from the East, enriching Basra or Balsora[1] and Baghdád, gilded Asia with those imperishable legends which are embodied in the "Thousand and one Nights," and are responsible for Milton's "gorgeous East."[2] It was from Balsora that Sinbad set forth on his adventurous voyages which quaintly portray the ideas of the period when the world was but little known, and even to-day the lovely palm-groves and romantic creeks that render Basra an Eastern Venice retain a glamour of departed glory; and the same high-pooped *baggala* in which Sinbad and his companions launched forth upon the deep can be counted by scores in the Shat-el-Arab.

When misgovernment began to close the Basra route, the great caravan road *via* Tabríz to Bandar Abbás took its place. Hormuz, at first situated on the Mináb river, and, when the mainland became unsafe, transferred to the island of Jerun, became the emporium of the East, until perhaps one of the greatest events in history occurred—the arrival of European ships in Eastern waters.

Although it is impossible to doubt the ultimate benefit that has been derived from the opening of this great trade route, which perhaps saved Europe from Asiatic domination by a final severance of the two arteries of the world's commerce *via* the Persian Gulf and the Red Sea, yet it is hard not to feel hurt that our representatives first appeared as pirates, far surpassing in their methods the general cruelty of the times. The behaviour of Albuquerque in the Persian Gulf was atrocious, and it is difficult to read how he mutilated his prisoners "for the glory of God" without a deep sense of humiliation. For more than a hundred years the Portuguese, by holding Hormuz, kept their hands on the throat of Eastern trade, occasionally cruising up the Red Sea, until, at the beginning of the seventeenth century, the English appear on the scene.

The recently published diary of Sir Thomas Roe,[3] our first ambassador to India, is, I would venture to suggest, of immense historical value, as showing our actual position in those days. A most salient feature appears to be the smallness of the trade, the

[1] Balsora was the corruption of the Arab Basra.
[2] Cf. *Paradise Lost*, book ii.
[3] Edited by W. Foster, under the auspices of the Hakluyt Soc.

whole of India not being able to furnish more than four or five cargoes a year. It was on this account that a ship, the *James*, was sent to Jásk to try and open up trade with Persia;[1] but even so there were difficulties, not only on account of the Portuguese, but also because Sháh Abbás wanted little else than cash[2]—although he never refused presents—and in those days, to take bullion out of England was considered to be almost criminal.

In 1620 there were two sea-fights off Jásk, the first being indecisive; but in the second the Portuguese were defeated, and the English factory, which appears to have been founded in 1619, was saved from destruction. Two years later, in 1622, in alliance with Persia's great Sháh, Hormuz was taken, and the Portuguese power received a blow from which it never recovered.

From this date until to-day British trade and influence, although fluctuating, has been on the increase, and our responsibilities have been faced with a determination that has been unsurpassed in any quarter of the globe.

At the beginning of the nineteenth century, the Jowasmi pirates were strong enough to take H.M.S. *Minerva* after two days' fighting, and every sailor was put to the sword. This affront was only wiped out by some desperate engagements, which forced the truculent Arabs to abstain from sea-fighting and piracy. Since the middle of the century the *pax Britannica* has been maintained, although not without a heavy outlay. In the Bahrein group alone has this peace been broken in recent times, namely in 1895, when *Sheikh* Jásim attempted to invade these islands from Zobára on the opposite coast. However, the punishment meted out to him was short and sharp, forty-four of his ships being destroyed by H.M.S. *Sphinx* and *Pigeon*, and an even larger number towed off to Bahrein.

[1] Cf. Sir Thomas Roe, p. 330: "That the war with the Turks having blocked commercial intercourse with Europe, there must be in Persia at once a dearth of cloth and a plethora of silk; that it was absolutely necessary to find some vent for the large stock of English goods in their warehouse, for which no immediate sale could be hoped in India."

[2] *Ibid.*, p. 353: "And obserue one thing well: The parts of Persia that vent cloth, which in Steele's judgement will not exceed 500 a yeare—a small matter—and the rest wilbe expected to be supplyed in mony, are the same that produce the silke and are nearest Turky, as Gordgestan and Gilan; and to those parts cloth can be brought cheaper by Aleppo then by Jasques."

MASKAT.

[*To face p.* 86.

At the present time the Persian Gulf is crowded with British shipping, Hindustani is the prevalent language at most of the ports, and peace prevails everywhere. It must, however, be remembered that were the British gunboats to quit this land-locked sea, piracy would immediately be re-established; and, as an Arab naïvely remarked to me, the loot would now be ten times as valuable as it was a generation ago.

I now return to my journey. Before we left Bushire, Colonel (now Sir Adelbert) Talbot, the Resident, the importance of whose post has been demonstrated by Lord Curzon, came on board bound for Maskat. After a smooth run we touched at Linga, the prettiest port in the Gulf, with its fringe of palms, behind which rises a scarped mountain. Its trade, which is considerable, is mainly a transit business, goods for the Pirate Coast being distributed from this centre. The roads to the interior are most difficult, and the value of Linga as a port suffers considerably from this fact. An interesting stroll may always be taken along the shore, where large *baggala* are built with timber imported from Africa.

Until a few years previously, Linga was governed by a Jowasmi *Sheikh*, but the Persian Government imprisoned him and appointed one of their own officials. While I was at Shiráz in 1898, *Sheikh* Mohamed, the son of the dispossessed chief who had died, seized the port, and there was the greatest difficulty in ousting him. As usual, a local chief did the work, and the storm passed over.

Continuing down the Gulf, we touched at Bandar Abbás, which is described in chap. xxvi., and in considerable heat steamed into the black, rocky harbour of Maskat, at the back of which the rugged ranges are so close together that there is no road of any description into the interior, except from the commercial port of Mattra a few miles to the north. All communication with Mattra, indeed, must be carried on by water, there being but a difficult foot-track across the great spurs. Passing a black rock, the playground of the British tar, the eye is first caught by the grim old forts built by the Portuguese, one of which was completed in the year of the Spanish Armada. Its

[1] *Ancient Trading Centres of the Persian Gulf*, by Captain Stiffe, *Journal R. G. S.*, vol. x. p. 612.

failure indirectly hastened the downfall of Portugal, 1650 A.D. being the date of their final expulsion.

The population huddled inside the narrow strip occupied by the town, and occupying reed huts outside, may, perhaps, aggregate 8000, but no census has ever been taken to my knowledge.

The Sultán's family, at one time, ruled over Omán and distant Zanzibár, but by an arrangement made in 1861, the northern and southern states were divided, and the British Government now pays the Sultán some 7000 rupees a month in connection with this partition.

As a political appointment Maskat is so detested that orders to take up the post are said to be occasionally answered by an application for leave. During my eight years' connection with Persia there have been almost as many Consuls. The post, however, is not without importance, and the interior is but little known. The climate, on the other hand, is terrible, and all the heat absorbed by the rocks during the day is given out at night; moreover the fine Consulate has no garden, and riding is almost impossible. French and American Consular representatives now both fly their flags at Maskat, and in 1898 there was much excitement about the concession of a coaling-station to France.

Leaving Maskat, where even a day on board ship makes the thoughtful realise Rudyard Kipling's conception of "the white man's burden," we steamed across to the squalid port of Gwádur, and a day's run brought us to Karachi, which seemed delightfully cool after Maskat. The luxuries of the Sind Club too were highly appreciated, after six months of the roughest fare.

. lmiral Scylax descended the Indus, and,
. . . ., explored the shores of Gedrosia and
. n took place about 512 B.C., and, in a
. of Alexander the Great, who, however, was
: of the fact that Greeks had already sailed
. indeed they had done so.

Great's day Makrán was known as the country
as regards the sea coast, while the hinter-
. . drosia.[2] To deal with the word Makrán, we
authority of Sir Thomas Holdich[3] that it is
the two Persian words *Máhi* and *Khurán*,
. act equivalent of Ichthyophagi. However, the
. , much older, and I would offer the following
. riologists apparently differ as to whether Magan
peninsula or the coast of Arabia behind Bahrein,
Omán, but, in any case, there is the Maka of the
which term is reproduced in the Mykians or
Herodotus. Now Makrán was particularly notable
. ves and morasses, the country being similar to the
:, which is known as the Ran of Kach, this word being
: *aranya* or *irina*, signifying a waste or swamp. Is
. possible that in *Maka irina* (signifying the waste
we have at last traced the origin of this much-
. d? In Sind the modern pronunciation is *Makarán*;
. tly the expression which the above two words might
. ed to form.

. ally speaking, Makrán consists of the district stretching
. as far as the watershed of the first important range of
. l thus includes a strip of country averaging some sixty
. , width. For twenty miles from the coast, there is a
plain traversed by several rivers, and often covered with
. . k. Most of the rivers, except after rain, only run above
. l in parts, and then flow underground, which has the
. . tage of saving immense loss by evaporation. This district
. d be less poverty-stricken than it is, as the soil is good and

Cf Maspero's *The Passing of the Empires*, p. 694. *Vide* also page 167.
[2] Cf. Arrian, vi. 28, 5.
[3] *Vide* his *Notes on Ancient and Mediaeval Makrán*, *Journal R. G. S.*,
. . . l 1896, p. 387 *et seqq*. (vol. vii.)

at Bushire, we first touched at Gwádur. There, among other items of news, we heard that Major Muir's[1] would-be murderer, Sháh Dád, whose movements we were to report, was living at a little hamlet on the frontier, and that the Rinds of Mand, a nest of robbers to the north, were much annoyed by slaves escaping to Gwádur, which, as it was a possession of the Sultán of Maskat, secured their liberation.

The following morning, in beautifully calm weather, we steamed into the wide bay of Chahbár, which Captain Grier pronounced to be the safest and most accessible on the coast. It is sheltered from the south-west monsoon by the mainland of Omán, on which side, too, the *Ras* Kuhláb[2] runs out, while to the south-east there is a natural breakwater in the shape of a long reef. But with a width of seven and a half miles at the entrance, and a depth of twelve miles, the anchorage is only comparatively safe.

By means of slings we transferred our horses without much difficulty to a large native craft which Mr Lovell, the clerk in charge, had kindly ordered for us, but when we approached the shore the problem arose how to get them over its high sides into the sea, the *baggala* not being able to get within some 200 yards of the shore. My companion was in his element, and while I went on shore to make arrangements, he had all our grain shifted to one side, which not only heeled over the *baggala*, but formed a ramp, up which the unwilling horses were driven overboard, and they finally swam ashore in safety. Our *impedimenta* were carried up to the substantial Telegraph Office, which must serve as an excellent object lesson to the neighbouring Baluchis.

Before describing our journey I propose to give some account of the province we had just entered. Baluchistán is the generally accepted nomenclature of a huge but thinly-peopled country, divided between the British and Persian Governments. This desert province roughly corresponds to the 17th satrapy of Darius as mentioned by Herodotus.[3] The Great King invaded the Hapta Hindu or the Panjáb, probably by the Baluchistán route, while a

[1] *Vide* chap. xxvi.

[2] *Ras* is Arabic for cape; its primary meaning is head.

[3] Cf. Rawlinson's *Herodotus*, vol. ii. p. 485. "The Parikanians and Ethiopians of Asia furnished a tribute of four hundred talents. This was the 17th satrapy." I am inclined to believe that the Mykians or Maka in the 14th satrapy inhabited Western Makrán.

fleet under his Greek admiral Scylax descended the Indus, and, undismayed by the tides, explored the shores of Gedrosia and Arabia.[1] This expedition took place about 512 B.C., and, in a sense, lessens the glory of Alexander the Great, who, however, was probably quite ignorant of the fact that Greeks had already sailed the Erythrean Sea, if indeed they had done so.

In Alexander the Great's day Makrán was known as the country of the Ichthyophagi as regards the sea coast, while the hinterland was termed Gedrosia.[2] To deal with the word Makrán, we have the weighty authority of Sir Thomas Holdich[3] that it is a contraction of the two Persian words *Máhi* and *Khurán*, which are the exact equivalent of Ichthyophagi. However, the word is, I believe, much older, and I would offer the following suggestion. Assyriologists apparently differ as to whether Magan is the Sinaitic peninsula or the coast of Arabia behind Bahrein, and including Omán, but, in any case, there is the Maka of the inscriptions, which term is reproduced in the Mykians or Mekians of Herodotus. Now Makrán was particularly notable for its mangroves and morasses, the country being similar to the adjacent coast, which is known as the Ran of Kach, this word being the Sanscrit *aranya* or *irina*, signifying a waste or swamp. Is it not then possible that in *Maka irina* (signifying the waste of *Maka*) we have at last traced the origin of this much-debated word? In Sind the modern pronunciation is *Makarán;* this is exactly the expression which the above two words might be expected to form.

Physically speaking, Makrán consists of the district stretching inland, as far as the watershed of the first important range of hills, and thus includes a strip of country averaging some sixty miles in width. For twenty miles from the coast, there is a sandy plain traversed by several rivers, and often covered with tamarisk. Most of the rivers, except after rain, only run above ground in parts, and then flow underground, which has the advantage of saving immense loss by evaporation. This district should be less poverty-stricken than it is, as the soil is good and

[1] Cf. Maspero's *The Passing of the Empires*, p. 694. *Vide* also page 167.

[2] Cf. Arrian, vi. 28, 5.

[3] *Vide* his *Notes on Ancient and Mediaeval Makrán*, *Journal R. G. S.*, April 1896, p. 387 *et seqq.* (vol. vii.)

the water supply fair, while there is excellent camel-grazing. Behind this is a belt of low, rounded clay hills,[1] which, in their turn, are succeeded by rugged limestone ranges, whose crests form the watershed of Makrán.

This scenery is so exquisitely described by Sir Thomas Holdich, that I make no apology for quoting from his important work: "A dead monotony of laminated clay backbones, serrated like that of a whale's vertebræ, sticking out from the smoother outlines of mud ridges, which slope down on either hand to where a little edging of sticky salt betokens that there is a drainage line when there is water to trickle along it; and a little faded decoration of neutral-tinted tamarisk, shadowing the yellow stalks of last year's forgotten grass, along its banks—such was the sylvan aspect of a scene which we had before us only too often."[2]

The northern slopes of the limestone range drain into the Bampur and Mashkid rivers, neither of which reach the sea, although, until our journey set the question finally at rest, it was thought that the Bampur river might possibly discharge its waters into the Fánoch river, known as the Rapsh in its lower reaches. To the north, in its western section, the Lut runs down to the Bampur river, while east of the Fahraj plain the regular north-west trend of the Persian mountain chains gives place to the equally regular east-and-west lie of the ranges, which is so noticeable a feature throughout all Southern Baluchistán, and partly accounts for its backward condition, access from the coast being so difficult. Further north again lies the district of Sarhad, where two parallel ranges running north-west divide this upland country from the Lut on the west, and the equally low-lying desert of Khárán on the east.

In Sarhad, there is the remarkable Kuh-i-Taftán or Chehel Tan, running up to nearly 13,000 feet, with a partially active volcano some 200 miles from the coast; but in Eocene times the sea flowed over the whole of this country, and there are still legends connected with the Lut, of which an apposite example is mentioned

[1] Dr Blandford writes: "Along the sea-coast (sc. of Makrán) . . . a newer series of rocks rests upon the nummulitics. It is easily recognised by the presence of thick beds of hardened clay or marl; it is of great thickness, and abounds in fossils. . . . The exact age has not been ascertained." Sir F. Goldsmid's *Eastern Persia*, ii. p. 452.

[2] *The Indian Borderland*, p. 319.

CLAY FORMATION, MAKRÁN.

[*To face p.* 92.

1

by Sir Frederic Goldsmid, to the effect that the prophet Yúnus or Jonah was cast up at Yúnsi, some three stages to the south of Turbat, and hid for many days under a gourd. Again, further east, on the Herát road, is the village of Langar, signifying an anchor and so a port and, according to M. Khanikoff, there is an ancient tradition that Langar was a harbour on the great inland sea. Although legends are, as a rule, far from trustworthy, yet, in the two instances given, it is hard to understand how they came into existence, unless there had been an inland sea at some not very remote period.

The central belt of Persian Baluchistán is extremely hilly, but possesses a fair water supply which is little used, and also an almost unlimited extent of scanty grazing, while the Bampur river is quite capable of supporting a large population at the cost of a trifling outlay in irrigation works.

Sarhad,[1] until a few years ago a nest of robbers, and now but little better, possesses great potentialities, with high-lying plains running up to Taftán and Safid Kuh, which latter is also an elevated range. Yet the whole of this district has scarcely any population, although the few *kanáts* which have been dug have proved to be a great success, and there are many traces of ancient cultivation. However, the opening of the Quetta-Sistán road is slowly but surely having its effect, as we can no longer be indifferent to raids, and the Persian authorities are taking steps to put an end to what is now little more than a nuisance, although, until quite recently, Baluchis murdered nearly every one they captured, no slave-market being open to them. In exceptional cases, when captives were enslaved, they were mutilated in order to lessen their desire of returning to their homes.

Further east in what is now known as British Baluchistán, the northern portion of the province which runs up almost to the Helmand is a desert. Separating it from Sind is the great range, or rather mountainous belt, which forms the north-west boundary of India, and extends from the extreme north of the Panjáb to Cape Monze, near Karachi. Nor does it end there, for it curves away westward in long narrow parallel valleys, such as that of the Rakshán, up which we marched to Quetta in 1896. As, however, British Baluchistán will be referred to in a

[1] *Sarhad* implies frontier and also Cold Country.

later chapter, for the present the above brief description must suffice.

As to the origin of the Baluchis we possess no definite knowledge, as they have no ancient literature, are very ignorant, and pride themselves as much on this ignorance as any mediæval baron. Sir Henry Pottinger assigns them to a Turkoman origin, but, according to Professor Rawlinson, Baluch[1] is derived from Belus, King of Babylon, who is identified with the Nimrod, the son of Cush, of Holy Writ. These two names are reproduced in Baluch and Kuch, referred to later on in this book, and indicate the origin of the nomenclature of the Kech or Kej valley and perhaps also of Kach. Throughout the Sásánian period Baluchistán was known as Kussun, which may be a form of Cush.

The *Sháh Náma* of Firdusi distinctly mentions the Baluchis as a tribe occupying Gilán during the reign of Noshirwán, and apparently they migrated to Baluchistán *via* Sistán. They are, in all probability, an Aryan race, and if we accept this, together with an immigration of Arabs flying from persecution on the death of Husein[2]—Aleppo is constantly referred to in their ballads—we can, in my opinion, fairly account for the Baluchis, whose chiefs all claim an Arab ancestry, and are apparently members of a different race from the peasantry, as is, I believe, the case among the Lushai tribes. This theory is, to a certain extent, supported by the fact that the Bráhuis only rose to power in the seventeenth century, when they descended from the mountains under Kambar to aid the last Hindu *rája*, whose kingdom they usurped.

My knowledge of the languages spoken is small, but I understand that the Bráhui tongue is akin to Tamil, a Dravidian language, and is not related to Persian, whereas the Baluchi language belongs to the Iránian branch of the Aryan family. This is a very important point. Again the Bráhuis are short,

[1] Balus is the Arabic, and Baluj is old Persian. Vide *Ancient Monarchies*, vol. i. p. 61 *et seqq.*

[2] Cf. the Baluchi song :—

"When Yezid fought with the *Imáms* an angel said,
'The liver of the Prophet has been rent in twain,'
And so on all sides they now exclaimed,
'The head of Husein has been struck off and cleft asunder.'"

HINGOL RIVER, MAKRÂN.

[*To face p.* 94.

thick-set, and round-faced; the Baluchis, on the contrary, are tall and slender, with decidedly long faces.

To summarise, the Bráhuis are apparently Dravidian aborigines, and the Baluchis are of mixed Persian and Arab origin—the latter brought no women—and we also know that there is a medley of tribes which have settled in Baluchistán, some of them in historic times. Finally, Istakhri mentions that the Makránis resembled Arabs. One point of considerable importance to note is that there are thousands of Baluchis outside Baluchistán, their habitat indeed extending to the new frontier province of India.

Mr Longworth Dames has translated many of their fables and ballads, and I append an extract from one of the latter, which relates to the quarrel of the famous *Mir* Chákar and Gwaharám: "The bold Rinds came to Bampur, to Kech and fertile Makrán; the greatest family in the Baluch assemblies was the Domki. The Rinds and Lasháris met together, they took counsel among themselves. 'Come let us march hence, let us leave these widespread lands. Let us conquer streams and dry lands, and deal them out among ourselves. Let us take no count of rule or ruler.'

"They came to their own homes. The chiefs ordered their slaves to saddle their young mares. The men called to the women, 'Come down from Chajú, take out your wrappings and beds, carpets and red blankets, etc., Chákar will not stay in this country, he will go to his own far land.'"

* * * * *

"One day some madmen went forth from Gwaharám's city; they were mounted on fine chesnut mares, for the sake of hunting and exercise.

"They killed a pair of young camels (of Gohar's, a friend of *Mir* Chákar) to fill their bellies withal.

"The chief fell into a great rage; on both sides damage was done. On this side was Gwaharám with his sword, on that side *Mir* Chákar. For full thirty years war continued about these young camels. Then the Baluch rulers made peace among themselves, and Chákar, on account of this feud among brethren, passed away to Satghar."

The only pre-Mohamedan remains that I have come across are the *Gorbasta* or Infidel Dams, which have been compared with the Cyclopean walls of Greece. They are generally situated across the mouth of a defile, and were built to catch the water for purposes of irrigation. In some instances, they may be found on a declivity, and in the case of Eastern Baluchistán there was evidently a dense population dependent on these dams, which were perhaps the work of the Baluch and Kuch.

Colonel Mockler, however, when travelling forty miles to the north-west of Gwádur, excavated some ancient brick buildings and also saw stone dams. He found bones, pottery, and stone knives.[1] In other parts of Makrán he discovered stone houses, probably tombs, locally termed Damba Kuh, but draws no exact deductions from these discoveries or from the excavations at Bahrein, where stone-built tombs have also been found. I can only express the hope that some explorer may thoroughly examine and compare these ruins; the most valuable results would, I am confident, reward him.

NOTE

The following is an incomplete list of the chief tribes of Western Baluchistán and Makrán. It is impossible to give them in any order, as they are so scattered in many cases; moreover the tribes of each district I visited are given in the various chapters.

	No. of Families	Habitat
1. Gichki	600	Panjgur and Kej.
2. Bolídi	400	Bolída.
3. Malik	600	Kolwa.
4. Noshirwáni	1000	Khárán, Panjgur, Kolwa, Bolída.
5. Bezanju	1600	Kolwa, Kir, Ormára, Bír.
6. Nahrui	1000	Valley of Bampur, Sarhad.
7. Hot	1000	Báhu, Dashtiári, Láshár.
8. Akazai, Sadozai, Askani } Rind	1000	Mand, Pishin, and Dasht.
9. Kowda	1200	Dashtiári.
10. Jadgal	800	Báhu and Dashtiári.
11. Shahzáda	800	Báhu and Dasht.
12. Kalmatti	300	Kalmat, Pasni and Kolanch.
13. Ráis	100	Kej.
14. Med	1600	Ormára, Kalmat, etc.
15. Luti	1200	Báhu and Dasht.
16. Darzáda	1000	Pasni and Bampur valley.
17. Gurgij	400	Báhu, Dasht, Chahbár.
18. Luri	400	Scattered.

[1] *R. A. S. Journal*, N.S., ix. (1877), p. 121.

MAKRÁN CHIEFS.

[*To face p.* 96.

	No. of Families	Habitat
19. Sangar	1600	Ormára, Kalmat, etc.
20. Wardilis	120	Kolanch and Kej.
21. Band	1200	Kolanch, Kej, etc.

In the above list only the chief tribes have been mentioned, and of course many of them change their habitat at various seasons of the year. Even so we have an ethnological medley, which is of extreme interest.

To take the first tribe on the list, the Gichki are the descendants of a Rajput family which settled in Baluchistán as late as the seventeenth century. The Bolídi hail from Maskat, the Malik are descendants of the Saffár dynasty, as mentioned in the following chapter, while the Noshirwáni were dispossessed by Sháh Abbás, who drove them from the neighbourhood of Isfahán to make room for Armenian settlers.

The Bezanju are a branch of the aboriginal Bráhui, and the Nahrui are still the most influential tribe in Persian Baluchistán under *Sardár* Husein Khán. The Hots are a branch of the turbulent Rinds, who resemble Arabs more closely than any other Baluchis, and are proud of the fact; while the Akazai, Sadozai and Askani Rinds, the Kowda and Jadgal, the Kalmatta and the Gurgij, claim to be descended from Aleppo exiles, but Jadgal merely signifies Jat speech. The Shahzáda tribe claims descent from the princes of Kandahár, and the Ráis are, I understand, descended from the famous or infamous Ghazz. The Meds are aboriginal pirates, the Darzáda are serfs. The Luris represent the gypsies, and the Wardilis immigrated from Sind.

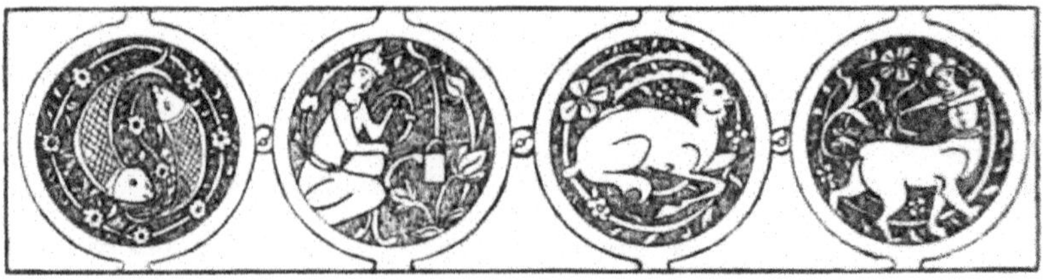

FROM AN ANCIENT BRASS BOWL.

CHAPTER IX

BALUCHISTÁN—(*continued*)

"Thou showest me the road to Makrán, but what a difference there is between an order and its execution! I will never enter this country, as its name alone terrifies me."—*Lament of Sinán Ibn Seláma.*[1]

In the previous chapter I have, to the best of my ability, dealt with Baluchistán as we find it to-day, with its interesting physical and ethnological problems, and I now turn to what is known of its history.

In the *Sháh Náma*, a contingent of Kuch and Baluch appear to have served under Kei Khusru, and are described as being as fond of fighting as rams, as never fleeing, and as being armed *cap-à-pie*. Their standard represented a tiger *rampant*.[2] As parts of India owned allegiance at times to Persia in these early days, it is probable that Baluchistán, with its Dravidian population of "Ethiopians of Asia," was also a tributary whenever the Sháh was strong and had no internal troubles to contend with. The province was undoubtedly traversed from east to west by Alexander the Great, but is again lost to sight for hundreds of years.

According to the *Sháh Náma*, Ardeshír was unable to make any impression on the Baluchis then inhabiting Gilán, but no details are given. A few centuries later Bahrám Gur, the Coeur de

[1] Sinán was the second Arab Governor of Makrán, which post he held for two years.

[2] If Baluchis inhabited the province which is now known as Gilán, a tiger was a most suitable emblem.

. marched to India, whence, according
;ht back the gypsies to amuse his
. t have travelled across Baluchistán,
·f the fact. In consequence of their
! the Baluchis wholesale, which no
at least a generation, after which they
atory habits, their independence being
·d.

.t of the Mohamedan era, Chach, the
· but one, is related to have marched
· hich formed the limit between Makrán
. ks he planted date-trees and set up a
This was the boundary of Hind in the time
."

..n was conquered in the early years of
n soon shared the same fate. In Muir's
: Mohamed bin Kásim was Governor of
. and during the following years conquered
:d's death arrested his triumphal progress
: hamedan supremacy was, however, estab-
y—a fact of great importance. Whether
permanently governed by the Mohamedans
.r as I can learn, it was first subdued by
Saffár dynasty. He ruled an empire which
.s to the Shat-el-Arab, but this brilliant
l, his brother Amr being captured by Ismáíl
. and put to death at Baghdád.

· Saffár held Baluchistán for many centuries,
·f Táhir, grandson of Amr, who ruled Fárs,
until A.H. 295 (907), the dynasty grew weaker,
·d by Mahmud of Ghazni.[2] In Baluchistán
·y became, in the course of centuries, a con-
I have seen many of their tombs, and all I
· Baluchis was that they were *Keiáni Malik*.
·hief and *Keiáni* is probably a reminiscence of

· ·.on).

· . mud of Ghazni was despatched to chastise the Baluchis
.n ambassador of his. He inflicted a severe defeat on the

the ancient royal family of Persia, whose descendants still inhabit Sistán.

An interesting account of Makrán can be gleaned from the pages of the tenth-century Arab travellers, of whom Masudi,[1] Istakhri and Ibn Haukal are the most famous, while in the middle of the twelfth century there are the records of Idrísi and of Benjamin of Tudela.

From the pages of these worthies we learn that Makrán was vast but barren, and that the largest town was Kir[2]—Idrísi terms it Kirusi—which was of about the same size as Multán. As Kir is described by Istakhri as a port, it is evident that Kir, now a squalid fishing hamlet west of Chahbár, was the important city referred to. Idrísi mentions the large output of sugar, and although his estimates of distance are too untrustworthy for detailed identification, Makrán was evidently a great highway, and much more prosperous in the tenth than it is in the twentieth century.

The Deilami dynasty seem to have held Baluchistán under partial control, as in A.H. 403 (1012), it is mentioned that Abul Favàris collected troops from Kermán and Baluchistán, and attacked his brother *Sultán-u-Dola.* Again in A.H. 419 (1028) he led a force from Kermán and Makrán to operate against Shiráz, but died on the way.

In his *History of the Seljuks*, Mohamed Ibráhim, who partly derives his information from Afzal Kermáni, relates how, in the eleventh century of our era, the chiefs of the Makránat or Makráns were assembled at a wedding of the Kufij and Kufs in Jíruft, where *Malik* Káward annihilated the latter tribes. Makrán, however, evidently submitted, as the historian Ahmad Ali Khán mentions that in the reign of Toghrul Sháh[3] the duty on silk in Makrán was 30,000 *dinárs* or 15,000 napoleons, while the harbour dues of Tíz were farmed for half that amount. Baluchistán must therefore at that period have been ruled from Kermán. A few years later, when the province was divided between two of his

[1] Masudi wrote about A.D. 913, while Istakhri, whose work was included in that of Ibn Haukal, flourished a little later. Idrísi's date is A.D. 1150, and Benjamin of Tudela travelled from A.D. 1160 to 1173. To complete the list Abulfeda flourished about A.D. 1273.

[2] Sir T. Holdich considers that Kiz or Kech is referred to. The difference in writing Kir or Kiz is small, but Kech is not a sea-port.

[3] He reigned from A.H. 551 (1156) to A.H. 563 (1167).

WEST ENTRANCE TO LUK PASS, MAKRÁN.

[To face p. 100.

sons, Arslán Sháh received Bardsír, Sirján, Jíruft and Khabis, as being equivalent to four shares, while Bam and Makrán, or two shares, fell to Bahrám Sháh.

Afzal Kermáni, who wrote at the close of the twelfth century, during the reign of *Malik* Dinár, does not say much of the position of Baluchistán, but the following extract from his work is of considerable interest: "Another important city in Kermán is Tíz, and the inhabitants of Hind, Sind, Abyssinia, Zanzibár, Egypt, and the country of the Arabs from Omán and Bahrein trade there. Every kind of musk, ambergris, indigo, and logwood, and aromatic roots of Hind, and slaves of Hind and Abyssinia and Zanzibár, and also fine velvets, shawls, sashes, and the like rare products have their market at this port. Near Tiz is Makrán, the mine of candy and sugar, which they export to all countries of the unbelievers and of Islam." Idrísi, on the other hand, discounts this description by writing of Tíz as being a small port. In the history of Mohamed Ibráhim it is recorded that caravans from Irák used to reach the sea at Tíz whenever the Hormuz route was unsafe, and, generally speaking, it may be said that Makrán has retrograded in civilisation, there being no silk or sugar grown there to-day.

At the beginning of the thirteenth century the Kuj and Baluch are mentioned as the tribes inhabiting the *Garmsir*, who made peace with Táj-u-Din, Sháh-in-sháh, *Amir* of Hormuz. Istakhri writes: "The Balujis live in the desert of Mount Kufs, and Kufs in the Zoroastrian tongue is *Kuj*, and they call them *Kuj* and *Baluj*."

Just before Chengiz Khán swept across Central Asia, *Malik* Shujá-u-Din, of Zuzan, a nominee of the last Sháh of Khiva, captured Bampur; in the following year he proceeded to Kech and Tíz, gaining possession of both towns. It is particularly stated that from the time of Toghrul Sháh, son of Mohamed Sháh, a period of forty-five years, Baluchistán did not obey Kermán, but each district had its own chief.

It has already been mentioned in chap. v. that Jalál-u-Din of Khiva marched from India *via* Makrán to contest the possession of Asia with the Mongol hordes, and we read that, in A.H. 620 (1223), after the destruction of Herát, Chagatai was despatched by Chengiz Khán to lay waste Makrán in order to cut Jalál-u-Din's lines of communication.

At the end of the thirteenth century Marco Polo, on his return journey from China, sailed past Makrán, and although it is improbable that the great Venetian touched anywhere on the coast, he gives the following account of it: "Kesmacoran is a kingdom having a king of its own, and a peculiar language. Some of the people are Idolaters, but the most part are Saracens. They live by merchandise and industry, for they are professed traders, and carry on much traffic by sea and land in all directions. Their food is rice and corn, flesh and milk, of which they have a great store."[1] It is to be noted that Kesmacoran is a combination of Kech or Kej and Makrán, and the term is even to-day occasionally used. Marco Polo further says that it is "the last kingdom in India as you go towards the west and north-west," herein corroborating Pliny, who wrote: "Many indeed do not reckon the Indus to be the western boundary of India, but include in that term also four satrapies on this side of the river, the Gedrosi, the Arachoti, the Arii, and the Paropamisadae."[2]

During this period we hear little for some years about Baluchistán, but Sultán Hajjáj, a pretender to the throne of Kermán, under the Kara Khitei dynasty, is known to have fled to and returned from India through the country.

At the beginning of the fifteenth century, when Tímúr had exterminated the Muzaffar family and bestowed Kermán on *Amir* Adugui, the latter sent Jalál-u-Din Jamshid to Baluchistán, which he plundered as far as Kech, but made no permanent impression on the province. Abdur Razzák, ambassador from Sháh Rukh to the Samuri, who passed through Kermán in 1442, mentions that he met the *Amir Háji* Mohamed on his return from an expedition into the province of Benboul. This is probably a corruption of Bampur or Bunpoor, as Pottinger terms it.

Towards the end of the fifteenth century Baluchis began to arrive at Multán, and early in the sixteenth century there is a great migration eastwards from Makrán under *Mir* Chákar, Rind. It was about this period that they were found in the Panjáb. Mr Longworth Dames considers that this migration was caused by Mongol pressure. *Mir* Chákar's tomb is at Satghar, in the Montgomery district, and apparently Baluchi ballads mostly date from this period.

When Sháh Abbás came to the throne, Ganj Ali Khán, the

[1] Cf. Yule's *Marco Polo*[2], vol. ii. p. 334.

[2] *H. N.*, vi. 78.

second great ruler of Kermán, marched in A.H. 1022 (1613) to attack Baluchistán by Jíruft, there being no desert in those days, to judge by the considerable ruins I saw when travelling in those parts. *Malik* Shams-u-Din[1] collected forces from all Makrán, but was defeated and taken prisoner at Kuchgardan, one stage from Bampur, and Ganj Ali Khán appointed *Malik Mírza* of the same Saffár family to succeed him. Later on, *Malik Mírza* made the Sháh a large present, and Baluchistán became once again independent.

Commodore Roggewein,[2] who sailed round the world between 1721 and 1723, mentions that in 1701 Bandar Abbás was attacked by the Baluchis with four thousand men, but that they were beaten off.

When the Sefavi dynasty waned, and Persia was invaded by the Afghán Mahmud, several Baluchis joined him, but upon the defeat and flight of his successor Ashraf, it was again Baluchis who murdered and plundered the refugees.

About the middle of the seventeenth century, Kambar, leader of the Bráhui shepherds, was summoned to aid a Hindu *rája* against Afghán encroachments. Apparently he usurped the throne, but everything remains obscure until the reign of Abdulla Khán, his great-grandson, who was ruling when Nádir Sháh invaded India. Nádir Sháh confirmed Abdulla Khán in his position, but a few years later he was killed in battle.

His second son Nasír Khán finally seized the throne, and upon the assassination of Nádir Sháh, fought for his independence with Ahmad Khán, Duráni. However, upon being defeated, he acknowledged Afghán suzerainty, and devoted himself to extending his sway in Baluchistán with much success.

In A.H. 1150 (1737), or by another account three years later, and more than a century after the last Persian invasion, Pir Mohamed, formerly *Beglerbegi* of Herát, accompanied by *Amir* Mahabbat[3] of Kasarkand, marched by way of Jíruft towards Bampur. *Malik* Shir Khán, of the same Saffár dynasty, collected troops from Kech and more distant Khárán, and the two armies met at what is now known as Chil-i-Nádir. The Baluchis made a desperate onset, but probably Nádir's artillery was too much for them, and *Malik*

[1] I saw his tomb at Kuhak. *Vide* chap. xx.

[2] *Vide* Kerr's *Voyages and Travels*, vol. xi. p. 159.

[3] His descendant, Abdulla Khán, was recently Governor of Geh

Shir Khán being slain, the army fled with a loss of seven hundred warriors. However, *Malik* Ardeshír, son of the dead chief, held Bampur successfully, and after a few days, the Persians raised the siege and captured Fahraj. Lashár was next conquered, and *Amir* Mahabbat installed as Governor of Baluchistán at Kasarkand. Pir Mohamed then marched to the south and captured Tíz, but on his return journey he lost a number of men from thirst. A few months later several of the forts in the Jálk oasis were captured by the aid of artillery, and even to-day the ruin that fell upon the district is indelibly impressed on the minds of the Jálkis.

Pir Mohamed and Aslam Khán having quarrelled and separated, the campaign towards Khárán was abandoned after an unsuccessful start, and Aslam Khán's complaints to Nádir Sháh resulted in Pir Mohamed losing his head, Fath Ali Khán, the Chief Falconer, being sent from Kandahár to carry out the sentence. He accepted the submission of *Malik* Ardeshir, who agreed to recognise *Amir* Mahabbat as his overlord, and after receiving presents the Persian army departed.

About the same time, in 1736, a force sent by Nádir defeated the nomads of Khárán, and two years later, the *Beglerbegi* of Fárs was ordered to bring his troops to Sind, and marched through Makrán. He captured the Kech fort, and it was apparently on this occasion that the natural fortress of Mihán[1] resisted all his efforts, tradition averring that Nádir's army failed to capture it. The winter was spent in Kech, and, as Sind was already in the hands of the ruthless Afshár, the *Beglerbegi* received instructions to rejoin his royal master.

During the period of anarchy that followed the death of the Nádir Sháh, Eastern Baluchistán, as mentioned above, finally acknowledged the suzerainty of Nasír Khán, whose power was felt as far west as Bampur. But his successors were degenerate rulers of a shrunken kingdom, and what is now known as Persian Baluchistán was independent when that indomitable traveller, Sir Henry Pottinger, crossed it in 1810. At the time of his visit, the sway of *Sháh* Mehráb Khán of Fahraj was acknowledged from Dizak to Bazmán. He was a Nahrui by birth and of no position, but on his marriage with the daughter of Seiid Khán, chief of

[1] *Vide* chap. xxvi.

Bampur, he had gradually established his rule over the surrounding districts. He boasted to Pottinger that he was outlawed by the Governments of Persia and of Afghanistán, and that some years previously he had raided and kept possession of Láristán for a period of three months.

In 1839, *Háji* Abdul Nabi, an intelligent traveller, found Mohamed Ali Khán, Nahrui, in possession of the Bampur fort, and reported that Mohamed Sháh of Sib was the most powerful chief in Baluchistán; but that he occupied no paramount position, and was, in fact, generally at war with some of the other independent chiefs, who, whenever inaction became oppressive, united to raid Narmáshir or Rudbár, and laughed at the threats of the Governor-General of Kermán. This state of affairs might have continued indefinitely, as raids on distant provinces of the Persian Empire would not have been likely to affect a Government that tolerated the Turkoman terror, but a new factor appeared, which changed the whole situation.

Reference has been made in chap. v. to the final flight of Ághá Khán across Baluchistán to India, where he rendered good service to the British Government. In 1844, his brother, Abul Hasan, known as the *Sardár*, marched through Makrán to Chahbár, and was everywhere warmly welcomed. By dint of diplomacy, he soon gained possession of Bampur, where, in 1845, he was besieged by a strong Persian force. He made a daring sortie, and killed and wounded almost all the gunners, but when he returned to the fort, their cries were so loud, that he thought that they came from his own stronghold, which, he concluded, must have been captured. He thereupon rode off south with a single servant, who deserted him, and was finally captured by Baluchi levies, and sent to Tehrán, where he was kindly treated. He lived to a green old age, and is still remembered as a heroic soldier, whom no climate or fatigue could affect.

This irruption of the Ághá Khán party brought about the downfall of Baluchi independence. Mohamed Ali Khán, the Nahrui chief, was seized by the treachery of a relation, and imprisoned for five years at Tehrán. He was then released, and upon returning to his home captured Bampur, surprising its Persian garrison. However, this was his last success, as, being unable to stand a siege, he fled to Mináb and died in the desert. His sons,

Chákar Khán and Husein Khán, were imprisoned at Tehrán for two years, and then released.

Two members of the Kájár tribe were appointed to rule the turbulent district, but were a failure as Governors, and it remained for Ibráhim Khán, the son of a baker at Bam, to achieve the permanent subjugation of what is now known as Persian Baluchistán. His methods were said to be cruel and he had a propensity for slave-dealing, but, no doubt, there was a constant call on him for revenue and presents, which he had to meet the best way he could. Sir Oliver St John, in 1872, describes him in the following terms: "The redoubtable ruler of Bam, Narmáshir and Baluchistán is a short punchy man of any age from forty-five to sixty, with a full and well-dyed beard, and small sharp eyes. . . . There seemed nothing in his face to indicate the really superior man he must be, not only as having risen to his present position by sheer merit, unaided by money or interest, but as having reduced one of the most turbulent countries in Asia to a state of order and tranquillity."[1]

As might be expected, the Commission that was appointed to delimitate the Perso-Kalát frontier in its Southern section, in connection with the Makrán telegraph line, was not welcomed by Ibráhim Khán, and when the Kalát envoy arrived unexpectedly at Bampur, General Goldsmid was placed in a rather awkward position. The Persian representative proving impracticable, the Commission broke up, and the award was made mainly from Sir F. Goldsmid's observations during a former journey. The *Saad-u-Dola*, to give him his title, was quite incapable of understanding the objects of the mission, and as soon as it had quitted Baluchistán he seized Kuhak, which had not been awarded to Persia. He further rounded off Persian territory by attacking and defeating Seiid Khán, Kurd, who was known as the *Sardár* of Sarhad, and lived at Kwásh.

In 1881, the Bráhuis of the Afghán *Garmsil*,[2] which is situated along the lower reaches of the Helmand, raided across the Lut to the gates of Tehrán, carrying off a quantity of camels and other property from Verámin, and then disappearing in the desert. The *Saad-u-Dola* tried to cut them off near Shurgaz, but was himself defeated and his camp taken; however, he finally avenged himself

[1] *Eastern Persia*, i. pp. 77-8.

[2] *Garmsil* is the same as *Garmsir*. Cf. Helmand and Hírmand.

on the Bráhuis by massacring the members of one of their caravans on its way to Jálk to buy dates. When the enormous distance, exceeding 700 miles, is considered, this *chapao* explains how the Turkoman were so successful in raiding into the heart of Persia.

Ibráhim Khán died in 1884, after having been Warden of the Marches for thirty years, as, although occasionally dismissed, he was speedily re-instated. His son died a few months later, and Zein-ul-Abidin Khán, his son-in-law, became Governor of Baluchistán, but in 1887 was succeeded by Abul Fath Khán, a Turk. This worthy in 1888 conducted a successful campaign against the Yarahmadzai[1] of Sarhad, during the course of which the Kurds observed a strict neutrality. In the spring of the following year they sent to the *Násir-u-Dola* to the effect that they were loyal, but fear had impelled them to stand aloof from Abul Fath Khán. The Governor-General apparently accepted these excuses, and proposed to give them some lands at Fahraj in exchange for their Sarhad property. This was agreed to, and the same spring the whole tribe moved to Fahraj.

The *Násir-u-Dola* having quitted Baluchistán, Abul Fath Khán treated his intended victims with distinction, until their suspicions were lulled, when he seized them, their women and property. This roused the Baluchis under *Sardár* Husein Khán, and Fahraj was besieged, but a sortie put to flight the cowardly assailants, and the Kurds were all subsequently executed. Abul Fath Khán was, however, dismissed, and Zein-ul-Abidin Khán was re-appointed to Baluchistán. In 1891, after an absence of two years, the Governor-General again visited the district, making solemn promises that he would imprison nobody; but these were broken, and the Baluchi chiefs were seized, many of them being in prison when I first visited the province. Baluchistán, its chiefs in bondage, relapsed into quiet under Zein-ul-Abidin Khán, and this was the position of affairs in 1893, but to complete the chapter, I propose to bring it up to date.

In 1896, the Perso-Baluch Commission on which I served effected the delimitation of the frontier, and scarcely were its labours completed when the dastardly assassination of the Sháh threw the province into a state bordering on anarchy. Zein-ul-

[1] The Yarahmadzai was originally a section of the Dámini tribe, but is now distinct. *Vide* chap. xi.

After luncheon it was necessary to take decided action, and we ourselves apportioned the loads, which had to be tied on by our servants, the Baluchis trying to hinder them as much as possible. The late Sir Oliver St John, whose knowledge of the Baluch was second to none, wrote that, "beyond making his camel kneel down to receive the load, and remonstrating in tones barely more melodious than those of his beast, if he thinks the latter too heavily laden, the Baluch takes no interest or trouble in the transaction." [1]

Finally, late in the afternoon, our camels started, and turning our backs on the hospitable clerk-in-charge of the Telegraph Station, we marched to Tíz, distant but seven miles. We first passed through the village of Chahbár, the home of numerous Indian traders, with its squalid hovels, partly redeemed from utter ugliness by a few trees, and then steadily rose across the rocky range dividing it from the famous mediæval port of Tíz. The latter place occupies a better position than Chahbár, as it is situated at the mouth of the main route into the interior *via* Kasarkand, and also absolutely commands the coast road, which on the east side winds down a very rough mountain path, and on the west has to pass through a gate in a wall running across from the cliffs to the sea, a distance of only a few yards.

It was too late to fully examine the ruins, which now consist of thousands of graves and little else, but we had just time to see over the modern Persian fort which had been built some twenty years previously to protect Chahbár, after it had been seized by the Persians, who dispossessed an Arab *Sheikh*. They, however, soon deserted it, but I recollect that when I reached Tehrán, H.M. Násir-u-Din specially questioned me about it, and was apparently under the impression that it was still garrisoned.

In 1188 A.D. Tíz was evidently a great port,[2] caravans using that route from the west when, owing to local disturbances, the Hormuz road was blocked. The line which they followed would probably have run from Irák to Kermán, and thence to Bampur, Kasarkand, and Tíz, the alternative route *via* Geh being impracticable for caravans. This journey was, however, much longer, and Tíz must have mainly depended on its being the centre of the Makrán sugar trade, and perhaps the outlet for the wheat of Sistán; it was certainly a resort of merchants, who probably

[1] *Eastern Persia*, vol. i. p. 21.

[2] *Vide* previous chapter.

objected to travelling as far as Hormuz. In the work of Afzal Kermáni the port is referred to as the "Gap of Tíz," and it is probably the Talmena of Arrian.

We found our camp pitched in the narrow valley, where the only water-supply consisted of a few holes containing a limited supply of muddy liquid, and we were proportionately grateful to the Baluchis, who had emptied our water-barrels on the ground that the Tíz water was excellent.

Being determined to start early, we finished breakfast before sunrise, but it took hours before the Baluchis who, to use my companion's expression, "snarled like a pack of jackals," were ready, and it was already terribly hot when we rode along the sea-shore towards Parag, a tiny squalid hamlet of Ichthyophagi, which is also used as a harbour. Here we turned our back on the sea, and also on the telegraph line, which, running close to the coast, suffers considerably from the humidity. Our horses were out of condition from the railway journey and subsequent sea-voyage, and we had been unable to procure them even a little chopped straw, but had been obliged to feed them entirely on grain at Chahbár; as therefore they began to give in, we decided to rest in the partial shade of some tamarisk bushes and let the caravan go on ahead. When at length it passed us, most of our servants were walking, the motion of the camel making them sick, but, as may be imagined, they soon got accustomed to it.

In the cool of the evening we rode across a lava-strewn plain, passing some tiny plots of ground with crops of cotton, and found our camp pitched at Nur Mohamedi, a small hamlet with the usual mud hole for our drinking supply. However, but half of our camels were in, and it was not until late at night that the remainder turned up, the men threatening to leave us, alleging that we had taken them, or tried to take them, seventeen miles in a day. The following morning they refused to stir, on the ground that a Baluchi camel cannot be allowed to march by night, and must also be grazed all day!

We perforce gave in, and explored the country in the morning in different directions. I rode towards the high cliffs, up which our track lay, while Brazier Creagh went off in the opposite direction, lost his way, and caused us all anxiety, as a day in the sun without water was a dangerous experience. However, about 1 P.M. he turned up, not much the worse, after having visited several hamlets all of the same type. We obtained some Indian corn stalks for our horses, which took to them most kindly, but throughout the journey forage was our chief anxiety.

In spite of a day's rest and a start in the false dawn, our horses became distressed, and more than one camel collapsed before we accomplished the fifteen miles to Pish Mant or Place of the Dwarf Palm. The leaves of this bush are used for many purposes, such as sandals, matting, baskets, thatching, bedding, and ropes. In *Eastern Persia*,[1] caps, sword-belts, gun-slings, and pocket-books are also mentioned, and even a *Kalián* or water-pipe was seen by General Lovett. Further, the berries are threaded and used as rosaries, the young shoots are edible, and the roots will apparently always burn, a great boon to travellers in a country where fuel is apt to be scarce.

Leaving the soft level plain, which is evidently of comparatively recent formation, the cliffs being a continuation of those at Tíz, we entered a stony desolate valley known as the Pir Ghurík or Grassy Defile, and crossing a low pass, rose on to a plateau. We had to walk more than half the distance, and at the stage the water was so vile that even the camels would not face it. To relieve the monotony, a swarm of hornets ate our lunch for us, cutting up and carrying off all the meat.

The next march, longer than the others, was to Ziárat, a shrine built in honour of Pir Shámil, a holy inhabitant of Sind, who died some three centuries ago. The track wound for some miles through low clay hills, and finally crossed a wide plateau, beyond which we were gladdened by the sight of running water, and our exhausted horses were soon gulping down as much of it as we thought good for them. Just before getting into camp, two wolves were sighted within easy rifle-shot, which was an interesting occurrence, as they are supposed to keep to the uplands; unfortunately, I had only my shot-gun with me. Another day's halt was imperative, although we had only grain to give our horses, but having reached the Geh river,[2] we had no more fears about water.

[1] Vol. i. p. 128.

[2] On the map, this appeared as River Kir, which is erroneous. *Kaur* is the Baluchi for a river, and the word *Kir* is evidently a corruption of this, to which some compiler prefixed "River."

I may here mention that our only European predecessor was Captain Grant, one of the band of explorers despatched by Sir John Malcolm in the first decade of the nineteenth century. His notes were of the scantiest, and as we had a most unintelligent Baluchi as guide, we did not feel at all sure whether we should find water in the *Kaur*. As a matter of fact, it was only running for a few hundred yards, the river-bed being dry both above and below; but digging will almost always disclose water in the Baluchistán water-courses.

At Ziárat, we had reached the northern limit of the *Dasht* or Coast district, which, we were told, was assessed at about £200 per annum, the districts of Geh and Bint each furnishing a similar sum in taxes. Continuing the march five miles up stream, the river-bed again held water, and we passed a succession of small hamlets and date-groves, finally halting at Nokinjá, where, having procured bundles of green rice for our horses, and eggs and milk for ourselves, we decided on yet another halt.

We were at last clear of the round clay hills, the ranges through which we were now passing throwing out fine bluffs which overhung the river-bed. Just above Nokinjá is the junction of the main tributary, the Sirhá, which, partly in this and partly in my fourth journey, was explored throughout its length. Higher up, we were delighted to reach Geh, the chief town of the district, and, in our eyes, "quite a place." After seeing hundreds of Baluchi villages, Geh—the Bih of the Arab traveller—remains fixed in my mind as the prettiest. There is a beautiful date-grove lying in the fork of two streams, the Gung and the Kishi, with a picturesque old fort perched on a bluff, and desolate hills all round enhancing the emerald green of the rice-fields; its altitude was 1500 feet. Supplies were to be procured, but although we were at the end of October, the noonday readings were still nearly 100 degrees.

Geh, with Kasarkand on the east, and Bint on the west, form the three towns in Persian Makrán first reached by the traveller from the coast, and are each said to possess the same population, which scarcely exceeds 2000 inhabitants, so far as we could judge. Captain Grant in 1809 wrote of Geh, "that it was reckoned the second city in Makrán, Kej being the first." The Governor of Geh, Mohim Khán, is a Kuh Baluch of Lashár, and half-brother of its chief. The old ruling family was that of the Bolídi.

We were visited by Chákar Khán, elder brother of *Sardár* Husein Khán, who represents the old order in Makrán, and recollects Baluchistán when it was independent of Persia; not unnaturally, he dislikes the changes which have occurred. A few of the inhabitants spoke Hindustani, and we learned that there was a small trade carried on with the coast, fish, in a very strong condition, being a favourite article of commerce. Upon the whole, the condition of the people seemed wretched, the local Governor, unchecked as in Persia by growing public opinion and the telegraph, grinding them so terribly that there was a large and increasing emigration to Karachi, Maskat, and Zanzibár.

Our first task was to pay off our camels, after which we engaged a few from Lashár, the hardiest and best for hill-work in Baluchistán, and, leaving our main camp at Geh, we marched off into the unexplored district lying between us and Fánoch. Starting before dawn, we stumbled for some miles up the stony river-bed of the Gung, and then bore up a side valley to the watershed separating the Gung drainage from that of the Sirhá, which we crossed at Khushk, a small village. At this point it has a bed some 200 yards in width, but the running stream was perhaps thirty yards wide by a foot deep; both banks being lined with villages, we were enabled to add considerably to our estimate of the population of the district. We should have been better advised to camp at Khushk, but rode on for a few more miles to the tiny stream of Sorhin, where, as we lay for hours under a rock waiting for our transport to come in, we realised the beauty of Isaiah's words, "the shadow of a great rock in a weary land."

The next stage to Malurán was interesting, as we were rather doubtful, not only as to the distance, but whether there was a river as stated, and if so, whether it belonged to the Geh or Bint basin. After a rugged march, we found a really fine river, Malurán being one of many villages and hamlets lining its banks. It is a tributary of the Rapsh river, which it joins below Bint.

The inhabitants, who had apparently never heard of Europeans, treated us with suspicion, and even after they came within talking distance, our usually successful plan of giving a man a rupee, as a proof that we meant to pay for supplies, was a failure. An animated discussion arose, I, on my part, explaining that we wished to pay and were their friends, but the headman, a particularly evil-looking rascal, remained obdurate. Finally one of our party made a spring and tripped him back into the stream, from which he emerged with his mouth full of mud, and supplies were at once brought in. It may be objected that we had no right to use *force majeure*, but I would advise any such objector to put himself into a similar position, and then see what he would do.

We finally found the people of Malurán so friendly that we decided to halt a day, during which, as usual, we rode off in different directions. My companion started along the Geh road, and thereby brought out all the elders of the village, who feared that he was riding back to complain. Taking in the situation, and in order to give them a lesson, he spent a long time in listening to their persuasions, and when he finally left the Geh road, the old men toddled home happy. We both noticed one remarkable fact at Malurán, which was that its inhabitants whistled, a rare accomplishment in the East, I fancy, as it is generally considered to be "devilish speech."

A very rough march brought us to the Fánoch or Rapsh river, the track, after crossing a low watershed, gradually approaching the particularly fine mass of the Band-i-Nilág or Blue Range. We were compelled to camp near a stream of very dubious water, and during the weary hours that we waited for the camels, whose pace rarely exceeds two miles an hour, we took lessons in natural history, and observed how the big frogs swallowed their smaller brethren. Almost all our servants suffered from fever, the result, I am sure, of not walking in the cold of the false dawn, but, in any case, we were not fortunate in our staff, some of them afterwards refusing to eat wild sheep, because it was *jungly*.

The final march to Fánoch was a unique experience. Winding up the river-bed, which runs between cliffs, the waterway being cut through the Band-i-Nilág, we first passed a superb blood-red rock, underneath which lay a deep pool; it is known as the Giri. Thenceforward, the colours of the rocks, some of which weighed hundreds of tons, were most gorgeous, varying from dazzling white to jet black; but the track was heart-breaking, and our horses had to be driven along it; we also greatly felt the absence of a guide. Accordingly it was with much satisfaction that we reached the top of the gorge, and saw the date palms of Fánoch a mile up-stream.

Our reception there was most friendly, the sons of Chákar Khán being Governors,[1] and they expressed immense delight at seeing our rifles, while six shots fired quickly from a revolver were quite too much for them. During a pause in the conversation, I was asked whether we wished to buy any stone. This rather puzzled us, until we saw that Brazier Creagh's geological researches had prompted the question. In reply, I said that we were not merchants, but that if he would send a few of the hundred-ton boulders to the coast, they would sell well. This he agreed to do, but did not explain how he proposed to set about it!

One object, and that a main one, of our trip was to gain some knowledge about the wide unexplored tract to the west, and with this in view, we decided to scale the Kuh-i-Fánoch, which looked as if the ascent would take an hour. However, it took four, and as the heat was intense, and the water-carrier lagged behind and lost us, we had a somewhat trying time, especially as the last 500 feet is a solid cliff of white limestone, and almost perpendicular. The summit once reached, we could easily trace to their sources the five separate streams[2] which form the Fánoch river, thus finally disposing of the theory of older travellers (as shown in General Goldsmid's *Eastern Persia*) that the Bampur river reached the sea. At the same time, we enjoyed a superb panorama, which gave us what we so much wanted—an idea of the lie of the country. To the west, our view was partly shut in by higher peaks; but to the north we caught the first glimpse of beautiful Bazmán, rising up in solitary state to a height of 9000 feet above the plain (11,200 feet above the sea); to the east were massive Azbag[3] and the district of Lashár which we were soon to explore.

Our plane-tabling finished, the descent of the almost sheer cliff

[1] Geránkash is the name of the chief tribe of Fánoch. For many years the district was ruled by a Ghilzai Afghán, who espoused Ághá Khán's cause.

[2] These are, counting from the west:—

1. The main stream, on which lies Mirábád, which we travelled down some five years later when coming from Rámishk.
2. Kaur-i-Kantakán.
3. Kam Kaur with Kam just above Fánoch.
4. Kaur-i-Magen, with Magen and Band-i-Bengi.
5. Kaur Ispid, joining in below Fánoch, with Ispid some six miles up it.

[3] Possibly this name is a corruption of Uzbeg. Mr E. G. Browne suggests that the last syllable represents the Sásánian *Baga* or God. Cf. Bagdád, a contraction of *Baga-dáta* or God-given.

had to be tackled by the aid of a rope manufactured from pagaris, and when we finally reached the river bank, we were all exhausted from thirst and fatigue. We found nine hours' climbing in a temperature of 118 degrees amply sufficient to strain our endurance, though it was well worth the effort, to obtain such a grand view of the features of the country. The White Hill, as it is sometimes termed, was only 4700 feet by the hypsometer, and as Fánoch is 2836 feet, everything was plainly seen and not dwarfed, as in the case of higher mountains.

Fánoch, where we rested a day to "eat" our fatigue, as the Persians say, has a much more prosperous look than Geh, several of the houses being substantially built of stone. There is a fort apparently of great antiquity, but, as is ever the case in Baluchistán, no information was forthcoming, although a most intelligent man gave me a fairly good and accurate description of the roads to the west, which I found useful five years later. Sheep, fowls, eggs, milk, barley, rice, and wheat were all plentiful, and the dates are famous throughout Baluchistán, but jaunty little skull-caps embroidered with red silk are the sole manufacture. I asked whether Fánoch was in Makrán, but was told that the watershed of the Band-i-Nilág was the boundary, to the north of which Fánoch lay; Bashákird on the west is not considered to form part of Baluchistán.

A return visit was paid to the slow-witted sons of Chákar Khán, after which we rode through the village and date-grove, returning to camp to pack up for the journey back to Geh. Our first stage lay down the Fánoch pass, which we thus had the chance of travelling through in both directions. The Giri pool proved too attractive, and we bathed in the hot sun, which gave me the only touch of fever I suffered from throughout the journey, and also a strong hint that bathing in the heat of the day is risky.

From Sartáb,[1] the stage in the river-bed, we took a more northerly line, striking the Malurán river at Abgá, whence, after a march which took us through a curious valley, with perpendicular slate rocks on each side, we descended the dry Jakán river, again striking the Sirhá at Ichán, which lies on the Geh-Fahraj route and was termed Hochan by Captain Grant. It was a large and prosperous village with a population of at least a thousand in-

[1] Or Cold Water.

habitants, and, in addition to a fine grove of palms, there were a few mango, fig, and mulberry trees.

The march back to Geh included crossing the watershed from the Sirhá, which is really the main stream, to the Gung, and, after rather less than a fortnight's absence, we found our main party all the better for the rest, its members having recovered from their various ailments.

Two days after our return, as we were preparing to start on towards Fahraj, we were agreeably surprised by the arrival of *Mir*[1] Khán Mohamed of Aptár and *Mullá* Basham, who said that he had been Post-Master of Gwádur, but was, in reality, a *farrásh* or sweeper. These two worthies brought a letter from H.H. the *Farmán Farmá*, welcoming me back to his province, and Zein-ul-Abidin Khán, Governor of Persian Baluchistán, also wrote to the effect that the two Baluchis had been instructed to smooth the way and escort us to Fahraj.

Our heavy boxes were sent *via* Chámp to the east, as being a less difficult track, and as we were determined to cross into Lashár, we retraced our steps to Ichán, where we met a Baluch who had been to America. From Ichán the track at first followed up a tributary of the Sirhá, but we finally reached the main stream, on the banks of which were some tiny plots of cultivation; the valley swarmed with partridges, some of which Brazier Creagh bagged. At this point the Kaur-i-Ziár-Nadán joined in from the north-east; up it runs a short cut to Lashár, said to be worse than the route we followed, but just passable for an unloaded donkey! We camped in the river-bed, and the following morning tackled the worst bit of road I have ever seen, in comparison with which the famous Bushire *kotals* are metalled *chaussées*. The gorge narrowed to a width of about thirty yards a mile after leaving camp, and the first obstacle met with consisted of a series of rocky steps, down which the river formed a cascade, with deep pools at intervals, which however the track avoids. The next novelty consisted of boulders of every size, from an omnibus to a football, across which our horses somehow scrambled, losing many a shoe.

A deep pool then confronted us, filling up the whole stream, and my waler tried it, but it was well out of his depth. Instead of waiting for our guide, whose ass had a terrible time climbing over

[1] *Mir* is a contraction of *Amir*.

the boulders, Brazier Creagh tried to skirt the pool, with the result that when some feet above it, his mare fell in, sinking under water and not improving the saddle. The guide came up at this moment, his face wreathed in smiles, and said that there was a track above. When we saw this, we could hardly believe that horses could climb it, and I remember "Cotmore's" look of bewilderment when he looked up and saw the mare above him. To my surprise, however, there were no casualties, though I should never have believed that laden camels could use such a goat track, and I still believe that only the Lashár camel could do so with impunity. The *crux* was passed, and yet the going was infamous; but we were cheered by seeing the smiling guide disappear, donkey and all, into a pool, which we felt was but just retribution for his untimely mirth. The bed of the river was of ruby-red rock, and we also saw many other colours, but nothing which rivalled the savage impressiveness of the Fánoch gorge.

Our horses being worn out, we were delighted to reach the source of the river, which is in the extensive but utterly neglected date-grove of Sirhá, and camping at an elevation of 3300 feet, we enjoyed the first day which had passed with a temperature of less than 90 degrees; it was also pleasant to hear that no limbs and no boxes had been broken, as we fully expected would have been the case.

We should all have liked a day's halt, but, as ever, the forage question was to the fore. Accordingly, in distinctly cooler weather, we rose across the watershed bounding Makrán, some three miles from our camp, at an altitude of 3600 feet, and then marched downhill, skirting the eastern slopes of the great mass of Azbag, which we had seen from the summit of Kuh-i-Fánoch. The track appeared delightfully smooth, and we struck a stream at Oghin or Hugin, which runs through Misk Hután on the Fánoch-Fahraj road, and is said to water several hamlets on its banks, which are inhabited by the Sarhái tribe. Oghin had a particularly fertile soil, and a little weaving was carried on; but we could not linger, and, after crossing miles of glaring shingle, we camped at Pip, the capital of Lashár.

The Governor came to see us, but was very shy until we asked him about his family history, when he brightened up considerably. He was a boy of sixteen, and son of *Mir* Hoti, who was something of a character in his day. Pip, or Paip, as it is also pronounced is a village of two hundred houses, clustering round a fort, and lying some distance away from its fine date-grove. In Baluchistán houses are always built in the open, probably because the space under the dates is all wanted for the crops. The change of atmosphere from the dry heat of the desert to the comparatively cool moisture of the date-groves is extremely pleasant, but probably apt to induce fever. After hours in the pitiless glare, however, shade is so grateful that we always pitched as close to the grove as possible, and did not suffer, so far as I know.

We both thought that the Lasháris were superior to any other Baluchis we came across. Possessed of better physique, they were wild specimens of humanity, but we always found them cheery and manly, which is not the case with the ordinary Baluch, who is greedy, conceited, unwilling, and unreasonable as a camel. I was constantly asked what rates of salary prevailed in India, and when I said that it was a question of ability, and that some men received 5 rupees a month, and some 10,000 rupees, my interlocutor would generally smile and remark, *sotto voce*, that he would probably earn the higher salary, being particularly *sarang* or slim. In engaging camels, servants, or guides, we often had to submit to their ridiculous pretensions, which tended to increase our expenses considerably.

At the same time, it is only fair to mention that the Baluchis are extremely honest, and, if entrusted with valuables or letters, will defend them with their lives: also, they are extremely moral, and treat their women more or less as equals. In fact, they have a code of honour and generally live up to it. Their honesty is exemplified by the fact that a bag of rupees, containing the pay of all the telegraph employés, used to be sent along the line, each man, in turn, taking out his wages. Only once was this confidence abused, and the thief had to leave the country, which is the heaviest of punishments for a Baluchi.

After a well-earned rest of a day, we continued down the fertile Pip valley, passing several villages, while for a mile or more reeds and water, from which rose a few duck, lay alongside the road. At Ispaka[1] we were in the Fahraj district, and saw the first signs of the detested Persian element, in the shape of two or three soldiers

[1] The Persians term it Isfaka: its inhabitants are of the Gabari tribe. It is referred to as Asfaka by the mediæval travellers.

AGRICULTURE IN MAKRÁN.

[*To face p.* 120.

and a sergeant. Baluchis call all Persians *Gajar*, a corruption of Kájár, the reigning dynasty, and, as they have only seen them as tax-collectors, the hatred is something extraordinary, although I think that it has diminished in virulence of late years. Another cause of dislike is the fact that the Baluchis, being rigid Sunnis, detest the Shia tenets of their conquerors. As a matter of fact, few people grind each other more thoroughly than Baluchis, but they nowadays tell their unhappy peasantry that they are collecting taxes for the Persian Government, and thus the odium is intensified, often unjustly. Grant had reported that the drainage flowed away from the Bampur river, and on this point we were enabled to prove him mistaken, unless, as is probable, it was due to a slip of the pen.

A belt of sand, quite as bad as any part of the Lut, lay between us and the Bampur river. Our advanced camp had been pitched off the road, and I missed it and rode on, until I could scan the whole country, but not seeing tents I retraced my steps. Brazier Creagh wisely struck the camp and followed. On meeting we decided to camp at Geshkok, a stage marked by two wells of brine, in a wide valley covered with saline efflorescence, which practically limits the belt of sand-dunes stretching for many miles east and west. Our water-barrels having been sent with the heavy baggage, we should have fared ill but for a bottle of distilled water in the medical panniers; yet our servants drank the well water and were none the worse, rather to our surprise.

To reach a river in Baluchistán is always a treat, so we pushed on across the north side of the ridge above Geshkok, from which we could see the long line of tamarisks that bordered the river, and in a very short time reached the village of Kasimabád, whose inhabitants are termed *Darzáda*,[1] which signifies a Negro-Baluch parentage. They are *adscripti glebae*, and in a miserable condition, nominally receiving a third of the crop, but really, as their appearance showed, only enough to keep body and soul together. They came in an almost naked state before our tents and said: "Look at and pity us." Brazier Creagh was indefatigable in attending to their ailments, but he said that what they wanted was proper food. We enlisted the good offices of the *Farmán Farmá* on their behalf, but anything that was effected was merely temporary, I fear.

[1] Bampur, Kuchgardan, etc., are all inhabited by these serfs.

The track to Bampur crosses to the right bank of the river by a ford, which was dangerous, owing to quicksands; the width was forty yards and the depth two feet. We were rather excited on reaching what we supposed to be the capital of Baluchistán, and were proportionately disgusted to find the grim old fort nearly deserted, the date-grove almost extinct, and only some two hundred squalid huts. Our camp was pitched in what had been a garden but was now a rubbish-heap, the supply of drinking-water being drawn from a muddy irrigation channel.

However, Bampur was an ancient capital of Baluchistán, probably because it possessed a mound, on which a strong fort could be built. According to a well-informed Persian, its original name was Bin Fahl. Pottinger, it is to be noticed, speaks of Bunpoor, and so this derivation may be correct. Bam Putr or Lesser Bam is the derivation given by the late Sir O. St John, who was not enamoured of the climate. Our later experience corroborated his statement that the "highly-irrigated land to the south and the burning sandy desert to the north cause sudden changes of temperature, and alternations from intense dryness to complete saturation, that make Bampur a by-word for unhealthiness, even in Baluchistán."[1]

The district, which practically includes the basin of the Bampur river,[2] is the richest in Persian Baluchistán, and, were proper use made of the water-supply, perhaps ten times the population could be supported, but, as elsewhere in Persia, almost continuous wars have caused the irrigation works to fall into decay. The land bordering the river is Government property, the crops being used to supply

[1] *Eastern Persia*, vol. i. pp. 75-6.

[2] The tribes are divided into dwellers on the right and left banks of the Bampur river.

Nahrui	left bank
Bámari	right "
Sábaki	" "
Abdulláhi	" "
Dakáli	both banks
Hut	left "
Zein-u-Díni	" "

No numbers are available but, in 1900, the tribes of Persian Baluchistán ranked in the following order:—(1) Nahrui; (2) Dámini; (3) Bámari; (4) Yarahmadzái; (5) Bolakzái; (6) Ghamshadzái; and (7) Hamáli. The three latter live in the eastern part of the province.

the Persian garrison, which is nominally five hundred strong. Anything left is used by the Governors-General, who frequently visit Bampur and Fahraj, but practically never go further east, owing to the scarcity of supplies. As in Egypt, the cultivated zone consists only of a narrow strip along the river, the desert to the north being just as close as on the south side.

Zein-ul-Abidin Khán, with whom, under his title of *Asad-u-Dola*, I was to have many dealings, wrote to say that he was expecting us at Fahraj, and the following day we rode on, Brazier Creagh keeping to the river, while I went by the track which skirts the cultivation, securing a bustard on the way. Passing a fortified *caravanserai*[1] which has replaced Bampur, the walls of the latter fortress having tumbled to pieces when its guns were fired, I was ushered into a spacious tent, where I had my first interview with Zein-ul-Abidin Khán.

The son-in-law of the redoubtable Ibráhim Khán, Zein-ul-Abidin Khán possesses great capacity of a practical nature and a particularly good grasp of frontier questions. Until he came to know me, I am afraid that, in his heart, he wished us not to see too much of the country, but, after many a "deal," we are now firm friends. Indeed, to the Oriental mind, our thirst for information seems uncanny, and in out-of-the-way places we were thought to be looking for mines or buried treasure.

Fahraj,[2] as the Persians term it, but Pahra, according to the Baluch pronunciation, is the Poura of Arrian, as demonstrated in a later chapter, and lying some four miles away from the river, is both healthier and cooler than Bampur, although the stream which runs through it is slightly sulphurous. Being the capital, its population has, no doubt, lately increased, and perhaps numbers two thousand souls, including the garrison. The date-grove is particularly fine, and as the land is mostly owned by free Baluchis, there is not the same misery as at Kasimabád and Bampur, although the Baluchi lady, in her long, black, shapeless garment like a nightgown, is a distinctly squalid individual, ageing very soon.

[1] It is termed the Kala Násiri.

[2] Its inhabitants include Borhánzái, Dámini, Kalkali, Bijárzái, Aduzái, Mahmudzái, Dikizái, Ráisi, Bámari, Sáhibki and Nahrui, besides a few gypsies, known as Luri, who are musicians and carpenters.

There were the ruins of two forts to examine, but no coins or seals were forthcoming, and we consoled ourselves with the thought that any Greek remains must be many feet below the surface. A few large kiln-burnt bricks were dug up when the foundations of the Kala Násiri were laid. We had frequent intercourse with Zein-ul-Abidin Khán, and one afternoon, by special request, we photographed him sitting on an iron bedstead, surrounded by his staff. During our rides, we found that the sources of the Bampur river were some springs lying almost due south of Fahraj. These were the haunt of much game, and almost every day we saw a wolf in some broken ground north of the village, but never within 200 yards.

One of my walers broke down utterly and was shot, and we bagged a number of foxes and jackals over its dead body. Our heavy baggage arrived in due course of time, and as we had no trained servant, everything required personal supervision, but at last the necessary stores were packed for a month's consumption—we decided to leave our heavy baggage at Fahraj—and we continued our journey.

A LUSTRED TILE. "HAIL OMAR!"

CHAPTER XI

SARHAD

"A territory
Wherein were bandit earls and caitiff knights,
Assassins, and all flyers from the hand
Of justice, and whatever loathes a law."
—TENNYSON'S *Geraint and Enid.*

THE *Farmán Farmá* having written to say that he would not reach the capital of Baluchistán until January, we were enabled to carry into execution the exploration of Sarhad, which still largely figured on the map as a blank, although Captain Jennings, R.E., had in 1885 given it a partial geographical existence.

We found that by entering the district from Magas we should have the largest section of unknown country to explore, and accordingly set to work to engage transport. This was a difficult task, as Sarhad bore an evil reputation, besides being a Cold Country, but after much waste of time we finally hired sufficient camels, and on 1st December started upon the second section of our journey.

The first stage, Aptár,[1] is a typical Baluch village, with its mud keep round which several huts clustered, while its date-grove and belt of cultivation were both good of their kind. There were also several gardens, and, to our joy, we were able to purchase some onions, one of the great deprivations in Baluchistán travel being the total absence of vegetables. Potatoes are not to be had, and should be brought from India, but, in our case, we had not tasted any vegetables, except at Fahraj, for weeks, and we obtained no more until we joined the *Farmán Farmá's* camp.

As for several stages there was no food or forage to be procured, we laid in a stock with great difficulty, and began a pleasant march up the Konár Rud, passing the first of the *Gorbasta* or Infidel Dams, which pointed to a date when the water-supply was carefully husbanded and not allowed to run to waste. Every few miles there were springs in the river-bed, with high grass, and we should have all enjoyed the march, but unfortunately Brazier Creagh had contracted an attack of dysentery, and at Során had to lie up for some days. From want of experience, we had no tinned milk, and the country had to be scoured for the fresh article, which was finally procured in small quantities.

While halting, *Guru*[2] Gopal Dass, a Hindu accused of murdering his wife, came to see me, and for two days I was enquiring into his case, which was so extremely complicated that when he was afterwards tried at Karachi, he was released on giving security, which, to the best of my knowledge, he has not since claimed. As far as I could make out, there was an enormous amount of falsehood and forgery; among other documents, one purported to be written in 1889, but bore an 1891 watermark, which discovery was distinctly interesting.

Brazier Creagh's recovery was remarkably rapid, to my intense relief, and the journey was resumed. Following Sir Oliver St John's example, I climbed the Kuh-i-Ispidán,[3] a fine limestone crag, but from its summit I saw that I must scale the far loftier peak of Hamant if I wished to obtain a really good idea of the country. We accordingly made a short march to a spring at a

[1] Its inhabitants are Hamáli and Zard Kuhi: the latter also inhabit Sarbáz.

[2] *Guru* signifies a religious teacher, I believe.

[3] *Ispid* is the ancient Persian form of *Sufid* or white. Cf. Pahlevi *spet*.

APTÁR. A TYPICAL BALUCHI VILLAGE.

[*To face p.* 126.

point which appeared to be close to the base of the mountain. Here we were shown the tomb of the father of *Mir* Khán Mohamed, our late *Mihmandár*, which is looked upon as a shrine, and I enquired what his virtues were. "He did not oppress the poor," was the prompt and most instructive reply.

Mountaineering in Baluchistán is always trying work, but in this particular case we were four hours distant from the base, and no guide was forthcoming, Hamant, according to all accounts, having never been scaled. Brazier Creagh very wisely after his illness did not attempt the climb, and we started up with a couple of camelmen to carry water, food, and the plane-table. Until 1 P.M. we toiled most painfully up the loose slate hillside, having constantly to retrace our steps, but at length we reached the crest. Hamant has erroneously been termed a volcano, but is simply a serrated ridge rising to an elevation of 7600 feet, and so narrow that we had to sit astride it. However, we had a view over the unexplored district to the south, which appeared to be little more than a weary maze of low hills, while in every other direction we enjoyed a magnificent panorama, although we could not, as we had hoped, catch a glimpse of the great volcano of Sarhad. The descent was most unpleasant, and personally I reached the base with only one boot and in rags, as we had to slide down many places. The dried-up pools in the limestone rock contained a deposit of lime just like blotting-paper, of which we took specimens, while, as elsewhere, the crags were of variegated colours. It was dark, and we were quite ten miles from camp, but delay being useless, we stumbled along hour after hour, not feeling at all sure as to whether we were going in the right direction.

A young camelman was the first to give in. He was not very plucky, as he had tried to turn back during the upward climb, but this move I had defeated by threatening to report him to his village, saying that I felt sure that no girl would marry him. This time he was dead beat, as indeed we all were. Sultán Sukhru, who showed up splendidly, got the boy up again, but five minutes later the second man declined to budge. Although our food-supply was exhausted, I felt inclined to agree to light a fire and spend the night, especially as I was barefooted, but just as we were finally settling down we caught a glimpse of a distant light, which revived our hopes, and, about 9 P.M., after having been fifteen hours on the climb, we reached camp. Rain beginning to fall a little later, we felt delighted to have had a clear day for our expedition, and, speaking for myself, I have seldom been more glad of a night's rest.

The next morning, although there was a steady drizzle, we could not wait, owing to the chronic forage question, and marched up the narrowing valley to Cheb, where, to keep warm, we collected bushes until those deadly-slow beasts of burden, the camels, arrived, and we camped in a genuine Scotch mist. The following day we crossed the watershed at an altitude of 4800 feet. It is known as Sar-i-Pahra, which seems to point to the fact that Pahra was the ancient capital of the district. The watershed divides the drainage flowing into the Bampur river from that which joins the Mashkid, the valley of which is known as Sarawán,[1] as is also a part of British Baluchistán. The range itself is the first of those in which the Baluch plateau meets the north-west ranges of the Persian mountain system.

After having been so long in the wilderness, it was quite pleasant to descend to the village of Magas, where we received a warm welcome from the white-bearded chief, who was a brother of Pasand Khán, a well-known raider at the time of the Goldsmid mission; and indeed Diláwar Khán had many a story to tell of those days, proudly showing us the mark of a bullet in his chest, which ought to have killed him.

The village of Magas, with a population of some two thousand inhabitants,[2] possesses the best climate in Baluchistán, lying, as it does, at an altitude of nearly 4000 feet; as, moreover, it is a hereditary property like Fánoch, there were all the signs of comparative prosperity. Diláwar Khán informed us that once, during a severe winter, the date-palms had all perished, and that Magas was about the highest elevation at which they could grow.

We should have liked to pay a flying visit to the district of Irafshán to the south, which was totally unexplored, but the claims of Sarhad being paramount, after a day's halt, during which we organised a shooting-match for the villagers, we started for the north. We marched towards the Kuh-i-Birk, which runs up

[1] Sarawán signifies a highlander as opposed to Jhalawán or a lowlander. The terms are practically equivalent to upland and lowland.

[2] The chief tribes in the district are Nákhudzái, Chahárizái, and Abdizái Dámini. In Sarbáz, to the south are Naskanti, Sagári, Kishi Kauri, Sir-i-Kauri, Kuh Ruki, and Zard Kuhi.

THE CHIEF OF MAGAS.

[*To face p.* 128.

into Sarhad, although its northern continuation is known as Kuh-i-Paskuh, and, after riding for a short time, we caught the first glimpse of Taftán, distant about 100 miles, and wondered whether we should be able to scale it. In the extreme distance it resembled a white cone, which is by no means its real shape.

Thanks to our guide, we camped at a pool of filthy water, although to our annoyance the next morning we found a beautiful spring a mile or two distant, known as Chashma-i-Pír. However, that is one of the drawbacks of exploring, but there are many compensations, as it is intensely interesting to form theories as to the lie of the country and the trend of the drainage; moreover, in parts where a European has never been seen, it was amusing to see how we struck the inhabitants.

In the course of the next march we crossed from the valley we had followed into one of more importance, known as the Kaur-i-Gerisht, and, to our surprise, found a large village called Paskuh.[1] The very dark inhabitants declined to give us supplies, on the ground that they were in rebellion. However, we pointed out that that did not affect their relations with us, and, after assuring them that we had nothing to do with the unpopular Governor of Sib, we were taken into their confidence, Brazier Creagh, as usual, winning their affections by dosing the sick. He noticed a flail at work, which is the only one we saw in Baluchistán. We both agreed that there must be much negro blood to cause the remarkable darkness of the people, but as it was just the same in Sarhad, I have since come to the conclusion that, being so remote, these people are the aborigines referred to in chap. viii.

The onward road lay up a wide open valley, and the second stage from Paskuh brought us into Sarhad, the mysterious and dangerous, as we had learned—quite wrongly—to consider it. From the watershed, which we crossed at 4600 feet, an altitude not much greater than that of Magas, we looked down on one of the wide expanses of savage scenery which are typical of this part of Asia. Not a village, not even a nomad tent, was to be seen, but in every direction tier upon tier of rugged barren ranges rose up, giving the idea of unlimited space, which somehow or other is always pleasing, there being, at any rate, no feeling of confinement.

[1] The inhabitants comprise Nodzái, Sandakzái, Chahárizái, Mazárzái, Gamshazái, and Shádádzái.

Riding on and suddenly turning a corner, we came upon a party of armed men, and thought that our adventures were about to begin, but upon our approach an old gentleman, who said that he was a member of the Kurd tribe of Sarhad, saluted us most amicably, and gave us the news of the district. The following day we marched round the base of the Kuh-i-Panj-Angusht or The Five Fingers Mountain, and, although we saw the fort of Kwásh in the distance, we halted at the new *kanát* of Nasrábád, where we found a group of black tents, termed *hasham* in these parts. The inhabitants were most friendly, and we took several photographs, but none of the plates developed well.

The plain between us and Kwásh bore signs of former cultivation, and the ruins of more than one village proved that Sarhad was not always as to-day; we were also informed that the Persian soldiery had cut down all the orchards for firewood.

Near the fort we met with our usual reception, and shortly after camping were visited by the Governor, Asad Ulla Khán, who showed himself most hospitable; indeed, ever since that date we have been friends.

The ancient capital of Sarhad is some two miles to the south-east of the modern fort, and Kwásh, the present capital, has hitherto appeared as Washt on the few maps that have taken any notice of this wild frontier district. For some time the name puzzled me, and it was not until I learned that the Persian word *Khosh* is pronounced *Khásh*[1] by the aristocracy, and *Kwásh* by the lower orders, that I understood that the meaning was simply "sweet," as applied to its water, which issues at a temperature of 70 degrees from underground. Situated at an altitude of 4500 feet, Kwásh should have been surrounded by cultivation, but consisted of nothing except a fort, constructed like a *caravanserai*, its garrison of perhaps 150 infantry and cavalry from Bam and, at most, 100 black tents. In fact, had the Governor been unfriendly, we should have been in great straits, as there was no grazing whatever, nor was flour or barley to be bought in the village.

Sarhad is an upland country, as described in a former chapter, and is, in fact, the only district between Quetta and Kermán that can be described as cool, there being low-lying deserts of an appalling width to its east and west. The ruins of numerous

[1] In Persian poetry the word is still *Khásh* as far as rhyming is concerned.

kanáts testify to the fact that water is abundant, as the proximity of Kuh-i-Taftán would imply; thus, in the future, we may expect Sarhad to form an important link, connecting Southern Persia with Quetta, and not to remain, as at present, the haunt of a few thousand families of nomads.[1]

After a day's rest I left my weary horse in camp, and started across the plain on foot to scale the Kuh-i-Panj-Angusht. We had engaged a guide, but a second man insisted upon following us, and it was not until four hours later, when the summit of the hill was reached, that he disclosed his purpose. "Sáhib," he began, "we have all heard of British justice, and I wish to lay a case before you." After this flattering exordium I could not turn a deaf ear, and the Sarhaddi went on to say that two years previously he had been betrothed to a maiden, but that the marriage was not to come off until he had provided a certain amount of cooking vessels and clothes. Recently he had heard from home that a rich man had wanted the girl, who was to be handed over to him in total disregard of her betrothal. He said that he had followed me from Kwásh to hear my decision, and swore to abide by it. I referred him to the Governor, but on his begging me to decide, I asked him whether he had paid in any of the dowry since the betrothal, which he confessed he had not. I then said that, at that rate, he could never marry the girl, and as it seemed unfair for her to be kept tied, I thought that he had better accept the position. This decision was rather a blow to him, but he acquiesced in it, and started off at once, apparently to release the lady.

Our host in vain tried to dissuade us from attempting the ascent of Kuh-i-Taftán, on the ground that in midwinter it was impossible. However, finding us inflexible, he sent orders to the various headmen, and rode out with us for many miles. On our bidding him good-bye, and expressing our gratitude for his

[1] The most influential tribe is one of the smallest, the Yarahmadzái only aggregating some 50 families, but, owing to their raiding propensities under the notorious Jiand Khán, a hegemony has been established, so that the Yarahmadzái control, perhaps, 1000 families. Next in importance are the Rekis, who aggregate 600 families, while the Ismáilzái clan is rather stronger, numbering 800 families. The Kurds, who were at one period the leading tribe, are now almost lost, in consequence of the tragedy related in chap. ix. They number perhaps 20 families. In 1900 it was estimated that the entire population of Sarhad was about 8000 families, say 40,000.

hospitality, he professed a hope that we should meet again when the *Farmán Farmá* reached Baluchistán.

Shortly after parting from Asad Ulla Khán we were accosted by a well-dressed Baluch, who was accompanied by five followers, and stated that he was a British subject. In answer to my enquiries, he informed me that he was a cousin of Jiand Khán, who owned some date-groves to the north of the Mashkel groves, which were, he alleged, in British territory. I asked whether he paid any taxes, but he answered in the negative, and said that he had come to see me in the hopes of being given a rifle for proclaiming himself a British subject! This modest request I felt myself quite unable to comply with, but I wrote down all that he said, and, two years later, on the Perso-Baluch Boundary Commission, his information proved to be of considerable value.

We camped near a well almost under the great volcano, and the following morning marched parallel to the range, until we struck the main drainage channel, up which we turned. The ground in parts had been carefully terraced, and this was evidently at one time a fertile centre, but nowadays the fine water-supply runs to waste, a melancholy sight in Persia, where water is so scarce. The terraces were called *Gorbasta*, like the dam on the Konár Rud.

Partridges swarmed here, and, indeed, the whole range was full of them. In the valley we came upon Kosha, the property of Kerím Khán, the ill-starred *Sardár* of Sarhad, and every one wished to stop, but we decided that the higher up we camped the better. Accordingly, at sunset, we pitched our tents at Wáráj, a tiny hamlet, where, at an altitude of 6500 feet, the cold was bracing enough to please anybody. We found a cave large enough to hold all the horses, which was a great boon, as they would otherwise have suffered more than they did.

Brazier Creagh, most unfortunately, was lame from an ulcer on his foot, and as the weather was working up for snow, I determined to make an attempt to scale the mighty volcano on the following morning. Starting before dawn was somewhat trying, and we had the utmost difficulty in persuading our guides to come. For the first seven miles the track lay up the valley, and we might have ridden but for the cold. We then reached a most extraordinary fissure known as the Band-i-Gelu, up which we

KUH-I-TAFTÁN.

[*To face p.* 132.

scrambled, to find ourselves in quite a new country above it, which recalled *Jack and the Beanstalk* to my mind. We next walked up a valley strongly impregnated with sulphur, and at an elevation of some 10,000 feet the actual climb began.

We first rose over the side of a hill and descended to a spring of excellent water, termed Ab-i-Kwásh, where we rested for a few minutes. Thence the ascent was stiff, and I had much difficulty in keeping to it, and still more in driving the guides, who felt the cold infinitely more than I did, as they were miserably clad. Huge boulders had to be surmounted for some distance, but the last 1000 feet was covered with deep white ash, which, when sighted from a distance, has given rise to the belief in the existence of eternal snow on the range.

It was not until 2 P.M., after eight hours' climbing almost without a rest, that we were able to rejoice in the fact that we had reached the summit. We found that the Kuh-i-Taftán was double-headed, the northern and slightly higher peak being known as the Ziárat Kuh or Mountain of Pilgrimage, while on the southern one was the volcano we had come so far to see, the surface of both being level, and separated by a slight depression. This latter is known as the Mádar Kuh or Mother Hill; to the west, separated by a precipitous ravine, is the Nar Kuh or Male Hill, and to the south-east, the Subh Kuh or Morning Hill. None of these hills are of importance, and only the Mádar Kuh is a volcano which, according to General McMahon, Vice-President of the Royal Geological Society, to whom I described it, is in the *solfatara* stage of its existence.

The crater, which was belching out blinding clouds of sulphurous smoke, consists of two apertures, each some three yards in circumference, which apparently unite close to the surface, as there was only a narrow strip of ground a yard wide between them. There was no fresh lava stream, and there is no record of the volcano ever having been in eruption. Yet it was not without considerable difficulty that we collected samples of the sulphur and sal-ammoniac[1] which form part of the revenue paid by Sarhad.

The view was the finest that I have ever enjoyed in Persia, every peak within a hundred miles standing out distinctly, as we looked across to Sistán and the Zirra in the dim distance. The cold

[1] These specimens are in the British Museum.

was intense, but I gladdened the hearts of the guides by allowing them to warm their hands on the hypsometer, which showed the altitude to be 12,452 feet. Although the day was bright, it was freezing so hard that when our work was done, our hands felt as if they would drop off, and as the sun was sinking fast, we raced down the cone, which had taken us hours to climb.

Hurrying against time, we reached the Band-i-Gelu after sunset, and, swallowing down an egg and some chocolate, I stumbled down the valley, reaching camp at 9 P.M., after spending a really pleasant Christmas Eve in scaling *the* mountain of Baluchistán. The volcano is locally known as the Kuh-i-Chehel-Tan or Mountain of the Forty Beings, who visited the range and disappeared; Taftán or Daftan signifies "boiling." The same legend is told at Quetta, and indeed is common in this part of Asia. So far as I could learn, the inhabitants of the valley have worshipped the volcano from earliest times, and it seems probable that the Forty Beings, in whose honour sacrifices are now made, were but an afterthought. My guide, an intelligent man of his class, said that they called themselves Mohamedans, but knew nothing whatever about the tenets of the religion, and that they worshipped the volcano.

There were numerous dams and terraces, together with remains of orchards in the valley in which we were encamped, and while exploring a parallel valley, we discovered a small lake in what, I think, must be an extinct crater. It is said to be very deep, contains sweet water, and was full of duck, as, strangely enough, it was not frozen over. Above it we scaled a perpendicular-looking hill of fantastic shape, known as the Kuh-i-Legwár, as we wished to have yet another view across the wild scene, which a heavy fall of snow had much beautified.

Opposite many of the ruined forts in the valley were oval caves, cut out of the cliff, and for a while I thought that they might be humble imitations of the tombs at Persepolis, but it seems more likely that they were the chief's granaries, although in troublous times somewhat exposed. One that I visited was eight feet in length, six feet in width, and five feet in height. None of them bore any signs of smoke and all were very difficult of approach. The inhabitants said that they were excavated in the time of Kudru Pádsháh, by which they may mean Khusru of the Indo-Iránian epic. In any case, this valley was evidently at some remote period an important centre, and it is a pity that there is no mention of the volcano by any of the early travellers.

A product of the range is *Mak*, which is a yellow marl, resembling in appearance the barley dampers which we were reduced to eating. It contains sulphate of iron, and when mixed with the leaves of a shrub termed *khanjak* yields a strong black dye.

Minerals may abound, but Brazier Creagh found none. We, however, heard of a certain Kuh-i-Ganj or Treasure Hill, with an unapproachable cave said to be full of gold. The cliff overhangs so much that men who have been let down to its level have not been able to reach it for want of further appliances, but have seen two great jars. I imagine that there may be a substratum of truth in this story. Well-carved tombstones, none however with very ancient dates, were to be seen in various parts, and it is evident that the country has not advanced in the path of civilisation, as nothing of the sort is achieved to-day.

On New Year's Day, 1894, we broke up camp and started off to find the village of Bazmán, where we had ordered our heavy baggage to meet us. As we had been delayed by the snowfall, a famine was imminent, and we were all on reduced rations of flour. The abundance of hill partridges, however, kept us in meat, as we had no less than forty in hand at one time. We skirted the range which runs more or less east and west, and after crossing several valleys, emerged on to a boulder-strewn plain, and camped at a pool of bitter water, opposite the Kuh-i-Ganj referred to above. The elevation was 5500 feet, but after the intense cold at Wáráj we all felt slack, which proves how everything is, after all, comparative.

The following day we steered for the conspicuous Gwárkuh range. The plain is termed Gálángaur, and under the hill were a few families of Rekis, but, alas! no supplies were forthcoming. Rounding Gwárkuh, we came upon a *tághur*,[1] known as Kal Mazár, and crossed Captain Jennings' route. He had been informed that the water of Kal Mazzár, as it is termed, had an exit to the west, but this is not the case. This *tághur* forms a triangular swamp which should afford grand shooting, the west end being some six feet deep.

[1] *Tághur* is the Baluchi for a *hámun*, an area receiving drainage from all sides without an exit.

We camped in the desert, and that night our guide absconded, averring that one of the camelmen had threatened to poison him. The fact was that, having been away for more than a month, all had earned what, in their eyes, was wealth, and were anxious to follow the shortest route back to Bampur. Our position was unpleasant, as all our stores except an ounce of tea were exhausted, and we were living on partridges and barley damper. Worse than this, we had only one feed left for our horses. However, we knew that Bazmán could not be more than forty miles off—it proved to be thirty-nine—so Brazier Creagh stayed with the camelmen, to prevent them from deserting us, while Sultán Sukhru and I went ahead to find a road. Climbing a hill, we noted a valley running out on to the plain, beyond which the Bazmán peak rose up in stately majesty. Most fortunately, it was practicable for camels, and we gradually descended to the wide plain, skirting yet another *tághur*. We finally hit a track which ran due south, camping for the night near three wells of drinkable water, termed Shuráf or Salt Water, where a heavy gale blew down most of our tents, and so secured an early start in the morning.

We had eaten our last morsel of bread and the horses their last grain of barley, and we must perforce either reach Bazmán or else go hungry. At any rate, our loads were light enough, and starting off early, we soon crossed the watershed, which separates the drainage flowing into the Bazmán *tághur* from that reaching the Bampur river, by the Rud-i-Kaskin. We sighted a black tent inhabited by Nahruis, who would not guide us, but pointed to a break in the hills to the south of the peak. Feeling once again that we knew the way, we marched on and entered the hills at about sixteen miles. Sultán Sukhru kept too far north, and struck a track which finally brought him to the village of Pansára, lying under the great peak, where he wisely spent the night. Hour after hour we scrambled down rocky valleys, and, hungry as we all were, it seemed as if we must stop, the camels being worn out, when, to our joy, we caught a glimpse of date-palms, and by an hour after dark were encamped at Bazmán. Here our stores and two posts met us, and we felt easier in our minds than we had been for many a day, as hunger is by no means agreeable, while to see one's horses daily growing thinner is simply heart-breaking.

The record of the five last stages will show that at present

Sarhad is almost uninhabited, but the water-supply is comparatively abundant, and it only requires a greater sense of security, combined with just rule, to make it a splendid country. Although raiding seemed still to be much in fashion, we did not suffer from it, being welcomed by all classes when it was known who we were; and thanks to this, our exploration of Sarhad was brought to a successful conclusion.

into Sarhad, although its northern continuation is known as Kuh-i-Paskuh, and, after riding for a short time, we caught the first glimpse of Taftán, distant about 100 miles, and wondered whether we should be able to scale it. In the extreme distance it resembled a white cone, which is by no means its real shape.

Thanks to our guide, we camped at a pool of filthy water, although to our annoyance the next morning we found a beautiful spring a mile or two distant, known as Chashma-i-Pír. However, that is one of the drawbacks of exploring, but there are many compensations, as it is intensely interesting to form theories as to the lie of the country and the trend of the drainage; moreover, in parts where a European has never been seen, it was amusing to see how we struck the inhabitants.

In the course of the next march we crossed from the valley we had followed into one of more importance, known as the Kaur-i-Gerisht, and, to our surprise, found a large village called Paskuh.[1] The very dark inhabitants declined to give us supplies, on the ground that they were in rebellion. However, we pointed out that that did not affect their relations with us, and, after assuring them that we had nothing to do with the unpopular Governor of Sib, we were taken into their confidence, Brazier Creagh, as usual, winning their affections by dosing the sick. He noticed a flail at work, which is the only one we saw in Baluchistán. We both agreed that there must be much negro blood to cause the remarkable darkness of the people, but as it was just the same in Sarhad, I have since come to the conclusion that, being so remote, these people are the aborigines referred to in chap. viii.

The onward road lay up a wide open valley, and the second stage from Paskuh brought us into Sarhad, the mysterious and dangerous, as we had learned—quite wrongly—to consider it. From the watershed, which we crossed at 4600 feet, an altitude not much greater than that of Magas, we looked down on one of the wide expanses of savage scenery which are typical of this part of Asia. Not a village, not even a nomad tent, was to be seen, but in every direction tier upon tier of rugged barren ranges rose up, giving the idea of unlimited space, which somehow or other is always pleasing, there being, at any rate, no feeling of confinement.

[1] The inhabitants comprise Nodzái, Sandakzái, Chahárizái, Mazárzái, Gamshazái, and Shádádzái.

hospitality, he professed a hope that we should meet again when the *Farmán Farmá* reached Baluchistán.

Shortly after parting from Asad Ulla Khán we were accosted by a well-dressed Baluch, who was accompanied by five followers, and stated that he was a British subject. In answer to my enquiries, he informed me that he was a cousin of Jiand Khán, who owned some date-groves to the north of the Mashkel groves, which were, he alleged, in British territory. I asked whether he paid any taxes, but he answered in the negative, and said that he had come to see me in the hopes of being given a rifle for proclaiming himself a British subject! This modest request I felt myself quite unable to comply with, but I wrote down all that he said, and, two years later, on the Perso-Baluch Boundary Commission, his information proved to be of considerable value.

We camped near a well almost under the great volcano, and the following morning marched parallel to the range, until we struck the main drainage channel, up which we turned. The ground in parts had been carefully terraced, and this was evidently at one time a fertile centre, but nowadays the fine water-supply runs to waste, a melancholy sight in Persia, where water is so scarce. The terraces were called *Gorbasta*, like the dam on the Konár Rud.

Partridges swarmed here, and, indeed, the whole range was full of them. In the valley we came upon Kosha, the property of Kerím Khán, the ill-starred *Sardár* of Sarhad, and every one wished to stop, but we decided that the higher up we camped the better. Accordingly, at sunset, we pitched our tents at Wáráj, a tiny hamlet, where, at an altitude of 6500 feet, the cold was bracing enough to please anybody. We found a cave large enough to hold all the horses, which was a great boon, as they would otherwise have suffered more than they did.

Brazier Creagh, most unfortunately, was lame from an ulcer on his foot, and as the weather was working up for snow, I determined to make an attempt to scale the mighty volcano on the following morning. Starting before dawn was somewhat trying, and we had the utmost difficulty in persuading our guides to come. For the first seven miles the track lay up the valley, and we might have ridden but for the cold. We then reached a most extraordinary fissure known as the Band-i-Gelu, up which we

KUH-I-TAFTÁN.

[*To face p.* 132.

scrambled, to find ourselves in quite a new country above it, which recalled *Jack and the Beanstalk* to my mind. We next walked up a valley strongly impregnated with sulphur, and at an elevation of some 10,000 feet the actual climb began.

We first rose over the side of a hill and descended to a spring of excellent water, termed Ab-i-Kwásh, where we rested for a few minutes. Thence the ascent was stiff, and I had much difficulty in keeping to it, and still more in driving the guides, who felt the cold infinitely more than I did, as they were miserably clad. Huge boulders had to be surmounted for some distance, but the last 1000 feet was covered with deep white ash, which, when sighted from a distance, has given rise to the belief in the existence of eternal snow on the range.

It was not until 2 P.M., after eight hours' climbing almost without a rest, that we were able to rejoice in the fact that we had reached the summit. We found that the Kuh-i-Taftán was double-headed, the northern and slightly higher peak being known as the Ziárat Kuh or Mountain of Pilgrimage, while on the southern one was the volcano we had come so far to see, the surface of both being level, and separated by a slight depression. This latter is known as the Mádar Kuh or Mother Hill; to the west, separated by a precipitous ravine, is the Nar Kuh or Male Hill, and to the south-east, the Subh Kuh or Morning Hill. None of these hills are of importance, and only the Mádar Kuh is a volcano which, according to General McMahon, Vice-President of the Royal Geological Society, to whom I described it, is in the *solfatara* stage of its existence.

The crater, which was belching out blinding clouds of sulphurous smoke, consists of two apertures, each some three yards in circumference, which apparently unite close to the surface, as there was only a narrow strip of ground a yard wide between them. There was no fresh lava stream, and there is no record of the volcano ever having been in eruption. Yet it was not without considerable difficulty that we collected samples of the sulphur and sal-ammoniac[1] which form part of the revenue paid by Sarhad.

The view was the finest that I have ever enjoyed in Persia, every peak within a hundred miles standing out distinctly, as we looked across to Sistán and the Zirra in the dim distance. The cold

[1] These specimens are in the British Museum.

Shahabád. A few miles to the east of it is a shrine in honour of *Mir* Mikdád, the standard-bearer of the Prophet's army, and in the cemetery were some particularly well-cut tombstones, one of which bore the following inscription : "*Mir* Ráis Halif son of *Mir* Khodá Dád." The date was A.H. 1059 (1649).

After a day spent in drying our kit, we marched on to Bijenabád, where we were once again on a known route, after having crossed a desert stretch of more than 150 miles with comparative ease as the *Farmán Farmá's* guests. Forage had been stored in advance at every stage, and after the grinding anxiety of the question of supplies in Sarhad, it was delightful to have that care off our minds, the whole party being rationed by our generous host.

It had been intended to cross the Halíl Rud, and march to Kermán *via* Isfandaka, but the river was in flood and impassable. It was consequently decided to proceed through Jíruft and Ráin, and we swung north towards the Jabal Báriz range, marching parallel to the Halíl Rud, which above Bijenabád flows almost at right angles to its lower reaches.

The first stage lay through a comparatively fertile district, and near the Jíruft boundary, which we crossed at eighteen miles, we passed a warm spring possessing healing properties, and known as Chashma Abbád. The following day we reached Dusári, the capital of Jíruft,[1] where most of the land is Government property. Rough rugs and saddle-bags were brought for sale, the latter costing about five shillings a pair, with a not unpleasing design, and there was a brisk trade, prices ruling only half as high as at Kermán. The date-grove of Dusári lies under a high limestone range, a lovely spring welling out from the cliff in which we had a swim, while close by was a most picturesque old mill, constructed of palm logs, the village lying some distance from the grove out in the open. As usual, we carefully examined the cemeteries, where some of the tombstones bore inscriptions dating from the seventeenth century, which were beautifully inscribed.

The whole of the mighty range which divides the hot country of Jíruft from the cold uplands of Ráin and Sárdu is termed

[1] Jíruft is full of nomads, who will be referred to in connection with their summer quarters. Váli Oshághi, an offshoot of the Afshárs, live in the district all the year round.

Jamal Báriz on the latest maps, but this is erroneous. The correct name is Jabal Báriz and is applied to the section of the range with a great peak, termed Amjaz, towering above Dusári, and also to the mountains running down to the Kermán road. A little further east is the Zurnák pass, which has hitherto not been explored; across it runs a direct but hilly route to Narmáshir.

After halting for *No Rus*—it is considered most unlucky to travel on the Persian New Year's Day—we continued our march parallel to the great range, passing a low hill known as Khar Pusht or Donkey Back. The country was so stony that shooting from horseback was considered too dangerous, even by the reckless Persians, but twenty-nine gazelles were bagged, mostly on foot.

At Dasht-i-Kuch we were opposite the famous City of Jíruft, but the day after our arrival the river was quite impassable for horses, so we crossed the river Shúr which flows down from Sárdu, and lunched on the bank of the Halíl Rud, across which some villagers swam to amuse their ruler. As the flood was falling we determined to remain a day after the departure of the *Farmán Farma*, and, being placed in charge of Husein Khán, the chief of the Mehni, we forded the fast-flowing torrent, which was some 200 yards wide, and explored the city termed *Camadi* by Marco Polo.[1] We slept in a *kutuk*, a primitive tent manufactured of goats' hair, and a distinctly airy domicile. After a long day spent in exploration, we returned to find our tents, which had been left standing when the Persian camp was struck, black with flies.

In consequence, we made an early start, but, even so, a cloud of flies accompanied us, which, do what we would, we could not shake off, and life was perfectly miserable. Altogether, we were glad to be leaving the Hot Country, where the noon temperature was rising unpleasantly, although we both considered the Halíl valley to possess much potential wealth. After skirting the main range for some miles, we turned up a *nala*, and ascended a narrow gorge overgrown with oleander, a deadly poison for camels.[2] Thence we descended into the valley of the Saghdár,[3] the scenery recalling the low hills on the Simla road, and camped near a fine brawling

[1] *Vide* chap. xxiii.

[2] Cf. Strabo, bk. xv. cap. ii. 7: "There was a plant resembling the laurel, which if eaten by the beasts of burden caused them to die of epilepsy, accompanied by foaming at the mouth."

[3] *Sagh* is the blackberry.

stream, the water of which tasted delicious. We were at an elevation of just under 5000 feet, and but for the flies, we should have enjoyed the cool air as well as a superb view of the snow peaks to the west.

We overtook the *Farmán Farmá* at Maskun, one of the numerous hamlets in these delightful well-watered highlands,[1] which swarm with partridges in the autumn. Gudár-i-Deh-Bakri, so called from a district of that name, which forms the summer retreat of the *Kháns* of Bam, was crossed at 7380 feet above the sea; in these regions, as may be imagined, it is never hot. From its well-wooded summit we could see across the low Kuh-i-Kafut which bounds the Bam plain, and our vision included endless leagues of the Lut.

From Marghak we marched towards the Kuh-i-Jupár, catching a glimpse of Bam fort on the way, and halting at the storm-tossed village of Sarbistán,[2] where the force of the wind had destroyed the half-grown crops. In our case, we could hardly sleep, so violent was the gale, and we left full of pity for the inhabitants.

A short march brought us to Pábana,[3] during the course of which we crossed the Sárdu river, a fine stream some thirty yards wide flowing towards Bam, and the next day we reached the little town of Ráin, where the acres of walled garden afforded a pleasant contrast to the squalor we had left behind. We there had the first sight of the white-robed women, a colour peculiar to Kermán, white being reserved for Jewesses in Yezd, and dark blue being the rule for Mohamedans. Ráin,[4] with a population of 5000 inhabitants, and lying at the junction of several roads, has been of importance for many generations, and was the site of a battle between *Malik* Arslán and his half-brother, Bahrám Sháh of the Seljuk dynasty, in the twelfth century.

[1] There are three divisions of the Jabal Bárízi—(1) Maskun, (2) Amjaz, and (3) Gava Kán. The *Kalantar* has a pedigree, showing him to be the twenty-fourth in descent from Sultán Sanjar.

[2] *Vulgo*, Sablistán. The correct form is Sarvistán or the Place of Cypresses.

[3] Lit., "At the foot of the wild pistachio tree."

[4] The nomads of Ráin are as follows:—

Mukbali	100 families
Noshádi	70 "
Hábil	30 "
Ághá Rezá	20 "
TOTAL	220 families.

For many days there had been a somewhat animated discussion as to the relative swiftness of Persian and English horses. The *Farmán Farmá's* doctor, who had been educated in Paris, had evidently not attended any race-meetings, as he gave it as his deliberate opinion that Persian horses were the fastest, and so persistent were they all, that I offered to run my waler, poor and thin as he was, against any of the *Farmán Farmá's* ninety horses. This challenge occasioned much excitement, which was increased when a large wager was proposed, but, as we declined to run for money, every one thought that our defeat was certain; we were also much chaffed at racing a horse like a camel (as they said) against the famous Arab horse "Gazelle Slayer," which was finally selected to run for the honour of Persia.

Brazier Creagh, who weighed considerably less than myself, agreed to ride the waler, while the *Farmán Farmá* was to be judge, and I occupied the post of starter. An objectionable uphill course[1] with a quantity of scrub was first measured, the length being rather less than a mile, and I mounted a horse of the *Farmán Farmá's*, as I wished to see the race, and was afraid that if I rode one of my own ponies, "Cotmore" might not start properly. After much waste of time, the *Farmán Farmá* riding down twice to give his final instructions, the start was successfully accomplished, and, as we expected, "Cotmore" galloped off, leaving the famous Arab far behind, and Brazier Creagh rode very easily past the winning post, about fifty yards ahead. In the meanwhile, after the start, I rode behind, and, to my surprise, saw that after half-way I was steadily gaining; I managed finally to come in second. This was too much for His Highness, who said that he fully realised that walers were much faster than Arab horses, but that my coming in second would ever be a puzzle.

Ali, the *Farmán Farmá's* jockey, was in a piteous state, and said, "May I be your sacrifice, how could I get near a horse which looks like a camel, but gallops faster than the wind?" I was puzzled at the utter failure of the "Gazelle Slayer," but it was perhaps partly to be accounted for by the inferior nature of Persian bits[2] and saddles, and the fact that Ali started off riding all he

[1] The elevation was 8000 feet, which might, I feared, affect my horse.

[2] The Persian bit has a terribly high port, while, in addition, there is a strong ring attached to the cross-bar. As a result, horses fear to lengthen their stride, and star-gazing is common.

knew, and pounded his horse. Moreover, we heard that their stable management was very poor, the horse having been overfed for several days, but given nothing, not even water, for ten hours before the race! Altogether, the match was the necessary ounce of practice, and opened the minds of His Highness and suite more than anything else could have done, while the result of the race was, of course, known all over the province.

That night our servants, who had won many bets, which, by the way, were never paid, enjoyed their triumph, and one of them who had studied the works of Sadi kept reiterating, "In the day of contest one lean horse is better than a stable full of asses."

The Hanaka *caravanserai* where we halted lies at an altitude of 7500 feet, at a point where the pass is somewhat shut in, although not exactly narrow. The ride down to Máhun being short, we started late, and, clearing the hills, saw the blue *minárs* of the famous shrine in the distance, and in a short time were comfortably established in the beautiful garden of the *Farmán Farmá*. Coming out of a stony desert, the contrast afforded by fountains, running water, and shady trees was almost overpowering, and when we were seated in the cruciform room overlooking the plashing jets of water, the murmur was so soothing that we could hardly keep awake.

We were readily shown over the shrine, which was erected in honour of *Seiid* Nur-u-Din, Yezdi, better known by his title of *Sháh* Namat Ulla. He was a descendant of *Imám* Bákir, and was born at Aleppo in A.H. 730 (1330). He acquired much learning, and began a course of travel, spending eighty days in meditation on the summit of Demávend in mid-winter, and a similar period on Mount Alvand—the Orontes of the Greek geographers. He thence proceeded to Kerbela, where he lived on dust for forty days, from which shrine he visited Najaf, and resided for a period of seven years at Mecca. He then joined *Sheikh* Abdulla Jafar, and travelled with him for some years, during which he probably visited India. At Samarcand Tímúr showed him much honour, but as his followers increased too rapidly, the Great Conqueror built a house for him at Máhun and sent him there, to keep him at a distance. However, he was a born rover, and soon started off to Shiráz, where it is stated that every one showed him great respect. Ahmad Sháh Bahmani, king of the Deccan, sent him such valu-

THE MÁHUN SHRINE.

[*To face p.* 148.

able presents that the custom dues amounted to £70,000; this sum Sháh Rukh remitted, as his wife pointed out that, if exacted, it would not look well in history! He finally died in A.H. 834 (1430), at the age of one hundred.

The prophecies of the *Sháh* (here used as a religious title of honour) are still current. The most famous of them Mrs Steel, in *On the Face of the Waters*, has rendered into verse as follows:—

"Fire-worship for a hundred years,
A century of Christ and tears,
Then the true God shall come again,
And every infidel be slain."

This prophecy was on every one's lips a generation ago, and was a cause, if not a main one, of the Indian Mutiny. A second prophecy was to the effect that the last Sháh of Persia would be called Násir-u-Dín, and this, as I know from what came under my own observation, was much quoted by the Baluchis, although it was happily proved incorrect.

Seen from a distance, the blue dome and *minárs* are most beautiful, but the entrance to the shrine would be disappointing were it not for some of the superb plane-trees which go so far to redeem the landscape in Persia. Inside, the courtyard was charming with shade, water, and blue tiles, but the interior of the shrine was not imposing, the walls being in need of repair. The floor was covered by a fine old carpet with large medallions presented to the shrine by Sháh Abbás, which has since been bought by M. Rakovsky. The date woven in it is A.H. 1067 (1656), whereas the great monarch died some years previously.[1] A fine shawl concealed the tomb, and on the walls I noticed a pair of black-buck horns from India. There was said to be a good library, but I heard that all the manuscripts had been allowed to rot; there are also other tombs in the same building, among them that of the son of the *Sháh*.

Mohamed Sháh assigned half of the land of Máhun to support the shrine, but, as usual, the money is partly misappropriated, although I believe that pilgrims are entertained free of cost, and there appeared to be a permanent population of dervishes.

[1] Probably the date shows when it was finished.

Between Máhun and Kermán we crossed a belt of sand-hills, which, as M. Khanikoff remarked, rival the Lut. At the same time, the sub-soil must be firm enough, as most of the *kanáts* run under these sand-hills. There is a half-way house termed Paiáb, and in order to let our camels get ahead, we rested for a few hours. It was close upon sunset when, passing the Sar Asiáb range and the ancient forts, I reached Kermán for the second time, exactly a year after my first visit.

SIGNS OF THE ZODIAC.

CHAPTER XIII

THROUGH CENTRAL PERSIA

Fabian.—"I will not give my part of this sport for a pension of thousands to be paid from the Sophy."—*Twelfth Night.*

AFTER halting for ten days, during which we received numerous visitors and added somewhat to our knowledge of Kermán, Brazier Creagh returned to India, and I started for Yezd. Thus, after six months of constant travelling, our party finally broke up.

To the city of Yezd there are two routes, nearly equal in length. The more southerly one is well known, having been travelled over by many Englishmen, including the members of the Goldsmid Mission; whereas on the route *via* Zarand and Báfk I had only one predecessor, Captain Keith Abbot, of whose travels there is but little record.

I found that to the north of Kermán there were villages in considerable numbers, while forage was so plentiful that, although I marched at considerable speed, the horses almost improved in condition. The first stage was Aferábád, one of a group of prosperous villages lying in the open plain; but the following day we passed through low hills, and entered a saline tract, which became very boggy when rain began to fall. We missed our camels, which had been sent further west in order to travel by an easier route, and after waiting for them in vain until dark, we had started forth on the unpleasant task of finding our camp when the heaviest hailstorm broke that I have ever experienced. My waterproof was torn off my shoulders, and the plain became a shallow lake. However, thanks to the flashes, we caught sight of some distant trees, and finally found our washed-out party at Aliabád. As we could not be wetter than we were, we soon had a tent up and a trench dug, but our kit had to stay as it was until the morning, when everything was opened and dried.

It was fortunately only a few miles to Zarand,[1] which has a population of 4000 inhabitants, and lies in a most fertile plain. Sad to say, the people seemed to be miserably poor, and our camp was crowded with beggars. The history of Zarand dates back at least as far as the twelfth century, when it was captured by *Malik* Dinár. It is no doubt of great antiquity, and lying as it does at the junction of several roads, must at one time have been a place of importance. Nowadays it derives its wealth from opium, fields of poppies extending in every direction.

Beyond the decayed town there was a succession of villages for some six miles, then five miles of sandy desert, after crossing which we camped at Akbarábád. Here we were again in a fertile oasis, the chief village, Yazdanabád, engaging in a considerable felt and carpet-weaving industry. The country was now very saline, and before reaching the stage of Sang, we crossed two salt streams flowing north-west to Báfk. Thence to Khudabád, which is eighty-six miles from Kermán, the road was said to be unsafe, Siríz and Khojabád, two important villages, having been deserted *en masse* two years previously when raided by Husein Khán Bahárlu. Khudabád is fed by a stream of salt water, but the crops were excellent. Our party excited extraordinary interest, but the people were friendly, and said that they frequently saw caravans, as there was a desert road across the Lut to Tabas.

Continuing our monotonous march, with a daily increasing temperature, we recrossed the salt stream and rested for a few hours under some tamarisks, wishing to see our camels safely past the jungle, which was said to be the haunt of robbers. As a matter of fact, only very small and weak caravans are held up. We camped for the night at Hauz-i-Dak, after a stage of eighteen miles, and next morning visited the village of Khudrán, occupying the narrowest of valleys, which is walled across. The houses are built on a little ridge, rising tier upon tier, and at the summit grew the finest *chinár* that has ever gladdened my eyes. Its gigantic

[1] The nomads in this district consist of a thousand families of Baluchis.

ALEXANDER THE GREAT CONSULTS THE SPEAKING TREE (ELIAS AND KHIZR ARE CATCHING FISH IN THE SPRING OF ETERNAL LIFE).

[*To face p.* 152.

roots surrounded a *hauz* of water, while its height and spread were colossal, and I can quite imagine how these solitary giants came to be considered sacred. At the same time, living in an enlightened age, it is difficult to understand how largely the legend of these trees entered into mediæval ideas. They were termed the "*Arbre Sol*, which we Christians call the *Arbre Sec*," by Marco Polo, who possibly rested under the one at Khudrán; and another name is the *arbre qui fent*, with reference to their shedding their bark. In connection with the term "Sun Tree," we read in the legendary history of Alexander, one of the few books known in mediæval England, how he meets two old peasants, and is told:

"Thou schalt fynde trowes two:
Seyntes and holy they buth bo;
Hygher than in othir contray all.
ARBESET men heom callith.

. . . .

"'Sire Kyng,' quod on, 'by myn eyghe,
Eythir Trough is an hundrod feet hygh,
They stondith up into theo skye;
That on to the Sonne, sikirbye;
That othir, we tellith thè nowe,
Is sakret, in the Mone vertue.'"[1]

These trees Alexander kissed, and began to wonder whether he should conquer the whole world and return to Macedonia. The Sun Tree replied: "Alexander, thou wilt be King of the whole world, but Macedonia thou wilt never revisit."

The origin of the *Arbre Sec* or *Sec Arbre*, as Odoricus terms it, is undoubtedly a reminiscence of the cursed fig-tree, which became confused with, or perhaps gave place to, the story of the oak at Mamre, which dried up at the death of Our Lord. These two legends were evidently mixed up by Marco Polo, and probably by most of the mediæval travellers, with the delightful vagueness of those early days.

To resume, we bivouacked in the desert, and then descended to the little town of Báfk, where dates flourish at an elevation of 3200 feet. The water-supply was brackish, but we camped near the *kanát*, which we ascertained to be the sweeter, and halted a

[1] Weber, *Metrical Romances*, i. p. 277.

day to rest our exhausted camels. At Khudrán we had crossed into what is nowadays Yezd territory, although Báfk was formerly a town belonging to Kermán, and its infantry was renowned throughout Persia in Sefavi times.

Rather over forty miles of desert lay between us and the Yezd plain, but the hope of seeing fellow-countrymen was a great incentive, and clearing Báfk, which appeared to be half deserted, we descended to the salt river, which we crossed at an elevation of just under 3000 feet, my lowest altitude between Kermán and Tehrán. It is apparently soon lost in a *Kavir*, as we could see a glittering expanse of salt some miles to the north. My subsequent explorations have proved that it is the lower reach of the Lálazár River. The passage of our caravan was taken advantage of by quite a dozen travellers, and as they spoke of robbers, we instituted sentry-go at night; also, owing to the long marches, we always bivouacked. After a march of thirteen hours, we halted at Hauz-i-Tabarku, and the following day stopped for a few hours at Chah Káwar. This well, as the history of the Seljuks shows, was dug by *Malik* Káward in the eleventh century, and that truly great ruler, the *Vakil-ul-Mulk*, began the construction of a *caravanserai*, which, owing to his premature death, has never been completed.

A steady rise brought us to the watershed, from which, in the setting rays of the sun, we could distinctly make out Yezd, and descending an arid slope covered with black gravel, we finally reached Fahraj, after a march of sixteen hours, our camels being utterly exhausted. An easy march, the last few miles of which lay across sand-hills, brought us to the desert city of Persia, lying at an altitude of 4020 feet, where I was received by Mr Ferguson, the manager of the Imperial Bank of Persia, with the hospitality which is so pleasing a feature of Persian travel, and for a few days enjoyed rest.

Life was not, however, a bed of roses for the tiny European community,[1] as not only was there no Governor, but the fanatical element was rather in the ascendant, and, but for fear of retribution, an Englishman's life would not have been safe for a week. The latest excitement was that a notice had been anonymously

[1] It included representatives of Messrs Hotz and Ziegler, which firms had recently established branches.

posted up, in which it was stated that Europeans who rode in the city would be "shot with revolvers," and, in fact, so threatening was the attitude of the Yezdis, that for some days the *bázár* office of the bank was kept closed. It may be urged that the fears of my countrymen were exaggerated, but when it is known that a Zoroastrian had been shot in broad daylight, without any attempt being made to arrest the dastardly assassin, and that murders were of nightly occurrence, I think that it spoke highly for the nerve of those who consented to stay in such a place with wife and child. I am glad, however, to say that since I first visited Yezd, matters have changed for the better. Much credit is due to the civilian pioneers, who here, as in so many parts of the world, have endured more hardships, and run greater risks than usually fall to the lot of a soldier, who is but rarely isolated.

The forward section of my journey as far as Kum was travelled by Marco Polo in the thirteenth century, followed by Odoricus in the fourteenth. In the fifteenth century it was used by Athanasius, Nikitin of Twer, and Josafa Barbaro, the latter explorer's description being as follows:—"Thense (sc. from Yezd) ye go to Meruth, a little towne, and twoo daies jo^r^ney further is a towne called Guerde, in the which there dwell certein men called Abraini, which in myne opinion either be descended of Abraham orells haue Abraham's faith, and they weare longe heare. Twoo daies jo^r^ney further, there is a toune called Naim, evill enhabited, not exceading v^c^ houses; and twoo daies jo^r^ney thense is a towne called Naistan, and from thense twoo other daies jo^r^ney is Hardistan, a little towne that maketh a v^c^ howses. Three daies jo^r^ney thense ye come to Cassan."[1]

Quitting Yezd at the end of April, our road ran across a sandy tract, which was, however, cultivated in parts, to Hujetabád, where a fine *caravanserai* and reservoir for water had been recently constructed. All round was a sea of sand, which the worthy Odoricus describes as "une mer moult marveilleuse et moult perilleuse." It is interesting to conjecture in what terms he would have commented on the Lut. A year later a European lost his way in this waste, and was obliged to walk about all night, to avoid being frozen.

[1] *Travels of Venetians in Persia*, p. 82 (Hakluyt Soc.).

The small town of Meibut, which lies some thirty miles from Yezd, is the *Meruth* of Barbaro; it boasts of a fine *caravanserai*, and the chaotic condition of its city walls can only be compared to those of Kuchán. Nowadays it is famous for the manufacture of *galim*, a very durable hand-woven cotton drugget, the usual colours being red and blue. There being no suitable camping ground, we rode through Meibut, with its adjacent villages, all bearing a look of great prosperity, and stopped for the night at the tiny hamlet of Kuchil. Thence we passed the fertile oasis of Ardakán and reached Agdá in one long stage; it is evidently the Guerde of Josafa, and his remark anent the "Abraini" is of considerable corroborative value, as I find that I wrote in my notes that the *Seiids* of Agdá considered the Parsis their kinsmen, and were, in fact, converted Zoroastrians.

As Ardakán,[1] a famous Parsi centre, was off Josafa's route, he probably only met Zoroastrians at Agdá, although why they were termed *Abraini* it is difficult to say, except that Zoroastrians sometimes identify Zoroaster with Abraham. The fact that it is still the custom to give a title of honour to those who become Mohamedans would satisfactorily account for the inhabitants being *Seiids*.

In the adjacent hills is a shrine in honour of the *Bánu*[2]*-i-Fárs*, the mother, or more likely the daughter, of Yezdijird. The legend runs that when fleeing from the Arabs, she begged some refreshment of a peasant. He immediately fetched and milked his cow, but the malicious beast kicked over the bowl when filled, and the royal fugitive departed thirsty. Until a few years ago, cows were sacrificed at the expense of the Zoroastrians, the killing and eating being done by Mohamedans. The act was evidently retributive, and the sacrifice was only stopped after a reference to Bombay. It was certainly a curious custom.

Two more stages brought us to Náin, the Naim of Josafa, where Nikitin spent a month. It is a small town, and of some importance, as the telegraph line branches off to Kuhpá and Isfahán, although the main road keeps further west, avoiding the

[1] The writings of the *dastur* of Turkábád in the Ardakán district are preserved at Bombay. The ancient faith was forsaken early in the nineteenth century, and only in one village, Sharifábád, is it still maintained.

[2] *Bánu* signifies Queen.

angle. Its ancient fort is known as Kala-i-Gabr, and even the *kanáts* bear Zoroastrian names.

Náin lies at an altitude of just over 5000 feet, and the track gradually rose in two short stages to Naiistanak,[1] the Naistan of Josafa. An almost imperceptible watershed lay between us and Jogand, or Zaferkand, famous for its plaids, and a fourth march brought us to the thriving town of Ardistán, the Hardistan of Barbaro, where our altitude was only 4000 feet. It is one of the most thriving towns in Persia, with rich soil and a population of over 12,000 inhabitants. Its gardens are particularly fine, and I have grateful recollection of the shade they afforded.

As time goes on Ardistán will increase in importance, especially if the Central Persia telegraph be constructed and the line running over the Kohrud be dismantled, as it surely will be; it will then be the station from which the two lines will bifurcate, its only rival, Káshán, being notoriously hot and unhealthy.

Four[2] stages more, and we reached Káshán, there being large villages every fifteen miles, while the track, which runs up the centre of the wide level plain, has nothing to break its even monotony, except a small belt of sand-hills, near the third stage of Abu Zeidabád. At this town the British Telegraph line, with its strikingly neat appearance, is reached, as also the main route through Persia, so that there was a stir and bustle quite novel to the traveller from distant Baluchistán. Throughout this part of my journey, *dari*, the Zoroastrian *patois*, was spoken, and it appears that a somewhat similar language is used in Luristán and Láristán. The heat was very trying, Káshán lying little more than 3000 feet above the sea; it is notorious for its climate, the number of its scorpions, and the cowardice of its inhabitants. It is, however, famous as the home of the beautiful lustred tile termed *káshi*, and the commercial activity of its citizens is proverbial.

The scholarly Herbert, after a learned dissertation about the scorpions, in which he quotes the ancient curse: "May a scorpion of Káshán sting thee," sums up as follows: "This noble city is in compass not less than York or Norwich, about four thousand families being accounted in her. The houses are fairly built, many of which

[1] The suffix *ak* is diminutive.

[2] The distance is about 70 miles, and was accomplished by Josafa in three stages.

are pargetted without and painted; the *Mosques* and *Hummums* are in their cupoloes curiously ceruleated with a feigned turquoise. . . . The silks in such plenty that one Cartwright, an English merchant, who was there about the year 1600, spares not to averr, that there was then more silk brought in one year into Káshán, than broadcloths are into London." [1]

To give an instance of the cowardice of the citizens, it is always cast in their teeth that, when dismissed from Nádir Sháh's army, their contingent asked for an escort home! A second story was told me of a particular individual, to the effect that he was such a coward that he never left home until he was summoned by the Sháh to Tehrán. On the advice of a friend, he converted himself into a walking arsenal, and started off on his journey. However, the Fates were against him, as he met a man with a big stick in his hand, who called upon him to bail up; this he did, handing over his sword, gun, pistols, and horse without any demur. Before returning home he asked the robber for his stick, and, bursting in upon his friend, cursed him for not knowing that a stick was superior to all other weapons! The following proverb with its delicate wit is a further illustration: "A dog of Káshán is the superior of the noblemen of Kum, though a dog is the superior of a Káshâni."

My recollections of the town are of a mass of shabby buildings, topped by a solitary *minár*. As I was anxious to reach Tehrán in time for the celebration of Her Majesty's birthday, and my quarters in one of the very fine *caravanserais* were somewhat public, I did not halt a day, but pushed on to Sinsin, where the *caravanserai* was unspeakably filthy and dilapidated. To Pasangun was another long march, and thence we reached Kum with its golden-domed shrine rising out of a mass of greenery. This town, lying at an altitude of 3200 feet in a barren and salt desert, bordering on the Lut, has had its vicissitudes, and probably only enjoys even moderate prosperity by virtue of its containing the shrine of Fatima, sister of the *Imám* Reza, which draws crowds of pilgrims, especially from Tehrán. It is also the sepulchre of many sovereigns of Persia, among them Fath Ali Sháh, who covered the dome with plates of gilt copper; the father of the present Prime Minister has also contributed largely to the adornment of the shrine. The

[1] *Some Yeares' Travels in Africa and Asia the Great*, p. 223.

THE SHRINE AT KUM.

[*To face p.* 158.

clock, from which may be heard delightfully mellow chimes, was, according to General Schindler, taken from a convent in the Caucasus.

I spent the day at the rest-house of the Road Company, there being a fine wide metalled track from Kum to the capital, but alas! the scale was far beyond the requirements of Persian traffic, and the road, which cost some £80,000, one way or the other, can scarcely be deemed a success. The original concession was from Tehrán to the Kárun at Shuster, but too much money was spent on the section to Kum.

It was about ninety miles to Tehrán, a journey of four days, the country, until quite close to the capital, being extremely desolate, although the recently-formed lake is certainly curious, and I seldom felt happier than when I saw the Union Jack flying inside the leafy groves of the British Legation. I received the most hospitable reception from Mr Conyngham Greene, who, a few years later, was destined to play a prominent part at Pretoria.

After seven months in the wilds, Tehrán life was quite bewildering, but it was immensely interesting to be able to acquire some knowledge of the Persian capital. Mr Conyngham Greene presented me to H.I.M. Násir-u-Din, who enquired in detail about the distant provinces of his Empire which I had visited, and was graciously pleased to remark that I had given him much useful information. The same afternoon I was introduced to H.H. the Sadr Ázam, who, two years later, on the occasion of the dastardly assassination of the Sháh, proved himself to be the most capable subject of the throne, his wise dispositions ensuring order, which is generally conspicuous by its absence when a monarch dies in Persia. Two or three days were spent at Gulahak, a village some six miles from Tehrán, and the property of the British Government; then, leaving Fakir Mohamed in charge of my horses, I started on the last section of my journey early in June.

A carriage was engaged to take me along the unmetalled road as far as Kazvín, whence there is a ride of just 100 miles to Resht, but some 40 miles out of Tehrán a wheel broke, obliging us to ride almost the whole distance, and make up time as well. Kazvín, which lies some 4000 feet above the sea, is now a town chiefly distinguished for possessing a broad avenue, but in history it has played a part that appeals to all Englishmen, and carries us back to the days when traveller and hero were interchangeable terms, and when Horace's *Illi robur et aes triplex* was even more applicable than when he wrote the lines.

During the reign of Queen Elizabeth, before the defeat of the Armada, the Indian Ocean was a *mare clausum*, and our mariners were driven to try for a north-east or north-west passage to India, the trade with Southern Asia having been from earliest times a commercial question of the greatest importance. It is not too much to say that upon it hinges the policy of all the Empires that the world has ever seen, except perhaps that of China, even the Transvaal War being connected with it, owing to the importance of South Africa as the half-way house to India.

One of the greatest, albeit less famous, Elizabethan heroes was Antony Jenkinson, who, upon the discovery of the White Sea by Richard Chancellor (who was, unfortunately, drowned shortly afterwards), opened up a trade with Russia, which resulted in great mutual profit, and the Englishman so pleased Ivan the Terrible that he sent him as his ambassador to Bokhára. Afterwards, he permitted British goods to pass free through the country, Jenkinson having conceived the audacious design of trading with Persia across Russia; a truly colossal scheme, when it is recollected that the Tsar had not even control of the Volga, and that the Crim Tatárs burned Moscow about that period.

Jenkinson, however, knew no fear, and launching into the unknown Caspian, which he roughly surveyed, landed at Shemákha,[1] a little to the north of Báku, whence, having gained the friendship of Abdulla Khán, king of Shirván, he proceeded to Kazvin, and presented himself before Sháh Tahmásp, whom he quaintly terms *Shaw Thomas*. To quote the Englishman's words: "Comming before his majestie with such reverence as I thought meete to bee vsed, I deliuered the Queenes majesties letters which he accepting demaunded of me of what countrey of Franks I was: vnto whom I answered that I was of the famous Citie of London within the noble realme of England, and that I was sent thither for to treate of friendship." The Sháh was cordial enough until religion was touched upon, when Jenkinson proudly avowed himself a Christian, and the fanatical monarch replied:

[1] Quite recently I have read a notice of its destruction by an earthquake.

"Oh thou vnbeleeuer, we haue no neede to haue friendship with the vnbeleeuers."[1]

Jenkinson's life was indeed in jeopardy, as the Sháh had just concluded a peace with the Sultán, and thought of sending him the infidel's head as a token of friendship, but the influence of Abdullah Khán of Shírván averted this danger, and he was able to establish a trade which, but for shipwrecks and robbery, would have been a success, "London clothes being much talked of in Persia."[2] However six journeys, all unfortunate, succeeded one another, and as Persia was again reduced to anarchy by Turkish inroads, this heroic enterprise was wisely allowed to lapse for a century and a half, after which, as has been already shown, it was revived with even less success.

It is interesting to know that Jenkinson is commemorated in Marlowe's *Tamburlaine*:

> "And Christian Merchants, that with Russian stems
> Plow up huge furrowes in the Caspian Sea,
> Shall vaile to us, as Lords of al the Lake."—ACT I. *Scene* 2.

Furthermore, it was Sháh Tahmásp who formed the theme of Milton's—

> "As when the Tartar from his Russian foe
> By Astracan, over the snowy plains
> Retires; or Bactrian Sophie from the horns
> Of Turkish crescent, leaves all waste beyond
> The realm of Aladule, in his retreat
> To Tauris or Casbeen."
> *Paradise Lost*, book x. line 431.

Leaving Kazvín, which the merchants accurately described as but "euill builded, and for the most part all of bricke, not hardened with fire, but onely dried at the Sunne,"[3] we procured most indifferent horses for the onward journey. First of all, that belonging to the postboy lay down and was left; as the others followed its example, we finally ended the stage on foot, carrying our saddles, the one luggage horse most fortunately holding out. At Mazra, where three years later I was snowed up, we procured good horses, and although there was no moon, we decided to press on, and finally

[1] *Early Voyages to Russia and Persia* (Hakluyt Soc.), p. 147.
[2] *Ibid.*, p. 394.
[3] *Ibid.*, p. 432.

reached Pá-i-Chinár[1] at midnight, after having ridden sixty miles, which had taken us twenty-two hours to accomplish. However, we were now in plenty of time for the steamer, and so went to bed to enjoy a well-earned sleep, only three hours having been our lot on the previous night.

This range of hills crossed by the Kharzan pass is famous as having been the headquarters of the Assassins, and as perhaps some of my readers share my former belief that they were a myth, a demonstration to the contrary may be of interest.

To be quite correct, it was in the latter half of the third century of the *Hijra* that a seventh and last religion was started in the name of the seventh in succession from Ali, the divine Mahdi or Guide, Mohamed, son of Ismáil.[2] Karmat, an early leader, committed horrible excesses. The Assassins were an offshoot of this sect, and were led by a certain Hasan Sabbáh, who was a school-fellow of the *Nizám-ul-Mulk*, the great minister of the Seljuks, and also of Omar Khayyám, one of Persia's sweetest singers. These fanatics appeared to spread mostly in Persia and to the west, and it was with the Syrian branch that the Crusaders were brought into unpleasant contact, Raymond, Count of Tripoli, being murdered in 1149, and Conrad of Montferrat, titular king of Jerusalem, in 1192.[3]

The account given by all mediæval travellers being practically identical, I will quote from the simple Odoricus: "Quant il trouvoit aucun bel homme et vigoureux, il lui monstroit tellement que cilz jouvenceaulz cuidoit estre en Paradis, car par soutilz engins et conduis, il y faisoit venir et plovoir vin, et faisoit à ces jounes hommes toutes les délices que corps d'homme pouvoit demander. Quant cilz vieillars vouloit aucun homme faire morir, il faisoit à aucuns de ces jouvenceaulz donner à boire buvraige qui le faisoit fort dormir, et tout en dormant le faisoit porter hors du Paradis et quant ilz estoient esveillié, il leur disoit que jamais en Paradis n'entreroient s'ilz ne mettoient à mort tel homme."[4]

[1] At the foot of the *Chinár* or Plane-tree.

[2] Some of the questions propounded to enquirers were: "Why did God take seven days to create the world when He could just as easily have created it in one moment?" "What, in reality, are the torments of hell?" "How can it be true that the skins of the damned will be changed into a fresh skin, in order that this fresh skin, which has not participated in their sins, may be submitted to the tortures of hell?"

[3] *Vide* Yule's *Marco Polo*, vol. i. p. 151.

[4] Cordier's *Odoricus*, p. 474.

The sleeping draught contained *cannabis Indica*, or *hashish*, whence the name of assassin. This delightfully simple plan of making every ruler a neutral, under pain of being murdered, flourished for about two centuries, and was finally crushed by Huláku Khán in the middle of the thirteenth century. Hoping to avert their doom by forming an alliance against the Mongol hordes, the Assassins despatched an embassy to the Courts of Europe, one member actually visiting England. It is interesting to note that the descendants of these romantic mediæval *Sheikhs*, after being defeated in a campaign in Baluchistán, became British subjects, with their headquarters at Poona.

To resume the thread of our wanderings, some thirty miles from the coast we entered the lovely forest which, sad to say, reeks with malaria, and arrived at Resht the night before the steamer sailed. To reach Pír-i-Bázár and then be rowed slowly across the lagoon to Enzeli occupied fully six hours, but, to my relief, the steamer was only just coming in, and was boarded in plenty of time. This was my first run along the west side of the Caspian, which must be terribly unhealthy, although the luxuriant vegetation was most attractive after the sterile wastes of Persia.

At Astára, where we crossed the Perso-Russian frontier, and at Lenkorán, there was no time to go on shore, but it was interesting to see how all the officers with their wives came off to the vessel, this evidently forming their only recreation. I felt how thankful we ought to be for our polo, cricket, and other games, which make even the smallest station in India a pleasant place of sojourn, and prevent that feeling of *ennui* which is stamped in large letters on Russian officials, whose fate takes them to distant corners of their mighty Empire.

At Báku I crossed the line of my first journey, intending to visit Derbent, and then travel along the recently opened line from Petrovsk to Moscow. Derbent (*Dar Band*, the Stop Gate) was certainly one of the most famous cities of the world, and probably, owing to its advantageous site, one of the oldest, as the great Caucasus range almost touches the sea, the city picturesquely lining its slope; its walls, which are still perfect, entirely and absolutely bar all passage.

Caterino Zeno, ambassador from the Republic of Venice to the Court of Persia in the fifteenth century, gives the following description of this world-renowned fortress: "Berbento is a city which was built in the passes of the Caspian mountains by Alexander, to resist the incursions of the Scythians, where the pass is so narrow that one hundred resolute soldiers could bar with their pikes the passage of a million of men."[1]

Some fifty miles to the north we arrived off Petrovsk, to enter which our steamer had to execute a left-about wheel, which would be quite out of the question in rough weather. The tiny harbour is formed by two piers, 150 yards and fifty yards in length respectively, with an opening of thirty yards, and there is but room for one ship to discharge at a time. The hills rise above the town, which consists of a main street, ending in the garden which is so pleasing a feature in Russia, and high above, huge white barracks show that there is a strong garrison. As may be supposed in such a hilly country, the Russian Government still has its hands full in repressing brigandage, and stories were afloat that all Russian officers who were caught were cruelly tortured.

No one who has visited the Caucasus, and has read the accounts of mediæval travellers, can doubt the benefits accruing to its inhabitants, who, if they lose their liberty, which was chiefly employed in murdering each other, or in selling their peasants as slaves, are, nevertheless, being slowly civilised. As a reward, Russia reaps undoubted advantages from the construction of this line, which has now been continued to Báku. Hitherto her commerce had been practically suspended during the winter, the Volga freezing up in November, while the military route between Vladikavkaz and Tiflis was also liable to interruption, and never could be used for goods bound to distant Persia.

Nowadays all this is changed, especially since the completion of the Resht-Tehrán road in 1899, and Russian goods can be poured into the land of Irán by routes which contrast more than favourably with those running from the Persian Gulf. This railway is also an additional chain wherewith to bind the Caucasus, which appears to have inherited the defiant restlessness of Prometheus, and finally Transcaspia is brought into closer connection with Russia, Samarcand being to-day less than a week's journey from Moscow.

Three days were spent in the railway, passing through

[1] *Travels of Venetians in Persia*, p. 44 (Hakluyt Soc.).

monotonously level steppes, and we finally reached the ancient capital of Russia, with its interesting associations of Ivan the Terrible and Peter the Great; it struck both myself and Sultán Sukhru, whom I took home as a reward for his faithful service, that it bore a distinctly Asiatic aspect, and the contrast at St Petersburg was quite startling. There, thanks to the great kindness of Mr (now Sir Henry) Howard and Major (now Sir Edward) Law, I spent two delightful days, after which the train rapidly bore me home *via* Berlin and Flushing. I thus completed nine months of constant travel and unfailing enjoyment.

DESIGN FROM A KERMÁN SHAWL.

CHAPTER XIV

THE MARCH OF ALEXANDER THE GREAT FROM THE INDUS TO THE KÁRUN.

"Comparisoun myght never yit be maked
Bitwixe him and another conquerour;
For al this world for drede of him hath quaked,
He was of knyghthode and of fredom flour."

—CHAUCER, *The Monke's Tale.*

THE unrivalled exploits of Alexander the Great still form a theme which, in the East at any rate, will never pall, while we, as Europeans, may well feel proud that a Greek conqueror should have made a deeper impression on the imagination of Asia than any Persian, Arab, Mongol, or Turk. In consequence, everything connected with the World-Conqueror's journey is, I venture to think, of great and enduring interest. Before, however, discussing his famous expedition, it may be as well to touch upon the services which he rendered to geography, both directly and indirectly.

For centuries anterior to the rise of Greek civilisation, Phoenician keels had explored to the western extremity of the Mediterranean

Sea, and evidence of the existence of a still earlier race of navigators is being gradually collected. But the Phoenicians so jealously guarded their secrets that the Greeks learned little or nothing from them: thus geography actually came into existence long after the Phoenicians had established a commerce in tin with the far-distant Cassiterides, although no Greek vessel had even sighted the Pillars of Hercules.

In the sixth century B.C. Hecataeus, the Father of Geography, displays an intimate acquaintance with the lands bordering on the Mediterranean Sea as far west as Sardinia, while to the east he possesses a general acquaintance with Asia as far as the Indus, making special mention of Caspapyrus, the town on the Indus, from which, under orders from Darius, Scylax of Caryanda was said to have travelled down to the Erythrean Sea. Egypt, too, is described from the writer's personal experiences.

A century later Herodotus, the Father of History, collects an immense amount of geographical knowledge, although his work was primarily historical. The range of his ken was indeed hardly wider than that of Hecataeus, and he declines to believe in the existence of a sea, either to the north or to the east of Europe; on the other hand, he regards the Caspian as an inland sea, whereas Alexander treated it as connected with the ocean. He refers to the reputed voyage of Scylax from the Indus to the Erythrean Sea, and also to the still more doubtful circumnavigation of Africa by the orders of Necho, in connection with which he names the Atlantic—for the first time so far as we are concerned. Western Asia being at that period almost entirely included in the Persian Empire, it was possible to obtain satisfactory information about its political geography, and thus Herodotus is able to give an account of the twenty satrapies into which Darius divided his vast possessions. As in the case of Hecataeus, India[1] made a great impression on the writer, who mentions cotton as well as gold. The voyages of Sataspes, who explored the coast of Guinea until driven back by the trade-winds; of Hanno, who followed in his footsteps; and of Hamilco, who explored Western Europe, are all authentic, but our attention must rather be directed to the

[1] India only included the valley of the Indus, so far as Herodotus and the writers for many centuries after him were concerned. For much of the above information I am indebted to the *History of Ancient Geography*, by H. F. Tozer.

Retreat of the Ten Thousand, the successful issue of which was evidently a main factor in determining Alexander the Great to throw down the gauntlet to the immense but unwieldy Empire of Persia. After the battle of Cunaxa on the Euphrates, in which the younger Cyrus had fallen, the comparatively small force of Greek infantry was in a position of the greatest difficulty, fearing to return by the open country, on account of their weakness in mounted troops. It was finally decided to march almost due north to the Black Sea, and this stupendous feat was accomplished, mainly by the genius of Xenophon, who safely led his army across the Armenian plateau in midwinter.

The battle of Cunaxa having taken place in B.C. 401, and that of the Granicus in B.C. 334, many of Alexander's councillors must have come in contact with the soldiers of Xenophon, and it was doubtless in full reliance on the proved superiority of the Greek shock tactics that the momentous expedition was undertaken. As its result an extraordinary expansion was produced in the field of geography by the exploration and subsequent colonisation of the country lying between the Tigris and the most easterly tributary of the Indus, a huge expanse of Asia, bounded to the north by the Syr Daria, and to the south by the Indian Ocean.

Alexander was accompanied by the most scientific men of Greece, whose writings alone must have appealed to all civilised Hellas, but perhaps still more was effected by the constant stream of adventurous Greeks passing across Asia, whose minds must have been widened by personal observation of its stupendous ranges, or, again, by its vast salt deserts and sandy wastes. In short, it may be considered that the horizon of the Greeks was as much enlarged by the conquests of Alexander the Great as was that of Europe by the discovery of America.

It has been my good fortune to be the first European to follow in the footsteps of the mighty Iskandar-i-Rumi,[1] through certain portions of his campaigns, and having also studied various authors on the spot, I am in a position to elucidate much that, from lack of geographical knowledge, has hitherto of necessity remained obscure. Alexander's passage across Eastern Persia being alluded to in another part of this work, I now propose to take up the

[1] *I.e.* Alexander the Greek.

H.I.M. MUZAFFAR-U-DIN, SHÁH OF PERSIA.

[*Frontispiece.*

narrative at the point when, after successfully traversing the Panjáb, a halt was made on the banks of the Hyphasis, the modern Bias.

Seeing that, before crossing to the Ganges valley, he must ascertain whether his army would support him, a subject on which he had doubts, Alexander made a spirited harangue, which is fully given both by Arrian[1] and Curtius. This, however, produced no effect on the war-worn veterans, who were only anxious to reach home safely with their wealth, and after waiting for three days in the hope that the impulsive Greeks might change their minds, the Great Soldier finally suffered himself to be conquered by his army, and the return journey was ordered. Retracing his steps past Lahore and Wazirábád, constructed and fortified by Hephaestion, and now the prosaic junction for Sialkot, he formed a standing camp on the Hydaspes, the modern Jhelum, where a large fleet was rapidly constructed for sailing down what were at first believed to be the upper reaches of the Nile. This misapprehension shows that the study of geography was less advanced than in the days of Herodotus, and also increases the improbability that Scylax was Alexander's predecessor. The number of men carried on board ship being only 8000, out of a total of 120,000, it is evident that the fleet was built for exploration, but the absence of dockyards must have been severely felt.

After pouring a libation not only to the Hydaspes but also to the Akesines (the modern Chenáb), into which it flowed, the Conqueror of Asia started off on a voyage which was destined ever to rank among the greatest. At the junction with the Chenáb, the eddies were apparently a cause of much danger, two ships foundering, and further down the hero nearly lost his life in storming Multán. Continuing his voyage, he founded a city at the junction of the Chenáb with the mighty Indus, subduing also the various adjacent kingdoms, but not without considerable trouble and loss.

[1] v. 25, *et seqq.* Arrian is, *facile princeps*, the historian of Alexander; he wrote early in the second century after Christ. For references to him, and to other ancient writers, I have used Mr J. W. M'Crindle's *Invasion of India* and *Periplus of the Erythrean Sea*, and I would beg to acknowledge my indebtedness to their editor. I am perhaps still more beholden for notes on the section of Alexander's journey through British Baluchistán to Sir T. H. Holdich, Vice-President of the Royal Geographical Society.

Upon reaching the apex of the Indus delta, Krateros, of whom more anon, "was despatched into Karmania," while Alexander, after exploring the delta, sailed out into the open sea, in order to place to his record the navigation of the great outer ocean, as Arrian shrewdly remarks. He then parted from his admiral, Nearchos, who was instructed to await the termination of the monsoon before attempting his sea voyage, and, all possible preparations having been completed, Alexander commenced his disastrous journey through Gedrosia.

Most writers on Alexander appear to be somewhat at a loss to account for his choice of such a desert route, as Krateros with the elephants, invalids, and heavy baggage, apparently met with no special hardships, and rejoined his royal master in Karmania by what was evidently a comparatively well-known road. In my opinion, the great Greek, who evidently "thought in continents," had determined to explore the Arabian Sea, the coasts of which he had learned were barren and inhospitable, and therefore the extraordinary policy of marching his army through the desert arose, in all probability, not from any wish to rival mythical journeys of Semiramis[1] and Cyrus, as Arrian makes Nearchos say, or from ignorance of the hardships to be encountered, but from the necessity of supplying his fleet by means of his army. This surely must have been the reason why the main caravan route was not adopted by Alexander, who faced the horrors of the desert rather than let it be said that he deputed to a subordinate a task which he dared not carry out himself.

Quitting the Delta, he advanced to the river Arabios, now the Purâli, upon reaching which he struck down to the coast, dug wells, and collected provisions for the fleet. This having been successfully accomplished and a force left in occupation of the district, the country of the Gadrosi was now entered "by a route mostly desert," as Arrian[2] says. For some stages he maintained touch with the coast by means of the cavalry, and a further supply of provisions was stored for the use of the fleet, part of which was looted by the soldiery, who already felt the pinch of hunger.

About a hundred miles from the Arabios, the Málán range, which abuts on the coast, forced the army to turn inland up the Hingol

[1] Semiramis is the Hindu Sami Rama.

[2] Arrian, vi. 22, 3.

RAS MALÁN, MAKRÁN.

[To face p. 170.

river; the hills are indeed practically impassable, and, in recent times constituted the *crux* of the difficulties which confronted the telegraph line in Makrán. In fact, Sir Thomas Holdich proves beyond doubt that the horrors suffered by the army were concentrated into this section, a distance of more than 150 miles.

The description given might have been written by a modern traveller, and powerfully appeals to every one familiar with Makrán. "For they met with lofty ridges of deep sand, not hard and compact, but so loose that those who stepped on it sunk down as into mud or rather into untrodden snow. . . . . The great distances also between the stages were most distressing to the army, compelled, as it was at times by the irregularity of the water-supply, to make marches above the ordinary length. When they traversed the whole of an allotted stage by night and came to water in the morning, their distress was almost entirely relieved; but if, as the day advanced, they were caught still marching, owing to the great length of the stage, then they were bound to suffer, tortured alike by raging heat and thirst unquenchable."[1]

During my journey from Chahbár to Geh in October 1893, which was also the time of year that the Greek army traversed Makrán, the temperature in the shade—whenever there was any shade—was generally about 100 degrees, while water was almost non-existent, and what little there was we could hardly drink. If the depressing feeling of not knowing the length of the stage or the chances of finding water be considered, then the misery of the situation for the Greek army, wending its weary way among sand-hills, where to take a rest meant almost certain death, can be readily realised.

To make matters worse, a *seiláb* or flood, so much to be dreaded in Baluchistán, added to their misfortunes, and again I cannot do better than quote from Arrian, who writes: "When the army on one occasion lay encamped for the night near a small winter torrent, for the sake of its water, the torrent which passes that way about the second watch of the night became swollen by rains which had fallen unperceived by the army, and came rushing down with so great a deluge, that it destroyed most of the women and children of the camp followers, and swept

[1] Arrian, vi. 24, 4-6.

away all the royal baggage, and whatever beasts of burdens were still left."[1]

Alexander, having lost his way, did not take the most direct route leading down the Basol, but, there is every reason to believe, regained the coast at Pasni, or perhaps a few miles to the east of it. Riding in advance of his army with only five men, he scraped away the shingle on the beach, and found good water, thus terminating the terrors of the desert. From Pasni,[2] which is to-day an evil-smelling hamlet of Ichthyophagi, the route lay along the coast for seven days to Gwádur, a distance of perhaps eighty miles; this village, which lies behind the hammer-like headland, being termed Barna by Nearchos.[3]

From Gwádur, the only comparatively fair track to the Bampur valley is struck; elsewhere, range after range of rugged hills has to be crossed at right angles, as I know to my cost; but between Gwádur and Fahraj the route mainly lies up and down river-beds, which constitute what Baluchis consider to be an excellent road, and it is to-day the only caravan route leading into the interior of Persian Baluchistán from the coast. Arrian simply writes:—"As the guides by this time knew the way, he led his expedition thence into the interior parts."[4] Alexander undoubtedly felt that to continue along the coast would involve the annihilation of his army by famine; he therefore decided to march inland, intending, after he had re-victualled his starving force, again to establish connection with the coast and his beloved fleet.

Poura, the capital of Gedrosia, is the name of the first town, which was sufficiently well stocked to warrant a long halt. As to its situation, there are two villages of that name (termed Fahraj by the Persians, and Pahra by the Baluchis), one in the Bampur valley, and the other in Narmáshir, between which a choice must be made. The word in its various forms signifies "a town," appearing elsewhere as Fara, and being also compounded as in Sultanpor, Jabalpor, and so on.

[1] Arrian, vi. 25, 5. A Governor-General once told me that he always "sticked" his tent-pitchers if he found his camp pitched in a *nala*, and more than once I have had occasion to thank my friend for the advice contained in his remark, as these floods may be generated a hundred miles away, and sweep past with an irresistible fury which is proverbial in Baluchistán.

[2] *Vide* chap. xxv.

[3] Arrian, *Hist. Ind.*, 27, 2.

[4] vi. 26, 5.

THE HINGOL RIVER, MAKRAN.

[To face p. 172.

Alexander's main object being first to rest his army, and then regain touch with his fleet while it was midwinter, he would certainly have taken advantage of the Bampur valley, where supplies were abundant, to re-organise his forces. He would then surely have followed the Hot Country fertile route, running direct to Rudbár, rather than take a line further inland which would involve the traversing of two sides of a triangle, running mainly across the desert. The latter must have been the route followed in part by Krateros, which fact would presumably have been mentioned. Again, this desert, 150 miles wide, has from time immemorial formed a natural division between Gedrosia and Karmania, and if ever a valley has been inhabited from early times, it is that of the Bampur river, with its abundant supply of water and rich loamy soil. Fahraj, in the Bampur valley, also possesses the ruins of two deserted forts, and was in any case a stage on the route. As it is also considered to be of great antiquity, I have no hesitation in selecting it as the capital of Gedrosia, where Alexander rested his army for sixty days. Indeed, if we accept the other site, we are involved in insuperable difficulties, as we must ignore Bam,[1] which was always a noted town, and the capital of the district.

To resume the journey, upon quitting Poura the Bampur river was followed down to where its waters commingle with those of the Halíl Rud, up which river the Greeks then marched. Nowadays, this district is inhabited by a few wild nomads, but numerous ruins testify to a state of departed prosperity, and this was the invariable route by which Baluchistán was invaded from Kermán, as appears in all native historians.

Only one writer, Diodoros Siculus, mentions the name of the city where Alexander formed his standing camp, which he gives as Salmous.[2] Now we know that it was five, probably long, stages from Hormuz, and therefore certainly in Rudbár or Jíruft. In this connection, it is intensely interesting to note that we have a Cono Salmi or *Kahn* of Salmi mentioned by Marco Polo as being six or seven stages from the same port: it is thus probable that the two greatest travellers in classic and mediæval times respectively have crossed one another's routes in the valley of the Halíl Rud.

[1] Bam is only two stages west of Fahraj.

[2] xvii. 106. He quite erroneously places it on the coast.

In chap. xxxvii. reference is made to an alabaster unguent vase of Greek manufacture, which was brought for sale at the hamlet of Bágh-i-Babu. It is hardly possible to doubt that it was left behind by this ever-victorious army, and this chance purchase is indeed of the highest historical value as furnishing what is known as a "fixed point" in survey parlance.

Having thus brought the illustrious Macedonian to Salmous in Rudbár or Jíruft, I now propose to deal with the route followed by Krateros. After being once recalled, he was finally despatched from the Indus delta by the route through the Arachotians and Sarangians. Kandahár, one of the many cities founded by Alexander, was the point first made for, and Sir Thomas Holdich is unquestionably right in his view that the Mulla, and not the Bolán Pass, was traversed. A few years ago, when excavations were made at Quetta in connection with its fort, a bronze statuette of Herakles was dug up, and we may thus feel satisfied that the route lay from the Mulla pass to this point, as indeed the lie of the country would suggest. Similarly from Kandahár the Helmand or Etymander would be followed to Sistán, which then extended to the Shela.

Between Sístán and Narmáshir lies the desert which I traversed in 1899, and, as the range bisecting it has but one pass,[1] opposite Ispi, now known as Nasratabád, we can confidently conduct Krateros over it. The Narmáshir Fahraj would possibly be the first village struck after 180 miles of desert, although a little off the road, and, continuing the journey, we can, with equal certainty, lead Krateros along the modern caravan route which crosses the Sháh Sowarán range by a pass barely exceeding 4000 feet, known as the Kotal-i-Gíshu. Arrian simply says: "When he (*i.e.* Alexander) arrived in Karmania, Krateros joined him, bringing the rest of the army and the elephants."[2]

We next read of the dramatic scene when the ragged, weather-beaten Nearchos visited his lord, who at first wept for the supposed loss of his fleet, but became supremely happy at hearing of its safety. Sacrifices were offered to the Gods, and especially to Poseidon, upon the completion of which ceremony the journey was resumed towards royal Susa. Nearchos was sent back to the fleet, which safely rejoined the army at Ahwáz, while

[1] *Vide* chap. xxxv.

[2] Arrian, vi. 27, 3.

Hephaestion was despatched through the *Garmsir*, because "as he was to make the journey in the winter season, not only was the sea-coast of that country the mildest, but the fleet abounded in all things necessary for the army on board."[1] In this last section, then, we apparently find the *venue* changed, and the fleet supplying the army.

To quote Arrian again: "Alexander, with his best and fastest Light Infantry and his Light Cavalry, marched towards Pasargardae."[2] This probably points to cross-country marching off the regular track; from Rudbár therefore I would lead the hero up the Tang-i-Murdán or Myrtle Defile to Soghun, whence the Kala-i-Sang, an ancient capital, was probably visited. The great *Kavir* was then crossed, and after traversing the rolling downs of Boanat,[3] Pasargardae with its royal gardens was reached, where the Great Conqueror was much distressed on discovering that the tomb of Cyrus had been desecrated.

Appointing Aristobulus to see the monument restored, he next visited Persepolis, where Orsines, the acting Governor of Persia, was crucified for tyrannical administration, and Peukestas, who had behaved so heroically at the storming of Multán, was nominated his successor.

Susa was to be the goal of this truly scientific expedition, the great army being finally concentrated at Ahwáz, where a bridge was built across the Kárun. This section of the long and eventful journey, during which some 28 degrees of longitude were traversed, ran direct from Persepolis to Behbehán, near which town Baron de Bode found traces of the royal road, which, however, still awaits the explorer. From Behbehán to Ahwáz and Susa the country is quite open, and presents no geographical difficulties.

Here, then, we may fitly take leave of perhaps the greatest man ever born, in Shushan the palace, where, to quote from the book of Esther,[4] "were white, green, and blue hangings, fastened with cords of fine linen and purple to silver rings and pillars of marble; the beds were of gold and silver, upon a pavement of red, and blue, and white, and black marble."

[1] Arrian, vi. 28, 7.

[2] *Id.*, vi. 29, 1.

[3] The route by which I travelled from Khára to Aravirjun, Munj, and so down to the Polvár plain, is probably the line followed by Alexander the Great.

[4] Esther i. 6.

FROM LUSTRED POTTERY.

CHAPTER XV

THE FOUNDING OF THE KERMÁN CONSULATE

"Near Spahawn the Vizier, with a Calvacade of about four thousand Horse and innumerable Foot, came out to meet us; The high-way for full 2 miles from the Town was full of Men, Women, and Children: here also we found the *Bannyans* in great numbers; who all altogether all the way, in a volley of acclamations welcomed us; this with the Kettle-drums, Fifes, Tabrets, Timbrels, and other anticks past my remembrance, ennobled the entertainment."—SIR THOMAS HERBERT.

IN October 1894, I was offered the task of founding a Consulate for Kermán and Persian Baluchistán, and although the post was to be unsalaried, and there was but a small office allowance, I was only too glad to continue my travels; I therefore accepted it with readiness. My sister, whom I was fortunately able to persuade to accompany me, has since given her impressions of the country in a book, entitled *Through Persia on a Side Saddle*.[1]

After a few hurried preparations, we started, travelling *via* Constantinople and Batum to Enzeli, which we reached early in December. We met Mr J. R. Preece, then the British Consul, but now the Consul-General at Isfahán, on board the steamer, and enjoyed a pleasant journey together to Tehrán. We were fortunate in crossing the Kharzan pass on a fine day, but, even so, it was hard enough to keep the ponies on their legs, the frozen snow being as slippery as ice, while the wind was bitterly cold. At

[1] Second Edition, 1901. John Macqueen.

Tehrán we were most kindly received by the Minister and Lady Durand, and a delightful winter was subsequently spent there.

We duly visited the ruins of Rei, which are situated some three miles to the south of Tehrán. Nowadays, there is little left except ruined walls and shapeless tumuli, but there is no doubt whatever that excavations would yield a rich harvest. Rei is the Rhages of Parthia and the Rages of the Apocrypha to which Tobias travelled from Nineveh, guided by the angel Raphael, to recover the ten talents deposited with Gabael by his father. Indeed, the book of Tobit has quite a Zoroastrian flavour, as evidenced by the kindly tone adopted towards the dog, an animal which the Jews held to be most unclean. As this curious old work was probably written in the second century B.C., when Rei was a great city, we can fairly claim for the latter a high antiquity, even if its alleged foundation by Cyrus the Great be incorrect.[1]

In Persian eyes Rei was accursed from its connection with Omar Saád, who was deputed by Yezid to slay the martyr Husein. A conference was held, at which he was nearly induced to change his purpose, but the fact that the Governorship of Rei had been promised to him steeled his heart against all better feelings. He has himself left some Arab verses on this subject, of which I append a translation:—

> "Shall I govern Rei, object of my desire? Shall I be accursed for slaying Husein? The murder of Husein damns me to inevitable flames; but yet sweet is the possession of Rei."

In Mohamedan times Rei reached its apogee in the tenth century, when Istakhri remarked that "excepting Baghdád there is no more flourishing city in the East than Rei." The great city suffered horrors from the Mongol hordes, 700,000 of its inhabitants being put to the sword, since which time it has been quite superseded by Tehrán,[2] and owing, no doubt, to the wasted condition of the land, became so fever-stricken that it gave rise to the well-known saying, "I was in a trance and saw the Angel of Death

[1] Mr E. G. Browne informs me that Rei or Ray, as the R.A.S. spells it, is mentioned as Raghâ in Vendidad, chap. ii., and as Ragâ in the Achaemenian inscriptions.

[2] In Yákut's great work, written in the thirteenth century, Tehrán is mentioned as an insignificant village, with inhabitants who occupied underground hovels.

fleeing barefooted from the fever of Rei." A quaint variation of this is given by Chardin, who, for "barefooted," substituted "nud en chemise."

To resume, Tehrán was visited by Ruy Gonzalez di Clavijo, an account of whose embassy to the court of Tímur has been edited by Sir Clements Markham.[1] He wrote: "This city of Tehrán was very large, but it had no walls, and it was a very delightful place, well supplied with everything."

In *Through Persia on a Side Saddle*, my sister wrote: "I confess that I was a good deal disappointed with Tehrán, regarded as the capital of Persia. The gateways look imposing at a distance from their size and colouring, but are crude and ill executed when seen near at hand. Upon entering the city, we drove through a scantily-populated district, squalid booths alternating with waste places or new mud buildings in course of erection, showing that the city had not, as yet, spread out to the full extent of its walls."[2]

The European quarter bears to other towns in Persia the same relation that Pera does to Stamboul, there being an Avenue des Ambassadeurs, which has the makings of a fine street, but there are the same number of dogs as at Pera, and the same lack of neatness, giving a squalid tone to everything. At the time of my visit there was a beautiful garden, known as the Bágh-i-Lálazár, which would have constituted a good lung for the capital, but it has since been broken up into lots and built over. The European quarter occupies most of the north of the city, with many extensive gardens belonging to Persians surrounding it. The palace is in the centre, and to the south are the important *bázárs*. Nor must I omit the magnificent parade-ground where through the kindness of the Sháh, who is particularly obliging in all such matters, polo was started at a later date. Thanks to the great hospitality showered on us, we both enjoyed our stay immensely, paper-chases on horseback, skating, and tent-pegging, all adding to the delights of Tehrán. Indeed, we quite felt as if we were once again leaving home when our mules were loaded up for a fresh start, *Mirza* Nasrulla Khán, a connection of the Nawáb family of Shiráz, who had been educated in England, accompanying me as secretary.

[1] Page 98 (Hakluyt Soc.). I wish also to acknowledge my great indebtedness to his *History of Persia*.

[2] Page 15. (First Edition.)

Even in Ladakh I do not recollect colder days than those which we experienced before reaching Kum, Karizek, where a large sugar manufactory built with Belgian capital now breaks the monotony of the desert, being an especially bleak spot.

At Kum the climate was comparatively springlike, and we decided to start tent-life; while further on at Kashán, always a warm corner, the heat was quite relaxing. Here an afternoon was spent in visiting the beautiful garden of Fin, which is typically Persian. This pleasaunce was beautiful with cypresses of a great size, and clear water running over the light blue tiles for which Kashán has so long been famous. However, the garden bears an ill name, for in the bath-house attached *Mírza* Taki Khán, who attempted to inaugurate reforms by refusing the customary bribes, was doomed to have his veins opened, Persia at that period not being prepared for a Vizier of liberal views.

Leaving Kashán behind, we took up a south-easterly direction, hugging the lower hills of the Kohrud range. A short march brought us to Khurram Dasht, or the Happy Plain, shortly beyond which, while wandering in the hills, we caught the last glimpse of peerless Demávend, the magnificent cone being thus visible at a distance of close upon 150 miles.

During the second day's march, we passed one of the numerous ruined *caravanserais* of Sháh Abbás, and as mile after mile was left behind, we began to think that we had lost our way, when, without warning, we found ourselves looking down an almost sheer cliff 800 feet high, and sighted our destination, the village of Hinján. After a difficult descent we reached this happy valley, where huge masses of conglomerate of every imaginable shape added to the fantastic unreality of the scene. The brook running through the village comes from a delightful hill country, and its two branches[1] are bordered with villages; the district belongs to the Sháh's sister. In these parts a remarkable kind of carpet is woven, the ground being brown, with dull black and red as the chief colours in a somewhat intricate pattern. We bought a specimen, but it showed up so badly in the company of Kermán carpets, that we were glad to get rid of it on any terms.

Continuing to Natanz, there was a gentle ascent, the hamlet

[1] The east branch is known as Chemur Rud, the west branch is the Burz Rud. Abiána on the Burz Rud was said to be the chief village.

of Abbásábád, with a group of superb firs, forming an unusual feature in the landscape. Crossing a watershed, we enjoyed a pleasing view, an uninterrupted succession of orchards lining the valley to the little town, which is the capital of a small district containing seventy-seven villages. Natanz, famous for its climate and fruit, was a favourite summer resort of the *Sefavi* monarchs, a hunting-box of Sháh Abbás still being pointed out on the neighbouring hills. Just as Isfahán is renowned for melons, so Natanz has given its name to a pear rivalling those of the Channel Islands in size, but perhaps hardly equalling them in flavour. There is a mosque still standing, which must formerly have been magnificent; at any rate, I believe that some of the finest lustred tiles in the South Kensington Museum once adorned its walls. It was built in A.H. 715 (1315).

Lying on the winter or lower road to Isfahán and avoiding the Kohrud Pass, Natanz was visited by some of the early travellers. The Magnificent Ambrosio Contarini passed through Nethos, as he terms it, in 1474, and remarked that "it is situated in a plain, and that more wine is made than anywhere else."[1]

For the next 100 miles we were doomed to drink brackish water, although we were still in the hills. Our route to Kuhpá[2] should have run almost due south, but our guides led us along the Isfahán road until, after passing Pábokh and Margh, we emerged on to the open plain. At the latter stage a halt was made to try for an ibex, but, owing to the heavy gales, only one head was seen, and that was too small to shoot. From a distance of perhaps thirty miles, we could descry the great mosque of Isfahán, which city we hoped to visit at some future date.

At Vártun, which lies in the middle of the plain, the water was scarcely drinkable, and we pitied the villagers condemned to such a brand. However, they probably resemble certain old inhabitants of Karachi, who, when a supply of pure drinking water was produced, complained that it was tasteless and insipid!

At Kuhpá we struck the Isfahán-Kermán telegraph line, and halted a day near a *kanát* outside the town, during which time such a gale blew that our tents could never have remained standing, had it not been for a sheltering wall. In 1898, when I again

[1] *Travels of Venetians in Persia*, pp. 129-130 (Hakluyt Soc.).
[2] Or "Foot of the Hill."

halted at Kuhpá, the *kanát* was reduced to half its former volume, giving an example, on a small scale, of the way in which population is forced to shift in Persia, the reduced supply irrigating less land, and thus feeding fewer mouths.

To the south of Kuhpá the map was a blank, and, as often happens in Persia, no reliable information could be obtained, but as we carried two days' supplies in reserve, we determined on exploration. Our route lay across a thickly-inhabited plain, towards a low range of hills, which we entered at thirteen miles, and, after following a stony track for a short distance, we camped at Guchkun, where we all revelled in the first drink of sweet water since leaving Natanz. Guchkun consists of two hundred houses, and can boast of a very picturesque old fort, which we scrambled up to inspect. From it we enjoyed a glorious view across the lake in which the Zenda Rud is absorbed. This *Kavir*—for its sides are coated with glistening salt—is generally termed *Kavir* Isfandiárán, from a large village of that name on the western edge, but other names are also given, Gávkháneh, its title on the map, being possibly an alternative to Gaukhána, from *Gaud*, signifying hollow.

The next stage led us to Ushk, lying in the outer hills of the same range, and we thence made for the Kuh-i-Chirás, an isolated peak which I was anxious to climb. From its summit, at 7400 feet, the view was most extensive, especially to the north, where peak after peak was recognisable. To the south-west I could clearly see the great ranges to the west of the Shiráz-Isfahán road, thus connecting with my first journey, and between us and Yezd lay a snow-clad range, which hitherto had received no adequate attention from the traveller.

To Serv, the route lay across a plain covered with the richest grazing, on which herds of camels with their new-born offspring were browsing. A flock of sheep having been carried off by Bakhtiáris on the previous day, we all marched in one column, but, as it happened, the only incident that occurred was that we were mistaken for raiders ourselves, an error which caused a general stampede of herdsmen.

Nodushán, our next stage, we found to be almost a town, and we consequently halted for a day. On our departure the muleteers and villagers had a great battle over some clothes which had been given to a laundress and not returned. We dubbed it "the battle of the shirt," as two of those garments were carried off by way of compensation.

We steadily rose from Nodushán until we entered the Yezd Alps, fresh glistening peaks showing up as we wound our way along the valley, down which ran a delicious mountain stream. After a somewhat weary ascent, we crossed the Gudár-i-Khat at an altitude of 8500 feet, from which we could look down the valley that leads to Yezd. We passed hamlet after hamlet, forming ideal summer retreats, and at sunset reached Násirábád, a large village situated at an elevation of 7100 feet. Marching downhill the next morning, we passed a succession of hamlets, the valley with its beetling cliffs gradually closing in until at Táft we camped in a garden, whence we could almost have thrown a stone across the narrow valley, and in the distance we could see Yezd, bathed in a yellow haze. We had here joined the main Shiráz-Yezd road, by which Josafa Barbaro had also travelled to Taste, as he calls Taft, "from whense folowing that waie an other daies jorney ye come to Jex."[1] Nowadays, Taft is famous for its felts.

The march to Yezd was a short one, and we were soon being welcomed by the Fergusons in their beautiful garden, where we were only too glad to rest for a few days. About two-thirds of our journey was now accomplished, only some 220 miles remaining to Kermán. As before mentioned, there are two parallel roads connecting the cities, along the most northerly of which I had previously travelled. I therefore decided on this occasion to use the southerly route, which is that followed by the telegraph line and post, and bidding adieu to the hospitable Yezd community, we continued between the parallel ranges, which we should never have quitted had we kept to the caravan track from Kashán southwards.

The second stage of Sar-i-Yezd, as the name implies, is the border of the district. From Sar-i-Yezd to Anár, if the caravan route be followed, there is a desert stretch of nearly seventy miles to be negotiated. Yet, by making a slight detour to the north, which adds at most six or seven miles to the distance, two of these undesirable stages can be comfortably avoided. Gird-i-kuh, which lies behind the hill of that name, not only furnished sweet water, but supplies in small quantities were obtainable, while at the next stage of Bandárun,

[1] *Travels of Venetians in Persia*, p. 82 (Hakluyt Soc.).

a corruption of Baháddrán, we found a cluster of seven small villages.

The desolate stage of Shims could not be avoided, but we were able to supply the whole camp with sweet drinking water from our barrels, that at Shims being so bad that it upset all our horses, and I felt sure that no self-respecting coachman at home would allow it to be used even for washing the wheels of a carriage. In *Eastern Persia*[1] Sir Charles Euan Smith waxes eloquent over this stage, and writes: "The scene of desolation, as it rises to our memory, could hardly be surpassed even in the desolate scenery of Persia. A stony, unbroken desert, intersected here and there by low ranges of barren, bleak, and rocky hills, stretches on every side, as far as the eye can reach; and neither beast, bird, shrub, tree, twig, nor human being, breaks the impressive monotony." After visiting Shims more than once, I can cordially attest the accuracy of the above description. However, upon this occasion, a gale relieved the "impressive monotony," and such was its violence that it burst open the doors of the *bálákhána*, which we had barricaded with two portmanteaux, tents, of course, being quite out of the question.

At Anár we were met by a guard of honour, dressed in blue cotton tunics with red shoulder-straps, who interested my sister by their attempts at combining a salute and a bow, while their officer carried a walking-stick, with which he belaboured any of the populace who dared to cross the procession. This little town is the head of a small district with a population of 3000 inhabitants, and produces a considerable surplus of grain, which, as a rule, is exported to Yezd. It boasts of a shrine, dedicated to Mohamed Sálih bin Musá Kázim. This commonplace mud building contains an exquisitely-carved Korán stand made of sandalwood, with a length of 50½ inches and a breadth of 17 inches. Round the outside are strips and rosettes of ivory. The upper panel has ALLAH carved along the top, the work being beautifully fine and deeply cut, and in the lower panel the names of the twelve *Imáms* form a most artistic tracery. The date, A.H. 761 (1359), is inscribed on the inside, and the inscription states that the stand was carved for the shrine.

In the history of the Seljuks of Kermán, it is stated that

[1] Vol. i. page 177.

Seljuk Sháh, brother of *Malik* Mohamed, the seventh Seljuk ruler, rebelled, was defeated, and escaped to Katíf and Omán. Returning to Kermán upon his brother's death, "he was seized at Anár and killed. His tomb is there." I made enquiries on this point and finally discovered that at the stage of Beiáz, in the Anár district, there is a garden known as the Mazár-i-Sháh, which is almost certainly the tomb of the adventurous Seljuk, who was put to death nearly eight hundred years ago.

After passing Kushkuh on the following day, we found our caravan in difficulties, owing to the flooded state of the road. The two leading mules had fallen, with the result that my uniform, packed in a so-called air-tight case, was partially ruined. Our horses, with their larger hoofs, fared better, and we gradually got the caravan across the floods two miles wide; but the experience cost quite £30 in ruined kit and stores.

We decided to call for lunch on a fine old *Khán* at Mehdiábád to the west of Bahrámábád, who had entertained me on my visit two years previously, when I was travelling as the guest of the *Farmán Farmá*. He was asleep when we arrived, but soon came out to welcome us, and my sister acquired her first experience of a Persian meal, as in her honour we were introduced into the *anderun*.[1] There, after a long delay, we started on *mást* or curds, which required no preparation, while plates of sweets were grouped all round; at last an omelet, *kabábs*, and all sorts of *pilo* were brought in, with which we drank sherbet cooled with lumps of ice.

As may be imagined, the ladies were all on the *qui vive* to catch a glimpse of the first English lady whom they had ever seen, and I regretted that etiquette forbade me to act as interpreter, although in this respect Persia is rapidly changing. An infant was brought in for inspection, tightly bandaged, as is the custom, and I recollected her again, when I stayed with Mahmud Khán three years later. On that occasion he had just come back from Mecca, where he had gone, partly at any rate, to avoid the importunities of Nasrulla Khán, who demanded payment of a British subject's claim. He whimsically acknowledged that he was now a *Háji*, "owing to the kindness of Nasrulla Khán."

Before entering Bahrámábád another flooded area had to be crossed, and in riding through the town we saw where the water had

[1] *Anderun* signifies the women's quarter.

A PARSI PRIEST.

To face p. 184.

cut a thirty-foot way, destroying the Hindus' *caravanserai* among other buildings. Bahrámábád is the head of the district termed Rafsinján, and the centre of a considerable trade in cotton. In 1893, and again at the time of this visit, most of the crop was exported to India, but in 1898 every ounce was sent on camels to Russia, *via* Shahrud, although at first sight the cost of transport would appear to be prohibitive.[1] Owing to this change the Hindus had all deserted the district, and the trade was in the hands of Zoroastrian agents of the Russian firm of Tomaniens. Messrs Hotz's agent at Yezd, who had spent a night with us at Anár, again put in an appearance, having been delayed by the floods. He described how building after building had been swept away by the irresistible rush of water.

The district of Rafsinján is not without interest from the antiquarian point of view, as iron spear-heads a foot long with a broad head are often picked up. Also, I was informed that an underground chamber was once broken into and found to contain a coffin, resting on china supports. An inscription was said to refer to a tribe called Bázil, of which, however, I know nothing.

On the road to Kabutár Khán we had another unpleasant experience, for, although the Lálazár river was fordable, we were nearly blinded by a gale of sand, and I experienced the greatest difficulty in keeping on the track. That night we were all knocked up—men, horses, and mules, while the three or four watches in the party stopped!

At Robát I received a visit which my sister described as follows:—"An old friend of my brother's rode from his eyrie in the hills to greet the Consul. He was a gaunt figure in long top-boots, with a blue smock showing beneath his short brown jacket, his costume completed by a huge flapping felt hat. These men resemble mediæval barons, sole lords of villages at long distances apart, their society consisting of their families and retainers. They ride forth after game with hawk and hound, followed by a horde of attendants, sons of the house, poor relatives, and servants, all mixed up together and treated much alike, without any fine distinctions of person."[2]

At Bághin we found excellent quarters in a pleasant garden house, and the day before entering Kermán we halted some six

[1] In 1900 it was again exported to India. [2] Page 79 (First Edition).

miles out, to allow the *istikbál* or reception to take place. This very ancient Persian custom is apt to be tedious, but as so much stress is laid on it, it must be submitted to; even ministers upon entering Tehrán are not spared. The theory is that when an official approaches a town he should be met by a party of welcome: and as I was founding the Consulate the reception party was of great dimensions.

The Governor-General, when discussing the question with Nasrulla Khán, who had preceded us from Yezd, wished the procession to wind round the city walls, but that did not meet with acceptance, and it was finally arranged that it should traverse the whole length of the main *bázár*. Upon the auspicious day I rode to a tent some four miles from the town, and was there welcomed by a General, with whom tea was taken. The appearance of a pony 13 hands 2 inches high, covered with gorgeous velvet and gold trappings, on which I was to make my entry, was an unexpected surprise. On demurring, I was informed that the *Sáhib Diwán* had sent it out specially for me, but I extricated myself from the dilemma by saying that in full uniform I must ride on a military saddle, and as my saddle obviously would not fit the pony I was obliged to decline the mount!

These preliminaries having been duly arranged a medley of riders, some two hundred in number, with numerous led horses, preceded us, and we rode at a snail's pace towards the city, the Hindu traders and the Zoroastrian community welcoming us on the road. At the west gate a fanfare was sounded, and about a hundred *farrashes* and mace-bearers joined in, the whole procession slowly passing along the narrow *bázárs*, in which all traffic was suspended.

The garden which had been engaged for the Consulate lay a mile beyond the walls, but in due course of time we reached it, and were ushered upstairs to undergo a second tea-drinking; after which, to my relief, the members of the *istikbál* departed. Although nothing could have been more cordial than the demeanour of the crowds, I think that most Englishmen do not enjoy processions, thereby differing from their mercurial neighbours across the Channel, with whom it appears to be a popular amusement.

DESIGN FROM A KERMÁN SHAWL.

CHAPTER XVI

THE CITY OF KERMÁN

"Who comes, embower'd in the spears
Of Kermán's hardy mountaineers?—
Those mountaineers that truest, last,
Cling to their country's ancient rites,
As if that God, whose eyelids cast
Their closing gleam on Irán's heights,
Among her snowy mountains threw
The last light of His worship too!"
—MOORE, *The Fire-Worshippers.*

THE capital of the province of Kermán was, from the dawn of history, an important centre, but the ancient Karmana did not occupy a site on or near the city of to-day. To demonstrate this fact I cannot do better than quote from Afzal Kermáni, who, it must be remembered, wrote in A.H. 584 (1188), and is therefore a sufficiently weighty authority.

Referring to the visit of Hajjáj-bin-Yusuf in the first century of the *Hijra*, he says: "It is possible that, at this date, Bardshír[1] was not a city nor well known, as Jíruft and Bam are more ancient than Bardsír." Further on we read: "And they say that Bardshír was founded by Ardeshír, son of Bábak, and that Kermán was

[1] Bardshír or Bardsír is now the name of the district to the south of modern Kermán, which was, when it first became the capital, known as the "City of Bardshír."

divided into two divisions. That to the east was Bam, the western was Sirján, and Bardshír is newly founded, and Abu Ali Mohamed ibn Iliás, whose name is inscribed on the Khabis gate, built the houses and the wall, as also the ditch and the hill fort; and the new fort and some of the old forts are his work." At first sight there is a contradiction in these passages, but I am inclined to believe that Ardeshír very possibly founded a city near modern Kermán, but not as the capital. Idrísi, too, states that the most ancient capital was in Jíruft.

In the early years of the *Hijra*, Arab colonies were planted in the province, and especially in Jíruft, as Afzal Kermáni states, and we may fairly believe that as the uplands were too cold for the conquerors, their centre would be Narmáshir[1] or Jíruft.

That Kermán was made the capital by Ibn Iliás is certain. His object was clearly to be as far distant as possible from the too powerful Deilami family in Fárs, as Sírján, for many centuries the capital, apart from the drawback of being on the western edge of the province, is more fertile, and occupies a better position for trade than Kermán. At the same time, it is most improbable that Ibn Iliás would have selected a site in the desert, and we may feel confident that Guwáshír,[2] as our own city is also termed, was already a centre of population. In proof of this I cannot do better than again quote from our author, who writes: "And they say that, belonging to the old fort is a dome, which is termed the Gunbud-i-Gabr;[3] it is of ancient date, and it is not known who built it, and they relate that the founder of it said, 'I built a tower between two paradises,' since on the one side is a garden, and Asai and Sháhiján, and on the other side the hamlets and gardens of Deh Zirlif and Farmitán."[4]

Abu Ali Mohamed Ibn Iliás was an adherent of the Sáman

[1] We know that Narmáshir was the seat of the first Arab Governor, but, as stated in chap. xxxvii., there is every reason to believe that the classic Karmana was in Jíruft.

[2] Guwáshír is a corruption of *Khurra-i-Ardeshir.* In the *Pahlevi Kárnámak-i-Artakhshir-i-Pápakán*, Ardeshír is made to say that the climate is healthy and the streams run with milk. As he refers to having founded it, we cannot reasonably deny its antiquity.

[3] This signifies "The Dome of the Fire-worshipper."

[4] This should probably be Zirisf and Farmitan, the manuscript being very obscure and difficult to read.

PLAN OF KERMAN

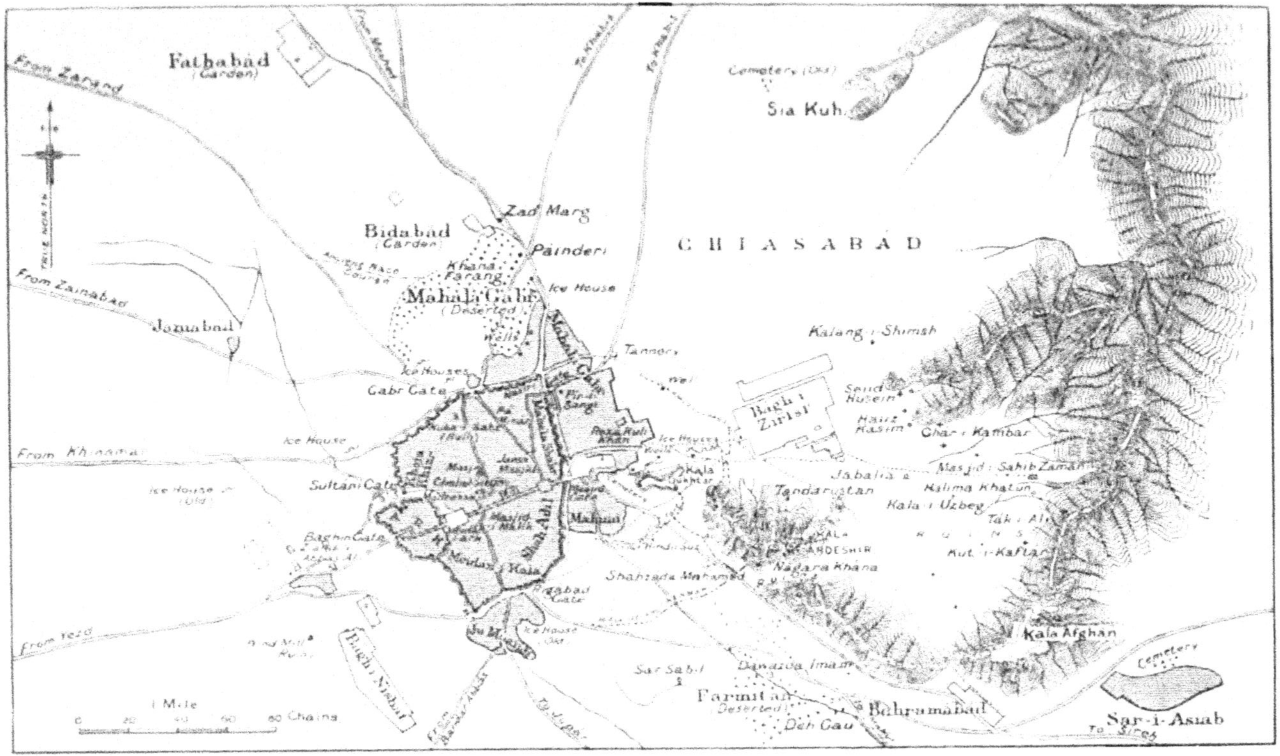

[*To face p.* 188.

dynasty, and raided in the desert between Fárs and Khorasán. Twelve times he brought a force from Khorasán to Kermán, and he built the Hill Fort in which to store his booty. Over its gate the following verses were afterwards inscribed:[1] "The son of Iliás built thee, but another inhabited thee. The world is thus, at one time it goes forward, and again it comes back."

Having then disposed of this somewhat knotty question, we can proceed to deal with the city, which has only partially changed its site.

As is often the case in Persia, Kermán is dependent on *kanáts* for its water-supply, lying as it does in a hollow, at an altitude of 5680 feet, while a limestone range, which was once very strongly fortified, dominates the town. It is mainly surrounded by desert, which is absolutely naked, all bushes being rooted up for use in the brick kilns and baths, but lying at the junction of many roads,[2] its position naturally makes it a trade centre. The Jupár mountains running up to 13,000 feet, at a distance of about 20 miles to the south-east, form the main feature in the landscape, and the range buttressing the eastern corner of the Irán plateau is of almost equal altitude, but less prominent. To the north lies the high scarped Kuhpaia chain, and further west is the distant peak of Sháh Tímorz.

The two routes to Yezd pass on either side of low regular hills, known in this particular section as Bádámu, and the Bandar Abbás road crosses an insignificant range before rising to the uplands of Bardsír. With the exception of the limestone crags referred to above, Kermán is some eight or more miles from every range, while to the south-west, south, and south-east, there is a wide belt of sand-hills, which make life unpleasant when gales are blowing. This, and perhaps the scarcity of water, together with its considerable altitude, accounts for the great healthiness of the city, but at the same time interferes with its prosperity, as, with so little land under cultivation, cheap bread is almost out of the question. Indeed, the surrounding sterility prevents the growing of crops in the immediate vicinity, and the task of supplying even the fruit stalls of the capital devolves mainly on Jupár and Máhun.

Approaching Kermán from the east, the city presents a somewhat confused appearance of wind-towers and mosques, surrounded

[1] Probably by the *Izzad-u-Dola.*

[2] *Vide* the plan.

by ruins almost on every side, but somewhat redeemed by the ice-houses with their high walls, in the shade of which the water is frozen. However, except by moonlight, the approaches are squalid in the extreme, as is generally the case in Asia.

The forts, two in number, were the centre of the life of ancient Kermán. That known as Kala Ardeshír covers the crest and spurs of a crag which rises some 500 feet above the plain. The walls, built of sun-dried bricks of colossal dimensions, are almost perfect, and in part rest on stone foundations. Below on a westerly spur is a second keep, which was formerly connected with the main work by a passage; of this traces can still be seen. A road winds up a watercourse on the north-west side to the castle on the crest, which possesses a triple line of defence, and there is a deep well, somewhat similar to the one in the Kala-i-Bandar of Shiráz, legend averring that it was connected with Khabis. So many murders were committed by throwing the victims down it that the *Vakil-ul-Mulk* ordered it to be filled up. The actual crest covers a small area, and although it has been trenched, nothing of interest was discovered, to the best of my belief.

Between this fort and the smaller one, known as the Kala-i-Dukhtar or Virgin's Fort, were the principal buildings, including the palace and mosque; it is in a portion of this area that numerous lustred tiles have been dug up and brought me for sale. The fact is that the ruins are considered to supply such excellent manure, that at certain seasons of the year many cultivators load their patient donkeys with the soil, and there is always a demand for old bricks, which are sold for building purposes.

The finest specimen of lustre that I saw measures 24 inches by 18½ inches, and consists of sapphire blue lettering an inch wide in parts, with a relief of half an inch projection on a ground of shot brown, with turquoise blue conventional leaves. Unfortunately, I could not fit together a perfect tile, but even as it is, this has been pronounced to be an iridescent tile of the highest quality. Other tiles were stars of various sizes, which were fitted in with crosses of turquoise blue, several specimens which were brought me showing the exact arrangement. I never obtained more than fragments of iridescent bowls or vases, but one of these with a figure must have been of surpassing magnificence when whole. Small bronze fishes and buckles, together with seals and coins

THE ANCIENT FORTS OF KERMÁN.

[*To face p.* 190.

of the *Caliphate*, conclude the list, although fragments of letters containing accounts, bills, and complaints of robbery were not without interest. Ancient jars and sherbet bowls were occasionally brought for sale, but their bulk forced me to curtail my purchases, the jars running to two feet in height and bowls to twenty-two inches in diameter. They are, however, most beautiful.

The Kala-i-Dukhtar is much lower, lining two ridges which form an obtuse angle, and is so narrow that it was mainly used as a covered way, whereas Kala Ardeshír was very strong.

On the southern spur of the main crag is a detached cliff, which is ascended from about half way up by one hundred and forty-three steps hewn in the rock: it was possibly a *Nakkára Khána*, whence weird music was discoursed at sunrise and sunset, although the marks of the chisel appeared to be fresh, and the steps may have been cut, as one account relates, for the use of the first Kájár Sháh. Anyhow, it stands above the ancient city, the wall of which ran from a point almost underneath it, while further south is the deserted quarter of Farmitan, with its acres of mud houses almost intact; it is stated to have been destroyed by the Afgháns at the same period as the Zoroastrian quarter.

The description given of Kermán in the twelfth century by Afzal Kermáni is worth quoting, if only as an example of Oriental hyperbole: "Its wall is like Alexander's barrier,[1] with a ditch resembling a vast ocean,[2] so that neither a vulture with its wings, nor a boat with its sails can cross it. Among believers and unbelievers such a city and such a wall, with two forts touching the city and a ditch like an ocean, can nowhere be seen."

At the southern angle of the range is a gap, with a platform built out from the cliff, surmounted by a tomb in honour of Reza Kuli Beg.[3] Below are the remains of a great ruined tank, which was formerly filled by the Bahrámjird river, the waters of which now run to Bághin, while above, a stiff climb leads to a small fort, constructed as a watch-tower, to warn the citizens of Afghán and Baluch raids.

[1] The Persian name for the great wall of China, which, although popularly considered to have been a colossal waste of money, was of extreme value.

[2] The wall was, at most, thirty-five feet high, and the ditch is forty feet wide at the bottom!

[3] Kuli Beg was a servant of Ibráhim Khán, *Záhir-u-Dola*.

Skirting the almost inaccessible frowning hills, a cave known as Kut-i-Kaftar or Hyena's Home is passed. It was evidently inhabited at one period, a tank being visible just below, while steps lead up to it. Continuing along the skirt of the hills, high up is a recess, in which *Ya Ali* appears in huge white characters, and beneath it there is a stone building near a tiny spring, *Ták-i-Ali*, or the Arch of Ali, being the name of the shrine, whose two stunted trees are decorated with thousands of votive rags. The miniature source is said to have run red at the time of the massacres at Isfahán during the eighteenth century, and it is firmly believed to be connected with the Zenda Rud.

In the plain the ruins lie thick, a mound being known as The Uzbeg's Fort, and close by is the tomb of Halima Khátun, sister of Persia's patron saint, the *Imám* Reza, behind which again is a mosque in honour of the *Sáhib Zamán*.[1] Neither of these buildings possess any importance.

A little further on, passing through a deserted cemetery, is an octagonal stone building, surmounted by a bracketed dome, with an interior diameter of thirty-eight feet, each face measuring eighteen feet. The apex is of brick, and there is a circular opening by way of finish; a mud ruin touches its western side. It is vaguely known as *Jaballa*, and is about the only stone building in Kermán. By the Persians it is firmly believed to be the "Dome of the Gabr" referred to above. It was said to have been the tomb of *Seiid* Mohamed Tabashíri, but this is denied in some quarters. When the graveyard was destroyed, the tomb it contained was wrecked, and, no doubt, the stone was employed for building purposes. To the south of it, close to the naked limestone range, is a group of mud buildings, known as Tandarustán, which are frequented mainly by Zoroastrians, but also by Mohamedans. Offerings of food are set out, and if the *Peris* or "good folk" eat them, the accompanying wish will be fulfilled. This is possibly a corrupt survival of the Parsi practice of making offerings to the dead.

In this remote corner, a low wall encircles a solitary European grave, that of the Rev. Henry Carless of the Church Missionary Society, who died at his post in 1898, deeply regretted, not only

[1] *Sáhib Zamán* or Lord of Time is the *Imám*, who is considered to be ever alive, and who will finally reveal himself as the *Mahdi* or Guide.

by his European friends in Persia, but also by many inhabitants of Kermán, over whom he had considerable influence.[1]

Moving westwards, the Bágh-i-Zirisf, the pleasaunce of Kermán, is approached. It consists of several gardens, and covers an area of perhaps half a square mile. Beyond it the ancient city walls are again struck, and keeping along them, the modern Zoroastrian quarter is reached. Touching it to the north is their ancient suburb, laid desolate by the Afgháns, the chief ruin of which is known as Khána Farang or European House, and just outside is what is known as the race-course, about half a mile in length.

On the south-west side are the remains of the lines of investment of Ághá Mohamed Khán; but as there is nothing further of interest in the outskirts, except the blue-domed shrine of Husein Khán in the graveyard to the east of the city, I now propose to describe the interior of Kermán.

The city is surrounded by a wall in a good state of repair, which is pierced by six gates, one of which, known as Sultáni, is said to be the work of Sháh Rukh. It was by the *Masjid* Gate that the Kájár conqueror entered Kermán. The shape of Kermán is irregular, its diameter being just a mile from east to west, and rather more from north to south. It is divided into five quarters as follows:

1. Shahr, which includes part of ancient Kermán.
2. Khoja Khizr.
3. Kutbábád.
4. Meidán-i-Kala.
5. Sháh Ádil.

There are also three extra-mural quarters:—(*a*) Gabrí; (*b*) Mahúni; (*c*) Ju Muiidi (*vulg.* Mehdi).

Touching it on the west side is the Ark or Fort, in which the Governor-General resides; it includes the Telegraph office,[2] barracks and arsenal. These buildings are mostly of recent construction, and are distinctly fine and in a fair state of repair, and there is a large garden surrounding His Excellency's private quarters.

The mosques are not without interest, the oldest being that

[1] Since writing the above, I have heard with deep regret of the death of Mr Patrick Duncan, late P.W.D., who was engaged in experimenting in artesian wells.

[2] There is a single line running to Yezd and Isfahán, and a weekly post from Tehrán and Bandar Abbás.

known as Masjid-i-Malik. It was founded by the Seljuk *Malik* Turán Sháh, who reigned from A.H. 477 (1084) to A.H. 490 (1096). In the sixteenth century the historian Mohamed Ibráhim mentions that he saw it still standing but in ruins, and since that date it has been practically rebuilt, but can hardly be deemed a fine building, although covering a large area.

The Masjid-i-Jámi, known also as Masjid Muzaffar, was built, as the inscription shows, in A.H. 750 (1349) by *Mobáris-u-Din*, Mohamed Muzaffar, who ran a somewhat meteoric course, as described in chap. vi. The third mosque of any interest, the Masjid-i-Pá-Minár, was founded by another member of his family, *Sultán Imád-u-Dín*, about A.H. 793 (1390). In all there are said to be ninety mosques in Kermán and six *madáris*[1] or colleges, the finest of which is that founded by the *Záhir-u-Dola*, consisting of a beautifully tiled court and entrance; it is well worth a visit. There are also fifty baths and eight *caravanserais*, that built by the first *Vakil-ul-Mulk* being quite a model. The *bázárs* are good and extensive, but are inferior to those of Shiráz.

Until 1896, when an earthquake completed its ruin, the Kuba Sabz or Green Dome was by far the most conspicuous building in Kermán. It was the tomb of the Kara Khitei dynasty, and formed part of a college, known as the *Madrasa* of Turkábád. The *Kuba* was a curious cylindrical building, perhaps fifty feet high, with greenish-blue mosaic work outside, the plastered interior showing traces of rich gilding. An inscription on the wall was read for me as follows:—"The work of *Ustád*[2] Khoja Shukr Ulla and *Ustád* Inaiat Ulla, son of *Ustád* Nizám-u-Din, architect of Isfahán." The date was A.H. 640 (1242), which would be eight years after the death of Borák Hájib, the founder of the dynasty. At the same time, I cannot vouch for the exact accuracy of my informant, and the tomb, which was partly destroyed by the *Vakil-ul-Mulk* in a search for treasure, is now a shapeless mound, thanks to an earthquake in 1896.

Not far from it is a stone, exquisitely carved, with verses from the Korán in Kufic and Naskh[3] set in the wall of a square domed building, which was ornamented in the same style as the Kuba Sabz,

[1] The plural of *madrasa*.
[2] *Ustád* signifies master craftsman.
[3] *Naskh* is what we should term copper-plate writing in Arabic.

fragments of blue tiling still adhering to the pillars. Underneath is a vault, showing that it was evidently a tomb, but no one in Kermán could give me any information on the subject, except that it is known as Khoja Átábeg or Sang-i-Átábeg.[1]

In the history of Mohamed Ibráhim it is told of *Malik* Mohamed, the seventh Seljuk sovereign, that "on the outskirts of Bardsír, he built in one line hospital, college, *caravanserai*, mosque and his own grave." It is just possible that the Kuba Sabz may also have formed part of this imposing group of buildings, and this would account for its date as given in Lord Curzon's work, 1155 A.D.,[2] but, at the same time, my informant was a well-educated man, and apparently read the inscription quite accurately; and as local information also corroborates the date he gave, it may be that the *Kuba* was built by *Malik* Mohamed and appropriated by the Kara Khitei dynasty. There is little else of interest, with the exception of a fine square touching the *Ark*, and a smaller one called after Ganj Ali Khán, Kermán presenting a maze of the usual narrow lanes and high mud walls. I will now turn to its inhabitants.

Known in Oriental phraseology as the *Dár-ul-Amán* or Abode of Peace, Kermán with its suburbs can claim a population estimated at just under 50,000. This may be divided according to the various religious sects as follows: —

Shia Mohamedans	37,000
Sunni Mohamedans	70
Babis (Behai)	3,000
Babis (Ezeli)	60
Sheikhis	6,000
Sufis	1,200
Jews	70
Zoroastrians (Parsis)	1,700
Hindus	20
TOTAL	49,120

Shia Mohamedans differ from the Sunnis in that they

[1] Or Stone of the Átábeg.

[2] *Malik* Mohamed died in A.H. 551 (1156).

[3] These numbers are only approximate, and represent the mean of several estimates.

consider Ali, the Prophet's son-in-law, to have been the first *Caliph*, whereas his three predecessors Abu Bekr, Omar, and Othman are execrated. As regards doctrine, the special Shia tenet is that of the *Imámate*, Ali its first holder being ordained by Mohamed, while his successors rule by divine right, and are believed to be immaculate, infallible, and perfect guides to men. The few Sunnis are mainly traders from Aváz, near Lár.

The sect of the Bábis was founded by *Mírza* Ali Mohamed of Shiráz, who in 1844 began to declare that he was the *Báb*[1] or Gate of Grace between some great person still behind the veil of glory and the world. As he was of the merchant class, and not erudite, his claims and writings appeared to be supernatural, and gained him many adherents. He was finally imprisoned, and in 1850 was sent to Tabríz for execution. Nearly a whole regiment fired at him, but when the smoke of the volley cleared away, there were no traces of the *Báb*, who was however eventually found quite unwounded, and was again bound and shot. In 1852, four Bábis attempted to assassinate the Sháh, and the sect was put down in the sternest fashion, the victims being allotted to the officials of all classes to be done to death.

The *Báb* had appointed *Mírza* Yáhyá, *Subh-i-Ezel*,[2] to succeed him, and for ten years he was acknowledged, but his position was challenged by his elder half-brother, *Mírza* Husein Ali, *Beha Ulla*,[3] who in 1866 proclaimed himself as "Him whom God shall manifest." Since this declaration his party has been in the ascendant, and that of the *Subh-i-Ezel*, who is living in Cyprus, has waned. Friendly relations among mankind, abolition of religious wars, and the study of all beneficial sciences, are inculcated, and these enlightened views are gaining thousands of converts, although mostly in secret. It is to be hoped that the doctrines of the *Báb* will eventually aid the cause of civilisation in Persia.[4]

The Sheikhi sect, albeit this is stoutly denied, holds almost identical views on many subjects with the Bábis. It was founded by *Sheikh* Ahmad of Ahsá or Lahsá in Bahrein, who was born about 1750. He gained a great reputation for learning at Kerbela,

[1] Cf. Báb-et-Mandeb and also The Sublime Porte.
[2] Or Dawn of Eternity.
[3] Or The Splendour of God. He died in 1892.
[4] Vide *The Episode of the Báb*, by E. G. Browne.

ÁGHÁ MOHAMED KHÁN (CHIEF OF THE SHEIKHI SECT).

[*To face p.* 196.

THE FOUNDER OF THE SHEIKHI SECT.

[*To face p.* 196.

and being invited to Persia by Fath Ali Sháh, finally settled at Yezd. He taught that at the resurrection men would not rise in the flesh, but only spiritually, and he believed that he was under the special guidance of the *Imám*. A "Master of the Dispensation" was expected, and accordingly many of the sect followed the *Báb* when he revealed his claims. A majority, headed by *Háji* Mohamed Kerim Khán, son of Ibráhim Khán, Kájár, *Zahír-u-Dola*, utterly declined to accept the new teacher, and became his bitterest opponents. The Sheikhis claimed that there must always be a *Shia-i-Kámil* or Perfect Shia, to serve as a channel of grace between the absent *Imám* and his church, and that *Háji* Mohamed Kerim Khán was that channel. His son, *Háji* Mohamed Khán, is now head of the sect, which numbers 7000 followers in the province of Kermán, and perhaps 50,000 in Persia.[1] He is a distinguished-looking man, possessing charming manners and a knowledge of the outer world which makes his society most agreeable, especially as he is entirely free from fanaticism.

The Sufi creed is a form of religious mysticism which has from earliest times deeply appealed to mankind in the East. Even Plato[2] drank of its fountains, and thereby influenced all Western thought. It is difficult to define, but a pure theism and the immortality of the soul are inculcated in allegorical language, wherein human love typifies that love of God which is alone real, everything else on earth being illusory. The *Murshid* or Spiritual Guide at Kermán, who is the religious head of the Máhun shrine, is a typical Sufi, frankly maintaining that all religious fanaticism is the result of ignorance, and should be swept away to make room for universal love. In any case, a Sufi is tolerant, and the spread of such doctrines would do much to remove the ignorance and fanaticism still so rife in Asia.

We next come to the Jews of Kermán, who are in a wretched condition, and yet, as petty dealers, are absurdly grasping, their ideas of profit being extortion. They are an offshoot of the larger Yezd colony, which is said to have travelled east from Baghdád.

Among the most ancient religions is that of the Zoroastrians, which appeals so strongly to our interest as having survived from a

[1] Hamadán and Tabríz are, after Kermán, their chief centres.

[2] Still more so the Neo-Platonists of Alexandria.

hoary antiquity, whereas Baal, Osiris, and Zeus no longer can claim even a single worshipper. Although starting with the same root-ideas as Hinduism, it avoided Pantheism, and evolved a religion so near to Monotheism, that Zoroastrianism certainly ranks close after the three religions of Judaism, Christianity, and Mohamedanism, in the purity of its creed. Its main doctrine consists in the eternal struggle between the powers of good and evil, in which every worshipper plays his part, while fire is considered to be sacred, and there is a complicated system of purification.

Zoroastrians are noted for their integrity, and are pure Iránians, in opposition to the mixture of Arab, Mongol, and Turkish blood which successive invasions have brought into Persia. On this account, perhaps, they are a finer and healthier race than their Mohamedan fellow-countrymen, but their co-religionists at Bombay are an example of the physical deterioration which India so surely produces. Agricultural and commercial pursuits are usually followed, the Zoroastrians being landowners and merchants. Generally speaking, they are not ill treated nowadays, although still forced to wear sober-coloured clothes, and forbidden to ride in the *bázárs*.

The women wear the ancient many-coloured Persian garb, which is extremely picturesque, and the sight of their healthy faces is quite a treat in a land where veiling is still the unwholesome practice. There is, however, a reverse side to the picture, and that is the deep ignorance in which the community is sunk, while their love of money is a vice that prevents a response to the most obvious calls on their charity. There is also, as ever, a steady falling away to Mohamedanism, and the Korán is taught in their schools.

The small Hindu colony hails from Shikárpur in Sind, its members generally spending three or four years in Persia and then returning home. Being British subjects, their trade flourishes, but as money-lenders of the most voracious breed they are unsurpassed, one claim brought into my court bearing interest at the rate of 40 per cent. for a loan, the security for which consisted of gold!

As to their appearance, it is not prepossessing, but I hardly agree with Mr Stack, who bluntly writes: "I never was more forcibly reminded of the physical inferiority of the Hindu race.

THE STONE OF THE ÁTÁBEG, KERMÁN.

[To face p. 198.

They looked like withered black apes."[1] At the same time they have their good points, and are certainly keen in business matters, and ready to accommodate almost any one.

I now propose to deal with the industrial side of the city. Kermán was, until quite recently, more especially famous for its shawls, but to-day, in dealing with its manufactures, its carpets claim precedence. These unrivalled products of the loom are woven in silk and wool, and, owing to their fineness and brilliant colouring, are incontestably the choicest the world has ever seen. A single Kermán rug will indeed make almost any other carpet appear tawdry and common. The patterns are very ancient, and evidently date from pre-Mohamedan days, as figures are frequent, but it is rather the conventional flowers and the exquisite blending of colours that are so admirable. The usual size is about 7 feet by 4 feet 6 inches, the unit of measurement being the *zar*, which is 39 inches by 19½ inches in the trade. The ordinary quality, 640 stitches per 39 inches for woollen carpets, is quite fine enough for most Europeans, but Persian connoisseurs are seldom content with this. The price per *zar* being about £1 sterling for the quality given above, these articles are certainly of the *de luxe* order. When at Constantinople a few years ago, one of them was shown to me as a great bargain for £26!

The *Farmán Farmá* introduced some ugly European patterns, but these, at my instance, were given up, and by rigorously insisting on adhesion to the old patterns, as well as by opening out new markets, I have assisted in bringing the industry to a thoroughly healthy condition, the carpets only requiring to be more widely known to become the fashion, especially for drawing-rooms and dainty boudoirs.

In Kermán itself[2] there are about one thousand looms, each carpet being superintended by a master-weaver and two or more little boys, who work entirely from a pattern which is recited, and contains many obsolete words; it is said that these patterns have been handed down orally from father to son for many centuries. Few women or girls are employed, which keeps the work at a high

[1] *Six Months in Persia*, i. p. 213.

[2] At Ráwár there are one hundred looms, and in the district round Kermán thirty looms. This is apart from the carpet-weaving carried on by the nomad tribes.

state of excellence, and aniline dyes, which have almost ruined the trade in nomad carpets, are carefully eschewed. It is difficult to estimate the output, but approximately it is 200,000 tománs or £40,000 per annum.

As to the silk carpets, "than which I do not think that a more exquisite fabric has ever been woven by human hands," as Lord Curzon writes, their prices are about two to three times as high as those of the woollen article, £10 to £15 pounds being the local price for a rug of the same measurements as given above. They make *portières* of surpassing beauty, which even the blindest Philistine admires, and, as time goes by, I hope to see them appreciated in England, and not, as now, sold in the *bázárs* of Cairo for over £100.

The *Shál* of Kermán (whence our word "shawl") is either woven from the down of the goat or from wool. Like the carpets, the patterns are learned by heart, and the work is much finer, and can only be executed by children; at the same time, owing to the invincible distaste of the Kermáni to steady application, the boys do not appear to be overworked or unhealthy. There has certainly been a change for the better since Sir Frederic Goldsmid's Mission, when a pitiable picture was drawn of the conditions under which the work was done.

This manufacture includes many varieties, the finest of which, woven in a fir-cone pattern of rich colours, is generally used for the *khalat* or robe of honour, which constitutes the Governor's re-investiture at *No Rus*.[1] A white or grey quality closely resembles merino, and the striped varieties are exported to Constantinople and used for wearing round the waist, or for ladies' dress. The product of the Kashmir loom is, however, superior in the finer qualities, and has affected the industry to such an extent that much down and wool is exported, especially to Amritsar, but it is stated that nothing can vie with the Kermán raw article, the quality of which is, no doubt, enhanced by the dryness of the climate. The looms at work are said to number three thousand, with an output of 300,000 tománs or £60,000.

After these two staple industries there is the minor manufacture of felts, which are made by washing and rolling masses of wool or down. In Persia a room is generally covered by a huge felt; above

[1] The Persian New Year's Day.

this is a blue and white drugget, which is used for sitting on during the summer, but in winter a carpet is preferred. Small felts, generally of a delicate fawn-brown, are also used during journeys, and these are particularly suitable for bedrooms. An intricate and frequently artistic pattern in many colours of worsted is sometimes hammered into the surface, and, generally speaking, but for its weight, a Kermán felt would be a popular article of export; it is sold at the rate of 4s. per 6¾ lbs. for the coarsest quality manufactured of wool, while the same weight in *kurk* or down fetches 10s. Two thousand felt cloaks are annually sent to Tehrán for the use of the troops, this payment in kind being provided by the State domains.

The usual overcoat of a Persian is the Arab *aba*, for which Kermán is also noted, five thousand of these brown articles, which are cut somewhat like a professor's gown (and perhaps served as its model), being made every year; their value is about £4000. Homespun, known as *barak*, is also woven to the value of £1000 per annum. It cannot, however, vie with the much cheaper and more durable *puttoo* of Kashmir.

The brass work of Kermán is also highly esteemed, and indeed it is remarkable that a city whose antecedents have been so unfortunate should be able to produce such valuable, varied, and artistic wares, which are steadily developing and restoring prosperity to its inhabitants.

I cannot do better than conclude this chapter with the Persian couplet—

> "On the face of the earth there is no place like Kermán;
> Kermán is the heart of the world, and we are men of heart."

FROM LUSTRED POTTERY.

CHAPTER XVII

LIFE AT KERMÁN

"Oh, East is East, and West is West, and never the
twain shall meet,
Till Earth and Sky stand presently at God's great
Judgment Seat." —RUDYARD KIPLING.

AFTER our arrival at Kermán, as related in chapter xv., there remained much to be done before we could consider ourselves finally settled. First of all, I paid my respects to the Governor-General, and had the pleasure of making the acquaintance of the *Sáhib Diwán*, an aged gentleman of eighty, who was considered the type of a Persian of the old school. Dressed in his official robes of Kashmir shawl, with jewelled clasps, His Excellency was most friendly, and asked particularly that when he returned my visit it might be regarded as private and informal, so that he might see my sister.

This disposed of another question, many Europeans not permitting Persians to meet their families, on the ground that the jealous *anderun* is closed to Europeans of the male sex. There is indeed much to be said for this opinion, but I thought that its observance would only widen the gulf between East and West, a gulf that I was anxious, even if in a very small way, to bridge over; and we finally found that by judiciously choosing our guests, and always inviting one or two who had been to Tehrán, there was nothing disagreeable for my sister, who preferred these arrangements to almost entire isolation, as she did not know enough Persian to mix with the wives of my friends.

A few days after our arrival M. de Rakovzky, an Austrian traveller of varied experience, became our first guest, and as the Rev. Henry Carless of the Church Missionary Society also came to settle, we were by no means so exiled as we had expected. I soon organised a weekly Gymkhana, with tent-pegging and lemon-cutting, etc., which was enthusiastically taken up, and our sports finally culminated in an organised race-meeting. We also practised the Persian sport of shooting from horseback at eggs with a rifle or gun, and the older Kháns enjoyed the pastime of galloping past buckets and throwing in stones.

In no part of the world could we have been treated with more consideration, and in my opinion the abuse heaped on Persians by travellers who have never even learned their language is altogether unmerited. The Persians are, as a nation, extremely courteous and witty: indeed from highest to lowest this is eminently the case. Their extreme readiness in retort is exemplified by the well-known story of a merchant of Isfahán who complained of harsh treatment to the Governor, son of a famous Vizier, whose family ruled all Persia. The Governor advised him to go to various other cities, but the Isfaháni objected that he would still be persecuted by other members of the family. Finally he was told to betake himself to the lower regions. "But the *Háji*, your father, is recently deceased," was the prompt reply. I will give a few of their proverbs:

"The jackal dipped himself in indigo, and then thought he was a peacock."

"A cut string may be joined again, but the knot always remains."

"Often to be kind to the tiger is to be cruel to the lamb."

"War at the outset is good, if it ends in peace."[1]

As with agriculturalists in other lands, parting with money comes very hard, and I met with some examples of exceptional meanness, one of which, at any rate, makes an amusing story. The individual in question, a royal Governor, was under considerable obligation to a European, and repeatedly expressed his intention of making him

[1] *Vide* paper by Miss E. C. Sykes in *Folklore*, vol. xii. No. 3.

a present. One day a long string of servants was seen approaching, headed by the Prince's steward, and upon reaching my friend's house, a silver tray, covered with a costly shawl, was set down. When the covering was withdrawn the gift was displayed—two lettuces from His Highness's private garden! The fees amounted quite to £1. As a rule, however, Persians are most hospitable, and if, on the one hand, their courteous manners and love of compliment be Gallic, on the other, they are decidedly British in considering food and clothes[1] the best investment for their money. Compared with natives of the Panjáb, of whom I have had many years' experience, the Persians possess much finer physique, are better fed and better clothed, and, among themselves, are incomparably more liberal. To give an example, the *Kalassies*, who carry the plane-table, sometimes refuse to don their clothing until after repeated orders, even when it is provided free, their idea probably being to sell their outfit in India. Such men, too, will never spend an anna to supplement their rations. Now my servants all spent their money on food and clothing, and it required pressure to persuade them to save even on a journey, when they receive a special allowance. My limited experience of Indian *sowārs* is practically the same, their main object in life being the saving of money.

Again, in settling claims, I have only once met with discourteous treatment, and in my district, writing at the close of 1900, I can say that every single claim has been fairly settled, reasonable compensation having been paid in cases of robbery. Of course delays are unavoidable, and I owe much to the tact of Nasrulla Khán; but even so, dealing with five Governors-General, there have been no instances of a dead-lock, with constant appeals for support to the Legation, and I can honestly say that British claims have always been readily acknowledged by each successive Governor-General. All has not been smooth sailing, however, and I have often found myself in opposition to vested interests. For instance, on informing the head of the Custom House that he was entitled by treaty to no more than five per cent., the first reply I received was, "Treaty! What treaty? *I* have signed no treaty!"

[1] A wealthy Persian's wardrobe includes several fur coats, averaging £50 each, while a good *kola* or lamb-skin hat costs £5.

Allowances have also to be made for the delicate position of the Governor-General in respect to the *mullás*; but here again I was fortunate in having most friendly *mullás* to deal with, and having once grasped their standpoint, I generally found that reasonable terms could be made without difficulty. The British subjects were mostly Hindus of a low class, who were engaged in money-lending, and were not at all anxious for cases to be brought to a conclusion, as their victims, once free, are very careful to have no further dealings with this community. They exhibited their ingenuity chiefly in flat refusals to deliver up original receipts, and also in raking up old claims after a lapse of years. In addition, there were a few Indian Mohamedan traders, a few Persians acting as agents to British subjects, and a stream of pilgrims. Many of these latter came from the Khurram Valley, and begged their way across Persia, even when provided with funds. This, as may be imagined, only tends to increase the Persian's hereditary contempt for a *Hindi*, which is as ineradicable as his hatred for an Afghán.

Education has generally been shamefully neglected, but there is a healthy discontent, which will, in time, lead to teaching the boys something in addition to a few chapters of the Korán, which, being in Arabic, cannot be understood. At present, a teacher holds as bad a position as in the England of the seventeenth century, and is paid about as much as a waiter. It is therefore hardly surprising that they still teach that London is the name of a country, and that one of its cities is the Atlantic Ocean!—an error dating at least from early Sefavi times.

Every week we took a long ride, and in due course of time thoroughly explored the environs of Kermán. As there are little mounds with ruins of forts at intervals in almost every direction, I imagine that the city was once encircled by a belt of villages, it being hardly conceivable that Kermán could itself have covered so great an area. Some ten miles away to the north is a Kala-i-Dukhtar occupying a high hill, and elaborately fortified. No one could give any clue as to its history. There are also gardens within easy riding distance, and as the level sandy waste formed ideal going, we could cover considerable distances in a few hours.

In addition to all this, we always enjoyed the sense of novelty, and the feeling that we were acting as pioneers, while almost every day we acquired some fresh knowledge about the country, or were brought an interesting curio for sale. Thus life passed pleasantly enough in this superb climate, mainly because every one made us feel welcome, even the country people being invariably polite, although an English lady must have been to them something of a new experience.

In June the nights grew hot, and my sister suffered much from the attacks of sandflies, as I did not then know that by sleeping away from walls, it is possible to avoid them almost entirely; we therefore determined on a change of scene. Many cool regions were recommended to us, but as I was particularly anxious to trace out Marco Polo's route, and also to obtain some stalking, we finally decided to proceed in the first place to the Kuh-i-Lálazár or Tulip Mountain, and then visit Sárdu, across which I felt sure that the great Venetian had travelled.

Our first stage led due south among the sand-hills to a garden lying underneath the Jupár range; thence, on the following day, we ascended the Bahrámjird river, and enjoyed a night of delicious coolness; at the third stage of Kariat-el-Arab or The Arab's Fort we were out of the heat altogether. A fourth stage brought us close to Lálazár, and we lunched by the way in a most delightful spot, the description of which, in *Through Persia on a Side Saddle*, runs as follows: "A deep gorge, on both sides of which shale cliffs rose magnificently, their base washed by a rippling stream, bordered with tamarisk and sweetbriar, and we lay under the willows and drank glass after glass of the delicious water, watching the delicate blue dragon-flies skim over the rivulet."[1] To appreciate a mountain stream properly, a previous course of indifferent water is a necessity.

Finding that at the village of Lálazár we were too far away from the hills, we camped at over 11,000 feet in the heart of the mountains. The shooting was of the very best, as the range was preserved for the Governor-General, and had not been shot over for many years.

[1] *Through Persia on a Side Saddle*, p. 147 (First Edition).

At the same time, the climbing of steep hills at a high elevation was most exhausting, especially at the outset. Stalking from this centre, I secured four fair rams and lost a fifth, although it was tracked by its blood for two days. As the situation was unpleasant for my sister, we decided to remove to the west *nala*, where we camped at a slightly lower elevation. We all suffered from drinking the water just as it emerged from the snow, but I afterwards found that to remedy this, it is only necessary to boil and then expose it to the sun.

Here the shooting was even better, and I secured six rams in as many days, one of which was a particularly fine head. This was the first good stalking I had enjoyed in Persia, as hitherto I had only been able to spare an odd day now and then, which is very little use; moreover, as no grazing was allowed on the hills, there was plenty of game, and had I wished it, I could have increased the bag.

One day my sister and I scaled the great peak, termed Kuh-i-Sháh-Kutb-u-Din-Haider or The Mountain of the Saint, the Polar Star of the Faith, Haider. We left our tents, which had been pitched in a willow grove beside a brawling brook before sunrise, and a mile above them we were on a snow bridge, an object so familiar to travellers in Kashmir. At about 11,000 feet the valley opened out, and we approached the platforms which had been constructed by H.H. *Násir-u-Dola*, the late brother of the *Farmán Farmá*. In this secluded retreat he had spent the summer months for many years, and as, like all Persians, he considered females and young to be fair sport, there was at that period but little game left in the hills.

Soon after this we had to scramble up a stiff slope, above which patches of snow were still lying. A rest and another ascent, this time over rocks, and we reached the summit of the second highest mountain in South-east Persia, at an elevation of 13,700 feet, no small feat for a lady to accomplish. Fortunately, the day was beautifully clear, and after inspecting the shrine with its collection of coins (among which figured a token of the Queen, dated 1837), beads, and scraps of iron, which lay in a rude circle of boulders, we turned to enjoy the glorious panorama.

To the north we could just espy the squat range under which

Kermán lay, mighty Jupár almost filling up that corner of the landscape. To the east we saw, close by, the giant Kuh-i-Hezár, which I climbed five years later, rising to an elevation of over 13,000 feet.[1] It is a beautiful mountain, and, being visible for well over 100 miles on the Baluchistán road, must have cheered many a returning Kermáni. South of it lay Sárdu, and the succession of grand ranges which, under different names, buttress up the great Irán plateau, while in almost every direction we looked across practically unexplored country, in which only the main roads appear on the map, the districts a few miles on either side of them not having been visited.

We asked our guide for details about *Sháh* Haider, but all he could tell us was that throughout the summer he made known his presence by loud detonations at night; but as this was easily explained by the splitting of the rocks, due to the enormous difference between the day and night temperatures, we returned to camp not much the wiser. I afterwards identified him with the saint who is buried at Turbat.

Loth as we were to quit this delightful range, the unexplored plateau of Sárdu proved too strong a temptation, and we decided to continue the march to Ráhbur to the south of the range, on the way to which we stopped in a fine grove of walnuts, and watched the women of the Mehni tribe weaving their carpets. The village of Ráhbur lies on the upper reaches of the Halíl Rud, which drains all this district; it has a good climate, but as the surrounding country is intolerably stony, we only halted a day to see the Governor and the Mehni Chief, both old friends. The latter, who was a man of considerable character, had, somehow or other, obtained possession of a mare with English or waler blood, and bred some very fine stock. News of this soon reached the Governor-General of the time, and the upshot of it was that a party was secretly despatched to seize the mare and her offspring. My friend heard this just in time, and escaped into the wilds, leaving his household gods to the disappointed myrmidons, who were severely "sticked" for their failure.

When returning the Governor's visit, an old man was introduced, also a Mehni, who said that he was one hundred and twenty-

[1] The difference in altitude between these two giants is very trifling.

five years old. His face was of the colour of wax, and his hair like spun silver, and I could only regret that I was no painter, for a more interesting subject I have never seen.[1]

Upon quitting Ráhbur, we marched approximately east, continually crossing branches of the Halíl Rud, one of which was unpleasantly deep, and halted for the night near a garden round which were camped some fifty families. It was the month of Moharram, and for hours we listened to the wailing cadence of the Passion Play.[2] At last it ended, and as a relief to the feelings the whole thing was turned into comedy, thus recalling the plays in Ladakh, where the same course is pursued. In Persia this is the only time that I have ever witnessed anything but the most sincere devotion, but nomads are always considered to be somewhat less strict in religious observances.

The next march brought us into Sárdu. Throughout the day we were continually crossing small rivers and passing through hamlets, and we had lunch in an orchard full of ripe apricots. There was also a thick sprinkling of trees in parts, which was a delightful contrast to the usually bare hillsides. This is the district of Henza, through which we were, in a tortuous fashion, making for the watershed lying between the Kuh-i-Henza and the Kuh-i-Bahr-Asmán; in the latter range are copper mines, which are worked spasmodically. We finally crossed a pass at an elevation of 9000 feet and thence gradually descended through waving wheat-fields to Dar-i-Mazár.

This is the capital of Sárdu, and possesses a well-endowed shrine in honour of *Sultán Seiid* Ahmad Saghir, son of *Seiia* Kabír, a descendant of the *Imám* Musá. *Seiid* Kabír[3] was said to have been the first preacher of Mohamedanism in India, where he died a martyr's death. His son lived and died in Sárdu, and the shrine was built by one of the Seljuk sovereigns of Kermán, probably by *Malik* Mohamed. The adjacent land is the property of the shrine, and its peasants (known as *Sheikh*) constitute almost the only permanent inhabitants of the district,

[1] He died in 1898.

[2] These plays, dealing with the martyrdom of Ali and his sons, are recited throughout the month of Moharram. Their influence is extraordinary.

[3] *Kabír* and *Saghir* signify Great and Small.

the nomads[1] merely spending the few summer months in these regions. Round the shrine half a dozen shops and a bath have been erected, and there were several Kermánis enjoying the beautifully cool climate.

We marched across the plateau, where in parts there was actually turf, and camped near the Sarbizan Pass; close by were the ruins of the *caravanserai*, built by the seventh Seljuk ruler, *Malik* Mohamed, and from an adjacent hill we looked down on the large village of Dilfárd, the track descending very rapidly. According to Afzal Kermáni, Moez-u-Dola, of the Deilami dynasty, was surrounded in these passes, his army being annihilated, and he only escaping himself with a few servants, and with the loss of his right hand.[2] The chief of the nomads in the history of Mohamed Ibráhim is made to say that he is defended by "many mountains, difficult passes, and thickly-wooded spurs." This latter statement would no longer be true, although the range is less bare than many others. Sarbizan provided excellent partridge-shooting, and a fine bracing climate, both of which we thoroughly enjoyed.

While halting, some nomad ladies came to call, headed by a very determined old party. After presenting us with some cheese, a demand was made for medicine, but our tabloids were not at all

[1] The nomads of Sárdu are very numerous; their governor is *Mír* Morád Ali Khán:—

1. Faráshi	40 families
2. Kafashi	45 "
3. Mír Saláhi } 4. Kuchami }	100 "
5. Salandari	12 "
6. Makbali	50 "
7. Digoi	15 "
8. Buz Surkh	10 "
9. Sheikh	12 "
10. Sarbizani	7 "
11. Ar Pallu	10 "
12. Kásimu	10 "
13. Kurd	20 "
14. Karái	10 "
15. Sarhaddi	25 "
16. Deh Kuna	10 "
17. Tírgar	15 "
18. Gurvi	15 "
TOTAL	406 families

The winter is spent in Jíruft.

[2] This latter fact is denied in other histories.

favourably received, the idea that anything so small could be potent being rejected with scorn. In fact, so much was this the case that our visitors were not mollified until a bottle of some decoction, mainly water, was mixed for their edification. The whole business reminded me of a Cape doctor, who said that if you gave a Boer less than a quart of medicine, he would decline to pay the fee!

We should have enjoyed a stay of a month at Sarbizan, but as the *Sáhib Diwán* had been dismissed after a very short tenure of office, and the *Farmán Farmá* re-appointed, we decided to return to Kermán before His Highness's arrival. The first stage again lay across the plateau, and we camped on what I termed the Sárdu river, which is formed by the Dar-i-Mazár and the Sarbizan branches, although lower down the Kuh-i-Hezár contributes largely to its volume. Our next stage of twenty-three miles brought us out at Ráin, situated in the open plain, where I struck my second journey. Thence we marched approximately west, passing a ruined *caravanserai* and some warm springs of sulphurous water at Ab-i-Gaz. Shortly afterwards the track ran between two somewhat prominent hills, and we skirted the range until we reached a stream of sweet water, by the side of which we lunched. We then entered the Band-i-Gudar, as this section of the Jupár range is termed, and gradually ascended to an easy open pass at 8600 feet. An equally easy descent brought us to another ruined *caravanserai* at the hamlet of Sang, and we finally halted at Ab-i-Garm. From this village down to Máhun was only a few miles, the track skirting the spurs of the range. At Máhun we were on a familiar road, and that night found us back at Kermán.

The arrival of the *Farmán Farmá* took place shortly afterwards, and thenceforward picnics and shooting-trips, interspersed with days spent at Máhun, enabled us to spend a very pleasant time until we quitted Kermán.

His Highness was anxious to relieve the poverty of Kermán, and advocated bread tickets, whereas I proposed that a road should be built. However, as no engineer was forthcoming, the former plan was adopted, every *Khán* being induced to subscribe; but although as far as possible the charity was honestly administered, the numbers of beggars seemed to quadruple. In any case, it was a novel departure in Persia, and tended to keep down the price of bread, which generally rises at the coldest time of the year.

Just before Christmas (1895) two Germans, who were begging their way round the world for a wager, arrived at Kermán. As it would have been a great source of discredit to have Europeans asking for alms, I was obliged to help them in every way, but I cannot say that I was sorry to hear that they had finally failed, as such people, in the East at any rate, do no good. Surely the inaccurate information collected in this way is not of much value, but on the contrary harmful; moreover, there is no Oriental whose idea of a European is not lowered when he sees travellers unaccompanied by servants, and sleeping in any hovel. At the same time a German cavalry officer, a guest of quite another stamp, came on to Kermán from Isfahán, and we were once again in touch with the outer world.

For some months negotiations had been carried on with the Persian Government as to the desirability of delimitating the undefined strip of border running from Kuh-i-Malik-Sia to Kuhak, but the winter set in without anything definite being fixed. Late in December, however, the Persian Commissioner, Ali Ashraf Khán, with the title of *Ihtishám-u-Vizára*, passed through Kermán, and a few days after his departure, my appointment as Assistant-Commissioner was telegraphed from Tehrán.

My sister was very kindly offered a temporary home by Lady Durand, but in the true traveller's spirit she preferred to face all fatigue and discomfort, and immediately set to work to empty our store-room of its very mixed contents, and to insure that the supply department, at any rate, should be thoroughly well organised.

DESIGN FROM A WATER-PIPE.

CHAPTER XVIII

FROM KERMÁN TO KUHAK

> "Out, *taylards*, of my paleys!
> Now go and say your tayled king
> That I owe him no thing."
> —*Romance of Richard Coer de Lion*, l. 2112 (Weber, ii. p. 83).

STARTING on an indefinitely long journey in Persia is no light task. Our *lares et penates* had, of course, to be left behind, but to calculate, purchase, divide into loads, and pack up supplies for a large party is a very heavy undertaking. On the one hand, economy in transport is desirable, but, on the other, to run the risk of a breakdown would be fatal; and if arrangements for forage to be ready on the road, for extra camels to carry it, and for securing a water-supply in the desert, be taken into consideration, it becomes evident how much preparation is needed.

In our particular case the servants were all averse to travelling in Baluchistán, and required much humouring, while every single article had to be checked and noted down, as otherwise we might have started off without such an essential as horse-shoes.

However, thanks to my sister, everything was accomplished the day after the arrival of the *gholám* from Tehrán with the written instructions, and finally we started off on our first long stage of twenty-three miles, the *Farmán Farmá*, with characteristic kindness, lending us his own transport, without which all our labour would have been in vain, as in mid-winter few caravans arrive at Kermán.

It was cold enough at Máhun, but at Hanaka, where the *caravanserai* is situated at an elevation of close on 8000 feet, it was positively arctic. As, however, we wisely combined the Chinese method of adding to our clothing with the English habit of plenty of exercise, we did not feel the frost at all acutely; at the same time, we were very grateful to the *Vakil-ul-Mulk*, the builder of the *caravanserai*. Ráin lies at an altitude exceeding 7000 feet, but the temperature was higher than at Hanaka, no snow having fallen on the southern slopes of the Jupár range: it is the Rábin of Ibn Haukal. We were much cheered by hearing that the Persian Commissioner had halted a day at the little town, as we were determined to overtake him, in spite of his long start.

From Ráin we marched down the banks of the Sárdu river, here termed the river of Bam, and after thirty miles, or rather more, lost our way in the dark, but finally found our advanced camp pitched near that of the *Farmán Farmá's* regiment, where we had to exchange some mules for camels; the district is named Tahrud or River-bottom, but there is no village of the name nowadays. The next stage to Abárik was a short but trying one, as it lay across broken ground, and having descended to Hot Country, we all felt relaxed and unfit for exertion.

Storm-tossed Abárik and Tahrud are famous throughout Persia, which fact is recorded in the following lines: "They said to the Wind, 'Where is thy home?' He replied, 'My poor home is in Tahrud, but at times I visit Abárik and Sarbistán.'" This latter is the village on the right bank of the river at which I had halted in 1894 in the midst of a very severe gale.

At Abárik, locally known as Averk, there is a hot spring which is covered in and used as a bath, and specimens of lead and zinc were brought to us from the hills to the north-west; the ruined fort is also of considerable antiquity.

The stage to Dárzin was not long, but as it was utterly monotonous, lying close to the pebbly waste of the river which held no water, we were glad to terminate it. The village is famed in local legend as the spot where Farámurz, son of Rustam, was hanged by Bahman; and we were informed that the right name was *Dárzanán* or Gallows-

Erecting.[1] As an instance of what changes there have been since the 12th century, I will quote from Afzal Kermáni, who writes: "We sat on the roof of the palace at Dárzin and looked at the number of villages touching each other, and the fragrant scented trees. . . . Zein-u-Din, who was with us, said, 'It is commonly reported that Fárs is a great and fertile country, and it is known as "Half the World." I have seen it all, and I swear that in the whole of Fárs I have not seen such a spot.'" To-day, alas! all is changed, Dárzin standing in the midst of a dreary waste, but even so there is improvement, as one of the old *kanáts* has been repaired, and will, it is expected, greatly increase the cultivated area.

Resuming our march, the track lay down the river-bed, with several ruins, mute witnesses of a prosperous past, close to both sides of the road; we passed Bídarán, with the dilapidated shrine of *Khoja* Asghar and a belt of reeds, and missing the *istikbál*, rode down the river-bed which divides Bam into two parts; we were finally ushered into a newly-built house in a shady palm garden.

Bam from early times has been of note in Persia. The district was designated *Arba* or Four, from its four cities of Bam, Rígán, Narmáshir, and Nisa. Of these, Bam and Rígán were founded by Bahman, Ardeshír can claim the credit of building the city of Narmáshir, and his wife constructed the dam on which Nisa depended. It was also the home of Haftán-bokht,[2] Ardeshír's great rival, in connection with whom a curious legend is recounted in the Pahlevi *Kárnámak-i-Artakshír-i-Pápakán* and also in the *Sháh Náma*.

His daughter, when spinning with other maidens, picked up an apple within which she found a worm. She thereupon vowed that if she completed her allotted task before the others, she would save the worm alive. Almost at once her spinning was miraculously completed, and, faithful to her promise, she cherished the worm. From this time the family of Haftán-bokht prospered until its chief became the ruler of the province of Kermán.

According to the Pahlevi work, "the army of Haftán-bokht

[1] As a matter of fact, the defeat of Farámurz took place at Gurába, to which place he had advanced from Bust and Zábul. *Vide* Macan's *Sháh Náma*, vol. iii. pp. 1245-6.

[2] Haftán-bokht signifies in Pahlevi "the seven have delivered," the "seven" being the seven planets. Firdusi, probably for metrical reasons, terms him Haftwád.

attacked a caravan of Ardeshír, and brought the spoils to Guzárán, a borough of Gulár, where the worm had its abode. Now as regards the (worm) idolatry, it (grew) so powerful that five thousand men, who composed its forces in the different frontiers of Sind, assembled, and Haftán-bokht too collected his army. Ardeshír sent to battle with the worm, but its supporters took refuge in the hills, and, falling on his army at night, routed it. Ardeshír then took the field in person, but was also routed, and barely escaped with his life." However, the worm and its supporters were finally defeated by a ruse, Ardeshír or one of his adherents visiting Guzárán in disguise, and pouring molten tin down the worm's throat, which effected the death of the monster and the overthrow of Haftán-bokht.[1]

At one time I thought that this fable of the worm was a poetical description of the introduction of the silk-worm, but I then came to the conclusion that it must be a legend of snake worship. Mr E. G. Browne, however, makes the happy suggestion that perhaps both these ideas were embodied in the legend, and this seems extremely likely.

Guzárán of the Pahlevi and Kujárán of the *Sháh Náma*, which is probably the site of ancient Bam, is situated about a mile above the fort on the river. It is now a ruin, and known as Kuzárán, which is almost exactly the same as Guzárán, and even to-day one of the gates of the fort is known as Kut-i-Kirm.[2]

At the time of the Arab conquest Nisa must have been of great importance, as it was made the capital of the whole province by Mansur-u-Din.

A few years later Abdulla Ámir founded the Masjid-i-Hazrat-Rasul,[3] which is still standing on the outskirts of the modern town. Bam has sustained numerous sieges, but although on one occasion, in Seljuk times, it was nearly captured by damming up the river, I do not think that any impression was ever made on the garrison except by a blockade.

[1] I would express my sense of obligation to the Parsi editor, and may he follow up this work with others of the same value. It is of great importance to have access to the material used by Firdusi. Professor Nöldeke's German translation, too, is of great critical value.

[2] *Kirm* signifies worm. *Kut* is corrupted from *Kot*, a fort, or *Ked*, a house. Cf. *Kut-i-Kaftar*.

[3] *I.e.* "The Mosque of His Holiness the Prophet."

The description given by Idrísi is of considerable interest: "Bam est grande, commerçante et riche ; on y cultive la vigne et le palmier ; beaucoup de villages en dépendent. Il y a un château dont les fortifications sont réputées les meilleures de toutes celles du Kerman ; ses habitants se livrent au négoce et à l'industrie ; on y fabrique quantité de belles étoffes de coton, ce qui forme un objet considérable d'exportation." [1]

In modern times the city was the scene of the tragedy which terminated the Kájár-Zand struggle, when Lutf Ali Khán, who had fled from Kermán, was basely surrendered to his hereditary foe by its Governor, to whose hospitality he had entrusted himself. Yet once again, in the middle of the nineteenth century, Bam was besieged by a mixed force of Afgháns and Sistánis. When the ammunition was all expended, and no hope remained, the women of Bam, headed by *Bánu* Husein Fathá, heated cauldrons of water, and gave the assailants such a *warm* reception that the city held out until help came from Kermán.

A few years later, Ághá Khán seized the fort and was blockaded therein for the best part of a year, until sickness broke out, and he was forced to retreat to India. After this the erection of the modern town was commenced. It lines both banks of the river, and would, I imagine, suffer from floods in years of heavy snowfalls.

Lying at an altitude of 3600 feet, with a population of thirteen thousand inhabitants, and possessing a fertile soil and a climate equally suitable for palm-trees and for many upland products, Bam is the centre of a wealthy district. A cool north wind mitigates the summer heat, the mountain villages of the Jabal Báriz range are close at hand, and the importance of the town is enhanced by its being the last commercial centre in this part of Asia until Quetta is reached.[2]

Thus situated on the frontier of Persia (Narmáshir being under its jurisdiction), Baluchistán is generally garrisoned by soldiers raised in the district, the Governor being usually a Bami. It, however, owes its wealth to the fact that it is the henna city, almost all of that valuable dye being produced in the district. The town is of considerable extent, almost every house, as at

[1] *Geographie d'Édrisi*, vol. i. p. 423.
[2] The distance is not far short of 700 miles.

Isfahán, standing in a garden, and new *bázárs* are springing up to support its affluence.

By one of the writers of *Eastern Persia*,[1] Bam is considered to resemble an Indian town, but I must say that I failed to notice this. Thirty years ago there were, perhaps, no palm-trees, which may account for the opinion then expressed. We visited the famous fort by special invitation, and found that the old town was still standing, the whole being surrounded by a high wall and ditch. We passed through the deserted *bázárs* for some 600 yards, the fort occupying the northern end of the enclosure, and, ascending a steep incline in the rock, which has never been smoothed, we passed through a strong gateway and a 40-foot wall, which is built of sun-dried bricks, as indeed is the whole fortress. We then found ourselves facing a second and equally high wall, some 20 yards up the hillside, and, turning sharply to the left, approached the second gateway, a square surrounded by stables being below us as we moved along. A second equally steep incline, leading up to a similar gateway brought us to the Artillery Park, where we saw some muzzle-loading field-guns mounted on unserviceable carriages; the date of one, I remember, was A.H. 1254 (1838). A third and steeper passage led up from this square to a platform, on which is a well, which we calculated to be some 180 feet deep; it is alleged to have been dug by Rustam, under orders from King Solomon! It now only supplies the water for a bath. A short flight of steps, and we reached the summit of the fort, a *Chahár Fasl*[2] or Four Seasons, evidently constituting the Governor's quarters.

From the roof of this building, we enjoyed a wonderfully beautiful view. Looking back, Kuh-i-Hezár with its mantle of freshly fallen snow riveted our gaze, and on each side of the valley the hills showed up against the turquoise sky, the Sháh Sowárán range to the south forming another vision of beauty. Below us lay the date-groves of Bam, and we could trace its river to the north-east; we also indistinctly saw the greenery of Narmáshir. Far away, Bazmán, loveliest of peaks, rose up

[1] Vol. i. page 196.

[2] A *Chahár Fasl* is a set of rooms, so arranged that they enjoy whatever breeze is blowing, being open in every direction.

THE FORT AT BAM.

[*To face p.* 218.

grandly in solitary state, and we could not decide which was the finer of the two great giants. Bazmán, however, rears its head some 9000 feet above the plain, whereas Hezár, albeit loftier, rises but 7000 feet above Ráin, and is surrounded by other if lesser peaks.

In the town several wealthy families are resident, chief of whom is Suliman Khán, who thirty years ago was in charge of Sir Frederic Goldsmid's escort. Next in importance and related to him was my friend the *Asad-u-Dola*, who has governed Baluchistán intermittently for many years.

Upon leaving Bam, which, I may remark, the Persian Commissioner had only quitted the day of our arrival, we passed through the ruins of *Chehel Kura* or Forty Colts. Upon demanding the reason for this name as applied to a garden, we were told that it was formerly so vast, that a mare which had been lost, was not found until accompanied by a brood of forty colts! I afterwards learned that the same legend was related about a garden near Kermán, which, lying between two ranges of hills, could not have been more than 100 acres in extent, so that it is evidently a stock legend, like that of *Chehel Tan*. Forty is a favourite number in the East, as, for instance, in the tale of *Ali Baba and the Forty Thieves*.

Four miles from Bam, we made a short sharp descent, and the track passed between the two portions of the very important village of Bora, which is said to be a corruption of Beravát. As it has a population of 5000, and exports annually 120,000 lbs. of henna, besides grain and dates, it is remarkable that this, the largest centre of population after Bam, should never have been noticed by any of the members of the Sistán mission. Nor is this its only title to fame, as in the vicinity lives a tribe of men, who are believed to be *taylards*. Originally there were two tribes, (*a*) *Dumdár*, or those having tails, and (*b*) Nártígi; only the Nártígi are now left. It may perhaps be news to most of my readers that we English were considered to possess caudal appendages (as the heading to this chapter shows); in the same way, all Shia boys are taught that Sunnis are similarly favoured.

To Vakilábád we marched along a fine stream of water, which, with its palms, willows, and waving grasses, afforded a pleasant contrast to the arid monotony of the greater part of Persia.

We had now reached the district of Narmáshir,[1] the name being possibly a corruption of *Narímán Shahr* or the City of Narímán, who was the great-grandfather of Rustam. With its graceful tamarisks and mimosa, this tract might be a slice cut out of Sind, and it is much warmer than Bam. Until almost the middle of the nineteenth century, parts of it were held by the Afgháns, and it is only now beginning to recover its prosperity.

From Vakilábád we enjoyed about the pleasantest winter stage in Persia, graceful tamarisks, not bushes but trees, and the *Kahur*, a species of mimosa loved by the camel, together with numerous little streams, affording the senses an immense amount of pleasure. Half-way, we crossed a sluggish river, which is lost near Fahraj, and there our guest, Count Magnus, left us, proud of being the first German who had penetrated so near to the eastern confines of Persia. A few miles up the right bank are the ruins of the city founded by Ardeshír, now known as Chigukábád or Sparrow-town.

Plenty of francolin called from the jungle, but I had wisely packed away my gun, as our only business was to push on, and at night we halted at the little village of Burj-i-Ághá-Mohamed, after lunching by a stream which would have justified the *Rusticus* of Horace by the fact of flowing down and leaving a dry bed.

The following morning we traversed a mile of jungle, and then suddenly emerged on to hard, bare, open desert, which continued for some five miles, after which scrub was seen, followed by tamarisks, and we were again in a jungle, in the middle of which lies Rigán. This place is shown on the map in large type, but it merely consists of a mud fort, garrisoned by ten soldiers, and possesses a population of perhaps two hundred. All round, however, are hamlets, whence supplies may be procured in abundance, while the grazing

[1] Nomads of Narmáshir:—

1.	Ráis	700 families
2.	Gurgendi	300 ,,
3.	Palangi	40 ,,
4.	Mohamed Ghulámi	50 ,,
5.	Sarhaddi	40 ,,
6.	Sheikhi	300 ,,
7.	Nidati	100 ,,
8.	Hot	150 ,,
9.	Mír Reki	50 ,,
10.	Sukhta	50 ,,
	TOTAL,	1780 families.

for camels is considered to be the best in Persia, and is resorted to from every part of the province.

The Persian Commissioner, whom we had once again almost overtaken, had left us a despairing message to the effect that, if we did not slacken our pace, we should wear him out, but this admission, as may be imagined, only stimulated us not to relax our efforts, and as both forage and camels to carry it were all ready at Rigán, we decided that it was not necessary to halt even for a day.

Between us and Bampur lay 160 miles of Lut, but as heavy rain had fallen only two days previously, we enjoyed much better water than generally falls to the lot of travellers, and traversed the distance in nine days, with scarcely a hitch, the only *contretemps* being the loss of fifteen camels for half a day.

The Goldsmid Mission had followed a southerly route, to avoid Sarhaddi raiders, and Sir H. Pottinger, the first European explorer of Baluchistán (if we except Alexander the Great), had travelled by Bazmán, which village I had previously visited, but the main route lay between, and had water at every stage. Indeed, were it otherwise, it would be almost impossible to march the reliefs across the desert, and, even as it is, a withered corpse is not unfrequently seen, bearing witness to the difficulties of the route. Each stage was monotonously like the rest, but at Dar-i-Kishkin, about halfway, we not only had a heavy fall of rain, but found a tiny perennial stream, which might be taken advantage of to form a hamlet.

At Gazak we had traversed two-thirds of the desert, and were delighted to find some nomad tents and a palm-grove. We finally struck the Bampur river at Kuchgardan, through which I had already passed, and I need hardly say that we fully appreciated its shady tamarisks and sweet water.

An escort of camelry here met us and a wilder-looking or more irregular force is scarcely conceivable. One man in particular, with a great reputation for courage, boasted of a scarlet beard of wondrous size. Doubly protected, as we had also a detachment of Bam cavalry, mounted on tiny starved ponies, which were mercilessly galloped about, we marched on to Bampur, and thence to Fahraj. At this latter place our reception was most ceremonious, the garrison lining the road, and the band playing the National Anthem; and when we espied the Persian Commissioner's camp, we felt well pleased to have overtaken him scarcely more than half-way.

Social functions, including visits from and to the *Ihtishám-u-Vizára* and the *Asad-u-Dola*, occupied two days, during which time we engaged thirty Baluch camels. It was agreed that I should march a day ahead, in order to be present on the frontier when the Persian camp arrived.

As far as Magas, where I was welcomed by the same old chief as two years previously, we were on a familiar route, but as this had been my furthest point east, I was only too anxious to go beyond it. Surán, where we halted a day, had plenty of snipe, but they were very wild in the morning, and later on the heat was too much for me, as, although it was early February, we had daily noon temperatures of 86° in our tents. Hitherto only vague rumours as to the British party had reached us, and I was beginning to wonder whether, after all, I had not pushed ahead so fast to no purpose, when a messenger came from Colonel Holdich to the effect that he was nearing Panjgur, and hoped to be on the frontier about the middle of February. As may be imagined, he too was equally anxious to know the whereabouts of the Persian Commissioner, as I had not been able to despatch a messenger until reaching Fahraj, and he evidently had not arrived.

From Surán we passed through Sib,[1] and thence marched to the south of Dizak, and so on to Isfandak. There we found a charming date-grove, a stream of crystal water, but—no inhabitants, the fact being that the headman felt uneasy in his mind at the prospect of meeting the *Asad-u-Dola*, as he had been concerned in various raids and other misdemeanours. In consequence, he and the villagers were bivouacking in the Siahán range to the north, watching the development of events, and, no doubt, accusing the Commission of being the cause of their exile.

We were now on the left bank of the Mashkel or Mashkid river (the latter being the Baluchi pronunciation). Its great river-bed and towering banks all point to its having been originally a mighty river, whereas now, even in spate, the torrent is readily forded after the first rush, yet the proverb, "He who

[1] This is the capital of a district which includes Paskuh. Its inhabitants are Arbábi, who are, I think, the aborigines. Later on, in the spring, its Governor rebelled.

THE PERSIAN COMMISSIONERS.

[*To face p.* 222.

stops to tie the latchet of his shoe in the Mashkel is lost," must have had its reason. Its waters discharge into the desert to the east of Jálk and partly supply the Mashkel date-groves.

We were now but two stages from our main body, a messenger having announced that the British Commission had just arrived. After a halt at a pool in the river-bed, we finally rode past Kuhak, saw the gleam of symmetrically-arranged tents, and were soon shaking hands with fellow-countrymen, after a journey of 600 miles mainly across deserts, at an average including halts of 15 miles a day, which must almost constitute a record for a lady marching with a caravan.

FROM LUSTRED POTTERY.

CHAPTER XIX

THE PERSO-BALUCH BOUNDARY COMMISSION.

"Lordynges, also I fynde,
At Mede so bigynneth Ynde;
Forsothe ich woot it stretcheth ferrest
Of alle the londes in the est."
—*Romance of Alisaunder*, line 4824 (Weber, i. p. 201).

BY way of preface to this chapter I propose to give some account of what was officially known as the Perso-Baluch Boundary Commission, although the *Ihtisham-u-Vizárá*, with greater accuracy, termed it the Perso-Kalát Commission.

Rather more than thirty years ago, when an overland telegraph line to India was under consideration, and it was important to know with whom to treat, this sealed land was visited by Sir Frederic Goldsmid, the final result of his enquiries being that a boundary was drawn from Kuhak[1] to the sea. Kuhak, which was considered a strong fortress, was at that time independent, and remained so; to the north, as far as Sistán, the country was unexplored, and of unknown ownership; no steps were therefore taken to determine the boundary. The Persian Government at that time was fortunate in having an excellent Governor in the shape of Ibráhim Khán, who indeed did his best to prevent the determination of any boundary, but, failing in that, he seized on Kuhak as soon as the English Commissioner was well out of the country. This step was not recognised by our Foreign Office,

[1] Kuhak is the diminutive of *Kuh*, a hill.

but as for some ten years longer our protectorate over Kalát and interest in its affairs was slight, the matter was allowed to remain quiescent.

When, however, our troops were stationed at Panjgur, raiding was felt to be intolerable, and it was suggested to H.I.M. Násir-u-Din that the undefined section of the frontier, together with the Kuhak question, should be finally settled. This occasioned much correspondence, during which a Kermáni wrote to the Persian Government that, just as Isfahán was half the world, so the Mashkel date-groves were half of Baluchistán, producing the finest fruit in the world. The negotiations were, I believe, on the point of falling through, the Sháh not caring for the expense of a commission that would not bring in an increase of revenue, when Naoroz Khán of Khárán suddenly occupied the groves, which had only recently been visited by the *Asad-u-Dola*, and declared by him to belong to Persia. Upon news of this reaching Kermán, the *Farmán Farmá* wrote me an official letter, asking me to eject the invaders of Persian soil. In reply, I pointed out that such incidents were unavoidable until the frontier was fixed, and that, in the meanwhile, I could take no action. A copy of this correspondence was sent by the *Farmán Farmá* to Tehrán, and brought home to His Majesty the inconvenience of doing nothing; he thereupon promptly agreed to the Commission, which met at Kuhak towards the end of February.

Our party was not a very large one, Colonel, now Sir Thomas, Holdich being Chief Commissioner, while Captain A. C. Kemball and myself were Assistant Commissioners. Lieut.-Col. R. Wahab, R.E., was in charge of a full survey party, and the escort of two companies of Jacob's Rifles and a few *sowárs* were under Lieut. C. V. Price. To conclude the list of British officers, Lieut. Turnbull, I.M.S., was medical officer in charge.

We found that we had reached Kuhak only four days after the British Commission, and the Persian Commissioner arrived the next day, but, had it not been for our promptitude, it would have been impossible to finish the work during the cold weather. Even as it was, after 10 A.M. the sun was much too powerful to be safe or agreeable, while the clear weather, so requisite for survey, ends in March, to be succeeded by six months of haze.

During the afternoon I was able to explain to Colonel Holdich the etiquette of an *istikbál*, and the following morning the Persian Commissioner and the *Asad-u-Dola* marched in amid the blare of trumpets and band, headed by our *sowárs* and some led horses. The Persian camp was pitched on the left or Persian bank of the dry river-bed, and the great question immediately arose who should pay the first call.

I must here explain that the *Ihtishám-u-Vizára*, who was thoroughly versed in European etiquette, was only too ready to act correctly throughout, but as the Governor of Baluchistán supplied him with everything, including the food he ate, he had to be guided to a certain extent by the truculent Warden of the Marches, who, however, I must say, was only standing up for what he considered his rights. Our view was, that as first arrivals we should be called on; but unfortunately Persian etiquette is just the reverse. The question was then debated in the Persian camp on the lines that Colonel Holdich was only sent by the Queen's Viceroy, whereas the Persian Commissioner was representing the King of Kings, and the *Asad-u-Dola* was his Governor.

In short, this question, ludicrous as it may seem, was all important, as being the actual test of relative official importance, and the assembled Baluchi chiefs from both sides of the frontier watched eagerly to see who would score first blood. It might have dragged on for days, when it was settled by the fact that both the Persian Commissioner and the Governor of Baluchistán had called on me first at Kermán and at Fahraj; they were consequently bound to do as much for my superior officer.

When the day came, the escort was drawn up in two lines, and as the Persian *cortège* approached, all possible honours were rendered, and the two Persians walked into the tent together, it being out of the question for one to precede the other, for that would have implied seniority.

A short visit with little conversation took place, partly owing to the fact that the Persian of India and that spoken in Irán are entirely different languages, as I have mentioned before. This was evidently not entirely grasped in India, and the result was that the official *munshi*, who was receiving a high salary and allowances, was not able even to carry a message, so that the whole work of interpreting and writing fell upon my small office.

NO. I. BOUNDARY CAIRN.

[*To face p.* 226.

The starting-point of the Commission was on the Mashkel, opposite Kuhak, and to save time an artistic cairn was already being constructed on the left bank. This was at once questioned, but the explanation that the opposite bank was low, and that the next one would be on our side, smoothed over that difficulty, although an invitation to be photographed at the cairn was declined, the astute *Asad-u-Dola* thinking that "presence gives consent."

At the proposed site of No. 2 pillar there was a full meeting. We afterwards heard that, had it not been for the fact that my sister had reached the top of the hill on which the cairn was placed, nothing would have tempted the portly Governor of Baluchistán to make the ascent. Once there, after recovering his breath, he became cantankerous, and said that we were robbing him of a valuable and fertile district, which proved to be half an acre in extent. The fact that the line to be followed had already been decided at Tehrán went for nothing, and we had to leave him to his representative to be calmed down.

The tireless Colonel Wahab left us in order to pillar the Siahán range, and we suggested that Suliman *Mírza*, the *Farmán Farmá's* representative, should accompany him, which he did most unwillingly, climbing peak after peak with his English colleague, and finding it, as he confided to me, heavier work than had ever before fallen to his lot. Colonel Wahab happens to be an extraordinarily accomplished mountaineer.

The two Commissions now marched to Isfandak in three stages, and thence we proceeded towards Jálk by the Bonsar pass, just below which we encamped. Here a second crisis occurred, the Persian Commissioner sending word that the Baluchis had reported to him that a boundary pillar had been erected to the west of the pass, and that this was causing much excitement. Having first carefully ascertained that the erection in question was only a triangulation point, a message was sent back to the effect that surprise and pain were felt at the idea that we could have done such a thing, and so crestfallen were the objectors that for a time there was no more trouble.

The various details of the two parties formed the most incongruous medley imaginable, what with British, Persians, Baluchis, and soldiers, regular and irregular. Camels, mules, and donkeys, were also a very prominent feature, and last but not least came our flock of sheep and goats.

All down the Kalagán valley were palm-groves and a green luxuriance of maiden-hair fern, while at Laji, on the top of a tower, I recollect a stuffed dummy, exactly like one of the giant warders which still ornament Alnwick Castle. We were told that it had been manufactured by a dervish, who guaranteed immunity from capture so long as the tireless watcher kept guard! However, it was for its gale that Laji will always be memorable. At 11 P.M. one night it began to blow so hard that a new tent was ripped right down its centre in a few minutes. By dint of great efforts our tents were kept up, or most of them, but the Persian camp was prostrate, and next morning we were asked to halt a day for repairs. To guard against any recurrence of such a disagreeable incident, the *Asad-u-Dola* made a soldier lie in charge of each peg for the rest of the journey!

The inhabitants of Kalagán were a wretched-looking people, but little better than the Bampur slaves, and throughout we were struck by the fact that the chiefs were much finer physically, and also fairer. There appears to be but little doubt that they are members of a different race, as mentioned in chap. viii., although, of course, their cleaner and handsomer clothes would make a considerable difference; the cultivators are said to be almost all Arbábis, a subject tribe not far removed from serfdom. Sir Henry Pottinger passed through Kalagán on his way from Nushki to Bampur.

At Jálk we halted for a fortnight, while the pillars were erected by which the Mashkel date-groves passed to Kalát, as already agreed upon at Tehrán. The district to the north was practically desert, and Colonel Holdich deemed it best to save a second cold weather's work, by suggesting that the ranges running down south-east from the Kuh-i-Malik-Sia should be accepted as a boundary, without doing anything more than sending a flying party to travel along them.

As this was agreed to by the Persian Commissioner, it only remained to visit and decide upon the ownership of some few groves of no great value, lying to the north of the others. As luck would have it, I had first heard of the existence of these unimportant groves when in Sarhad in 1893, and had taken full notes, so that Wahab and Kemball had only to see to the erection of boundary mounds, which at the best were a makeshift, being composed of sand and bushes, and one at least had disappeared by 1899.

The Jálk oasis is of considerable extent, covering quite four square miles. Everywhere there are date-palms, under which were growing barley, wheat, and beans, and in the gardens were pomegranates, fig-trees, and vines. Down the centre ran a marshy *nala*, full of reeds, which we explored one day for pig, and scattered about were eight considerable villages.[1] A remarkable phenomenon, observed by Colonel Holdich, was that the Mashkel date-groves, some forty miles to the east, were fed by springs from Jálk, which run underground to the edge of the *hámun*. I may mention that these groves, far from being "half of Baluchistán," are of but little value, but this did not prevent their being a source of constant annoyance.

In this oasis there were several domed buildings, mainly built of sun-dried bricks, inside which were the tombs of a departed race of chiefs, known as the Keiánian *Maliks*. This is, however, a mistake, there being little doubt that these chiefs were members of the Saffár family, which ruled in Baluchistán for more than five centuries.[2] Some of the mausolea consisted of but one chamber; others also possessed an antechamber, while a third kind had two stories. There were remnants of tiling under the line of the dome, and occasionally there were crude drawings of elephants and peacocks, but everything was of the lowest order from an artistic point of view.

The Persian New Year's Day (March 21st) most unfortunately came round just before our work was finished. The British Commissioner proposed to call with his staff on his Persian colleague, as representing the Sháh, but as the *Asad-u-Dola* said, "Where do I come in?" Nasrulla Khán was once again kept on the move between the camps, and we unavoidably offended the Governor of Baluchistán by pointing out that the Persian Commissioner was, in our eyes, the Sháh's representative, but that, if he desired, a visit would be paid to him later on. This waving of the olive branch was, however, of

[1] The inhabitants of the district, which is ruled by Abdulla Khán, Bolakzáí, comprise Ghamshadzáí, Rekí, Arbábi, Shiáhi, Umrái, Sipáhi, Ráis, and a Hindu or two, who live much like Mohamedans—except when fellow-countrymen arrive.

[2] *Vide* p. 99.

little avail. It was a good thing that our labours were so nearly terminated, as the breach between the *Asad-u-Dola* and the *Ihtishám-u-Vizára* grew daily wider, culminating in a threat on the part of the former to leave the latter without supplies in the desert on the return journey, if Colonel Holdich's demand that the Persian authorities should be responsible for the Yarahmadzái[1] was accepted. Matters were thus at an *impasse.* However, an arrangement by which the obnoxious agreement was partly signed by the two Commissioners in my tent, saved the situation, and at the formal meeting only the description of the various pillars was detailed, and the maps duly signed and sealed. The *Asad-u-Dola*, quite ignorant of the ruse, beamed with triumph, and I tried hard to look dejected as the longitude and latitude of each pillar was solemnly read out—and nothing else!

The day before the Commission broke up athletic sports were organised, commencing with a camel race, which suggested a series of "prehistoric peeps." I have not the slightest doubt that the camel is the origin of the ancient dragon, at least as regards the head and neck. Everything went off well until the wrestling match, when, owing to the different styles and rules, a long delay ensued, and as soon as the combatants were hard at it, the crowd broke in and began to belabour the unhappy champions. In a moment stones and sticks were in active circulation, and many of us had a bad time while separating, or trying to separate, the conflicting parties.

The Bami soldiers then raised a cry that rifles were necessary, and made off to their camp, although a percentage took advantage of the confusion to belabour their general. As they all knew me, I galloped off to their camp, and kept them from touching their rifles, or rather insisted that they should be put down, and then, to prevent a fiasco, instructed competitors, but no others, to go back to the ground. The *Asad-u-Dola* and the Persian Commissioner were then persuaded to return, and I proceeded to find Colonel Holdich, who had kindly taken my sister to the camp. He at once mounted a spare pony and cantered back, and the races were concluded in a most friendly spirit. The Baluchis fully thought

[1] This Sarhad tribe was constantly raiding across the frontier, and it was partly on that account that we so gladly gave up the date-groves owned by them.

TOMBS OF KEIANIAN MALIKS, JÁLK.

[*To face p.* 230.

that war had been proclaimed, and assembled in large numbers—to help us, they said. One lesson I learned, and that was to avoid wrestling competitions in mixed sports; it arouses as much feeling as a football match in Lancashire.

The sequel was amusing, as the *Asad-u-Dolá* announced his intention of "sticking" everybody all round, whereupon my tents, which lay apart from the British camp, were invaded by the whole regiment, seeking *bast* or sanctuary round my charger. The *Asad-u-Dola* harangued his men, but in vain, and then appealed to me for assistance. Acting on Colonel Holdich's instructions, it was finally arranged that one man should be punished on both sides, as I had noted two particularly outrageous offenders, and so the incident closed.

A great banquet was the last event to commemorate the fact that the frontier, 300 miles in length, had been delimitated in just a month, a fact which speaks volumes for the excellence of the plan adopted by the Chief Commissioners. On this occasion, to quote my sister, "Fat Háji Khán, the Persian Commissioner's interpreter, came to the front, electrifying us, when he suddenly struck up the *Highland Laddie*, which had been taught him, so he told us, by an English lady, to whom he had become tenderly attached during his stay in London."[1]

The next morning at an early hour we started back towards Kuhak, after the most cordial of leave-takings, and thus terminated the Perso-Baluch Boundary Commission.

[1] *Through Persia on a Side Saddle*, p. 283 (First Edition).

COUPLET FROM HÁFIZ.

CHAPTER XX

ACROSS BRITISH BALUCHISTÁN TO QUETTA

"Until another night in night
I enter'd, from the clearer light,
Imbower'd vaults of pillar'd palm,
Imprisoning sweets, which, as they clomb
Heavenward, were stay'd beneath the dome
Of hollow boughs."

—TENNYSON, *Recollections of the Arabian Nights*.

BRITISH Baluchistán has, so far, lacked a historian, although in the reports drawn up by various officials, the material is all ready, and only awaits the man. Geographically speaking, the western section consists, in its northern division, of desert running up to the Helmand, the centre and south being occupied by long but narrow valleys, trending with the greatest regularity from north-east to south-west. Further east the Baluch Highlands, which are an offshoot of the mighty Hindu Kush, are entered, and it is on the great plateau held up by them that both Kalát and Quetta are situated. As may be supposed, the climate of the western section is much the same as that of Persian Baluchistán, Panjgur in particular supplying some of the finest dates in the world; but between Kalát and Quetta the cold is sometimes intense, and I recollect Colonel Wahab pointing out a spot where his party had been overtaken by a blizzard. In the dark they had pitched their tents under the lee of a mound, which in the morning was discovered to be composed of commissariat draught bullocks, frozen to death!

As far as my journey is concerned, it is merely necessary to recapitulate from chaps. viii. and ix. that Khárán is peopled by Noshirwánis and various subject races, Panjgur by Gichkis, and Kalát by a very mixed population of Bráhuis, Rinds, Afgháns, Dehwárs, slaves, and Hindus.

It is not generally known that it was less than two decades ago that a British representative first appeared at Panjgur, in the person of that great frontier officer, Sir Robert Sandeman. The Government of India, not wishing to incur a large and totally unremunerative expenditure, began by sending an officer on tour for several cold seasons; but this was not sufficient, as the Baluchis only waited until the escort had gone, to recommence their feuds.[1] In 1891, Major Muir was holding a court out of sight of his guard, and incautiously ordered the arrest of *Mir* Shahdád, a noted blackguard. Resistance was made, an unarmed servant being killed, and Major Muir severely wounded, while Shahdád escaped for the time being, but as my presence at Kermán made Persian Baluchistán too hot for him, he finally surrendered to Kemball in his 1894-95 tour. For a year or so after this outrage a small garrison was maintained at Panjgur, but this was withdrawn in 1893, the country having settled down to some extent, although, as later chapters will show, the struggle against the restraints of civilisation was not quite at an end.

To resume, as far as Kuhak we halted at the same stages as before, the weather daily becoming hotter, but at Laji the monotony was relieved by two bears, the first I had seen in Baluchistán, chasing Turnbull back into camp. We all turned out and raced up the hill, but, as may be supposed, we only got a glimpse of Bruin, who was quite out of shot, and we had to be content with recovering Turnbull's helmet. I think that bears must be very rare, as I have only on one other occasion seen their tracks; indeed, the food question must be a difficult problem for them to solve.

At Kuhak we camped near the pretty little village, where, while examining a mausoleum, similar to those described at Jálk, I found

[1] The Rinds, in addition to giving trouble in other ways, attacked a telegraph party in 1893, looting everything and carrying off five captives.

a brick with an inscription, mutilated in places, but with a few lines legible, to the effect that *Malik* Shams-u-Din, who died in A.H. 1027 (1617), was the individual in whose honour the tomb had been built. He was almost certainly the opponent of Ganj Ali Khán.[1]

From Kuhak we crossed the Mashkel with its coffee-coloured flood, little more than a foot deep, and then entered the valley of the Rakshán. It is wide and shallow, and runs east for some 200 miles with a northerly trend. At the second stage we underwent our worst experience of salt water, which not even the most hardened campaigner could swallow, and we bitterly regretted a case of beer which we had presented to our Persian colleagues. Our flour, too, was musty and almost inedible.

The following day brought us to Panjgur or Five Tombs, so called from its five chiefs slain at the time of the Arab Conquest; it is a lovely oasis, consisting of several hamlets and extensive date-groves. Indeed, the dates of Panjgur are considered to surpass all others. However, the district bore rather a sinister reputation, as in the previous year a *Ghási* had, in a most cold-blooded and treacherous manner, attacked Lieut. Parker, who was in command of a section of a mountain battery. The dastardly assailant professed to be anxious to show off his horse's paces, and asked Parker to canter ahead, whereupon he rushed up and stabbed him. It is satisfactory to know that he was quickly caught by the gunners, and, after trial, was duly hanged and burnt. Kemball having been the judge on that occasion, an attempt at vengeance was highly probable; we were all therefore forbidden to go out, except with an orderly, and we took the extra precaution of strolling about with shot guns, which would stop a *Ghási* better than any revolver.

We halted for Easter Sunday, and the following day we passed the deserted barracks, occupied until 1894 by infantry of the same regiment as that composing our escort, "Jacob's Rifles," which has since greatly distinguished itself in Uganda. The heat was trying and the days long, as the march was always over by 8 A.M. and a siesta was quite out of the question.

However, we were steadily rising, as our aneroids showed, and although the marches were intensely monotonous, day succeeding day without a sign of life being anywhere visible, yet we could interest ourselves by speculating on the causes that had swept away

[1] *Vide* chap. ix.

KUHAK.

[To face p. 234.

the population from this valley, which for mile after mile was carefully terraced, while here and there were mounds littered with pottery. War, no doubt, had had much to do with it, but, even more probably, ruthless deforestation in this and adjacent districts had decreased the rainfall, after which the springs dried up and the population was driven away. At the same time, water is to be procured, and artesian wells would, no doubt, be of great service, but what particularly struck me was that we were passing through a most magnificent country for camel breeding. Everywhere the richest scrub covered the ground, while the climate and soil resembled that of many parts of Afghanistán. Consequently there would be no fear that the camels raised here would break down on trans-frontier service, as is invariably the case with those bred in the plains. Even in the last Afghán war, neglect of this question is said to have caused the loss of 36,000 camels, which not only dislocated the transport service, but also bred the most terrible amount of sickness; nowadays perhaps all this is changed, but, even so, it seems a pity that use cannot be made of this "Great Lone Land," where we saw no sign of life for quite 200 miles.

At Nágha Kalát, which we reached by a 35 mile march, we halted a couple of days to recuperate our camels, and utilised the delay to inspect the immense ruins. The great reservoirs, of which we saw frequent remains, were prominent objects; as already mentioned, in Baluchistán they are termed *Gorbasta*. After this we rose more rapidly, and were soon on the Baluch Highlands, where the level plains were a mass of flowers, and where, thanks to the greater altitude, it was no longer necessary to march at night.

Towards the end of April we reached Kalát, the capital of Baluchistán, which is situated at the considerable elevation of 7000 feet. As mentioned in chap. ix., a great ruler of this province was Nasír Khán, who accompanied Nádir Sháh to Delhi. Upon returning to Kalát he found that his brother's tyrannical behaviour had ruined the country, all the Hindus having fled in a body to save their property. Nasír Khán killed his brother, *Háji* Mohamed Khán, and received the title of *Beglerbegi* from Nádir Sháh, who evidently approved of his action. In a few years he restored prosperity to Baluchistán, and it is related that he marched *via*

Panjgur to Kasarkand, every chief apparently submitting to him and becoming his tributary.

Upon the assassination of Nádir Sháh he opposed Ahmad Sháh, and, at first, successfully. He was, however, defeated at Mastung, and forced to retreat to Kalát, where he was besieged. After beating off three assaults peace was made, and Nasír Khán bound himself to furnish troops whenever called upon to do so. In return for this he was excused the payment of tribute.

Not long afterwards he aided Ahmad Sháh against Persia, and headed his Baluchis in a desperate charge which decided the day in a battle fought near Meshed. Again, at Tabas, by an ambuscade of his planning, the Persian army was annihilated. Returning home in triumph, his kingdom was extended as far as distant Karachi, and Baluchistán enjoyed a period of prosperity which has never since been equalled.

Kalát possesses a population of perhaps 50,000 inhabitants, which however fluctuates, the town being almost deserted in the depth of winter. Its *bázárs* are very mean, and altogether Kalát shows that it is owned by a race which is far lower than the Persians in the arts of civilisation. Its fort was, I understand, mainly the work of Nasír Khán, and at the time of its construction must have been almost impregnable, its situation being excellent.

In this work I have made no mention of the games played by Baluchis, but it seems that we owe the now popular exercise of tent-pegging to this people. In support of this I give an extract from Pottinger: "Before I close this enumeration of their diversions, I may describe a very hazardous, though popular one among all classes, which they perform on horseback, and call Nezuh Bazee or spear play. A wooden stake of moderate thickness is driven into the ground, and a horseman at full speed pierces it with the point of his spear in such a manner as to force it out of the earth and carry it along with him. The difficulty and danger in accomplishing this feat is evidently augmented or decreased according to the depth that the stake is in the ground."[1]

Nasír Khán died in A.D. 1795, and it was during his successor's reign that Pottinger passed through the country, and noted that since his death even Kej had ceased to pay tribute. His unworthy successor, Mahmud Khán, was a drunken creature, and died in

[1] *Travels in Beloochistan*, p. 66.

THE KHÁN OF KALÁT AND COURT.

[*To face p.* 236.

1819, being succeeded by his son Mehráb Khán, during whose reign Kalát was first brought into contact with the Government of India.

In 1838 that most "wild, ill-considered, and adventurous" expedition, as Sir Henry Durand justly termed it, to force a weak and worthless sovereign on the Afghán people, was undertaken, and British officers were deputed to Kalát to secure the co-operation of the Khán, whose territories were traversed in the advance on Kandahár. Suspicions of treachery on his part arising, in November 1839 a British force attacked and stormed Kalát, and Mehráb Khán was killed. His papers, when found, proved that he was innocent of disloyalty, but was the victim of an intrigue. His successor and the British representative were both murdered a few years later, and a second Nasír Khán was appointed chief, being succeeded in 1857 by *Mir* Khudadád Khán.

His career was distinctly chequered, as for nearly twenty years he was at war with his *Sardárs*. In 1877, Quetta was bought by the British Government, and during the subsequent Afghán war Khudadád rendered yeoman's service. Later on his doings aroused dissatisfaction, and after having murdered his Vizier and family in a somewhat atrocious fashion, he was deposed, and Kalát was again occupied by British troops.

On this occasion the immense treasure that was seized was laid out at interest, and is now being spent in improvements. It is wonderful how generally throughout Persia the confiscation of these cases of rupees was noticed, and the Khán commiserated. It rather reminded me of an Armenian, who, being in a Consulate at the time of the massacres, and hearing from refugees that his relations and friends were all being murdered, appeared quite unmoved. Later on in the day, a fresh arrival mentioned that the *Pasha* had seized all the money of one victim, and then, but not till then, my acquaintance tore his hair and bewailed the calamities that had befallen his nation.

To conclude this short sketch, Khudadád Khán's son, Mahmud Khán, was appointed to succeed him, and is now the Khán of Kalát and *Beglerbegi* of Baluchistán.

To resume, we rode over a low pass in the hills, and came in sight of the picturesquely-situated fort, where the British Commissioner was met by the Khán's brother and some recently-raised Lancers. The camp was pitched near the miserable-looking building which houses the political agent; however, we had no reason to grumble, as from its garden we procured the first vegetables that we had tasted since leaving Jálk, where we had enjoyed a solitary dish of beans. We were once again on the telegraph line, which we had quitted at Kermán, and two stages further on, beyond the delightful Mastung valley, we struck the road in course construction to Kalát, which, however, has never been finished.

At our last camp of Sariáb we could see the nearly-completed Bolán pass railway, and our Persian servants, in order to air their knowledge, came to inform us what it was. Our uncivilised horses did not take kindly to cantonments, and were nearly driven wild, first by a wheel-barrow, and then by the railway-station. We, for our part, revelled in the green avenues, and when we finally reached the Agency at Quetta, felt inclined to exclaim, as Sádi does of Shiráz, "This indeed is Paradise!"

The kindly welcome of Sir James Browne, the beautiful English-like house, and all the unwonted luxuries of every kind, were a fitting end to a most successful journey, which enables my sister to claim to have been the first lady to ride from the Caspian Sea to India, a distance of close upon 2000 miles.

FROM A PERSIAN BRASS BOWL.

CHAPTER XXI

A MISSION TO THE KÁRUN VALLEY

"And dear as the wet diver to the eyes
Of his pale wife who waits and weeps on shore
By sandy Bahrein, in the Persian Gulf,
Plunging all day in the blue waves, at night,
Having made up his tale of precious pearls,
Rejoins her in their hut upon the sands."
—MATTHEW ARNOLD.

THE two days we spent at Quetta were fully employed in social duties and selling off horses and mules. Fortunately, I had already disposed of three horses at Mastung, and we took on three to Simla, while the transport authorities bought most of my mules. In fact, after using my horses for about a year, I made a considerable profit on them, prices in India ruling very high and remounts still being of a poor quality. I understand, however, that there is a steady improvement, but, after living in Persia, the country-bred horse seems a very "three-cornered" animal.

We determined to leave most of our servants temporarily at Quetta, while the heavy baggage was despatched by goods train to Karachi, and, after saying good-bye to our genial host, whose almost sudden death shortly afterwards was a great loss to his country, we started for Simla. The Bolán line was just completed, but not open for traffic, and we travelled *via* Humái through a belt which for wildness can only be compared to the Bushire *kotals*. A communicative guard pointed out a mountain of mud which may at any time destroy the line,[1] and altogether the run was extremely interesting, although the temperature steadily rose hour after hour.

At a roadside station a Tehrán telegram overtook me, containing the terrible news of the assassination of H.I.M. Násir-u-Din. The ill-fated monarch was visiting the shrine of *Sháh* Abdul Azím, near Tehrán, when *Mírza* Rezá, a follower of the notorious Jamál-u-Din, who plotted against Persia from Constantinople, stepped forward with a petition. As the kindly Sháh was in the act of taking it, the assassin fired his revolver which was concealed behind the paper; his victim fell, mortally wounded, and died shortly afterwards. H.H. the Prime Minister rose to the occasion, and giving out that the Sháh was only slightly wounded, drove back to Tehrán, and took all the necessary steps to secure order before the sad news was known. This decided action, which was supported both by Sir Mortimer Durand and the Russian *Chargé d'Affaires*, undoubtedly saved Persia from a period of anarchy. The Imperial Bank of Persia also rendered great service, as, acting on instructions from Sir Mortimer Durand, it advanced money to pay the troops and to enable H.I.M. Muzaffar-u-Dín to reach the capital without undue delay.

Our servants were quite stunned at the news, and, as residents in the country, we were able to sympathise keenly with them on the heavy loss suffered by the land of Irán. We fully expected that the whole country would be in a turmoil, and that I should very soon be recalled, and although it was my intention to pay only a flying visit to Simla, I began to wish that my camp equipage had been sent to the coast by passenger not by goods train.

In due course of time, the familiar station at Kalka was reached, but, as our servants were demoralised, and, like many Persians abroad, homesick, we prudently resolved to march up to Simla in three stages, instead of leaving our horses to follow us.

I had spent little more than a fortnight at the lovely but somewhat cramped hill-capital of India, enjoying much hospitality the while, when orders came for me to proceed to

[1] If the railway be continued to Nushki, it could then be united to Karachi by a line running through a much less difficult country — at least, so I understand.

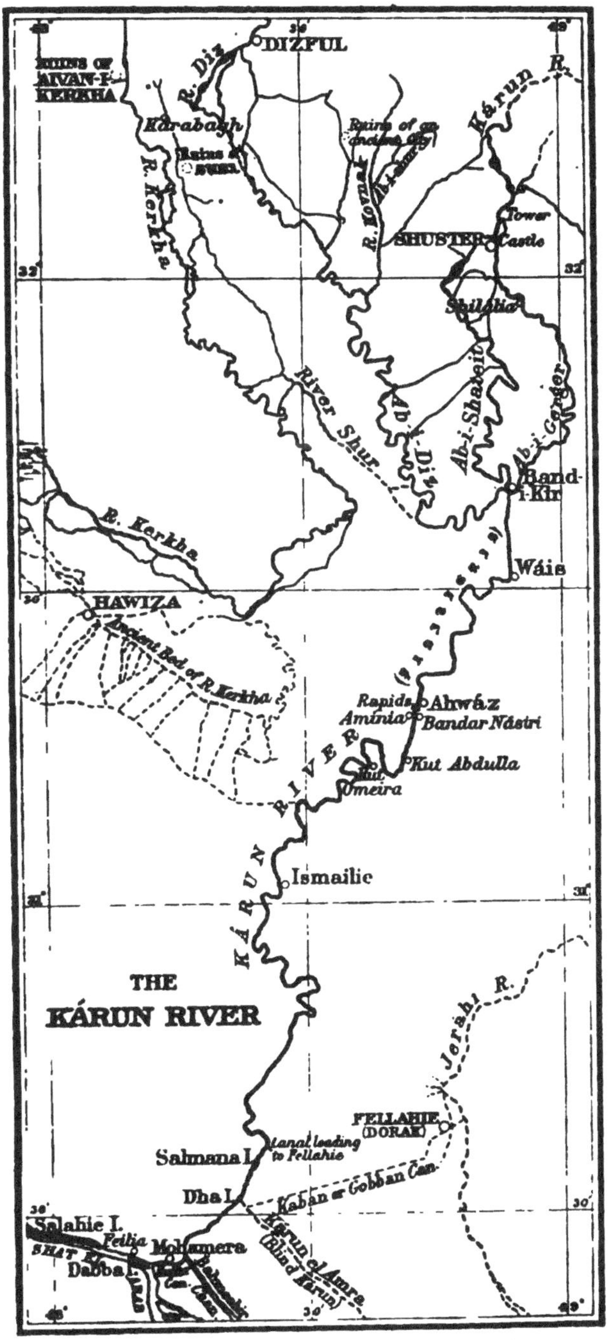

MAP OF THE KÁRUN VALLEY.

[To face p. 240.

the Kárun valley, and my work at Simla being finished, we left somewhat hurriedly, hoping thereby to escape the monsoon. Not only did we fail in this, but we also were unlucky in having a notorious roller in the ss. *Kapurthala*. After two days of misery we reached Jásk, where the monsoon was not felt, although the boat with the mails was a good deal tossed about, while at Bandar Abbás and Linga there was a dead calm.

It was my first visit to Bahrein, and I was naturally anxious to make the best of the short time at our disposal. Bahrein (literally "the two seas") consists of a group of islands, the largest being termed Bahrein, and the second Moharrag. They are the centre of immensely valuable pearl fisheries, which are carried on more or less all along this coast, but the banks round the islands are by far the richest. Some five thousand boats take part in the harvest, of which perhaps a third belong to Bahrein itself, and these vessels with their remarkably artistic rig give the sea a very animated appearance.

The method pursued is so accurately described by Ludovico di Varthema at the end of the fifteenth century, that I cannot do better than quote his description:—"They throw down a rope with a stone to the bottom. In the middle of the boat is one of these fishers, who hangs a couple of bags round his neck, and ties a large stone to his feet, and goes fifteen paces under water, and remains there as long as he is able, in order to find the oysters in which are pearls. As he finds them he puts them into the bags, and then leaves the stone which he had at his feet, and comes up by one of the said ropes."[1]

The yearly output of pearls is valued in the Persian Gulf at a million sterling, half of which sum represents the harvest of the Bahrein banks. On returning in the autumn, Hindus dressed in extraordinarily tight white nether garments, with jaunty little caps, brought insignificant-looking packets on board, which were valued at thousands of rupees, the wily Hindu apparently absorbing most of the profit of the fisheries by making large advances to the Arabs.

We landed in spite of considerable heat, and rode off on the superb asses for which the islands are noted, to the ruins of a mosque and some wells, which were not of much interest, but we had not sufficient leisure for visiting the Phoenician tombs, which

[1] *Ludovico di Varthema*, p. 95 (Hakluyt Soc.).

Panjgur to Kasarkand, every chief apparently submitting to him and becoming his tributary.

Upon the assassination of Nádir Sháh he opposed Ahmad Sháh, and, at first, successfully. He was, however, defeated at Mastung, and forced to retreat to Kalát, where he was besieged. After beating off three assaults peace was made, and Nasír Khán bound himself to furnish troops whenever called upon to do so. In return for this he was excused the payment of tribute.

Not long afterwards he aided Ahmad Sháh against Persia, and headed his Baluchis in a desperate charge which decided the day in a battle fought near Meshed. Again, at Tabas, by an ambuscade of his planning, the Persian army was annihilated. Returning home in triumph, his kingdom was extended as far as distant Karachi, and Baluchistán enjoyed a period of prosperity which has never since been equalled.

Kalát possesses a population of perhaps 50,000 inhabitants, which however fluctuates, the town being almost deserted in the depth of winter. Its *bázárs* are very mean, and altogether Kalát shows that it is owned by a race which is far lower than the Persians in the arts of civilisation. Its fort was, I understand, mainly the work of Nasír Khán, and at the time of its construction must have been almost impregnable, its situation being excellent.

In this work I have made no mention of the games played by Baluchis, but it seems that we owe the now popular exercise of tent-pegging to this people. In support of this I give an extract from Pottinger: "Before I close this enumeration of their diversions, I may describe a very hazardous, though popular one among all classes, which they perform on horseback, and call Nezuh Bazee or spear play. A wooden stake of moderate thickness is driven into the ground, and a horseman at full speed pierces it with the point of his spear in such a manner as to force it out of the earth and carry it along with him. The difficulty and danger in accomplishing this feat is evidently augmented or decreased according to the depth that the stake is in the ground."[1]

Nasír Khán died in A.D. 1795, and it was during his successor's reign that Pottinger passed through the country, and noted that since his death even Kej had ceased to pay tribute. His unworthy successor, Mahmud Khán, was a drunken creature, and died in

[1] *Travels in Beloochistan*, p. 66.

THE KHÁN OF KALÁT AND COURT. [*To face p.* 236.

1819, being succeeded by his son Mehráb Khán, during whose reign Kalát was first brought into contact with the Government of India.

In 1838 that most "wild, ill-considered, and adventurous" expedition, as Sir Henry Durand justly termed it, to force a weak and worthless sovereign on the Afghán people, was undertaken, and British officers were deputed to Kalát to secure the co-operation of the Khán, whose territories were traversed in the advance on Kandahár. Suspicions of treachery on his part arising, in November 1839 a British force attacked and stormed Kalát, and Mehráb Khán was killed. His papers, when found, proved that he was innocent of disloyalty, but was the victim of an intrigue. His successor and the British representative were both murdered a few years later, and a second Nasír Khán was appointed chief, being succeeded in 1857 by *Mir* Khudadád Khán.

His career was distinctly chequered, as for nearly twenty years he was at war with his *Sardárs*. In 1877, Quetta was bought by the British Government, and during the subsequent Afghán war Khudadád rendered yeoman's service. Later on his doings aroused dissatisfaction, and after having murdered his Vizier and family in a somewhat atrocious fashion, he was deposed, and Kalát was again occupied by British troops.

On this occasion the immense treasure that was seized was laid out at interest, and is now being spent in improvements. It is wonderful how generally throughout Persia the confiscation of these cases of rupees was noticed, and the Khán commiserated. It rather reminded me of an Armenian, who, being in a Consulate at the time of the massacres, and hearing from refugees that his relations and friends were all being murdered, appeared quite unmoved. Later on in the day, a fresh arrival mentioned that the *Pasha* had seized all the money of one victim, and then, but not till then, my acquaintance tore his hair and bewailed the calamities that had befallen his nation.

To conclude this short sketch, Khudadád Khán's son, Mahmud Khán, was appointed to succeed him, and is now the Khán of Kalát and *Beglerbegi* of Baluchistán.

To resume, we rode over a low pass in the hills, and came in sight of the picturesquely-situated fort, where the British Commissioner was met by the Khán's brother and some recently-raised Lancers. The camp was pitched near the miserable-looking building which houses the political agent; however, we had no reason to grumble, as from its garden we procured the first vegetables that we had tasted since leaving Jálk, where we had enjoyed a solitary dish of beans. We were once again on the telegraph line, which we had quitted at Kermán, and two stages further on, beyond the delightful Mastung valley, we struck the road in course of construction to Kalát, which, however, has never been finished.

At our last camp of Sariáb we could see the nearly-completed Bolán pass railway, and our Persian servants, in order to air their knowledge, came to inform us what it was. Our uncivilised horses did not take kindly to cantonments, and were nearly driven wild, first by a wheel-barrow, and then by the railway-station. We, for our part, revelled in the green avenues, and when we finally reached the Agency at Quetta, felt inclined to exclaim, as Sádi does of Shiráz, "This indeed is Paradise!"

The kindly welcome of Sir James Browne, the beautiful English-like house, and all the unwonted luxuries of every kind, were a fitting end to a most successful journey, which enables my sister to claim to have been the first lady to ride from the Caspian Sea to India, a distance of close upon 2000 miles.

FROM A PERSIAN BRASS BOWL.

CHAPTER XXI

A MISSION TO THE KÁRUN VALLEY

"And dear as the wet diver to the eyes
Of his pale wife who waits and weeps on shore
By sandy Bahrein, in the Persian Gulf,
Plunging all day in the blue waves, at night,
Having made up his tale of precious pearls,
Rejoins her in their hut upon the sands."
—MATTHEW ARNOLD.

THE two days we spent at Quetta were fully employed in social duties and selling off horses and mules. Fortunately, I had already disposed of three horses at Mastung, and we took on three to Simla, while the transport authorities bought most of my mules. In fact, after using my horses for about a year, I made a considerable profit on them, prices in India ruling very high and remounts still being of a poor quality. I understand, however, that there is a steady improvement, but, after living in Persia, the country-bred horse seems a very "three-cornered" animal.

We determined to leave most of our servants temporarily at Quetta, while the heavy baggage was despatched by goods train to Karachi, and, after saying good-bye to our genial host, whose almost sudden death shortly afterwards was a great loss to his country, we started for Simla. The Bolán line was just completed, but not open for traffic, and we travelled *via* Hurnái through a belt which for wildness can only be compared to the Bushire *kotals*. A communicative guard

miles by river, and rather less than 80 by land, so that the whole distance from Mohamera to Shuster is less than 200 miles by river, and at most, 140 miles by land.

From Mohamera to Wáis, a village some 12 miles above Ahwáz, both banks of the river, which here divides an immense alluvial plain, are under the jurisdiction of *Sheikh* Mizal, the hereditary chief of the Kab Arabs, and it is this district that we are first called upon to discuss. The *Sheikh*, the almost independent overlord of a considerable territory, viewed the opening of the Kárun with much disfavour, not from any feeling of hostility to the British, but from a perfectly natural dislike to the curtailment of his independence by the presence of Persian troops and officials. Nor has his opposition been merely passive, as he started his own service of two steamers, and by applying a strict boycott to Messrs Lynch's boat, for some time prevented the booking of cargo or passengers.

Mohamera is a filthy little town surrounded by palm-groves, and, somehow or other, has not profited as much as was expected by the new state of affairs. However, it is the residence of a British Vice-Consul, and the terminus of a telegraph line, which hitherto has not effected a junction with the Turkish system, relations between the two powers not being particularly friendly along this section of the frontier. On the opposite or left bank of the river are barracks only inhabited by a handful of soldiers. To save confusion, I have not hitherto referred to the fact that Mohamera is situated on a canal known as the Haffar, which was cut at some remote period, and has become the main mouth of the Kárun; indeed, the numerous rivers which roll through this tract of soft alluvial country have constantly changed their courses, to the despair of any one who attempts to locate them from the ancient writers.

It was mid June when we joined the *Malamir* and began our ascent, passing the Bahmeshir or natural channel of the Kárun, which still carries off part of its waters to the Persian Gulf. in ancient times it formed the eastern mouth of the Tigris, and the Shat-el-Arab the western. In 1841, it was successfully navigated by Lieut. Selby in the *Assyria*, but since then it has not, to my knowledge, been examined, which is to be regretted on account of its importance to Persia.

Above Mohamera the palm-groves stretched for some miles, but then suddenly ceased, and thenceforward the outlook was bare and monotonously level, the growth of timber mentioned some fifty years ago by Selby having been eradicated. Numerous nomad villages studded the banks, and in no other part of Persia have I seen such numbers of buffaloes, mares, mules, and donkeys. I should mention that, as in Baluchistán, stallions are generally killed, and so far does this absurd practice prevail, that to make a present of a stallion is an insult.

We moored for the night, and the following afternoon, after having steamed twenty hours from Mohamera, we reached Bandar Násiri, so named in honour of the late Sháh. Bad news greeted us before landing, as we were informed that Mr Tanfield, Messrs Lynch's agent at Shuster, had been murderously attacked by a servant, and had just been brought down more dead than alive by Mr Parry, who represented the firm at Ahwáz. It was hoped that we might have a doctor on board, but as the telegraph line had been broken, news of the outrage had not reached us. By dint of hard work, the *Malamir* was ready to start back on the following day, and we did what we could for the victim by dressing his terrible wounds, which included the total severance of the left hand. He finally reached Basra in time to be operated upon, and recovered, thanks to his remarkable pluck, and the skill of Dr Scott.

Ahwáz is a site of antiquity, being in all probability the point where Nearchos, after ascending the Kárun, then known as Pasitigris or Lesser Tigris, joined Alexander, who had thrown a bridge of boats across it on his way to Susa. For many centuries it was the capital of Khuzistán, and of considerable importance, partly owing to its trade with India, but still more on account of its large output of sugar, and it is sad indeed to see but a squalid village on the site of so much prosperity and civilisation. At the same time, there has been much improvement since Lord Curzon's visit some six years before. For instance, he described Messrs Lynch's agent as paying "a rent of £170 a year for quarters (a mat-hut) that would be exorbitant at £7,"[1] where now rises the finest warehouse in Southern Persia; a wharf too has actually been constructed, not to mention a wool press, and machines to separate wheat from barley. In addition to this, Messrs Hotz & Sons have established

[1] *Persia*, vol. ii. p. 353.

the Kárun valley, and my work at Simla being finished, we left somewhat hurriedly, hoping thereby to escape the monsoon. Not only did we fail in this, but we also were unlucky in having a notorious roller in the ss. *Kapurthala.* After two days of misery we reached Jásk, where the monsoon was not felt, although the boat with the mails was a good deal tossed about, while at Bandar Abbás and Linga there was a dead calm.

It was my first visit to Bahrein, and I was naturally anxious to make the best of the short time at our disposal. Bahrein (literally "the two seas") consists of a group of islands, the largest being termed Bahrein, and the second Moharrag. They are the centre of immensely valuable pearl fisheries, which are carried on more or less all along this coast, but the banks round the islands are by far the richest. Some five thousand boats take part in the harvest, of which perhaps a third belong to Bahrein itself, and these vessels with their remarkably artistic rig give the sea a very animated appearance.

The method pursued is so accurately described by Ludovico di Varthema at the end of the fifteenth century, that I cannot do better than quote his description:—"They throw down a rope with a stone to the bottom. In the middle of the boat is one of these fishers, who hangs a couple of bags round his neck, and ties a large stone to his feet, and goes fifteen paces under water, and remains there as long as he is able, in order to find the oysters in which are pearls. As he finds them he puts them into the bags, and then leaves the stone which he had at his feet, and comes up by one of the said ropes."[1]

The yearly output of pearls is valued in the Persian Gulf at a million sterling, half of which sum represents the harvest of the Bahrein banks. On returning in the autumn, Hindus dressed in extraordinarily tight white nether garments, with jaunty little caps, brought insignificant-looking packets on board, which were valued at thousands of rupees, the wily Hindu apparently absorbing most of the profit of the fisheries by making large advances to the Arabs.

We landed in spite of considerable heat, and rode off on the superb asses for which the islands are noted, to the ruins of a mosque and some wells, which were not of much interest, but we had not sufficient leisure for visiting the Phoenician tombs, which

[1] *Ludovico di Varthema*, p. 95 (Hakluyt Soc.).

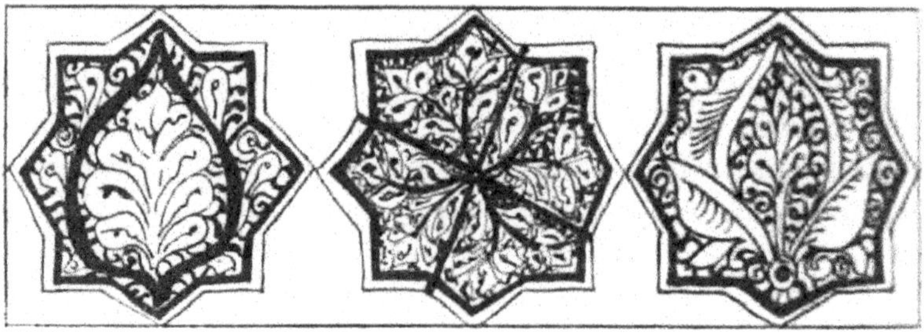

FROM LUSTRED POTTERY.

CHAPTER XXII

A MISSION TO THE KÁRUN VALLEY—(*continued*)

> "From Atropatia and the neighbouring plains
> Of Adiabene, Media, and the South
> Of Susiana to Balsara's haven."
>
> —MILTON, *Paradise Regained.*

BEFORE resuming our journey I propose to give some account of the navigation of the Upper Kárun, which, as has been stated before, is but a stretch of eighty miles. This insignificant length of water-way was considered by the late Sháh, who appears to have been badly informed by interested individuals, to possess such potentialities that it was expressly reserved for exploitation by Persian subjects. A means of escape from this predicament was discovered by making a present to the Sháh of the ss. *Shushan*, a boat originally built for the Nile Expedition, which was to be worked by Messrs Lynch Brothers as H.I.M.'s agents. This gift was accepted, but since 1890 has been worked at a small but constant loss, the fact being that a 30-ton steamer cannot earn the wages of an English captain and engineer, unless allowed to tow barges, for which permission has, so far, been refused. At the same time, the necessary Ahwáz-Shuster link, without which all hopes of northern development would be futile, has been maintained.

A concession was sold to the Násiri Company (which practically meant the *Moen-u-Tajár* of Bushire), which obtained land at Ahwaz, Mohamera, and elsewhere on the understanding that wharves and warehouses should be constructed. This, to a limited extent, has been done, and, at any rate, the *Moen-u-Tajár* built the tramway and runs a steamer on the Upper Kárun. His prospects are alluded to later on in this chapter.

After spending a day or two at Ahwáz, where I left my sister in charge of Mrs Parry, I embarked on the ss. *Shushan*, accompanied by Mr Parry, who had decided to visit Shuster. The inhabitants of the river above Wáis are under various petty chiefs, and the *Red Pig* (as the *Shushan* was termed), and Europeans in general, were received with much abuse. Catching the name of Omar more than once, I asked for an explanation, and was informed that we were being cursed as Sunnis, it being evident to the Arab mind that we were members of that section of Mohamedanism, for the excellent reason that we were not Shias. This will give some idea of the level of intelligence reached by these Arabs, who are of a lower type, or less civilised than the Kab.

We moored for the night at Band-i-Kír, where, as before mentioned, the Ab-i-Diz, the Shuteit, and the Gerger all unite. In the early morning we strolled on shore, and put up a sounder of pig, but it seemed useless to fire at one, as we could not have eaten it. In the tongue of land formed by the Shuteit and Gerger are the remains of an ancient city, described by Layard[1] as dating from Keianian times, Band-i-Kír, or the Dam of Pitch, no doubt supplying the water to irrigate its lands. The only erection we saw was a huge tank, constructed with the view of working the steamer with oil, as the growth along the Kárun is nearly all cut down, and serious inroads have been made on the Ab-i-Diz supply. Captain Plant informed me that he had taken the *Shushan* some miles up the Ab-i-Diz, but that it would not pay to navigate it.

Remembering that Lord Curzon had heard a lion roar at this point, we hoped for a similar act of courtesy on the part of the king of beasts, but we only saw one lion, and that was a dead one floating down the river. On the other hand, we saw more than one shark right up the Ab-i-Gerger, and it appears that during the summer they choose the Kárun in preference to the Tigris, owing to the cooler temperature of its waters. At any rate, bathing is freely indulged in at Basra, whereas in the Kárun, men, women, children, horses, sheep, in fact almost every living thing

[1] *Early Adventures*, vol. ii. p. 28.

except the well-protected buffalo, pays a heavy tribute to the shark.

The Ab-i-Gerger is a canal some thirty yards wide, commanded by such high cliffs that the day was monotonously hot, and we were glad to moor to the bank near Shilália, although we wisely waited until nearly sunset before cantering into Shuster. Crossing the Minau canal by a rather fine bridge, we found ourselves in the *bázárs*, and, after riding for some distance through the streets, which form the common sewer, and are almost impassable for a European, we pulled up at Messrs Lynch's house, which, like many of those in Shuster, is surrounded by very high walls.

I had, as is customary, sent on to inform the Governor-General of my arrival, but this was to be the solitary occasion on which I found myself treated with marked discourtesy. Persian Governors elsewhere have always shown a perfect readiness to meet my very reasonable requests as soon as they understood them, and I have never suffered from irrational behaviour in any other part of Persia, a fact which speaks well for the courtesy of the many officials with whom I have had to transact business.

Early the following morning I proceeded to the fort, and was received by H.E. the *Nizám-u-Sultana*, and his brother, the *Saad-ul-Mulk*, with a refusal to recognise me officially. I pointed out that I had already sent them a letter from the Resident at Bushire, who was deputing me by the Minister's orders; this point was, after some discussion, yielded.

The case of poor Tanfield was at first referred to, but as I was awaiting instructions from Tehrán, I only discussed it in general terms, both brothers professing themselves entirely indifferent at the outrage. Meeting with no encouragement, I broached my main case, and said that I had been instructed by the Minister to ask for an indemnity for an assault committed by Persian soldiers at Ahwáz on Messrs Taylor, Adey, and other British subjects. This, too, His Excellency refused to discuss, on the ground that the soldiers would not obey him, and had nearly thrashed their general to death. I endeavoured to intimate suavely that the Minister could not accept such an answer, but the *Nizám-u-Sultana* would not change his views. I was, in consequence, obliged to express my deep regret that he should be acting so blindly against his own interests, and inform him that I could only report his refusal to

SHUSTERFORT AND VALERIAN'S BRIDGE.

[*To face p.* 252.

Tehrán. To cut a long story short, H.H. the *Sadr Ázam* paid me the great compliment of telegraphing to the *Nizám-u-Sultana* through me to pay the indemnity—the equivalent of £300—without delay, and, shortly afterwards, both brothers were dismissed for their incapacity and want of courtesy.

Shuster in the summer is almost inexpressibly hot, our daily reading at 8 A.M. being 108 degrees, while 128 degrees was the usual reading at noon. However, for all its filth and heat, it has a great history, its derivation being similar to that of Susa or Shushan,[1] and it can boast of grander public works than perhaps any other city in Western Asia. It is situated on rising ground just below the point where the Kárun bifurcates. The Ab-i-Shuteit with its diminished stream washes the base of the cliff on which stands out the finest fort I have ever seen in Persia, and still more of its waters are drawn off through a tunnel into the Ab-i-Minau, which irrigates the land close to Shuster. Below the fort is the great dam and bridge, a splendid monument of Sásánian enterprise, the design of which has been attributed by an improbable tradition to the Emperor Valerian. Its total length is said to be 570 yards, but, as there was a wide gap, we could only visit one end of it. The dam consists of great blocks of stone with sluices, the picturesque winding bridge being built over it. It was undoubtedly the chief work of Shápur, and it is more than probable that the Gerger canal was cut to permit of the double operation of building the dam and paving the bed of the river. The Ab-i-Gerger, as mentioned above, runs between high cliffs, and gives every appearance of having possessed a greater volume, its dams having been constructed with the endeavour to force back the river into its ancient bed.

Close to Shuster are several caves, and in one place a square room is hewn out of the rock, while the water rushing through the numerous tunnels and turning mills was always a pleasant sight.

Layard, in his *Early Adventures*, highly praises the Shusteris, but nowadays they are extremely fanatical, and it was very hard to act with the moderation demanded by my official position, knowing, as I did, that these half-Persian, half-Arab creatures had stoned poor Tanfield when he was being carried down to the river. One of their leaders, a most fanatical *mullá*, who had blackmailed Messrs Lynch Brothers, expressed a wish to see me, and as Parry

[1] Shushter is the correct form of the word.

pointed out that my refusal would probably involve him in trouble. I agreed, and passing through the *bázár*, where the scowling inhabitants spat on the ground as we passed, we were ushered into a great conclave. After the usual compliments, I said in honeyed tones that I understood that the Shusteris were very amenable to their *mullás*, very much under control, and so forth, which remarks produced many a complacent stroke of the beard and loud ejaculations of "Thank God." Having put these facts in more than one way, in order that all present might understand, I changed my tone, and said that I should like them to explain how it was that in such a town, a stranger, known to be severely wounded, was stoned by its inhabitants, who had never dared to annoy him when well. I shall never forget the look of surprise that passed round. Having concluded my remarks, I left the crestfallen assembly, home-truths being evidently rare in Shuster and therefore, perhaps, more telling.

Among our annoyances was the news that the brother of Tanfield's would-be assassin—the latter had been thrown into chains and despatched to Tehrán—had vowed to take revenge on me. As he was known to be half-witted, it was necessary to take precautions, and, during the day, I always faced the door and kept a revolver in a drawer. At night we slept on the roof still stained with the victim's blood, and as there was no door, we placed a table across the opening, on the near side of which Sultan Sukhru slept. A move of the table would awake him, and while affording him protection, would give me ample time to shoot.

Mr Kipling writes of Lahore as the "City of dreadful night," but I think that Shuster was infinitely more disagreeable, as, in addition to the heat, every night bullet after bullet flew across us, as a gentle hint to quit. We both caught the pernicious local fever, and when our work was done, and we started back to Shilália, made bets as to whether we should be able to sit our horses. Having heard that Arabs were looting close to the town, and that an attack on the steamer was to be expected, upon reaching it, we surrounded the tiller with bales, though with little hope of success against a determined assault. As we were at dinner a volley whistled overhead, and the passengers replied with their Martinis. This went on for some time, and as no shots came in reply, a victory was claimed. Far into the night paeans and war

SHUSTER.

[*To face p.* 254.

dances precluded all chance of sleep, although for a time the scene was weirdly interesting, lines of white figures advancing and retreating, while volleys were fired by way of chorus.

On my return to Ahwáz, after having spent three weeks at Shuster, I was able to gain a better insight into local affairs. To my amusement, I found that the Deputy *Kargusár* was the same *Mírza* who had given Lord Curzon so much trouble, and it was quite refreshing to hear how, according to his account, he had done everything to forward that distinguished traveller. The Governor was *Sheikh* Ibud, nephew of *Sheikh* Mizal, one of the few Arabs with whom I have become acquainted, and he struck me both as a gentleman and as anxious to be educated.

Local politics in Ahwáz were distinctly of a complicated nature. *Sheikh* Mizal had seized the tramway, the property of the Násiri Company, with which Messrs Hotz & Sons were connected; he had further threatened to shoot the *Moen-u-Tajár* on sight if he visited Arabistán. The *Nizám-u-Sultana*, on the other hand, was not only Governor-General, but a large landowner, and Messrs Lynch's landlord, while the *Moen-u-Tajár*, who had known him as a clerk at Bushire, wrote him insulting letters. To complete the picture, Lord Curzon's friend, the *Mírza*, was fishing in troubled waters.

At Ahwáz the nights were cool, but the temperature rose to 118 degrees during the day. As no vegetables or fish were forthcoming, our kind hostess, Mrs Parry, was forced to feed us wretched invalids on a diet of egg-flips until, early in August, my work being finished, I was able to run down to Basra and consult a doctor.

Before quitting the Kárun it may perhaps not be out of place to state what my recommendations were. In the first place, I strongly urged that an arrangement should be made by which the Kárun should be bridged on the Isfahán road, and the track made sufficiently good for caravans. I deprecated any large expenditure, but suggested that Messrs Lynch Brothers would probably be willing to advance the money, execute the work, and receive a fair rate of interest from the Persian Government or from the Bakhtiári chiefs, who in return would be allowed to charge some small toll. This tribe annually loses twenty or thirty men and hundreds of live stock from want of a bridge; their sympathy was therefore already won, and they were extremely anxious to see it built. My chief point was that it would only strangle commerce if a large sum were spent, whereas, when the trade had come, money could be laid aside for improvements.

When I reached Tehrán in the autumn of 1896, acting upon Sir Mortimer Durand's instructions, I fully explained the question to the *Farmán Farmá*, who gained the Sháh's willing consent to the principle of this proposal. However, before everything was settled the Legation had to take an immense amount of pains, and it was finally decided that Messrs Lynch Brothers should advance and spend £5500 on a permanent girder bridge at or near Gudar-i-Bolatak and on a smaller bridge at Pul-i-Imárat, besides improving the track where necessary, and building a *caravanserai* or two. The Bakhtiári chiefs, who are enthusiastically in favour of the scheme, will pay six per cent. and have the right to charge up to 5 krans or 2s. per load, which was the exact sum I suggested. I do not wish to indulge in any forecasts of great success, but of one thing I feel sure, namely, that in Persia most of our schemes have been ruined from doing things on too large a scale at first, and from expecting an immediate return on the capital invested.

The second point that I urged was that for a Vice-Consul tied to Mohamera, there should be substituted a Consul for Arabistan and Luristán, who should make his headquarters at Ahwáz, and spend at least six months every year in travelling. At first he could use his influence to open up the Bakhtiári road, and then devote his attention to the Luristán route, besides, of course, keeping an eye on Shuster and Mohamera. I selected Ahwáz as the headquarters of such a post, because it is the centre of all communications, whereas Shuster is not a desirable place of residence, and its importance to British trade will decrease with the growth of Ahwáz. The effect of the advent of British merchants is already considerable, grain being grown in increasing quantities, and even the poor Bakhtiáris are securing comparative affluence by collecting gum, and no doubt the traffic across their uplands will bring a silver harvest.

One pleasing trait in the Arabs is their honesty in fulfilling their contracts. When money is advanced against a certain quantity of grain, that quantity will always be forthcoming up to date, the head of the tribe making up for any deficiency or failure. As the years roll by, fanaticism will doubtless give place to the feelings of friendliness which are such a pleasing feature in the Kermán province, where a close and increasing intercourse with India has afforded object lessons which are unmistakable.

Perhaps the greatest characteristic of English people in the East is the intense kindness shown to strangers, especially in illness, a fact which on this particular occasion I proved to the hilt, and not for the first time. Leaving Ahwáz, where I could not throw off my illness, I was met at Mohamera by Captain Whyte, and we nearly sank on the way up to Basra, our launch running into a vessel laden with grain. Dr Scott pronounced my case to be a bad attack of pleurisy, and until I left, I could make no improvement. My sister kept marvellously well, although the climate naturally told on her, but, as many of our fellow-countrymen were also ill, I now look on the beauty of Basra as distinctly baleful. Even when lying on cushions on the river, the moist heat was overpowering, and I felt amazed at the energy shown by every one when the date-harvest began. Indeed so great is it that friction occasionally ensues, the agreements between the various firms, who form a sort of syndicate, being sometimes differently interpreted. With sterling common-sense, when it is all over and the last load of dates is disposed of, they hold a dinner which wipes out all disputes of the past.

The dates are packed in boxes, which are sent out from Norway all ready for nailing together, whole families of Arabs being engaged to pack them, and the merchants superintending on the spot. A large percentage of the crop is exported to America, and in England the Black Country absorbs most of the fruit that is eaten. The date strikes me as a somewhat neglected fruit, and I would recommend it for Army candidates who wish to put on weight, but it ought to be eschewed by the stout.

At the beginning of September, as it was out of the question for me to ride across the Bakhtiári mountains to Tehrán, and Dr Scott recommended a sea voyage, we embarked on board the *Assyria* for Bombay. After the punkahs and comforts of the Consulate, the heat was more than trying as we steamed down the lovely river, in addition to which the cargo of Arab horses made the ship roll whenever we anchored. At Bushire we heard that Captain Piffard was dying of heat apoplexy, but I am thankful to say that I met him a year later, looking perfectly well. Going on shore was out of the question, and it was a case of possessing one's soul in patience; but I have always felt how much better off we are than the early travellers to India, when, to quote Mr Whiteway, "Sleep was hardly possible lest the scanty dole of water should be stolen. The mortality was frightful; men crept away to die in corners and were sometimes not found for days. On the average not 60 per cent. reached India."[1] This being an account of an average voyage, we may well be thankful for the changes effected, by which a sea voyage is frequently the means of restoration to health, as it was in my case.

We waited a day at Bahrein, at Bandar Abbás, and at Maskat, all equally hot, after which we reached the open sea, and were soon at Karachi, where we enjoyed the Director's hospitality, and a few days later we boarded the P. and O. *Peninsular*, bound for Egypt. The plague broke out just about this time, but did not affect us in the shape of quarantine. However, at Aden the telegrams reported that there was cholera in Egypt, and we decided to proceed to Brindisi, and thence travel Eastward Ho, instead of crossing Egypt and picking up the Constantinople boat at Alexandria. Our voyage was as pleasant as voyages always are on a P. and O., although we roused much indignation on board by our contempt for the heat of the Red Sea, which, indeed, struck us as agreeably cool after the Persian Gulf!

After enjoying a day at Brindisi, where the vintage was in full swing, we picked up an Austrian-Lloyd, which coasted to Athens. We thus, while fresh from Maskat, visited both Aden and Corfu, and were struck by the happy description given by Lord Curzon of the first-named rocky harbour as "a mixture of Corfu and Aden, combining the romantic outline of the one with the forbidding desolation of the other."

We spent a few days at Constantinople, waiting for a steamer, during which time we visited the Ottoman Bank, guarded like a fortress after the recent outrage,[2] and by the middle of October we were once again at Tehrán. Shortly after our arrival the Perso-Baluch agreement was signed, setting the official *imprimatur* on our work, and it was very pleasant to meet the *Ihtishám-u-Vizára*,

[1] *Rise of the Portuguese Power in India*, p. 46.

[2] It had been seized by Armenians, with the object of blowing it up, in order to attract attention!

KUDUM ON THE RESHT ROAD.

[*To face p.* 258.

who was resting after his long journey. Thanks to the warm support tendered on every side, polo was instituted, and when my report was finished, and we started for home in February 1897, it was evident that the game had come to stay.

After crossing the Kharzan pass for the last time—the Russian road which is now finished avoids it—we just caught the steamer, in spite of worse weather than anything I had experienced in Persia. On the Black Sea, too, we were frequently storm-bound, the timidity of the Austrian-Lloyd Captain rousing my sister's ire. A few hours only were spent at Constantinople, and we next stopped for a day to see Sofia, which is certainly a curious town, its streets being absurdly wide for the traffic. We remained two days at Buda-Pesth, and I took the opportunity of calling on the "ex-dervish" Professor Vambéry, whose thrilling experiences of Asiatic travel are unrivalled. From the capital of Hungary he disseminates the truth about British action, which monstrous criticisms on the Transvaal War have shown to be no unnecessary task. A day or two at Vienna and a few hours at Munich, with a short sojourn in Paris, brought us finally home, after an absence of roughly two and a half years.

I generally find that I have more work to do during my leave than at any other time, but on the present occasion I had the pleasant task of taking charge of H.E. Abul Kásim Khán, *Násir-ul-Mulk*, who came to the Court of St James's to announce the accession of H.I.M. *Muzaffar-u-Dīn*. His Excellency, whom I already knew, was an Oxford graduate, and when his official duties were terminated, he returned in a private capacity to spend some weeks in England, and take his M.A. degree. As is always the case, the summer passed at express speed, and in the autumn, to use the Persian expression, the drum of departure was beaten, and I quitted England for my fourth journey in Persia.

DESIGN FROM A LEAD PLAQUE.

CHAPTER XXIII

MARCO POLO'S TRAVELS IN PERSIA.

"I am become a name;
For always roaming with a hungry heart
Much have I seen and known; cities of men
And manners, climates, councils, governments,
Myself not least, but honoured of them all."

—TENNYSON'S *Ulysses*.

IN the present chapter I propose to describe the journey (so far as it relates to Persia) of Marco Polo, the Father of Modern Geography. Throughout, I shall freely use Sir Henry Yule's great work, wherein is stored a wealth of knowledge, which enables me to elucidate much that thirty years ago was perforce undecided, as our geographical knowledge of Persia at that date was extremely vague; at the same time, I have undertaken two tours mainly to solve difficulties which required a full knowledge of the local topography, and it will, I think, be conceded that the man on the spot, who has also studied the literature, is more likely to be correct than one who is limited to imperfect small-scale maps in Europe.

To avoid plunging *in medias res*, I will give a very brief account of the state of Europe and Asia at the period, which accounted for the route taken by the illustrious Venetian. In the latter part of the thirteenth century, when the story commences, the Mongol invasion had reached its western limit, and Christendom had recovered from its alarm, at one time so great, according to Matthew Paris, that even the people of Gothland and Friesland did not dare to come to Yarmouth for the herring fishery.[1] Nor was the panic without foundation, for while the Tatárs,[2] as they are generally termed, were conquering Hungary, Pope Gregory IX. and the Emperor Frederic II. continued their suicidal wars, and, humanly speaking, only the death of Ogdei or Ogotay, the *Kaán*, saved Western Europe from thraldom of the most debasing character. Meanwhile the Empire of Constantinople was growing feebler, the Latin dynasty tottering to its fall, and at a time when Europe should have been united, practical impotence prevailed, the result of local jealousies and enmities. Notably the two sea powers of Venice and Genoa, which acted as middlemen in the great trade between East and West, were bitter rivals and generally at war with one another. Both states held possessions and settlements throughout the Levant, but Venice alone traded in the Black Sea, Genoa not founding her flourishing commerce until a Greek dynasty was once again established at Constantinople.

Alexandria was, when the Mamelukes allowed it, the great emporium for the treasures of the East, but as Asia and Eastern Europe were in the hands of the Mongol, trade was being gradually drawn to the ports of Cilician Armenia and Trebizond, thereby establishing the northern caravan routes from India to Europe, while distant China was, for the first time, open to those European travellers, who had the courage and inclination to spend a considerable portion of their lives on such a colossal journey.

The two brothers, Nicolo and Maffeo, of the Polo family were evidently cast in a heroic mould, and in 1260 started from Constantinople on a trading venture to the Crimea, which was prolonged to Sara,[3] the capital of Russia on the Volga, or, to be

[1] *Chronica Majora*, iii. 488.

[2] The spelling Tartar was at first adopted, whence St Louis' pun, "Ad sua Tartara Tartari detrudentur."

[3] The word is simply *sarai*, better known as *caravanserai*, and is the scene of Chaucer's—

> "At Sarra, in the Londe of Tartarie,
> There dwelt a king that werried Russie,
> Thurgh which ther deyede many a doughty man;
> This nobil kyng was cleped Cambynskan."

more exact, the chief residence of Barka Khán, who ruled the empire of Kipchak or Southern Russia.

Owing to an outbreak of war, which severed their communications, the two brothers determined to extend their journey, and descending the Volga, they struck east and crossed the desert to Bokhára. There they were seen by envoys of the *Kaán* returning from the court of Huláku Khán, the founder of the Mongol dynasty of Persia, who persuaded them to become their companions; to this they consented, and continued their great enterprise, finally reaching distant China.

Kublei, or Khubilay, the *Kaán*, received them with great kindness, being delighted to meet European gentlemen, and he was so much pleased with what he heard of the Christian religion, that "he took it into his head that he would send them on an embassy to the Pope," and begged that a hundred teachers might be commissioned to convert himself and his people. The brothers, having received a golden tablet from the *Kaán*, started back on what proved to be a three years' journey, finally reaching Ayas, on the Gulf of Iskanderun, in safety. They thence proceeded to Acre, arriving there in 1269.

It is interesting to speculate as to what might have been the result had Christendom risen to this appeal, the Mongol being, like their kinsmen of modern Japan, in search of a religion, and even as it was, Christianity was adopted in more than one instance. But it was not to be, and when the brothers, after visiting Venice and staying there a couple of years, decided to return to China, this time accompanied by Marco, the only assistance they finally obtained was that of two Dominican monks, who never even left the sea-coast. In this ignominious fashion was perhaps the greatest chance of spreading Christianity that occurred in mediæval times allowed to fall through.

To return to our travellers, who started on their second great journey in 1271, Sir Henry Yule, in his introduction,[1] makes them travel *via* Sivás to Mosul and Baghdád, and thence by sea to Hormuz, which is the itinerary shown on his sketch map. This view I am unwilling to accept for more than one reason. In the first place, if we suppose, with Sir Henry Yule, that Ser Marco visited Baghdád, is it not unlikely that he should term the river Volga the

[1] Vol. i. p. 19 (Second Edition).

Tigris,[1] and yet leave the river of Baghdád nameless? It may be urged that Marco believed the legend of the re-appearance of the Volga in Kurdistán, but yet, if the text be read with care, and the character of the traveller be taken into account, this error is scarcely explicable in any other way than that he was never there.

Again, he gives no description of the striking buildings of Baudas, as he terms it, but this is nothing to the inaccuracy of his supposed onward journey. To quote the text, "A very great river flows through the city, . . . and merchants descend some eighteen days from Baudas, and then come to a certain city called Kisi,[2] where they enter the Sea of India." Surely Marco, had he travelled down the Persian Gulf, would never have given this description of the route, which is so inaccurate as to point to the conclusion that it was vague information obtained from some merchant whom he met in the course of his wanderings.

Finally, apart from the fact that Baghdád, since its fall, was rather off the main caravan route, Marco so evidently travels east from Yezd, and thence south to Hormuz, that, unless his journey be described backwards, which is highly improbable, it is only possible to arrive at one conclusion, namely, that the Venetians entered Persia near Tabríz, and travelled to Sultánia, Kashán, and Yezd. Thence they proceeded to Kermán and Hormuz, where, probably fearing the sea voyage, owing to the manifest unseaworthiness of the ships, which he describes as "wretched affairs," the Khorasán route was finally adopted. Hormuz, in this case, was not visited again until the return journey from China, when it seems probable that the same route was retraced to Tabríz, where their charge, the Lady Kokachin, "moult bele dame et avenant," was married to Gházán Khán, the son of her betrothed Arghun. It remains to add that Sir Henry Yule may have finally accepted this view in part, as in the plate entitled *Probable View of Marco Polo's own Geography*[3] the itinerary is not shown as running to Baghdád.

Accompanying the party, we find Tabríz to be fully described, as also a monastery on its borders, and the next city mentioned

[1] *Vide* vol. i. p. 5. It is noteworthy that John de Plano Carpini, who travelled 1245 to 1247, names it correctly.

[2] The modern name is Keis, an island lying off Linga.

[3] Vol i. p. 107 (Introduction). In the first edition the routes are not shown on either of the above-mentioned maps.

is Saba, now Sáva, from which the three Magi were supposed to have set out to worship the new-born Saviour.[1] Sáva is now a little district to the west of Kum, with a small town of the same name, and was undoubtedly passed through by the travellers, the main road, which was followed by the worthy Odoricus and others, running *via* Sultánia to Kum and Kashán.

After a somewhat inaccurate chapter on the divisions of Persia, of which Tabríz is not considered a part, Yezd or Yasdi is next described as "a good and noble city," where "they weave quantities of a certain silk tissue known as Yasdi, which merchants carry into many quarters to dispose of." This city is so fully dealt with in other parts of this book that we will continue our traveller's narrative. "When you leave this city to travel further, you ride for seven days over great plains, finding harbour to receive you at three places only. There are many fine woods (producing dates) upon the way . . . .; there are also wild asses, handsome creatures. At the end of those seven marches over the plain you come to a fine kingdom, which is called Kerman." There are two roads uniting Yezd to Kermán, each some 220 miles in length, along both of which I have travelled. The choice between them in the present case happens to be quite simple, as the mention of date-palms fixes it to the northern of these two routes, there being extensive groves at Báfk.

It may be urged that this is not final, but there is yet another proof, and that is the altitude of the two roads. On the southerly, now the main road, with its telegraph line and posting-stations, the altitude after leaving the Yezd plain is never less than 4000 feet, and generally about 5000 feet, and therefore dates are quite out of the question in so elevated a district and such latitudes. On the northern road, however, the drainage from the main road, after passing behind Bahramabád, runs through the hills and becomes a salt river, which is crossed a few miles to the west of Báfk, at an altitude of 3100 feet, the difference being therefore very marked. At this point, looking to the north, I saw a wide glittering expanse of *Kavir*, the home of the wild ass. This section of the journey may then be considered to be settled. Marco Polo

[1] Cf. "The multitude of camels shall cover thee, the dromedaries of Midian and Ephah; all they from Sheba shall come: they shall bring gold and incense, and they shall show forth the praises of the Lord."—Isaiah lx. 6.

KUBA-I-SABZ, KERMÁN.

[*To face p.* 264.

must have travelled very long stages, averaging over 30 miles a day, and, oddly enough, I took exactly the same time on the main road, when pressed for time in 1900. As to the "three places only," Báfk is certainly one, and Khudrán, with its perennial stream, perhaps a second, but further east there are, nowadays, villages all along the route, where Ser Marco found a desert, and, as will appear later on, the ancient town of Zarand must have been deserted at this particular period.

Kermán in 1271 A.D., and for some years subsequently, was ruled by Turkán Khátun, the energetic daughter of Borák Hájib.[1] Marco says, truly enough, that the kingdom was not hereditary, but Kermán was continuously ruled by a member of this Kara Khitei family for another thirty years. If on his return journey from China he again passed through the city, he would have found Padsháh Khátun, daughter of Turkán Khátun, ruling as energetically as her mother. She was the wife of Kei Khátu, and had a somewhat stormy career, as, after strangling her brother Surkátmush, his widow and her own sister rose against her, and she too was strangled in turn and laid to rest in the Kuba-i-Sabz.

To return from this digression, Marco in the first place mentions the turquoises of Kermán, and in the note reference is made to a manuscript treatise, in which those of Shebavek are noticed. Until quite recently, the only mines I knew of were those a little to the north of Páriz, but in 1900 a mine was visited twenty-four miles to the north-north-east of Shahr-i-Bábek, which is no doubt the Shebavek referred to; none of the mines are worked to-day, being filled up by the silt washed down by rain.

As to the "steel and ondanique," or "Indian steel,"[2] there is much iron in the Kermán district, but the mines are neglected, the metal being imported from India. Nowadays, Kermán is not famous for "harness of war," as the European rifle has killed the trade in swords and so forth, while the population is, generally speaking, unwarlike and spurs are not worn. Nor is the city especially noted for its needlework, but almost throughout Persia most exquisite embroidery is still produced at what seems an absurdly low price. Perhaps also reference is made to the famous shawls

[1] *Vide* chap. v.

[2] *Vide* p. 272. *Ondanique* is doubtless a corruption of *Hinduwáni* or Indian. The word found its way into Spanish as Alhinde and Alinde.

or *shál*, which are only exceeded in beauty by those of Kashmir. Marco Polo was evidently a keen sportsman, and his description of the *sháhín*, as it is termed, cannot be improved upon.[1]

As a separate chapter is devoted to Kermán, we leave it for the present, and again quote the traveller. He says: "On quitting the city you ride on for seven days, always finding towns, villages, and handsome dwelling-houses, so that it is very pleasant travelling; and there is excellent sport also to be had, by the way, in hunting and hawking. When you have ridden those seven days over a plain country, you come to a great mountain; and when you have got to the top of the pass you find a great descent, which occupies some two days to go down. From the city of Kerman to this descent, the cold in winter is so great that you can scarcely abide it, even with a great quantity of clothing. After you have ridden down hill those two days, you find yourself in a vast plain, and at the beginning thereof, is a city called Camadi, which formerly was a great and noble place, but now is of little consequence, for the Tartars in their incursions have several times ravaged it. The plain whereof I speak is a very hot region; and the province that we now enter is called Reobarles."

In tracing this section of the journey, the first point is to identify Camadi, which, until quite recently, could not be done with any certainty. However, in the recently-printed history of

[1] A Khán has given me the following list of the hawks of the province, which I have enumerated in the order of their size:—

(1) *Karagush*, black and white with black eyes; is seldom used, being difficult to train; it is also held accursed for having killed the chief hawker of Shah Abbás.

(2) *Gush*, formerly termed *báz*, black and white, yellow eyes. This is the favourite hawk, and numbers are caught and sent to Tehrán; it is principally flown at partridges.

(3) *Sháhín*, red on the breast, under the neck and between the thighs, is smaller than the *gush*, but faster. It has rightly been identified by the late Sir O. St John as the falcon referred to by Marco Polo; it has yellow eyes.

(4) *Charkh*, black and white, red eyes; about the same size as the *sháhín*; it soars and strikes bustard.

(5) *Lachin*, black and white, reddish eyes; is used for hunting small birds.

(6) *Karaghi*, black and white, yellow eyes; used as No. 5.

(7) *Tarantar*, the smallest species, resembles the *Karaghi*, but it has black eyes; it is only used for hunting sparrows.

the Seljuks of Kermán by Mohamed Ibráhim, we read that "Komádin was a suburb at the gate of Jíruft, a resort of strangers, from Turkey and Hind, and a meeting-place of travellers by sea and land, the treasury of the wealthy and the storehouse of the East and West." In 1170, just a century before Marco Polo's journey, it was looted for the first time by Bahrám Sháh, one of the Seljuk princes. A few years later it was again raided, but had apparently recovered, as it is described as "the abode of men from every quarter, and the storehouse of the valuables of China, and Cathay, and Hindustán, Abyssinia, and Zanzibár, and Dariabár,[1] Turkey, Egypt, Armenia, Azerbaiján, Transoxania, Khorasán, Fárs, and Irák." This description is of great interest, not only as vindicating the accuracy of the great Venetian, but as showing how widely traders travelled at that period. The Ghazz completed the ruin of Camadi, and when Marco passed through it, it was, as he remarked, "of little consequence."

In 1894, and again in 1900, I spent a couple of days on the site of the city of Jíruft, of which Komádin was a quarter, occupying a huge area on the right bank of the Halíl Rud, close to Sarjáz. The ruins consist of millions of kiln-burnt bricks, eight inches square, and the surface is littered with fragments of pottery. I was shown what was evidently the fort, as the ditch was distinctly traceable; it was square, each side measuring 286 yards. There are some underground chambers that would repay excavation, and I bought a quantity of seals and coins of the Sásánian or later periods. There were no lustred tiles, nor could I find a cemetery. A legend runs to the effect that the city of Jíruft was destroyed by a flood, and this is probable, as not a wall is standing, which would hardly be the case if the city had been sacked and deserted. It is now in common with other ruins in Persia, known as *Shahr-i-Dugiánus* or City of Decius, the Roman Emperor with whom the story of the seven sleepers of Ephesus is connected.[2]

Having thus described our "fixed point," to use the survey

[1] Dariabár is the old name for the sea-coast to the south of Láristán and Kermán.

[2] In the *Journal of the R. A. S.* (N. S. vol. xiii. p. 490) General Houtum Schindler, C.I.E., gives a most valuable contribution to the itineraries of Marco Polo in Southern Persia. I am glad to find that, after having closely followed in the footsteps of the great Venetian, I have arrived at almost the same conclusions as General Schindler, to whom I would here express my thanks.

expression, it remains to find the road leading to it. In 1895, and again in 1900, I made a tour partly with the object of solving this problem, and of giving a geographical existence to Sárdu. I found that there was a route which exactly fitted Marco's conditions, as at Sarbizan the Sárdu plateau terminates in a high pass of 9200 feet, from which there is a most abrupt descent to the plain of Jíruft, Komádin being situated about thirty-five miles or two days' journey from the top of the pass.

Starting from Kermán, the stages would be as follows:—

	Intermediate	Total
1. Jupár (small town), . .	16	16
2. Bahrámjird (large village), .	17	33
3. Gudar (village), . . .	16	49
4. Ráin (small town), . .	16	65

Thence to the Sarbizan pass is a distance of 45 miles, or three desert stages, thus constituting a total of 110 miles for the seven days. This is the camel route to the present day, and absolutely fits in with the description given. Just as Marco in the previous section travelled 220 miles in a week, obviously with mules as transport, so, on this occasion, he as certainly used camels, and only travelled 110 miles in the same period.[1] Had he used the faster means of transport, he would have proceeded either by Máhun and Huseinabád, or by Máhun and Hanaka, the former route being used in the summer, and the latter in the winter, but as both include a high pass, they are out of court.

Nowadays Sárdu is only inhabited during the summer months by nomads, but there are ruins of villages inhabited many centuries ago by the Gil tribe, which has almost disappeared, only a few families being left.

Apart from the geographical proofs given above, I can also furnish historical evidence, as the Seljuk monarchs generally spent the five winter months in Jíruft, and in the history of Afzal Kermáni, and also in that of Mohamed Ibráhim, it is mentioned that, on one occasion, fearing an attack from Bam, the king marched to Kermán *via* Báft, instead of following the main road *via* Ráin; other proofs of a similar sort abound. The question to be decided by this section of the journey may then, I think, be

[1] A camel stage is considerably shorter than that of a mule.

considered to be finally and most satisfactorily settled, the route proving to lie between the two selected by Colonel Yule as being the most suitable, although he wisely left the question open.

The district of Jíruft, which bore the same name at the time of Marco's journey, is bounded to the south by Rudbár, which is undoubtedly the Reobarles of our author, and his error of only remembering the one name is very natural. His description of Jíruft holds good to this day, as far as dates and pistachios are concerned, but there are no "apples of Paradise" or plantains[1] further north than Mináb, the whole magnificent plain, with its almost unlimited potentialities, being inhabited by a few nomads, mainly of the Mehni tribe, whereas, according to the *Násikh-ul-Tawárikh*, the silk dues alone brought in half-a-million tomans. The francolin is the *dorraj* or black partridge, which is splendid shooting, and equally good eating. The description of the large humped oxen, which kneel to be loaded, is true to life, and equally so is the account of the fat-tailed sheep, which are common all over the land of Irán; I have been told by a Persian gentleman that he thought sheep in England decidedly incomplete!

On resuming their journey the Venetians were attacked by brigands only seven members of the party escaping to the shelter of Conosalmi, which Colonel Yule identifies with Idrísi's Kanát-ul-Shám. The word much resembles the Salmous of Diodoros Siculus. Here I again quote from our traveller, who says: "The plain of which we have spoken extends in a southerly direction for five days' journey, and then you come to another descent, where the road is very bad and full of peril, for there are many robbers and bad characters about. When you have got to the foot of this descent, you find another beautiful plain called the plain of Formosa. This extends for two days' journey; and you find in it fine streams of water with plenty of date-palms and other fruit-trees, . . . and on the shore you find a city with a harbour, which is called Hormos."

In 1900, I travelled along this route for three or four stages, which lay in the Jíruft or Rudbár districts. Two marches from Camadi was Kahn-i-Panchur, and a stage beyond it lay the ruins of Fariáb or Pariáb, which was once a great city, and was destroyed

[1] I induced the Mehni chief to send for a few plants from Mináb, which are doing very well. General Schindler considers that the fruit of the *Konár* is referred to.

by a flood, according to local legend. It may have been Alexander's Salmous, as it is about the right distance from the coast. Continuing on, Gulashkird, mentioned by Idrísi, is the next stage; the road then descends to the Duzdi river, and after passing through a belt of hilly country, emerges on to the level plain. which in every way differs from the uplands of Persia.

The description of this plain of Formosa, as Rusticiano quaintly styles it, is most accurate. Even the mariners of Nearchos found it "pleasant and agreeable, and abounding in everything except olives," and to-day Mináb not only boasts of the finest and most extensive date-groves in Persia, but is the only district where mangoes, plantains, and other tropical fruits are produced in any abundance. The account of the climate and its effects is delightful, and, moreover, very true; even in February the heat is most exhausting to a European, and a summer's day spent on board a steamer off Bandar Abbás is an experience that needs no repetition.

Some unrecorded event, probably the sight of the unseaworthy craft, which had not an ounce of iron in their composition, made our travellers decide that the risks of the sea were too great; we therefore have the pleasure of accompanying them back to Kerman and thence northwards to Khorasán.

Remembering the Caraonas, the brigands who captured most of the party in Jíruft, they followed a more westerly road, which is rather scantily described as follows: "On the road by which we return from Hormos to Kerman you meet with some very fine plains, and you also find many natural hot baths; you find plenty of partridges on the road; and there are towns where victual is cheap and abundant, with quantities of dates and other fruits. The wheaten bread, however, is so bitter, owing to the bitterness of the water, that no one can eat it who is not used to it."

The above description probably refers to the main winter route, which runs *via* Sirján. This is supported by the fact that under the Kuh-i-Ginao, the summer station of Bandar Abbás, there is a magnificent sulphur spring, which, welling from an orifice four feet in diameter, forms a stream some thirty yards wide. Its temperature at the source is 113 degrees, and its therapeutic properties are highly appreciated. As to the bitterness of the bread, it is suggested in Sir H. Yule's notes that it was caused by being mixed with acorns, but, to-day at any rate, there are no oak forests in this part of Persia. There is, however, a bitter plant termed *Khár* which grows in the wheat.[1]

Having brought the party back to Kermán, we now enter on the last and most difficult section of their Persian wanderings. To quote the text: "On departing from the city of Kermán you find the road most wearisome; and I will tell you how this is. The first three days you meet with no water, or next to none. And what little you do meet with is bitter green stuff, so salt that no one can drink it. . . . In all these three days you meet with no human habitation. After those three days of desert (you arrive at a stream of fresh water running underground, but along which there are holes broken in here and there, etc.). You then enter another desert which extends for four days; it is very much like the former except that you do see some wild asses. And at the termination of these four days of desert the Kingdom of Kermán comes to an end, and you find another city which is called Cobinan."

I will begin by frankly stating that in a paper which I had the honour of reading before the Society of Arts,[2] I led the travellers along what is now the main road, as at three stages from Kermán there was a running brook, and near Darband, three marches further on, ruins of a city were pointed out to me. This fitted in exactly as regards the next section, but involved the ruin of Ráwár, and also the non-existence of the modern Kubanán. This group of five villages, however, with Kubanán its centre, still exists some ninety to a hundred miles north-north-west of Kermán, and as it is a "fixed point" to which there is only one road, we are bound to follow it.

When describing Marco's journey from Yezd to Kermán, I mentioned that I should on *prima facie* evidence have given Zarand as one of the three inhabited spots referred to, but, although mentioned often in the previous century, we must presume it to have fallen into ruins, which is quite possible, when we take into account the constant fighting and the ravages of the Ghazz. Zarand being about half way, we must suppose that near it a deserted *kanát* was struck, where the party watered. The whole

[1] Gen. Schindler favours the most direct route *via* Urzu and Báft, on which he mentions the existence of sulphurous springs. If, however, Marco returned in midwinter, as seems probable, this route would not have been open.

[2] No. 2324, vol. xlv. June 4th, 1897.

district is salt, as I can testify as far as Zarand, and beyond that Mr Stack speaks of salt streams.[1]

This being probably the route, we will now give our traveller's account of Kubanán. "Cobinan is a large town. The people worship Mahommet. There is much iron and steel and ondanique, and they make steel mirrors of great size and beauty. They also prepare both Tutia (a thing very good for the eyes) and Spodium; and I will tell you the process. They have a vein of a certain earth which has the required quality, and this they put into a great flaming furnace, while, over the furnace, there is an iron grating. The smoke and moisture, expelled from the earth of which I speak, adhere to the iron grating, and thus form Tutia, while the slag that is left after burning is the Spodium."

I translated Marco's description of tutia (which is also the modern Persian name) to a *khán* of Kubanán, and he assured me that the process was the same to-day; spodium he knew nothing about, but the sulphate of copper is found in the hills to the east of Kubanán, and it is from this that tutia is prepared.

Kubanán of to-day, to quote Mr Stack, who, unfortunately, mentions nothing about Marco Polo, "lies almost at the foot of the hills, is embosomed in mulberry trees, and maintains a small manufacture of silk. On a spur above are the remains of an old fort, and a little lower, a mile from the village, stands a platform of hewn stone with two low towers above it, called the Throne of Latif-Shah." Kubanán or the Hill of the Wild Pistachio was scarcely "une cité grant," as Marco terms it, but it was important as being the frontier district of Kermán, although often seized by the ruler of Yezd. Alp Arslán, one of the great Seljuks, is stated by a native chronicler to have returned to Khorasán by this route, which fact clearly shows that it was a main road. It is mentioned that his army nearly perished from thirst between Kubanán and Tabas. *Malik* Dinár too, more than a century later, invaded Kermán *via* Kubanán, and I am informed that the road is still largely patronised, the camel grazing being better than on the Tun-Duhuk-Naiband route, which was explored by me in 1893.

[1] Vide *Six Months in Persia*, vol. i. p. 231 *et seqq*. General Schindler considers that Marco followed a circuitous route to Kubánan, but there seems to be no necessity for adopting this view, especially if the conditions under which our traveller wrote his work be remembered.

To continue, "When you depart from the City of Cobinan, you find yourself in a desert of surpassing aridity, which lasts for some eight days; here are neither fruits nor trees to be seen, and what water there is is bitter and bad, so that you have to carry both food and water. The cattle must needs drink the bad water, will they nill they, because of their great thirst. At the end of those eight days you arrive at a Province which is called Tonocain."

This section of the Lut has not hitherto been rediscovered, but I know that it is desert throughout, and it is practically certain that Marco ended these unpleasant experiences at Tabas, 150 miles from Kubanán. To-day the district is known as Tun-u-Tabas, Káin being independent of it.

Here we take farewell of the illustrious Venetians, as, probably owing to a lacuna in the manuscript, the onward route to Balkh, the Mother of Cities, cannot be traced. We may, however, feel sure that Nishápur or Herát would have been mentioned, if only because of the cataclysm that had befallen them when Chengiz made his murderous invasion. At the same time, it is satisfactory to have been able to establish the substantial veracity of the great traveller, whose character, like that of other benefactors of the world, suffered from the ignorance of mankind and the tendency to belittle what could not be understood.

FROM A KÁIN CARPET

CHAPTER XXIV

THE KARWÁN EXPEDITION

"In this plain (sc. Reobarles) there are a number of villages and towns which have lofty walls of mud made as a defence against the banditti, who are very numerous, and are called Caraonas."—MARCO POLO.

AT the end of November 1897 I found myself once again at Bushire, but before I had been there a week, information was received that Mr Graves, who was in charge of the telegraph line between Jásk and Gwádur, had been murdered on the Rapsh river. This outrage brought home to many, for the first time, to what dangers an isolated Englishman is exposed when travelling in Makrán, with only a few cowardly servants to protect him, but it also showed how high British prestige had hitherto stood, as this was the first murder in the history of the telegraph line, now in its third decade.

It generally happens, when such events occur, that there is some local cause which tends to release the savage tribesmen from the fear of stern retribution, and in the case of Makrán there were two very potent factors at work. The first of these was the assassination of H.I.M. Násir-u-Dín in May 1896, and the fact that since the accession of H.I.M. Muzaffar-u-Dín, the present Sháh, no Persian force had appeared in Baluchistán. One of the leading chieftains, *Sardár* Husein Khán, took advantage of this state of affairs, and gave out that there was no new Sháh, to prove which point he referred to the saying of *Sháh* Namatúlla of Máhun, who prophesied more than four hundred years ago, that the last Sháh of Persia would be named Násir-u-Dín.

In the second place, there is not the slightest doubt that the victory of the Sultán, the religious head of the Sunnis, over Greece was the cause of intense rejoicing among Mohamedans. In the eyes of a European who reads the papers, and has possibly travelled in Greece, that power does not to-day represent a potent force, but as in the East perhaps the greatest name of all is that of Alexander the Greek, so for the Sultán to have conquered the world-conqueror's nation meant an enormous addition of prestige, of which the fanatical *mullás* would take the fullest advantage.

Thanks to the energetic representations of the Resident, which were strongly supported at Tehrán, within a few days of the murder Ahmad Khán, the *Daria Begi*, or Lord of the Ocean, embarked on the *Persepolis* with sixty soldiers, while the "man in the *bázár*" could talk of nothing else but the promptitude with which the expedition started. The Resident having instructed me to conduct the preliminary enquiry into the murder, and, if possible, to commence operations for bringing the guilty to justice, I was soon on my way to Makrán on board H.M.S. *Pigeon*, commanded by Lieut. and Commr. Mowbray.

It was my first experience of travel on a gunboat, which in rough weather resembles the lightest of corks, and when it is smooth, the space appears so limited to a land-lubber's eyes that a feeling of cramp never leaves him. However, pleasant society and pleasanter anticipations make up for much greater discomforts, and after calling in at Jásk, where we communicated with Bushire, and where I picked up a guide, Abdul Azíz by name, of whom more anon, we steamed on to the mouth of the Rapsh river, anchoring some three miles off a miserable fishing hamlet termed Galag.

We were by no means the first arrivals, as we found H.M.

Cable ss. *Patrick Stewart* and the *Persepolis* both at anchor, the former of which we soon boarded, and found Mr Ffinch, the Director-in-Chief, Mr Sealy, the Director of the Persian Gulf Telegraphs, and many other friends. Mr Ffinch, who had just returned from the shore, told me that the Persians had arrived off Galag three days previously, an hour after the *Patrick Stewart*, and had landed the following morning. They were, however, unable to procure any transport, as every camel had been driven into the interior by its owner, and it was only owing to his exertions, and by sending out the telegraph line guards to reassure the timid Baluchis, that the *Daria Begi* had been able to procure the ten camels he required, as he had brought no tents, believing that the scene of the murder was on the coast, and not eleven miles inland, as it proved to be.

Acting with great promptitude, Mr Sealy had already begun to connect Galag with the main line, a piece of work which was eventually completed in some three days, and, needless to say, proved invaluable to us.

After a consultation it was decided that our best plan would be, in the first place, to join the *Daria Begi*, who had marched to the scene of the murder at Rapsh on the previous day, and with the promise of eight camels, which Mr Ffinch expected that night, we began to disembark. This proved no easy task, as there was a bar, and the channel was very tortuous. However the officers of the *Patrick Stewart* having already buoyed the channel, and lending us their steam launch and boats, the whole party of four officers and twenty-six blue-jackets and marines, with a few Sidi boys and servants, were safely landed by about 4 P.M., and our baggage, consisting of water-barrels, ammunition, and blankets, was carried to a camping ground about half a mile distant, where two tents were already pitched. These we were glad to take possession of, as the dew at night was extremely heavy.

About 9 P.M. we were delighted to see our camels, and by 3 A.M. on the following morning we were afoot and struck our tents. The bluejacket, with his usual versatility, started loading the camels as if it were his daily occupation, taking no notice of the protests of the camel-drivers. When, however, the "Ship of the Desert" arose, its load fell off behind, after which experience

THE KARWÁN EXPEDITION. THE START.

[*To face p.* 276.

the Baluch was given a greater share in the proceedings, and we got off about an hour before sunrise.

Our course lay across an absolutely level plain, dotted over with fine tamarisks, while every now and then we caught sight of a clump of date palms. When the sun rose, it at once became unpleasantly hot, and the bluejackets were much relieved by having their blankets stowed away on the spare camel, which had been reserved for emergencies. In spite of the hot sun the tamarisks were dripping with dew, and great care had to be taken to avoid a shower bath when resting in the shade.

After a four hours' march we reached the scene of the murder, underneath what is technically known as a "mast," which means a sort of Eiffel Tower, some eighty feet high. The wire is attached at this elevation whenever a considerable river has to be crossed, such being the vagaries of rivers in these parts that, in addition to the necessity of a single span at a considerable elevation, the masts have to be at some distance from the banks, to provide against a possible change of course.

Our first care when we reached the river was to select the best possible site for a camp, as we were within reach of the Karwánis, and had to be prepared for the possibility of an attack. In front of us the wide river-bed offered a splendid field for fire, but in every other direction there was a thick growth of tamarisk; in fact, there was little choice, so we settled ourselves down near the Persians, and, after a rest, the energetic bluejackets set to work to cut down tamarisks and construct *abattis*.

Mowbray and I went off to interview the *Daria Begi*, whom I was naturally anxious to meet, as upon his friendliness much depended. I found him to be a very fine-looking dark man of about fifty, with bluff but courteous manners, whose almost European quickness at seizing a point and making up his mind was very pleasant.

"After compliments," as Indian *Munshis* always begin the translation of a letter, the *Daria Begi* told me that upon his arrival off Galag some camel riders were seen to trot off into the interior, and therefore he was not surprised that the Karwánis[1]

[1] Is it not possible that the Karwánis are the Caraonas of Marco Polo? They are distinct from the surrounding Baluchis, and pay no tribute to any Governor.

were ready to enter into negotiations with him as soon as he arrived at Rapsh. He had left his camp, where booths had been constructed to supply the lack of tents, and met a party of forty of them on the right bank of the river. At first they declined to regard the killing of Mr Graves as a serious matter, and even after they had acknowledged that it was wrong, they promised in a very half-hearted manner to hand over the murderers, the *Daria Begi* giving them until sunset on the third day.

We arrived on the second day, and it was accordingly arranged that, if there were no signs of surrender on the part of the tribesmen when the date expired, we should march to their villages, and by bringing home to them the disagreeable prospect of the threatened destruction of their homes and date-groves, persuade them to change their views. Before, however, taking this somewhat decided step, we made careful enquiries as to how the Karwánis were armed, their numbers, and whether they were united. We were told that the tribe possessed but few breech-loaders, and that they could muster about eight hundred fighting men, of which perhaps a third would stand aloof. We also learned that there were three sections viz. Sháhozáí, Hassadzáí, and Hotukzáí.

The murderers belonged to the Sháhozáí clan, and the fact that Sháí Mohamed, their chief, had been principally concerned in the outrage, indicated that it would be no easy matter to seize the guilty. It appeared that they, to the number of sixteen, attacked Mr Graves's camp at midnight, and that before he was aware of what was going on, he was severely wounded and despatched in bed, while speaking in a dazed fashion. The chief of the Hassadzái, Mírdost by name, was the negotiator, as his clan was little concerned in the murder, and the Hotukzáí section maintained a strict neutrality, their chief, Pír Dád, a magnificent whitebeard of eighty, visiting the Resident upon his arrival later on.

Our united forces included thirty wild hillmen from Tangistán These highlanders are usually the dread of Bushire, which town, according to a local Governor, they would have looted long ago, were it not for British gunboats and the Residency escort. A light Krupp carried in sections on camels and manned by sailors of the *Persepolis* formed a veritable fetish to the Baluchis, who think that a cannon is not fair play, while some twenty or thirty Persian *sarbás*,[1] literally "men who risk their heads," completed a total of rather under a hundred. Half-a-dozen Sidi boys, a certain number of whom are attached to every man-of-war in the Persian Gulf, and who revelled in such names as "Ropeyarn," "Hammock," and "Bilgewater," formed a stretcher party, and were armed with cutlasses.

Before leaving the coast we had landed a further supply of stores, which arrived on the following day, and in the evening Messrs Sealy, Townsend, and Carnegie, who had completed the line, came into camp with some ten lascars, to all of whom Mr Ffinch gave permission to accompany the expedition, which we then thought would not receive any further additions. At nightfall, however, a solitary camel-rider was seen trotting up from the coast, and this proved to be Mr Wood of the Imperial Bank of Persia, to whom I am indebted for the illustrations of these parts.

At midnight every one was afoot, and the camels, which were now about eighteen in number, were loaded up. When I went across to see how the Persians were getting on, the *Daria Begi* told me that every Baluch expressed the profoundest ignorance of the Karwán district. Our maps were a blank, and all our enquiries on the previous day had elicited very little truth, the fact being that the natives, with considerable wisdom, were looking forward to a day of retribution, when we should have left the country.

The local chief, *Mír* Isá by name, a fine-looking Baluch, had been to see me on the previous day, and had been profuse in protestations of willingness to help. As it was impossible to break up our party, we had decided to engage some of his people to guard Mr Campbell, the new Inspector, who remained at the telegraph line. The *Daria Begi* suggested that I should take the chief himself to act as guide, and, if necessary, as a go-between; but when I informed Isá of this, he demurred. It was really quite comical to note what wild excuses he gave; at one time he averred that he did not know the way, and when this was received with incredulity, he swore that his wife was dying. Finally, he tried to make off, but this was defeated by

[1] Cf. *jámbás*, a corruption of *jánbás*, a man who risks his life. In S.-E. Persia this term is applied to a camelry soldier, but elsewhere it signifies an acrobat.

my instructing Sultán Sukhru not to let him out of his sight, and he eventually yielded to the inevitable.

One of the *Daria Begi's* camels, which carried part of the field-gun, delayed us for more than an hour, and it was not until nearly 3 A.M. that we crossed the river, after which we marched north-west. There being a late moon, it was easy enough to see for some distance, and after a mile or so we perceived that Isá was pursuing very tortuous tracks, first bearing to the right and then again to the left. We remonstrated with him, but he pleaded the darkness as an excuse; I think, however, that he must have led us several unnecessary miles, as when we marched back to Rapsh we found well defined tracks, whereas Isá took us mainly across country, and Nasrulla Khán had to be constantly trotting up and down to keep the whole party in touch. At sunrise we halted for half-an-hour and then continued the march towards a range some 700 feet in altitude, underneath which we imagined that the villages would lie. At about 7 A.M. we reached a bifurcation, and in the distance saw a date-grove. Isá was so anxious for us to go there that we wisely decided to continue along the other path, soon after which we descried a party of some sixty camelry riding out of shot, to our left. The tamarisk, which had so far been thick, here began to dwindle, and we were soon in the open plain.

Isá now became so violently agitated that his knees knocked together, and he expressed his intention of leaving us. This, however, we did not want, as we thought that he might be useful later on. He and his six followers then half drew their swords, with the foolish idea (as he afterwards explained) of killing the *Daria Begi* and myself, but as they were all instantly covered, they would have had little chance of success. He finally swore that if we allowed him to meet the Karwánis, he would bring about the surrender of the murderers, and as we were anxious to avoid bloodshed, and also thought that the tribesmen, seeing that we were in earnest, might throw up the sponge, we called a halt, and sent off Isá, along with a lame *Sheikh* whom the *Daria Begi* had brought from Jásk, and who rode Isá's ass.

For two hours we waited in the grilling sun, until we saw the lame man slowly returning on foot; he informed us that the Karwánis were professedly ready to catch the murderers in a few

THE KARWÁN EXPEDITION—A COUNCIL OF WAR.

[*To face p.* 280.

days' time, if we would not enter their villages but return to the Rapsh, and, as we had anticipated, Isá did not show up again.

The order to continue the advance was given, and as we were only a few miles from the villages, and resistance was possible, we took even greater precautions than before. For the first time I mounted the riding camel, to secure a good view, and told Abdul Azíz to drive. That worthy, however, had developed an alarming toothache, which he averred the shaking of the camel would render a martyrdom, so, wishing to keep both hands free, I told him to lead my "charger." To this, too, he objected, and I at last saw that the man was actually green from fear, after the manner of Isá.

About noon we approached a large village, and the Tangistáni scouts, who advanced by rushes at quarter-mile pace, were soon collected at the last ridge, where they rather hesitated to enter the village, as each matting hut and enclosure might contain an armed Baluch. Nothing moved, however, except a few fowls and goats, so in they rushed, and were soon engaged in the thoroughly congenial occupation of looting. First the kids, then the fowls, were captured, and after that a few sacks of flour and some baskets of dates, but the two hours' delay had given the Karwánis time to clear out most of their property, which was perhaps just as well. The village was a collection of several groups of three or four mat huts, each surrounded by a thorn enclosure for the sheep, and, as we afterwards discovered, was called Kárkinde, being the home of the Hassadzáí. I had offered a reward for any relics of the ill-fated Mr Graves, and some of the spoilers brought me his pocket-book, a newspaper, and other trifles, all found in the various hovels.

When the bluejackets arrived, the question of water was most urgent, but, oddly enough, although there is generally a defined track to the village well, we could not find it for nearly two hours, in spite of having men out searching in every direction. The discovery of a well thirty feet deep, holding perhaps three feet of water, was hailed with delight, and after a drink all round, water-bottles and barrels were refilled, the whole party marching over to where the *Daria Begi* had fixed up his gun, on the only commanding ridge near at hand. It was a great sight to see the Lord of the Ocean distributing the spoil; two or three men received a goat, and every one a handful of flour and dates. He also very kindly presented us with a couple of sheep, which were speedily converted into mutton, and by 3 P.M., after being fifteen hours on the march, we were able to get some food.

Nothing could exceed the gaiety of the bluejackets, many of whom suffered terribly from sore feet, but the joy of being on shore, after a summer spent in patrolling the Shat-el-Arab, made all aches and pains quite a treat, and they naturally had a hope of being able to enjoy a bit of a fight.

We had hardly settled down when a large party of camelry rode round our position, at a distance of half-a-mile, by their leisurely movements evidently judging themselves out of range. The *Daria Begi* very wisely did not commence hostilities, and after circling round, the *lashkar* or war party made off towards the hills, in the direction in which we imagined the villagers to have fled.

The site of our camp consisting of a long ridge, rather too narrow to occupy, except where the *Daria Begi* had taken possession of the highest point, we camped just behind it, keeping sentries on the summit, whence they could enjoy a good view. As, however, there was thick scrub on two faces, we decided to utilise every one for that night, posting a lascar or a servant between each sentry, while both officers and volunteers were continually going the rounds. At 10 P.M. a shot was fired at a sentry, and a murmur was heard, as if there were a number of men. Mowbray fired a Verrys light, which illuminated the whole camp, and it was probably this that prevented an attempt to rush us. One of the officers, when going round the sentries to the rear, saw a figure rushing in. He challenged, and getting no reply, was about to fire, when he fortunately perceived that it was a lascar, who had lost the use of his tongue from fright! Nothing else disturbed the stillness of the night, the moon rising shortly after; but the following day we decided that our first care must be to find a better site for the camp. This took some time, but at last a small ridge was found, with a well handy and a clear field of fire all round, and thither we marched by relays, some of our camel-drivers having deserted.

Abdul Azíz also was not to be found in the morning, and two days later he arrived at Jásk, having, as he stated, been seized by Karwánis, and beaten within an inch of his life. An examination, however, showed no marks of violence, and the wretched coward was dismissed from telegraph employment, a severe but merited punishment. He was rather a loss in one way, as his was the only name that any of the naval party could even approximately seize, "Abdul's Ashes" being considered quite a linguistic triumph! On the other hand, Nasrulla Khán's servant, dressed in a short, pleated Persian coat, excited much mirth, and whenever he appeared on the scene, "Eh, Bill! look at that Tyrolean gal!" was invariably repeated with infinite gusto.

At a meeting to decide what step should next be taken, it was agreed to send out the Tangistánis to scout and to make a reconnaissance in force on the following morning. At nightfall the news came that the tribe was at a date-grove in the hills to the west, so, leaving the gun and a small guard for the camp, we marched off an hour before sunrise.

Just as the dawn was breaking, we reached a precipitous cliff, up which there appeared to be no road, but a shot fired from above showed that we were in the right direction. The Tangistánis and bluejackets scrambled up the rocks, the former keeping ahead, thanks to their light kit of rolled-up trousers, a jacket, a Werndl rifle, and perhaps one hundred cartridges. The Baluchis, foolishly enough, waited for us to reach what proved to be a plateau, and then a running skirmish commenced, the Tangistánis taking cover splendidly and advancing at a great pace. There were, perhaps, some sixty Baluchis firing away most wildly, but with our glasses we could see swarms of them behind—spectators apparently. A check, caused by the enemy's lining the dry bed of a *nala*, gave the bluejackets the chance of joining in. However, upon seeing them, the Baluchis ran like hares, and the few volleys fired took very little effect, although we saw that two or three men were hit.

The *Daria Begi*, who had experienced the utmost difficulty in scaling the cliffs, being far behind, we induced the Tangistánis to wait for him, and after about half an hour the admiral, who was much shaken owing to a nasty fall, put in an appearance, and we advanced on the date-grove of Tolada, which we saw in the distance. On our way, the scouts pounced on a Baluch hidden behind some rocks, but, proving to be a traveller, he was released.

We found the well at once, surrounded by heaps of date-stones and the ashes of numerous fires, which showed that it had been occupied the previous night. The Tangistánis, who had no water bottles, were much exhausted, and so were we all. An hour's halt was therefore decided upon, during which we explored the date-grove, which consisted of perhaps two thousand palm trees, the Persians in vain looking for any hidden supplies of wheat.

Having heard that there was an easy way down to the plain, we marched to the south, and came on to a beaten track which led us to the cliff, down which we scrambled by hanging on to steps cut in the rocks. We were then perhaps four miles from Kárkinde camp, where we arrived about noon. On sitting down to breakfast, I received a note from the Resident, who had reached Rapsh; I thereupon decided to ride in on a running camel, and arrived in two and a half hours, which makes the distance about twelve miles. The camp, where we had left Campbell almost alone, was now a scene of activity, some thirty bluejackets of H.M.S. *Lapwing*, a section of Bombay Infantry, and the Residency servants, all tending to give it life.

Colonel Meade told me that he had sent for the head of the Hotukzáí section, which was not implicated in the murder, and on the following day two grand old whitebeards appeared. To my amusement Isá also attended under safe conduct, but looked utterly wretched as soon as he saw me. The Hotukzáí chief bewailed the murder, and agreed with us that it was wicked, but as he neither offered any assistance whatever, nor made any suggestions, after an impressive warning the Resident dismissed him. I naturally wished to ask Isá a few questions, but he rather prudently begged to be allowed to say his prayers, and we saw him no more.

Two or three days were spent in ciphering and deciphering telegrams, and I remember that one day Major Fagan, H.M.'s Consul at Maskat, to whom the actual enquiry and taking down of evidence was entrusted, and myself were hard at work from 4 A.M. until nearly dinner-time, one portentous telegram which arrived occupying many hours. The Resident then marched to Kárkinde, where nothing much had occurred except a little sniping, in the course of which Mowbray, a son of Anak and consequently a good mark, had been nearly hit.

The following day being Christmas, Colonel Meade invited Messrs Ffinch, Barker, and Campbell to come up to his camp. In the morning I made a long reconnaissance, during which I

THE FUNERAL OF MR GRAVES.

[*To face p.* 284.

stalked a caravan, only to find that they were friendlies, but the fact that the cattle were aimlessly wandering about showed us that the entire district was deserted. In the evening we all dined with the Resident, and enjoyed the best of dinners, in spite of the great difficulties his servants must have had to contend with; and we retired to our crowded tents, hoping that, at least, some sniping might occur as a satisfactory conclusion to the day. Sure enough, a sentry fired at a moving object, but as no shot was returned, we imagined that it must have been a camel-driver trying to desert, and nothing else happened to entertain our guests.

The water-supply at Kárkinde being insufficient for our augmented party, the Resident decided to move the camp to the date-grove of Gao, where there was more water. Meanwhile the *Daria Begi* threatened, if the Karwánis still continued recalcitrant, to cut down their palm trees—a terrible punishment, as no trees bear what is their staple food until seven years old. It is needless to say that the villages were all fired, as the force marched through each portion of the district.

At night, our piquet beyond the Gao date-grove opened fire, but it was never ascertained whether the enemy was in force or not, and as the Resident received a letter from Seiid Khán, the Governor of Geh, promising to secure the murderers if the date-groves were spared, our next move had to be decided. We had, by Major Fagan's enquiry, clearly established the names of the murderers, and had driven the tribe from its villages, which had been burnt; it was also possible to destroy their date-groves, although the Resident was reluctant to consent to this course. On the other hand, there were no signs of the murderers being given up, and the two gunboats could not be left indefinitely at Galag. Moreover, it was the business of the Persian Government to seize the murderers, and our position was mainly that of onlookers anxious for results. Finally, more important business called us elsewhere. Consequently Colonel Meade decided to accept Seiid Khán's offer, and to leave an escort at Rapsh for the protection of Campbell until the murderers were captured. Thus the first phase of the Karwán expedition came to an end, and there being insufficient transport for the whole party to move together, we marched back to the coast by relays.

FROM A KERMÁN CARPET.

CHAPTER XXV

A WINTER CRUISE IN THE PERSIAN GULF.

" High on a throne of royal state, which far
Outshone the wealth of Ormus and of Ind,
Or where the gorgeous East with richest hand
Show'rs on her kings barbaric pearl and gold,
Satan exalted sat." —*Paradise Lost*, book ii. line 1.

I QUITTED Makrán on board H.M.S. *Lapwing*, and after putting in at Maskat for coal, we steamed across to Hormuz. Before describing our visit, it may be of interest to outline the history of this island, which during mediæval times was one of the greatest emporia of the world; and retained its position as such for more than a century after the rounding of the Cape of Good Hope by Vasco di Gama.

In ancient times Hormuz was situated on the mainland, on what is now known as the Mináb river, and, as related in a former chapter, it was at this port that Nearchos landed and proceeded to report his arrival to Alexander the Great. It was also from this harbour that, after the Arab conquest, the persecuted Zoroastrians commenced that emigration, the results of which have been to increase the population of India by a numerically small, but commercial and highly-progressive race. In a Parsi history we read that "the emigrants first fled into Kuhistán (in Eastern Persia), where they remained a century, and afterwards travelled to Hormuz, where they dwelt fifteen years, and then sailed to Diw." This latter is an island to the south of Kathiawár. Marco Polo, towards the end of the thirteenth century, twice visited Hormuz, but shortly afterwards a new Hormuz was built on the island, which has since borne the name, the mainland having become unsafe.

For two centuries the island city was the theme of the East, and is fully described by the travellers of the time. Among the earliest was the monk Odoricus, who merely writes, "Orenes (sc. Hormuz), est toute enclose de murs, et moult y a de grans et de grosses marchandises."[1] He then expatiates at length upon the heat. Abdur Razzák, who became a traveller, much against his will, says that "Ormuz, which is also called Jerun, is a port situated in the middle of the sea, and which has not its equal on the surface of the globe. Travellers from all countries resort hither, and, in exchange for the commodities which they bring, they can without trouble or difficulty obtain all that they desire."[2]

The appearance of the Portuguese under Albuquerque, who grasped the importance of its strategic position, finally resulted in Hormuz becoming a Portuguese possession of immense value, as the officials of that nation established a monopoly of everything, and forced all traders to buy of them on the spot. As the years passed, the Portuguese became so unpopular with their neighbours that Sháh Abbás, who felt galled that the King of Kings should have the profits of his commerce drained by a European nation, made a treaty with the English, then a steadily rising people, and Hormuz was captured in 1622 by a combined Anglo-Persian force, the Portuguese being expelled; from this the emporium never recovered, the modern Bandar Abbás absorbing the bulk of the traffic.

We landed on the island (which is some twelve miles in circumference), close to the fort, which occupies a peninsula and is washed on three sides, the sea having receded, as testified by the remains

[1] Cordier's *Odoricus*, chap. ix., p. 69.

[2] *India in the Fifteenth Century*, p. 5.

of the quays, which are now high and dry. This grand old fortress is still practically intact, and is approached by a massive door, studded with iron spikes. It was protected in front by a bastion of great strength, flanked by a second bastion, after which the guard-house was passed, beyond which the main lower portion of the fort was visible. It consisted of a square with a large tank, now empty, round which were barracks and store-houses, built into the massive forty-foot wall, which has a parapet eighteen feet wide. A steep rise led to the inner work, in which we saw a superb reservoir, an oval forty feet high and fifty feet long, with a passage encircling it about twenty feet above the bottom; it was, however, empty. A final rise brought us to the summit of the fort, some sixty feet above the ground level. There, overlooking the ruined city, was all that was left of a sumptuous palace, while numerous cannon lying about bore mute witness to the stormy past. We calculated that the fort covered some three or four acres, and looking at its strong high walls, one felt proud that the British tar of the day had been able to capture it, although the garrison, after a heroic defence, surrendered mainly from want of water in the tanks. The Persians, our allies, lost a thousand men at a single assault.

Strolling among the ruins of the city, it was impossible not to regret the destruction of such a proof of human energy, for Hormuz itself produces only salt and red ochre, fresh provisions, and even water, having to be imported. Thus to found a great city amid such arid surroundings was indeed an achievement. The description given by Sir Thomas Herbert, who visited the fort a few years after its capture, runs: "And both within and without the castle, so regularly built and so well fortified with deep trenches, counterscarp and great ordnance, commanding both city and haven, that none exceeded it through all the Orient."[1]

Skirting the bay, we passed a tombstone roughly inscribed:

"THOMAS FULLER. Aged 14. 1897"

a pathetic memorial, which somehow brought back the forcible words of a Frenchwoman: "Ah yes, the English scatter their bones about like cigar ends."

Beyond the site of the town, now a mere village with two

[1] *Some Yeares Travels into Africa and Asia the Great*, p. 106.

hundred inhabitants, who dry fish and possibly smuggle, we visited the ruined chapel of Santa Lucia,[1] the walls of which are still standing, albeit in a shaky state. It was never a very fine building, I imagine, but, with its crypt still intact, it forms an interesting relic of the past.

The bluejackets took much more interest in collecting sea spinach, which lined the little bay, and in drawing a seine net. Soles, whiting, smelts, a young ground shark, deadliest of the tribe, barracouta, conger eels, and a fine 9-lb. hake were all hauled on shore. On seeing this latter fish, a shout arose of "Beat him and pay the harbour dues!" while all the tars, west countrymen, and worthy descendants of Kingsley's heroes, sang:

> "Lardy Edgecumbe, Earl divine,
> All the hakes fish be thine,
> All the fishes of the sea,
> Lardy Edgecumbe, belong to thee."

This reference to a disputed fishing due at Plymouth made the party as merry as crickets, and we left them picnicking on shore.

From Hormuz we had intended to make Kishm, but as the weather was unfavourable, we coasted the island, and finally anchored in the grand harbour which lies between Kishm and Henjám. The earliest mention of Kishm appears in Arrian, and runs: "It produced plenty of vines, palm trees, and corn, and was full eight hundred stadia[2] in length. . . . In this island, the sepulchre of the first monarch thereof is said still to remain, and his name was Erythras, and from him the sea was called the Erythraean Sea."[3] Strabo, however, makes the site of this tomb to be at Bahrein.

It was in connection with the capture of Hormuz that Englishmen first appeared at Kishm, its fort being reduced as a preliminary operation. Our artillery practice was extraordinary, a gun on the fort being dismounted at the first shot, but one of the Arctic heroes perished during these operations, the event being described as

[1] It is so termed on the map in Astley's *Collection of Voyages*.

[2] This would come to rather less than 100 miles, which is approximately correct.

[3] *Indika*, 37.

follows in Purchas' *Pilgrims*:[1] "Master Baffin went on shoare with his Geometricall Instruments, for the taking the height and distance of the Castle wall; but as he was about the same, he received a small shot from the Castle into his belly, wherewith he gave three leapes, by report, and died immediatly."

At the north-west corner of Kishm is the station of Bassidu or Bassidore, where, until some twenty years ago, a considerable British garrison was maintained, in order to subdue the pirates, and after accomplishing this, to patrol the Persian Gulf. However, the climate was very trying, the thermometer rising to incredible heights, and as steam had practically brought the Gulf close to Karachi, the garrison was withdrawn to Jásk. In Moore's poem, "Kishm's amber vine" seems to suggest a delightful spot, yet there are few more unhealthy corners of the world than this section of the Persian Gulf, where everything is barren, squalid, and sun-scorched to a degree that can only be realised by being seen. The island, in the winter of 1896, was the scene of a terrible earthquake, in which 1200 people were killed, and almost every house destroyed.

Henjám is another island with a past, and although now occupied by only a few savages, was formerly densely inhabited, the hills being carefully terraced, while there are ruins of a large town. Near the landing-place we found the remains of a telegraph station, Henjám at one time being used as a half-way house between Bushire and Jásk.

The gunner of the *Lapwing* discovered a bed of oysters, which were excellent eating. In the harbour we found nineteen *bagalas* loaded with salt from mines on the mainland, waiting for the ss. *Tresco*; and also a very large sailing vessel,[2] loaded with rice and bound for Koweit, which had put in for shelter from the gale.

At Bandar Abbás we purchased some delicious oranges, picked up the post, and then returned to Maskat, where we found the Resident. The town was in a state of great excitement, as on January 1st 1898 the Sultán, instead of firing a salute in honour of the Queen-Empress, as he had invariably done since the great Dehli *Darbár*, had fired the usual number of guns, but "in honour

[1] Vol. ii. book x. chap. ix. p. 1792.

[2] These vessels, many of which are built at Linga, make but one voyage a year, and are owned by Arabs.

of all Christian nations." The Resident arrived on the very day, and upon explaining to the Sultán his breach of courtesy, the latter fired the salute on 3rd January, and hoisted the British flag for twenty-four hours.

During the next two or three days I visited Mattra, the commercial port of Maskat. It is an open roadstead, and so should be much cooler. Dr Jaykar, the Agency surgeon, who resides there,[1] has made a study of the zoology of this part. His name will not be forgotten, as his discovery of a new mountain goat, the "Hematragus Jaykari," which no European has hitherto shot, ranks as one of the most interesting finds of the century. As this goat has its habitat within thirty miles of Maskat, I am surprised that no official has yet tried to bag one, to my knowledge. The Gulf climate apparently saps all energy, as even in midwinter at Maskat walking is a weariness to the flesh, owing to the relaxing heat.

On 8th January the British India ss. *Kilwa* came in, after having taken a reinforcement of one hundred Tangistánis to the *Daria Begi*; their chief had been a prisoner for fourteen years on board the *Persepolis*, and had been released to lead his tribe. The latter ship having run out of all supplies, their arrival was most opportune.

Quitting with much regret the *Lapwing*, whose officers formed a most united party, I transferred myself to the *Lawrence*, where I was among old friends, and we were soon on the way to Jásk; there we handed in telegrams, and I picked up Sultán Sukhru and my heavy baggage, which had been landed by mistake. We also enjoyed an excellent afternoon's tennis at the Telegraph station, after which we bought some of the quaint Bashákird rugs, and then returned on board, waking up to find ourselves off Galag once more.

We landed in smooth weather, and rode up to the camp at Rapsh, from which horses had been sent down for our use, the Resident having left four behind. We found Campbell in a formidable earth-work, with wire entanglements all round, and the *Daria Begi* next door had burrowed to such an extent that he was almost underground. The news was not cheerful, as information had just been received of the cutting up of Captain Burne's survey party in British Makrán, and of the destruction of the

[1] He retired in 1900.

telegraph line for many miles to the east of Chahbár. This, we knew, would speedily re-act on Persian Makrán, and as the *Daria Begi* was not allowed to act on the offensive, the capture of the murderers did not appear to be much nearer achievement.

Upon reaching the seashore, after a most enjoyable day, we found that some members of the *Lawrence* had had excellent fishing, the young ground-sharks in particular having afforded good play. The boat stuck when crossing the bar, and we all got rather wet, but on the whole the weather at Galag was excellent, especially compared with what other parties had experienced.

Arriving at Maskat, we found that Colonel Meade was nearly ready to proceed to Chahbár, which was to be garrisoned by a detachment of the Bombay Marine Infantry, while a larger detachment under Lieut. Waller was sent to Jásk.

Before leaving, I accompanied the Resident to pay a farewell visit to the Sultán. The palace is the old Portuguese factory, a three-storied building, and at its entrance His Highness met us and shook hands. He then led us up a rickety flight of stairs, and we entered a furnished room, with a black and white mosaic floor, a round table, and an old-fashioned clock, which was not working. Greatly to Colonel Meade's amusement, my uniform delighted the Sultán so much that he could not take his eyes off it. He asked how many of the officers of the Queen-Empress wore such a uniform, and on being told "many hundreds," said: "What a happy sovereign she must be!" with such feeling that we all laughed. Upon leaving, I was earnestly invited to call whenever I passed through Maskat. The scene was somewhat embarrassing, and bordered on the ludicrous, but, at the same time, I think that our officials are somewhat apt to forget how great a power display still is in the East. In Baluchistán a traveller's status is partly determined by the number of his loads, in Persia by his servants and his general turn-out, while everywhere, as far as my experience goes, the greater the show, the greater the effect. Travellers on more than one occasion have told me that they had only brought rough shooting clothes with them; all such I would refer to Lord Curzon's work, where it is laid down that a dress suit is the most essential article of outfit, even for those who would attempt to reach Lhassa.

To resume, the *Lawrence* weighed anchor amid the roar of a salute, and the next morning we found ourselves at Chahbár

THE SULTAN OF MASKAT.

[To face p. 292.

which I had not revisited since my second journey in 1893-4. The *Patrick Stewart* came in a few hours later, so that we were a large party on shore, especially as the detachment of Bombay Marine Infantry under Captain Creagh, an old school-fellow, had also arrived on the previous day.

As I was most anxious to visit the small ports east of Gwádur, I asked Mr Ffinch for a passage on board the *Patrick Stewart*, which he readily granted, and at sunset I took a seat in its launch. We passed through shoals of *garfish*, dozens of which leapt on board, attracted by the lantern. They had pointed noses, and one of our party was nearly blinded, the point only just missing his eye.

The following morning found us at Gwádur, where we saw a curious phenomenon. Either a storm or some noxious gas or both together, had lined the beach with tons of fish, which had quickly decayed and formed a kind of bog. A track had been prepared across this, which we were warned to keep to, but a member of the party disregarded the advice and sank into the fish bog almost up to his waist.

Since my visit to Rapsh, when I had received the first news of the outbreak in the Kej valley, matters had become comparatively serious. It would appear that authority in the valley of Kej was represented by a Hindu, Udu Dass, more generally spoken of as the *Násim*. The Baluchis, headed by a spendthrift and dissolute member of the old ruling family, had formed a party, and, as the drought had produced much want, were able to collect a large number of men and seize Udu Dass, who, in my opinion, could never have been popular. At first Mehráb Khán, their leader, vowed that he would "colonise hell" with the *Násim*, but he finally agreed to release him, if the fort of Turbat were evacuated. This was done, and Udu Dass betook himself to the fort of Abdul Kerim Khán, cousin of the rebel chief, who protected him.

In the meanwhile part of the survey party which was divided up was attacked and Captain Burne, R.E., who had been suffering from fever and was sleeping on a hill some distance off, heard of this, and returned to find his camp looted and his followers dispersed. Although on the sick-list, he walked some twenty-five miles and rode another hundred miles on a camel to Ormára, whence he telegraphed the news of the outbreak to Karachi.

Captain Turner had better luck, his camp being escorted in by yet another relation of Mehráb Khán. As may be imagined, the hinterland of Gwádur was much disturbed, the Rinds having joined the rising, and the Parsi postmaster told me confidentially that every morning he expected to find his throat cut!

Having encouraged every one with the news that troops were being sent to Ormára, we returned on board, and steamed on to Pasni. We had heard that a body of Mehráb Khán's men were holding that village, whose *Naib* had been seized, but allowed to escape, and was now being brought back in triumph by us. We tried to surprise the party by landing before daybreak, and doubling round behind the village, but we were just too late, our arrival having been observed.

Pasni lies due south of the Kej valley, and was the centre of the havoc committed, the line having been destroyed for many miles, the wires cut and carried off, and the posts knocked down. Since the construction of the line nothing of the sort had occurred, but so far every one, even the line-guards, had kept quite cool. We learned that there had been about a dozen of Mehráb Khán's men in Pasni, who had only just escaped us. Fortunately, the telegraph station, a substantial block of buildings, had not been touched, and adjourning thither we tried to communicate with Ormára, but in vain, although messages between Ormára and Karachi were easily tapped.

The village of Pasni is a squalid collection of huts, reeking of decaying and decayed fish, but I was very glad to have visited it, as it was there that Alexander first reached the coast, and commenced digging wells for his thirsty soldiery. The harbour is not at all bad as harbours go in Makrán, although inferior to Gwádur.

It was only a few hours' run to Ormára, which consists of a hammer-headed promontory like Gwádur. We landed at about 9 P.M., and Mr Ffinch and I proceeded to the camp, which was some two miles from the telegraph station. We there found Colonel Mayne of the Baluchis with three hundred men, and also Captains Knox and Tighe of the Indian Political Service; the camel question had been settled, and the force was about to proceed along the coast to Pasni, where two mountain guns and other reinforcements joined them. From Pasni they marched inland, and found about one thousand Baluchis occupying one of the low but rugged passes. A cleverly planned attack was successfully carried out, and the rebels, who showed much pluck, as they had very few rifles among them, were shot down by scores. Mehráb Khán escaped, but Baluch Khán, a noted firebrand, and the actual leader in the field, with many other chiefs, was killed.

So ended the first, and, in all probability, the last engagement in Makrán in which the Baluchis stood. The result was excellent, as hitherto rebellious chiefs had been treated with much leniency, and had consequently ceased to regard rebellion in its proper light. Moreover, a Baluchi battle is considered severe if two or three warriors bite the dust, so that the fact of the list of the slain running into three figures produced a stupendous effect throughout Baluchistán, and, without doubt, indirectly aided the work on the Persian side of the frontier.

The next day we reached Karachi, where I enjoyed the hospitality of the Director, but my work was soon done, and in far too short a time I was once again running up the Gulf on board the ss. *Assyria*, commanded by one of the smartest and brightest of British India captains, who, however, fell a victim to the climate, dying of heat apoplexy at Bushire a few months later.

At Maskat I was in quarantine, much to my disgust, as the *Cossack*, *Lapwing*, and *Pigeon* were all in harbour. The great event had been the capture of arms on board the ss. *Baluchistán*, four hundred and eighty huge cases having been seized and conveyed to the Consulate. This question has been such a burning one, and so much that is inaccurate has been written about it, that it may be as well to give the facts.

In or about the year 1883, a firm at Bushire started dealing in arms in a small way, and made such profits that most of the houses trading to the Gulf gradually followed suit. There was, indeed, a nominal prohibition, but the traffic was encouraged by the Persian custom-house authorities, as no objection was made by the importers when the treaty five per cent. was raised. The net result, as may be imagined, was to arm the whole province of Fárs and Arabistán with rifles much better than those possessed by the Persian troops; consequently at the present time South-west Persia is at the mercy of the nomads, did they but realise it, or could they combine. The Arab coast is also full of rifles, which fact naturally increases brigandage and strangles trade. Maskat became the distributing centre for South-east Persia and Arabia, thousands of rifles of all sorts being landed,[1] and as the customs increased in value the Sultán profited by the traffic, not at once realising the necessary consequence, that his subjects would pass entirely out of control.

The Persian Government had for many years endeavoured to put a stop to the trade, and it sought the assistance of the British Government, which suspected that arms were conveyed to the tribes on the North-west frontier, at that time in revolt, in order to arrange with the Sultán of Maskat to seize all arms bound for the Persian Gulf. The confiscation was first carried out at Bushire, where some seven thousand rifles were seized and finally despatched to Tehrán. Again, at Bahrein, owing to a private dispute, the *Sheikh* had taken into his custody a large depôt while at Maskat, as before stated, four hundred and eighty cases of rifles and ammunition were seized on board the *Baluchistán*. As may be supposed, a proportion of the firms received timely warning, but any impartial onlooker could judge by the number seized what harm the trade was doing. To take an instance, suppose that the Baluchis had been all armed with these rifles, which they could easily have procured at Maskat, the position would have been one of extreme difficulty for Major Mayne: or again, had the Karwánis been armed with breech-loaders, our advance with less than one hundred fighting men would have been far too hazardous, and, in any case, the loss of life would have been great. Of course, from the manufacturer's point of view, the closing of this promising market was hard, but can any one honestly say that he thinks that modern arms of precision should be put into the hands of men who will invariably use them to disturb the peace, and keep whole countries in the backward state from which we are slowly and laboriously trying to raise them?

The theory that the arms are sold to respectable merchants will not hold water, as no merchant knows what becomes of his wares. It was hotly denied that arms could or did reach the frontier tribes through Persia, and an Indian newspaper the *Pioneer*, was most sarcastic with reference to any one who held contrary views: however, as a matter of fact, small but

[1] The figures for 1896-7 were 19,261.

increasing consignments were being bought at Bandar Abbás and at Maskat, and were carried to the Indian borderland by the Afghán tribesmen, who own some hundreds of camels, trading between Bandar Abbás, Eastern Persia, and Afghanistán. As H.H. Abdur Rahman was not likely to favour this trade, it is probable that the rifles were smuggled in, the fact that a rifle could be sold for six times its cost price on the North-western frontier making the game worth the candle.

After being weather-bound in Maskat for three days, we continued our voyage up the Gulf, arriving at Bushire a few hours before the Resident, who had completed his tour by a visit to Bahrein. At Bushire the effects of the arms question were very much to the fore, as the Persian official entrusted with the post of confiscator was the well-known *Malik-u-Tajár*, who, it was whispered, had applied for the task to gratify his personal animosities, while the "man in the street" gave it as his opinion that in Persia "Martini Khán" was Sháh.

FROM LUSTRED POTTERY.

CHAPTER XXVI

ACROSS BASHÁKIRD

Prospero.—"We must prepare to meet with Caliban,
A devil, a born devil, on whose nature
Nurture can never stick."
—*The Tempest*, ACT iv., *Scene* I

I WAS not left inactive at Bushire very long, for on reporting my arrival, I received orders to join the Governor-General of Kermán at Fahraj, and march down with him on to the rear of the Karwánis. It was decided that Bandar Abbás should be my starting-point, and final instructions from Tehrán only reached me a few hours before the return of the ss. *Assyria*. As the officers of the B. I. Company were on strike, this was, so far as I knew, the last chance of proceeding down the Gulf for an indefinite period. However, in spite of the short notice, my plan of keeping everything ready and packed for a six months' journey stood me in good stead, and that evening found me once again on board the *Assyria*, with servants, tents, and stores all complete. As generally happens, we had a particularly rough passage to Bandar Abbás, where I boarded the *Lapwing*. The sea rose suddenly in the afternoon, and going on shore was risky, but my luggage had all been landed in the morning, and I was bound to follow.

It was really very rough, and the boatmen somewhat lost heart, the anchorage being a good two miles off shore. We were distinctly glad to reach *terra firma*, and I could not help thinking of Sir Dodmore Cotton and Sir Thomas Herbert, who also "landed safely, though Neptune made us first dance upon his liquid billows, and with his salt breath seasoned the *Epicinia*."[1]

The purchase of camels here occupied nearly a week, and this being the first occasion on which I had spent more than a few hours at Bandar Abbás, I will take the opportunity to give a description of it.

The port of Gombrun was always of importance, and during the period of prosperity enjoyed by the island of Hormuz, would naturally form the starting-point for caravans. Upon its capture from the Portuguese, it was renamed Bandar Abbás or the Port of Sháh Abbás, to commemorate the victory. A study of the map will show the importance of this harbour, the whole of the overland trade between East and West, at one period, being attracted to it by the fact that further west the route was flanked throughout by nomads of the most predatory type, and further east caravans would have to undergo, to some extent, the horrors of the Lut. For a short time the port of Tíz was also in favour, but there is no doubt that the additional land journey to reach it must have made transport more expensive.

Outside the modern town, which lines the beach, are fast vanishing remains of masonry buildings, and the present Government and Custom House was in past times the Dutch factory. This was a grand edifice, and its massive beams and flooring still look as strong as ever. However, appearances are deceptive, as the *Daria Begi*, who must weigh sixteen stone, had broken through a few months previously, and fallen some fifteen feet, miraculously escaping injury. The importance of Bandar Abbás to-day, is, as yet, scarcely appreciated. Its drawback is a terribly bad climate, upon which all travellers have commented, in more or less quaint and forcible language. Of these no one can surpass Dr Fryer: "But I proceed to acquaint you that nothing is left here but a sensible Map of Purgatory, if that may please some to be a Road to Paradise; to see how the Fiery Element makes the Mountains gape, the Rocks cleft in sunder, the Waters stagnate, to which the Birds with hanging Wing repair to quench their Thirst; for want of which the Herds do low, the Camels cry, the Sheep do bleat, the barren

[1] *Some Yeares Travels into Africa and Asia the Great*, p. 111.

Earth opens wide for Drink, and all things appear calamitous for want of kindly Moisture." [1]

The Kuh-i-Ginao, which rises to a height of some 7000 feet, thereby cutting off all air from the port, is easily accessible, being but a night's ride from the town. I sent Sultán Sukhru to explore the range, and he found gardens and plenty of water at an elevation of some 5000 feet, which shows that at any rate Bandar Abbás possesses an adjacent hill station, which Bushire does not. It can also boast of a comparatively fair harbour, whereas at Bushire ships lie in an open roadstead far away from the land, vessels of heavy draught hardly being able to get within sight of the town.

At the end of the last century the Bushire-Shiráz route was less unsafe than those leading inland from Bandar Abbás; therefore the British Residency was established at Bushire, and it became the headquarters of trade, Kerim Khán, the great Zand, making efforts to protect it. I venture to forecast that in twenty years' time, Mohamera and Ahwáz on the west, and Bandar Abbás on the east, will be the two great ports of Southern Persia, while Bushire will sink into comparative insignificance, and will only be used for local traffic.

From Bandar Abbás four [2] caravan routes radiate into the interior, and these I now propose to deal with, as no description that I have read is even approximately accurate. The most westerly runs to the district of Sirján, and is, generally speaking, a winter route. In Sirján it bifurcates, the main branch running to Yezd, and striking the Kermán-Yezd road to the west of Rafsinján, while a less important track runs to Kermán. As much of the through traffic changes hands in the Yezd *bázárs*, this route is naturally the most important, but, owing to the absence of security, it is at times almost deserted.[3] The second through route, which we followed for some stages, runs *via* Manuján to Narmáshir. Thence the major part of the traffic is carried across the Lut to Neh and Meshed.

Between these main trunk lines, if they may be so termed, lie the direct Kermán tracks. These run together for some four or

[1] *Travels into Persia*, p. 228.

[2] I do not count the ancient route *via* Lár to Shiráz, which is only used for local traffic.

[3] This was the case at the end of 1900.

BANDAR ABBÁS.

[To face p. 300.

five stages, to a point south of the famous or infamous Tang-i-Zindán or Prison Defile, where whole caravans are occasionally drowned by a sudden flood. A few miles east of the village of Niu the winter road, *via* Gulashkird and Jíruft across the Jabal Báriz range, breaks off from the summer route *via* the Tang-i-Zindán, Báft, and Bardsír. In addition, there is a rough route *via* Rahbur, and the route across Sárdu, which was followed by Marco Polo, neither of which is open for traffic until May. From Kermán goods are forwarded to Birjand or Meshed, but Khorasán is mainly supplied by the other routes, although the Nushki-Sistán road threatens to divert the traffic to one where the *Pax Britannica* is being enforced for about half the distance.

The above details will show the great importance of Bandar Abbás. In addition to its native population, which fluctuates from 8000 to 4000 inhabitants, it is also the temporary home of some 50 Hindus, while the beach presents a varied scene in which Baghdád Armenians, Persians, Arabs, Afgháns, and Baluchis, all play their part, not to mention an occasional European. It is not under the province of Kermán, as its geographical and commercial position would lead one to expect, all the ports being ruled by the Governor of Bushire, an arrangement due to the desire to farm the customs to the greatest advantage. Indeed, it was never in modern times a part of Kermán, Persian authority being delegated to the Sultáns of Maskat, who ruled the district for about a century, until, some thirty years ago, the reigning Sultán was too weak to maintain himself even at his capital. Persia then resumed control of the port and its customs, the trade of Kermán, no doubt, benefitting by the change. In the spring of 1900 Captain Hunt of the Indian Political Service was directed to found a Vice-Consulate at the port.

To return to my journey, I was forced to spend some days in buying camels, as it was impossible to hire, and there was even more difficulty in engaging drivers at a reasonable rate, the local authorities wanting to make too much profit for themselves. However in time everything was arranged, and on 23rd February we started off, in spite of considerable heat, toward Mináb (*vulgo* Minao).

A special riding-camel, an Arab thoroughbred, had been bought for my use, as horses were out of the question in the famine-stricken desert that lay before us; but not only did she turn out a jibber, but when we halted for a few minutes at the hamlet of Nákhodá, some five miles on our way, she absolutely declined to be ridden any further, and flung herself down on the ground, thereby materially damaging her rider. I was finally taken in tow by a servant, and even then she backed at every favourable opportunity; consequently, I did not enjoy the first stage.

There are two roads to Mináb, and we followed the northern or longer one, as there are no villages on the direct track, which hugs the coast. As it was, we had to cross two inlets with treacherous bottoms, while in parts the going was greasy. We camped near some wells in the district of Deh No, which is inhabited by sixty Baluch families, owning thirty wells and four hundred date-trees. The main caravan came in very late, and we were then informed that it had been held up by eight Bahárlus armed with Martinis. They had begun to loot, but the servants told them that it was very dangerous to touch a Consul's things; after discussing this point, they finally concluded that they had better run no risks, and went on their way, having taken only a basket of dates. Finding, however, that one camel had taken advantage of the confusion to bolt with its load, we decided to halt a day and send out a search-party, which discovered the missing animal with load intact.

Three long but level stages brought us to Mináb, which possesses the most extensive date-groves in Persia. The palms were being fertilised by the process of inserting a spathe of the male tree into that of the female, one male palm sufficing to fertilise thirteen female trees. That this is a very ancient custom is shown by the figures of eagle-headed deities found in the palace of Assur-násir-pal at Nimrud, which carry a basket in the left hand, and an uplifted palm-spathe in the right, ready for insertion.[1]

We were once again on classic soil, the river being the Greek Anamis, and close by was Harmozia, the landing-place of Nearchos, since the period of whose journey the river has evidently shrunk in volume. Mináb is the metropolis for Bashákird, whose savage inhabitants barter skins and wool for copper vessels, and occasionally for sugar. Tea is not yet appreciated, as will be seen later on. The Bandar Abbásis mostly come to Mináb for the summer, not, I opine, because it is much cooler, but in order to be near the dates. Henna, indigo, mangoes, oranges, limes, and plantains are all

[1] British Museum, Nimrud Gallery, slabs 30, 33, 34, 39, 40.

grown in considerable quantities, and matting and rough plaids are manufactured. The inhabitants number five thousand, among whom two British Indian Mohamedans born in Mináb, and some Hindus, appeared to handle most of the trade.

As Sultán Sukhru was due to follow us with final orders, we halted two days, and tried to find out something about Bashákird, while we completed the number of our camels and laid in four loads of dates for their fodder. Camels are, however, not ordinary beasts, and although almost all of our strings[1] ate dates greedily, two or three camels would not touch them, and even to the end of the journey resisted most violently when balls of the obnoxious fruit were forced down their throats.

Our last night at Mináb was among the worst that I have spent in Persia, a furious gale blowing, which brought down palm after palm round our tents, while, even worse, the foul dust and insects from the filthy camping-ground filled our mouths, noses, and ears, and for days we could not get our belongings clean.

The route led up the Mináb river, where we were perhaps following in the footsteps of Alexander's admiral. The track was very rough, the weather hot, and at sixteen miles, near the Gardan-i-Pichal, a low tortuous pass, we met a peasant, who informed us that the road was blocked by forty brigands from Márz, in Bashákird, and that he was hastening in to report the fact. As may be supposed, the so-called escort of villagers was all for a strategic movement to the rear, but I freely discounted the number, and we pushed on in skirmishing order. The only four men sighted vanished among the hills, and we were not disturbed, much to my relief.

At some eighteen miles, the Rudkhána Duzdi[2] or the River of Theft, effected a junction with the main stream, and late at night we reached Birinti, which is in Rudán, a sub-district of Fárs, the traveller thus passing through two districts before Kermán territory is reached. The following day we reached Jagin, which figures largely in Baluch legends, as the place where the Kinds (who claim to be Arabs, and were expelled as supporters of Ali) first met the rulers of the province. They say that they travelled to Kermán

[1] A string of camels consists of seven, attended by two men.

[2] More water is brought down by this tributary than by what is considered to be the main river; its basin is also much more extensive.

"between the earth and the sky," which probably means that they took ship at Basra.

Here I was once again in my district, Jagin being a village of Rudbár, whose ruler I had known for many years. Another easy stage brought us to the famous fort of Manuján, which, even in decay, is a formidable-looking work. Mohamed Ibráhim, in his history, mentions its capture by *Malik* Dinár at the end of the twelfth century of our era. Its garrison was tortured to death, and the stores of indigo and Brazil wood were all burnt. Some two centuries later it was seized by Afghán and Jermán[1] mercenaries. Owing to its position on the borders of Bashákird, its walls have, no doubt, seen numberless sieges.

We camped in a date-grove, where our camels enjoyed excellent grazing for the first time, although there was also some poisonous vegetation, which caused the death of one of them. At Manuján, although there is a considerable population, nothing could be procured on account of the drought; we were therefore able to congratulate ourselves on being practically independent of the country.

As I could gain no reliable news of the *Ásaf-u-Dola's* movements, I determined to march on towards the north-east, especially as Durrán Khán, Governor of Rudbár, was living some two stages off in that direction, and would, I felt sure, bring me the latest information. The route lay at first across reedy scrub, and at about a mile we reached the Mináb river, here some twenty yards wide; thence we entered more open country, which continued as far as our camp at Khána Sháh. As we were now close to Márz, we kept a careful look-out all night, and although we were once alarmed, we found that the supposed brigands were peaceable travellers.

The next stage lay throughout among low hills, and as it was there that we expected an attack, every precaution was taken in the way of scouting and patrolling, although I felt that it was a bit of a farce. I had been instructed to procure an escort from the Governor of Bandar Abbás, but, as I anticipated, he had no soldiers himself. I consequently engaged some armed villagers, who, I hoped, would keep watch at night, and on this occasion I kept the head of the escort close to me, telling him that I should shoot him if his people bolted, but they were in such a state of panic, that even this "en-

[1] The Jermán were Mongols, originally sent to garrison Kermán, in the time of the Kara Khitei dynasty.

couragement" would have been of little avail, had I ever dreamed of carrying out my threat.

Near the crest of a low pass we saw a cairn marking the site of a murder committed four days previously. A large party of Afgháns, armed to the teeth with Martinis, was carrying sugar and tea to Rigán, when a band of brigands, taking advantage of the darkness, fired a volley, killing one man and wounding two others. Before their comrades could come up, seven camel loads of sugar and tea were carried off. By a curious coincidence, the sugar belonged to a British subject, and when the *Ásaf-u-Dola* asked me out of whom he ought to squeeze the compensation, I was able to inform him that the headman of Rámishk had sold sugar to my servants at about half Bandar Abbás rates, and was a cousin of the leader of the *chappao*. The tea was at once thrown away as useless!

The sun was very trying—we were now well into March—and I was quite knocked up when we reached our halting-place at Káhn Mírza, a small hamlet situated on the last stream of sweet water that we were destined to see for some days. Durrán Khán came down from a village some miles off, and informed me that the Governor-General had already left Rigán, and was only four or five stages from Bampur, and I had in consequence to make up my mind as to what course I ought to adopt. My orders were to proceed to Fahraj to join the Governor-General, but as his instructions were to march to the coast immediately, it was obviously out of the question to indulge in a stern chase. Finally, after looking at the question from every side, I determined to send the *Sadr Ázam's* letter, containing orders for the *Ásaf-u-Dola*, together with a letter from the *Chargé d'Affaires*, and one from myself, explaining the position on the Rapsh, by a running camel across the desert to Fahraj, and to march east across the blank on the map[1] and find Rámishk, as I knew that by so doing I should cut across the Governor-General's route.

Durrán Khán departed somewhat annoyed, as I had declined to give him a rifle which he had asked for as a present. This I had refused, because, in the first place, I had none to spare, and in the second place, I had determined not to give away any rifles, which might possibly be used "agin the Government."

[1] It was not until long after my journey that I found that that eminent Indian traveller, *Khán Bahádur* Yusuf Sharif, had visited Bashákird.

We now began to march across the tract of country which lies between the mountains of Basháкird and the Jáz Morián. As I had fixed many of these peaks four years previously, when travelling to the north of this lake, in ordinary circumstances this section of my journey would have been immensely interesting. However, much to my annoyance, I was prostrate with fever, and consequently remembered very little of what I saw, although both Nasrulla Khán and Sultán Sukhru noted down everything as we marched along. The country was covered with rich camel grazing and was perfectly level, but the well water was vile; moreover, it rained heavily every day, though perhaps it was owing to this that I was able to continue the march.

Rámishk, which I was the first European to visit, is situated on the outer or northern edge of the Basháкird hills, lying in a fork between two branches of a *nala*, both of which held water at the time of our visit. There is a fair-sized date-grove, and, counting the adjacent hamlets, a population of two thousand. We were still in Márz territory, and also almost due north of, and not very far from the district of Karwán, where we heard that a night attack had been delivered, and that the British and Persian forces had been driven out of the country.

Although I did not believe this, the Basháкirdis did and in consequence we received information that we should be attacked. My illness made me reckless, and, failing to realise the seriousness of the situation, I told my informant that if a British Consul were murdered, the heads of a thousand Basháкirdis would have to be cut off by way of compensation, not counting the forty or fifty that our party would certainly kill! This bluff, I afterwards heard, saved the situation, as it struck the Basháкirdis as particularly hard that those who were killed in the attack would not be allowed for in calculating the thousand. A second report came in that the *Daria Begi* had been wounded in a skirmish, and only two Tangistánis shot, and it was also rumoured that four hundred camelry were on their way from the north to Rámishk, whence they would be able to operate on the rear of the Karwánis. However, no letter came from the *Ásaf-u-Dola*, although we heard that a messenger had missed us, but when we knew that the troops were actually coming, we felt sure that the Governor-General had received the *Sadr Ázam's* instructions, and was carrying them out. We consequently decided to proceed to Fánoch, where we hoped to meet His Excellency. Accordingly, I was once again hoisted on to my camel, and we continued the march, this time through hilly country.

We followed up the Rámishk *nala*, passing several hamlets and date-groves, the district being thickly populated for Baluchistán, and, crossing the watershed, we descended to the hamlet of Daggaz. The next march was along a track so difficult to find that we lay down perforce by the road, and slept till the false dawn; we then crossed miles of the most broken and rugged ground, finally arriving at the important village of Kutáich. I was at last in Fánoch territory, and very soon the Governor, an old acquaintance, appeared, and expressed much pleasure at seeing me. He told me that his uncle, *Sardár* Husein Khán, was at Mihán, some thirty miles to the south, where there was a strong natural fortress which had never yet been taken.[1] His father, Chákar Khán, an old friend of mine, was close by, but was too ill to come in and see me.

I was given a very friendly message from *Sardár* Husein Khán, but this I declined to receive, and at the same time sent him a reminder that he could expect nothing from me, as he had not only failed, but had not even tried to seize the murderers. I said that the British Government did not forget, and that it would never relax its efforts until justice was done, nor would the Persian Governor-General rest until the guilty were brought to the gallows. As an instance of this, I pointed out that *Mir* Sháhdád, whom they all knew, had attacked and wounded Major Muir, and then for years had wandered about, until, utterly worn out, and without a place to lay his head, he had finally surrendered in despair. In accordance with their custom, the Baluchis, who are a feckless, lazy, and almost hopelessly backward race, made promises which I knew they would not keep, as they rarely carry out an agreement except from fear, and I marched on towards Fánoch, without having accomplished much as regards Husein Khán.

Two marches before reaching that village, the long expected messengers from Fahraj arrived with a letter from the *Ásaf-u-Dola*, to the effect that he had received the *Sadr Ázam's* instruc-

[1] There is said to be an inscription giving the names of the Generals who attacked it, probably under Sháh Abbás and Nádir Sháh; their names were Ali Kuli Khán and Haider Kuli Khán.

tions, and, although unable to move owing to fever, he had at once despatched an influential Baluch and a Persian General to point out to the Karwánis that they must surrender the murderers, or else be attacked both in front and rear; also, that he had sent a large force to Rámishk ready to march south, if necessary, and finally, that he hoped to see me at his camp.

Once again I had to decide as to my plans. Everything had already been set in motion satisfactorily, and my mission had so far been accomplished, but I was daily growing weaker, the terrible heat, which was generally over 100 degrees from 11 to 4, preventing my recovery. These circumstances united in directing my journey towards the coast, and I wrote to the Governor-General, thanking him for his prompt action and regretting that I could not proceed to Fahraj. I then continued the march to Fánoch, where I struck my 1893-4 journey, after having safely travelled across Basbákird, which is yet another striking instance of the rule that inaccessible regions possess a savage population.

The Bashákirdi is, I would venture to suggest, the original inhabitant of Baluchistán, with a skin rather darker than that of a native of Bombay, and a very low level of intelligence. His dress is not peculiar, except that it is scantier than in other parts of Baluchistán. On the coast there is a mixture of negro blood as elsewhere. Geographically speaking, Bashákird consists of one main rugged range running from east to west, which serves as a watershed to streams draining either into the Arabian Sea or the Jáz Morián. North of this is the open plain running down to the *hámun*, while to the south are numerous low rocky hills, the district forming a barrier between Persia and Baluchistán.

Lying apart from caravan routes, ancient or modern, until some twenty-five years ago its fastnesses had never been penetrated. Mr E. Floyer, the author of *Unexplored Baluchistán*, saw its hills when stationed at Jásk, and the longing grew in his mind, until he had carried out an adventurous but successful journey to Anguhrán. In 1888 Lieut. Galindo, of the Sussex Regiment, travelled from west to east through the heart of the country, and in June 1894 Major Massy and Captain Medley, both of the 19th Bengal Lancers, marched to Kermán from Jásk in the middle of the hot weather. These latter officers I met at Karachi just as they were starting, and I felt very anxious as to their safety, unt-

I heard from the *Farmán Farmá* that he had sent down to meet them, which was fortunate, as their camelmen had deserted, and they were stranded.

My own line lay mostly to the north of the hills, and consequently I came but little into contact with the aborigines, the people at Rámishk being comparatively civilised. On making a present of a knife, I was asked whether it came from *Karkhána Rájers*, which I finally understood to mean Messrs Rodgers and Sons, the famous cutlers, who have, I feel sure, seldom received a higher proof that their "Sheffield whittles" are appreciated in remote corners of Asia.

As a sign of the poverty of Bashákird, I may mention that until a few years ago no attempt was made to levy taxes, and even now its revenue, paid irregularly and at the rifle's muzzle, amounts to only Ts. 800, or about £160 per annum. Durrán Khán of Rudbár farms the district, but I do not think that his post is an enviable one, especially as he is held responsible for raids.[1]

The hill country is very rough and difficult for laden camels, the traveller constantly marching up or down stony valleys full of dwarf-palm, with here and there a grove of half-wild dates. As a set-off to this gloomy picture, which is deepened by the intense heat in summer, there is, generally speaking, a plentiful supply of sweet water. A very rough estimate would give the district eight thousand inhabitants.

At Fánoch I congratulated myself that fate had been kind in allowing me to march across the last blank on the map of Persia, which I had gazed across with longing eyes from the summit of Kuh-i-Fánoch some four years previously, and, after a halt of a day, we commenced our rush down to the coast.

My reasons for moving quickly were partly to frustrate a band of Karwánis, which was said to be lying in wait for us, and

[1] Starting from the west, there are four sub-divisions, all of which pay £40 per annum, and so may be considered to contain an approximately equal population. Sindark consists of some fifteen villages and hamlets, and as it borders on Mináb, whither its inhabitants occasionally resort, it is the least savage sub-district. Jakdán, further east, was visited by Galindo, who describes the village as infinitely squalid and miserable. The district contains twenty-four villages and hamlets, some of which are close to Jásk. Anguhrán was visited both by Floyer and Massy, and has fourteen villages, while finally Márz, with its capital of Rámishk, boasts of twenty-two villages and hamlets.

partly to reach the coast without a breakdown, as my weakness was increasing daily. For two stages we followed our 1893 route, but as we were not making for Geh, we marched down the Sirhá river, which we struck at Pothán; Sultán Sukhru laid in a stock of Mokht bangles as we passed by that village, and at Naokinjá we again joined our 1893 route.

Our mode of travelling was to start directly after dinner, which was served at 4.30 to 5 P.M. One guide and the servants accompanied me on running camels, our march taking from four to seven hours, according to its length. On the guide's camel was strapped my bed and bedding, and upon arrival this was set up, and I immediately fell asleep.

Daily it grew hotter and daily our camels broke down, but the end was near. The last night we travelled to Parag,[1] some fifteen miles from Chahbár, and there saw the welcome telegraph line, while I intercepted a packet of letters which was on its way to me from Rapsh. Hearing that the Salt River was too high to cross until 2 A.M., we lay down for a few hours, and then on again, one camel after another giving in, although their loads had been reduced to almost nothing. At the gap of Tíz only three camels out of eight were able to move, and it seemed as if we must break down almost within sight of Chahbár. At last, however, I looked down on the Telegraph Office, and in a short time was once again with fellow countrymen, and delighted to be able to rest. My hosts, Messrs Wilson and Keelan, were of course able to give me the news, and I was also in communication with Tehrán.

Two or three days after my arrival, we heard the good news that the Karwánis had thrown up the sponge, the *Ásaf-ud-Dola's* plans having worked to perfection, and we finally heard that Shái Mohamed, the chief murderer, had been captured, while *Malik* Jind had been shot in attempting to escape. Shái Mohamed was duly hanged at Jásk before an assemblage of chiefs, thereby pointing the indelible moral that British officials cannot be murdered with impunity, and that the Persian Government is both ready and able to ensure that stern retribution follows upon all such outrages.

Often good comes out of evil, and I cannot but think that the friendly co-operation of the two Powers has been an important

[1] Near this hamlet in the summer of 1900 M. Flün, a member of a Russian survey party, died and was buried at Chahbár.

MAKRÁN SCENERY.

[*To face p.* 310.

factor in allaying the spirit of unrest on both sides of the frontier. Baluchis have often asked me what pay they would receive were they to migrate, and although I have done my best to impress on them that it is hopeless to try and play off one frontier official against another, the sight of mutual and continued co-operation will, I am convinced, tend more than anything else to prove that the old order has changed, and that there is nothing left for them but to settle down and till their fields.

During my stay at Chahbár I lived principally upon fish and turtles' eggs, the latter being so common that the Baluchis feed their camels on them! I telegraphed to Karachi for the mail to pick me up, and on 14th April said good-bye to my kind hosts, wishing them a speedy change of station, as Chahbár, although perhaps a shade better than Jásk, is no place for a white man in the summer. At Maskat I was, as usual, in quarantine, but Colonel and Mrs Meade, who were also there, very kindly visited me at a distance, and I was also fortunate in being with my old skipper, Captain Simpson. At Bandar Abbás we set our happy homesick camelmen on shore, and again came in for bad weather up to Bushire, where I was welcomed by a day's quarantine, to be spent on the island of Abbásak. However, I had as companion a Swiss traveller, M. Veillon, and we rejoiced that we had escaped the fate of the *Patna*, whose passengers, owing to a case of plague, had not been allowed to land at Bushire, and, consequently, had proceeded to Basra; the steamer stuck on the bar, and then, after a considerable detention, they finally underwent nine or ten days' quarantine on Abbásak, taking up their quarters the day after we left.

Early the following morning we landed at Bushire, whither I was glad to return after an exciting trip of two months' duration.

DESIGN FROM A PLATE.

CHAPTER XXVII

FROM BUSHIRE TO SHIRÁZ

"Here Art-magick was first hatched: Here Nimrod for some time lived: Here the great Macedonian glutted his Avarice and Bacchism. Here the first Sibylla sung our Saviour's incarnation. Hence the Magi are thought to have set forth towards Bethlehem."

—SIR THOMAS HERBERT on Shiráz.

I HAVE not hitherto described Bushire, which served so often as my starting-point, and is at the present time of such commercial and political importance.

It is situated on a peninsula, which sometimes becomes an island, as the *mashíla* or swamp which connects it with the mainland is frequently under water. The town itself, like its inhabitants, is half Persian, half Arab in character, and gradually rose into importance when Bandar Abbás became unsafe as a commercial *entrepôt*. The Residency is a spacious building, guarded by Bombay Marine Infantry, and contains offices, treasury, and stables, besides living rooms, but it possesses no garden, and the only lawn tennis court is in front on the beach, where the game has to be played *coram publico*.

Colonel Meade generally lives at Sabzabád, the highest part of the island, and seven miles south of Bushire, with which his office is connected by a telegraph line. At that hamlet there is a nice airy house with a garden, and outside is the open desert. Not far away, perhaps two miles, is the Telegraph Station of Reshire, with its neat blocks of buildings, and scattered about are other houses, that occupied by the bank being the most spacious. Although society suffers to some extent from these long distances and the rough tracks, yet British hospitality triumphs over this, and there are constant re-unions for lawn tennis and golf. Polo should also flourish, but that driving is preferred to riding, no doubt owing to the exhausting heat. During the winter the climate is occasionally bracing, but the long summer is very trying, although not so unhealthy as might be supposed. It is interesting to know that the peninsula was less barren some two thousand years ago than to-day, for Nearchos says, "This country is a peninsula, and called Mesambria; in it they found many gardens, and in them fruit-bearing trees of all kinds."[1]

Besides the Resident, who from his position of influence naturally leads the European colony, there are German, French,[2] and Dutch Consuls, the first two possibly for the purpose of creating trade, as they have few interests at present; Messrs Hotz's agent is Consul for the Netherlands, the appointment being *honoris causa*.

At Bushire I found my old host, Dr Scully, who had arranged to return to Shiráz with Colonel and Mrs Meade. I was invited to join the party, but as the accommodation was limited as far as Kazerun, and there was every prospect of unpleasant heat, it was decided that Veillon and myself should precede the main body as far as that little town, to which there was a choice of routes.

In 1893 I had marched by land to Borázjun, but this route was now unsafe, owing to the Tangistánis, who indeed robbed and murdered with more or less impunity all round the town. I therefore adopted the alternative way to Shif, a landing-place on the mainland a few miles to the north of Bushire, to which we were conveyed in the Residency launch, and as a strong *shamál*[3] was

[1] *Indika*, 39.

[2] In 1900 it was decided to open a school under the charge of the French Consul.

[3] The *Shamál* or North Wind is the most trying in the Persian Gulf.

blowing, we were only too glad when we finally turned our backs on the Persian Gulf.

At Shif there is a tower, but no *caravanserai*, so after tea we mounted our "hirelings," and were soon cantering across the level *mashíla*. Owing to the heat, we had not started until 5 P.M.; night therefore still found us on the road, and our guides, who apparently knew their way only by day, tried to persuade us to follow a road running due west. After many disappointments, we finally reached our camp, which was pitched at Kasho (Khosháb), the site of the only battle in the Anglo-Persian War of 1857. This campaign merits an account, as many people are not aware that such an event ever took place.

Early in that year General Outram had landed at Bushire, after storming Reshire, which had been magnificently held by Tangistánis, our loss being extremely heavy, and had then marched with two mixed brigades to Borázjun. There a Persian force under the *Shuja-ul-Mulk* was encamped, which retired on his approach, leaving everything at his mercy. After blowing up the powder magazine, the British force retired towards Bushire, having no intention of marching up the *kotals* to Shiráz. The Persian army[1] boldly attacked at Khosháb by night, but was repulsed with heavy loss, as against a very trifling list of casualties on our side.

At Borázjun, we stopped at the Telegraph Office, where I was soon visited by my old friend of the Boundary Commission, Suliman *Mírza*, who was on the war-path, blowing brigands from guns, and generally endeavouring to inspire the Tangistánis with terror. At the time of our visit he was preparing to instal a new Governor, the former one having taken to the hills after robbing a member of the Persian Gulf Trading Company, for which he was called upon to pay an indemnity. A second visitor was an aged *Seiid*, who remembered the British occupation of Borázjun. He told us how the General had posted a sentry over his house, to ensure his being unmolested, for which long-past act of kindness he is still, not unnaturally, grateful.

The temperature in the airless room was ninety-nine degrees, which, combined with the exposure to the sun, brought on a return

[1] I have been informed that the attack was made by Kashgai nomads, and not by the regular troops.

of fever, and we decided to march the following evening, instead of in the morning. Our advance party was a stage ahead, but in the afternoon I was horrified to learn that a valuable waler, which I had purchased at Bombay, but had not had time to break in, had galloped back from Daliki. With much difficulty he was caught, and we afterwards learned that the stable floor had collapsed under his weight—he stands sixteen hands two inches—and poor "Dragoon's" quarters had fallen bodily into a well, which so alarmed him that upon scrambling out he had broken away.

At Borázjun is a *caravanserai* which Lord Curzon describes as the finest he saw in Persia; I there returned Suliman *Mirza's* visit, and was glad to find that he had risen in the world. He was now at the age of twenty-eight a field-marshal, had two silver maces carried in front of him, and was surrounded by quite a staff of officers.

To Daliki the track was level but very stony, as Colonel Meade, who tried it a few days later in a *tonga*, found to his cost, and I had additional reason to be thankful that "Dragoon" had not broken his knees during his flight. Just before reaching this stage, we crossed a stream smelling strongly of sulphur and running emerald green. Unsuccessful borings for petroleum have been made on this spot, but so far the only product consists of bitumen, which is used for dressing camels' backs and for horses' hoofs. Daliki lies in a charming date-grove, and is on the banks of the Shápur river, an important body of water, but undrinkable at this point. We put up in the tiny rest-room and gasped all day, although the temperature was only ninety-seven degrees, but Daliki is one of those choice spots, like Sibi, which, lying at the foot of ranges, can get no air, and are in consequence very much worse than stations in the open.

We were now about to enter the world-renowned defiles, but as Veillon was badly chafed and I was as weak as a rat, we decided to break up the first long march into two, and sleep for a few hours on the way. Two miles after quitting Daliki we entered a network of low, rugged hills, and were very glad to reach the river-bank; there the air was fresher, and near the fine bridge built by the *Mushir-ul-Mulk* dinner was awaiting us. At 1 A.M. we continued our march through the grandest scenery, the frowning cliffs on each side faintly lit up by the moon impressing me more than anything we passed during the other stages. At the foot of Kotal-i-Mallu[1] the idea forced itself into the mind that we were climbing into a new land, so sheer is the precipice, up which a corkscrew path is cut in the soft earth by the mules, the engineers of Persia. The ascent was much steeper than any that is laid down for cavalry in drill books, but as we met no descending caravans, it only took some three hours to arrive at the top, where, in the cool of the dawn, the difference in the flowers brought the delightfully simple lines of Browning's *Pied Piper* to memory, or rather the words haunted me, and I found myself repeating:

> "And flowers put forth a fairer hue,
> And everything was strange and new."

The altitude was only 1700 feet, but we were once again in the open, and the rest-room at Konár Takhta was quite palatial. The next "ladder," the Kotal-i-Kamárij, is the steepest of all and the worst, especially if, as has been my fate on both occasions, it is crowded with mules. The road is worn in the naked rock, millions of hoof treads having formed steps, up which our ponies picked their way.

The *kotal* is famous as the scene of one of Kerím Khán's victories at a time when this extraordinary man, who rose by sheer force of character and rectitude from being a common soldier to the throne of Persia (although he always termed himself *Vakil* or Regent and not *Sháh*), was fleeing from an Afghán claimant. He and his troops were at the bottom of the pass, and Asad Khán half-way down, when the local tribes, who were concealed in the crags above, attacked the Afgháns, who were thus caught like rats in a trap.

The track runs parallel to a gorge for most of its distance, but finally enters it, the road filling up the whole of the distance between the cliffs. From the summit there is a slight descent, and we found ourselves at Kamárij, a village with an elevation of 3000 feet; the climb was therefore well worth the labour. From this point our course lay through the Tang-i-Turkán, famous for its mention by Sadi, who, in addition to suffering from the difficulties of the road, was robbed in the Turk's Defile.

Upon clearing the defile, we rode north-west, instead of swing-

[1] *Mallu* is a corruption of *Malun* = Accursed.

DALIKI.

[*To face p.* 316.

ing round east to Kazerun, and, traversing the pretty village of Diriz, with its graceful palm-grove and ruined fort, we marched up the left bank of the river. The district is very fertile, with irrigation channels every hundred yards until we approached Shápur, which is grandly situated at the mouth of a gorge. For nearly a mile we passed through ruins, which were more interesting than the shapeless mounds which mark most ancient sites in Persia. Here and there were the remains of a round arch, and we also saw battlemented towers, the solid masonry of which promised to hold good for many a year.

As we drew near the gorge, which is less than a hundred yards wide at its west end, we saw the famous rock sculptures on the right bank, while the fort rose on the left, commanding the road. The rock on which its walls are still standing is carefully scarped in parts; elsewhere Nature has made it inaccessible, and we quite felt that the site was worthy of the city.

No sovereign belonging to the house of Sásán has left such works behind him as Shápur, the bridge at Shuster, which has already been referred to, the rock sculptures near Persepolis, and the similar works of art which I am about to describe, besides other ruins which I have not visited, forming a remarkable series of undertakings for a single sovereign to execute.

Passing the fort we entered the gorge, and in the first place visited the tablets on the left bank, two in number. The first of these represents the triumph of Shápur over the Roman Emperor Valerian, of which an example in a much better state of preservation is to be seen at the *Naksh-i-Rustam*. The second tablet, which we did not notice at first, owing to its being a short distance further on, portrays the investiture of Cyriadis, also in the presence of Valerian. Shápur, who rides a charger which resembles engravings of the ancient British war-horse, but gives the impression of not being up to his weight, is surrounded by soldiers chiselled in other divisions of the tablet. I asked our guide what the scene represented, and he promptly replied, "A school"!

Fording the river, which runs with a swift current and is deep in the gorge, we proceeded to examine the four tablets on the right bank, which represent similar scenes. The Sásánians were evidently men of few ideas, the submission of captives, and, in particular, the captive Valerian, playing the chief part in most of their sculptures. In a cave in the cliffs high above the valley is the great statue of Shápur, but as neither of us was in a fit state for the hour's climb we left that for a future date.

We found the tents unpleasantly warm, with a temperature of ninety-eight degrees, and most of the party bathed in the dangerously cool river. A swarm of young locusts on the left bank was apparently bent on suicide, to the evident approbation of the fish assembled just below who gobbled them up by thousands as they hopped into the water; it would be interesting to know why the locusts insisted on this method of being devoured.

We rode into Kázerun, parallel to the range on which Shápur is built, which soon sinks into insignificance, and made for a magnificent garden, the Bágh-i-Nazar, lying a mile to the south of the small town. Here we were among the finest orange trees I have ever seen, forming as they did an avenue some 200 yards long. In the afternoon the Governor came to call, bringing a letter of welcome from the *Farmán Farmá*, as well as a telegram to enquire how we were getting on, and the following morning the Resident's party arrived. It was unanimously agreed to halt a day or two and enjoy a rest, together with the post which was delivered at the same time.

Upon quitting the beautiful orange garden, one of the choicest spots in Persia, we rode for eight miles to the foot of the Kotal-i-Dukhtar or Daughter's Pass, her mother presumably being represented higher up in the Old Woman's Pass. The rise was very sudden, and the naturally stony track had been made worse by attempts at paving, but there was nothing very bad, as there were numerous paths, and we had not to wait for descending mules, nor was there any difficulty in passing caravans going the same way as ourselves. We camped in the oak forest, which it is to be hoped will not be burnt for fuel or used for building, although it seemed thinner than five years previously, the trees not being close enough to afford much shade. The Kotal-i-Pira-Zan or Pass of the Old Woman lay before us, and we could descry the *caravanserai* of Mián Kotal perched 2000 feet above our camp. The road was really not at all steep, and I remember that one member of the party walked most of the way up.

We pitched tents on the roof of the *caravanserai*, generally the only clean spot, the very nice set of private rooms being too malodorous for English noses. Our noon temperature was seventy-eight degrees, or some ten degree cooler than down below, and our altitude was 6000 feet, or rather higher than Shiráz itself. The following morning from the summit of the pass (7500 feet), we enjoyed a grand view to the south, looking across tier upon tier of dwindling hills, beyond which lay the sea, the whole clothed in that heat-mist so well known to Anglo-Indians.

The descent to the Arjan plain was rough, but we found yet another variety of scenery, green turf of a somewhat marshy order covering the whole *Dasht*. Were it not for the gigantic mosquitoes and the malaria, this valley would be a delightful place of residence, the surrounding hills being full of game—notably the maneless lion which haunts this locality—while the marsh and lake also afford excellent sport in the winter. Many of the tombstones, I noticed, were carved to represent a lion, or rather what was intended for a lion, either as a compliment to the king of beasts, or as extolling the valour of the villagers. The altitude of the Telegraph Office being about 6600 feet, we were enjoying a cooler climate than we should experience at Shiráz, the thermometer at 6 A.M. the next morning reading thirty-eight degrees.

Leaving this bit of Kashmir behind, we rose through low hills, until at 7200 feet we commenced our descent into the valley of the Kara Aghach, the classical Sitakos. The scenery vividly brought back Kalka, the starting-point for Simla, the high bushes in flower much resembling the jungle of the low hills, where the Himalayas rise from the plain. At Khán-i-Zinián, the *Farmán Farmá's* camel *jemadár* came in to see me. As he had been with me on the 1896 Commission, we were old acquaintances. He spoke very highly of the grazing, and generally thought Fárs a richer province than Kermán, which is emphatically the case.

This was our last cool camp, and we halted for two days, Veillon and Nasrulla Khán marching ahead to Shiráz, where the latter was naturally anxious to see his family. We broke up the long stage into two, and early on 19th May, after a continued descent, rode into Chinár-i-Rahdár, where we were met by Mr King Wood and Haider Ali Khán, the British Agent. We thence drove to Afifabád, the *Kawám-ul-Mulk's* garden, with its avenues of great cypresses and running streams, where his son welcomed the Resident. After this we again entered the carriages, and, escorted by some *sowárs* and clouds of dust, drew up at the Telegraph Garden, where the sight of trees, flowers, and neatly-kept paths formed a delightful termination to this section of my wanderings.

DESIGN IN COLOURS ON CLOTH OF GOLD.

CHAPTER XXVIII

FROM SHIRÁZ TO ISFAHÁN

"In trauell thitherwards he grieves, in wonder, to behold
The down-Fals of those stately Townes and Castels which, of old,
Whilst Persia held the Monarchie, were famous ouer all.
Nor Alexander wonne of these one Peece with labour small.
The mightie Citties Tauris and Persipolis he past;
Two ruin'd Gates, sundred twelue miles, yet extant of this last."
—JENKINSON, from *Albion's England*, cap. lxvi.

I NOW propose to give a brief account of Fárs, which will complete my mention of the provinces of Southern Persia, as I have already dealt with Kermán, Persian Baluchistán, and Arabistán. Fárs is the same word as the Greek *Persis*, from which, as mentioned above, the title of Pársi is also derived, as well as the term Persia, which we apply to the land of Irán. The province was the cradle of the Achaemenian dynasty, and it was from the rugged hills of Fárs that, after asserting his supremacy over Media, Cyrus the Great led those irresistible hosts to prey on the effeminate inhabitants of Babylonia.

Physically speaking, the province presents more or less the same characteristics that I have described at some length in chap. v., but it may, generally speaking, be laid down that the rainfall in Fárs is much heavier than in dry Kermán. A proof of this is given by the vineyards lining the hills in many parts, which depend entirely on the rainfall; this would be quite out of the question further east. There is also much better grazing, and in every respect Fárs is richer than Kermán.

Shiráz, the capital of Fárs, and the city which "turns aside the heart of the traveller from his native land," has a population of rather less than 50,000 inhabitants, and lies at an altitude of 5200 feet in a particularly stony valley, which has a width of perhaps twelve miles. It was the camp of the Arab invaders at the time of the conquest of Persia, and was founded as a city by Mohamed bin Alhakam, on whom the government of Fárs was conferred by the famous Hajjáj bin Yusuf. As, however, it boasts of remains of both Achaemenian and Sásánian sculptures, it was evidently a more ancient site. There are also the traces of a great fort, known as the Kala-i-Bandar or Port Fort, with two wells hewn to an immense depth in the solid limestone. One of these was, until quite recently, used for the execution of women taken in adultery, and the legend runs that some straw thrown down it appeared at Bushire! This stronghold certainly dates from pre-Mohamedan times, and the sculptures which adorn it are feeble specimens of the same art that is so gloriously displayed on the Mervdasht plain.

To-day Shiráz offers no imposing appearance, but we would fain believe that it was far otherwise when its elder poet indited:

> "Sadi, night and day, sorrowing over Shiráz, says:
> That all cities are hawks, but our city a royal eagle."

While immortal Háfiz, with equal love and pride, sings:

> "May every blessing be the lot,
> Of fair Shiráz, earth's loveliest spot!
> Oh, Heaven! bid Time its beauties spare,
> Nor print his wasteful traces there."

In fact to-day Shiráz is mainly famous as the former home of Irán's greatest bards, whose tombs are still to be seen, although much neglected.

As the city is too well known to require a full description from my pen, I will confine myself to remarking that the *bázárs* and palace well repay a visit. Nor should the traveller omit the splendid gardens, termed Masjid-i-Bardi, where the pleasure-loving citizens, the only Persians who really seem to enjoy life, spend most of the summer, every one entertaining in turn.

In a Shirázi's eyes his town is the acme of perfection, but most Europeans suffer considerably from the climate, fever and sleeplessness being common maladies. However, although I could not regain my health, the few months I spent at the capital of Fárs were pleasant enough. We had the best of lawn tennis, and I was also able to start polo, and had the roads not been so atrociously stony, our surroundings would have been everything that could be desired. In addition to this, the fact that the *Fárman Farmá* was Governor-General ensured that everything went smoothly, and many were the occasions on which we talked over what had happened since we last met, the Diamond Jubilee naturally interesting His Highness to no small degree.

Early in August Colonel and Mrs Meade marched to Kuh-i-Bamu, a high hill to the north of the city, where I joined them a few days later. The camp was pitched in a hollow near the only spring, and although we were at an elevation of 6700 feet, it was rather hot during the day. As compensation we ate the most delicious figs and grapes that I have ever tasted, and generally enjoyed *dolce far niente* for several days, until unexpected orders came for me to proceed to Luristán. Delighted to be once again on the move, and that towards a district I had not seen, I immediately returned to Shiráz, said good-bye to my friends, and at the end of August drove off north, the *Farmán Farmá* kindly lending his carriage to start me on the first very long stage. We stopped for tea at about seven miles from Shiráz, when Nasrulla Khán rejoined me, his faithful servant riding on a mule with saddle-bags crammed to bursting-point with sweets and bottles of sherbet.

For many a mile we followed the course of a diminutive stream, the famous Ruknábád which Háfiz celebrated in the following verse:

> "Still be thou blest of Him that gave
> Thy stream, sweet Ruknabád, whose wave
> Can every human ill assuage,
> And life prolong to Chizer's [1] age."

---

[1] Chizer or Khizr drank of the waters of eternity. He appears in the corner of the illustration facing p. 152.

Although we halted twice, for tea and dinner respectively, the route seemed interminable, and when we reached Zárgun at 1 A.M. every one dropped asleep until the mules came in.

The next march was a delightful contrast, and I much enjoyed long gallops on the Mervdasht plain, crossing Moore's Bendemeer[1] at about six miles from Zárgun. It runs in a dull muddy stream, some thirty yards wide, and with its bare banks chilled all my feelings of romance. The giant columns of Persepolis soon showed up on the opposite side of the valley, but I bore rather to the right, and, crossing a rich plain, as much cut up by great irrigation channels as Sistán, pulled up at Kinára, where I again rejoined my kind hosts, the Meades.

The marvels of this neighbourhood occupy some eighty pages in Lord Curzon's work, which I would strongly advise all travellers to read through carefully and then take with them to the *Takht-i-Jamshid*, as the Persians term it; otherwise, they are sure to miss a great deal. I would also suggest that more than one day be spent among the ruins of Persepolis, which, like the peerless Táj, show best by moonlight. If not, the traveller may leave, as I did after my first visit, with much bewilderment and little profit.

We reached the foot of the great platform early in the morning, and were first struck by the fact that some of the stones used in facing it were as large as many a room. "Dragoon" too was easily ridden up the shallow steps. The porch of Xerxes with its colossal bulls, which at once reveal their kinship to Assyrian art, was first passed through; then, turning to the right, we approached the northern staircase, leading up to the hall of Xerxes. Although it is partly buried, one could never tire of gazing on speaking likenesses of the various classes of people who lived more than 2000 years ago, as they came in procession, bearing gifts to honour the King of Kings on New Year's day, the vernal equinox.[2]

Desisting with difficulty from the fascinating amusement of guessing at the identity of the various peoples and offerings, we mounted the staircase and entered the great hall, covering nearly an acre. Here, perhaps, in the moonlight, the magic weirdness of

[1] Bendemeer is Band-i-Amir or The Amir's Dam; the altitude at the bridge is 5200 feet.

[2] Dividing up the groups are what I believe to be hill cypresses; at this period the garden cypress was probably unknown.

THE PORCH OF XERXES.

[*To face p.* 324.

the ruins appeals most fully to the imagination, the great seventy-foot fluted columns still standing to the number of twelve, all eloquently speaking of a mighty past. The "Babylon is fallen, is fallen" of the book of Isaiah was nowhere so forcibly evident as in this pillared waste, formerly the palace, where the *Sháh-in-sháh* showed himself to adoring multitudes from every clime.

Proceeding further, the palace of Darius, a comparatively small building, but in a better state of preservation, is reached. The doorways and other blocks of great size and high polish show clearly that this was the central hall of a building where the monarch resided. Personally, I had the feeling that such enormous blocks were rather wasted, especially as the intervals were evidently filled up with bricks, as in the buildings of to-day. I espied Professor Vambéry's name clearly cut in one corner, and when I wrote to inform the "ex-dervish" of the fact, he said that some of his happiest days were spent on the platform, with a donkey for his only companion, on whose back he used to visit the surrounding villages to procure bread and cheese.

Beyond, the palaces of Xerxes and Artaxerxes do not attract the visitor, as they cannot vie in interest with the other ruins, so turning towards the hill, we entered the Hall of a Hundred Columns, the largest structure on the platform, covering a full acre, but, alas! not a single pillar remains. The bas-reliefs on the doorways are, however, of the greatest interest and beauty. Apart from the king stabbing a griffin, which appears almost everywhere with monotonous reiteration, there is on the southern doorway a beautiful clearly-cut series of figures, representing the various subjects, who support the Great King. The monarch is seated on a throne, much resembling a high-backed chair, while above is shown a delicately-carved canopy, and the god Ormuzd hovers on high.

It may be of interest, before quitting Persepolis, to quote the account of this last piece of sculpture, as given by Josafa Barbaro.[1] "For upon this plaine there is a mighty stone of one peece, on the which arr many ymages of men graven as great as gyaunts, and above all the rest, one ymage like vnto that that we resemble to God the Father in a cercle, . . . and before hym the image of a man leanyng on an arche, which they saie was the fygure of Salomon."

After dinner in the porch of Xerxes and a moonlight reverie

[1] *Travels of Venetians in Persia*, p. 81 (Hakluyt Soc.).

among the columns, I said good-bye to the Resident and Mrs Meade, with whom I had been associated for the better part of a year, and with whom so many stirring and pleasant days had been spent, and the next morning, by sunrise, I was at the *Naksh-i-Rustam*, on my way north.

The Sásánian rock-sculptures which we saw here would, were it not for the greater attractions of Persepolis, fill the traveller with wonder; but before dealing with them, a few lines must be devoted to the Achaemenian tombs, below which they figure; these latter are elaborately decorated, the door being divided into four compartments, of which the three uppermost are solid, while the fourth is now open, the stone that originally formed it having in each case disappeared. None of these sepulchres are easily accessible, and travellers should not trust to the local guides, who are ill provided with ropes, and have probably never heard of a ladder.

Below are the rock sculptures of the Sásánians, seven in number, which will readily be recognised as more or less portraying the same subjects that we had seen at Shápur, but on a more grandiose scale.

While engaged during the summer in collecting references to the ancient game of *Gu-u-Chogán* or Polo, among the pieces of poetry brought to my notice was one from Firdusi's great epic, in which Zál, praising the prowess of Mehráb of Kábul, says

"In figure none approach him,
Not a man is his peer with the *Gu*."

This appeared to me to refer not to polo, but to a weapon, and probably the pear-shaped pendant which swings at the royal charger's quarters is intended for a mace. Against the usual theory that it was a tassel, I would urge that such ornaments are not fastened by chains, that it would be too heavy to serve such a purpose, and also that it does not appear in all the sculptures, as it otherwise probably would. In fact there is little doubt that it was a weapon which was either held in the hand and thrown, or else swung round the head and used as a mace. As all the Persians whom I have asked hold this view, and many term it *topuz* or mace, it would seem that Chardin was not very far out when he described it as a bullet used as a sling. It was, in fact, what is known as a "Morning Star." The solution of ancient problems is

THE HALL OF XERXES.

[*To face p.* 326.

often at our door, and at Yezd a game is played which consists in collecting a chain in the hand and throwing it at a friend. It is then jerked back and again prepared for action. This, I imagine, was the use of the pendant described, and, indeed, it must have served some such purpose, as it was certainly uncomfortable for the charger, and there was apparently only one, not two, to each horse.

Opposite the tombs is a small square building, the use of which has been explained in many ways—it resembles the early Lycian tomb in the British Museum—and further west are two fire altars, which I had altogether missed upon the occasion of my first visit. Our guide, when asked what they were, assured us that they were barber's tables, and grew angry when we threw doubt on the explanation. However, European travellers were not much better informed until this century, and there are few subjects on which more has been written wide of the mark than on these remains, anent which I cannot refrain from again quoting Josafa Barbaro: "A little further, there is a great ymage on horsebacke, seemyng to be of a boysterouse man: who they saie was Sampson; about the which arr many other ymages apparailed of the frenche facon, with longe heares."[1]

The sun soon grew hot, and hoping to return in the future to scenes of which it is impossible to tire, we kept up the right bank of the Polvár, the Medus of the ancients, and evidently the Eufra of Ludovico di Varthema,[2] who mistook it for the Euphrates. We passed the caves of Hajiabád, where we did not stop to inspect the famous bilingual inscription, and, crossing the river, were very glad to gain the shelter of the Telegraph Office at Sivand, the village from which our muleteers hailed. It is inhabited by Lurs, who industriously keep up their reputation as thieves, the treasury of a dismissed Governor-General having been their latest booty.

The march to Mashad-i-Murgháb, a distance of some thirty miles, which can be easily broken into two if desired, is one of the most interesting in Persia. At some five miles the track up the Polvár, which here gives a twist at right angles, opens on to a wide fertile plain, full of villages. After skirting this the gorge is again re-entered, the river flowing between frowning cliffs with fresh green reed beds. Trees abound wherever there is room for them,

[1] *Travels of Venetians in Persia*, p. 81 (Hakluyt Soc.).
[2] *Travels of Ludovico di Varthema*, p. 101 (Hakluyt Soc.).

but the gorge soon narrows to such an extent, that the track follows a passage cut in the solid rock, the construction of which must have been a great engineering feat in its day. Shortly after we emerged on to the Polvár plain, and looking back, wondered on which bank was the "very high hill," from which the Persian women and children looked down on one of the decisive battles of the world, whereby the Persians, from being a tribe of needy nomads, succeeded to the wealth and civilisation of Media, and to the rule of Western Asia.

From a military point of view, I felt inclined to favour the high precipitous hill on the left bank, which is steeper, and commands a better view than that on the right, but in any case we were again on classic ground, as by the river bank we found a tent pitched close to the mausoleum of Cyrus the Great, who perhaps of all the monarchs of Persia interests us the most.

The tomb, which has been the cause of so much discussion, and was certainly designed by a Greek architect, was originally surrounded by a colonnade, of which M. Dieulafoy gives a restored plan; indeed, the bases of many of the columns are still visible. Known for centuries as the Mashhad-i-Mádar-i-Sulimán, or The Tomb of the Mother of Solomon, the mausoleum stands on seven courses of white limestone, composed of enormous blocks, the lower steps being hard to climb, but the upper ones are shallower. The walls and roof are built of great blocks, beautifully fitted together, and still standing, in spite of the fact that the metal clamps have been scooped out by the nomads. To effect an entrance, we had to crawl through a very narrow doorway, which has been graphically described by Arrian.[1] The interior, which is blackened with smoke, was found to be ten feet five inches long by seven feet six inches wide and six feet ten inches high. This chamber was quite empty but for a string of votive offerings, while an Arabic inscription adorned the wall.

Arrian, who gives a description of Alexander's visit, says that the following inscription was on the tomb, "O man, I am Cyrus, the son of Cambyses, who founded the Empire of Persia, and was King of Asia. Grudge me not therefore this monument."[2]

[1] vi. 29. "And above was a house of stone, roofed, having a door that led within, so narrow that hardly could one man, and he of no great stature, enter, even with much difficulty."

[2] *Ibid.*

THE GOD ORMUZD HANDS THE KIDARIS TO SHÁPUR.

[*To face p.* 328.

SHÁPUR AND THE [illegible]

[*To face p.* [illegible]

In the early afternoon, we inspected the ruins of Pasargardae, consisting of a bas-relief of Cyrus, which is becoming indistinct, a column, a pillar, a building in ruins, resembling that at the *Naksh-i-Rustam*, and a second platform. This latter is built into the side of a low hill, and is not therefore dwarfed by its surroundings as the Persepolis platform is, when seen from a distance, but it has never been finished.

From Mashad-i-Murgháb, at which village I had struck the main road five years previously, we marched first across stony ranges, and then over open plains to Dehbid, the "Dehebeth" of Barbaro. This stage, which is famous for its length, was shortened by the kindness of Mr Jefferies of the Indo-European telegraphs, who met me in a smart dogcart some miles out. Since I had made his acquaintance in 1893, he had undergone a siege, the occasion being the death of H.I.M. Násir-u-Din, when the Arabs,[1] who believed that the Telegraph Station contained wealth beyond the dreams of avarice, the very instruments being of gold, according to rumour, determined, once for all, to settle this question.

Fortunately for the English community, consisting of Mr and Mrs Jefferies, who were joined by Mr and Mrs Dalton of the Imperial Bank, travelling with specie from Shiráz, the station is

[1] The following list of Arab tribes was given me by Mr E. J. Blackman in 1900:—

JABBAURA.

		Summer quarters	No. of Families
1.	Lo Mohamedi	Boanat	2000
2.	Marídi	"	2000
3.	Shíri	"	500
4.	Ghani	"	600
5.	Lavrduni	"	100
6.	Bahuli	"	100
7.	Kambari	Plain to east of Mashad-i-Murgháb	100
8.	Jábari	Dehbid	200
9.	Hindi	"	100
10.	Pir-i-Salámi	"	60
11.	Safari or Kuchi	"	450
12.	Nakd Ali	South of Dehbid	100
13.	Darázi	"	300
14.	Shikári	"	90
15.	Mahári	"	100
16.	Sabáhi	"	100
17.	Karái	"	400
	TOTAL		7300

surrounded by a seventeen-foot wall, and stands in a small garden, enclosing which is a second low wall, poplars growing between the two, which helped to screen the defenders. The *caravanserai* was first rushed by four hundred footmen, armed mainly with sticks, and some sixty cavalry, a large body of Arabs keeping up a fire on the Telegraph Station, to prevent any diversion from that quarter. Jefferies, in the meanwhile, had been reinforced by a few Persian soldiers, and when an attempt was made to rush the station, a sufficiently hot fire was kept up to prevent the Arabs doing anything more than scale the outer wall.

The telegraph lines were not cut, and the *Kawám-ul-Mulk*, the official head of the nomads of Fárs, on being communicated with, sent a message to the chief of the Kuti tribe, Yádulla Khán. This was conveyed in safety, and the besiegers were attacked by Yádulla Khán's tribe, and finally driven to plunder elsewhere, which they did with much thoroughness, the whole district being ravaged, and many villages burnt.

This same hamlet is also the scene of an act of heroism, which hitherto has been unnoticed. On the arrival of a telegraph inspector, Mr Blackman, one winter's afternoon, a man came in to report that his servant had been bitten by a mad wolf. This beast, after biting many other people, all of whom are reported to have died, next seized the cook in the dark passage leading into the

SHEIWÁNI.

		Summer quarters	No. of Families
1.	Kuti (Fársi)	West of Dehbid	500
2.	Kuti (Abdul Yusufi)	Kergun	250
3.	Amala	"	300
4.	Labu Háji	South of Dehbid	200
5.	Ammádi	"	150
6.	Palangi	"	50
7.	Vali Sháhi	Mashad-i-Murgháb	150
8.	Alwáni	"	200
9.	Beni Abdulláhi		150
10.	Khush Námi		50
11.	Hasani		50
12.	Tigriti		50
13.	Hannái		50
14.	Chahár, Bunichi, Burbur, Jelodár		200
15.	Lur		100
16.	Ali Sadi		150
		GRAND TOTAL of Tribes,	9900

YEZDIKHÁST.

[To face p. 330

station, whereupon Blackman ran out, felt for the heart of the brute, and shot it with his revolver.

Dehbid is noted for being the highest telegraph office in Persia. It has an elevation of close on 8000 feet, and I was only too glad of a day's rest in its bracing atmosphere, during which I visited the Tal-i-Kháki, which is stated to be the ruin of one of Bahrám Gur's hunting lodges.[1] It is furthermore justly noted for its excellent cheese, loaded with which the march was resumed, after a pleasant rest. From Abáde, an important village, famous for its exquisitely-carved sherbet-spoons, a most artistic article, and also for having been the prison of the Sefavi puppet during the rule of Kerim Khán, we marched to Shulgistán and thence to Yezdikhást, which is a village built on a rock, shaped like a steamer, in the middle of a valley. There is only one entrance with a drawbridge, and a well of brackish, but drinkable, water inside enables its inhabitants to defy any assault not supported by artillery. The houses are built over the precipice, rickety balustrades of wood projecting over the abyss. Nowadays half the population lives outside, which should be healthier, especially as the percentage of children who tumbled down the cliff must have been great.

This was our last stage in Fárs, and upon reaching Maksud Beg, we were met by the adjutant of H.R.H. the *Zil-i-Sultán*, who had been sent to escort our party in.

At Kumisha we found a considerable town and comfortable quarters in the Telegraph Station, but as Isfahán was too close for us to delay, we rode on to Meiár, our last stage. The *caravanserai*, which has recently been repaired, is now undoubtedly finer than that of Borázjun, and possesses two excellent sets of rooms upstairs. All this is the work of an energetic Persian, to whom also we were indebted for our first taste of an Isfahán melon, the fruit in which Persia need fear no rival. The best melons are grown at a hamlet called Gurgáb, which has brackish water. In the early morning a ripe melon will burst if a horse gallops by. This I have seen doubted, but it is so much of a fact that gardeners will

[1] From this hamlet branched off the road to Yezd, followed by Josafa Barbaro, who travelled by Vargun (now Aravirjun), Deiser (now Dehshir), and Taste or Taft. In 1873, when the volume of the Hakluyt Society dealing with the early Venetian travellers was brought out, Boanat was a blank on the map; it is interesting to note that Dehebeth was a "towne, wheare they vse tillaige and making of fustians."

run out to present melons to riders, and beg them to move at a walk.

An early start was necessary, as we meant to accomplish two stages to the ancient Sefavi capital of Persia, and only stopped for lunch at Kala-i-Shur, where Wood overtook me, having ridden nearly a hundred miles a day from Shiráz. After clearing a chain of low hills, we eagerly approached the Khaju bridge, which is so luxuriously constructed that there are stepping-stones below the broad roadway from pier to pier across the Zenda Rud;[1] thence a noble avenue of plane trees which would be a feature in any capital, a long vista of *bázárs*, and finally the Consulate, kindly placed at our disposal by its absent owner, and one of the most comfortable and best appointed houses in Persia.

The sights of Isfahán have been so minutely described, that more than a passing reference would be out of place. The two world-renowned bridges ending in avenues of mighty planes, and the *Chehel Sutun* or Forty Pillars, the acme of Sefavi art, are perhaps the most striking remains of past grandeur, but I must confess that the *meidán* or polo ground, with its stone pillars still standing, fascinated me more than anything else, and I was not content until I had knocked a goal between the posts and carefully measured them.

During my stay I had two audiences with H.R.H. the *Zil-i-Sultán*, with whom I also had the honour of dining. His Royal Highness struck me as a somewhat smaller edition of the late Sháh, and his keen sense of humour was much in evidence. His reception of me could not have been more gracious, and I was much struck by his knowledge of international politics, and by the care he takes to keep the road safe, his officers being really trained to carry out orders to the letter.

On more than one occasion Wood and I visited the Armenian village of Julfá, on the right bank of the Zenda Rud, the head-quarters of the Church Missionary Society and of the European colony. This village, if its sanitation were looked after, should be a delightful place of abode, but its odours vie in my recollections with those of Shuster. It maintains a close connection with India where a proportion of the young men are educated, but, on the

[1] This river is also termed Zaienda or Life-giving, but General Schindler writes that Zenda is correct, the word signifying great, not living.

MASJID-I-SHÁH, ISFAHÁN (SHOWING ANCIENT GOAL-POSTS ON POLO GROUND).

[*To face p.* 332.

other hand, the fact that many of the families receive remittances from relations in Calcutta has not tended to increase the energy of the residents.

Towards the middle of September my plans were all changed, and orders came for me to proceed to Sistán, Wood on the following day being instructed to accompany me, much to our mutual satisfaction. As may be supposed, his was a telegraph mission, the first part of which consisted in finding a route by which the Kohrud pass could be avoided, so I gave him some days' start.

The evening before my departure I said good-bye to M. de Morgan and staff, who were marching back to their excavations at Susa, where the greatest success has attended them, and the following evening I was once again bound Eastward Ho!

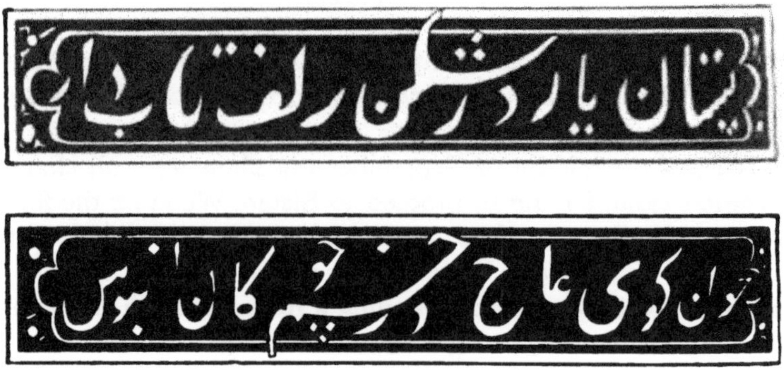

A COUPLET ON POLO.

CHAPTER XXIX

POLO IN PERSIA

"The ball no question makes of Ayes and Noes,
But Here or There as strikes the Player goes;
And He that tossed you down into the Field,
He knows about it all—He knows—He knows!"
—FITZGERALD'S *Omar Khayyám*.

THE origin of the fascinating game of *Gu-u-Chogán*,[1] as Persians term polo,[2] is so ancient that a poet sings:

"As long as the world has been spinning round
The *Gu* has been twisting away from the *Chogán*."

I propose to lay before my readers a summary of the mass of references that I have collected, which (allowing for the poetical licence, excusable in a bard of Irán, the cradle of polo) will at any

[1] *Gu* signifies the ball, and *Chogán* the polo-stick. The latter word has found its way into Europe under the form chicane, which was used for the *jeu du mail* in Southern France. It apparently then had reference to practices connected with the game, and has in the long run become the English word chicanery. Mr A. G. Ellis of the British Museum, who has kindly assisted me in this chapter, informed me that *shagharán* is the word used in Tibet for polo ground. *Chogán* is, no doubt, a contraction of the Pahlevi *Chavigan*.

[2] *Polo* or *Pulu* is a Tibetan word for a ball manufactured from willow-root.

rate prove what a position the great game held in Persia from before the dawn of history down to the eighteenth century.

Historically speaking, the most ancient reference to the game is contained in the Pahlevi history of Ardeshír; but even then the game was so ancient, that we can well accept the testimony of Firdusi, and carry this sketch back to earlier times, when the game was as well known in Turán as in Irán.

Before, however, plunging *in medias res*, it may be as well to discuss briefly the original nature of the game and the method of playing it. We may assume that the ball was always approximately of the same size and shape, but the *Chogán* appears in two distinct forms. In early times it was shaped like the Persian letter د *dál*, and somewhat resembled a gigantic mustard-spoon. At this period the game had two phases, in the first of which the players struck the ball as high into the air as possible, and then caught it again in the bowl of the *Chogán*. After these preliminaries, four players a-side, as to-day, formed a *mêlée*, and the ball was struck between the goal-posts by one party or the other.

In illustration, I give a free translation of a passage from Firdusi's *Sháh Náma* or *History of the Kings*. The player of the day was Siawush, father of Kei Khusru,[1] who sought the protection of Afrasiáb, the King of Turán.

"If the King orders me, let me bring some of my Persian *sowárs* on to the ground. Let them be my partners in striking the ball, and let us divide into two parties.

"The War Lord (sc. Afrasiáb) agreed, and Siawush chose seven Persians, who were good and experienced players. The rattle of the drum rose up from the plain; the dust ascended straight to heaven.

"From the clang of the cymbals, and the braying of the trumpets, you might say that the earth was quaking.

"They threw the ball on to the royal polo ground. The shout of the heroes reached the moon.

"The War Lord smote the ball on the plain, it must have reached the clouds, so hard was it hit.

"Siawush galloped forward and rushed his horse, so that when the ball descended he suffered it not to touch the dust. He smote it when it reached the plain, so that it disappeared out of sight.

[1] Kei Khusru was already a mythical hero in the seventh century B.C., when the Zend-Avesta was probably written.

"The Great King ordered that the ball should be brought to Siawush. Siawush bent down and kissed the ball. The sound of the horn and drum arose.

"Siawush changed his horse, and for a moment let the ball fall to the ground. After that he so struck the ball, that it ascended to visit the moon. From his stick the ball flew so far out of sight, that you might say the heavens attracted it.

"On the ground there was no player like him, nor any one with such a bright smile. Afrasiáb laughed to see that stroke; his famous men were astounded.

"They all swore with a shout that such a famous rider had never been seen in the saddle."

The second part of the game is thus described:

"The men of valour and the heroes approached the ball; from every quarter they galloped their horses.

"When the Persian heroes galloped on the ground, they soon bore off the ball from the Turks.

"Siawush was delighted with his Persians, and with heart full of pride, he bore himself like a cypress."

As this is presumably the earliest polo match on record, I need not apologise for having given a practically full translation of the narrative.

Next, we appropriately find a mention of the game in connection with Alexander the Great, the story running that when, as a youth, he succeeded his father, the King of Persia sent him a *Gu* and *Chogán*, with the idea of pointing the moral that he should not occupy himself with anything more serious than polo. His reply was that he accepted the gifts in the sense that the *Gu* was the earth and himself the *Chogán*. History shows how he kept his word.

In the old English romance of *Kyng Alisaunder*,[1] "a scourge and a top of nobleys" replace the ball and polo stick. These were sent to Alexander by "Darie, the Kyng of Kynges," who is made to say:

> "Therefore, Y have the y-sent
> A top and a scorge to present,
> And with gold a litel punge
> For thow hast yeris yonge:
> Wend thou hom therwith, and play."

---

[1] Weber, *Metrical Romances*, vol. i. p. 74. See also Budge, *Life and Exploits of Alexander*, p. 35.

SIAWUSH PLAYS POLO BEFORE AFRASIÁB.

[*To face p.* 336.

The Parthian dynasty, which ruled Irán from shortly after Alexander's death, for a period of five hundred years, has left little in the shape of records, and I have not been able to find anything about their prowess at polo, but under the succeeding Sásánian dynasty the game flourished mightily.

In the Pahlevi history of Ardeshír[1] it is related that the future conqueror was sent for to the court of Ardavan, where he accompanied the king's sons to the chase, and to the polo ground. As may be imagined, the hero far surpassed his companions in both fields of action. This is the earliest *historic* reference, and would date from the middle of the third century of our era. We next read that when doubts were entertained as to the identity of Shápur, the lad was summoned to court with a number of companions. To test him a polo ball was thrown near the Sháh's feet; Shápur alone dared to follow it up, and was immediately acknowledged to be of the blood royal.

Under Shápur II., about A.D. 358,[2] a certain Kardagh was king of Assyria. During a game of polo a holy man, Abdishu by name, crossed the ground and was roughly handled, whereupon he made the sign of the cross. As a consequence, the ball clove to the ground, and no force could move it. Needless to say, this miracle converted Kardagh and his court. Tracing the further fortunes of the house of Sásán, we read that Bahrám Gur, the great hunter-king, was given three professors, whose duties were to teach him—(1) reading; (2) hunting; (3) polo and skill in weapons. This would still be a popular programme if introduced at home! Tabari, who confirms the *Sháh Náma* on this subject, adds that there was an appropriate kit.

Khusru Parviz, almost the last monarch of the dynasty, whose love for his wife, Shirin, is a favourite theme of Persian poets, was evidently fond of the game. During or perhaps before his reign, ladies took it up, and apparently held their own, as the following extract from *Nizámi* shows:

"Seventy maidens like lionesses presented themselves before Shirin, all blazing with ardour. In courage, each one resembled

[1] *Kárnámak-i-Artakshír-i-Pápakán.*

[2] The history of this event was written in the sixth century. In the seventh century, in the Sanscrit *Harsha Charita of Bana*, it is mentioned that hares were struck like polo balls.

Isfandiár; in archery, they were the equals of Rustam the Horseman. In shooting, Siawush was comparatively unfit to carry their horse-rug, and they played polo so well, that they filched the ball from the spinning world.

"The cypress-like maidens bound sheaves of arrows to their sides; they sat their saddles like cypresses. They all had moon-like faces veiled, and thus proceeded to the presence of the Sháh.

"The royal gatekeeper came out and passed them in. The King of Kings was overcome at seeing them. He showed condescension, and rose up before Shirin, whom he seated at his right hand. He really was delighted at the sight of their persons, abodes of sweetness and cities of sugar, but was ignorant of their strength and courage, and that they could perform feats of horsemanship.

"In order to inspect the black-veiled houris, he, with happy heart, proceeded to the plain.

"When he reached the polo ground, the fairy-faced ones curvetted on their steeds with joy.

"They started play, when every Moon appeared a Sun, and every partridge a hawk.

"When Khusru perceived those sweet-singing birds like doves in a meadow, but yet resembling hawks in their attack, he said to Shirin: 'Let us gallop, *Raksh*,[1] and play polo for a while on the plain.'

"They threw a *Gu* into the royal *Chogán*; the graces flew about the plain.

"The whole country from the number of *Chogán* resembled a grove of willows. . . .

"At times the Sun bore off the ball, at times the Moon.

"Now Shirin won, and now the Sháh."

From the above delightful account, it will appear that there were more players than four a-side, but I would urge that this was rather a practice game than a match, and, as will be seen further on, four was the regulation number, in later, as in the earliest times. That polo was really a fashionable game for ladies at this period is also shown by the story of Gurdiya, the beautiful sister of Bahrám Chúbín, who slew a too importunate lover, and being asked by Khusru to describe her achievement, exhibited her skill in military

[1] *Raksh* was the name of Rustam's great war-horse; hence its frequent use for favourite steeds.

exercises and in polo. Shirin was apparently out-classed, as she warns the king against "this she-devil,"[1] but was unable to prevent her marriage to Khusru.

The death-knell of Persian independence had already sounded, and the land of Irán became a province in the hands of Arab savages, who, for some generations, were far too busy in securing their position to find any leisure for adopting the games of the conquered race. However, by the end of the second century of the *Hijra*, polo was restored to its former popularity, and it is related that the famous Hárun-al-Rashíd was so small that when on horseback he could not reach down to the *Gu* with his *Chogán*.

In the following century Amr-i-Lais of the Saffár dynasty is used "to point a moral and adorn a tale" in the *Kábus Náma*,[2] a work written about the time of William the Conqueror, which anticipated not only Shakespeare's Polonius, but also the Badminton Library. As it gives the rules of the game, I quote in full:

"*The Etiquette and Rules of Polo.*—Listen, my son, if you enjoy polo, do not contract the habit of always playing the game, as in it there is much danger and risk to the players.

"As they tell the story, Amr-i-Lais, who was blind in one eye, when he became the ruler of Khorasán, proceeded one day to the polo ground to knock about the ball, where he found his Commander-in-Chief, Azhar Khar by name. This latter came forward and seized his rein, saying: 'I cannot allow you to knock about the ball and play polo.'

"Amr-i-Lais replied: 'Since you knock about the ball and play polo, and it is all right, why is it not right for me to play?'

"Azhar Khar answered: 'Because I have two eyes, and if by accident, the ball should fall on one eye, I have another eye with which to see the world. Your Majesty has but one eye, and if the *Gu* should fall on that one eye, we should have to bid farewell to the *Amir* of Khorasán.'

"Amr-i-Lais said: 'Although you are an ass,[3] you are quite right, and I agree never to play polo while I live.'

"But if you play occasionally, so as to show off, there is no

[1] *Journal*, *R.A.S.*, April 1900, p. 243.

[2] The writer was "Unsuru" 'l-Ma'áli' Kei Ká'us ibn Iskandar ibn Kábus, who wrote in A.H. 475 (1082).

[3] This is an execrable pun on the name, *Khar* signifying an ass.

harm, but do not join in the game too often, and thus avoid danger and risk. And there should not be more than eight players, and you should stay at one end of the ground, and place some one else at the far end; and have six players galloping about in the centre of the ground.

"Whenever the *Gu* comes to you, hit it back into the game and pretend to ride hard, but do not go into the *mêlée* and avoid danger and risk by keeping your distance and looking after yourself to preserve your safety."

From the above extract it will be seen that matches were four a-side, with the post of back clearly defined.

About a century later than the reign of Amr-i-Lais, polo claimed a royal victim in Abdul Malik, of the Sámán dynasty, who was killed by a fall from his horse in A.H. 350 (961). The house of Sámán was succeeded by that of Ghazni, one of whose rulers, Masud, had a bitter enemy to the game in his vizier, who did his best to stop it, but fortunately failed.

In the twelfth century of our era, Constantinople became a great centre of polo, which is fully described by the historian Cinnamus. Nur-u-Din, the inveterate enemy of the Crusaders, was a fine performer, and so enthusiastic that he frequently played by torchlight. As may be supposed, the chivalrous Saladin also excelled in the game, and we can only regret that the Crusaders did not learn it from their adversaries.[1]

In the fourteenth century Tímúr gave a ghastly exhibition at Damascus, in which his men used the heads of the citizens as balls. The works of Sadi, who flourished rather before this time, and those of Háfiz, who had a historical interview with the terrible Tímúr, both abound in references to polo.

Sadi writes:

> "I would fain fall at her feet like a *Gu*,
> And if she smites with her *Chogán*, keep silent."

And again:

> "Every heart inflamed with love that has fallen into the curl of thy tresses,
> Than that thou canst not see a better *Gu* in the cup of the *Chogán*."

[1] On some pottery of this period dug up in Egypt, two polo sticks are shown as the crest on several of the fragments. I understand that the polo stick bearer was a high official.

"O PRINCE OF RIDERS! HÁFIZ WELCOME CALLS
"SO RIDE APACE AND SHREWDLY SMITE THE BALLS."

[*To face p.* 340.

Háfiz sings:

"I said, 'I will enquire as to the welfare of the *Gu* of the world.'
It replied, 'I suffer much in the cup of the *Chogán*, so ask me not.'"

Mysticism too, as may be supposed, was quick to use the game as a vehicle of expression, and there is actually a poem by Mahmud Árifi, in which a "confidential conversation" is carried on, the *Gu* leading off with:

"Oh may my head be the sacrifice of thy foot:
May I give my head to the winds for thy sake.

. . . .

"I am without religion if I turn my head from thee.
Except my head I have nothing in my hand."

The *Chogán* replies:

"O thou that like myself art tired of the world,
Around thy head are a thousand like myself.

. . . .

"My figure that is bent like a و
Is a proof of my friendly soul.

. . . .

"Behind thee my head ever follows:
So long as my head lasts, I will ne'er forsake thee."

The finale is:

"In the service of the Sháh like a crescent and a full moon,
Gu ran along on its own head and *Chogán* behind kindly bent."

We have now reached the period when European travellers appear on the scene. Sir Anthony Sherley, an adventurer of the time of James I., who succeeded in winning the affection of Sháh Abbás in the most extraordinary fashion, gives an interesting description, which is, I imagine, the earliest English account of the game. "Before the house there was a very fair place, to the quantity of some ten acres of ground, made very plain; so the King went down, and when he had taken his horse, the drums and trumpets sounded; there was twelve horsemen in all with the King; so they divided themselves, six on the one side, and six on the other; having in their hands long rods of wood, about the bigness of a man's finger, and at one end of the rods a piece of wood nailed on like unto a hammer. After they were divided and turned face to face, there came one into the middle, and threw a wooden ball between both the companies, and having goals made at either end of the plain, they began their sport, striking the ball with their rods from one to the other, in the fashion of our football play here in England." [1]

A generation later Chardin witnessed games on the Isfahán Square, which is 560 yards in length and 170 in width, whereas to-day 300 yards by 200 constitutes a full-sized ground. This must have given the players plenty of room, although, as will be seen, there were more than eight. The goal [2] posts are still standing, and as they are of solid stone, cut like a mitre at the top, accidents must have been of frequent occurrence. Their height is nine feet, and the distance between them is twenty-four feet, which is the same measurement as at Hurlingham.

Chardin's description will, I feel sure, appeal to all players:

"On se partage (pour l'exercice de mail à Cheval) en deux Troupes égales. On jette plusieurs boules au milieu de la Place, et on donne un mail à chacun. Pour gagner il faut faire passer les boules entre les piliers opposés, qui sont aux bouts de la Place, et qui servent de passe. On se moque de ceux qui la frappent au pas du cheval, ou le cheval étant arrêté. Le jeu veut qu' on ne la frappe qu' au galop, et les bons joueurs sont ceux qui, en courant à toute bride, savent renvoyer d'un coup sec une boule qui vient à eux!" [3]

In a later volume further interesting details are given: "Comme le mail est court, il faut se pencher plus bas que l'arçon, pour l'atteindre, et dans les règles du Jeu, il faut assener le coup au galop. Ce jeu se fait par parties de quinze ou vingt contre autant." [4]

After Sefavi times Persia was so harried by invaders and internal disorders, that polo died out, as indeed was the case in India, although, fortunately for the world, it was still played in some remote border states, such as Skárdu, Hunza, and Manipur Sir John Malcolm, referring to the game, said that it was introduced

[1] *The Travels and Adventures of the Three Sherleys*, p. 70.

[2] To-day in Persia, at "tip and run," the boy who catches the ball shouts "*Goal Giriftam.*" This former word is perhaps a corruption for *Gul*, and so the expression means, "I have won the flower."

[3] Chardin, vol. i. p. 363. Amsterdam, 1735.

[4] *Ibid.*, vol. iii. p. 58. Amsterdam, 1735.

and played in Scotland in the eighteenth century, under the name of "Horse Shindy." If so, the 10th Hussars were not the original introducers of the game into the United Kingdom, but this is apart from my subject, and I will now briefly refer to its renaissance at Tehrán.

In 1897 I brought sticks and balls to the capital, but was assured that no one would play. However, aided by Mr Horace Rumbold, who, by a coincidence, had played at Cairo with the "Bays," a trial game was organised, and shortly after the Legation was full of both players and ponies. Among the players was Sir Mortimer Durand, and thanks to the general keenness displayed, mighty Demávend can now again look down on the ancient game of *Gu-u-Chogán*. I have since organised the game at Shíráz and Kermán,[1] while players who learned at Tehrán have started clubs at Vienna and Constantinople, and thus the seed sown has borne fruit.

In conclusion, by permission of Sir Mortimer Durand, I quote one of his poems, which is connected with the game, and was written in memory of the late Baron Von Gaertner, German Minister at Tehrán, who played it so vigorously:

"HURLINGHAM, *June* 1897.

"Renton was playing a wonderful back,
He had 'saved,' when the ball had a yard to roll,
Turned on it, carried it right through the pack,
And driving and galloping landed a goal.

"Behind me a thundering shout 'Well played!'
'Well played!' and I turned to a voice that I knew,
And a strong brown hand on my shoulder was laid,
A big-limbed Teuton of six foot two.

"And oh! it was pleasant on Hurlingham Green,
That long bright day of an English June,
And he sat there enjoying it, happy and keen,
And the last merry gallop came all too soon.

"And then I remember he rose with a sigh,
'Aho! I am sorry—a grand game done,'
And he held my hand and he said 'Good-bye,'
'Good-bye, we shall meet in the Land of the Sun.'

[1] Great games are now also played by the Persian boys on donkeys, and considerable skill is displayed.

"PERSIA, *March* 1898.

"Close to the crest of the desolate pass,[1]
A lone broad plain where the snow lies deep,
Not a tree, not a bird, not a tussock of grass,
The great hills sleeping a deathlike sleep.

"Two mules down on the treacherous road,
Over the stream where the snow-bridge sank,
Short mad struggle to lift their load,
Bloodshot eyeball and labouring flank.

"Little is left of the fading day.
'What are they carrying, Akbar Khán?'
'The Almán[2] minister's corpse,' they say,
'They are bearing it back to Farangistán.'

"Dead!—And I saw it, the soft June sky,
And the smooth green sward when the game was done,
And I stood bareheaded, and said 'Good-bye,
'Good-bye'—We had met in the Land of the Sun."

---

[1] The Kharzan Pass.
[2] Almán is the Persian for German.

DESIGN ON BRASS BOWL.

CHAPTER XXX

FROM ISFAHÁN TO THE BRITISH FRONTIER

"Chanting of order and right, and of foresight, warder of nations;
Chanting of labour and craft, and of wealth in the port and the garner."
—CHARLES KINGSLEY, *Andromeda.*

OUR first stage from Isfahán was Gulnabád, the scene of Persia's shame, where, in the middle of the eighteenth century, the troops of the degenerate Sefavi monarch were defeated by a body of less than 20,000 Afgháns, who, before they were driven out, either killed or murdered more than a million Persians, and dealt a blow to the royal city from which it has not yet recovered. We marched due east across a wide uninteresting plain, crossing my 1895 route at Kuhpá. Thence we rose into the hills, where I halted a day to climb a somewhat high peak, the Kuh-i-Sáru, being desirous of obtaining a good idea of the surrounding country, through which it might be decided to run the telegraph line.

At Náin, where I waited a day for Wood to rejoin me, there was a shrine inhabited by *Hájí* Agha Hasan, an extraordinarily well-read and travelled dervish.[1] He told me that the original saint was *Hájí* Abdul Waháb, and that when Abbás *Mírza*, the heir of Fath Ali Sháh (who predeceased his sire), was travelling through Náin, the *Pír* visited his sons and asked to see their swords. All refused with the exception of Mohamed *Mírza*, of whom the saint prophesied that he would one day sit on the throne. Since the time

[1] He died in 1899.

that the prophecy came true, the shrine and its guardians have wanted nothing from Mohamed Sháh and his descendants.

In the course of our conversation Nasrulla Khán, who, like almost all educated Persians, is pessimistic, said that his feelings had been hurt at seeing that more than two thousand years ago chairs were in use, as the Persepolis sculptures proved, whereas to-day Persians sat on the ground. "Be of good cheer," replied the sage, "we in those early days cared only for material progress, which we have now abandoned for higher things, whereas Europeans have just reached the stage of material progress."

Wood, to whom I narrated this, said that once in discussing religion with a *mullá*, he had urged that the English were at any rate known throughout Asia as being truthful, whereas in Persia that virtue was not conspicuous. "Agreed," was the reply, "but why is it so? The devil has got the English in his claws, and so does not object to their speaking the truth, but he has not yet got the Persians, and so is striving to corrupt the true religion."

Our chief interest at Náin was the behaviour of Wood's Armenian clerk, aged twenty-two, whom he had engaged at Julfá to keep his accounts and generally make himself useful. This youth, who had been educated in India, was a remarkable mixture of cowardice and home-sickness, and although he had only left Julfá a week, was falling ill from the separation from his family. Wood told me that ever since the first stage he had wished to go back, but had not dared to face the perils of the way, and that at night he paid the servants to sleep round him in a circle! On reaching Náin, he burst in upon Nasrulla Khan, and, with floods of tears, said that whenever he quitted Julfá to visit Isfahán, his mother never left the garden gate until his return, leading him to suppose that in the present case also the poor old lady was glued to her post of observation until he re-appeared.

This was my first experience of an Armenian on the road, and I can only trust that the youth in question, who is a member of one of the respectable families in Calcutta, may not be a fair sample of his race. It was finally decided to send him home, and after praying for an escort in addition to the muleteers and a *farrash*, he departed, relieving the party of a very useless member.

From Náin to Yezd, and indeed to Kermán, I was travelling along familiar routes, but this was unavoidable, as I wished to show my companion what I conceived to be the best line for the Central Persia Telegraph to pursue.

At Hujetabád, one stage from Yezd, Mr Stuart Ferguson, the manager of the Bank and an old friend, came out for the night, and in his company we rode into Yezd, the Governor sending out a carriage drawn by six black horses for our reception. No sooner were we inside the Bank than a crowd clamouring for bread surrounded the house, the bad harvests in Fárs having caused a great scarcity, since Yezd itself at no time grows more than a three months' supply within the district. Ferguson went out and appeased the mob, but throughout our stay we could never count on bread in the morning. This is the first time I have ever actually been so near to wanting the staff of life in a town.

The Yezd community had been augmented since my last visit in 1895, Dr and Mrs White of the Church Missionary Society having settled there, and it is mainly owing to his, or I might say their, energy in healing the sick that Europeans are now comparatively popular.

Quitting a most united and hospitable community with much regret, we continued our march on 17th October. At Sar-i-Yezd I was met by an escort sent by the Governor-General of Kermán, which was rather fortunate, as stones were thrown at my Indian *syce* while he was watering the horses. The Headman was thereupon seized by my escort, and as he refused to produce and punish the culprits, I sent him in to the Governor with a note. As a sequel, the guilty were brought into Yezd, and "sticked" in the presence of the Bank interpreter, which will secure Europeans against molestation in Sar-i-Yezd for many a year to come. The fact that this has been the only occasion during my travels on which a servant of mine has been assaulted testifies to the invariable friendliness of the villagers. In the present case the stones were thrown by some young *Kháns*, who probably thought it fun.

As in 1895, we avoided the main road and kept to the north, which was fortunate, as the two *sowárs* who had gone into Yezd with the Headman were attacked on the caravan road by brigands. These worthies had taken possession of the *caravanserai* of Zein-u-Din, and one of the men was shot in the thigh. I sent him back to Yezd, and Dr White's treatment probably saved his life.

Throughout the journey we had the greatest difficulty as regards bread and forage, and at one stage, although my camp was a full mile from the town, it was surrounded by hundreds of women, who complained that the landowners possessed plenty of wheat, but were holding on for still higher prices. In order to hear what they wanted me to do, I asked that two ladies should come forward and speak, which they did, bringing me specimens of a perfectly inedible composition of bran and millet, together with some lucerne, which they assured me—and I believe them—was their staple diet. Persians have absolutely no idea but that of hoarding in time of scarcity, and I am afraid that they care nothing, as a class, for the sufferings of their own fellow-countrymen. The Shirázis are notorious sinners in this respect, and perhaps the only way to cure them is that adopted by the Afgháns, who, having captured Shiráz by starving out its defenders, discovered several months' supplies of wheat hidden away in the various storehouses. So disgusted were they at this treachery, that they hanged the various owners by hooks inside their granaries, and allowed them to die of slow starvation in sight of plenty, a barbarous but effectual lesson to their fellow-citizens.

All along the road old friends had met me, and near Kermán, where the usual *istikbál* took place, the Rev. A. R. Blackett, of the Church Missionary Society, also rode out in the friendly fashion that Europeans have adopted from the Persians.

More than two and a half years having elapsed since I had left Kermán, I was nearly overwhelmed with visits to pay and receive, and cases to go through and settle, although I was delighted to revisit a town where I had spent so many happy months. My most important business was to persuade H.E. the *Ásaf-u-Dola*, whom I met for the first time, but who could not have been more friendly, to despatch an officer to Chahbár, in order to enquire into the long-standing claims for compensation due to British Indian subjects. As the Perso-Baluch Boundary Commission had upset my first attempt at such an arrangement, I was extremely anxious to have everything put on a proper footing, especially after the recent disturbances. I am afraid that I was somewhat too prompt for His Excellency, as the moment he agreed to my proposals, I walked across to the Telegraph Office, where it had been arranged that I should talk to the minister, and shortly afterwards I was able to convey Sir Mortimer Durand's thanks for the arrangement so speedily effected—much to the *Ásaf-u-Dola's* surprise, as he had all the Oriental idea of *festina lente*.

Another case connected with Makrán was that of Abdi Khán of Dashtiári, a district near Chahbár, to whose threats it was mainly due that the Telegraph Station had been garrisoned by Indian troops. I had written to the *Ásaf-u-Dola* on the subject, and he had ordered the arrest of Abdi, and had kept him in prison at Kermán, pending my arrival. On being brought before us and permitted to speak, he said that when his Sháh died, he understood that every chief became independent,; that the Governor of Baluchistán had ordered him to pay taxes, but that he had declined, as he knew that there was no new Sháh, and that the Governor wanted the money for himself; that the British Government used to pay him one thousand rupees per annum, as an indemnity for the injury done to his land by the telegraph posts, but that this had been stopped, as the Persian Governor had written to say that it should be paid to his brother.

The *Ásaf-u-Dola* here interrupted him sharply with the remark that he was simply asked why he had written letters threatening to massacre the telegraph officials at Chahbár. At first he denied point-blank; he then said that his brother had written the letters and stolen his seal, but finally blurted out, "I did write the letters, but I never carried out the threats," as if he had done nothing wrong whatever. When the prisoner was withdrawn we had a consultation, and I told His Excellency that Mr Ffinch had often stated that he would give "anything in the world to be shut up in the same room as Abdi with a thick stick." This amused the *Ásaf-u-Dola* hugely, and he suggested that Abdi should be sent to Mr Ffinch for correction, but as the Director-in-Chief was once more in London, this could not be carried out.

His Excellency then said that Abdi's brother would pay no taxes, and that as Abdi had had the educational advantages of several months in prison, he proposed to send him back to Dashtiári. I left the matter in his hands, upon the condition that he should undergo a year's imprisonment, and pay compensation in all cases proved against him before being released, which was finally done.[1]

[1] His behaviour has since been exemplary.

We stayed some three weeks at Kermán, during which time riding-camels were bought, all provisions laid in, and we left for the frontier on the 19th November, in threatening weather. After a day's halt in the beautiful garden at Máhun, then looking somewhat forlorn, we marched to the north of the caravan road, which goes by the Kotal-i-Hanaka, a pass I had twice crossed. This new route, which I had only seen from a distance when shooting in the hills, proved to be a great success, there being no pass whatever, but only an open watershed, which was crossed at an altitude of 8450 feet, and so lower than the Kotal-i-Hanaka. It also possessed the additional advantage of being some six or seven miles shorter.

The stage of Zein-ul-abád, twelve and a half miles from Máhun, as well as that of Neibid on the far side of the watershed, being both above 7000 feet, we revelled in many degrees of frost, from which our horses with their extra felts did not suffer. But this was too good to last, as we were steadily descending to Bam. In this thriving centre two busy days were spent in social functions, there being almost as many *Kháns* as at Kermán.

Bam being the last town for about 700 miles in this direction, we constructed sheep pens to carry live stock for the journey, and Wood bought some riding camels. We were soon on the way to Narmáshir, where we hoped for a little shooting. We camped on the banks of the river of Azizabád, which I had marked down in 1896 as a likely spot, nor were we disappointed, black and sand partridges, hares, pigeon, and snipe, all being bagged. Again, near Rigán, where we halted to make our final arrangements, we found a fair number of black partridges, but, as must always be the case, lost a large percentage for want of a dog.

We were now at the edge of the desert, which Wood had been ordered to cross to Ládis, and as may be supposed, I was only too glad of a companion. Upon quitting Rigán, our first march lay to the north of east, and we halted at the tiny hamlet of Deh Yághi Khán, and filled up every empty bottle, besides our barrels, with the somewhat brackish water. Deh Yághi Khán was built some thirty years ago by a Baluch chief of the Sheikhi tribe, who was settled there to defend Narmáshir against raiding-parties of his countrymen, and at this hamlet an escort of eight camelry was due to meet us, but as is always the case with Baluchis, only four men were procured and

GARDEN OF H.H. THE FARMÁN FARMÁ MÁHUN.

[*To face p.* 350.

that with the greatest difficulty. Yár Mohamed Sultán, their leader, was anxious for his brother to accompany us, but as the youth in question had been our guide from Rigán, and knew practically no Persian, we soon sent for Yár Mohamed himself, who was the best Baluch we had to deal with on this journey. But the shameless mendacity of this people, and the grumbling at whatever is given, checks the growth of any liking for them, whereas, on the contrary, there is often warm attachment between Persian servants and their English masters.

I had already crossed the desert which lay before us further to the south, and hoped to experience nothing very bad in the way of salt water, but although we had suffered from rain on the way, not a drop had fallen east of Rigán, and we were consequently dependent on the spring rains, which had been very scanty.

In spite of the fact that it was the first week in December, we found the sun's rays very powerful, especially as we had descended more than 6000 feet since leaving Kermán, and at the stage of Deh Yághi Khán we were just below 2000 feet. We therefore started off in the dark, and for three miles stumbled through a tamarisk grove. Beyond that we entered the utterly bare desert, covered with stones of volcanic character. This continued for fifteen miles, until, in the very heart of the desolation, we crossed a low pass, which Nasrulla Khán, after enquiring of a Baluch, assured me was the Dahána-i-Bulbulán or the Nightingales' Gorge. This struck me as irony indeed, until Wood came in and explained that *Bulbulak* or Hissing Water was the proper and indeed most suitable term, considering the volcanic surroundings.

At eighteen miles we found our camp pitched in the middle of nowhere, the disconsolate camels in vain hunting for a few bushes, and there was no water. The following day, however, we found some tamarisks in a torrent bed a few miles from camp, much to the joy of our camels, just beyond which the direct track to Ládis branched off, a route that still awaits the explorer.

We passed a brackish spring, where there were tracks of the wild ass, and then crossed a level plain covered with salt efflorescence, on the eastern edge of which we found our advance camp at Cháh Ráis, a well of dubious water. I may mention that even our best water was pronounced undrinkable when analysed in India. I suddenly recollected that evening that this very spot had been pointed out to me from the summit of the Kuh-i-Bazmán, nearly five years before.

From Cháh Ráis our direction lay due east, and at first through fine sand, the Tal-i-Rubá or Fox's Hill being a conspicuous landmark. We were consistently making for the northern continuation of the Bazmán range, and encountered the insignificant hills into which it dwindles at fifteen miles, crossing a low watershed at an altitude of 3100 feet soon afterwards. We then made for a black, flat-topped hill, finally reaching Samsor. Here we encamped on the left bank of a desert river of very brackish water and of considerable volume, full of reeds. Were it only sweet it could support hundreds of families, but as it is, it takes its source in the desert, and flowing north-west in an aimless way, discharges into one of the salt *hámun*, termed Shurgaz, which lies near the Sistán road.

Our guide informed us that the black hill was associated with prodigies of valour wrought by himself, when, after the Sháh's death, raiders from Sarhad drove off all the flocks from Narmáshir. On this occasion he had pursued and surrounded the Sarhaddis, who took refuge on the Tal-i-Samsor, where they agreed to abandon their booty and return home. "What about the sheep?" I asked. "Oh! none of those were restored, I and my relatives dividing them among ourselves as compensations for our risks!"

The *Gur-i-Khar* or wild ass has always interested me, perhaps owing to the numerous references made to it in Eastern books,[1] or perhaps because I have never been able to shoot one, and as our camels were worn out for want of grazing, we decided to halt and try our luck. We started off at daybreak, in eight degrees of frost, and after looking all round from a mound, discovered two of the desired quarry making for the hills. We followed them up for miles, but in vain, the sight of our tents having evidently scared them.

We had sent for drinking water to Cháh-i-Hanjerá, some twelve miles to the south-west, but when it came there was not much difference between it and the Samsor brand. However, the camels had enjoyed a rest, and when we resumed the journey, a short march brought us to the edge of the Sarhad range, which we had seen for

[1] Cf. Job xxxix. 5 and 7: "Who hath sent out the wild ass free? or who hath loosed the bands of the wild ass? He scorneth the multitude of the city, neither regardeth he the crying of the driver."

the last week. At Áb-i-Gajjari there was a limited water-supply of the same salt description, and plenty of firewood; the camp was pitched in the stony river-bed, as no better site could be found.

The next day's march lay right across the Siá Band, and as we wasted several hours in a futile stalk after wild sheep, the twenty-two miles seemed interminable. We first bore towards Kuh-i-Tacháp, which is flat-topped and used as a sanctuary in troublous times; this we passed at thirteen miles, close to the point where my 1894 route crossed our road. Thence we ascended mile after mile, passing beds of reeds and many wild pistachio trees. The last rays of the setting sun struck Taftán as it suddenly rose before us, but not in its majesty—it is a disappointing mountain when seen from a distance—and by sunset we reached the Gardan-i-Jauri, at an elevation of 6350 feet. Near this we expected to find our camp, but the springs had all dried up, and we were obliged to march on, lighting beacons to help our servants and camels. Clearing the hills we entered a wide plain, but saw no signs of our camp until, turning a corner, we espied a beacon being lighted. About 9 P.M. we found our advance tents at Jauri, near a stream of what we thought was sweet water—at any rate it tasted so to us—and, as may be supposed, it was very late before the whole party was in.

From Jauri to Kwásh, the capital of Sarhad, are two routes, the one we followed being the most southerly. A short stage brought us to the wells Cháhán-i-Asháhi,[1] and the following day we wended our weary way across the plain; indeed the march would have been extremely monotonous, but that I was able to recognise familiar landmarks as peak after peak rose up into view. At twenty-four miles we left the plain, which drains into a *hámun* to the south-east, and entered the hills, skirting the Panj Angusht range. An easy watershed was followed by a rough descent, and at twenty-nine miles we reached Chashma Ziárat, where we found really sweet water, the first since leaving Rigán. A long sleep and a rest for every one was the order of the day, the advance camp not leaving till the morning. A five-mile ride brought us to Kwásh, where a few camelry under the Governor rode out to receive us. These were the first human beings we had seen for eight days, and we had almost the feeling of passengers coming into port, with the difference that we were

[1] "The Royal Wells" is the translation.

expected to give not to receive news. Everywhere we heard the same story, that the drought had compelled the nomads to flee to Sistán, and the reduced number of black tents testified to the truth of this. It was with the utmost difficulty that we procured a few pounds of wheat, and we grew very anxious about the supply question, as we had counted on Kwásh for something more than this.

As any one who can read is a *rara avis* in Sarhad, Nasrulla Khán was asked to decipher the last two letters from the Governor of Bampur, which were to the effect that Mahmud Khán of Sib had died, and that all the Sarhad chiefs were to attend the Governor, who was marching there to "arrange" the succession. Among others, Jiand Khán, the owner of the frontier date-groves, who had been given the rank of *Sultán* or captain, was ordered in, but I felt sure (and, as the sequel proved, correctly) that he would politely decline.

A long halt was out of the question as our supplies had run so low, and as we intended to try and scale Kuh-i-Taftán from the east. Accordingly, after a day's rest, during which we scraped together a little wheat, barley, and some dates, we again marched off into unknown country.

Our route lay round the base of the great volcano, and at the second stage of Sangun we decided to leave our camp for two or three days. This little village was the property of Abdul Kerím, then the chief of the Kurds of Sarhad,[1] a small body of nomads having been planted as "Wardens of the Marches," by their own account, although the general legend is that they are the descendants of a family of travelling wrestlers. In any case, they are not nowadays distinguishable from the surrounding population, and one of Wood's servants, a respectable Kurd, would not allow that they were fellow-tribesmen. To our surprise we saw in this remote hamlet perhaps one of the largest cypresses in the world. Its girth at about 5 feet from the ground was 25 feet, and just above huge limbs like those of an oak branched off. From a distance it resembled a big plane tree except for its colour, and it was quite worth a long journey to inspect it.

Our camp having been pitched at Sangun, at an elevation of rather less than 6000 feet, we marched with small light tents

[1] He was killed shortly afterwards by his cousin.

towards the great peak, which rose some 7000 feet above us. At ten miles we had risen 1500 feet, and as the camels could go no further, two donkeys and some twenty guides and servants carried up our kit to 8500 feet, where we camped near a spring of water, in threatening weather. In the afternoon we went in different directions, but saw no game and no fresh tracks. At night we lit a bonfire, but the bush being thick, we did not find it as cold as we had expected, probably because we had stacked brushwood round the tents.

The following morning we started at sunrise, and after two hours of steady tramping, reached a natural amphitheatre at an elevation of 10,000 feet. Another rise of 1000 feet brought us to the foot of the cone, opposite a sulphur spring and close by a frozen waterfall of sulphur-tainted water. Up to this point the climbing had been easy, but once on the steep cone, we had to toil up yard by yard, often using the hands as an aid.

From Sangun we had noticed thin white vapour curling out of the mountain side, and at about 12,000 feet we passed the lowest and most important of several orifices, the first group including two small and one large aperture; 300 feet higher up was a second group of four. Upon approaching the large orifice, which is, however, smaller than the one on the summit, the ground grew hot, the stones all round being coated with a mixture of sulphur and sal-ammoniac. My thermometer, which only registered up to 170 degrees, burst when inserted in the vent from which the white vapour issued with a noise exactly like that of a locomotive letting off steam. Some thirty feet from the summit cliffs rose sheer and barred the road, causing us the exasperating sensation of failure at the last moment, which was naturally much worse for Wood than for myself, although I should have liked to have visited the craters again. The descent was easy enough, and, after tea at the "icefall," we returned to camp, suffering from bad headaches as a penalty for approaching the orifices; the following morning we returned to Sangun.

The night temperatures were now delightfully cold, and we generally started in eight degrees of frost, but to reach Ládis we had once again to descend, camping half-way at the Jangal. *Omne ignotum pro magnifico* is a bad rule in the East, as Ládis, which had been represented as a cluster of thriving villages, proved to be a collection of seven hamlets,[1] in which supplies were almost unprocurable, the little we managed to scrape together being sold at about six times Sistán rates. The district can, however, boast of a very nice stream, with sufficient water to irrigate many hundreds of acres; there is also plenty of suitable land and the climate is good. With an altitude of 4200 feet, and Kuh-i-Taftán as a neighbouring hill-station, Ládis must in time rise to importance as forming the only cultivated area lying between Rigán and Nushki, although it is hopeless to expect development so long as Sarhad is unsettled and liable to raids.

We had fixed upon this spot as our halting-place for Christmas Day, and although supplies were difficult to come by, we shot plenty of game, including black and hill partridges, snipe, pigeon, teal, and a woodcock.

Mohamed Rezá Khán, the Reki chief, who, like all Baluchis, considers himself of Arab extraction through Hamza, an uncle of the Prophet, gave us much of his society. He supplied men for three or four posts on the Nushki road, and on the strength of this his self-importance was extreme. However, like all Baluchis, he would not raise a finger to procure forage or flour, while protesting his intense desire to serve us, and I had to exert considerable pressure before he would settle the case of a Peshin Afghán, who had been robbed by members of his tribe in 1896. The individual in question had been hanging about since that date in the hope of obtaining justice, which my opportune arrival secured for him.

After our Christmas dinner Wood left me for a few days in order to discover a better route through the hills to the west, while I marched north-east, in order to strike the Kacha Kuh post as soon as possible, as there I hoped to obtain news of my next-door neighbour, Captain Webb Ware, Political Assistant of the Chágai district. Upon leaving Ládis, we crossed the river close to the fine old fort, which is now deserted owing to the undermining action of water on the cliffs, and after a stiff rise, descended a *nala*, which drains

[1] Commencing from the west is Dizak, a ruined fort, on the right bank of the river, with no population; then Barziár, surrounded by thirty tents, and Bangán, where we camped, with eight tents; Ládis and Alinján come next, the whole population of the former and half of the latter having disappeared, only twenty families being left. Further south and away from the river, M- Kuh with forty tents and Anda with twenty tents. Total, one hundred and eighteen tents, or a population of about six hundred, all miserably poor.

towards Mirjáwa (properly Mirjabád), the frontier village. It is the property of Mohamed Rezá Khán, who insisted upon being my guide.

The range of hills to the east, towards which we were marching, is, it is interesting to note, the exact counterpart of the Siá Band on the west. We halted in the waterless desert, where a letter arrived from Webb Ware, to the effect that my escort would reach Robát in a few days, but that he himself could not be there until the middle of January. Much to my surprise, the camels broke down on the next day's stage, which shows that they cannot go for very long without water, except after training. We entered the range obliquely and camped at Bugsár, the sweet-sounding Baluchi term for a meadow.

A telegram from Kermán, which had been despatched only a week after my departure, reached me at this stage, and I calculated that if it took as long on its return journey to the Telegraph Office at Kermán, it mattered very little what answer I gave, as the question would be pretty sure to have been settled weeks before. A second letter also came in from the Mashkel, as Webb Ware, who is nothing if not thorough, had sent copies to three points on the frontier. The present missive was brought by a nice-looking boy, the brother of the chief, *Mír* Kiá. When it came to the question of paying for the messenger, the boy begged us not to say what we gave him, as otherwise his brother would annex it, the usual custom in a patriarchally organised family, which appears to stifle all individuality.

The march of the following day led across a broken-up country, and a little snow fell. We gradually approached a black, forbidding-looking range, and after a long stage, reached the post of *Seiid* Langar, under the Kacha Kuh, on the Nushki-Sistán road.

The opening up of this route has been so recently accomplished that no excuse is needed for giving some account of it. As a result of the Baluch-Afghán and Perso-Baluch Boundary Commissions, a large slice of desert, with little, if any, population, had to be recognised as part of the Indian Empire. This somewhat unpromising "No man's land," the refuge of most of the border ruffians, who periodically sallied forth to plunder and lay waste, was handed over to Webb Ware, who had been on the Boundary Commission, and he at once started to open up a caravan route appointing some of the prominent brigands as guards. A difficult country to develop can hardly exist, as from Nushki, then a mere village, to cultivated Sistán is a distance of, approximately, 500 miles, and nowhere along the road was there even a hamlet. When it is realised that a camel caravan marches but little more than ten to twelve miles a day on an average, the extent of this appalling waste can be more accurately appreciated, and further, if the almost total absence of water, the terrible summer heat, the prevalence of brigandage, and the want of population are all considered, it may tend to show what difficulties had to be overcome.

However, although it was at first a case of "hastening slowly," there now exists a rude stone building occupied by a few levies at every stage, while *bannias*, who sell supplies at fixed rates, are stationed at the more important *thanas*, where branch post-offices have been opened. A post now runs twice a week as far as Sistán, and what is known in India as a *kacha* road, fifteen feet wide, has been constructed from Nushki, to which point there is a metalled road, and also a telegraph line. If, as is rumoured, the railway line were to be prolonged to Nushki, not only would the cold bleak Baluch highlands be avoided, but Nushki might become an extremely important centre, as I understand that between it and Karachi the country is comparatively easy for railway construction. In this case, a Karachi-Nushki line would be substituted for the terrible Quetta-Sibi section, ever a weak line of communication, and any junction with a Persian or an Afghán railway would probably take place at Nushki.

In 1900 the interests of the *Khán* of Kalát in the Nushki district were bought out by the Government of India, and prosperity is now advancing by leaps and bounds. At the time of my journey all this was in an embryonic condition, as the question was, whether the through Khorasán trade could be attracted to the route, or, in other words, whether the new road could compete with the old-established routes from Bandar Abbás, as otherwise a large expenditure was unjustifiable.

The routes from the coast, as mentioned in chap. xxvi., run via Narmáshir to Neh, or Naiband, and are at least a hundred miles shorter, while the country is more fertile, the greatest stretch of desert being some 200 miles in width. In addition, the camel-grazing is better, and the track is throughout, as far as the district of Káin, in Hot Country, whereas Quetta lies at an elevation of

5500 feet. Consequently, the natural advantages were against the new route, and at first the few people who travelled along it expressed strong hopes that they might never use it again.

Thanks, however, to the wise liberality of the Government of India, headed by a Viceroy who is also a Persian traveller, and had previously studied the question in all its phases, a considerable expenditure was decided upon, all tolls and duties being abolished, with the happy result that where I only met one small caravan, hundreds of camels now pass. Such a success is it, that the merchants at Bandar Abbás are losing much of their business, and the desert is literally teeming with life, nomads from every quarter settling down in proximity to the road. Hamlets, too, are springing up as the disused *kanáts* are cleaned out and fresh ones dug, while a brisk local trade has already been created by the inhabitants of the lower reaches of the Helmand and of Sistán, who find a profitable market for their wheat and barley.

When the history of India in the last decade of the nineteenth century comes to be written, I venture to think that high praise will be awarded to a Government which has made such a desert "blossom like the rose." The moral effect on the neighbouring countries is not easily reckoned, and every Sistáni now wishes for a trip to Quetta; there is also a safe refuge for the harassed trans-frontier nomads, who are gradually filling up what was five years ago a blank, in every sense of the word. The value of the trade now aggregates £100,000, and is increasing.

Before, however, quitting this subject, I would point out that the natural line for through traffic runs *via* Kandahár and Herát, and that if Habíbulla Khán adopts a more liberal trade policy than his father, the Nushki-Sistán route would lose most of its importance; it is, in fact, an artificial channel of trade, called into being by the prohibitive dues levied by the late Amir, who as it were built a wall round Afghánistán.

To resume, at Kacha Kuh I was joined by some *sowárs* of the 6th Bombay Cavalry. Their horses were much exhausted by almost continuous marching, and they found no words too strong to paint the desert stages they had traversed. I was much struck by the bales of compressed forage which they had brought from Quetta, enabling them to perform a journey which otherwise would have been almost out of the question in midwinter, a camel being unable to carry a greater load than 150 lbs. of *kah* or chopped straw, owing to its enormous bulk.

Upon continuing the journey, we moved parallel to the range in bitterly cold weather, the thermometer registering many degrees of frost, while our moustaches froze hard even in bed. We arrived at Bug on the last day of 1898, and thence crossed the range, twisting up and down a veritable labyrinth of *nalas* with precipitous cliffs. I was very glad to hear that Webb Ware subsequently discovered a track which kept entirely to the east of the Kacha Kuh, as whenever heavy rain fell, or the snow melted, no caravan could pass by the route that I travelled.

On 2nd January 1899 we reached Robát Kala, approaching it along the Afghán frontier, where the neat boundary pillars were apparently intact. Winding up a stony valley, we sighted a *caravanserai*, not unlike an old peel tower, with its background of frowning black hills, and in a few minutes were encamped on the north-western extremity of the great Indian Empire, whose south-eastern limits are more than 2000 miles distant.

FROM A BRASS TRAY.

CHAPTER XXXI

SISTÁN

> "And thou hast trod the sands of Seistan
> And seen the river of Helmund, and the Lake
> Of Zirrah." —MATTHEW ARNOLD, *Sohrab and Rustum.*

BEFORE entering the province of Sistán it may perhaps not be out of place to outline the various interesting historical and physical problems by which we are confronted.

In the *Sháh Náma* Sistán is the home of the famous family of champions, who seated the Keiánian dynasty on the throne of Persia. Their most brilliant scion was Rustam, whose matchless daring forms the main theme of Firdusi's great epic, and who is as much the national hero to-day as he was a thousand years or more ago, everything in Persia that is not understood, such as the Sásánian rock sculptures at Persepolis, being attributed to this champion, who, like the Homeric heroes, was as mighty a trencher-man as warrior, and almost equally respected for his prowess in both fields.

At the period referred to above, Sagistán, as Sistán was then called, practically meant the low country to the west of Kandahár, Zabulistán being the name for the upland country, now the home of the Berbers. During the latter years of Rustam—he lived well over a century—the Persian capital was shifted from the banks of the Helmand to Fárs, and in due course history takes the place of legend.

With regard to the historical existence of Rustam, I think we may at all events admit that there was a champion, or a family of champions, who led the hosts of Irán, and furthermore, that as their history is given so circumstantially almost down to historical times, there is every probability that their exploits have a substratum of truth. Moreover, in those days, a man bigger and heavier than his adversaries always inspired a very wholesome fear, for not only could he deal deadlier blows, but, equally important, he could carry heavier armour; in fact he was like a battleship, and his opponents resembled cruisers.

The Sarangians, mentioned by Herodotus as belonging to the 14th satrapy, occupied Sistán during the reign of Darius, and the Greek historians who narrated the conquests of Alexander the Great, gave the name of Drangiana to what is now, roughly speaking, Southern Afghánistán. This province was traversed by the world-conqueror on his way to Bactria and by Krateros on his march from Karachi to Karmania. But the most ancient traveller who actually visited and described these provinces, albeit very briefly, is Isidorus of Charax, who was a contemporary of Augustus, and whose account is of such value that I quote it in a footnote.[1] We thus see that Fara and Neh were important towns, while Γαρὶ may be Girishk. Zarangia is the same as Sarangia, and includes Persian Sistán. The town of Zirra is apparently the same word which still survives in the name of the great lagoon mentioned below.

Sakastani or the Land of the Sakae is evidently the same word as the Sistán of to-day. The Sakae have disappeared from this part of Asia, but I understand that the theory connecting them with the Saxons is held in certain quarters.

According to Mr Hogarth,[2] Alexander the Great wintered in Sistán, and thence marched up the Helmand, and I am inclined to think that, after crushing the revolt of Satibarzanes and his family at Artacoana, the modern Herát, he marched to Tabas Sunnikhána, and from Tabas[3] proceeded to Fara, striking the upper Helmand

[1] Ἐντεῦθεν Ἀναύων χώρα τῆς Ἀρείας, σχοῖνοι νέ, ἐν ᾗ πόλις μεγίστη Φρὰ καὶ Βὶς πόλις καὶ Γαρὶ πόλις καὶ Νιὴ πόλις· κώμη δὲ οὐκ ἔστιν.—ISIDORUS OF CHARAX. 16 (Müller's *Geographi Graeci Minores*, vol. i. p. 253).

[2] *Vide* his *Philip and Alexander of Macedon*, p. 217.

[3] *Vide* p. 407.

about Girishk, near which village I would locate the tribe of Euergetae. It must be borne in mind that Alexander was bound for Bactria, but was forced to keep to the main roads, admitting which, we can practically fix the route as given above.

In the catalogue of Bactrian coins at the British Museum (Pl. vi. fig. ii.) there is a silver coin of Plato Epiphanes, a contemporary of Eucratides of Bactria, who reigned in the middle of the second century, B.C. It has been surmised that Plato Epiphanes was King of Sistán, and although not proved the theory is most suggestive, and certainly deserves mention.

We may pass over the Parthian and Sásánian dynasties, only remarking that the Arab conquest is perhaps responsible for the final destruction of the very ancient cities of Keikobád and Garshásp, and the foundation of Arab towns in their stead, but this is merely conjecture, especially as the invading hordes at first caused the nomadisation of the country.

It was from Sistán that the Saffár dynasty went forth to win an empire, and the province is described by that illustrious traveller, Istakhri, who gives a detailed account of Zaranj or Zirra, which was evidently immensely strong. He concludes his description of Sistán as follows: "Some land in the vicinity of this city is barren and sandy. The air is very warm. Here they have dates: there are no hills. In winter there is no snow: in general there is a wind, and they have windmills accordingly."[1] When one reads of the numerous bridges and boats, it is lamentable to reflect that to-day both are equally unknown in Sistán, which has indeed retrograded in every way.

In A.H. 764 (1362), Tímúr, at that time a fugitive, entered the province at the head of a thousand horsemen[2] and captured many villages, but was eventually wounded in the hand and foot and compelled to retreat to Makrán. It was from this wound that he received the *soubriquet* of *lang* or lame, which accounts for the name of Tamerlane by which he is still known in Europe.

In A.H. 785 (1383), Tímúr again invaded Sistán, after massacring man, woman, and child in Khorasán, and carried Zirra by assault the same day that he appeared before it. He then marched on

[1] Sir W. Ouseley's *Ibn Haukal* (p. 205), which is generally considered to be a record of the travels of Istakhri.

[2] Cf. Markham's *Persia*, p. 193 *seq.*

the capital, which was Záhidán, so far as I can learn. There the resistance was desperate and the Sistánis fought like lions, but they were no match for the irresistible Tatár, and the capital was finally captured, the entire garrison being put to the sword. The whole of the loot was sent to enrich Samarkand, the *mullás* were conveyed to Herát, and Záhidán was given over to the jackals, who still form its inhabitants. To complete the catastrophe, the great dam, then known as the Band-i-Rustam but later termed the Band-i-Akva or the Afghán's Dam,[1] was destroyed by the merciless Tímúr, or, if local legend be accepted, by his son Sháh Rukh.

It is at this point that I would refer to the physical problems of Sistán,[2] as Sháh Rukh's action tended to change the conditions of the province so materially that it still presents more or less the same appearance to-day. Sistán, that is to say, the lake and delta formed by the discharge of the Helmand and other less important rivers, was at some remote period one vast lake. Land was formed by the *detritus* brought down by the various rivers (of which the Helmand is by far the most important) along the northern portion of this lake, but this is now desert, while inhabited Sistán to the south was formed by the drying up of the lake itself, owing to the decreased volume of the river, and perhaps also by the use of the water for purposes of cultivation.

In another part of this book I have ventured to express my opinion that Alexander's march with a large army and a huge camp tends to show that Asia was, in his day, not so arid as at present, and it would seem possible that, in a sense, my observations in Sistán support this contention, as some of the dry *nala* courses have banks more than 200 feet high, while elsewhere they are less than 30 feet; also to the south of the district the water-worn cliffs are very striking.

If we turn to modern travellers, we find that M. Khanikoff was particularly struck by the fact that the Birjand river, or rather its bed, runs right across the Lut, giving evidence that the rainfall was, at no very distant period, much greater. Nowadays, none of its water ever reaches the desert, even in flood time. Again, Sir

[1] General Houtum Schindler, who is so great an authority on Persia, pointed out to me that the Afgháns were termed Aghváns in Sefavi times.

[2] Vide *From the Indus to the Tigris*, by Dr Bellew; Ferrier's *Caravan Journeys*; and Colonel Yate's *Khorasán and Sistán*.

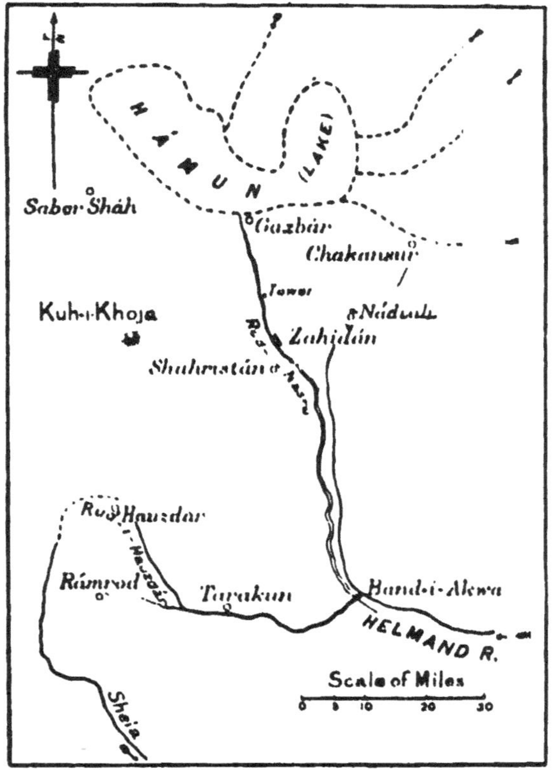

SKETCH No 1

THE HELMAND DELTA. [To face p. 364.

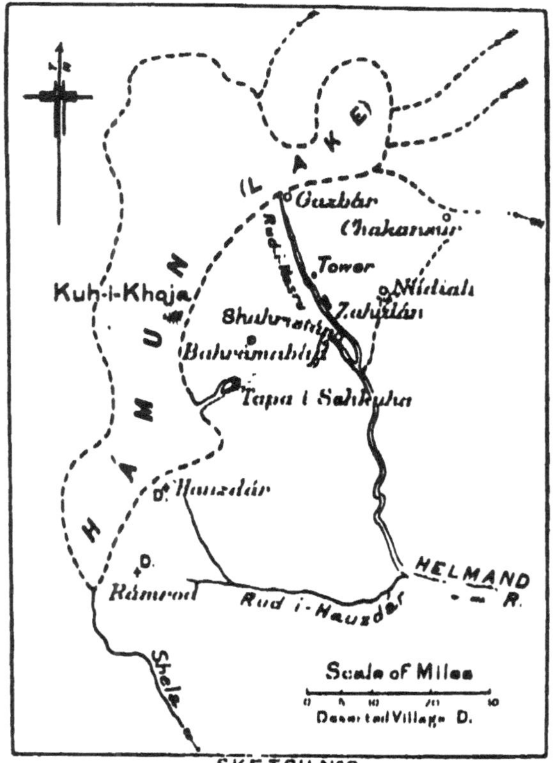

SKETCH No 2.

THE HELMAND DELTA. [To face p. 364.

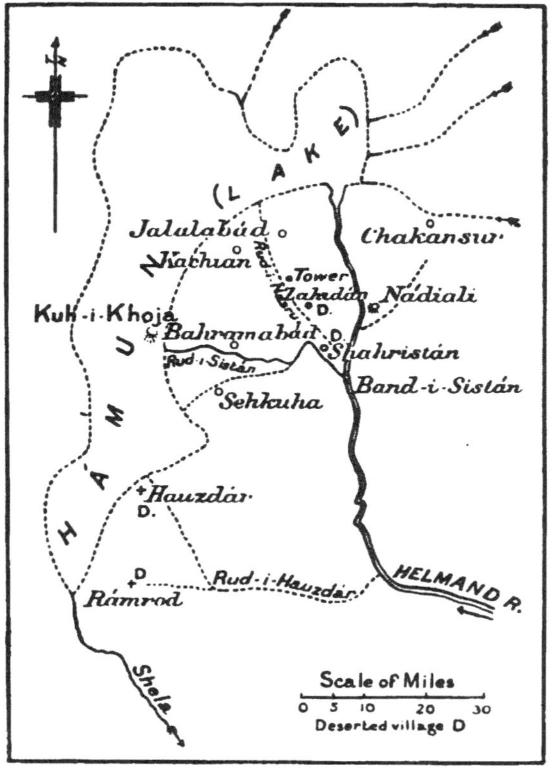

SKETCH No. 3.

THE HELMAND DELTA. *To face p.* 364.

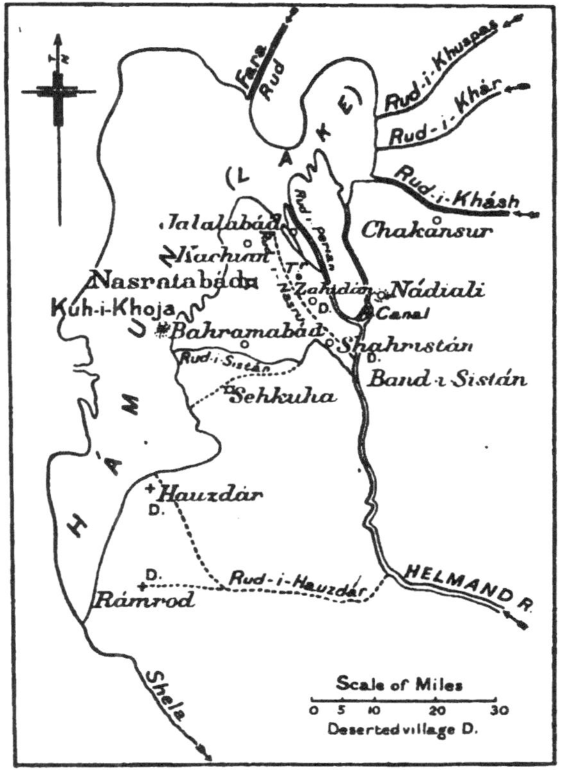

SKETCH No. 4.

THE HELMAND DELTA. [*To face p.* 364.

George Birdwood informed me that India was being ruined in the same manner, by the destruction of her forests, when Great Britain appeared on the scene just in time.[1] I could give much more evidence of a similar character.

Sistán of to-day has water on three sides for part of the year, the Helmand forming its eastern boundary, while to the north and west lies the *hámun* or lagoon, which will be described further on. To the south-east of inhabited Sistán is situated the Gaud-i-Zirra or Hollow of Zirra, which is connected with the lagoon by the Shéla, a watercourse 350 yards wide, with banks 50 feet high where I crossed it. The great trough itself is at least 100 miles in length by 30 miles in width, and appears to have received either the whole of the present water-supply or the overflow of the old and greater flood; otherwise it is impossible to account for its vast area. The Shéla runs in a briny stream when there is a large accession to the lake, and Captain Jennings describes the parallel waters of the Shéla and Helmand flowing in opposite directions, with the lowest of sand-ridges intervening. Nowadays, as a rule, there is little more than a marsh in the lowest portion of the *Gaud*, not ten per cent. of its area being covered, even in springtime. If Istakhri be correct, it would appear that in his day the Hirmand, as he always terms it, ran down to the Zirra Lake, which he describes as being 30 *farsakh* or about 100 miles in length when full. This would seem to settle the question.

Before the advent of Tímúr the lame, the Helmand was dammed to the south-west of Rudbár, not far from the modern Bandar Kamál Khán, by the Band-i-Avk or Akva, which is shown in Conolly's map as the Bund-i-Burmakoa.[2] From the Avk or Akva dam (the modern spelling is apparently the latter form) the Rud-i-Hauzdár, a wide and deep canal, was drawn off to water the district south of the modern inhabited Sistán, where the traveller of to-day passes deserted towns of considerable size. The chief of these was Hauzdár, which is said to be the spot where Rustam's son, Farámurz, was impaled by Bahrám.

The main river then ran north-north-west past Shahristán and Záhidán, villages lining its banks for many miles. This

[1] It was not, however, until comparatively recently that scientific forestry was introduced, and to this delay recent famines may be partly attributed.

[2] *Journal of Asiatic Society of Bengal*, vol. ix. p. 724 (1840).

was the position of matters before the Tatár cataclysm, but when Sháh Rukh destroyed the great dam, the Hauzdár district, as may be imagined, finally lost its water-supply, and although the Rud-i-Nasru remained the main stream, a new channel was formed near the modern dam, which encircled the "three hills" of Sehkuhá, then uninhabited, but later on the capital of Sistán.

As far as is known, there was no further important alteration until some sixty years ago, when, according to Conolly, who was there shortly after, the whole of the water united in forming a course to the west of Nád-i-Ali, striking off near the modern dam, and consequently Sistán was left waterless. In despair, all classes united and constructed a dam which, however, the river avoided, and in Conolly's time—he travelled in 1839—nothing more was done. Later on, perhaps in the forties, the present tamarisk dam was constructed, and the Mádar Áb excavated, no light task.

The course of the river remaining unchanged, when Sir Frederic Goldsmid was appointed to arbitrate between Persia and Afghánistán, he constituted it the boundary from the dam down to where its waters discharged into the lake. Eight years ago however, probably as the result of deposited silt, the river began to work out a passage further west, until at the time of our visit the main Helmand, under the name of Rud-i-Perián,[1] ran parallel to, and to the east of the ancient Rud-i-Nasru, destroying Jahanabád (mentioned by Ferrier), Ibrahimabád and Jalalabád, the home of the Keiáni family. It is expected that the unbridled stream may finally seek its original course, and as it is the Afgháns can fairly complain that they are left high and dry, the Nád-i-Ali branch holding little water.

To resume the history, after Tímúr the Keiáni tribe, which claims descent from the Persian royal family of twenty-five or more centuries ago, appears to have generally ruled the province. Its chief was sometimes independent, but when the Sefavi dynasty was at its zenith, he naturally acknowledged the overlordship of Persia, just as his ancestors had probably paid tribute to the Uzbegs.

When Isfahán was besieged by the Afgháns, *Malik* Mahmud, the reigning prince, came to the rescue with 10,000 followers, but as the invaders promised him the possession of Khorasán, he left

[1] Rud-i-Perián signifies "River of the Fairies."

the royal city to its fate. Shortly afterwards he was captured in Meshed by Nádir, who was beginning to force himself to the front, and his heirs, who were two brothers, sustained a seven years' siege on the Kuh-i-Khója, but were finally conciliated and submitted.

Upon the death of Nádir Sháh, the kingdom of Afghanistán was founded by Sháh Ahmad, who held all Eastern Persia, including Káin and Sistán, both of which provinces were administered from Herát. The Keiáni tribe was gradually waning, owing to family quarrels, and to its espousal of the losing side at the death of Ahmad Sháh, and at the end of the eighteenth century, the Nahrui[1] tribe of Baluchis was invited to settle in Sistán as a counterpoise to the Shahrekis[2] and Sarbandis.[3]

In 1833 the Sistánis took part in the defence of Herát against the Persians, but some twenty years later Ali Khán, the chief of the Sarbandi tribe, who treated Ferrier with true hospitality, in spite of pressure from his neighbour of Chakansur to rob and kill him, gave in his adherence to Persia, and received a royal bride, the daughter of Bahrám *Mírza*,[4] who was escorted to Sehkuha, his stronghold. Ali Khán's hands were unfortunately not clean, as he had blinded his eldest brother's son, Lutf Ali Khán, in order to seize the chiefship, and he was besieged and killed by another of his nephews Táj Mohamed, the Sháh's cousin being wounded while endeavouring to defend her husband, after which she returned to Tehrán, and is, I believe, still alive. As an interesting souvenir I bought a carpet that was looted at this time, and was the property of Ali Khán. It was sold to me by one of his grand-nephews. Táj Mohamed was at first allowed to hold the chiefship, but being summoned to pay his respects to the Sháh at Meshed, he was imprisoned, but escaped, and thence-

[1] The Nahrui tribe claims descent from the Arabs of Nahrawán. In Sistán there are perhaps 2000 families under its chief, Seiid Khán, son of *Sardár* Sharif Khán.

[2] The Shahrekis to-day have no importance, but may include 500 families.

[3] The Sarbandis, now the most influential tribe, were connected with the Bráhuis, and may thus be aborigines; they were almost annihilated by Tímúr, who transported the few survivors to Burujird. Nádir Sháh brought back a section of the tribe to Sistán, where it has taken fresh root, and numbers 3000 families.

[4] This I learnt from M. Khanikoff's *Mémoire*, which I have found to be most valuable.

forward led a roving life, being employed by the late Sir Oliver St John at Kandahár, and finally dying at Quetta.

After this the Persian Government gradually took possession of Sistán, and began to occupy forts across the Helmand, but meanwhile Shir Ali had been able to strengthen his hold on the throne of Afghánistán, and was consequently in a position to oppose this process of absorption. To avoid a Perso-Afghán war, Her Majesty's Government finally agreed to arbitrate in accordance with the treaty of Paris, and the Sistán Mission, which first drew British attention to the district, was the result. Its record is embodied in General Goldsmid's *Eastern Persia*, which is a veritable mine of information.

The position was one of difficulty, owing to the hostility of the local authorities, which was mainly the result of ignorance. The arbitrator had to decide, not so much as to claims—both the Afgháns and Persians having laid the district under tribute at various periods—but as to the actual *status quo*. The *Amir* of Káin, however, imagined that the British Commissioner was trying to seize as much territory as possible for his Government—Afghánistán being always regarded by Persians as a province of the Indian Empire—and as the Persian Commissioner was apparently only anxious to make money,[1] he saw that by fostering this mistaken idea he could advance his private interests.

Reading through the account, one is mainly struck by the hostility displayed by the *Amir* of Káin, who was in charge of the province, and still more by the extraordinary forbearance shown by the British Mission, which was thrown away on the rough people they had to deal with. Not being able to make a full enquiry, General Goldsmid returned to Tehrán, where he gave his decision by which, as before stated, the Helmand was made the boundary, thus giving to Persia practically the whole of the revenue-paying portion. However, an appeal was made to the Secretary of State by both parties, but the decision was upheld.

Sistán was again more or less lost sight of, although occasionally visited by British[2] and Russian officers, until the opening up of the

[1] For his bad behaviour he was punished by the Persian Government.

[2] In the winter of 1893-4, Colonel Yate made a tour in the district, the impression he produced being so great, that I heard that the "Lord Sáhib" was in Sistán.

Quetta-Nushki-Khorasán road, which was one result of the Perso-Afghán Boundary Commission, and in this connection it was visited by Captain Webb Ware in 1897. A Russian Vice-Consul was appointed in the autumn of 1898, and about the same time I was instructed to found a Consulate, which accounts for my presence in the district.

DESIGN FROM A KERMÁN SHAWL.

CHAPTER XXXII

THE FOUNDING OF THE SISTÁN CONSULATE

"There is a history in all men's lives,
Figuring the nature of the times deceased;
The which observ'd, a man may prophesy,
With a near aim, of the main chance of things
As yet not come to life, which in their seeds
And weak beginnings lie intreasured."
—SHAKESPEARE, *Henry IV.*, PART II.

HAVING in the previous chapter given a brief account of the province for which we were bound, I will again take up the thread of my narrative.

I thought that I was ahead of Wood, but having no news of him, we quitted Robát Kala, and after crossing an open watershed, effected a junction with the track from Fahraj, which I carefully scanned, hoping to see signs of my fellow-traveller. However finding none, I erected a pile of stones in which I inserted a note. At thirteen miles we passed a spring of sweet water at the stage of Kuh-i-Malik-i-Siá,[1] and there, at last, I found the unmistakable tracks of the cyclometer, and so knew that Wood was in touch with the advance camp.

At this point we were skirting the base of a low, black commonplace hill, such as one sees in thousands throughout Sarhad, and it was with quite a sense of disappointment that we

[1] Or Hill of the Black Chief.

noted that this was the point where the British and Persian Empires met the state of Afghánistán, the name of Kuh-i-Malik-i-Siá being a familiar one to frontier officers, although it had never, I believe, been visited until about fifteen years ago. It was selected by Sir Frederic Goldsmid, who remarked that it was the first hill met with to the south-west in a suitable position for terminating the Sistán boundary, which was accordingly delimitated in a direct line from the Sistán dam to this low black hill, but no boundary pillars were erected. It was not until 1896 that the Perso-Baluch and the Baluch-Afghán frontiers were demarcated, and not until after my visit that the longitude and latitude of this, the north-west boundary pillar of our great Indian Empire, was finally fixed by Mr G. P. Tate, of the Indian Survey, who has been more than fifteen years in Baluchistán.

At the stage of Hurmak I found Wood and party, the latter, including the camels, being quite worn out. After quitting me at Ládis, he had travelled due west as far as Galugán across unexplored country, finding the passage through the hills very easy. Thence, in order to gain the open level desert, he had crossed the Galugán plain, some thirty miles wide, but had found the Rud-i-Máhi, which leads through the western range of Sarhad, very difficult for a telegraph line, the road running down the river-bed, which is fringed by high precipitous cliffs. He had thence rejoined me *via* Duzdáp or the Bandits' Pool, a suggestive and appropriate name. As the pads of his camels were terribly worn, we calculated out our supplies and decided to halt a day, as at Hurmak was the last fresh water we should enjoy until we drank of the Helmand.

When the journey was resumed, the unending succession of stony *nalas*, up and down which our horses had been stumbling, came abruptly to an end, and we entered an apparently boundless level plain, the contemplation of which was at first quite oppressive. Strangely enough, its vastness, and perhaps the growing warmth of the day (although at 8 A.M. the thermometer stood at twenty-four degrees), produced the same feeling that is experienced upon landing after a long sea voyage. Even the horses were affected by lassitude, although they were soon able to appreciate the change. We halted in the waterless waste near some bushes suitable for fuel, and as these were the last we should meet with, all the spare camels were loaded up with firewood, and we prepared three or four sackfuls of charcoal.

The following morning we reached the banks of the Shéla,[1] erroneously termed Shelag, which held large pools of brine, on which a few duck were disporting themselves. One of these we hit, but so thick were its feathers that three or more barrels were necessary to bag it, and after all it was pronounced to be uneatable. Crossing the wide and deep river-bed diagonally, we ascended the left bank, and approached the first group of ruins, consisting of domes on an apparently artificial mound, from which we knew that we were in the district originally watered from the Helmand by the Rud-i-Hauzdár. We camped near Girdi Cháh, the half-way house at which my post was afterwards installed, visiting the immense ruins of Ramrud in the evening, where the mud houses, after being so long deserted, are still almost fit for habitation.

Girdi Cháh, as a glance at the map will show, is of importance, both from its position and also from the fact that it possesses the only drinkable water for many miles, and even that is much contaminated. It is therefore of necessity visited by the caravans which have cut across Afghán territory, as well as by those which have kept to Persian soil. My postal *sowárs* began cultivating a little grain and cleaned out the wells, so that in time a village may spring up, which will be the greatest boon to caravans, most of which avoid the cut-up surface of Sistán, and after sending in for supplies, skirt the western edge of the lagoon.

The next march ran through a district covered with deserted towns and villages, many of which are even now habitable, but, alas! there is no water. At the seventh mile we passed to the east of an artificial mound, which is covered with tombs. Its name is Khák-Mohamed-Dervish, signifying that on it are buried the remains of Mohamed, a saintly character. The country, when not bare, was covered with tamarisk, but at the time of the Sistán Mission roots of reeds were visible, and the country was, it is stated, annually flooded until about 1866.

We rose over a five-foot bank, which ran out of sight east and west, and was evidently used to limit the inundations, close by

[1] *Shéla* is an Arabic term for a body of water; cf. *Mashila*, signifying a swamp, the name for the district behind Bushire.

TRUE NORTH
HELMAND
NAIZAR
HAMUN
Mirgul
Tapa-i-Tilai
Hadimi
Gazbar
Karkusha
Dost Mohamed
Beiring
Kachian
Siadak
Rasul
Khán Táus
Bandán R.
Mil-i-Nádir
Rud-i-Perian
Nasrabád
Nasratabád
Bunjar
Pillar
Huseinabád
Iskil
Fort
Afzilabád
Zahidán
Nádi Ali
Milak
Kul
Kuh-i-Khoja
Deh Nawáb
Bahramabád
Kala-i-Arbáb
Shahristan
Sultan Mohamed
Jazinak
Chilling
Band-i-Jaruki
Khoja Ahmad
Mádar
Dolatabád
Kala No
Kala Kohna
Band-i-Sistán
Sehkuha
Helmand R.
Varmál
Chah-i-Asak
Hauzdár
Kundár
SKETCH MAP OF
SISTÁN
Scale of Miles
0 5 10 20
Nat scale 1:750,000 or 11·8 miles-1 inch.

[To face p. 372.

which was Kundar, presenting an imposing appearance when seen from a distance. Continuing on across the bare level plain, we kept to the west of Hauzdár, an important town in ancient days,[1] and camped at Asak Cháh, where we found several wells of indifferent water, with large flocks of sheep in the neighbourhood.

At length we were within a short march of inhabited Sistán, and so were desirous of completing the few remaining miles that intervened between us and supplies of flour and forage, the want of which had caused us much anxiety. We afterwards learned that a relief train had passed and missed us near Girdi Cháh.

We rode across a turfy plain, and soon reached the first irrigation canal, some fourteen feet wide and eighteen inches deep. Our horses at last were happy, and drank and drank until we forced them on from motives of humanity. Skirting the water-worn cliffs we soon sighted Varmál, a large village of perhaps one thousand inhabitants. On alighting at our camp, we beheld sack upon sack of barley and flour, which proved that we were once again in a land of plenty, and as we had not a day's rations in hand, our satisfaction was immense.

I have been much struck by the resemblance that exists between Sistán and Egypt on the one hand and Sarhad and Palestine on the other. Sistán absolutely depends on the Helmand, much as Egypt does on the Nile, both districts being the granaries of the surrounding tribes. Again, in Sarhad, just as in Palestine, drought renders the land uninhabitable, the flocks of sheep and goats dying from want of nourishment, and, during my journey across Sarhad, every enquiry as to absent tribes elicited the invariable reply of "Gone to Sistán."

In the same way as the patriarch Abraham, and later on Jacob, were forced to seek Egypt, to preserve their families alive, so to-day the nomads of Sarhad are collected in and round Sistán, although the skeletons that we passed proved that there had been a considerable loss of life on the road. To complete the parallel, just as the traveller to Egypt traversed the Arabian Desert, partly in sight of the Mediterranean Sea, so too the famine-stricken herds-

[1] Hauzdár, as we saw it, is comparatively modern, and consisted of an irregular, many-sided wall, inside which were hundreds of houses, the largest being two-storied. It was at one time the property of the Ráis tribe, but the Sarbandi chief, having gained a footing by marriage, seized the fort and dispossessed its previous owners, most of whom were probably killed.

men painfully urge their worn-out flocks across the desert to Sistán and see the great *hámun*, and then the glistening Helmand, which, like the Nile, guarantees the wanderer and his flocks from death by hunger.

From Varmál Nasrulla Khán proceeded to Nasratabád, the capital, to arrange for our reception, and we were very glad of a halt. Our first visit to the lake revealed a perfectly open sheet of water covered with myriads of wild-fowl, all of which were well out of range. While we looked on, feeling rather depressed as there are no rafts at Varmál, the birds rose with a roar exactly resembling the surf beating on a rocky shore.

Finding that our chances of the longed-for wild-fowl shooting were *nil* in this part of Sistán, we turned our attention to two or three gardens containing fine vines, which were said to be full of black partridges. After scrambling over thorn-protected walls and jumping from trench to trench (the vines being grown in this manner), we finally put up a brace of partridges which were being stalked by a jackal, and were fortunate in bagging all three.

Returning to the camp in triumph, we found that the Governor had sent down an official to look after us and escort us to Nasratabád. We marched in two stages to the capital, and although we made a detour to the west, to avoid the deeper irrigation channels, yet many of our camels fell and wetted their loads. The *abdári* camel which carried our lunch stuck so firmly that the bank had to be ramped, and the poor "ship of the desert," which is helpless and miserable in water, was hauled and lifted on to dry ground by a gang of men. Some of the channels were thirty feet wide and three feet deep, so that even one's saddlery suffered somewhat, although later on we underwent much worse experiences.

Two Turkoman couriers, who had come down from Meshed with the first home post since we left Yezd in October, headed the *sowárs* in the inevitable procession, and about four miles from the fort we were met by *Mír* Masum Khán, the Governor, a boy of nineteen, whom, however, I took to be at least twenty-five, partly because he wore blue spectacles. This being the night before the first day of Ramazán, the month of fasting, after being greeted by the garrison, armed with ancient guns resembling gas-pipes and headed by a band, which discoursed weird and plaintive music, we were left to settle into camp.

Having been somewhat puzzled by the discrepancies in the various accounts of the capital that I have read, I propose to explain how matters are to-day.

When the Persian Government was established in Sistán, a fortified residence for its ruler was a necessity. It was moreover important that his residence should be as near the Persian side of the province as possible, in order to provide for reverses, and naturally the question of supplies also came in for consideration. The present fortified village was accordingly built some thirty years ago by the *Amir* of Káin, almost touching the important village of Huseinabád, which now has some three thousand inhabitants.

At first apparently the name of the fort was Násirabád, and it is so termed by the members of the Goldsmid Mission, but its present name is Nasratabád. It consists of an enclosure about a quarter of a mile square, surrounded by thirty-foot walls of considerable thickness, with towers at close intervals. Running all round is a protected way, which is loop-holed, and there is a deep ditch, sometimes filled with water. Inside there are some fifty to one hundred shops, mainly occupied by soldiers, who, during their term of service in Sistán, devote themselves to trade, and are scarcely ever taken away from the fort. The interior is not entirely occupied by houses, and little patches of grain may occasionally be seen growing; as is always the case with Persian troops, donkeys are everywhere to the fore. At the north-west corner is the *Ark* or *Reduit*. Its profile is about the same as that of the rest of the fort, so far as I could judge, but as the matter was of no importance, I did not ask any questions, which are sure to arouse suspicion, the meanest mud tower being guarded as jealously as Mont Valérien.[1] The four gateways are closed at sunset, after which ceremony there does not appear to be any sentry-go, although, no doubt, some soldiers sleep in the guard-rooms.

Nasratabád is garrisoned by two Káin regiments, one of which is disbanded at home, while the other supplies the shop-keepers for the capital in the intervals of their military duties. They are armed with the useless *jezail*, although I understand that at Birjand there is a store of Werndl rifles, and, as may be supposed, they do not constitute a formidable body of fighting men. The score of gunners hail from Tabríz and hold a better position, of which they

[1] In *Eastern Persia* several anecdotes are given, bearing out this statement.

take the fullest advantage by carrying on a money-lending business and charging 500 per cent. as a minimum! To borrow from a gunner in Persia means more than to fall into the hands of the Jews in England.

We returned the Governor's call the day after our arrival, and, upon entering the village, turned sharp to the right and passed a rusty cannon, with its rammer stuck in its mouth, and about six gunners drawn up behind it. We thence rode through a second gateway, finally alighting at a low door and skirting a pool of water where two swans were swimming about, we entered a mean room in which *Mir* Masum Khán received us. He is the son of the *Hishmat-ul-Mulk*, himself the eldest son of the late *Amir*, and had been Governor of Sistán for the last six years, under the guidance of a vizier.

He was rather sallow and unwholesome-looking, and, as may be supposed, was ignorant and somewhat conceited, having been a Governor surrounded by menials all his life. However, we got on well enough, especially as I had no cases to settle with him, in which event I think that there would have been difficulties, as his mother, the daughter of *Sardár* Sherif Khán, must have been taken into account.

The political situation in Sistán at the time of our arrival was decidedly interesting, as, owing to *Mir* Masum Khán's close connection with the Nahrui tribe, *Sardár* Seiid Khán, his maternal uncle and its chief, had become the *de facto* ruler of Sistán, and, not unnaturally, made himself disliked by the leading men of the province. Upon being repeatedly petitioned, the *Hishmat-ul-Mulk* decided to send his eldest son by an inferior wife to replace his half-brother, putting him in charge of Abdul Waháb Beg, brother of Mohamed Rezá Khán's mother.

The new Governor and party reached Sistán early in January 1898, and asked to have the fort handed over to them. *Mir* Masum Khán, however, had no intention of throwing up the sponge, and pleaded illness as an excuse for delay. Thus matters dragged on for about three months, there being two Governors in Sistán. *Mir* Masum, however, had the advantage of possession, and the regiment was also on his side. To end the complication, Abdul Waháb collected his party with a view to rushing the fort, but after a conflict he was deserted, and had to surrender at discretion.

Meanwhile, a strong desire for his death had grown up, and the pretext was soon forthcoming, as he had been implicated in the assassination of a certain Dervish Khán, who was murdered on his return from Meshed, a short distance from Tabas, and whose family lived in Sistán and was clamouring for vengeance. Abdul Wahád Beg, however, swore to be a supporter of *Mir* Masum—the half-brother apparently counted for nothing—and it was arranged that he was to proceed to Meshed, in order to try and win over the Governor-General to his new views. In spite of this, as his fidelity was doubtful, it was finally decided to kill him, and one day, in broad daylight, he was shot with a revolver. He rushed off from the fort, pursued by his assassin to the Deputy-Governor's house, and, upon his promising to die speedily, no more shots were fired, but he was carefully watched to see that he did not break his word! The murderer then rode quietly off towards Birjand to be rewarded by the *Amir* of Káin—at least so it was stated—and every one considered that the atmosphere had been cleared!

It is appalling to note that murder is considered as a mere trifle, just like drinking a glass of water, as a Persian remarked to me; but yet I suppose that at the time of the Renaissance, only some four centuries ago, similar views were entertained, at any rate in Southern Europe, while in Chitrál it is only the successful assassin who is lauded.

The *Hishmat-ul-Mulk*, upon receiving information of what had happened, was furious, not only on account of the murder, but also at his orders being slighted, and instructed Purdil Khán, the one-armed Sarbandi chief, to drive out the Nahruis and to use force should *Mir* Masum decline to leave Sistán.[1] A sharp skirmish or two ensued, just about the date of my arrival, and the Nahruis finally crossed into Afghán territory, to await further developments, while *Mir* Masum tried to avoid leaving Sistán.

I may here perhaps anticipate events so far as to say that he finally did quit Sistán and visited his father at Tun, who merely said to him, "Masum, by killing Abdul Wahád you have knocked my staff from my hand." No further notice was taken of him, but his two chief advisers were seized and severely beaten, upon which he fled by night to Birjand, where his uncle showed him every

[1] The order was that he might resist so far as to kill one man, but that if he went further, he was to be killed himself.

kindness, and where he, too, was awaiting further developments, when I passed through in the autumn of 1899. I last heard of him at Quetta.

After spending but four days at Nasratabád, we returned to Varmál, where I had finally arranged to meet Webb Ware. We had hoped, as mentioned above, to have seen one another on the frontier, but owing to supply difficulties, he had been somewhat delayed, and so had very kindly crossed the desert and followed me up to Sistán.

Two days were spent in handing over papers, books, etc., and in exchanging news, after which Webb Ware, followed by Wood, marched off south. There were heartrending scenes between the servants, both camps being dissolved in tears, and Wood had great difficulty in getting his party to start. My feeling of loneliness was for a short time staved off, as Tate, who had also joined my camp, agreed to visit the Kuh-i-Khoja, and the following morning saw us on the march to the north-west.

If Sistán be the centre of the Persian heroic age, the Kuh-i-Khoja, its only hill, naturally plays a great part, and fully merits some mention. From whatever direction the traveller approaches the province, he descries a low, flat-topped hill like a dining-table, and if those articles were in use in Persia, I feel sure that we should have another "Table Mountain." Curiously enough, the Thabas Induna to the north-east of Buluwayo closely resembles the Kuh-i-Khoja. On its summit Mozilikatzi dealt out grim justice.

Kuh-i-Zor, Kuh-i-Rustam, or Kuh-i-Khoja, the latter term being almost universal nowadays, is generally more or less of an island, although at the time of the Goldsmid Mission the lake was waterless.[1] On the occasion of our visit, in order to approach it we employed *tutin* or reed rafts, which resemble bisected cigars, and are very fairly steady. The water being shallow, we had to wade in for some distance, and, upon reaching the raft, we sat upon a roll of felts. The ordinary *tutin* is some nine feet long and two feet six inches wide, and lasts about ninety days, after which the reeds rot. We occupied more than an hour in being slowly punted across the open water, which was brackish and perhaps four feet deep, there being very few reeds in this particular section.

[1] It was also dried up upon my return to Sistán in the autumn of 1899.

KUH-I-KHOJA SISTÁN.

[*To face p.* 378.

The Kuh-i-Khoja rises 400 feet above the plain, and is only accessible on the south and south-east. I may mention that it is apple-shaped, with a diameter of about a mile, albeit it has generally appeared in maps as an oblong, running from north to south. We landed near the ruins of the town of Kakaha, which is built into the cliff and was strongly fortified. There is an outer wall with bastions, and this lower fort is even now a formidable work, with a square in the middle. A road was formerly constructed up the face of the cliff, at the summit of which is another work, the key to the position, termed Kok. This was the scene of Rustam's first exploit, when as a lad he captured the fort and slew Kok the king. Further west there is a gorge, which also leads to the summit, and commanding this is a small fort termed the Keep of the Forty Virgins, the legend being monotonously common in this portion of Asia. The hill is mainly composed of black basalt, and in its forbidding sterility and absence of water somewhat resembles the island of Hormuz.[1]

The whole surface is dug up into pits, the remains of mines, and tanks for water now empty, yet another proof of a decreased rainfall, or it is covered with tombs, which are either constructed of boulders roughly laid to form places of sepulture, or are domes of mud, or else cairns with pillars. As thousands of people have been buried up here, one would suppose that the water from the tanks must have been poisonous, and this burial above ground struck me as a curious custom. In the south-west corner we espied a white patch, and found it to be covered with black stones of the size of peas all congealed together, which have since been pronounced botryoidal chalcedony.

At the northern end is the shrine of the *Khoja* Ghaltan, a domed building of rude construction, inside which the saint reposes under a tomb composed of sun-dried bricks, twenty feet in length, and at the entrance are two stone weights. If any one makes a petition to the *Khoja*, he sleeps on his doorstep, and if his desire be granted, he is thrown several feet by some supernatural force, otherwise nothing happens!

At the vernal equinox the lower classes run foot-races and put the weight with the stones referred to above, while the *Kháns* ride

[1] *Vide* paper by General Beresford Lovett, *Journal of the R. G. S.*, vol. xliv. p. 145 (1874).

races, albeit a worse race-course it is impossible to find. There is also a custom of throwing burnt wheat on to one of the little shrines, termed the Ziárat-i-Gandum-i-Pirán or Shrine of the Wheat of the Holy Men. This ensures a good harvest, but I could not learn the origin of the practice. As the remainder of the wheat is eaten, it is probably of pre-Mohamedan origin; in any case, it is a widely-spread custom, and perhaps a reminiscence of the days when the generative power was worshipped.[1]

Tate left on the following morning in a dust storm, and I spent a day on the lagoon, shooting coots from the *tutin*; they might have been numbered by thousands, and rose at about forty yards. Before leaving, I paid a second visit to "Table Mountain," and noticing that there were the marks of a dried-up spring in Kakkar, as also of a *kandt*, was told that Ali had destroyed the water-supply. Why and when, none could say. As we were examining the ruins, a wild cat, like a miniature tiger, sprang out of a hole, and nearly knocked down *Khán Bahádur* Asghar Ali, whom Tate had left with me, and who proved to be a most useful addition to my party.

From Kuh-i-Khoja I decided to march across to the Band-i-Sistán on the Helmand. At Dolatabád, the headquarters of the Sarbandi, the approaches had been flooded, and the village rendered practically an island, while sentry-go was the order of the day.

All the villages in Sistán are built on dung-hills, as I believe they generally are in Egypt, the reason being, that when the country is inundated, the villages form islands. Imagine a collection of squalid, dome-shaped mud huts, with a manure heap and a donkey in front, and the type of Sistán village is grasped. There are a few low-walled enclosures, with vines, mulberries, and pomegranates, but these are all quite young, and Sistán is still as treeless west of the Helmand as when Conolly drew attention to this fact.

From Dolatabád we marched to Sehkuha, distant but six miles, passing Kala-i-Sám on the way. This ruined fort, built by or named after the grandfather of Rustam, was destroyed by the new course adopted by the Helmand, as mentioned in the previous

[1] Cf. Frazer, *The Golden Bough*, 2nd ed. vol. ii. pp. 130 *et seqq.*, 190 *et seqq.* In the examples quoted Mr Frazer advances the theory that the killing of the corn spirit (represented here by the burnt corn) was necessary to ensure a good harvest in the coming year.

chapter. Sehkuha is shown in maps of Sistán as its chief town, but to-day it possesses a population of less than one thousand souls, including a garrison of fifty soldiers. On one of the three hills lies the somewhat pretentious abode built by Ali Khán for his royal bride. It is said that he owed his downfall to the fact that upon his return from Persia he wished to form a Court, and was not content with the free and easy Baluch manners. This naturally made him unpopular, and he seems to have been quite deserted at the critical moment.

The fort is still sufficiently strong to resist a Baluchi onset, and is rather picturesque, the irregularities of the ground enhancing its formidable appearance. One morning we rode to the water-worn cliffs to the south, which are composed of a very soft clay, so soft, indeed, that after rain their slopes must be impassable.

From Sehkuha, continuing the tour, we marched to Deh Sukhta or the Burnt Village. We had just reached camp when Purdil Khán came riding by with some forty *sowárs*, having expelled the rebels from Sistán. He is one-armed, the result of a fall off a donkey in extreme youth, and struck me as being frank and a gentleman. He is also very much better informed than his countrymen, by whom he is respected, although his enemies speak slightingly of him as "only three-quarters of a man."

Before reaching the next stage we had to cross the Rud-i-Sistán, which took the best part of a day. At Khoja Ahmad, some four miles from the dam, it was forty yards wide, and in parts over six feet deep. The horses and mules swam across, the kit being slowly transferred to the right bank in the one *tutin* of which the village boasted, and the camels managed to walk across in some five feet of water. About half-way through these operations, it was rumoured that *Sardár* Seiid Khán's party had crossed the Helmand to loot the village, whereupon an exodus took place, until we promised the frightened peasants our protection.

We paid more than one visit to the classic Etymander, as the Helmand was termed more than two thousand years ago. It is a fine river, apparently about as broad as the Thames opposite the Tower of London, and, after many months of travel in "a barren and dry land, where no water is," the sight of so noble a river filled the senses with the keenest exhilaration. Perhaps one of the greatest joys of travel is the extraordinary manner in which the simplest pleasure is appreciated. After a long march in the sun, a few trees and running water appear a paradise, and an omelet or vegetables, after long abstention, give much more pleasure than the most epicurean feast at home. Once back in England the good fare is revelled in for one or two days, after which the *status quo ante* is revived, and the cultivated palate regains its normal condition.

The Band-i-Sistán is a very trumpery concern, but perhaps its strength lies in its weakness, as it is easily repaired, and a stone dam might cause the river to change its course, if constructed at this point. At the time of the Sistán Mission the dimensions were—total length 720 feet, greatest breadth 110 feet, and depth 18 feet. At the period of my visit, its breadth and depth had been greatly diminished, and although the river was very low, water trickled through and over the *band*. The only material used was tamarisk, stakes of no great thickness being driven into the river-bed, around which were twisted smaller branches. Roughly constructed fascines are added to solidify the structure, which is, however, destroyed every year, and Sistán is practically waterless when the snow water from the Berber hills is exhausted, until thousands of villagers repair the dam.

There is said to be one excellent sort of fish in the Helmand, but the few we caught were most insipid. After being six years in Persia I unpacked my hooks for the first time, but with very little success. As in the *hámun* also fish are only caught at night, I came to the conclusion that the enormous number of birds of prey had perhaps altered their habits.

The banks of the Mádar-Áb or Mother Water, as the great canal is termed, are covered with the densest growth of tamarisk, one of the few jungles I have seen in Persia. A few black partridges were put up, but it was difficult to shoot them.

To the west of Khoja Ahmad lay the famous ruins of Shahristán, the Persian equivalent of The City, in order to visit which we had to cross some ten canals. As these were very deep in parts, we made a guide precede us, and if the water was only up to his chest, we crossed; if higher, we tried for a better ford. The ruins are certainly extensive, but less so than those of Záhidán. Istakhri relates that Rám Shahristán was the ancient capital, and that its inhabitants founded Zaranj.

At our next halting-place, Deh Nawáb, we had an unusual excitement. About 2 A.M. a shot was fired, and when we all turned out, the sentry told us that he had watched a party of twenty men stealthily approaching, at whom, as they took no notice of his challenge, and were apparently bent on rushing the camp, he had fired just as they were getting among the horses. We found footprints which corroborated this statement, but soon turned in again, nothing else happening.

There was little or no shooting to be enjoyed until we halted at Iskil, some miles to the south of which we were informed that the country was flooded and full of game. Upon riding there, we found that this was strictly true, and were soon wading in about a foot of water. Along the edge a few snipe were bagged, but they were very wild, although they have never been shot at before in these parts. Wading was not easy, as one constantly floundered into deep holes, and to keep cartridges and gun dry was a constant anxiety. Duck of all kinds rose, generally out of shot, and as those that were hit frequently fell into and remained under water, we picked up but few.

Another day we tried for boar, but although we saw some fresh tracks, we never got a shot. That night, after wading up to our waists for six or seven hours, we sat up for flighting duck, as it happened to be full moon; no luck, however, attended us.

Upon the whole, we did very well, and with more than one gun—the Sistánis only made "pot shots"—the sport would be excellent, although the wading is hard work. This whole district, which is now covered with tamarisk or high reeds, was, until a few years ago, under cultivation, and we saw the deserted fort of Guri, which is out of the reach of the invading water. It is these constant changes that cause the geographer to despair.

Close to Iskil is the famous city of Záhidán, which was situated on the left bank of the Rud-i-Nasru. The fort, built on rising ground, covered a large area, enclosing the space of 600 yards square, with a *reduit* 180 yards square. Ruins of sun-dried brick houses together with kiln-burnt bricks are scattered everywhere about, but the only interesting monument was a tower, which will, I fear, soon collapse. It is constructed of burnt bricks, and is now some 60 feet high. The circumference at the base is 55 feet, and there is a spiral staircase built entirely of bricks overlapping each other; a large gap on the south side threatens the stability of the whole *minár*.

Two inscriptions in Kufic are built in brick set into the tower, one perhaps sixteen feet above the ground, and the second near the top. Although not very clear, I thought that I could make out "Mohamed His Prophet" twice, and so came to the conclusion that the inscriptions were the Mohamedan Confession of Faith, "There is no god but God, and Mohamed is His Prophet." This tower was evidently a *minár*, belonging to a mosque which is now a shapeless ruin, and it is interesting to know that another such tower is to be seen outside Sabzawár, on the Tehrán-Meshed road. Upon enquiring the local name, the guide gave Mil-i-Kasimabád,[1] that being the nearest village, but I was told that the correct name is Mil-i-Kusanak, while the ruined town now termed Kala Tapa was formerly known as Arvakin.

The Headman of Iskil, *Mir* Abbás, visited us with seven brothers and a swarm of small children. He has collected numerous coins and seals from Nád-i-Ali, on the Afghán side, which is universally acknowledged to be of immense antiquity. Among the selection shown I saw Greek, Parthian, Sásánian, and coins of the *Caliphate*, together with a Venetian ducat. Some of the seals were also Greek, but I saw nothing of any great interest. One afternoon his son, who would have easily outweighed Dickens's "Fat Boy," brought his jewels for exhibition, chief among which was a bit of a chandelier, valued at thousands of pounds. Not to hurt his feelings, I said that I knew nothing about jewels. Some of the stones were from Neh, which was said to abound in gems, but they are all of light weight, and, as I understand, of no market value.

We returned to Nasratabád, passing Banjar, which is one of the most important villages, and was Sir Frederic Goldsmid's head-quarters in Sistán, and I could not help congratulating myself on my more favourable position with an escort of Indian cavalry, and practical independence of the local authorities. However, I was somewhat premature, as when, upon returning to Nasratabád, the flag was hoisted for the first time on a camp flagstaff, there was the greatest possible excitement, which somewhat surprised me, as, of course, it floats over the Consulates in the holy city of Meshed and elsewhere in Persia.

[1] Or Pillar of Kasimabád.

The Deputy-Governor first called, saying nothing to me but upon leaving he engaged in a long discussion with Nasrulla Khán, and tried to argue that as it was a fresh departure, special reference should be made to Meshed (which would have involved about two months' uncertainty), and that the flag should not be hoisted in the interim. This it was impossible to accede to, but two days later the Governor returned from a shooting trip, and was immediately threatened by the leading *mullás*. Their chief, *Háji* Ismáil, declared that he would give him three days in which to remove the cause of offence, after which he himself would do it. Messages were then sent up strongly urging me to lower the flag, pending reference to Meshed, and the bearers allowed me to see that *Mir* Másum Khán had charged them to threaten me. Finally, I declined to receive any further communications on the subject, except in writing, whereupon the Governor asked that Nasrulla Khán might visit him. He then cleared the room and said that the Sistánis were ignorant fools, and that he knew that Consuls were bound to fly their flags; indeed he finally confessed that he had been playing a part throughout.

After this the excitement calmed down, the son of *Háji* Ismáil having most sagely pronounced his opinion to the effect that, first of all, the flags should be torn down in Meshed, and after that in Sistán. Needless to say, it was a relief when the question was settled, as the position was delicate, no one being able to gauge an Eastern mob, but I was immensely amused when the redoubtable *Háji* Ismáil sent me a message to the effect that he was a great friend of mine, and had only used threats from fear lest the people might turn on *him*, had he not taken their view of the matter.

DESIGN IN GOLD FROM LINEN HEAD-DRESS.

CHAPTER XXXIII

THE SISTÁN LAKE AND MIÁN KANGI

"See how this river comes me cranking in,
And cuts me, from the best of all my land,
A huge half-moon, a monstrous cantle out."
SHAKESPEARE—*Henry IV.*, PART I. ACT. iii. *Scene* 1.

AFTER having satisfactorily settled the flag question, as narrated in the previous chapter, we started off on our second tour, a noon temperature of ninety-two degrees on 2nd March proving that any delay would entail much heat.

Our first stage was Hadími, situated close to the lagoon, which I now meant to explore thoroughly. Along its edges dwells a tribe of Saiáds or fowlers, who struck me as being perhaps aborigines, both from their appearance and from the account they gave of themselves. Living close to them, but entirely distinct, are the *Gaudár* or Cow-keepers, whose herds of cattle graze in the lagoon, feeding off the young reeds. Sistán is famous for its cows.

Naturally I took most interest in the Saiáds, who informed me that they were the only genuine Sistánis,[1] which is quite possible, as they and they alone could have escaped in a body from the Mongol hordes by taking food on board their rafts and hiding in the reeds. They pay six krans, or about 2s. 6d. per family, and also 1300 lbs. of feathers per annum in the way of taxes, the latter

[1] According to Sir H. Rawlinson, the only pure Aryans are the Sistánis and the Jamshídis of Herát.

amount being collected from the whole tribe, which numbers four hundred families. The feather trade is their chief interest, only one or two families engaging in fishing, but at present the results of their labour are entirely used for stuffing cushions, although, no doubt, in time, the sale of plumes will largely increase their incomes; the total output is 4000 lbs. per annum.

The birds are caught by means of nets held open by stakes, into which they are slowly driven, lanes being cut in the reeds or staked out in the open water as a further assistance. A man lying hidden on his *tutin* watches until his prey is swimming over his net, when he pulls a string, releases the stakes which form a rude spring, and the hapless fowl is his.

Early one morning we rode to the *hámun*, a dense jungle of reeds, down which runs the narrowest of creeks. Here we stepped on board our *tutin* and were slowly punted along an open lane about the width of a main road. On each side we heard the calls of countless birds, and many descriptions of hawks hovered above. The first bird shot was a *bostáni*, which is non-migratory. To some extent it resembled the *minaul* pheasant of Kashmir, with blue plumage and a scarlet beak. Then coots swam across the waterway and a tiny little blue bird darted about just like a kingfisher.

After being punted for three or four miles, we reached the hunting-grounds, which consist of a series of lagoons opening one into the other. Here a few duck were bagged, and we passed a fisherman on his way home with twenty or more freshly caught fish. Some were three or four pounds in weight, and they resembled a barbel, but I regret that I could not be sure of their species. The water averaged some three feet in depth, and although brackish, is drunk by the fowlers. It was very clear, but not a fish was to be seen, although I carefully watched all the day.

The total bag might have been considerable, but I calculated the meat-eating capacity of my party, and was careful to avoid any waste of cartridges so far from civilisation; but as it turned out, the ducks were poor eating. Altogether, the experience of being out of the dust and on the water with plenty of game to shoot at was very pleasant. In the evening we saw rafts propelled by tiny little boys, not three feet high, bearing home the bundles of reeds with which to prepare a new craft. Their nude bronze-coloured figures managing the unwieldy rafts without any sign of exertion presented a most graceful appearance, and would make a very pretty study for an artist. My fowler was most conversational, and told me, among other facts, that passengers occasionally went by this route to Lásh Juwain in Afghán territory, the *hámun* taking twenty-four hours to cross.

At the next stage of Gazbár, the shooting was of quite a different character, the lake being free from reeds, and on the mud flats were large flocks of geese. My last experience of a wild-goose chase was off the coast of Scotland, when a party of us, after crawling for a long distance, were preparing to fire a volley at about 500 yards. A lady, however, showed herself on the sky-line, and we were left lamenting! On this occasion, however, the game was much less wary, and we could generally fire our Martini and Lee-Metford carbines from a distance of about 400 yards. A volley knocked over on the average two or three geese, some of which were untouched by the bullet, but again our bag was limited by the number of mouths to feed, especially as the *sowárs* would not eat any bird shot dead, such being the very unpractical law of Mohamedanism. Another day we tried for wild boar, but without success, as we could not secure any beaters.

A report having reached me that the Rud-i-Perián was rising, I determined to cross it at once, or else I should have been obliged to forego visiting the district lying between it and the old Helmand, known as Mián Kangi. It is quite unlike other parts of Sistán since the change in the course of the Helmand, and, moreover, has not been fully explored since that date.

I accordingly marched to Jalalabád, formerly the property of the Keiáni tribe, but now a place of no importance. The head of the family has quitted Sistán for a home at Sarakhs. I enquired whether there were any ancient manuscripts in the possession of his family, but was informed that they had no records, except some *farmán* from the Sefavi sovereigns. The new river has spared the village, but all the cultivated zone has been cut off. We visited the ruins which lined the Rud-i-Nasru, among which were houses built of burnt brick, and all were of a higher style of architecture than the universal mud dome of to-day. Tímúr and Sháh Rukh undoubtedly dealt a lasting blow to Persian civilisation, and one which has changed the course of history.

THE HELMAND LAGOON.

[*To face p.* 388.

Heavy rain which had threatened for two or three days caught us on clay soil, absorbing little or no water, and our camp became a lake, with the usual disagreeable result. Trusting that my uniform-case was water-tight, I left it to the last, but it played me false, and my papers as well as a new aneroid were soaked. The camels could not move for a day, and we then started off to rejoin the advance camp, which had crossed the river before the rain. Dismal forebodings of being swept away were freely indulged in, but we took all precautions, engaging a party of men to assist the camels. After crossing some shallow channels we struck the main stream, a quarter of a mile wide and nearly four feet deep, flowing with a strong current. To give an exact idea of the depth, the water was some six inches above the saddle flaps of my sixteen hands two inches waler, and as the stream was strong, I felt very nervous about my loads.

We landed in a tamarisk swamp, but found it to be a small island, beyond which lay yet another branch of the river, at the sight of which Shavey, the fox terrier, sat down and howled. However, it was only sixty yards across, albeit quite as deep as the main stream, and we then had only two or three insignificant arms to negotiate. The river was rapidly rising, and heavy rain again fell; I was therefore very glad when the camels had crossed in safety. The only *contretemps* was that a servant known as the "Frog" had taken an appropriate header, his camel having stumbled.

We were now in Mián Kangi,[1] which is one dense jungle of tamarisk some twenty feet in height, the villages being situated in clearings. Although the treeless character of Sistán has been much commented on, yet this district is one continuous forest, any accurate exploration of which would be impossible, were it not that there are artificial mounds in parts, rising perhaps eighty feet above the surrounding country. On some of these were ruins of forts.

From Burj-i-Gul-Mohamed, the frontier village of North-east Sistán, inhabited by members of the Sahroni tribe, we rode to the dry bed of the Helmand, which was so shallow that I was at first inclined to throw doubts on the guide's statement. However, there is no doubt that the river, before reaching the *hámun*, moved slowly, and deposited its silt among the

[1] Mián Kangi, I was informed, is equivalent to Mesopotamia.

mass of reeds and tamarisks, both of which have almost disappeared, and now all that remains to mark the border is this dry, insignificant watercourse, still known as the Rud-i-Ashkán. Beyond is a low hill, the Tapa-i-Tilái or Golden Mound, whence there was not a sight of water, the eye ranging across miles of thirsty ground covered with the roots of reeds. A few nomads of the Buzi tribe, who are Persians, inhabit this wilderness which stretches up to Chakansur, watering their flocks from wells, otherwise there is the stillness of death, indicating most forcibly that there is no life in Persia without water.

The river rose day by day, compelling us to march to Milak,[1] where the Rud-i-Perián takes off, as there alone does the stream run in one branch. Two miles to the south-south-east of our camp we came upon extensive ruins, known as the Takht-i-Pul or Platform of the Bridge. Here three small arches of burnt brick were shown us as being the remains of a bridge across the Helmand, but their small size was sufficient to show the absurdity of the notion. Numerous bricks pointed to the existence in time past of a considerable town, and the bridge probably spanned its irrigation canal. However, as usual, we could learn nothing as to the history of the spot.

Before reaching the stage of Siadak, we had to cross the deepest channel that had, so far, lain in our path, our guide sinking in up to his neck. However, our horses were now so accustomed to the work that we only stripped off our nether garments, and crossed successfully, not a camel falling, to my astonishment. The headman of the village, which belonged to Khán Ján Sinjeráni[2] before he was expelled with the Nahruis, had recently returned from Quetta, where he had interviewed the Agent to the Governor-General. His venture had evidently been profitable, as he was contemplating another journey as soon as he could collect sufficient wool and clarified butter, which form the staple exports of Sistán.

Close at hand are the remains of Karkusha, said to have been

[1] Diminutive of *Mil*, a pillar.

[2] The Sinjeráni tribe is pure Baluch, with its headquarters at Chagai. In Sistán the nomad life has been mainly given up, and the chief of the tribe, which numbers about two thousand families, is Khán Ján, son of Ibráhim Khán, who murdered Dr Forbes many years ago. The Sahroni tribe mentioned above acknowledges Khán Ján as its overlord.

a Keiáni capital. Its bricks measured twenty-four inches by seventeen inches, but no antiquities were forthcoming. Half-way to Milak we came in sight of Nád-i-Ali,[1] across the old Helmand, here running some two feet deep. The remarkable hill has a wall all round, with towers on the north side, and contains a garrison of one hundred regulars from Kábul. The ancient town is said to lie on the south side. Two other hills to the east, Sufidak and Surkhdak or Little White and Red Hills, are unoccupied, and, as may be imagined, discount the military value of the fort. The Governor of the district, known as the *Akhundzáda*,[2] resides at Kala Kang, to the south of Chakansur. We were told that the chief place for finding coins and seals was Amirán, a few miles to the south of Nád-i-Ali, and I hope that in due course of time these cities with their ancient records of a little known period may be accessible to the excavator.

Owing to the dense tamarisk, we had to march for miles in the now shallow Helmand, crossing a very deep canal which has been cut across Mián Kangi from the Rud-i-Perián. Throughout this section of our journey, the tales that we heard of Afghán tyranny made one reflect on the great contrast between it and Persian rule. On the Afghán side no melons are sown, as they would all be seized by the rapacious soldiery; even tea and sugar are almost unknown, and only smuggled across in tiny quantities, according to report. Trade under such circumstances is promptly strangled, and there is practically no communication with Kandahár, although that town is only some ten stages distant.

Writers coming from Europe or from India are, in my humble opinion, much too severe on the state of Persia. To take Sistán alone, a few years before the Persian Government acquired it, no traveller's life was safe, as M. Ferrier testifies in his *Caravan Journeys*. Even at the time of the Sistán Mission the change was very great, not a single attempt at spoliation or violence occurring on the Persian side, and to-day, except for trans-frontier forays, the district is as safe as most parts of Europe. A steady immigration goes on from the Afghán side, and thus increases the cultivated area of the country, which has quadrupled under the rule of the Sháh.

[1] In ancient times No Kei. Vide *Eastern Persia*, vol. i. p. 299.

[2] Or son of the *Akhund*. An *Akhund* is a teacher or reader.

The swollen Rud-i-Perián had now to be negotiated, a foaming torrent 300 yards wide, with perhaps 40 or 50 yards unfordable. The *sowárs* rose to the occasion, the horses and mules being ridden across, although one or two were nearly carried away and drowned. Our gear, to use the comprehensive naval expression, was slowly taken across in rafts, and then came the turn of the camels. Each "ship of the desert" was divested of its saddle, six gourds being firmly bound in their place. They were then led up stream for a quarter of a mile by two swimmers, with gourds under their arms. Upon entering the torrent, one man tugged the camel in front, and the other sat on its tail to balance it. The *oont*, as Thomas Atkins terms it, apparently made no effort to swim, but, with an expression of dignified melancholy, was towed across like a log.

It took the whole day to accomplish the passage of the river, and we then returned to Nasratabád, marching through the ruins of Záhidán in a storm, which moved the sand-hills most unpleasantly, while poor Shavey being close to the ground had a very bad time, and required much lotion before he could see again. The servants, thanks to my insisting upon goggles as a part of their outfit, escaped without much discomfort, but they were also glad of the lotion.

The weather had now become hot, with noon temperatures of ninety-seven degrees, and the plague of flies and gnats commenced. The 1st of April brought us the sight of the first snake, "that harbinger of spring," and altogether we were glad that we were leaving Sistán for the upland province of Káin. As forage was 250 per cent. dearer in Birjand, we decided to take a two months' supply with us, which meant loading one hundred camels, to collect which from the outlying desert required about a week. I will, therefore, take this opportunity to summarise my impressions of Sistán, my two tours having practically covered the whole district, as from each camp I had ridden out in all directions, that nothing might escape my notice.

Sistán, as my account shows, falls into two sections, the treeless and the jungle. The soil in both is the same, and appears to be, generally speaking, a light loam. In several parts there are square miles of sand-hills, which could, however, be cultivated and got rid of, while round Nasratabád[1] the country is salt and hummocky.

[1] Nasratabád occupies a portion of the site of ancient Zirra.

with innumerable hollows. In this section in particular there are many shallow ponds, which must be grand breeding-places for mosquitoes and germs. In fact, were it not for the Bád-i-Sad-u-Bist-Ruz or Wind of 120 days, Sistán could scarcely be inhabited. This providential blast blows across the district from April to July, and although hot and disagreeable, carries away the malarial taint. When it dies away, the mass of the inhabitants, who struck me as a sickly race, suffer terribly from fever. However, with proper accommodation, the climate of Sistán, although the temperature in tents rises to an average of over 110 degrees during the summer, can be favourably compared with parts of Bengal, and its short cold weather is as bracing as can be desired.

In Lord Curzon's *Persia* the Sistán question is fully dealt with from a political point of view, but as I am not at liberty to do the same, I wish merely to draw attention to its geographical position. It has already been pointed out that it is a small Egypt, and a granary to the surrounding tribes, but this is accentuated by the fact that while it lies half-way between Russian territory and the Persian Gulf, with a thin population on both sides, it is also the only cultivated district lying between Quetta and the province of Kermán. At the same time arable Sistán, with a population aggregating but one hundred thousand, including some seven thousand nomads, only includes the Helmand delta, and I do not think that the grand water supply now running to waste can ever be controlled, except by the power holding the upper reaches of that river, nor can the zone of cultivation, under present conditions, be very greatly extended.

DESIGN FROM A KÁIN CARPET.

CHAPTER XXXIV

THE PROVINCE OF KÁIN

Εντεῦθεν Ἄρεια σχοῖνοι λʹ. Ἔνθα Κανδᾶχ πόλις καὶ Ἀρτακαύαν πόλις καὶ Ἀλεξάνδρεια ἡ ἐν Ἀρείοις.—ISIDORUS OF CHARAX, 15.

IF it be true that pleasure mainly consists in anticipation, the happiest hours in India must be those spent in the *tonga*, which rapidly carries the passenger from the plains where existence is a burden, to the heights where a white man can freely breathe and sleep. My feelings were somewhat similar during the last week or ten days in Sistán, as even the nights had been close, and dinner had become a penance, owing to the myriads of self-immolating insects. Consequently, although seven hot marches lay before us, the certainty of comparative coolness beyond enabled us to scorn the various little discomforts, so well known to many of my fellow-countrymen, although our horses were driven nearly mad.

Previous experience of Baluch camel-drivers having taught me what phenomenal patience is necessary to get them under weigh, I prudently arranged that all the camels hired from them should have a day's start, and in order to minimise their unreasonable complaints, I had the grain made up into equal loads some ten pounds lighter than what is considered to be the custom. Even so, however, a day was occupied in shouting and grumbling, the camel-drivers, as usual, having no ropes and no ideas as to loading.

Our first stage was a short one to Afzalabád, the last village in Sistán to the west. There a post overtook us, its bearer being full of the heroic deeds he and his fellow *sowárs* had performed in beating off a band of Baluch raiders, and taking great spoils in the shape of two donkeys. The next march lay across the *hámun*, but, fortunately for us, the spring floods had not reached the road, although we had to make a slight detour to the south, the direct track having been rendered impassable.

We started at 4 A.M., and almost immediately had to negotiate a wide and deep water channel, which is an unpleasant experience in the dark. I then formed the party into a line of connecting files, so as not to lose the way. Every half hour we lit a fire, and this, with passing the number down from front to rear, kept us all on the right track, which was extremely rough and full of traps.

When the day dawned we found ourselves opposite Kuh-i-Khoja, and were passing through the burnt reed-beds, among which the "freshe greene" of the young reeds looked delightfully bright. Seeing the *Mil-i-Nádiri*, which I had descried from the top of the Kuh-i-Khoja, I left the road which bends round a little to the north-west, and made across country to examine it. The *Mil* was placed on the west edge of the lagoon, and is roughly constructed of sun-dried bricks with a base circumference of just one hundred feet. There was originally a spiral staircase, and the tower is open about twenty feet from the ground on the Sistán side. According to local tradition, it was built by Nádir Sháh (who camped at Nasrabád, a little to the north of Afzalabád), to serve as a beacon and watch tower.

The stage of Beiring (the word means a "mound" in Sistáni, which may be the purest Persian) is only a section of the shore, and as the poisonous greyish fly was present in clouds, to be succeeded by the blasting hot wind, we revelled in the thought that it was our last day in Sistán. Indeed, although we quitted the land of Rustam before the summer had set in, we quite agreed with the Arab poet who wrote:

"O Sistán! may the clouds refuse their beneficent rain, may ruins and the desert cover thy soil! In winter, thou art a place of suffering and misfortune; in summer, a mass of serpents and insects. God has created thee as a punishment to men, and has made thee a hell."

To the north, some ten miles away, are the ruins of Sábar Sháh, which was destroyed at the same time as Záhidán, that portion of the lake being still termed Dariá-i-Sábari or the Lake of Sábar.

Two marches across the bare desert, where the loss of life during the summer is said to be very great, brought us to the hills, which are entered by a gorge perhaps a hundred yards wide. At its mouth is the hamlet of Bandán, lying on the edge of the only date-grove of these parts, and a mile or two further up lay Zein-ul-abád, our halting-place.

From this point there are three roads to Birjand, *via* Neh, Shusp, and Huseinabád respectively. The first is the longest and safest, the second is direct but rather dangerous, and the third is scarcely ever used except by large caravans. However, as our party was too big to be attacked, and I was bound to keep to the route followed by the couriers from Meshed, we used the third route and made three long stages to Duru, where we were once again at an elevation of about 4000 feet, and free from the tormenting fly and the heat of Sistán.

We spent a week at this village, discharging most of our camels, and thenceforward had to move by relays. However, there were numerous hamlets in the surrounding hills to explore, and the main peak of the range was well worth a visit. It rises to about 6000 feet, and on its summit is a fort very solidly built of stones fitted in with cement, or rather, in technical language, uncoursed rubble in cement, this being the style of most of the forts I visited in Eastern Persia. There are also two or three tanks, empty as they all are nowadays. Our guide spoke of Shekevand as the builder of the fort, but the headman of the village said that it was erected by Hoshang, the second king of the Peshdádian dynasty, which is hardly likely. We enjoyed a grand view, especially to the east, where the three ranges sank down to the Dasht-i-Náúmíd or Desert of Despair.

The headman informed me that his ancestors came from Bokhára some six generations ago. On this account they consider themselves saints, able to perform cures, but this did not prevent them from anxiously enquiring whether I had a doctor with me!

Upon continuing our journey, we marched obliquely across the plain, which swarmed with tortoises, to the huge delight of Shavey, who soon learned to turn them over, obliging one of us to dismount and set them right again. The Persian name for this animal of *Kása Pusht* or Cup-back, is very happy, and so is *Khár Pusht* or Thorn-back, for the hedgehog.

At Huseinabád the Birjand road branched off, but we decided to march north to Tabas Sunnikhána, as the courier who was due had not arrived. This district, as its name signifies, is inhabited by Sunnis, and was really more Afghán than Persian at the time when it was seized by the *Amir* of Káin. It contains about sixty villages, with a population of some fifteen thousand, and, lying on a level, fertile plain, supplies Birjand with wheat and forage. The fort at Tabas is said to be of the same pattern and designed by the same "Vauban" as those of Herát and Fara, while the one at Neh is very similar. It is now much broken down, but the *Amir* of Káin has built a round tower inside, where a handful of infantry are said to keep watch and ward. The site is probably one of antiquity, and the ancient name given is Mazinán, tradition averring that the builder was a general of Alexander the Great.

To the ordinary traveller perhaps the most striking feature is the immense number of windmills, of which we had observed very few in Sistán or on the road, whereas at Tabas there are twenty or thirty in a row. These windmills are mentioned in Sistán by Istakhri in the tenth century, long before they were introduced into Europe,[1] and here perhaps we see the original pattern, which merits some description, as, although rough, it struck me as extremely practical. Two mud walls are constructed parallel to the prevailing wind, one of which either curves or is inclined so as nearly to close the north-east entrance, from which the wind comes, while the other end is wide and open. The upper mill-stone has a stout pole fixed into it, which in its turn has flanges constructed of reeds. The wind entering the narrow end bears on each flange as it rotates, and thus a most efficient mill is produced at a minimum cost.

The courier duly reached us at Tabas, and it was then determined to march straight into Birjand, so as to be settled down before the month of Moharram, during which little or no work is done. Our route, which ran due west, lay across the Mainabád range, which consists of rolling hills rising to between 8000 and 9000 feet.

[1] Mr E. G. Browne informs me that windmills were known to the Persians at the period of the Arab conquest. This is shown by a story in Masudi's *Murúju'dh Dhahab*, ed. Barbier de Meynard, vol. iv. p. 227. I would here acknowledge my obligations to Barbier de Meynard's *Dictionnaire de la Perse*—a most valuable work.

The first stage of Furk was recommended as a summer retreat. It is built at the mouth of a gorge, and can boast of one of the most picturesquely-situated forts that I have seen. In the middle of a narrow valley a serrated hill rises to perhaps 500 feet, and on its summit is constructed an irregular and most formidable-looking castle. With Tabas, it shares the reputation of being almost impregnable, and on the strength of this, its Governor used to revolt periodically. For some years this was done with impunity, until a bright idea penetrated the somewhat obtuse brain of a besieging general, who dragged a gun on to the hills above, and then proceeded to open fire. Needless to say, the money-bags were speedily produced! We camped at about 5700 feet, just off the river-bed which forms the "High Street," but decided that it was too much shut in for summer quarters, as the hills on each side were very steep.

Just above Furk lies the larger village of Darmián, a corruption of Darra Mián or Middle of the Valley. The gardens lined the track for some two miles, the fruit-trees in blossom forming a sight which is always beautiful. Winding up and up, the hills became rounded and more open, while tiny hamlets with their miniature orchards were successively passed, the highest being situated at some 6500 feet, and containing but one house. Several passes cross the range, and the various sections of our party all appeared to have come by different ones. Everywhere the hills were one bright mass of tulips and hyacinths on the higher parts, the scenery being quite idyllic. Our guide informed us that the road was closed for at least a month in the winter, and that at the end of March a heavy fall of snow had damaged the orchards, the pomegranates in particular having suffered. Once across the pass, we gained a clear view of the valley in which Birjand lies, a curious range of low clay hills running down the centre, while opposite us rose the Bakarán range with numerous hamlets on its skirt. The Birjand valley itself is remarkably sterile, and firewood is at famine prices, none being procurable within about fifty miles.

As usual, Nasrulla Khán preceded me, both to arrange for a house or garden, and also to settle the wearisome, but important, reception ceremonies. The day before entering Birjand, we halted some seven miles off, at Bujd,[1] in a pleasant garden, the first we had

[1] Bujd is a Sunni village.

BIRJAND.

[To face p. 398.

entered that year, and the following day the usual *istikbál* took place, the *Amir* of Káin's brother being in command of the reception party.

Birjand, as we approached it, differs from other towns in Persia, inasmuch as it is built on the low hills referred to above, and divided by the broad bed of the river which passes through Khusp and is lost in the Lut. Its treelessness is very striking, but is explained by the fact that the town only boasts of one *kanát*, and even the water of this is undrinkable, the citizens relying upon tanks, which are filled with water from the hills. At the foot of the town and commanded by it, lay the fort, round which we made a circuit, and entering a garden of barberry bushes, with a few mulberries, were ushered upstairs into a fair-sized mud room. As is always the case, there were no windows and the doors were crazy to a degree, but it was a great improvement on anything we had seen for some months, and we were proportionately grateful.

Three days after our arrival we received a call from the *Amir* of Káin, who is one of the last feudal chieftains in Persia representing the old order. Although they have kept no record, they believe themselves to be of Arab descent, and of the Khuzái or Khuzaima tribe, which was ruled by Táhir the Ambidexter, a doughty warrior, who set Mamun on the *Caliph's* seat. Apparently forced to emigrate from Bahrein, they gradually became the ruling family of Káin, the districts of Neh and Bandán first falling under their control, when they marched up from the south. About the end of the seventeenth century the whole district of Káin was in their hands, and upon the decay of the Sefavi dynasty, they became practically independent, or, as a Persian would say, "they looked two ways." It was a chief of this family who blinded Sháh Rukh at Meshed in A.D. 1748. In recent times, the fortunes of the family were more or less bound up with Herát, and until the death of the infamous Yár Mohamed, the Vizier of Sháh Kamrán, there were few dealings with Persia.

However, the Persian Government waxed stronger and stronger, and, although Herát was not taken, the province of Khorasán, so long independent of Persia, was recovered, and the grandfather of the present ruler was seized after making an ineffectual resistance. Politic treatment converted him into a staunch adherent of the Kájárs, and it was his son, *Mir* Alam, who practically subdued Sistán. Although not courteous to the British Mission, he was in many ways an ideal ruler, keeping his province comparatively free from the scourge of Turkoman, Baluch, and Afghán raiders, and before his death in 1891 he must have experienced intense satisfaction in comparing the state of his province, as he left it, with its old condition of daily rapine and murder. During the latter part of his life, the *Amir* of Káin was perhaps the most powerful and independent feudatory of Persia.

Upon his death, he left Sistán to his eldest son, Káin falling to his second son, the present *Amir*, a division which, as may be supposed, has implanted an implacable feeling of hatred between the two brothers, probably augmented by the fact that the *Amir* of Káin succeeded to, or possessed himself of, all the stored-up wealth.

The *Shaukat-ul-Mulk*, to give him his Persian title, is aged forty-seven and of medium height; he has lost some teeth and wears spectacles. Although stiff at first, he was soon deeply interested in hearing about the Soudan, and the Cape to Cairo railway greatly took his fancy.

He was at Mecca when a boy, and reads the Persian newspapers, one of which, the *Habl-ul-Matin*, published at Calcutta, contains a considerable amount of information, enabling him to follow the course of the world with tolerable accuracy. He recounted some of the experiences of his early days, when there was much hard skirmishing, and dilated on the present peaceful state of affairs. His wife's sister being married to Sir Naoroz Khán of Kharán, he takes an interest in Kalát politics, and professed astonishment at my knowing so much about the various frontier tribes, until I pointed out that that was my business. The idea of wireless telegraphy, however, quite upset him. Even with wires it seemed to him most uncanny, but that without wires messages should be constantly passing through people's bodies was, he thought, a most uncomfortable notion!

Mohamed Ibráhim Khán, his younger brother and heir—for he has no children—is about eighteen, and appeared to be a very pleasant, gentlemanly young fellow. When I told him that I had organized polo at Tehrán and Shiráz, he implored me to start it at Birjand, but as all my polo sticks were broken, it was out of the question.

We explored many delightful gorges along the Bakarán hills,

and enjoyed exceptionally cool weather, my solitude being relieved by the advent of M. de Stroeff, the Russian dragoman at Meshed, who brought down silver samovars for the *Amir* and his younger brother as presents from the Tsar. Unfortunately, M. de Stroeff was so much knocked up by the journey that he constantly suffered from fever. As he persisted in wearing the usual Russian cloth cap, I must say that I was not surprised at his falling ill, as it offers no protection whatever to the back of the neck or temples.

Soon after his departure, early in June, intense heat suddenly set in, and I decided to follow my camp. From motives of economy it had been despatched by relays to Duruksh, which we were universally assured was *par excellence* the hill station of the province. It was a scorching afternoon when we started, and after skirting the town and clearing the low range we emerged on to the wide lifeless plain, our direction being almost due east. A pyramidal-shaped hill, known as Kuh-i-Már or Snake Mountain, was the most prominent object on our road, and although we passed the small village of Dastgird, it did not boast of a single tree, and consequently gave no relief to the weary waste. However, twelve miles from Birjand we entered the hills, and crossing a very steep pass, reached Ráhnish in the dark, and found our camp with some difficulty.

The courier from India having met us on the way, the following morning was spent in office work, and, even had it been cooler, which it was not, we were not ready to continue the march until late in the afternoon. An hour's climb brought us to the Sar-i-Cháh pass, after surmounting which we left the drainage of the Khusp or Birjand river behind, and descended that of the Fákh Rud, which river we had already crossed at Tabas. We passed the village of Sar-i-Cháh with its hundred houses, which is said to suffer much from the wind, and thenceforward hamlet succeeded hamlet until, just at nightfall, we quitted the valley and rose on to a level plain. Gásk was finally reached rather late, but our mules were not in until midnight. The *Khán Bahádur*, who had quitted Birjand some days before our party, told me that Duruksh was very little higher than our present stage, where his thermometer had daily registered over 90°, and we went to bed with the feeling that all swans were geese in this part of Persia.

From Gásk, a village of fifty houses, and boasting of thirty carpet looms, we swung due north, and there was a gentle descent to the Fákh Rud, after crossing which we entered the hills and saw Duruksh lying up a narrow valley. Passing Asiabán,[1] a large village no higher than Gásk, half-an-hour's ride brought us to our supposed hill station, and we were ushered into a filthy tumble-down building, which we were informed was the famous Bágh-i-Nazar. To remain in the vermin-haunted house being quite out of the question, we next examined the tiny garden, in which there was barely room to pitch our tents, and when at noon the thermometer rose to ninety degrees, we felt that Duruksh was a fraud. However, we were wrong, as in a day or two the north-east gales set in, and thenceforward it was pleasantly cool, although at times we could have wished for less wind with its concomitant of dust.

As we were settled down in the heart of Káin for a couple of months, I now propose to give some account of this province, which mainly consists of a belt of elevated, hilly, and comparatively fertile country, lying between the boundless Lut and the smaller Dasht-i-Náumid. To the south, as has been mentioned, it is separated by a barren strip of country from Sistán, while from Neh there is only one village[2] southwards until Narmáshir is reached. On the north alone is there an adjacent fertile country, but even so a high range has to be crossed. It is therefore evident that both Káin and Sistán are much isolated by nature, and the backward policy of the ruler of Afghánistán has discouraged all trade; there is indeed intercourse with Herát, but far less than there would have been, had it remained a Persian province.

The two special products of Káin are saffron, which is said to supply most of the provinces of Persia, and is mainly grown round the town of Káin, and barberry, which grows to perfection at Birjand. Wheat and barley, in good years, are produced in sufficiently large quantities to feed the province, although the districts near Sistán import its surplus grain to a considerable extent, but as a large percentage of the crop depends on irrigation, there is frequently a partial scarcity. Silk is a reviving industry, the output being sent to Meshed, and opium, alas! is widely grown, the pernicious influence of which is ruining Eastern Persia, especially the well-to-do classes. When both parents smoke their children are born with a craving for the drug, which is

[1] Asiabán signifies a miller.

[2] Nasratabád (Kermán).

smoked in its strongest form, the opium which has been once burnt being boiled two or three times and then smoked over a candle. This is considered so deadly that *Shír Afkan* or Lion Slaying is one of its epithets.[1] The autumn crop consists of large quantities of melons and beetroot. The potato has not as yet been introduced, and despite my efforts, the *Amir* would not take the question up, although he fully agreed with me as to the value of the vegetable, which is almost a necessity to us. The fruit is, if anything, worse than at Kermán, which is much to be regretted, as few parts of the world would produce better pears, peaches, apples, and quinces, if a modicum of trouble were taken.

The great expanses of desert lying to the east and west form ideal breeding-grounds for camels, thousands of which are reared in the province; and as each village can boast of a large flock of sheep and goats, there are some compensating advantages gained by inhabiting a thinly-peopled district.

The only manufacture of more than local importance is that of carpets, which are almost entirely woven in the Duruksh district, some 450 looms being employed, a hundred of which are in the village itself. It is a matter for much regret that aniline dyes have almost entirely taken the place of the lovely vegetable colours, and yet I was informed that there was practically no saving in cost, but only a little less trouble. Fortunately, however, one or two master weavers still clung to the native dyes, and I think that my example in purchasing somewhat largely for friends from them alone, not to mention my constant warnings on the subject, may have had some effect.

The patterns of conventional flowers are pleasing, but they look common by the side of a product of the Kermán looms. The export is exclusively to Meshed, whence the carpets are consigned to Constantinople, Egypt, and Vienna. I was told that only the cheaper qualities were in demand. As regards prices, a specially well-woven carpet, fourteen feet by eleven, cost just £20. It was, however, of much better quality than usual, and was said to be, not without truth, a masterpiece of the Duruksh looms. Other carpets, of the same size, with, of course, half the number of stitches, I

[1] I have been informed on good authority that horses accustomed to the smoke of this pernicious drug lose condition if a non-opium smoker be put in charge of them.

bought for half the price. The Beluri nomads, who inhabit Duruksh and Zírkuh, also weave small rugs, which bear almost a family likeness to those of the Turkoman, and this, so far as I saw, exhausts the list.

As to the inhabitants, I have already referred to the large number of Sunnis, and the Afghán element is also strong. Both in Birjand and among the nomads there is a large Arab-speaking population, and a debased *patois* of that tongue is preferred to Persian by the *Amir* and his family.

Rather to my surprise, there are but few nomads in the province. The Arabs, who number perhaps 400 families owning villages, round which they carry on agriculture, and the Baluchis who graze in the southern portion of the province, are but temporary visitors, returning to Sistán in the late summer. The Beluri are, I believe, gypsies, the word being a corruption of Luri, and this completes the list. The late Mr Ney Elias mentioned that there were some 2000 to 3000 families of Mongols in the province of Káin, but did not state in what district they lived, nor whether they still maintained a wandering life.[1] After a few days' sojourn at Duruksh we settled down, and our life was rendered more pleasant by the friendliness of all the inhabitants of the hill station. The leading family claimed descent from the Sefavi dynasty, from the shipwreck of which royal line they were left waifs a century and a half ago. A generation since they were reduced to beggary, but being *Seiids*, were spared the exactions which took place at the siege of Herát, when the villagers were driven to leave their property to be promptly annexed by the grandfather of our friends. Although they were more backward in their ideas than the *Kháns* of Kermán, it was interesting to gain a glimpse of a Persia which is fast vanishing, but was well represented by the gorgeous silks and velvets which the young princes donned, in contrast to the sober hues now prevailing elsewhere.

My thirst for information was not liberally quenched, but, at any rate, the derivation of Duruksh from *Darra Raksh* or The Valley of Raksh seemed possible, although I can hardly imagine Rustam's great war-horse being sent so far off for its summering.

The large village has a population of about a thousand, and is

[1] Vide *Tárikh-i-Rashídi*, p. 494*a*. (Second Edition.)

dominated by an old fort, while there are towers on all the hills. The only brick building is a mosque, called the Mosque of the Uzbegs, a nomenclature which is probably correct, the Uzbegs having held the province for two hundred years, until expelled by Sháh Abbás. Above the houses the narrow valley was a mass of gardens for some two miles, up which we could always find a shady ride. There were numerous tracks, all equally stony, and no hill shooting, but our time was fully occupied with the exploration of the district and attempts to collect information, not to mention the lengthy process of overhauling kit, necessitated by nine months' travelling.

To my delight, one morning Lieut. Wyatt, R.A., arrived with an Hospital Assistant, whom the Government of India, with their wonted liberality, had attached to the party. They had, indeed, performed a record journey, having travelled 800 miles from Quetta in thirty-eight days. Wyatt's account of the heat, which would have made sleep in the day a forerunner of apoplexy, will, I hope, be sufficient to deter other travellers from running such risks, and I quite understood the anxiety of the political authorities in Baluchistán until news of their safety was received. Life was now, naturally, much brighter, as I had not seen a fellow-countryman for six months, and soon we were busily engaged in putting the escort through their musketry course; a riding-school and jumps were also prepared, as the country was too stony for moving out of a collected walk.

The elevation of our camp was some 7000 feet, and the hills rose to 8000 feet, there being a high level plateau to the north of Duruksh. From the peaks which we scaled, we obtained a thoroughly comprehensive idea of the whole country, which to the east, west, and north consisted of rolling hills, all of approximately the same height; to the south the wide valley of the Fákh Rud lay between us and the Mainabád range, which we had crossed between Tabas and Birjand.

By the end of July it was once again time to resume our tramp's life, our first stage being Sháhkin, to which the route lay almost throughout across the high plateau previously mentioned. Descending first into the valley on the northern side, we came upon the village of Isno, a little fort lying in a wide valley, which reminded my companion of Tirah, the country and style of fort being identical. Continuing down the fertile valley, which narrowed considerably, we found our camp pitched beyond Sháhkin, a village of one hundred and fifty houses, which formerly gave its name to the district, and is the Shahva mentioned by Dr Bellew as one of the divisions of Káin, although not visited by him. The village, which lies at exactly the same altitude as Duruksh, bears a close resemblance to Sivand on the Shiráz-Isfahán road, and the ancient fort looks as if in days gone by it had been of great strength.

We were now in the centre of a square block of unexplored country, and, as is so often the case in Persia, we found the blank on the maps to be a very fertile and well-peopled district; the climate, judging by the looks of the villagers and the feel of the air, bracing even in August, must be extremely healthy. Our road ran down the main valley, across which tracks lay in every direction, enabling the *Khán Bahádur* to add quite a hundred villages to the map of Persia before he reached Káin. Throughout this short stage there was a steady descent, and at Khushk we were in a much warmer climate.

The third march to the ancient capital was a long one, and the road difficult to find, as upon clearing Khushk we quitted the main valley, and at nine miles entered the Rud-i-Shur, a deep *nala* with masses of tamarisk, draining north-east. Following down it, we missed the tracks of our mules, and finally discovered that the road ran up the steep cliff side, on the top of which we entered a wide open plain. To the east rose up the masses of the Kuh-i-Várizk, and passing the tiny hamlet of Kalát Kasáb, where a peasant ran out with an offering of a melon, we saw the *Khán Bahádur* like a black speck on the corner hill of the range bounding the Káin plain. A long-distance volley at some gazelle was, as usual, without result, and our interest was soon centred in the very ancient city which lay extended before us in the middle of the plain. Viewed from the south, the first thing that strikes the traveller is the extensive belt of gardens, which are especially agreeable after the treelessness of Birjand. The eye is then caught by a Masjid-i-Jáma, so extremely ugly that it has been compared to a factory, round which the ruined city walls can be traced.

We camped in a small garden about a mile to the north-east of the town, but the heat was decidedly trying, August being too early for tent life at Káin. Our first visit was to the Kala Kuh, which is probably the most ancient site of the city, and occupies the crest of two hills, rising some 500 feet above the plain. Approached from the north-east, a massive tower is passed, and the first line of bastioned walls is entered; thence there is a slight rise past a tank, which is cut in the living rock. The second line of defence is reached by passing through a domed guard room; inside there are many ruins, all of the same solid character as on the Kala Kuh near Duru. The keep, which occupies the second hill, forms a separate work, and is 30 feet higher than the exterior work, the total length of the work being 350 yards, while the width is 30 yards on an average. The highest fort was, we were informed, a stronghold long before the advent of Mohamedanism, but the lower works are comparatively modern, being constructed by Kerím-ibn-Jamshíd in the 14th century of our era; the mosque in Káin is also his handiwork. On a platform built out from the side of an adjacent hill is the shrine of Abu Turáb, a dervish, who flourished in the same century as Kerím-ibn-Jamshíd.

One afternoon we rode through Káin, which is, I think, the most desolate-looking town I have ever seen. The population numbers about 4000, the majority being *Seiids*, who, as a rule, strongly object to work, and so, although inhabiting a very rich valley, are content to remain miserably poor, in spite of their large output of saffron and the reviving silk industry.

Káin was considered by Dr Bellew to be identical with Artacoana, the royal palace of the Arian princes who revolted under Satibarzanes. Alexander, who was then on his way to Bactria, took some light troops, and having travelled seventy miles in two days, surprised the Arii, who fled. Curtius says that 13,000 of them defended themselves on a rock, which may well have been the Kala Kuh. Artacoana, or Artacoan, as it is written in some manuscripts, is very like Herát-i-Káin in sound; but this derivation may not be correct.[1] In any case, accepting Káin as Artacoana, it is almost certain that Alexander the Great travelled *via* Sháhkin and Duruksh to Tabas, this being the only direct route.

It had been my intention to stop geographical work at the

[1] Mr E. G. Browne thinks that Herát was Arabicised from the ancient *Harí*, cf. Zend-Avesta *Harôyu* (=Sans. *Sarayu*) and Achaemenian inscription, *H.riwa*. The question of Alexander's route is discussed on p. 362.

range bounding Káin to the north, as this appeared on the map as a solid barrier; but when it was discovered that the whole drainage of Nimbuluk, as the district towards Gunabád is termed, joined the Rud-i-Shur in the Káin plain, I decided to include Nimbuluk, and thereby carry my explorations up to the important range separating it from Gunabád. I was thus able to join up with my first journey in Persia, such connections being always satisfactory.

We crossed into Nimbuluk by the Gudár-i-Gaud. Rising to a height of 6800 feet, and lying at the angle where the Káin hills join the higher range which shuts off the desert from Nimbuluk and Káin, this pass, as its name implies,[1] consists of two ridges with a dip in between, the track skirting grey clay hills; in case of rain, the track would be scarcely practicable. We camped at Girimanj, which lies in the open plain, Dehishk and Buznabád, the abode of the Governor, being situated a few miles to the west and near the Khabísi pass, which is on the main Bandar Abbás-Khorasán road. Thence we could see Khidri and Dasht-i-Piáz lying on the skirt of the range, and realised how disheartened Persians must have been in the days of Turkoman forays, as this was one of the most dreaded stages in the whole long journey according to the account given in the record of the Sistán Mission. The inhabitants of Khidri are mostly Arabs, but wear the Herát sheepskin head-dress, and the immense numbers of donkeys and camels thronging it showed that we were on the main road, in fact, there was no camping ground unoccupied; we therefore moved up to Dasht-i-Piáz, which is also a large village lying at the entrance to the hills.

There are only three passes across this range—(1) the Darakht-i-Bana[2] pass, which debouches at Kákh; (2) the Sulimáni further east, a rather more direct and easier pass; and (3) the Gudár-i-Abbasabád, which leads to Kháf. Nimbuluk should therefore have been absolutely secure from the Turkoman terror, had not the road guards, who received no pay, become the partners of these man-stealers.

To complete our work, all three passes were visited in turn, and from the crest of the range we could look down on Kákh and Gunabád, which latter district I had crossed in 1893 when bound for Kermán; in the dim, hazy distance we could descry the range separating Turbat from Meshed, and I longed for a rail-

[1] *Gaud* signifies hollow.

[2] *Bana* is the wild pistachio.

BANA PASS (LOOKING NORTH).

[To face p. 408.

way which would enable me to visit my friends at the sacred city. The Sulimáni pass is, perhaps, a corruption of Suliáni, the name of a large village in the plain, or *vice versa;* its watershed is hardly higher than Dasht-i-Piáz, and it is mainly used by the through traffic, albeit pilgrims travel by Kákh, where there is a shrine. We had a long ride to the Gudár-i-Abbasabád, which was generally used by Turkoman. Our guide, when a lad, was carried off by them, but had escaped during a storm, and the account he gave of the abject state of fear in which every one lived was most instructive.

We returned to the Káin plain by the Dahána-i-Karkáb after halting for a night at Nokáb. The whole forms a superb camel-grazing district, of which Suliáni is the centre. This gorge, down which runs the united drainage of Nimbuluk, is about four miles in length and impassable after rain. We camped at Isfishád, six miles from Káin, and on the following morning visited the north-east corner of the plain and ascended to the Gudár-i-Chang-i-Kalak. In the evening I enjoyed some excellent pigeon-shooting along a line of disused *kanáts*.

Although it was now September we were glad enough to return to the hills, and, camping for a few days at each hamlet, we slowly moved south. At Sehdeh, which lies about half-way between Káin and Birjand, we came upon a colony of *Ághá* Khán's followers. Their head is a young man named Morád *Mírza*, and it is said that there are altogether 1000 families in these parts, who regularly pay tithes to the *Ághá*.[1] The last stage before returning to Birjand was Ghíp, a pleasant little hamlet just off the road, and, as before, we discovered village after village, the district of Alghur, as it was termed, being remarkably fertile.

It was the end of September when our work was done, and after crossing the Gudár-i-Samán-Sháhi, we once again looked down upon the valley in which Birjand lies, after having successfully explored the whole of the great backbone of rolling hills which constitute so conspicuous a feature of the province.

[1] *Vide* p. 163.

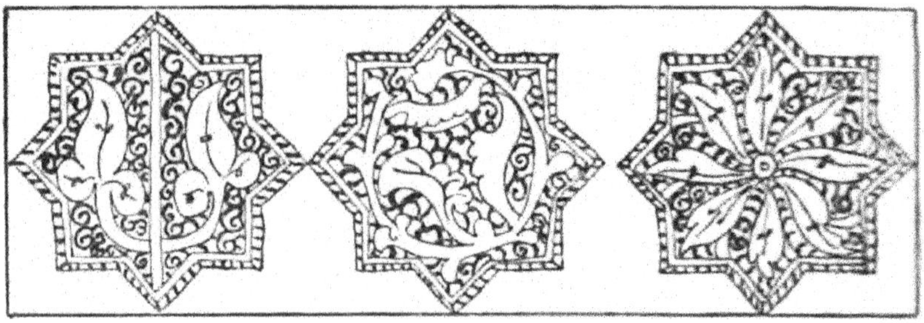

FROM LUSTRED POTTERY.

CHAPTER XXXV

FROM BIRJAND TO YEZD (*VIA* SISTÁN)

"C'est la désolation absolue, le grand triomphe incontesté de la mort. Et là-dessus, tombe un si lourd, un si morne soleil, qui ne paraît fait que pour tuer en desséchant ! . . . Nous n'avions encore rien vu d'aussi sinistre : on est là comme dans les mondes finis, dépeuplés par le feu, qu' aucune roseé ne fécondera plus."—PIERRE LOTI, *Le Désert*, p. 90.

MY instructions being to return to Sistán and Kermán, our mules had to be paid off and some forty or fifty camels engaged, while many an hour was spent poring over maps before we could decide which was the best route to follow.

My conclusion was that, as it was impossible to see the whole of Eastern Persia, I had better confine myself to visiting Neh, and to ascertaining what was really the main caravan route, information respecting which was vague to a degree. Finally, I wished to explore the mines of Kala Zarri, which had only been hastily examined by M. Khanikoff's geologist in the middle of the 19th century.

Our good fortune being in the ascendant, we found that there was a track across the ranges, leading direct to the Golden Fort from Mud, and enabling us to combine all the various objects of our journey, without materially increasing its length. Accordingly, the first week in October saw us once again on the move, the Hospital Assistant being left behind to look after the post, and from Birjand we retraced our steps as far as Bujd, passing on the way a new garden of the *Amir*, which had made immense progress during the summer, and should be a pleasant residence when finished.[1] From Bujd we bore south-south-east, and the rise was continued to the important village of Mud, noted for its homespuns, where we left the main road to Neh and Sistán, and struck south-south-west up a valley which was full of villages, Fánud and Heriván being the chief. The river-bed was very stony, but the pass over the Bakarán range was easy, and only 7300 feet in altitude, the high peaks suddenly terminating at this point. We enjoyed a splendid view across range after range of hills, and indeed there are few countries where a view is so satisfactory as in Persia, since not only is bad weather quite exceptional, but peaks can be recognised even at distances exceeding 200 miles.

We camped just below the pass in cold frosty weather, and sending the caravan down the steep stony valley to Mukhterán, branched off to the west in search of Chinishk, where we had news of a wonderful cave. After much up and down work we sighted the little town perched on a steep hillside, the houses nestling among great boulders, and passing through it, we reached a huge plane, beneath which we rested while making enquiries. We were informed that the cave was a shrine, and on the appearance of a little deformed man, who said that he was its custodian, we scrambled up for a few hundred feet until we reached a small platform built out from the limestone crags. Boots and sun hats were taken off, as we were warned that the cave was both narrow and slippery, and, preceded by our gnome-like guide, we entered it by a very small hole which had rough steps cut at intervals. After a descent of perhaps twenty feet, we proceeded in a lateral direction, squeezing past a rough box which was said to be full of bones. Just behind it came the *crux* in the shape of a small round hole, through which the guide scuttled like a rabbit, but it proved a tight fit for me, and I felt grave doubts as to whether I should not stick on the way back. The cave then opened out, and a small tank, cut in the living rock, showed that it had once been inhabited. We again zigzagged downwards, passing perfect skeletons at the corners, and were assured that this weird catacomb was of immense extent. However, our curiosity was

[1] I was pleased to hear that both doors and windows for the house were purchased in Quetta.

satisfied, and fully agreeing with Virgil's "*superas evadere ad auras hic labor hoc opus est*," we scrambled back, and reached the open air with some pleasure. The "gnome" informed us that the skeletons were the mortal remains of a band of pilgrims who, upon hearing at Turbat that the *Imám* Reza had been poisoned, ended their days in this cave.

Turning our backs on a quaint secluded corner of unexplored Persia, we followed down the valley until the plain was reached, but it was dark before we arrived at Mukhterán, which is a great centre for camel breeding.

The next range that we traversed was much lower, and at Sibcháh we struck the great caravan route which runs from Neh past Khusp and crosses into Nimbuluk by the Khabísi pass. Here we lost all our riding camels as well as one of the load camels, and it was not until the following afternoon that six out of eight returned, overcome with thirst. As we failed to obtain news of the other two,[1] in spite of having sent out searchers in every direction, we marched across a third range to Basirán, a village which is situated on the edge of the Lut at an elevation of 4800 feet.

A short ride of eleven miles to the south-west brought us to Kala Zarri, which is also known as the Kala Gabr, this latter name undoubtedly pointing to a pre-Mohamedan origin, which was corroborated by the style of architecture. Crowning a low rocky hill, the fort was undoubtedly built to protect the spring and smelting forges below it. Its shape was square, of unhewn stones fitted in mortar, with traces of mortar outside; indeed, the whole work, including the shape of the bastions, exactly resembled the fort we had seen at Káin, and one we were soon to inspect at Neh. Its outside measurement was sixty feet, height of walls twenty feet, thickness three feet, while the loopholes were nineteen by eight inches. Smelting is still carried on with the most primitive appliances, the tile bellows being delightfully unpractical.

The mines are two miles to the south on the skirt of the last black range, beyond which lay the level plain of the Lut stretching across to Khabis, the whole country vividly recalling to my mind the desert as I saw it when entering it from Tun. These ancient

[1] In 1900 one was found at Khabis, but died a few days later, thus falling a victim to its homing instinct, which had led it right across the Lut.

workings consist of colossal cuttings and a series of gigantic wells connected by galleries. The former, some fifty feet deep and twenty wide, were easily accessible, and we chipped off specimens of the copper. The shafts we measured by tying a stone to camel-ropes knotted together, the bottom being struck at a depth of seventy feet, while the average diameter was twelve feet. There was apparently no attempt at accommodation for the miners, who must have lived below or in booths, and to my disappointment there were no inscriptions. The mines, which, according to the learned M. Khanikoff, are mentioned by no Mohamedan geographer, were worked with an enterprise and skill quite unknown to-day, the degenerate successors of these mighty men of yore contenting themselves with re-smelting the slag. The annual output is said to be 6000 pounds, fetching 3d. per pound at Birjand. The smelters only work after the harvest is gathered, and when a tax of £20 per annum was levied by the late *Amir*, operations ceased, many families migrating to work the copper mine at Sabzawár. To the best of my knowledge, there are no other mines in the province of Káin.

After waiting a day at Basirán for news of the lost camels, we continued our march to Neh, halting at Deh No, which lies due north of the Sháh Kuh, a conspicuous peak some 8000 feet high, which must be almost visible from Khabis; on its summit is a shrine. From Deh No we made a short stage to Meighán, beyond which we joined the Khabis-Neh road, and crossing a range of clay hills, descended on to the Neh plain. The first object to catch our attention was the deserted fort, which bore a strong family likeness to the one at Tabas, and we counted exactly fifty windmills in a row, before reaching camp.

Neh, first mentioned as Nie by Isidorus of Charax,[1] is undoubtedly a site of great antiquity, and must have been a place of importance, lying as it does on the direct line between Bandar Abbás and the Khorasán, and within the first cultivated area struck by caravans after leaving Narmáshir. At the present time nine routes radiate from the town. Ancient Neh, which no traveller had hitherto discovered, is undoubtedly what is known as Kala Sháh Duzd, three miles to the east of the more modern fort; it is built on a hill only accessible on the west side, and is carefully

[1] *Vide* p. 362.

guarded by numerous *sangars*. The track about half-way up enters the line of bastioned wall by passing under a little fort which was almost a duplicate of Kala Zarri. Above, lying up the steep hill-side, were thousands of houses, built of unhewn stone fitted together with mortar, the summit being some 600 feet above the plain. The other faces are perpendicular, but the water-supply seemed insufficient, there being only tanks, so far as could be seen. The area covered was quite four acres, and these are certainly the most important ruins which I have examined in Eastern Persia.

Legend has it that Sháh Duzd or King Thief forced Zál to pay tribute, until Rustam grew up, when the overlord was challenged to single combat. All their weapons having been exhausted, they wrestled until, by mutual consent, a halt was made for refreshment. Rustam of subtlety indulged sparingly, but his less careful opponent drank his fill, and was easily worsted, thereby sealing his own doom.

Neh grows ample supplies for its own consumption, but as it feeds all the caravans passing in both directions, it imports grain largely from Sistán; this accounts for the number of its mills. Its population is perhaps 5000 or rather less.

Continuing the return journey, at the low ridge dignified by the name of Gudár-i-Zard[1] the direct road from Quetta to Meshed was crossed, and we swung round to the east, entering a wide stony plain which gradually sinks down to the south, and camping at Aliabád, whence there is also a direct route to Sistán, running to the south of Bandán and Beiring. We met 400 camels and donkeys, all bearing grain, which was the first sign of commercial activity that we had seen since leaving Dasht-i-Piáz. A long march across the Gudár-i-Ghinchi brought us to Bandán, where there was so much wind that we had to pull down our tents, and we were soon back again in Sistán, which we found as dry as we had left it water-logged. Upon the present occasion, we used the Surkh Gazi route and camped at Nasrabád, whence I took a long ride to the north and nearly crossed the *hámun*, there being no water except in the Dariá Sábari.

The new Governor, Mohamed Reza Khán, to whose tragic experiences I have before referred, rode out to meet me, and I found that we were quite regarded as friends, previous suspicions

[1] Or Yellow Pass; it is some ten miles from Neh.

having happily been dispelled. Abbás Ali, an especially smart Hospital Assistant, who had already visited Sistán, had also just arrived, and I had the pleasant feeling that I should leave everything in good working order for my successor. There was no shooting near Nasratabád, nor any cases to settle, and, as I was expecting a visitor at Kermán in the shape of Captain Napier of the Oxfordshire Light Infantry, I only remained a few days, during which I presented the Deputy Governor with a silver self-winding watch and chain, and heard that he approved of my gift, but would have preferred a watch with a key!

Early in November our transport arrangements for crossing the desert were all completed, and we slowly marched to Varmál, whence, for the second time, we turned our backs on Sistán.

Roughly speaking, the distance to Narmáshir is 200 miles, which is approximately bisected by the village of Isfe or Ispi, now called Nasratabád. We made two short stages to Cháh Lashkarán, which lies a few miles north of Girdi Cháh, and then the desert had to be faced. The line we took was the one used by the Sistán Mission some thirty years previously, and in good years there is water at distances of about twenty-five miles a little to the south of it, but as this was a dry year, we had to accomplish a stage of thirty-seven miles, mostly uphill, which means for the camels twenty hours' continuous marching. However, there was no help for it, so, giving the advance camp a good twelve hours' start, we rode across the level plain, which abruptly terminated at ten miles, and thenceforward we wended our weary way along very stony tracks. A low range of hills, a plain, and a descent into a river-bed occupied many hours, and when we reached running water, we thought that we were at the stage; but we were mistaken, as, after ascending through some reeds, from which a snipe got up, we left this stream, the water of which was intensely bitter, and were very glad to sight our camp lying in a tamarisk grove near the spring of Turshâb. Its altitude was 4200 feet, a great rise from Sistán. Between us and Garágha, evidently the Kilagh Ab of the Sistán Mission, lay a fairly high range of hills, and altogether we felt that this belt of country should not be a desert, as it is certainly fertile, and the camel-grazing is especially luxuriant. It is interesting to know that Garágha was one of Rustam's favourite hunting preserves, and it was here that Bahmán, when sent on an embassy to him, tried to make it a success by crushing the Champion of the World with an avalanche of rocks. Rustam, however, continued his occupation of roasting a wild ass whole until the stones were nearly on him, when he diverted them with a kick! Garágha once was a village, and given security would no doubt be so again, but population in Persia is very scarce, and the percentage of non-workers terribly high.

In the Malusán range, which now divided us from Nasratabád, are very ancient copper mines, which were intermittently worked until a big raid was made from Nushki, some thirty or forty years ago. Chehel Kura or the Forty Furnaces is the local name.

Nasratabád we found to be situated in a wide valley, and lying as it does at the junction of roads coming from all directions, it is of considerable importance. Both the ancient Isfe,[1] now partially dismantled, and the modern square fort are comparatively speaking strongly built. We decided to halt a day, during which I enjoyed excellent sand-grouse shooting, the birds coming in by threes and fours from the desert to drink at the stream, which, albeit brackish, is an excellent one, irrigating many acres. Having succeeded in procuring some chopped straw, we reloaded our forage camels and started off on the second desert section, rising towards the range, which has no particular name, although its highest peak is known as the Kuh-i-Khul. Entering the hills by a gradually narrowing valley, we reached at ten and a half miles what is locally known as Darwáza-i-Nádir. A limestone ridge runs at right angles across the valley, and a way has been cut through it, mainly, no doubt, by the agency of water, but as the cutting is faced with masonry, it must be partly due to human agency. On the Sistán side there are three towers, two of which probably supported a gateway, in which an iron door was hung.

That Nádir Sháh has no claim to the honour of erecting this and other public works, the following extract from the history of Mohamed Ibráhim proves: "On the Sistán road in the valley of Káward at four *farsakhs* from Isfe an iron gate was constructed and a garrison stationed. From the head of the valley to Fahraj was twenty-four *farsakhs*.[2] Every three hundred paces a pillar

[1] The Baluchis term it Ispi. It is said to have been founded by the mighty Isfandiár.

[2] It is actually ninety-one miles.

twice the height of a man was built in such a way that at night from each pillar a second one could be seen, so that no one could lose their way." Just above we found the traces of a spring, which was dry, and consequently would preclude the possibility of garrisoning the post.

The pass known as the Gudár-i-Surkwak is narrow, and from its summit we looked across the yellow Lut to the distant ranges behind Narmáshir that we knew so well. Below it we came upon a herd of wild sheep, which allowed us to approach within forty yards, and then were only driven off by Shavey, so little is seen of man in these hills. My rifle was of course a mile behind.

The *darband* we had passed through possesses quite another interest for the traveller. It would hardly have been built had there been other neighbouring passes, and as we were assured that there were none, it may be fairly inferred that every traveller from Sistán to Narmáshir is, and always was, bound to follow this route. This being so, it seems almost certain that we were treading in the steps of Krateros. Arrian (vi. 17) says that Alexander, before starting on his march through Gedrosia, "sent away Krateros into Karmania by the route through the Arachotians and the Sarangians." In chap. xxvii. he says that Krateros joined his sovereign "when he arrived in Karmania."

Krateros then travelled from the Indus to the Helmand, where he was in known country. He thence followed its course to Sistán, and must have traversed Narmáshir[1] in order to join his master in Rudbár or Jíruft; he therefore undoubtedly followed the road that I have described. It is a curious coincidence that he passed through Fahraj, which the late Sir Oliver St John, erroneously I maintain, identified with the Pura of Arrian.

We camped for the heat of the day near a ruined *caravanserai*, and as there were thieves on the road, we marched in one body to Gurg, which we reached at sunrise. Gurg is generally considered to be the worst stage in this part of the desert, the pools of water being quite undrinkable, and the bitter river, which has been wrongly shown on the map as the lower course of the Rud-i-Máhi, waters a jungle of tamarisks, haunted by Baluch brigands, who, if pursued, can find refuge in the broken ground

[1] This is Bunbury's Nurmansheer. Cf. his *History of Ancient Geography* vol. i. p. 522.

towards the hills. Even in November the mosquitoes were trying enough, but in summer, owing to the heat, Gurg is little better than a death-trap, and here more than elsewhere the abomination of desolation can be realised; I felt that this was indeed the terrible blighting Lut, which requires a Pierre Loti to describe it.

In the afternoon we again marched on, and after sleeping for a few hours on the road to let the camels get ahead, at twenty-one miles we passed the first so-called Mil-i-Nádiri. The column has, however, collapsed, the almost imperishable red bricks lying prone in three or four huge masses.

At Shurgaz the water was just a little better, but so scanty that there was none for the camels. We left it in the afternoon, and at thirteen miles passed the second column, which is still standing, although its base has been much eaten away. Its height, according to measurements made by the Sistán Mission, is fifty-five feet, with a base circumference of forty-three feet, and there is a staircase leading to the summit. It is mentioned in the history of Mohamed Ibráhim as follows: "At the top of the valley a *caravanserai*, a tank, and a bath were built of bricks, and two columns were constructed between Gurg and Fahraj, one forty *gaz*[1] in height and the other twenty-five *gaz*." As *Malik* Káward was strangled by his nephew in A.H. 466 (1073), these fine public works were erected just about the time of William the Conqueror.

As may be imagined, after marching just over a hundred miles in three days, we were very glad to turn our backs on the Lut (albeit the track was good enough upon the whole), and reach the green palm grove of Fahraj, where the sweet water tasted delicious.

A village with a thousand inhabitants from which the population of Nasratabád is drawn, Fahraj is of considerable importance as lying on the edge of the desert, and it was until some sixty years ago held by the Afgháns, who also apparently owned Khabis. A day's halt was imperative, as our camels could hardly move, and I shot a few black partridges, but they proved scarce, although the thick jungle, water, and cultivation promised excellent sport. At night a gale, so heavy that all our tents collapsed, made us thankful that we were on the right side of the desert, and the following day we reached the bridge of Azizabád, where, thanks to last year's experience, I enjoyed some excellent shooting, and then rode on

[1] A *gaz* is about the same length as a mètre.

THE PILLAR OF NÁDIR.

[To face p. 418.

for the night to Vakilabád. We did not rest at Bam, as I heard that Captain Napier was ahead of me, having travelled rather faster than I had calculated, and we finally met at Máhun, where I waited for a couple of days to allow Nasrulla Khán to make the necessary arrangements.

On the 2nd December, after being sixteen months on the march, I entered Kermán, where I enjoyed the pleasant novelty of having a guest to entertain, only however for a few days.

My first care after settling down was to organise and despatch a trial caravan to Quetta, Captain Webb Ware having kindly agreed to assist me in the matter. The exquisite carpets, the finest in the world, had never before been exported to India, and I felt that they should form the bulk of the venture; so for some weeks the merchant who agreed to embark on the enterprise (which I partly financed) brought up bales of carpets, all of which were carefully examined by me before being passed. Two Baluch levies came across from our frontier to act as a guard, and with samples of Yezd silks, saffron, homespun, and pistachio nuts, the little caravan, the pioneer of greater things, started. Fortune smiled on it, as His Excellency the Viceroy happened to visit Quetta at the period of its arrival, and the purchases he made were so considerable and drew such attention to the caravan that the carpets were all sold at a handsome profit. In 1900 the second and much more important caravan was despatched, and I now consider that a trade may be established to the mutual benefit of Indo-Persian relations.

Hearing early in January 1900 that the war in South Africa had attained much larger proportions than had been anticipated, I determined to send in a request to be allowed to proceed there. Meanwhile I travelled to Yezd, where, in order to pass the slow impracticable hours until my fate was decided, I procured two manuscript histories of Yezd, by the help of which, and a certain amount of enquiry, I was able to gain an accurate account of the interesting public buildings of the city.

Yezd is said to have been a desert when Alexander the Great conquered Persia, and the hero, being struck by its remoteness, built a prison near the site of the modern city for his royal captives, their dungeon being a deep well. Háfiz, in reference to Yezd, writes: "I was afraid of Alexander's prison, and prepared to go to the country of Sulimán."[1] In this, no doubt, he evinced a desire to be unpleasant, as the Yezdis did not treat him well, and his ire finds vent in the following lines:

> "O morning wind, say to the dwellers in Yezd from me,
> May the heads of the ungrateful be the balls of your polo sticks."[2]

The present name of the city dates from Yezdijird I. (A.D. 399-420), father of Bahrám Gur, who probably refounded it in the fifth century of our era. Lying near no frontier, its history has been comparatively peaceful, and no doubt it was on this account, together with its remoteness from the invader, that at the time of the Arab conquest Yezd, and in a lesser degree Kermán, became the refuge of those who adhered to the ancient religion. The former is still their headquarters, and in some measure a sacred city.

Yezd was visited by Marco Polo in the thirteenth century, by Odoricus in the fourteenth, and by Josafa Barbaro in the fifteenth, the latter's account being so interesting, that I cannot refrain from quoting it: "We came to Jex, a towne of artificers, as makers of sylkes, fustians, chamletts, and other like. This towne is walled, of V myles in circuite, with very great suburbes, and yet in maner they all arr wevers and makers of divers kindes of sylkes which came from Straua,[3] from Azzi, and from the pties towardes Zagatai: towards the sea of Bachu, the best whereof come from Jex, which, with their workes, do aftrewards furnishe a great parte of India, Persia, Zagatai, Cim and Macim,[4] parte of Catay, of Bursia,[5] and of Turchie; wherefore lett him that woll bie good silkes of Soria, faire and well wrought, take of these."[6]

Before referring to modern Yezd, I propose to describe its buildings, chief of which is the Masjid-i-Jáma, originally founded by *Sultán* Alá-u-Dola, Gursháasp, in A.H. 513 (1119). It was during his rule that Yezd received its title of *Dár-ul-Ibáda* or Abode of Devotion, Alá-u-Dola requesting Malik Sháh that it might be bestowed on him for that purpose. The mosque was

[1] *i.e.* Fárs.

[2] This may refer to Tímúr's action at Damascus when men's heads took the place of polo balls, as mentioned in the chapter on Polo.

[3] Astrabád. [4] Chin and Machin, or China. [5] Basra?

[6] *Travels of Venetians in Persia*, p. 73. (Hakluyt Soc.)

YEZD.

[*To face p.* 420.

rebuilt by *Seiid* Rukn-u-Din in A.H. 777 (1375), and its mosaic work bears the date of A.H. 877 (1472), in which year *Mir* Chakmák covered it with beautiful designs. It is entered by a lofty gateway of a type peculiar to Yezd, but the mosaic work has almost all fallen off, while the doors, which are exquisite specimens of wood-carving, will in a very few years disappear.[1] Passing through this erstwhile noble approach, the mosque lies at right angles. Its dome is indeed stripped nearly bare, but the interior is still perfect, the prevailing colour being blue, and the effect very striking.

The fort was built in A.H. 532 (1137) by Abu Jafar *Sultán*, Alá-u-Din, Kanjár, but beyond the strength of its profile, it is of no interest. Close to it is a dome fast falling into ruins, which is, however, beautifully ornamented in the interior, Kufic inscriptions in dark blue, light green, and brown blending most artistically with the white of the background. All the mosaics have fallen from the walls, and this is all that remains of the Vukt-i-Sáat, which consisted of a college, a library, and an unrivalled observatory, all built by *Seiid* Rukn-u-Din in A.H. 726 (1325). The latter is fully described in one of the histories referred to above, and I relegate the description of its marvels to a footnote.[2]

[1] An attempt was made by an enterprising official to send them to the Paris Exhibition!

[2] The description of this wonderful piece of mechanism runs as follows:—

"Opposite the entrance of the *madresa* are two columns, on one of which there is a copper bird, and this bird always looks towards the sun and swings round. On the other column is a flag which appears five times a day, when the drum should be beaten. On the column in the middle of the observatory, was a wooden wheel painted. It was divided into three hundred and sixty divisions; each division had degrees, showing every day when the sun rises, in letters representing numbers. On the four corners of the wheel four circles appeared. On each circle were thirty divisions, and the name of the month was written according to the Turki, Rumi, Arabic, and Jaláli calendars (*i.e.* Persian of the new era). Every day that passes has one division. From two little windows above the wheel two bronze birds appear, and throw bronze dice into a bowl that is placed below the birds. Then the wheel moves, and of twelve white boards that show the twelve hours one falls, and a black board comes into its place, and at the five times (*i.e.* of prayer), when the die falls, the drum inside the observatory is struck, and the flag appears on the column. The circle is drawn to the top of the wheel, and thirty white circles are placed on it. Every day of the month one of the circles will be black, and on these circles the whole of that month is written. And on another side, opposite the clock, twelve other boards are placed, and at night, when one hour passes, one lamp of the twelve that are placed appears again. In the middle of this wheel

It is rather sad to read that this public benefactor was accused of the murder of a rich Christian, on the theory that otherwise he could not have obtained so much money for his college! He "ate 1000 sticks," and was exposed to all sorts of insults, but finally was released and died, honoured by all, his tomb resting under the dome.

Outside modern Yezd, which lies partly to the south-east of the ancient city, is the shrine known as *Sheikh* Dád, which possesses a fresco representing Ali, his two sons, and favourite servants. Taki-u-Din, Dádá Mohamed, was born at Isfahán, and on his arrival at Yezd was at first treated as a rival by the *mullás*, but they finally accepted him as their chief. He died in A.H. 700 (1300), and his shrine was raised in A.H. 726 (1325), the term *Sheikh* Dád being a corruption or abbreviation.

The square of Yezd is known as the Meidán-i-Mir Chakmák.[1] This worthy, a Syrian by birth, governed Yezd under Sháh Rukh, and not only repaired the Masjid-i-Jáma, but also built the fine mosque known by his name. The square is entered by the second of the very lofty gateways referred to above, and in it stands an octagonal tile-covered pillar some nine feet high, which is known as a *kalak*. This puzzled me for some time, as the word literally means a clay bowl for holding hot charcoal. All the Parsi shrines include a pillar of this sort, and it would appear that the Mohamedans of Yezd and Kashán have adopted it from the members of the older religion. During the month of Moharram lamps and, if necessary, fires are lighted upon it, and it is the centre for the breast-beating ceremonies.

there is a zone or zodiac, on which the names of the forty-seven stages of the zone are written. Also, above the circle of the zodiac, the names of the five great planets, Zohal (Saturn), Mushtari (Jupiter), Otárid (Mercury), Marikh (Mars), and Zohre (Venus), were written, and the description of every day, and of every star (*i.e.* whether auspicious or the reverse).

"Inside the observatory was a cistern, twice the height of a man, made of copper Every day it was filled with water, and copper dishes were fastened by a chain on the surface of the water. And below that cistern an astrolabe of bronze was constructed, and from one side of the machine the water poured from the hole, and as the water of the cistern decreased the dishes sunk, and the whole of the works were moved by that water; and small bowls, hung up like trays, showed the minutes, and every minute a hammer was struck on them, and gave forth a sound, and low down in the observatory was a wooden window, with a wooden bolt, and it was from this that the sound came out."

[1] Mir Chakmák literally signifies Master of the Gun Hammer.

A PARSI FAMILY.

[*To face p.* 422.

But enough of ancient Yezd, and I will now devote a few lines to the city as I know it. Approached from Kermán the rider, after entering a belt of sand-hills, sees in the distance the two high gateways with their minarets and a forest of wind-towers, which, when viewed during a sand-storm, give a weird sense of unreality, recalling the *Arabian Nights*. Gardens are gradually dominating the sand, which is erroneously stated to be encroaching on Yezd, and these extend for a mile, until the somewhat mean but busy *bázárs* are entered, important business being generally transacted in the extensive *caravanserais* which open off them.

Possessing a population reckoned at 60,000, Yezd still keeps seven hundred looms busy weaving all sorts of silk. That known as *Husein Kuli Khán*, after its originator, who was a native of Kermán, consists of a fir-cone pattern on a plum-coloured ground, and is far from cheap, costing about 7s. 6d. per yard. The other silks are not particularly pleasing, and are mainly used for linings. White silk handkerchiefs are, however, cheap and fairly good, and the finest embroidery in silk can be purchased at almost nominal prices; it is known as *Rubandi* and is most effective.

Apart from its silk looms Yezd possesses almost a monopoly of the henna trade, the leaves of the shrub being imported from Narmáshir, where of late years enormous profits have been realised, its price having more than doubled. Opium, too, is largely dealt in, but I understand that adulteration has almost ruined the trade, temporarily, at any rate. There is also a considerable export of cotton, almonds, and pistachio nuts.

Yezd, however, owes its wealth to the fact that a large proportion of the imports from the south changes hands in its *caravanserais*, and also to the industry of the Parsi community, the members of which, cut off from India until some sixty years ago, are now striving to follow in the path of their co-religionists, who are British subjects. Numbering 7000 members, of whom 1000 live in the actual city, the Parsis, by dint of hard work and in the face of adverse circumstances, bid fair to outstrip their Mohamedan fellow-countrymen. Against improvement, however, the *Dastur* or priests set their face, so that two or three generations must elapse before enlightenment becomes universal.

In all this work our race is playing a great part. I have mentioned that in 1894 there was a strong anti-European feeling, but now time has changed all this, and Europeans appear to be not only respected but liked.

The fact that a *caravanserai*, given by Gudarz Mehrbán, a Parsi, has been turned into a well-equipped hospital by Dr White of the Church Missionary Society, appeals to high and low, and the Imperial Bank of Persia is no longer regarded in the light of an intruding institution.

My visit proved that the old order was changing, as the three leading religious lights, who between them hold Yezd in the hollow of their hand, broke through the ice and called on me. I found them all friendly, and was glad that public opinion had so altered that social intercourse between East and West was no longer a thing to be reprobated. In many other ways, too, there is progress, rich merchants who have spent many years at Bombay bringing back ideas which have already borne fruit in the introduction of new trees and shrubs and in building better houses.

The European colony consisted of two representatives of the Bank, five members of the Church Missionary Society, including a lady doctor, and a representative of Messrs Ziegler & Co., a Manchester firm.[1] Until my arrival their chief amusement was lawn tennis, but I was able to start a Gymkhana, which was warmly supported, several Persians taking part in the tent-pegging and jumping. When I said good-bye to my kind host, Mr Fothergill, and started back towards Kermán, my disappointment at not being allowed to proceed to Africa was only accentuated by the feeling that I was leaving so much of life and hospitality behind.

[1] Messrs Hotz & Sons closed their agency in 1898.

DESIGN FROM A WATER-PIPE.

CHAPTER XXXVI

AN ANCIENT CAPITAL OF KERMÁN

"The city of Sirján is watered by subterranean aqueducts: in the suburbs they raise water from wells. This is the largest of all the cities of Kermán. The inhabitants are Sunnis."—IBN HAUKAL.

To the south-west of Kermán is a triangle of upland country lying between the Báft road and that to Sirján. This I had wished to explore for many years, but it was not until April 1900 that the opportunity presented itself, both of travelling in this unknown district, and also of visiting Sirján, where I was anxious to find out something as to the site of what was said to be an ancient capital of the province.

Leaving Kermán, we struck the southern road near the shrine of *Sheikh* Ali Goheri, who is stated to have been a mystic, and, passing the gardens of Rigabád, soon found ourselves in the blighting waste of sand-hills which almost surrounds the city, and were proportionately grateful to reach our first stage of Jupár.[1] This little town, with a population of perhaps 4000 inhabitants, is visible from Kermán, its blue-domed shrine erected in honour of *Sháhzáda*[2] Husein forming a splendid landmark: its gardens are extensive and supply the fruit-stalls of the city.

[1] The derivation of Jupár is said to be a corruption of *Já-i-Pársál* or Last Year's Abode, which was given it by the nomads.

[2] *Sháhzáda* signifies Son of a Sháh, who may be either temporal or spiritual. *Sháhzáda* Husein was a brother of the *Imám* Reza.

Jupár lies under the lofty picturesque range of the same name, from which the major portion of the water-supply of Kermán is drawn, the *kanáts* running for miles under the sand-hills. As far as Máhun, villages line the skirt of the mountain at comparatively frequent intervals, and, after the city, this is the most important Parsi centre.[1]

The main caravan route, which was followed by Marco Polo, as a rule keeps a few miles to the west, striking the Bahrámjird river, as I would term it,[2] at Chári, but most travellers prefer to spend the night at Jupár, as there are no supplies to be obtained at the regular halting-place.

The second stage had alternative routes, the easier but more circuitous track keeping rather to the west, and uniting with the main road near Gulumak. We, however, chose the more direct track, which crosses a rugged spur of the Jupár range by a pass known as Gudár-i-Bacha-Mullái or The Pass of the *Mullá's* Boy. It would be too steep for camels, and is trying enough for mules, but the view looking up the valley is fine, the cultivation round the various villages and hamlets giving quite a fertile look to what is one of the richest districts of Kermán. Bahrámjird or Bahrámkird, as the peasants term it, is an ancient village situated mainly on the left bank of the river, which is some twenty yards wide. It was almost certainly one of Marco Polo's stages, in which connection it is interesting to note that a few years before his journey it was the meeting-place between Borák Hájib and Jalál-u-Din, the last scion of the Khiva family, who was murdered after vainly striving to stem the Mongol wave of invasion.

From Bahrámjird I decided to march to Nagar, which lies due west. The distance on the map was seventeen miles, whereas it proved to be exactly half that length, the intervening desert being monotonously bare and level.

Nagar contains a ruin of considerable interest, which was at one time used as a mosque, but has now only the walls left. These show unmistakable signs of having been built at two periods, to the latter of which the burnt-brick *minár* must be assigned. Only

[1] Jupár, Ismailabád, and Kerimabád count one hundred and ten Parsis among their inhabitants, while Kanát Ghastán has one hundred and seventy Parsi inhabitants and a "Tower of Silence."

[2] Like so many rivers, it has no one name, but Bahrámjird is the oldest and best known village on its banks.

some thirty feet of this are still intact, and round it is a belt of blue Kufic lettering. The *mihráb* bore an inscription dated A.H. 615 (1218) until quite recently. The orientation being towards Jerusalem, we may feel confident that this was originally a Nestorian church which had been converted into a mosque. We had now struck the main route to Bandar Abbás, which was henceforth followed as far as Báft, and leaving Nagar, for some miles we traversed a well-cultivated plain; then, passing a shrine in honour of yet another brother of the *Imám* Reza, we crossed the first and lower range which holds up the highlands. It has often struck me that in a sense Persia resembles a saucepan, as the plateau has a very distinct rim, which is generally at least 5000 feet higher than the centre, which again is as flat as a pancake.

After crossing the Gudár-i-Zárchi, as it is termed, we were only separated by a somewhat narrow valley from the main range, which rose up very grandly, this being as rugged scenery as any I know in the province. The hillside was aflame with the yellow flowers of the bush termed *durmun*, but when we camped below the pass, we found the gale too heavy for our somewhat crazy tents, and reading or writing was quite out of the question. Directly to our south lay a pass, known as the Gudár-i-Soghurk, and further east there is a wide break in the hills which the main route follows. The night was delightfully cold, and the following morning we thoroughly enjoyed crossing and re-crossing the Murgháb[1] stream. We were now travelling in a green land of meadows peopled by nomads, and down every valley raced a clear brook.

We left Kala Askar to the east, and rose to the pass which bears the ominous name of *Kafanu* or Shroud, but there was no snow left, and the gradients are so easy that a horse can cross it at a gallop. Indeed, although some 9000 feet in altitude, the Gudár-i-Kafanu could easily be kept open the whole year round, but as the nomads desert the highlands, there are no villages where caravans can purchase supplies, nor any organisation for clearing away or beating down the snow.

We met a large number of Baluchis marching up from the Hot Country to Bardsír. The sight is always of interest, and it is wonderful how friendly and sensible all the animals are, tiny children of three riding the camels, on one of which a newly-born

[1] Murgh-áb signifies Stream of Fowl.

mainly the property of the Ali Ghazalu, the chief Afshár division dotted the landscape to the south, and towards the main range to the north lay Balvard, the gardens of which are mostly owned by the Karái tribe. As we were in the heart of an unexplored district, it was pleasant to be able to fill what was a blank on the map with numerous villages; not that this is unusual, for main roads were shunned by the villagers, owing to the fact that Governors generally took supplies without payment. To-day, however, this extortion is becoming a thing of the past, and, in course of time, villagers will naturally seek the main routes, which, for the development of Persia, is much to be desired.

At the stage of Aliabád we were in the district of Sirjan,[1] the Kala-i-Sang being just visible in the distance. Next morning we turned our backs on the highlands and steadily descended. When we reached the level plain, we passed a low black slate ridge, on which is situated a dilapidated shrine in honour of *Sháh* Firuz, and at Izzetábád a tent was pitched for the midday halt, as we had overtaken the advanced camp.

Close by was the famous Kala-i-Sang, of which I made a preliminary inspection, and, continuing the march we passed a second shrine, which is much resorted to, known as *Imamzáda* Ali. Village after village was skirted, and we were feeling as if the stage would never end, when I was met by the *Khán Bahádur*, who

[1] Nomads of Sirján:—

1.	Shul Turki	90	families.
2.	Fársi and Namatulláhi	20	,,
3.	Khorasáni	700	,,
4.	Tairiári	15 ?	,,
5.	Yakúbi	20 ?	,,
6.	Bavúrdi	10 ?	,,
7.	Siá	10 ?	,,
8.	Bichára	15 ?	,,
9.	Bagzáda	20 ?	,,
10.	Sazanda	10 ?	,,
11.	Bucháikchi (a) Sarsaidáli	50	,,
	Bucháikchi (b) Kara Saidáli	50	,,
	Bucháikchi (c) Khursali	30	,,
12.	Ankali Buchákchi	40	,,
13.	Nuki Buchákchi	25	,,
14.	Arashlu and Siadu	100	,,
15.	Halvái	25	,,
16.	Karái	600	,,
	TOTAL	1830	families.

said that we had nearly reached Saiidabád. Twenty-four miles from Aliabád the main caravan route from the south joined in, and a few miles further on we were met by the mayor and chief merchants, under whose escort we rode through the narrow *bázárs*, and, at sunset, after a thirty-mile march or rather more, found delightful quarters in a fine garden. Its charms, however, we did not fully appreciate until the following morning, when two enormous sweetbriars in full bloom, backed by equally gigantic rose-trees—they were more than bushes—delighted the sense of smell, while the liquid melody of the *bulbul* filled our ears, and I quite endorsed the exquisite lines of Hafiz:

> "The *bulbul* at dawn lamented to the East Wind
> Of the havoc that the rose and its scent made.
> . . . .
> On every side have love-lorn *bulbuls* lamented,
> While the East Wind made merry at their grief."

I found the authorities extremely friendly, as is generally the case in South-east Persia, and my thirst for information was, for once, fairly assuaged as regards Saiidabád itself, but little was to be learned about the Kala-i-Sang; in fact I could not ascertain that it had ever been visited by any of the *Kháns*.

After a day's rest, I rode back in order to explore thoroughly what is undoubtedly an ancient capital of the province, though, to the best of my knowledge, it has been ignored by the very few travellers who have passed this way. Kala-i-Sang or Stone Fort is also known as Kala-i-Beiza or White Fort, and rises in glorious purity of colour some 300 feet above the level plain. Its direction is from north-east to south-west, and its length 400 yards, while its breadth is rather less than 200 yards; it is shaped like an egg. Approached from the north, this remarkable limestone crag is surrounded at some fifty yards from its base by a low wall of sun-dried brick, which bore traces of having been rebuilt on older foundations. Inside this we found a beautiful stone pulpit, some five feet high, on one side of which were four rows of *Naskh* inscription; a fifth row had been obliterated.

While the *Khán Bahádur* and myself were laboriously trying to make out the meaning, three ragged peasants appeared, and at once began to decipher the inscription. I was not much surprised to hear that their leader was the *mulla* of the village, and we learned from him that the pulpit had been constructed by Sultán Ahmad, *Imád-u-Din* of the Muzaffar dynasty of Kermán in A.H. 789 (1387).[1] We were furthermore informed that the headman of Izzetabád had wished to remove the pulpit to the village, and that in order to lighten it, the top row of the inscription had been hammered off, after which the task was given up, as the pulpit is a monolith, and must weigh two or more tons.

Under the *mulla's* guidance we moved round to the south-west corner, where, as also at the north-east angle, there is a high traverse wall, the intervening space to the south having evidently been the ruler's residence. On this side the inner wall is some forty yards from the cliff, while the outer is two hundred yards distant, so that the total area enclosed was very great.

The sole access to the fort is on the south-west, where we found a second inscription on the right-hand side, just below the remains of a brick dam. Nothing, however, could be read until I sent for a skin of water and carefully washed the surface of the rock, when we made out a few lines to the following effect: "In this blissful abode *Amir Ázam* Husein-ibn-Ali constructed the *Hammám*." The date was apparently A.H. 410 (1019), but as the third cipher was not clear, it may have been anything from A.H. 410 to 420 (1019-1029). The individual who thus perpetuated his memory was almost certainly the Deilami Governor, but I have not been able to identify him further. The ruins of the *Hammám* were, however, clearly visible, the foundations of the stove having remained almost intact.

On the crest of the hill the buildings have collapsed, and the same is generally true of the walls, but under the north-east and highest portion of the crag is a fine grotto, known as the "King's Seat," which is faced by the pulpit, and yet a third inscription giving the name of Mohamed Sháh was delicately chiselled in the rock. As there was no date, it was impossible to identify the particular sovereign thus commemorated.

Below is a second grotto, known as the *Anderun*, where the ladies spent the heat of the day; and as the cliff is quite inaccessible on this face, it must have formed an ideal retreat for a

[1] The inscription runs: "The Sovereign, great, just, glorious and victorious, Sultán Ahmad." The date is in Arabic. Sultán Ahmad is referred to in chap. v.

Persian ruler. No antiquities of any kind were forthcoming, but I picked up a lustred tile, which at once showed that this fort was inhabited during the thirteenth century. History relates that it was the prison of the founder of the Muzaffar dynasty in the middle of the fourteenth century.

Afzal Kermáni writes:—"Among the divisions of Kermán is Sirján, the ancient capital of Bardsír, a fine fertile district; and in Seljuk times they drew their troops thence, and kept a large garrison in it, as being on the Kermán-Fárs boundary. And in Sirján are many ancient graves, and travellers and Sufis term it Lesser Syria. And there is a great fort reaching to the clouds. During the reign of Arslán Sháh it was repaired, and again destroyed. To-day[1] it is occupied."

This, then, is an ancient capital of Kermán, although not the Carmana of Ammianus Marcellinus. Sirján is locally considered to be a corruption of Samangán, famous in Persian legend as the home of Rustam's mighty son. As, however, the *Sháh Náma* particularly mentions that Samangán was in Turán, it is impossible to accept this theory.[2]

So far as I could gather, the Kala-i-Sang was taken by Tímúr's forces, after plague had broken out among the garrison, and when the district recovered a new capital was built and termed Shahr Biumídi or the City of Despair, an appropriate designation. Upon the Afghán invasion the old fort was again occupied, but was captured by the enemy and, Shahr Biumidi having been destroyed, Saiidabád[3] was founded by a certain *Mírza* Saiíd in its immediate proximity.

When we returned to our garden we found an old woman and two girls making a great commotion, and, upon enquiry, it turned out that they claimed the cook as a member of their family, which Husein strenuously denied. The evidence brought mainly consisted of similarity of age, name, and dress, and it was finally remembered that we had once employed a groom called Husein many years before, which accounted for the error.

Saiidabád has some three thousand houses, and lies in a most fertile plain studded with villages; the soil is much richer than at Kermán, the trees especially being very fine. Although

[1] *i.e.* in 1188 A.D. [2] *Vide* p. 19.

[3] Saidabád is incorrect, but hitherto universally accepted.

its altitude is about 5300 feet, I was informed that roots of date trees were occasionally dug up, so that its climate must have changed, possibly owing to deforestation. Sad to say, there is no place where opium-smoking is so prevalent, and in despite of the natural richness, there is in consequence much poverty.

The only shrine of interest is that in honour of Kamál-u-Din, consisting of a neat building, which the *Farmán Farmá* had repaired. Kamál-u-Din was a descendant of the *Imám* Reza, and was killed with a spade. According to one account, he suffered from the same indiscreet zeal which impels the Hazára to kill immediately any traveller showing signs of sanctity. The explanation is given in Southey's *St Romuald*:—

"'But,' quoth the Traveller, 'wherefore did he leave
A flock that knew his saintly worth so well?'
. . . .
'Why, Sir,' the Host replied,
'We thought perhaps that he might one day leave us;
And then should strangers have
The good man's grave,
A loss like that would naturally grieve us;
For he'll be made a Saint of, to be sure,
Therefore we thought it prudent to secure
His relics while we might;
And so we meant to strangle him one night.'"

By the second week in May my work was done, and, although I should have liked to visit the great *kavir*, the course of which I had traced for many miles from the crest of the Kala-i-Sang, I was obliged to return to Kermán.

As usual, I tried to avoid the main route, and heard that there was a good track across the mountains, which was more direct than the caravan road *via* Khán-i-Surkh. Upon clearing Saiidabád, we shaped our course for a prominent flat-topped hill known as Takht-i-Tanbur, behind which we crossed a wide, deep *nala* and camped near the village of Amirabád, which was built some twenty years ago by the Karái nomads. Escorted by its owner, the following day we entered the hills, passing a hamlet of *Seiids*, known as Sukhta Chál, where we entered the river-bed, down which a chattering stream was flowing. Partridges abounded, and our guide was much upset at finding that we refused to shoot them, no Persian ever regarding the close season.

It was a pleasant change to be in the hills again, especially as we rose steadily and found our camp pitched at Tangru, the head-quarters of the Karái. As I was anxious to meet the chief of the Bucháкchi, we made a short march up to Takkia, which is also inhabited by *Seiids*, the nomads tilling some of the land, but leaving in the autumn. It contains a shrine in honour of *Sháh* Abdur Rahman, one of the innumerable brothers of the *Imám* Reza.

The district is the summer abode of Isfandiár Khán, chief of the Buchákchi, and it was not long before I received a visit from this Robin Hood of Persia. His latest feat had been the sudden seizure of Saiidabád and imprisonment of its Governor, on the pretext that such were his orders from the Sháh. He collected the taxes, and when a rising took place he sent for his secretary and solemnly composed a telegram in which he reported to Tehrán that he was being hindered in the execution of his duties by the disloyal citizens! This quite convinced the townspeople, and "Robin Hood" was allowed to make off with several bags of money.

Continuing the journey, a mile above Takkia we came upon an extraordinary spring bubbling like boiling water. I had no thermometer with me, but the temperature must have been about sixty degrees, and the water bubbled up from several holes with a considerable noise. Abbád, as it is termed, is evidently the spring described to Sir Oliver St John as "bubbling up to a great height with a noise that is audible a *farsakh* off, but which never overflows its basin."[1]

The mountains were thickly covered with scrub, in which we saw the stunted tree from which gum is extracted, and, after an easy ascent, we crossed the range by the Seh Gudári pass at an elevation of about 9000 feet. I sighted two rams on a distant peak, but a stalk was out of the question, so swinging round from north to west, we descended a narrow and rather steep valley.

After crossing the Rud-i-Zindán or Prison Brook, which flows down from Kuh-i-Chehel-Tan,[2] we edged obliquely towards

[1] *Eastern Persia*, i. pp. 103-4.

[2] This Mountain of Forty Beings has the same legend as the Sarhad volcano. The name is common, and such mountains almost always have a shrine on the summit.

the plain, and camped at a small village which is also known as Kala-i-Sang. Formerly it must have been of considerable importance, to judge by the extensive ruins, but to-day it is a hamlet. We were now on the edge of the Bardsír plain, and could look down on to the village of Mashiz, behind which rose the Kalba Gáv, or Cow's Head, the peaks of which are visible from Kermán.

The next day we gradually descended, and, after crossing the important Bahrámábád-Bandar Abbás road, reached the group of villages which cluster round Mashiz, where I struck the line of my first journey in Persia. A soldier whom I had taken to India in 1896, and who still sighs for the lemonade of Quetta, came to see me, as also the Lalazár shikarry with whom I made arrangements for the summer, and from Mashiz we crossed the range to Kheirabád, which lies a few miles to the south-east of Bághin.

It was now the middle of May, and heat and a dust-storm prevented us from regretting that this was our last day in tents. The following morning a short ride terminated this interesting tour, and I was once again back in my beautiful garden, and engaged in organising the Kermán Polo Club.

FROM LUSTRED POTTERY.

CHAPTER XXXVII

A MEDLEY—GYPSIES, THE BRONZE AGE, AND SOUTH AFRICA

"Royal the pageant closes,
Lit by the last of the sun—
Opal and ash-of-roses,
Cinnamon, umber, and dun."
—RUDYARD KIPLING.

DURING the summer of 1900 I spent some time in making enquiries about the gypsies of South-east Persia, my immediate object being to furnish information to Mr Albert T. Sinclair, who is better known as the great "Romany Rye" of Boston.

The question of their origin is such a vexed one that I propose simply to give a *précis* of the information that I gathered about this interesting people. In Persia they bear different names in different provinces, generally however speaking of themselves as *Fiuj*, which is said to be Arabic. In Kermán they are known as *Luli*,[1] but in Baluchistán as *Luri*. In Fárs *Kaoli*, a corruption of *Kábuli*, is their usual appellation, although *Gurbati* is also used. In Azerbaiján we find the name *Kara Chi*; in Khorasán *Krishmál*, a corruption of *Gheir-i-Shumár* or Out of the Reckoning, and, to go further afield, in the Chengyání of Turkey we find an approximation to, or the origin of the European *Zingari*.

Their occupations in Persia hardly differ from what we see in England, and I have frequently met them carrying round gaudily-painted spinning-wheels or pipe-stems for sale; occasional working in iron, and dealing in horses, camels, donkeys, or any

[1] In Central Asia the word is *Liuli*.

living animal, completes the tale of their trades. Their character is considered to be bad. The men cannot easily be distinguished from the surrounding peasantry, but, as the illustration shows, the women dress differently, while their features are certainly not those of the Persian peasant. The tribe is governed by the *Shátir Báshi* or Chief Runner of the Sháh, who keeps his deputies in every province.

Their language,[1] of which I compiled a vocabulary, is termed *Gurbati*, and is spoken with slight variations all over Persia. Their numbers are considerable, five thousand families alone inhabiting Azerbaiján, while the total in Persia may amount to twenty thousand families, or about a hundred thousand souls.

Kermán possesses from three hundred to five hundred families under Sháh Kerím, a terribly stupid man, whom I sent for to check the vocabulary which I had collected from two different sets of gypsies. He told me that the province was divided into beats, and that, what with a monopoly in turning and mending wheels, etc., they made a fairly good living. He also said that they rarely married outside their tribe.

I quite agree with Mr Sinclair, who points out that there is an immense field for a philologist, not only among the gypsies, but among those other tribes, such as the Lak, who are universally considered to be aboriginal inhabitants of Irán. The subject is, however, beyond the scope of this work.

. . . . . .

[1] The following are a few specimen words :—

[*N.B.*—A=Arabic. P=Persian. H=Hindustani.]

God	Pápari or Pábari.	Black	Sutai.
Man	Máris.	White	Safina.
Woman	Nadeo.	Bad	Náshigáb.
Eye	Nuhúr.	Good	Khábeh.
Mouth	Dahan Gás.	——	
Tongue	Zabán (*P*).	One	Yek hát.
Horse	Ghora (*H*).	Two	Do. hát, etc.
Ox	Tirang.	(Yek and hát are *P*).	
Cow	Tirang Mázitu.	——	
Dog	Sanaftá.	To do, say	Imáshtam.
Day	Ruz (*P*).	To beat	Taburdan.
Night	Lail (*A*).	To die	Meiti.
Food	Káti.	(*cf.* checkmate).	
Water	Ponu (*cf.* Pani in *H*).	To run	Palmídam.
Bread	Maná (*cf.* Manna).	To give	Banídam.

GYPSIES OF SOUTH-EAST PERSIA.

[*To face p.* 438

In July the temperature was, for Kermán,[1] unpleasantly high, and it was a relief when everything was arranged for my summer tour, during which I hoped to complete my exploration and survey of the Cold Country of the province. As far as Bahrámjird I followed practically the same route as in spring, but on this occasion, instead of turning west, I continued up the river-bank. A few black partridges have been imported from Jíruft, and it was pleasant to hear their strident click, which is the precursor of such good sport in the winter.

At the hamlet of Huseinabád the Ráin route followed by Marco Polo branched off, and after a trying march we reached Kariat-ul-Arab, with its two hundred houses and blue-tiled shrine in honour of *Sultán* Husein, a brother of the *Imám* Reza. The third day we accomplished the long stage to Lalazár, which I had visited in the summer of 1895, and where the barley was still green, whereas it had been reaped in May at Kermán. There are traces of three separate villages, the oldest being a little fort on a mound, and the shikarry told me that Khárzár[2] was the name of the village until some forty years ago, when the *Vakíl-ul-Mulk* invented Lalazár or Tulip Bed.

The march to the camping-ground under the great peak was delightful, if only for the wealth of flowers and running water, but the weather was most unfortunate, and, at an altitude of 11,000 feet, we shivered in our draughty tents. The sport, too, had deteriorated since 1895, as the game was no longer preserved, and owing to that and the incessant wind, I only secured four heads, a great falling off from my former bag, but, on the other hand, my stay was shorter.

Upon quitting Lalazár we passed through many acres of peas, and hugging the range, struck the main Kermán-Ráhbur road near Shirinak, a hamlet lying well above 9000 feet. In the Lalazár range the wild pea grows in great profusion to a height of about a foot. It resembles the sweet pea, and its pods are used as a relish. Of the cultivated peas, the *nakhod* much resembles the wild pea, and is most highly esteemed, selling at about the same rate as wheat; it has two species, the *Shámi* and the *Rasmi*. The *Karru Kudi* resembles the English pea, but is very hard. Bread is

[1] Ninety-one degrees was the average reading for about a week.
[2] Probably meaning thorny.

occasionally made from it, and its value is lower, being the same as barley. The *Karru* has long thin leaves, and is, I believe, a bean.

From Shirinak we marched across an open watershed some three miles from camp, and found that a narrow valley, down which ran the road to Ráin, separated us from the huge Kuh-i-Hezár, which we hoped to scale. The wheat of Chahár Tak, a hamlet in the valley, was being reaped as we crossed its fields and struck the Sárdu road. Leaving the track, we bore uphill towards the base of the mountain, and camped at the tiny hamlet of Urdigán.

The ascent of Kuh-i-Hezár was by no means arduous, as we not only rode to the base, but almost half-way up the deep valley, which penetrates to the heart of the range. The vegetation was luxuriant, an epithet that can rarely be applied in Southern Persia, and there was some difficulty in forcing our way through the thick growth of wild celery, the shoots of which are boiled and eaten with sour milk. Never have I noticed so many strange fragrant plants, and I am convinced that this would be a grand hunting-ground for a botanist, as is indeed implied in the term *Hezár* or Thousand, which is applied to the mountain, and is said to refer to the number of its vegetable products. Six miles from camp we left our mules and commenced a long climb up the south side of an immense valley. On reaching the ridge, a herd of wild sheep appeared, but as the wind was unfavourable for stalking, we plodded steadily up the hillside, which had been completely denuded by avalanches. Finally, five hours after leaving camp, we reached the summit, Kuh-i-Hezár being in reality a gigantic Hog's Back, though its slopes are steeper than those of the well-known ridge in Surrey. It also bears a distinct resemblance to the view of Mount Ararat, which forms the striking frontispiece to Mr H. F. B. Lynch's interesting work on Armenia.

As on the Kuh-i-Sháh, myriads of tiny moths fluttered round us, while the view was superb and, from the geographical point of view, extremely valuable, as we were able to take in the lie of the country, which was either a blank or drawn from fancy on the map. Black clouds rolled up, but too late to interfere with our view, which ranged to the great peaks above Jíruft, and, after reading the clinometer, which showed that we were at about the same altitude as the summit of Kuh-i-Sháh, we turned in search of the herd of sheep, which we had seen on the way up, but cloudy weather spoiled our stalking, as is ever the case in Persia. We found ourselves crossing very bad ground, but finally reached camp, after having scaled the second of the two Titans which guard South-east Persia.

From Urdigán, for a few miles the track lay almost due east among low hills, and we then turned south, striking the direct Ráin-Mazár road, which runs round the eastern base of Kuh-i-Hezár, and camped at Kur Gaz, a tiny hamlet inhabited by two families. The following day we skirted the eastern spurs of the ranges which drain into Sárdu, passing more than one delightful hamlet, and finally emerged on the plateau, joining our 1895 route at the capital of Sárdu.

From Dar-i-Mazár we marched to Sarbizan, where we halted for a few days and took long rides to the various points of interest. The partridge shooting was excellent, but we had but little time to indulge in it, and all too soon left the cool plateau and travelled east to Givar. This little district lies in a valley draining towards Jíruft, which is practically a *cul-de-sac*, and is so remote that it has not yet even appeared on a map. The track was almost as bad as those of Kashmir, but from time to time we came upon pleasant meadows, and our guide spoke of certain ancient inscriptions. These latter turned out to be grotesque delineations of ibex, which, for a while, quite deceived the *Khán Bahádur*, while the guide declined to change his views on the subject.

Finding the air of Givar very close, and its water tainted with sulphur, we were glad to leave its rugged ridges and retrace our steps homewards. Marching north towards Ráin, we reached a pass known as Zangal Murd, across which runs the road to Bam. This watershed we skirted, and, a few miles further on, recrossed into the Sárdu plateau, halting at the hamlet of Tutak. A march of nineteen miles brought us to the familiar Ráin, whence we hastened back to Kermán, bad weather having considerably lengthened the tour.

For a week after our return readings of ninety-two degrees were registered, but this was the dying effort of the summer, and the weather soon became pleasantly cool.

. . . .

A *Khán* on a visit to Kermán had told me that when breaking some ground to form a new garden, he had brought to light a quantity of bronze arrow-heads and vessels. I asked him to show me specimens, but he said that his servants had thrown them all away, except a few that were at his home. I had been so often deceived in my researches that I felt no desire for a fruitless errand, but as I found Khinamán to be a small district quite unexplored, I determined to pay my friend a visit. I first rode some twelve miles west to the district of Kavir, where I lunched in the beautiful garden of Husein Ali Khán at Fathabád, and inspected the seedlings and vegetables, raised from the seeds which I had given him. In the evening we continued the march, rising towards the Kuh-i-Bádámu, and passing not far from the medicinal springs of Ab-i-Murád, which are especially resorted to by the Parsis.

A very long rugged march brought us to our destination at nightfall the following day, and, after a warm welcome from the *Khán*, I was soon enjoying an excellent Persian dinner, and gaining information about the find. It appears that the village has been inhabited from time immemorial, and there is a legend that it furnished to Yezdijird a contingent of seven warriors mounted on bulls. My host said that hundreds of tombs were discovered some five feet below the surface of the ground. The corpses, however, had crumbled into dust, and it could not be ascertained in what direction they had been laid. In the tombs were jars of pottery, round bowls of two sizes, a pair of bracelets, two pins, and some arrow- and spear-heads, all of which were of bronze, except the vessels. In addition, two or three cornelian gems were found, and some small silver earrings and bracelets, which I did not see. The custom of placing a cornelian in a dead man's mouth, with the names of the twelve *Imáms* engraved on it, is one that still obtains.

An axe-head was also shown me, and there were, in addition, two handles which may have fitted some other weapon, but not the axe-head. This completed the list of the bronzes. The vessels were of three types, one being clearly a lamp, and of the others, one exactly resembled the modern Persian pocket-bowl, which is carried for drinking purposes. Some great jars, much like the *khom* of to-day, but shorter and wider, were also shown. In them a yellow dust had been found, possibly wheat or millet, but this had all been thrown away.

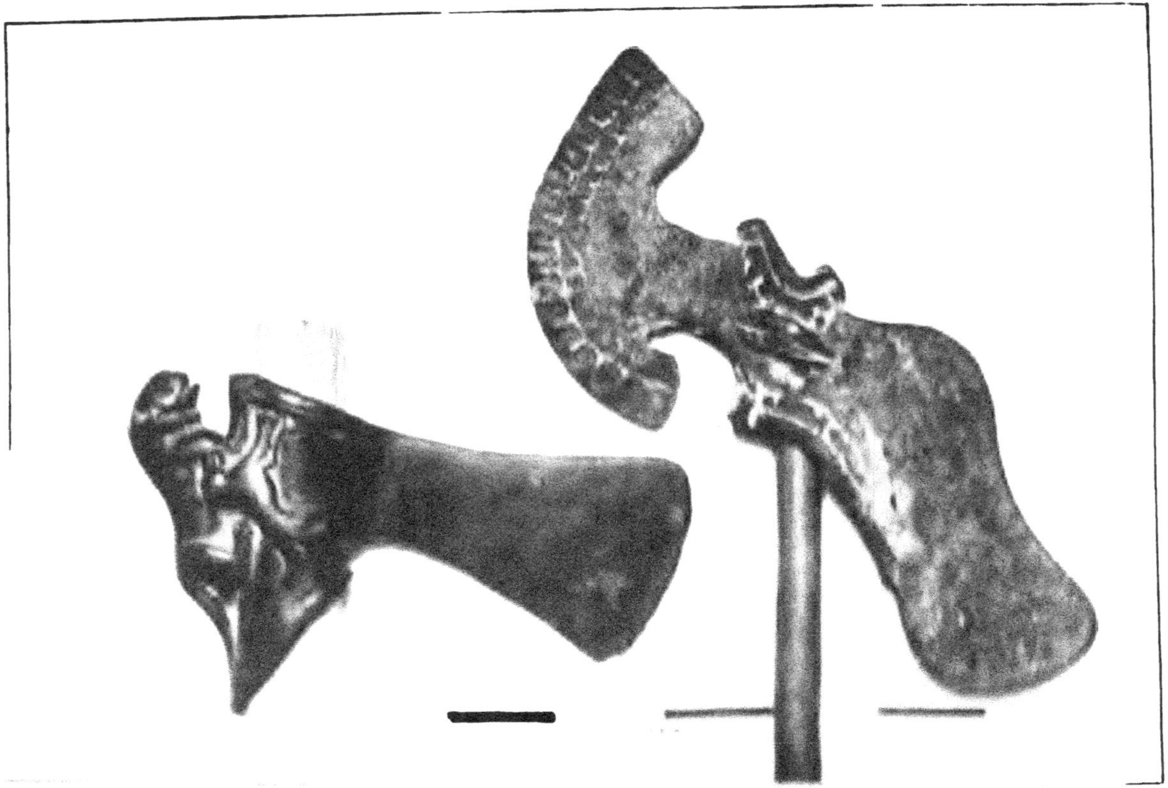

BRONZE AXE-HEAD FOUND AT KHUNAMAN (RIGHT), COMPARED WITH AXE-HEAD FOUND IN ARMENIA.

[*To face p.* 442.

Mr C. Hercules Read, of the British Museum, has very kindly furnished me with the following note on the axe-head: "The special interest of the bronze axe found at Khinamán is that its form shows it to be, not a useful weapon, but a survival or degradation of such an implement. The angle at which the blade is set to the handle shows that it can have no real utility, while, on the other hand, the exaggerated crest which forms a sort of counterpoise to the blade is out of all proportion to the mass of the weapon as such.

"The axe from Armenia, a fairly remote district, in Canon Greenwell's collection, has certain analogies with it, but differs essentially in being manifestly a serviceable weapon. The socket, in this case, is large enough to admit a stout strong handle, while the ornamental lion is small, and well adapted as an ornamental appendage. The angle at which the blade is set to the shaft is also a clear indication that it was intended for use. Widely different in general appearance as these two objects are, there seems to me to be a clear resemblance in essentials, and in time this may be made clearer by further excavations and discoveries in the country intervening between South-east Persia and the Black Sea. If the date of the axe be considered to be that of the alabaster vase found in its neighbourhood, this would furnish additional confirmation to the statement, that the use of iron came in in these countries at a date very much later than in the Mediterranean."

In the above note Mr Read makes no direct reference to the age of these bronzes, except that he hypothetically connects them with an alabaster vase, which is referred to later on in this chapter, dating from the fourth century B.C., but we may, I think, conclude that this most interesting find[1] dates from, at the latest, the Achaemenian era.

After a good night's rest we examined the garden, and I was shown what had once been a brick kiln, although only a few bricks had been found, none of which were forthcoming. We then rode from Kákh, the actual site of the garden, past Khinamán, of which it was formerly a suburb, and down to the village of Gulu Salár,

[1] The whole of the above can be seen at the British Museum. Canon Greenwell's axe, by kind permission of its owner, appears for purposes of comparison in the illustration.

which lies on the skirt of the range above Kabutar Khán. Gulu Sálár is an important village, and tradition avers that it was founded in the reign of Noshirwán by Azad Máhán, who also founded Máhun. On a lofty crag facing Khinamán is situated a massive stone fort, known as Kala-i-Dukhtar, which by its size indicated the ancient importance of the town.

The same day I was taken to see more tombs marked by four rows of stones forming a square. They contained masses of bones, some of which were two or three inches in length, while fragments of iron, which may have been arrow-heads, and a little jar with a handle were also produced. One fragment of iron was said to have been found inside the jar, and another in a skull.

When I left Kákh, my host rode up the valley with me, and we passed the ruins of a huge sun-dried brick fort, from which some years ago a cannon was unearthed. It is known as Kala-i-Ághá-Ali.

Turning my back with regret on such an interesting district, I returned to Kermán by a more northerly route, lunching near the shrine of *Bibi* Hefát, a sister of the *Imám* Reza. Close by are the ruins of Kala Máhr. I camped at the elevated village of Boj, and the next night found me back at Kermán, after a more than usually pleasant trip.

In November the drum of departure was beaten, and preparations for my winter tour began, but with servants as experienced as mine had become there was very little trouble, the muleteers whom I had employed in Káin having hurried down from Yezd to re-enter my service. A few busy days were spent in saying good-bye, and a cold day in November saw us once again on tour and bound for the Hot Country.

As far as Jíruft, where I had arranged to meet Lieut. Crookshank, R.E., I was travelling over a familiar route, and as my companion arrived later than myself, I had plenty of time to examine in greater detail the ruined cities which are so noticeable a feature of the district.

As I have mentioned more than once, neither the modern Kermán nor the Kala-i-Sang can claim to be the classic *Carmana*. Idrisi, however, refers to this subject when describing Jíruft, and I consider that his evidence is of the greatest value. The translation of his great work runs as follows: "Entre Djireft (Jíruft) et Fohredj

GREEK ALABASTER VASE FROM JÍRUFT.

[*To face p.* 444.

(Fahraj) est Hormuz el-Melik, aujourd'hui connu sous le nom de Cariet el-Djouz. Ce fut une résidence royale jusqu' à l'époque où le siége du gouvernement fut transféré a Chirdjan (Sírján); actuellement cette ville est de peu d'importance. De Hormuz à Djireft vers l'ouest, on compte une journée, et à la ville de Bam, une journée."[1]

This then must surely be the site of the *Carmana omnium mater* of Ammianus Marcellinus and, in the future, rich additions to our knowledge of the history of Persia will undoubtedly be made by some skilled excavator.

At Bágh-i-Bábu, a few miles south of Camadi an alabaster vase was brought for sale, which one of my servants purchased for a worn-out pair of trousers. When shown at the British Museum it was pronounced to be an unguent vase of Greek manufacture, dating from the fourth century B.C. As I had already proved the extreme probability that Alexander the Great formed a standing camp in this valley, and that here too he received the welcome report of way-worn Nearchos, the finding of this vase was particularly gratifying as proving beyond all reasonable doubt that the Greek host had indeed rested in the fertile valley of the Halíl Rud. It is interesting to note that the unguent vase is perhaps similar to the "alabaster box of very precious ointment" mentioned in St Matthew's Gospel.

Being joined by Lieut. Crookshank, we slowly marched towards Gulashkird, which was certainly on Marco's route, and then swung west to explore another Kuh-i-Sháh, which has the same legends as its namesake near Kermán. At Dolatabád, in Urzu, the objects of my tour having been accomplished, I sent back Nasrulla Khán to Kermán, and marched rapidly down to Bandar Abbás. A quantity of rain had fallen, and there was doubt as to whether the famous or infamous defile known as Tang-i-Zindán or Prison Defile would not be closed. For some twenty miles the track runs up and down river-beds, and many caravans have been swept away by irresistible floods. Fortune, however, smiled on us, as we were in the *tang* a day after a spate, and safely emerged on to a plain, quaintly termed Formosa by Marco Polo. The contrast between the population of this coast strip and that of the highlands was most noticeable, and the

[1] *Géographie d'Edrísi*, vol. i. p. 423.

Khán Bahádur said that, but for the palm groves, everything reminded him of the Panjáb, from the creaking water-wheels to the dress, or undress, of the peasantry.

At Bandar Abbás I stayed with Captain Hunt, who had been commissioned to found a Vice-Consulate, and two days later I started for South Africa. At Karachi, where I parted, with much regret from the indispensable Asghar Ali, a coolie ship was just starting for Mombasa, and by great good fortune I caught a Mauritius steamer at the lovely Seychelles, where I enjoyed the hospitality of Mr Harold Baty. At Mauritius, Mr Ireland entertained me, and early in March I finally reached South Africa. There I twice crossed the Karroo and imagined myself back in Persia, while the marvellous ruins in Rhodesia struck me as akin to the *gorbasta* of Baluchistán, which, indeed, is not at all impossible.

To conclude, until wounded I had the great honour of serving in command of Welsh Yeomanry under Lord Methuen, who was as much admired by his division as he was feared by the stubborn Boers.

DESIGN FROM A KERMÁN CARPET.

CHAPTER XXXVIII

CONCLUSION

"Behold! I see the Haven nigh at Hand,
To which I meane my wearie Course to bend;
. . . .
There eke my feeble Barke a while may stay
Till mery Wynd and Weather call her thence away."
—*The Faerie Queene*, I. xii. I.

AN old gentleman once asked me why the British Government "poked its nose" into Persia. In order to complete my task without laying myself open to the charge of neglecting this general question, I propose to give a few facts which may justify our attitude, and also, I hope, be of some service to those who realise the importance of the problem.

In the first place, a reference to any atlas will show that Persia emphatically lies in the "Highway of the Nations," which, until quite recently, left China in proud isolation, and ran from Europe to India. This is, I would urge, a fact of premier importance.

To illustrate its position it may suffice to point out that since the extension of the Russian Empire over the Caucasus and Transcaspia, the land of Irán is conterminous with that power along the whole extent of its northern and also for a portion of its eastern frontier. On the west again the Turkish Empire is touched, while on the east, although the Indian Empire only directly marches with Persia for a few desert stages near Kuh-i-Malik-Siá, the protected states of Afghánistán and Kalát constitute its border for several hundreds of miles; finally, to the south, the Persian Gulf bounds Irán. This brief survey, then, shows that Persia is of great interest both to Russia and to Great Britain, to the latter power especially, as the paramount power in India, Afghánistán, and Baluchistán.

To amplify, Transcaspia, which is now a Russian province, draws almost all its supplies from Khorasán, and much of the rice and dried fruits consumed in Russia are exported from Persia; in return, owing to its proximity and the exertions made by the Northern Power in the cause of communications, Persia is one of the few markets of the world in which Russian manufactures can compete with advantage against those of Western Europe. Neither Turkey nor Afghánistán is exactly progressive, nor do they trade to any great extent with Persia, and it remains to deal with the relation of Irán to Great Britain, and especially to the Indian Empire.

At the present time we are eminently in the position of *beati possidentes*, and only too anxious, not to extend, but rather to develop the Empire which has been so hardly won. Thus any reasonable man will acknowledge that it is to our obvious interest, from a commercial and every other point of view, that Persia should be strong and prosperous enough to form an effective barrier between the frontiers of India and of Transcaspia. Indeed, to be in close juxtaposition in Asia to one of the great military powers, would inevitably involve an increased army in India and the loss of that strength of remoteness which has recently stood the Boers in such good stead. It has been urged that were Russian railways to meet those of the Indian Empire, a difference of gauge would obviate all dangers of such a connection, but will this argument really hold water? A junction between the Transcaspian and Indian railway systems would certainly not pay commercially, and it would surely be unwise for Great Britain to countenance any such project, even if the Amir of Afghánistán were disposed to waive his objections.

Before quitting the subject of railways, I would give it as my opinion that the proposed scheme of running a railway along the coast of Southern Persia would end in failure, both because it could not compete with sea-borne commerce and also because the

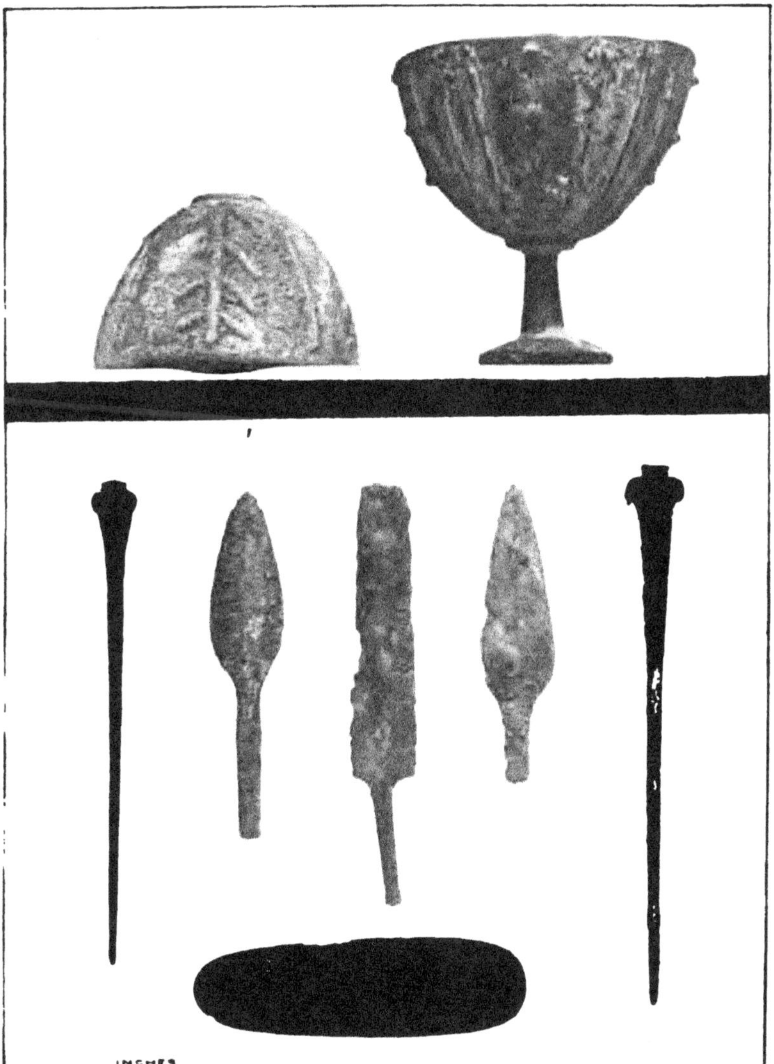

COPPER BOWLS FROM VICINITY OF KERMÁN, AND BRONZE IMPLEMENTS FROM KHINAMÁN.

[*To face p.* 448.

engineering difficulties would be very great. Finally, the climate is so torrid that very few passengers would use such a line for their journey to or from India. A study of the geography of Persia, as I understand it, shows most clearly that its railways, with perhaps two exceptions, should run in the same direction as the ranges, namely, from north-west to south-east, and few parts of the world can show country so suitable for railway construction as that lying between Tehrán and Kermán, while further east the desert is crossed at its narrowest part. Attempts to run railways in other directions will encounter considerable engineering difficulties, and, even under the most favourable conditions, how are the railways to pay? In this connection, it must be remembered that almost every Persian owns an ass, while the *Kháns* are obliged by etiquette to ride everywhere, and that, as they have but little sense of the value of time, they would seldom make use of the train for short journeys. Moreover, with an average of ten or more miles between villages, it is difficult to see how a passenger traffic could be maintained.[1]

To turn to the question of roads, on the southern coast Persia is by nature much isolated from the sea by a series of serrated ranges, which cause the engineer to despair, and, in my opinion, no metalled road from the coast of the Persian Gulf to the interior could possibly pay for many years, as the natural difficulties to be surmounted are out of all proportion to the volume of trade that the very sparse population can be expected to produce. I am therefore forced to the conclusion that *festina lente* is the highest wisdom in the South of Irán, and that small enterprises, such as the Bakhtiári track, should be made to pay, before constructing *chaussées* on a European scale, reminding one of Sofia, where the streets are so wide that it costs too much to water them.

It may be objected that the recently constructed Resht-Tehrán road is considered to be a success, and that Great Britain should not allow trade to suffer from lack of similar communications in the South of Persia. However, the case is not exactly the same, as if the *chaussée* does pay a fair rate of interest on the very heavy cost of construction—a point which is open to doubt—it is mainly

[1] In *International Geography*, edited by Dr Mill, Persia is shown as possessing a population averaging 15 to the square mile, while that of India is 182. Also the population is much denser in the north than in the south.

because it is used by all Russian merchandise destined for the capital, and has practically a monopoly of the passenger traffic with Europe. The fact, too, remains that this road was not completed without the financial support of the Russian Government. The British road running south from Tehrán to Kum can scarcely be considered a financial success, partly, I imagine, because the scale of its construction was far too ambitious for the amount of traffic which passes over it. Moreover, to the east of it lies the Lut, and nowhere is a fertile district tapped. The original intention was to continue the undertaking to Shuster, but this was never done.

Before discussing the question of commerce in detail, it would appear to be advisable to refer to the Indo-European Telegraph line and to the Imperial Bank of Persia, as constituting the most important British interests which we are called upon to discuss. The former is the Persian section of a telegraph line running across Germany and Russia to India. As far east as Tehrán this important enterprise is the property of a British company, but from Tehrán to India it is owned and worked by the Government of India. At present, from Tehrán it runs south to Bushire, whence cables have been laid to Jásk. The remainder of the distance is a land line, which joins the Indian system at Karachi. An agreement has, however, been come to with the Persian Government by which a purely land line will branch off at Kashán, and reach India *via* Yezd, Kermán, and Bazmán. Although the Indo-European Telegraph line does not supply the sole means of telegraphic communication with India, its importance is considerable and steadily increasing.

The only other British institution of any note is the Imperial Bank of Persia, which was unfortunately founded just before the occurrence of a decided and, to all appearance, a permanent fall in the value of silver. In spite of this and other difficulties, the chief of which is the prevalence of fraudulent bankruptcy in Persia, the Imperial Bank has gained its experience, even if at a heavy price, and it is to be hoped that its future may prove to be a prosperous one.

Perhaps the Resht-Tehrán road is the most important Russian undertaking in Persia, but, in addition, a bank has been founded, which is termed Banque des Prêts de Perse. Quite recently, in 1900, by furnishing a loan of two and a half millions sterling to the Persian

Government through the agency of the above bank,[1] the statesmen of the Neva have strengthened their financial and *pari passu* their political position in the land of Irán. It is understood that, for a long term of years, Persia can accept no financial assistance except from Russia. A second important agreement with Russia bound the late Sháh to grant no concession for railways within his dominions. In the north-west the railway line is fast approaching the Persian frontier, and on the north-east, Askabád is joined to Meshed by a somewhat rough but practicable road. Rumours of an Askabád-Meshed railway are rife, and it is also reported that a *chaussée* is to be constructed from Tabriz to Tehrán, but even as matters now are the position of Russia as regards trade avenues compares more than favourably with that of Great Britain.

To discuss the question of commerce, British trade reaches Persia *via* Trebizond and Erzeroum to the value of £200,000 (in 1900), the goods being carried by caravans of camels, and, in spite of the length of the journey and the primitive means of transport, Manchester calico still holds its own in the *bázárs* of Tabríz. On the south the weekly service maintained by the British India Steam Navigation Company distributes the manufactures of Europe at the various ports along the coast, Bushire, Linga, and Bandar Abbás being by far the most important.[2]

[1] A second loan of about a million sterling has just been negotiated.

[2] The following figures from Persian Gulf Consular Reports and from reports published by the Persian Custom House relate to the foreign trade of the year 1900:—

Ports	Imports from			Exports to		
	India	U.K.	Total	India	U.K.	Total
	£	£	£	£	£	£
Bushire . . .	277,542	715,437	1,323,063	135,974	155,174	710,338
Linga . . .	238,159	—	501,434	216,020	2,733	470,198
Bundar Abbás .	204,306	69,597	338,946	86,363	5,669	102,671
Mohamera . .	89,442	118,820	281,570	68,869	12,544	115,339
Totals . .	809,449	903,854	2,444,013	506,226	176,120	1,398,546

In 1900 the total tonnage entered and cleared at these ports aggregated 1,025,363 tons, of which 896,414 tons were British.

In addition, the British firms of Messrs Bucknall and of Messrs Strick & Co. run direct from England to the Persian Gulf.

In the Shat-el-Árab, connection is effected with the Kárun service; and at Basra imports and exports to the value of £1,000,000 are handled by the river steamers of Messrs Lynch Brothers, which run to Baghdád. From this famous city the markets of Western Persia are stocked with British goods. Add to this the recently opened caravan route, along which goods to the value of £100,000 reach Eastern Persia, and the list of the main arteries of commerce is complete.

At present, practically the whole of this trade, representing a total which exceeds four millions sterling, is carried in British steamers, but yet Russia, in 1900, made the experiment of organising a monthly service from Odessa, so that it behoves British merchants to beware. Still, however, the fact remains that this rich commerce is practically British, and if we add to it the trade of the other ports in the Persian Gulf and the trade of Maskat, the imposing total exceeds six millions sterling, and this without counting the profits made by the various shipping companies.

As accurate custom house returns are only gradually being introduced into Persia, it is impossible to say whether Russo-Persian trade possesses as great a volume as that of the British Empire with the Persian Gulf, but I am inclined to think that £4,000,000 to £5,000,000 would be a fair estimate. However, the next few years will undoubtedly see the publication of full and accurate returns, for which we must wait.

The immediate future will, it is to be feared, not show an improvement in the British percentage of trade. Indeed, considering the comparatively excellent nature of the avenues of approach which Russia has at her command, British trade occupies a most creditable position, and every decade shows a steady increase in its volume, which is most encouraging.

The newspapers some time ago were full of bitterness at the want of enterprise of British merchants. But the firms engaged in the Persian trade are certainly not to be included in this sweeping denunciation, as in every way the customer is carefully considered. I think at the same time that, generally speaking, British manufacturers might study commercial geography with immense advantage, as I am constantly receiving letters and advertisements which betray a grotesque lack of knowledge of the countries with which they propose to open up business relations. To give a single instance, I once received a beautifully got-up and well-bound book, giving illustrations and descriptions of the latest steam laundries and drying-rooms. With it came a letter asking me to furnish a list of firms who would be likely to take up agencies. In reply I said that in Persia clothes were washed by the side of any convenient brook, the water-supply of the town preferred, and pointed out that the cost of book, postage, and letter, say two shillings, was merely thrown away.

Having thus sketched the position of the Persia of to-day, as I understand it, I will now proceed to state the Persian question as it is viewed in England, where it is rightly considered in its general relation to our foreign policy in Western Asia. To put the matter in a nutshell, our publicists are divided on the question of whether or no it will pay us best to "deal" with Germany or with Russia, whereas a third party prefers us to maintain our "splendid isolation" and avoid "deals."

The first alternative we view is that Germany hankers after our place in the sun, and, generally speaking, cherishes ambitions which can only be satisfied at our expense, while her statesmen and press are unfriendly and even insulting. To put the case as stated in a recent article,[1] "It is the German Empire that is our real rival, the empire with the 'future on the water.' Germans are credited with the dream of an empire extending from the Bosporus to the Persian Gulf, and embracing territories in the enjoyment of an excellent climate, to which would be directed the stream of German emigration now wasted in the cities of America."

Accepting this view, and considering that we are already overburdened with responsibilities of government, it is argued that it is to our interest to "make Russia happy" wherever possible. It is held that by adopting this policy we shall obtain the friendship of the great Northern Power, and thus rest secure in India. Acting on these premises, increased activity on the part of Russia in Turkey, Persia, or China should be accepted by us without misgiving, and we should in every way regard a Russian advance with complacency. In short, it is held that Russia, with coaling stations and arsenals in the Persian Gulf and elsewhere in the East,

[1] Vide *Quarterly Review*, *Persia and the Persian Gulf*, January 1902.

would not threaten India, and that her aspiration to reach the sea, the intensity of which Captain Mahan in *The Problem of Asia* shows to be but natural, can be satisfied without detriment to British interests. To summarise this view, I cannot do better than quote the authority who writes under the name of "Calchas": "The writer is of those who conceive that while we retain the command of the sea, it would be an aid to the defence of India to encourage Russia to develop at the mouth of the Persian Gulf another vulnerable extremity." [1]

I will now turn to the party which favours an understanding with Germany, on the supposition that it would be more desirable in every way to have that state as our neighbour in India than to see the Muscovite power gradually surround and isolate the Indian Empire from Central Asia. A "Russian Diplomatist," who professes to represent the views held by the Russian Foreign Office, writing in the *National Review*,[2] states most categorically: "We therefore cannot see any serious possibility of England's preventing Russia from approaching towards the Persian Gulf. It is possible that this goal will not be reached to-morrow, but it certainly will be in the near future. In any event, a partition of influence in Persia between Russia and England appears to be outside the range of practical politics."

It is urged by some writers, the most illustrious of whom is Captain Mahan, that the interests of the three great Teutonic nations, viz. of Great Britain, the United States, and Germany, are so identical that these states will certainly work together for the open door in Asia. This being so, the acquisition by Germany of the port of Koweit as a terminus for her so-called Baghdád railway should presumably be encouraged by Great Britain, and the three Teutonic powers would bar the southern advance of Russia. Captain Mahan writes in reference to this: "Unless Great Britain and Germany are prepared to have the Suez route to India and the Far East closed to them in time of war, they cannot afford to see the borders of the Levant and the Persian Gulf become the territorial base for the navy of a possible enemy."[3] And again: "Russia, territorially situated in the Persian Gulf, is placed upon the flank of India; she controls one issue of any possible railroad

[1] *Fortnightly Review*, July 1901. [2] January 1902.
[3] *The Problem of Asia*, p. 77.

from the Mediterranean through the valley of Mesopotamia, and absolutely interposes between it and its prolongation to India."[1]

We finally come to that party which considers that any expansion on the part of Germany, either in Asia Minor or in South America, will attract to that power the bitter hostility of Russia and of the United States respectively.

Great Britain, on the other hand, supported by her daughter nations, and the benevolent neutrality of the United States, is held to be free to follow out her destiny, even if it signifies an Empire stretching from Egypt to Hong Kong. The recently announced Anglo-Japanese Treaty is considered to strengthen our hands immensely in the Far East, while the Transvaal War has proved that not only is the Empire one, but that no European power could subdue Canada, Australia, New Zealand, or South Africa, even if the Mother Country were defeated.

Holders of these views point out that Germany is practically impotent outside Europe from want of a navy which she can never afford, so that she will continue to seek the protection for her trade that the White Ensign offers. Russia, on the other hand, is financially weak and occupied with domestic questions, and it is therefore considered that she would not lightly throw down the gauntlet to the war-hardened legions and the limitless resources of the British Empire, an Empire which has been cemented by blood and foreign calumny.

To state the case in detail, it is asked whether Russia exports such valuable products from Transcaspia as to require an outlet to the south, or on what other grounds she seeks a port on the Persian Gulf, and it is considered that to occupy and fortify, say Bandar Abbás would constitute a direct menace to Great Britain in India. It is further considered that the necessarily heavy expenditure would be mainly incurred in order that Great Britain might be rendered pliable in Europe. To put the question in another way: "There is no motive, in the good of Russia, for the other (sc. Teutonic) states to consent to an arrangement which carries with it hazard to them."[2]

To approach other aspects of the case, it is asked what possible *quid pro quo* could Russia give to compensate the Indian Empire for its threatened security and loss of prestige, which would necessi-

[1] *The Problem of Asia*, p. 119.

[2] *Ibid.*, p. 120.

tate doubling the British garrison and the East Indian squadron? Again, to take the question of trade, has Russia done anything but strangle Indo-Russian trade, and does not the closing of the so-called "free" port of Batum teach Great Britain a lesson? Finally, in this connection, it is pointed out that there are other problems in Asia awaiting settlement, and it is held that Russia would show her "gratitude" by insisting on a settlement on similar lines, say in Tibet.

As regards the larger question of Western Asia, the plains of Mesopotamia are seen to be geographically connected with the Persian Gulf, and, to quote again from the article in the *Quarterly Review*, "When publicists, with bland indifference to the rights of the present possessors, whet their imagination with colonising schemes on a great scale; when Mesopotamia is apportioned to the Germans, and Persia to the Russians, we may put in a claim for the teeming millions of India, and with greater justice we may demand that this vast potential granary shall never be dissevered by means of a foreign occupation, from the markets of India, which it is plainly destined to supply."

To conclude this brief sketch, I cannot do better than quote the weighty words of Viscount Cranborne, who, speaking in the House of Commons on 23rd January 1902, declared that "you may roughly lay down that our object in Asia is to maintain the *status quo*. . . . We are anxious for the integrity of Persia, but we are anxious far more for the balance of power; and it would be impossible for us, whatever the cause, to abandon what we looked upon as our rightful position in Persia. Especially is that true in regard to the Persian Gulf. It is true not only of the Persian Gulf, but of the Southern Provinces of Persia, and those provinces which border on our Indian Empire. Our rights there, and our position of ascendancy, we cannot abandon."

In the above pages, I have conscientiously tried to give every point of view with absolute impartiality, and have throughout quoted the latest authorities, so that however feebly I have discussed this difficult question, I hope that it may attract if only a few of those who help to lead or form public opinion.

To resume, I have seen it stated that British prestige is low in Persia, but in Southern Persia at any rate this is far from being the case. Persians possess remarkable political acumen, an instance of which was the universal tendency to minimise the importance of the war in South Africa, and, thanks to fair dealing and love of sport, Englishmen are particularly popular in Persia, as a rule. I should, however, qualify my statement so far as to say, that any brusqueness of manner or brow-beating gives intense offence, and, indeed, if asked the most important qualification in dealing with Persians, I should unhesitatingly recommend a substitution of "*politesse*" for the word "*audace*" in Danton's famous utterance.

As the pages of this book have shown, I have almost everywhere been the recipient of ungrudging hospitality and courteous consideration, and, as I have constantly had dealings with all classes, my opinion is, I would urge, likely to be fairer than that of the casual globe-trotter. Several books on the land of Irán have been written by travellers who have rushed hastily through the country, have not learned Persian, have engaged some scoundrel as servant, and have encountered many difficulties at the post-houses. It would be equally fair to judge of Paris or London by the surliness of its cabbies!

In spite of the terrible corruption obtaining in Persia, which the Government are making efforts to suppress, in spite of the lack of education and the absence of progress in the shape of roads and railways, I have reason to consider the Persians to be the finest and most gifted race in Western Asia, a proof being that they invariably prosper when they emigrate. To this Bombay and Zanzibár bear witness, while even in the remote Seychelles I was welcomed by a Persian who was the wealthiest inhabitant of that group of islands. Moreover, my opinion merely repeats the views of Sir Henry Rawlinson, who, in his day, was an unrivalled authority on the land of Irán, and wrote "The Persian, considered as a mere animal, is very superior to any other Asiatic, to an Indian or a Turk, or even a Russian."[1]

The above quotation also represented the views of Sir Charles MacGregor, who travelled mainly in Eastern Persia, and wrote of some regiments that he saw near Meshed: "They are all composed of more or less fine material. They are dirty, slouching-looking ragamuffins certainly; but brought into trim by English officers, they would very soon become fine soldierly fellows. . . . They are,

[1] *Journal U.S. Instit.* vol. i. p. 29.

taken as a general rule, men of fine physique and very hardy muscular frames."[1]

Again, almost all over China a white man is liable to insult, and a distinguished diplomatist told me that he was looked on by his friends as extraordinarily lucky in having but one dead cat thrown at him while serving at Pekin, whereas in Persia, apart from a few fanatical centres, a European is generally welcomed by all classes, especially if he can speak the language.

Although by no means blind to the defects of a nation which was great and ruled the world when we were but savages, yet, sitting at home surrounded by trophies, the result of many an exciting stalk, with the walls covered with the exquisite old tiles and products of the loom which no European manufacture can rival, I feel that I can lay down my pen with all good wishes to my many Persian friends, and with a hearty and sincere **FLOREAT PERSIS**!

[1] Vide *Journey through Khorasán*, passim.

TAMÁM SHUD.

FROM A KÁIN CARPET.

INDEX

Abáde village, 331
Abárik (locally Averk), 214
Abbád, a hot bubbling spring near Takkia, 435
Abbás, *Mir*, headman of Iskil, 384
Abbás, Sháh, 9, 11, 13, 66, 86, 102, 143, 149, 179, 180, 287, 299, 307, 341, 405
Abbás Ali, a Hospital Assistant, 415
Abbás Kuli *Mírza*, 69
Abbás *Mírza*, heir of Fath Ali Sháh, 69, 345
Abbásábád, hamlet, 180
Abbasabád, Gudár-i-, 408, 409
Abbásak island, Bushire, 311
Abbáside dynasty, 51
Abbot, Captain Keith, 151
Abdi Khán, of Dashtiári, 349
Abdishu, a holy man, 337
Abdul Azím, Sháh, 240
Abdul Aziz, Author's guide, 275, 281, 282
Abdul Husein *Mírza*, *Farmán Farmá*, Governor-General of Kermán, 71, 75, 76, 118, 141, 142, 146, 147, 211, 213, 225, 256, 309, 318, 323
Abdul Kerím, chief of the Kurds of Sarhad, 354
Abdul Kerím Khán, 293
Abdul Nabi, *Háji*, a traveller, 105
Abdul Waháb, *Háji*, 345
Abdul Waháb Beg, 376, 377
Abdulla, *Mullá*, the *Imám Juma* of Kermán, 68
Abdulla Amir, 216
Abdulla Jafar, *Sheikh*, 148
Abdulla Khán, ruler of Jálk district, 229
Abdulla Khán, chief of Kalát, 103
Abdulla Khán, king of Shirván, 160, 161
Abdur Rahman, Amir of Afghánistán, 297
Abdur Rahman, *Sháh*, brother of the Imám Reza, 435
Abdur Rahman ibn Áshath, 50
Abdur Razzák, 64, 82, 102, 287
Abgá, 117
Abiána, 179
Abid (Water of the Willow), 39
Abraham, 373
Abu Seiid, last king of the house of Tímúr, 65
Abu Ali (Mohamed, son of Iliás or Eliás), 52, 53, 188
Abu Bekr, 196
Abu Jafar, 54
Abu Jafar *Sultán*, Alá-u-Din, Kanjár, 421
Abu Kálinjár, 54, 55
Abú Muslim, 51
Abu Nasr, 54
Abu Turáb, a dervish, 407
Abu Zeidabád, 157
Abubekr, *Mírza*, 64
Abul Abbás (known as Es-saffa or the Shedder of Blood), 51
Abul Fath Khán, Governor of Baluchistán, 107
Abul Faváris, 54, 100
Abul Hasan, *Seiid*, Mahallati, Governor of Kermán, 68, 69
Abul Hasan Khán, *Sardár*, 70, 105
Abul Kásim, *Amir*, 64, 65
Abul Kásim Khán, *Násir-ul-Mulk*, 259
Abulfeda, Arab traveller, 100

Achaemenian dynasty, 321; tombs of, 326
Acre, 262
Aden, 258
Adey, Captain, 243, 252
Adugui, *Amir*, 64, 102
Aeschylus, *Prometheus Vinctus*, 4
Aferábád village, 151
Afghán Boundary Commission (1885), 12
Afghánistán, invaded by Nádir Sháh, 67; and the arms traffic, 297; the railway question, 448
Afgháns, 66, 67, 69, 103, 217, 233, 235; the 1838 expedition, 237; seize Fort at Manuján, 304; defeat Persians at Gulnabád, 345; and the Shirázis, 348; besiege Isfahán, 366; in the Káin province, 404; and Fahraj, 418
Afifabád, 319
Afrasiáb, king of Turán, 335
Afshár, 104, 143
Afshárs, the, 428, 429
Afzal Kermáni, historian, 48, 52, 100, 101, 111, 187, 191, 210, 215, 268, 433
Afzalabád, 394
Agdá (the Guerde of Barbaro), 156
Aghá Ali, Kala-i-, Khinamán, 444
Aghá Hasan, *Háji*, a dervish, 345
Aghá Khán, Governor of Kermán, 69, 70, 74, 78, 105, 217, 409
Aghá Mohamed Khán, 69, 193
Agra, 66
Ahmad, Khalaf ibn, 53
Ahmad, Sultán, *Imád-u-Din*, of the Muzaffar dynasty, 63, 432
Ahmad of Ahsá or Lahsá in Bahrein, *Sheikh*, founder of the Sheikhi sect, 196
Ahmad Ali Khán, historian, 100
Ahmad Khán, the *Daria Begi*, 275-283, 285, 291, 292, 299, 306
Ahmad Khán, Duráni, 103
Ahmad Saghir, *Sultán Seiid*, 209
Ahmad Sháh, Amir of Afghánistan, 236, 367
Ahmad Sháh, Bahmani, king of the Deccan, 148
Ahmad Sultán Sufi, Oghalán, Governor of Kermán, 66
Ahwáz, 174, 175, 245, 247, 248, 250, 251, 255, 256, 300
Ajam Sháh, 59
Ak-Átabai, subdivision of the Átabai tribe, 12, 16
Akbarábád, 152
Akchánim, 18
Akesines river (modern Chenáb), 169
Akhund, teacher or reader, 391
Akkala, or White Fort, an ancient Kájár stronghold, 12
Ak-koinlu, or White Sheep, dynasty, 65
Aktá district, nomads of, 428
Akus, near Khabis, 41
Akva (or Avk), Band-i-, or the Afghán's Dam, 364, 365
Ála Dágh, 19
Áláchuk (áláchik), nomad dwellings of the Turkoman, 12
Alam, *Mir*, conqueror of Sistán, 399
Alá-u-Dola, *Sultán*, Gurshásp, 420
Albion's England, 321
Albuquerque, 85, 287
Aleppo, 94
Alexander the Great (Iskandar-i-Rumi), 49, 91, 98, 142, 153, 166, 175, 247, 275, 294, 303, 328, 336, 362-364, 407, 417, 419, 445
Alexandria, 261
Alghur district, 409
Ali, the Prophet's son-in-law, 50, 162, 196, 303, 380, 422
Ali, *Háji Mullá* Sultán, "teacher" of Beidukht, 30
Ali Ashraf Khán (Ihtishám-u-Vizára), Persian Commissioner, 212, 224, 226, 230, 258
Ali Ghazalu, chief of the Afshár clan, 430
Ali Goheri, *Sheikh*, 425
Ali *Imamzáda* shrine, near Sirján, 430
Ali Khán, chief of the Sarbandi tribe, 367, 381
Ali Kuli Khán, 307
Ali Mardán, 66
Ali Mohamed *Mirza* (the Báb, or Gate of Grace, founder of the Bábisect), 196
Aliabád, 152, 414, 430
Alinján, 356
Almán, Persian for *German*, 344
Almár range, 139, 141
Alp Arslán (Seljuk), 56, 272
Alvand, Mount (Orontes of Greek Geographers), 148
Alvand Beg, Governor of Fárs and Kermán, 65
Ament, ruined fort of, 19
Amír Khán, Governor of Kermán, 66
Amirabád, 434
Amirán, 391
Amjaz, a peak of the Jabal Báriz range, 145; a division of the Jabal Bárizi, 146
Ammianus Marcellinus, 48, 433, 445
Amr, 53
Amr-i-Lais (Saffár dynasty) ruler of Khorasán, 52, 99, 339
Anamis river (the Greek), 302
Anár, 182, 183
Anaristán village, 42
Anda, 356
Anderun, women's quarter, 184, 202
Anglo-Japanese treaty, 455
Anglo-Persian war (1857), 314
Anguhrán, 308
Aptár, a Baluch village, 126
Arab piracy, in the Persian Gulf, 86, 87
Arab tribes, list of, 329

Arababád, 35
Arabian Nights, 85, 219, 423
Arabian Sea, 308
Arabios river (now the Purâli), 170
Arabistán province, 245, 295
Arabs, their prosperity in the ninth century, 85
Arachoti, the, 102, 417
Arávirjun villages, 79, 331
Ardakán oasis, 156
Ardaván, 49, 337
Ardeshír, son of Pápak or Bábek, 49, 98, 104, 187, 215, 220, 335
Ardeshír, fort of (at Kermán), 190
Ardistán (Hardistan of Barbaro), 157
Arghún Khán, 62, 263
Arian princes, the, 407
Arii, the, 102
Aristobulus, 175
Aristophanes, 84
Arjan plain, 319
Armada, Spanish, 160
Armenia, Cilician, 261
Arnold, Matthew, 239; *Sohrab and Rustum*, 361
Arrian (*Periplus*; *History of India*), 91, 109, 123, 169,-175, 289, 328, 417
Arslán, *Malik*, 57, 146
Arslán Sháh, 56, 57, 101
Artabanus, or Ardaván, 49, 337
Artacoana (modern Herát), 362; (Káin), 407
Artaxerxes, 325
Arvad (Arados), 83
Asad Khán, 316
Asad *Pahlawán*, 63
Asad Ulla Khán, Governor of Sarhad, 130
Asad-u-Dola, 219, 226-231
Asaf-u-Dola, 70, 304-307, 310, 348, 349
Asak Cháh, 373
Asghar, *Khoja*, 215
Asghar Ali, *Khán Bahádur*, 380, 430, 431, 441, 446
Ashraf, the Afghán, 103
Ashukán, Rud-i-, 390
Ashuráda, Russian Naval Station, 6
Asiabán village, 402
Askabád, 451
Aslam Khán, 104
Assassins, the, 68, 162, 163
Assur-násir-pal, palace at Nimrud, 302
Assyria, British India ss., 291, 298
Astára, 163
Astatki, (oil refuse), 5
Astley, *Collection of Voyages*, 289
Astrabád (*Dár-ul-Muminin*, or Abode of the Faithful), 9-11, 49; (the Straua of Barbaro) 420
Astrabád Bay, 6, 13
Ata Illáhi nomads, 70, 78
Átabai tribe, of the Yomuts, 15; list of tribes under their protection, 16
Athanasius Nikitin of Twer, 65, 155, 156
Atrek river, 13-16, 18, 23, 24
Augustus, 362
Austrian-Lloyd Steamship Co., 259
Austrian Mission, 76
Aváz, near Lár, 196
Ayas, 262
Ázad Máhán, Governor of Kermán, 10, 49, 444
Azbag (Uzbeg), mount, 116, 119
Azerbaiján, 64
Azhar Khar, 339
Azizabád river, 350, 418
Azrakites, a section of the Khárijites, 50
Azzi, 420

Báb, Gate of Grace, 196
Bábak, 187
Bábis (Behai and Ezeli), numbers in Kermán, 195, 196
Báb-ul-Ábáb (modern Derbent), 49
Babylon, 84
Bacha Kuh, or Child Hill, 141
Bacha-Mulláі, Gudár-i-, or The Pass of the *Mullá's* Boy, 426
Bactrian coins, in British Museum, 363
Bádámu, Kuh-i-, 189, 442
Bád-i-Sad-u-Bist-Ruz, or Wind of 120 days, 393
Badránli, 19
Baffin, death of, 290
Báfk, 152, 153, 264, 265
Báft, 301, 427, 428
Bagdamál village, 22
Baghdád, 53, 66, 85, 262, 263, 452
Bágh-i-Bábu hamlet, 174, 445
Bágh-i-Lálazár, Tehrán, 178
Bágh-i-Nazar, Duruksh, 402
Bágh-i-Siá village, 80
Bághin village, 58, 67, 72, 185, 191
Bahárlu tribe, 81, 302
Bahmán, 214, 215, 415
Bahmeshir (natural channel of the Kárun river), 246
Bahr Asman range, 48, 209
Bahrám Chubín, General, 52, 338
Bahrám Gur, the Cœur de Lion of the Sásánian dynasty, 98, 331, 337, 420
Bahrám *Mírza*, 367
Bahrám Sháh (Seljuk), 57, 101, 146, 267, 365
Bahrámabád, chief town of Rafsinján, 77, 185, 264
Bahrámjird river, 191, 206, 268
Bahrámjird village (or Bahrámkird), 426, 439
Bahrein (The Two Seas), 83, 86, 91, 96, 101, 241, 258, 296
Baiis Sangar, Governor of Kermán, 64
Bakarán range, 398, 400, 411
Bakhtiári, tribe, 181, 255, 256; mountains, 245

Bákir, *Mírza*, 79
Bákir, *Imam*, 148
Baktash Khán, Governor of Kermán, 66
Báku, 5, 160, 163
Balaclava, 2
Balkh, 13
Baluch-Afghán Boundary Commission, 357; frontier, 371
Baluch Highlands, 232, 235, 358
Baluch Khán, 295
Baluchis, the, 67; as servants, 110, 111; their character, 120; hatred of the Persians, 121; of Kej valley, 293, 294
Baluchistán, 66, 89-108, 232
Balvard, 430
Bam, 47, 52, 63, 69, 70, 101, 146, 188, 214, 215-218, 350
Bampur (Bunpoor), ancient capital of Baluchistán, 33, 101-105, 110, 122, 141; river, 44, 92, 93, 116, 173, 221
Bamu, Kuh-i-, near Shiráz, 323
Bana, Pass, 408
Bandán hamlet, 396, 399, 414
Bandar Abbás, 85, 87, 103, 189, 241, 258, 270, 287, 290, 297-301, 311, 312, 359, 413, 446, 451, 455
Bandar Aminía, 248
Bandar Gaz, 7
Bandar, Kala-i-, or Port Fort, Shiráz, 190, 322
Bandar Kamál Khán, 365
Bandar Násiri village, 247, 248
Bandárun (Bahádárán), 182
Bangán, 356
Banjar, 384
Banque des Prêts de Perse, 450
Bánu, a queen, 156
Bar, Dasht-i-, 429
Bára Sing (stag) of Kashmir, 8
Barak, homespun, 201
Barbaro, Josafa, 46, 79, 155-157, 182, 325, 327, 331, 420
Bardshír or Bardsír, 101, 187-189, 301, 436; list of nomads in district of, 73
Bárjan (Bárchi), Kuh-i, 52
Barka Khán, ruler of Kipchak or Southern Russia, 262
Barker, Mr, Persian Gulf Telegraph, 284
Barlás tribe, 64
Barziár, 356
Bashákird, 117, 142, 302, 303, 308, 309; mountains of, 306
Bashákirdis, the, 306, 308
Basham, *Mullá*, 118
Basirán village, 33, 412, 413
Basol, 172
Basra, or Balsora, 85, 243, 244, 257, 304, 452
Bassidu, or Bassidore (Kishm), British garrison stationed at, 290
Batum, the Land of the Golden Fleece, 3
Baty, Harold, 446
Bázil tribe, 185
Bazmán village, 104, 136, 138, 139; range, 33, 116, 140, 218; *tághur*, 136
Behbehán, 175
Beiáz, Anár district, 184
Beidukht, 30
Beiring, 395
Beiza, Kala-i-, or White Fort, also known as Kala-i-Sang, or Stone Fort, 430, 431
Bellam, a raft, 244
Bellew, Dr, *From the Indus to the Tigris*, 364, 406, 407
Beluri nomads, 404
Belus, king of Babylon, identified with Nimrod, 95
Benboul, a corruption of Bampur, 102
Bendemeer (Band-i-Amir or The Amir's Dam), 324
Benjamin of Tudela, *Itinerary*, 58, 100
Bent, Theodore, 242
Berber hills, 382
Berberi (Hazára) tribe, 361, 429, 434
Berosus, 83
Bessus, 49
Bias (ancient Hyphasis) river, 169
Bíd Khán range, 429
Bidár pass, 28
Bídarán, 215
Bijenabád, 144
Bimurgh village, 30
Bint, district, 113; river, 114
Birdwood, Sir George, 365
Birinti, 303
Birjand, 37, 301, 377, 398, 399, 402, 404; or Khusp, river, 364, 401
Birk, Kuh-i-, 128
Bismarck, 60
Black Sea, 2, 259
Blackett, Rev. A. R. (Church Missionary Society), 41, 348
Blackman, E. J., 329, 330
Blandford, Dr., 92
Boanát district, 79, 175
Bode, Baron de, 175
Boj village, 444
Bokhára, 160
Bolán Pass, 174; railway, 238
Bolatak, Gudár-i-, 256
Bolídi dynasty, 113
Bombay, 457
Bonsar pass, 227
Bora (Beravát) village, 219
Borák Hájib, founder of the Kara Khitei dynasty, 60, 194, 265, 426
Borázjun, 313-315
Borhán-u-Din, *Amir*, 64
Bráhui tribe, 94, 103, 106, 233
Brasswork of Kermán, 201
Brindisi, 258
British trade in Persia, 451
British India Steam Navigation Co., 451
Bronze Age, the, 442, 443

Bronzes, found at Khinamán, 442, 443
Browne, Mr E. G. (*A Year among the Persians*), 12, 52, 79, 116, 177, 216, 397, 407
Browne, Sir James, 238
Browning, Robert, *Pied Piper*, 316
Buchákchi tribe, 435
Buchanan, Mr, of Basra, 244
Bucknall, Messrs, 452
Buda-Pesth, 259
Budge, *Life and Exploits of Alexander*, 336
Bugsár (Baluchi for meadow), 357
Bujd village, 398, 410
Bujnurd, 13, 20, 21
Bulbulak, hissing water, 351
Buluwayo, 378
Burj, a tower, 38
Burj-i-Ághá-Mohamed village, 220
Bunbury, *History of Ancient Geography*, 417
Burne, R.E., Captain, 291, 293
Burz Rud, 179
Bushire, 81, 87, 242, 274, 295, 297, 298, 300, 311, 312, 450, 451
Butcher, S., Indo-European Telegraphs, 243
Buzbar village, 30
Buzi tribe, 390
Buznabád, 408

Calo Johannes, Emperor of Trebizond, 65
Camadi of Marco Polo (Komádin), 266, 267
Camels, and their loads, 109
Campbell, Inspector, Persian Gulf Telegraphs, 279, 284, 285, 291
Campbell, Mr, of New Zealand, 77-79
Caraonas, brigands, 270
Carless, Rev. Henry (Church Missionary Society), 192, 203
Carnegie, Mr, of Persian Gulf Cable ss., 279
Carpets, Turkoman, 21; Káin, 28; Kermán, 179, 419
Cartwright, Mr, English merchant at Káshán, 158
Caspapyrus, on the Indu, 167
Caspian Sea, 5, 7, 160, 163
Cathay and the Way Thither, 84
Central Persia, 151-165
Chach, Hindu rája of Sind, 99
Chagatai, 101
Cháh Káwar, 154
Cháh Kuru, 38
Cháh Ráis, 351
Cháhán-i-Asháhi, the Royal Wells, 353
Chahár Fasl, or Four Seasons, 218
Chahár Gumbaz (Four Domes), 34
Chahár Tak hamlet, 440
Chahbár, 90, 100, 105, 110, 292, 310, 311, 349
Cháh-i-Hanjerá, 352
Chakansur, 367, 390
Chákar Beg, 55
Chákar *Mir*, 95, 102
Chákar Khán, 106, 114, 115, 307
Chakmák, *Mir*, 421
Chaldaea, 83
Chámp, 118
Chancellor, Richard, discovers the White Sea, 160
Chang-i-Kalak, Gudár-i-, 409
Chardin, M., 178, 326, 342
Chári, 426
Chashma-i-Pír, 129
Chát, ancient Persian fort at, 16
Chátrud village, 61
Chaucer, *Canterbury Tales*, 166, 261
Cheb, 128
Chehel Kura, or Forty Colts, ruins of, 219
Chehel Kura, or the Forty Furnaces, copper mines at, 416
Chehel Pái, or the Forty Steps, 37
Chehel Sutun, or Forty Pillars, at Isfahán, 332
Chehel-Tan, or Mountain of the Forty Beings, 92, 133, 134, 139, 435
Chemur Rud, 179
Chenáb (Akesines) river, 169
Chengiz Khán, 29, 60, 61, 101, 273
Chengyání, gypsies of Turkey (the European *Zingari*), 437
Cheshma Abbád, a warm spring in Jíruft, 144
Cheshma, or *Chashma*, a spring, 37
Chigukábád, or Sparrow town, 220
Chikishliár, or Russian frontier roadstead, 6
Chil, a pond, 143
Chil-i-Nádir, battle of, 103, 143
China (Cim and Macim of Barbaro), 420
Chinár, the *Arbre Sec* (Marco Polo's *Arbre Sol*), 152, 153
Chinár-i-Rahdár, 319
Chinishk, cave at, 411
Chirás, Kuh-i-, 181
Chitrál, 377
Chizer or Khizr, 323
Church Missionary Society, 41, 192, 203, 332, 347, 424
Cinnamus, the historian, 340
Cities of Lot (Shahr-i-Lut), 32
Clavigo, Ruy Gonzalez di, 25, 178
Cobinan (Kubanán), 271-273
Cold Country, the, 56
Comneni Emperors, of Trebizond, 65
Conolly, *Journey to the North of India*, 19, 76, 203, 365, 366, 380
Conrad of Montferrat, 162
Constantinople, 258; a centre of polo, 340
Contarini, Ambrosio, 180
Copper mines, in the Boanát district, 80; in the Bahr-Asmán range, 209; at Chehel Kura, 416

Cordier's *Odoricus*, 162, 287
Corfu, 258
Cossack, H.M.S., 291
Cotton, Sir Dodmore, 299
Cranborne, Lord, 456
Creagh, Major Brazier, Royal Army Medical Corps, 89, 111, 116, 118, 119, 121, 123, 126, 127, 129, 132, 135, 136, 140, 141, 147, 151
Creagh, Captain, Bombay Marine Infantry, 293
Crim Tatárs, the, 160
Crookshank, R.E., Lieut., 444, 445
Crusaders, the, 162, 340
Cunaxa, battle of, 168
Curtius, 169, 407
Curzon, Lord, *Persia*, 20, 23, 26, 31, 87, 195, 200, 242, 245, 247, 251, 255, 258, 292, 300, 315, 324, 393
Cypress, a gigantic, 354
Cyriadis, 317
Cyrus the Great, 48, 98, 170, 175, 177, 321; Mashhad-i-Mádar-i-Sulimán, or The Tomb of the Mother of Solomon, mausoleum of, 328
Cyrus the younger, 168

Dád, Sháh, 90
Dád, *Sheikh*, shrine at Yezd, 422
Dádá Mohamed, Taki-u-Din, 422
Daffadár Sultán Sukhru, Lance, 3rd Panjáb Cavalry, 89, 127, 136, 165, 248, 254
Daggaz hamlet, 307
Dágh, a range, 16
Dahána-i-Bulbulán, 351
Dahána-i-Karkáb, 409
Dak, Hauz-i-, 152
Daliki, 315
Damba Kuh, tombs in Makrán, 96
Dalton, Mr, Imperial Bank of Persia, 329
Dalton, Mrs, 329
Damascus, 340
Dames, M. Longworth, 94-96, 102
Dámini tribe, 107
Danton, 457
Daráb, 59
Darakht-i-Bana pass, 408
Darband (Derbent), 38, 163, 271
Dárghá, a magistrate, 38
Dárghá, Burj-i-Darband, 38
Dar-i-Kishkin, 221
Dar-i-Mazár, capital of Sárdu, 209; river, 211
Dar-i-Sábari, or Lake of Sábar, 395
Dari, the Zoroastrian *patois*, 157
Dariá Sábari, 414
Darius, 48, 49, 90, 167, 325, 336, 362
Darmián (Darra Mián or Middle of the Valley), village, 398
Darwáza-i-Nádir, 416
Darzáda, Baluch serfs, 121
Dárzin (Dárzanán or Gallows-Erecting) village, 214
Dashtiári, a district near Chahbár, 349
Dastgird village, 401
Dates, Panjgur, 234; Basra, 257
Decius, Emperor, 267
Deh village, 79
Deh-Bakri, Gudár-i-, 146
Deh Nawáb, 383
Deh No, 302, 413
Deh Rud, 42
Deh Shuturán, Village of Camels (Yezd), 63, 77, 78
Deh Súkhta, or the Burnt Village, 381
Deh Yághi Khán hamlet, 350, 351
Dehbid (Dehebeth of Barbaro), highest telegraph office in Persia, 79, 329, 331
Dehishk, 408
Dehshir (formerly Deiser), 331
Dehwárs, 233
Deilami dynasty, 53, 54, 56, 100, 188, 210
Demávend, Mount, 141, 148, 179
Derbent (*Dar Band*, the Stop Gate), 38, 163
Deregez, 13
Dervish Khán of Sistán, 377
Despina, daughter of Calo Johannes, 65
Dieulafoy, M., 96, 328
Diláwar Khán, 128
Dilfárd village, 210
Dinár, *Malik*, Ghazz tribe, 58, 101, 152, 272, 304
Diodoros Siculus, 173, 269
Diriz village, 317
Diw island, 287
Diz, Ab-i-, 245, 251
Dizak, 104, 356
Dolat Sháh, 63
Dolatabád, 380, 445
Dovoji, tribe, 16-18
Dravidians, the, 94, 96
Duhuk village, 35
Duke, Captain, Indian Medical Staff, 27
Dukhtar, Burj-i-, at Darband, 38
Dukhtar, Gudár-i-, 73
Dukhtar, Kala-i-, or Virgin's Fort, at Kermán, 190, 205; at Khinamán, 444
Dukhtar, Kotal-i-, or Daughter's Pass, 318
Dumdár tribe, 219
Duncan, Patrick (P.W.D.), 193
Durand, Lady, 177, 212
Durand, Sir Mortimer, Minister at Tehrán, 4, 19, 177, 237, 240, 256, 343, 349
Durrán Khán, Governor of Rudbár, 143, 304, 305, 309
Duru, 396
Duruksh (*Darra Raksh*, or the Valley of Raksh), 401, 402, 404; carpet looms at, 403
Dusári, capital of Jiruft, 144
Duzd, Sháh, or King Thief, 414
Duzdáp, or the Bandits' Pool, 371

Duzdi, Rudkhána, or River of Theft, 270, 303

Eastern Persia, 92, 106, 116, 218, 368, 375, 435
Edward I., embassy to Persia, 62
Egypt, 101, 167; resemblance between Sistán and, 373
Elburz river, 20
Elias, Ney, British Consul-General at Meshed, 23, 25, 26, 404
Elizabeth, Queen, 160
Ellis, A. G., of the British Museum, 334
Enceladus, 141
English and Persian horses, relative swiftness of, 147
Enzeli, 5, 6, 163, 176
Erythras, 289
Erythrean Sea (Persian Gulf), 83, 91, 167, 289
Erzerum, Treaty of, 242
Esther, Book of, 175
Etna, 141
Etymander (Helmand) river, 93, 106, 174, 381
Eucratides of Bactria, 363
Euergetae tribe, 363
Euphrates, 83, 84

Fadwand in Jíruft, 48
Fagan, Major, Consul at Maskat, 284, 285
Fahraj (Pahra, Poura), 69, 92, 104, 107, 108, 118, 123, 154, 173, 221, 417, 418
Fákh river, 401, 402, 404
Fakir Mohamed, author's servant, 89, 159
Fánoch river (or Rapsh), 92, 114-116; village, 309.
Fánoch, Kuh-i-, 116, 119, 309
Fánud village, 411
Fao, 242
Faramurz, son of Rustam, 214, 365
Fariáb or Pariáb, 269
Farmán Farmá, 71, 73, 75, 76, 77
Farmitan, 191
Farráshbáshi, chief carpet-spreader, 60
Fárs (Greek Persis), 49, 50, 52, 53, 56-58, 65, 295, 321
Fárs, Bánu-i-, 156
Fath Ali, *Ághá*, 67
Fath Ali Khán, Governor of Kermán, 67, 69
Fath Ali Khán, Nádir Sháh's chief falconer, 104
Fath Ali Sháh, 69, 81, 158, 197, 345
Fathabád village, 79, 442
Fatima, shrine of, at Kum, 158
Fazl Ali Khán, Governor of Kermán, 70
Feodosia, 3
Ferguson, M., Imperial Bank of Persia, 154, 182
Ferguson. Stuart, Imperial Bank of Persia, 347
Feridun, 141
Ferrier, M., *Caravan Journeys*, 78, 364, 366, 367, 391
Ferrukh Sháh, 59
Ffinch, Mr., Director-in-Chief, Persian Telegraphs, 276, 279, 284, 293, 294, 349
Firdusi, *Sháh Náma*, 19, 94, 98, 215, 216, 326, 335, 361
Firuz *Mírza*, Governor-General of Kermán, 70, 71
Firuz, *Sháh*, 430
Fitzgerald, *Omar Khayyám*, 45, 72, 334
Fiuj, Persian Gypsies, 437
Floyer, E., *Unexplored Baluchistán*, 308
Flün, M., 310
Folklore, 203
Formosa, plain of, 269, 270, 445
Fortnightly Review, 454
Foster, W., Editor of Sir Thomas Roe's *Diary*, 85, 86
Fothergill, Mr, of Yezd, 424
Frederic II., Emperor, 261
Fryer, Dr, *Travels into Persia*, 299
Fuller, Thomas, 288
Furk village, 398

Gabari tribe, 120
Gabr, Kala-i-, at Náin, 157
Gabrí, Káin city, 193
Gadrosi, or Gedrosi, the, 170
Gaertner, Baron von, German Minister at Tehrán, 343
Gajar, Baluch name for Persians, 121
Gajjari, Ab-i-, 353
Galag, fishing hamlet, 275, 291, 292
Gálángaur, plain of, 135
Galgazut, Gudár-i-, 42
Galindo, Captain, 33, 308
Galugán, 371
Gama, Vasco di, 286
Gán Yokmáz, sub-tribe of the Átabai, 15, 16
Ganges river, 169
Ganj, Kuh-i-, or Treasure Hill, 135
Ganj Ali Khán, Zik, ruler of Kermán, and Governor of Kandahár, 66, 102, 195, 234
Gao, date-grove, 285
Garágha (Kilagh Ab), 415
Gardan-i-Jauri, 353
Gardan-i-Pichal pass, 303
Garm, Ab-i-, 35, 211
Garmsir (*Garmsil*), the, 101, 106
Garshásp, 363
Gásk village, 401; carpet looms at, 402
Gaud, Gudár-i-, pass, 408
Gaud Ahmar, or Red Hollow, 74, 75, 77
Gaud-i-Zirra, 365
Gaudár, cowkeepers of Sistán, 386
Gava Kán, division of the Jabal Bárízi, 146
Gaz, a mètre, 418
Gaz, 40

Gaz, Ab-i-, 211
Gazak, 221
Gazbár, 388
Gazelle, *G. Benetii* and *G. fuscifrons*, 47; shooting in S. Persia, 76
Gedrosi, the, 102
Gedrosia (Makrán), 48, 91, 170, 417
Geh, 110, 113; river, 112, 114
Gelu, Band-i-, fissure (Taftán), 132
Genoa, 261
Geok Tapa, or Blue Mount, fort, 14, 22
Gerânkash, chief tribe of Fánoch, 116
Gerger, Ab-i-, 245, 251-253
Gerisht, Kaur-i-, 129
Germanii, the, 48
Germany, and the Thirty Years' War, 60; Persia and, 453, 454; Russia and, 455
Geshkok, 121
Ghaltun, *Khoja*, 379
Ghazal, *Sheikh*, chief of the Kab Arabs, 243
Ghárán Khán 62, 263
Ghazni dynasty, 340
"Ghazz coffee," 58
Ghazz tribe, 57-59, 267, 271
Ghiás-u-Din (Kaiaschirin), Governor of Kermán, 60, 64
Ghinán, Governor of Kermán, 51
Ghinchi, Gudár-i-, 414
Ghip, hamlet, 409
Gholám Husein Khán, Sipahdár, Governor of Kermán, 70
Gholam Riza Khán, *Háji*, Governor of Kermán, 71
Gichkis, the, 233
Gil tribe, 268
Gilán, 7, 98
Gill, Captain, 73
Ginao, Kuh-i-, 270, 300
Gird-i-kuh, 182
Girdi cháh, 372, 373, 415
Giri pool, the, 115, 116
Girimanj, 408
Girishk village, 363
Gíshu, Kotal-i-, 174
Givar, 441
Givi Dur river, 74
Gohar, a pearl or jewel, 80
Goklán Turkoman, the, 18-20
Gold, in Kermán, 48
Goldsmid, Sir Frederic, and the Goldsmid Mission, 92, 93, 106, 116, 128, 151, 200, 219, 221, 224, 366, 368, 371, 375, 384
Goloshes, Russia the land of, 4
Gombrun port, *see* Bandar Abbás
Gopal Dass, *Guru*, 126, 142
Gorbasta, or Infidel Dams, pre-Mohamedan remains, 95, 126, 132, 235
Gore, Colonel St. G., Surveyor-General, India, 39
Granicus, battle of, 168
Grant, Captain, 113, 117, 121
Graves, Mr, of the Indo-European Telegraphs, his murder, 108, 274, 278, 281
Great Lone Land, the, 235
Greece, 275
Greeks, 166, 168, 174
Greene, Conyngham, Chargé d'Affaires at, Tehrán, 159
Greenwell, Canon, 443
Gregory IX., Pope, 261
Grier, Captain, 90
Gu- (ball) *u-chogán*, (polo-stick), polo, 334-344
Gubi, 83
Guchkun village, 181
Gudar, 268
Gudar, Band-i-, section of Jupár range, 211
Gudarz Mehrbán, a Parsi, 424
Guinea, Coast of, 167
Gujar district, 38
Gulahak village, 159
Gulashkird, 270, 301, 445
Gulár, 216
Gul Mohamed, Burj-i-, village, 389
Gulistán, Treaty of, 6
Gulnabád, 67, 345
Gulu Salár village, 443, 444
Gulumak, 426
Gunabád, 30, 31, 408
Gung river, 113, 114, 118
Gúr Khán, Universal Lord, 60
Gur-i-Khar, wild ass, 352
Gurába, 215
Gurbati, gypsies in Fárs, 437
Gurchibáshi, chief scout, 66
Gurdiya, sister of Bahrám Chúbín, 338
Gurg, 417
Gurgáb, hamlet, 331
Gurgán river, 12, 14
Gurgur river, 429
Guri fort, 383
Guru, a religious teacher, 126
Guwáshír (corruption of Khurra-i-Ardeshír), 188
Guzárán of the Pahlevi, Kujarán of the *Sháh Nama*, 216
Gwádur, 90, 96, 172, 293, 294
Gwaharám, 95
Gwárk, 40
Gwárkuh range, 135
Gypsies, their names in various provinces, 437

Habíbulla Khán, Amir of Afgbánistán, 359
Habl-ul-Matín, Persian newspaper, 400
Hadími, 386
Haffar canal, Mohamera, 246
Háfiz, 64, 322, 323, 340, 341, 419, 431
Haftán-bokht, 215
Haider Ali Khán, 319
Haider Khán of Isfahán, 138

Haider, Kuli Khán, 307
Haider, *Sháh Kutb-u-Din*, a saint, 207, 208
Haideri, Turbat-i-, 29
Háji, a man who has performed the pilgrimage to Mecca, 30
Háji Ibráhim, 68, 81
Háji Khán, 231
Hájiabád, caves of, 327
Hájib, a chief guardian, 60
Hajjáj, Sultán, 102
Hajjáj-bin-Yusuf, 50, 187, 322
Hak Nafas, *Mullá*, 16–18
Hakluyt Society's publications, *Early Voyages and Travels to Russia and Persia*, 10, 160, 161; *Embassy to the Court of Timur*, 25; *Travels of Josafa Barbaro*, 46; *Travels of Venetians in Persia*, 79, 155, 164, 180, 182, 325, 327, 331, 420; *Sir Thomas Roe's Diary*, 85, 86; *Travels of Ludovico di Varthema*, 327
Hali or Halil river, 44, 142, 144, 145, 173, 208, 209, 267, 429, 445
Halima Khátun, 192
Halimu pass, 19
Hamadán, 54, 197
Hamant peak, 126, 127
Hamdi *Pasha*, 245
Hamid *Mirza*, Sultán, Governor-General of Kermán, 71
Hamilco, 167
Hamza, 356
Hanaka *caravanserai*, the, 148, 214, 268
Hanaki, Kotal-i-, 18, 350
Hanni hamlet, 40
Hanno, 167
Hanway, *Travels in Persia*, 10
Hari Rud, 24
Harmozia, the landing-place of Nearchos, 302
Hárun-al-Rashid, 339
Hasan Ali Khán, Garrus, *Amir Nizám*, Governor-General of Kermán, 71
Hasan Sabbáh, leader of the Assassins, 162
Hashimabád village, 79
Hassadzái, clan (Karwánis), 278, 281
Hassan Ali *Mirza*, Shuja-u-Sultana, Governor of Kermán, 69
Hassan Bey (Ussun, or Uzún Cassano), 65
Hassan Beg Baiendari, 65
Haus, underground water-tanks, 34
Hauzdár, 365, 373
Hauzdár, Rud-i-, 372
Hawiza province, 248
Hawks, of the Kermán province, 266
Hazára, or Berberi, tribe, 27, 429, 434
Hecataeus, the Father of Geography, 167
Heiat, Bibi, sister of the *Imám* Reza, 444
Heider, *Sheikh*, 65
Helmand (Etymander) river, 93, 106, 174, 232, 359, 362, 364-366, 372, 373, 381, 382, 389-391, 417; lagoon, 386
Hematragus Jaykari, mountain goat, 291
Hendabád, 30
Henjám, 289, 290
Henza, district, 209; Kuh-i-, *ibid.*
Hephaestion, 169, 175
Heracles, 61; his statue dug up at Quetta, 174
Herát, 52, 60, 65, 101, 359, 364, 404
Herbert, Sir Thomas, *Some Yeares' Travels in Africa and Asia the Great*, 157, 176, 288, 299, 312
Heriván, village, 411
Herodotus, 48, 90, 91, 138, 167, 362
Hezár, Kuh-i-, 208, 211, 218, 440
Hind, 101
Hindu Kush, 232
Hindu money-lenders, 205
Hindus, of Kermán, 195, 198; of Kalát, 233
Hingol river, 170
Hinján village, 179
Hishmat-ul-Mulk of Sistán, the, 376, 377
Hiwentsung, Emperor, China, 49
Hogarth, David G., *Philip and Alexander of Macedon*, 362
Holdich, Sir Thomas (*Notes on Ancient and Mediaeval Makrán; The Indian Borderland*), 91, 92, 96, 100, 169, 171, 174, 222, 225, 226, 228-231
Horace, *Odes*, i. 160, 220
Horde, corruption of Urdú, Mongol for army, 45
Hormuz, 48, 54, 56, 58, 62, 84-86, 101, 110, 263, 286
Horses, Turkoman, 19; relative swiftness of English and Persian, 147
Hoshang, second king of the Peshdádian dynasty, 396
Hot Country, the, 50, 56, 145, 173, 214
Hoti, *Mir*, Governor of Pip, 119
Hotukzái clan (Karwánis), 278, 284
Hotz & Sons, 154, 185, 247, 255, 313
Howard, Sir Henry, 165
Hugin, or Oghin, river, 119
Hujetabád, 155, 347
Huláku Khán, founder of Mongol dynasty of Persia, 61, 163, 262
Hunt, Captain, Indian Political Service, 301, 446
Hunza, 342
Hur village, 40
Hurmak, 371
Hurmái, 239
Husein, Sháhzáda, brother of the *Imám* Reza, 425
Husein, *Sultán*, brother of the *Imám* Reza, 439
Husein Ali Khán, 442
Husein Ali (*Beha Ulla*, or the Splendour of God), 69

Husein Ali *Mirza*, Governor-General of Kárs, 196
Husein Fathá, *Bánu*, 217
Husein-ibn-Ali, *Amir Âzam*, Deilami, Governor of Kermán, 432
Husein Khán, Bahárlu, 73, 152
Husein Khán, chief of the Mehni, 145, 193
Husein Khán, *Háji*, 70, 106
Husein Khán, *Sardár*, 107, 108, 114, 275, 307
Huseinabád, hamlet, 268, 375, 396, 439
Hushun, fort of, 429
Hydaspes (modern Jhelum), river, 169
Hyphasis (modern Bias), river, 169

Ibn Haukal, Arabian traveller, 100, 214, 363, 365, 425
Ibn Muávia, 51
Ibn Zobeir, 50
Ibráhim *Háji*, 68, 81
Ibráhim Khán, Governor of Baluchistán, 106, 107, 123, 138
Ibráhim Khán, *Záhir-u-Dola*, Governor-General of Kermán, 69, 191, 197, 224
Ibráhimabád, 366
Ibud, *Sheikh*, Governor of Ahwáz, 255
Ichán (Hochan), 117, 118
Ichthyophagi, 83, 91, 109, 111, 172
Idrísí (Geographie d'Edrisi), 100, 101, 188, 216, 217, 269, 270, 444
Ik, or Shabankára tribe, 59
Il Nakhái, nomad tribe, 38
Ilkháni, Head of Tribes, 21
Imád-u-Din, Sultán Ahmad, 63, 64, 194
Imám Juma, official *Mullá* who prays for Sháh's health, 68
Imám Verdi Beg, 67
Imárat, Pul-i-, 256
Imperial Bank of Persia, 28, 240, 424, 450
Inaiat Ulla, *Ustád*, 194
Inchá river, 19
India, 167
Indo-European Telegraphs, 108, 450
Indus river, 91, 96, 167, 170, 417
Indus Valley, Mohamedan supremacy established in, 99
Irafshán, 128
Irák, 64, 65, 101, 110
Irán Sháh, 57; Ireland, Mr, 446
Isa, *Sheikh*, 242; *Mír*, 279, 280, 284
Isaiah, 114, 264, 325
Isfahán, 63, 64, 332, 366
Isfahán-Kermán telegraph line, 180
Isfaka or Ispaka, 120
Isfandak, 222, 227
Isfandiár village, 35, 416
Isfandiár Khán, chief of the Buchákchi, 435
Isfandiárán, *Kavir*, 181
Isfe or Ispi (now Nasratabád), 174, 415, 416
Isfishád, 409
Isháq Khán, chief of the Kárai tribe, 29
Isidorus of Charax, 362, 394, 413
Iskanderun, Gulf of, 262
Iskil, 383
Ismáíl, of Sámán dynasty, 52, 99
Ismáíl, *Háji*, chief of the *Mullás* (Sistán), 385
Ismáíl Sháh, founder of Sefavi dynasty, 65, 66
Ismailabád, 426
Ismáilzái clan, 131
Isno village, 405
Ispidán, Kuh-i-, 126
Istakhr (Persepolis), 51
Istakhri, Arab traveller, 100, 101, 177, 363, 382, 397
Istikbál, a reception, 186, 226
Itinerary of Rabbi Benjamin of Tudela, 58, 100
Ivan the Terrible, 160, 165
Izzetábád, 430

Jabal Báriz range, 47, 144, 145, 217, 301
Jabal Bárízi tribe, 146
Jabalia in Kermán, 192
Jabbaura (Arab tribe), list of, 329
Jacob, 373
Jacob's Rifles, 234
Jáfar, brother of Ali, 51
Jáfar Bai, tribe of the Yomuts, 15
Jagin, village, 303, 304
Jahan, Shah, 62-64, 66
Jahanabad, 366
Jakán river, 117
Jalalabád, 366, 388
Jalál-u-Din, last Sháh of Khiva, 60, 63, 101, 426
Jalál-u-Din Jamshid, 102
Jálk, 227, 228
Jálk oasis, 104, 229
Jálkis, the, 104
Jamál-u-Din, 240
James I., 341
Jangal village, 30
Jáni Khán, Shámlu, Governor of Kermán, 66
Jargin, *Amir*, 64
Jásim *Sheikh*, 86
Jásk, 241, 275, 291, 308, 310, 450
Jats and Meds, the aborigines of British Baluchistán, 94
Jauri, 353
Jaykar, Dr, Agency Surgeon at Mattra, 291
Jáz Morián, or Haunt of Birds, 143, 306, 308
Jefferies, Mr, Inspector of Indo-European Telegraphs, 80, 329, 330
Jeffries, Mrs, 329
Jenkinson, Antony, *Early Voyages and Travels to Russia and Persia*, 10, 13, 66, 160, 161, 321

Jennings, R.E., Captain, 125, 135, 365
Jeraili Turks, 22
Jeremiah, 27
Jermán (Mongol) mercenaries, 304
Jerun island, 62, 85
Jews, 59; of Kermán, 195, 197
Jhalawán, a lowlander, 128
Jhelum river (ancient Hydaspes), 169
Jiand Khán, chief of the Yarahmadzái, 131, 354
Jihun *chil*, 143
Jind, *Malik*, 310
Jíruft (Shahr-i-Dugiánus or City of Decius), 43, 44, 52, 56, 58, 63, 100, 101, 103, 144, 188, 267, 269, 301
Job, Book of, 45, 352
Jogand, or Zaferkand, 157
Journal of Asiatic Society of Bengal, 365
Journal of the R.G.S., 379
Jowasmi pirates, 86
Jowasmi *Sheikh*, Governor of Linga, 87
Ju Muiidi (Kermán city) 193
Julfá, Armenian village on the Zenda river, 332
Jumein, 30
Jupár range, 61, 146, 189, 206, 208, 268, 425, 426

Kab Arabs, 243, 246, 251
Kabir, great, 209
Kabír, *Seiid*, first preacher of Mohamedanism in India, 209
Kabutár Khán, 185, 444
Kacha Kuh, 356, 357, 359
Kafanu, Gudár-i-, or Shroud Pass, 427
Kafir Kala, or Infidel Fort, 27
Kaftar, Kut-i-, or Hyena's Home, near Kermán, 192
Kafut, Kuh-i-, 146
Kah, chopped straw, 360
Kahn Mírza hamlet, 305
Kahn-i-Panchur, 269
Kahtaba, Abú Muslim's General, 51
Kaiaschirin (Ghiás-u-Din), Governor of Kermán, 60, 64
Káin, province and city (Artacoana), 37, 65, 399, 407; its products and factories, 402; carpets, 403
Káin, Amir of, the *Shaukat-ul-Mulk*, 397, 399, 400
Kájár dynasty, 68, 69, 106, 121, 191
Kákh, 408, 404, 443
Kakkar, king of the Shahr-i-Lut, 38
Kakkar, ruins of the town of, 379, 380
Kal Mazzár *tághur*, 135
Kala Askar, 427
Kala Kang, 391
Kala Kásim village, near Shahr-i-Bábek, 78
Kala Kuh, Káin city, 407
Kala Máhr, ruins of, 444
Kala Násiri (the fort of Fahraj), 123
Kala Sháh Duzd (ancient Neh), 413
Kala Tapa (formerly Arvakin), 384
Kala Zarri (or Kala Gabr) mines, 410, 412
Kala-i-Shur, 332
Kal-i-Salá river, 29
Kalagán, 228
Kalát, 31, 225, 232, 233, 235-237
Kalát Kasáb hamlet, 406
Kalba Gáv, or Cow's Head, 436
Kamal-u-Din, 434
Kamárij village, 316
Kamárij, Kotal-i-, 316
Kambar, chief of the Bráhuis, 94, 103
Kamrán, Sháh, 399
Kanát, an underground channel for water, 44
Kanát Ghastán, 426
Kanát-ul-Shám (Marco Polo's Conosalmi), 269
Kandahár, 66, 67, 174, 359
Kaoli (corruption of Kábuli), gypsies in Fárs province, 437
Kara Aghach (classical Sitakos), 319
Kara Khitái (or Khitei) dynasty, 60, 62, 102, 194, 265, 304
Kara Koinlu, or Black Sheep, dynasty, 64, 428
Kara Su, or Blackwater, river, near Astrabád, 12
Kara Tapa, or Black Hill, 15
Kara Yusuf, 64
Karabághi tribe, 70
Karachi, 88, 258, 295, 308, 446
Kárái or Karait tribe, 29, 430, 434, 435
Kardagh, king of Assyria, 337
Kariat-el-Arab, The Arab's Fort, 206
Karizek, 179
Kárkinde village, 281, 284
Karkusha, 390
Karmania. *See* Kermán
Karmat, 162
Kárnámak-i-Artakshír-i-Pápakán, 215
Karramzái tribe (Bazmán), 138
Karru Kudi, bean, 439
Kárun (Kuh Rang; Pasitigris or Lesser Tigris), river, 175, 243, 245-247, 255, 452
Kárun Valley, Mission to the, 241-259
Karwán, 108; expedition, 274-285
Karwánis, the, 277, 278, 280, 306, 308-310
Kasarkand, 104, 110, 113
Kasa Pusht, or Cup-Back, Persian name for a tortoise, 396
Káshán, 69, 157, 179, 263
Kashgai nomads, 314
Káshi, lustred tile, 157
Kasho (Khoshláb), 314
Kasimabád village, 121
Kasimabád, Mil-i-, 384
Kaskin, Rud-i-, 136, 141
Kathiawár, 287
Kauffmann, General, 13

Kaur-i-Gerisht, 129
Kaur-i-Ziár Nadán, 118
Kavir (from Arabic *Kafr*), a saline swamp, 31; the Great, near Robát, 78; district of, 442
Kavir, Dasht-i-, 31
Káward, *Malik*, 55, 56, 100, 154, 418
Kázerun, 313, 318
Kazvín, 159, 160, 161
Kech, or Kej (valley), 95, 101-104, 113, 293
Keelan, Mr, of the Chahbár Telegraph Office, 310
Kei Khátu, 62, 265
Kei Khusru, 335
Keiáni tribe, 366, 367, 391
Keiánian dynasty, 361; *Maliks*, 229
Keis (Marco Polo's Kisi) island, 263
Keikobád, 363
Keisar Bai, the abduction of, 142
Keiumárs *Mírza*, 70
Kemball, Captain A. C., 225, 228, 233, 234
Kennedy, J., *The Early Commerce of Babylon with India*, 83, 84
Kerbela, 148
Kerím, Sháh, ruler of the Kermán gypsies, 438
Kerím Khán, the great Zand, 68, 300, 316, 331
Kerím Khán, *Sardár* of Sarhad, 132
Kerím-ibn-Jamshíd, 407
Kerimabád, 426
Kermán, Province of, 43-71, 102, 110, 150, 151, 300, 301, 308, 348, 349; City of (Dár-ul-Amán or Abode of Peace), 187-201, 263, 265, 271; religious sects in, 195; carpets and shawls of, 199, 419; brass-work of, 201; life at, 202-212; the Consulate, 186
Kermán Sháh, 56
Kermán-Meshed route, 34
Kerr's *Voyages and Travels*, 103
Kertch, 3
Kesmacoran (Kech or Kej and Makrán), 102
Khabis, 33, 37, 41, 69, 99, 101
Khabísi pass, 408
Khabr, Kuh-i-, 429
Kháf, 408
Khafájai, nomad tribe in Rafsinján district, 77
Khaju bridge, over the Zenda Rud, 332
Khák-Mohamed-Dervish, 372
Khalaf ibn Ahmad, 53; captured by Mahmud of Ghazni, 99
Khalat, robe of honour, 201
Khalíl, Sháh, 65
Khalíl Ulla, *Sháh*, 64
Khán, *Ághá*, 409
Khán, Hauz-i-, 37
Khán, Mírza, of Isfahán, 138
Khán, *Seiid*, chief of Bampur, 104, 106; Governor of Geh, 285
Khán Ján, Sinjeráni, 390
Khán Mohamed, Governor of Kermán, 66
Khán Mohamed of Aptár, *Mír*, 118, 127
Khána Farang or European House, in the ancient Zoroastrian suburb of Kermán, 193
Khána Sháh, 304
Khanikoff, W., *Mémoire*, 33, 93, 150, 364, 367, 410, 413
Khán-i-Zinián, 319
Khanjak, a shrub, 135
Khar Pusht, or Donkey Back Hill, 145
Khár Pusht, or Thorn-back, Persian name for hedgehog, 396
Khar-i-Shikan, or Donkey Destroying defile, 41
Khára, also known as Herát district, 78
Khárán, 103, 104, 233
Khárijites (Separatist party), 50, 51
Kharzan pass, 162, 176, 259
Khat, Gudár-i-, 182
Khedr or Khizr, 141, 323
Khedr-Zenda, Kuh-i-, Mountain of Khedr the Living (Bazmán range), 141
Kheirabád, 436
Khidri, 408
Khinamán district, 442, 443
Khiva (ancient Khwárizm), 13, 60
Khizr or Chizer, 141, 323
Khoja, Kuh-i- (Kuh-i-Zor, Kuh-i-Rustam), 367, 378, 379, 395
Khoja Ahmad, 381, 382
Khoja Khizr, quarter of Kermán, 193
Khoja Shukr Ulla, *Ustád*, 194
Khojabád village, 152
Khorasán (Land of the Sun) province, 20, 37, 52, 56, 301, 363, 413
Khorasáni nomads, 70
Khosháb (Kasho), 314
Khuda Banda, Mohamed, 62
Khudá Murád Khán, 68
Khudabád, 152
Khudadád Khán, *Mír*, 237
Khudrán village, 152, 265
Khul, Kuh-i-, highest peak of range to S. of Isfe, 416
Khurram Dasht, or the Happy Plain, 179
Khusbáb (Sweet Water) well, 34
Khusháb, Gudár-i-, 42
Khushk village, 114, 406
Khusp or Birjand river, 401
Khusru Parvíz, of Sásánian dynasty, 58, 337, 338
Khuzái or Khuzaima tribe, 399
Khuzistán, 247
Kiá, *Mír*, 357
Kilagh Ab (Garágha), 415
Kilwa, Brit. India ss., 291
Kinára, 324
King Alisaunder, 224

Kingsley, Charles, *Andromeda*, 345
Kipchak, or Southern Russia, 262
Kipling, Rudyard, 88, 254, 437
Kir (Kiz, Kirusi), largest town of Makrán, 100
Kír, Band-i- (Dam of Pitch), 245, 251
Kirik village, 19
Kirm, worm, 216
Kirm, Kut-i-, 216
Kishi river, 113
Kishkin, Dar-i-, 221
Kishm, 48, 289, 290
Kiskán, 428
Kizil Alan ruins, 14
Knox, Captain, Indian Political Service, 294
Kohendil Khán, Governor of Shahr-i-Bákek, 78
Kohrud range, 179
Kokachin, Lady, 62, 263
Komádin (Marco Polo's Camadi), 57, 266, 267
Konár river, 126
Konár Takhta, 316
Koreish tribe, 51
Koti tribe, 330
Kotluk Turkán, 63
Koweit, port of, 454
Krateros, 49, 170, 173, 174, 362, 417
Krishmál (*Gheir-i-Shumár* or Out of the Reckoning), gypsies in Khorasán. 437
Kubanán (Marco Polo's Cobinan), the Hill of the Wild Pistachio, 271-273
Kublei (or Khubilay) Kaán, 62, 262
Kuch tribe, 94, 98
Kuch, Dasht-i-, 145
Kuchán district, 13, 22, 23, 66
Kuchgardan, 103, 142, 221
Kuchil hamlet, 156
Kudru Pádsháh, Khusru of the Indo-Iránian Epic, 134
Kufans, the, 51
Kufij tribe, 52, 56
Kufs or Kufus, the, 56, 100, 101
Kuhak, 70, 106, 212, 223, 224, 233
Kuhistán, 287
Kuhláb, *Ras* (cape), 90
Kuhpá, or Foot of the Hill, 180, 345
Kuhpaia range, 40, 42, 68, 189
Kuj, the, or Kufs, 100, 101
Kuk, 379
Kuli, Mustafa, 18
Kuli Beg, 67
Kuli Sultán, Sháh, Afshár, Governor of Kermán, 66
Kum, 155, 158, 179, 264, 450
Kumári pass, 29
Kumisha, 331
Kundar, 373
Kur river, 4
Kur Gaz hamlet, 441
Kurd Mahálla village, 9
Kurds, the, 13, 19, 107, 131
Kurk, 201
Kusanak, Mil-i-, 384
Kushk Burj, 429
Kushkuh, 184
Kut, from *kot* a fort, or *ked* a house, 216
Kutáich village, 307
Kutb-u-Din, Sultán, 61
Kutb-u-Din Haider, 29
Kutbábád, Kermán city, 193
Kutuk, goat's-hair tent, 145
Kuzárán (Gujárán), 216
Kwásh, capital of Sarhad, 130, 353
Kwásh, Ab-i-, 133

Ládis, 355, 356
Lagash (Shirpurla), in Shumer, 83
Lahore, 169
Laji, 228, 233
Lak tribe, 428
Lálazár (or Tulip Bed, formerly Khárzár) river, 73, 74, 154, 185, 206, 439
Lálazár, Kuh-i-, or Tulip Mountain, 206
Lament of Sinán Ibn Seláma, 98
Langar villages, 93
Langar *Seiid*, 357
Langley, Geoffrey de, 62
Lapwing, H.M.S., 284, 286, 291, 298
Láristán district, 87, 105, 157
Lashár, 104, 114, 118
Lasháris, the, 120
Lashkarán, Cháh, 415
Law, Sir Edward, 165
Lawrence, ss., 291, 292
Layard, Sir A. H., *Early Adventures*, 251, 253
Lazareff, Armenian General, 13
Legwár, Kuh-i- (Taftán range), 134
Lenkorán, 163
Linga, port in the Persian Gulf, 87, 241, 451
Lomakin, 6, 13
Longfellow, 53, 61
Lot, cities of, 32
Loti, Pierre, *Le Désert*, 32, 410
Lovell, Mr, 90, 109
Lovett, General Beresford, 112, 379
Luli, gypsies in Kermán province, 437, 438
Luri, gypsies in Baluchistán, 437
Luristán, 157
Lurs tribe, 327
Lushai tribes, 94
Lut or Lot, desert of, 31-42, 92
Lutf Ali'Khán, 66-69, 217, 367
Luti, Persian for buffoon, originally a Sodomite, 32
Lynch, H. F. B., 440
Lynch Brothers, 243, 245-247, 250, 252, 253, 255, 256, 452

Macan's *Shdh Náma*, 215
M'Crindle, J. W., *Invasion of India, Periplus of the Erythrean Sea*, 169
Macgregor, Sir Charles, 31, 457
M'Mahon, General, Vice-President, Ryl. Geolog. Socy., 133
Mádár Ab, or Mother Water, 366, 382
Mádár Kuh, or Mother Hill (Southern Taftán peak), 133
Madrasa, a college, 194
Magan, 83
Magas village, 128, 222
Magnus, Count, 220
Mahabbat, of Kasarkand, *Amir*, Governor of Baluchistán, 103, 104
Mahallát, 70
Mahan, Captain, *The Problem of Asia*, 454 455
Mahdi, or Guide, 192
Máhi, Rud-i-, 371, 417
Mahmud, leader of the Afgháns, 67, 103
Mahmúd of Ghazni, 54, 55, 99
Mahmud Arifi, 341
Mahmud Khán, *Mirza*, Ala-ul-Mulk, Governor-General of Kermán, formerly ambassador at Constantinople, 71
Mahmud Khán, ruler of Kálát, *Beglerbegi* of Baluchistán, 237
Mahmud Khán of Sib, 354
Mahmud Khán, *Mírza*, the *Farmán Farmá's* doctor, 75, 184
Mahmud, Sultán, Governor of Kermán, 66
Mahmud, *Malik*, prince of Sistán in 18th century, 366
Máhun, 148, 189, 211, 268, 350, 419
Mahúni, quarter of Kermán city, 193
Mainabád range, 397, 405
Mak, yellow marl, 135
Makrán (Gedrosia), 89, 91, 96, 99-105, 113, 171, 274, 364; telegraph line in, 106
Maksud Beg, 331
Málán range, 170
Malcolm, Sir John, *History of Persia*, 67, 113, 342
Malik, a chief, 55
Malik Sháh, 420
Malik-i-Siá, Kuh-i-, Hill of the Black Chief, 212, 228, 370, 448
Mallu, Kotal-i-, 316
Malurán village, 114, 115; river, 117
Malusán range, 416
Mangku Kaán, 61
Manipur, 342
Mansúr, Sháh, 64
Mansúr-u-Din, 216
Manuján, 300, 304
Már, Kuh-i-, or Snake Mountain, 401
Margh, 180
Marghak, 146
Markham, Sir Clements, *History of Persia*, 178, 363
Marlowe, *Tamberlaine*, 161
Marriage by capture among the Kurds, 22
Marvás village, 80
Márz, 303, 304, 306
Mashhad-i-Mádar-i-Sulimán, or The Tomb of the Mother of Solomon, Cyrus' mausoleum, 328
Mashad-i-Murgháb village, 80, 327, 329
Mashila, a swamp, 312
Máshiz, 69, 70, 73, 74, 436
Mashkel date groves, 228, 229
Mashkid, or Mashkel river, 92, 128, 222 234
Masjid-i-Bardi, gardens at Shiráz, 322
Masjid-i-Hazrat-Rasul (The Mosque of His Holiness the Prophet), at Bam, 216
Masjid-i-Jáma in Káin city, 406; Masjid-i-Jámi, or Masjid Muzaffar, in Kermán city, 194
Masjid-i-Jáma, in Yezd city, 420
Masjid-i-Malik, in Kermán city, 194
Masjid-i-Pá-Minár, in Kermán city, 194
Maskat, 87, 88, 258, 286, 290, 292, 311
Maskun, division of the Jabal Bárizi, 146
Maspero, Professor, *The Dawn of Civilisation*, 83; *The Passing of the Empires*, 91
Massy, Major, 19th Bengal Lancers, 308
Mastung, 236, 238
Masud, chief of the Ghazni dynasty, 340
Masudi, *Les Praires d'Or*, 84, 100; *Murúju 'dh Dhahab*, 397
Masum Khán, *Mir*, Governor of Sistán, 374, 376, 377, 385
Mattra port, Persian Gulf, 87, 291
Mauritius, 446
Mayne, Colonel, 294, 296
Mazanderán province, 7, 69
Mazár pass, 74
Mazár, Dar-i-, capital of Sárdu, 209, 211 441
Mazián, 80
Mazra, 161
Mazraán district, 59
Meade, Colonel, Resident at Bushire, 284, 285, 292, 311-313, 315, 323, 326
Meade, Mrs, 311, 313, 323, 326
Mecca, 148
Medley, Captain, 19th Bengal Lancers, 308
Meds and Jats, the aborigines of British Beluchistán, 94
Meh Kuh or Mist Mountain (Kuh-i-Zenda), 141
Mehdiábád, 184
Mehmán Khána, a *caravanserai* in Kuchán, 23
Mehni tribe, 145, 208, 269
Mehráb of Kábul, 326
Mehráb Khán of Fahraj, *Sháh*, 104; ruler of Kalát, 237

Mehráb Khán, leader of the Kej rising, 293-295
Meiár, 64, 331
Meibud (now Meibut), the Meruth of Barbaro, near Yezd, 63, 156
Meidán-i-Kala, Kermán city, 193
Meidan-i-Mir Chakmák, Yezd city, 422
Meighan, 413
Melukhhkha, 83
Merv, 13, 55, 57, 66
Mervdasht plain, 324
Merwan, 51
Meshed, 24-26, 236, 301, 367, 385, 451
Mesopotamia, plain of, 456
Methuen, Lord, 446
Meynard, Barbier de, *Dictionnaire de la Perse*, 397
Mián Kangi (Sistán), 388, 389, 391
Mián Kotal *caravanserai*, 318
Mihán, fortress of, 104
Mikdád, *Mír*, Standard-bearer of the Prophet's army, 144
Milak, 390
Milán *chil*, 143
Mill, Dr, editor of *International Geography*, 449
Milton, *Paradise Lost*, 85, 161; *Paradise Regained*, 250
Mináb (*vulgo* Minao), river, 85, 105, 270, 286, 301-304
Minau, Ab-i- (Shuster), 252, 253
Minerva, H.M.S., taken by Jowasmi pirates, 86
Mingal, chief Dravidian tribe, 96
Mir Kuh, 356
Mírdost, chief of Hassadzáí clan, 278
Mirjáwa (Mirjabád), Sarhad frontier village, 357
Mírza, "Secretary," when before a name, "Prince" when after, 9
Misk Hután, 119
Mizal, *Sheikh*, ruler of the Kab Arabs, 243, 246, 255
Mobáriz-u-Din, Mohamed Muzaffar of Meibud, 63, 194
Mockler, Colonel, 96
Moez-u-Dola, of the Deilami dynasty, 210
Moen-u-Tajár, of Bushire, 250, 255
Mohallab, 51
Mohamed the Prophet, 25
Mohamed, known as Abu Ali, 52, 53, 188
Mohamed, son of Ismáíl, 162
Mohamed, *Amir Háji*, 102
Mohamed, *Malik*, seventh Seljuk ruler, 57, 63, 184, 195, 209, 210
Mohamed, *Sheikh*, of Linga, 87
Mohamed Ali Khán, *Gurchibáshi*, Governor of Kermán, 66
Mohamed Ali Khán, Nahrui, 105
Mohamed Amin Garrus, 68
Mohamed bin Alhakam, founder of Shiráz, 322
Mohamed bin Kásim, Governor of Makrán, 99
Mohamed Hasan Ali, *Sardár*, Eriváni, Governor of Kermán, 70
Mohamed Hasan Kájár, 68
Mohamed Ibráhim, *History of the Seljuks*, 100, 101, 194, 195, 210, 267, 268, 304, 418
Mohamed Ibráhim Khán, 400
Mohamed Ismáíl Khán, Núri, first Vakíl-ul-Mulk, Governor of Kermán, 70
Mohamed Kerim Khán, *Háji*, 197
Mohamed Khán, Háji, head of the Sheikhis, 197, 235
Mohamed Rezá Khán, the Reki chief, 356, 357, 376; Governor of Sistán, 414
Mohamed Salih bin Musá Kázim, 183
Mohamed Sháh of Sib, 105, 149, 345
Mohamed Tabashíri, *Seiid*, 192
Mohamed Takí, Governor of Kermán, 69
Mohamed Yahya, 58
Mohamed II., Sultán of Turkey, 65
Mohamera, 243, 245-248, 300
Moharrag island, Bahrein, 241
Mohim Khán Governor of Geh, 113
Mokaddasi, 53
Mokht village, 310
Mokik, *Cheshma*, 37
Money-lenders, Hindu, 205
Mongol or Moghul invasion, the, 60, 101, 163, 177, 261, 426
Mongols, in Káin province, 404
Montferrat, Conrad of, 162
Montgomery district, 102
Monze, Cape, 93
Moore, *The Fire-Worshippers*, 187; *Lalla Rookh*, 290, 324
Morád Ali Khán, *Mír*, Governor of Sárdu, 210
Morád *Mírza*, 409
Morgan, M. de, 333
Morghib, ruins of Zoroastrian fire temple, 78
Moscow, 160, 165
Mosques in Kermán city, 193, 194
Mostasim Billa, *Caliph*, 61
Mosul, 262
Mountaineering in Baluchistán, 129
Mowbray, Commander, 282, 284
Mozilikatzi, the Matabele king, 378
Mud Village, 411
Muir, Sir William (*Caliphate*), 99
Muir, Major, 90, 233, 307
Muiz-u-Dola, the (member of the Deilami dynasty), 53
Mukhterán, 411, 412
Mullá pass, 174
Müller, *Geographi Graeci Minores*, 362
Multán, 100, 102, 169, 175
Munich, 259
Munj, 79
Mur, Kuh, 35

Murád, Ab-i-, 442
Murád, Sultán, 65
Murád Khán, 68, 139
Murdáb, or Dead Water, a lagoon, 6
Murdán, Tang-i-, Myrtle Defile, 175
Murgháb, Stream of Fowl, 427
Murshid, teacher, 30
Murtazá Kuli Khán, 66; of Zarand, 69; second *Vakil-ul-Mulk*, Governor-General of Kermán, 70
Musa, *Imám*, 209
Musa Khán, chief of the Ak Átabai, 12, 14, 15
Musab, brother of Ibn Zobeir, 50
Musáfiri tribe, 40
Muzaffar-u-Din, Mohamed Sháh, 62
Mustafa Kuli, 18
Muzaffar dynasty, 63, 64, 102, 432, 433
Mustakfi, Caliph of Baghdád, 53
Muzaffar-u-Din, Sháh of Persia, 240, 259, 275

Nád-i-Ali (ancient No Kei), 366, 384, 391
Nádir Sháh, 10, 23, 36, 67, 103, 104, 143, 158, 235, 236, 307, 367, 395, 416
Nádiri, Mil-i-, 395, 418
Nagar, ruined church at, 426, 427
Nágha Kalát, 235
Nahávand, battle of, 50, 51
Nahrui tribe, 104, 136, 367, 376, 377
Naiband, 36
Naiistanak (the Naistan of Barbaro), 157
Náin (the Naim of Barbaro), 156, 345
Najaf, 148
Nakhod, cultivated pea, 439
Nákhodá hamlet, 302
Naksh-i-Rustam, 317, 326, 329
Namat Ulla of Máhun, *Sháh*, 29, 64, 148, 275
Namati, the, 29
Naokinjá, 310
Naoroz Khán of Kharán, Sir, 225, 400
Napier, Colonel the Hon. G., 18, 19, 21
Napier, Captain, Oxfordshire Light Infantry, 415, 419
Napoleon, his plans for invading India, 11
Nar Kuh, Male Hill (W. Taftán peak), 133
Naramsin, son of Sargon I., 83
Narmáshir, 47, 58, 67, 69, 105, 174, 188, 215, 217, 300, 350, 402, 413, 415, 417; nomads of, 220
Narmáshir, Fahraj village of, 174
Nártígi tribe, 219
Násir Khán of Tárum, 68, 103, 104; ruler of Kalát and *Beglerbegi* of Baluchistán, 235, 236
Násir Khán II., 237
Násir-u-Din, Mohamed-bin-Burhán, *Amir* Governor of Kermán, 63
Násir-u-Din, Sháh of Persia, 110, 149, 159, 225, 240, 274, 329
Násir-u-Dola, 207
Násirábád village, 182, 375
Násiri company, 250, 255
Naskh, copper-plate writing in Arabic, 194
Nasrabád, 414
Nasratábád, 130, 174, 374, 375, 384, 392, 402, 416
Nasru, Rud-i-, 366, 383, 388
Nasrulla Khán, *Mírza*, 178, 184, 186, 204, 229, 280, 283, 306, 319, 323, 346, 354, 357, 374, 384, 398, 419, 445
Natanz, 179
Náúmíd, Dasht-i-, or Desert of Despair, 396, 402
Naushádir, Kuh-i-, 141
Nazar, Bágh-i-, at Kázerun, 318; at Duruksh, 402
Nearchos, Alexander the Great's admiral, 48, 49, 84, 170, 172, 174, 247, 270, 302, 303, 313, 445
Necho, 167
Neh, 300, 384, 396, 399, 402, 413, 414
Nejd, 49
Neo-Platonists of Alexandria, 197
Nestorius, patriarch of Constantinople, founder of the Nestorian sect, 49
Nikitin of Twer, Athanasius, 65, 155, 156
Nikruz, Governor of Kermán, 63
Nilag, Band-i-, or Blue Range, 115, 117
Nimbuluk district, 408, 409
Nimrod, Belus identified with, 95
Nimrud, 302
Nisa, 215, 216
Nishápur, 55, 60
Nituk (Bahrain), 83
Niu village, 301
Nizámi, 337
Nizám-u-Din, ruler of the Ik, 59
Nizám-u-Din, *Ustád*, 194
Nizam-u-Sultana, the, of Shuster, 252, 253, 255
Nizám-ul-Mulk, 57
No Rus, New Year's Day, 145, 200
Nobel, Messrs, oil refineries at Báku, 5
Nodushán, 181
Nokáb, 409
Nokinjá, 113
Noldeke, Professor, translation of the Pahlevi *Kárnámak*, etc., 216
Noshirwán, founder of Astrabád, 10, 49, 99, 444
Noshirwánis, the, 233
Novorossisk, 3
Nur Mohamedi hamlet, 111
Nur-u-Din, 340
Nur-u-Din, Yezdi, *Seiid* (Sháh Namat Ulla), 148
Nushki, 240, 356, 358, 416

Odessa, intense cold at, 2
Odoricus, 153, 155, 162, 264, 287, 420

Ogdei, Ogotei, or Ogotay Kaán, 61, 261
Oghin or Hugin river, 119
Omán, 56, 88, 90, 91, 101
Omar, 50, 196
Omar, S'aád, 177
Omar Khayyám, 45, 162
Ondanique, corruption of Hinduwáni or Indian, 265
Onesikratos, 48
Opium, in Káin province, 402
Ormára, 293, 294
Orsines, acting Governor of Persia, 175
Othman, 196
Ottoman Bank, Constantinople, 258
Ouseley, Sir W., *Ibn Haukal*, 363, 365
Outram, General, 314
Oweis, *Sultán*, 63, 64

Pábana, 146
Pábokh, 180
Pádsháh, Khátun, 62, 265
Pahlawán, professional wrestler, 63
Pahlevi Kárnámak-i-Artakhshír-i-Pápakán, 188, 215, 335, 337
Pahra, 128
Paiáb, half-way house between Máhun and Kermán, 150
Pá-i-Chinár, 162
Palestine and Sarhad, compared, 373
Palm, uses of the dwarf, 112
Palmer, Professor, 73
Panjáb, invaded by Darius, 90, 102
Panjgur, or Five Tombs, 225, 234
Panj-Augusht, Kuh-i-, or the Five Fingers Hill, 130, 131, 353
Pansára village, 136; Kuh-i-, 141
Pápak, or Bábek, father of first king of the Sásánian dynasty, 49, 78
Parag, hamlet of Ichthyophagi, 111, 310
Paris, 259
Paris, Matthew, *Chronica Majora*, 261
Páriz, nomad tribes, 75
Parker, Lieut., 234
Paropamisadae, the, 102
Parry, Mr, Lynch Brothers' representative at Ahwáz, 247, 251, 253
Parry, Mrs, 251, 255
Parsis, 156; in Yezd, 423; around Jupár, 426, and *see* Zoroastrians
Parthian dynasty, 336, 363
Partridge, black (*francolinus vulgaris*), 47
Pasand Khán, 128
Pasangun, 158
Paskuh, Kuh-i-, 129; village, 129, 222
Pasni, hamlet of Ichthyophagi, 172, 294
Passion Play, the, in Persia, 209
Patrick Stewart, H.M. cable ss., 276, 293
Paul of Russia, Tsar, his plans for invading India, 11
Pansára village, 136; Kuh-i-, 141
Pearl fisheries, Bahrein islands, 241
Perián, Rud-i-, River of the Fairies (name of Helmand), 366, 388, 390-392
Persepolis (Istakhr), 51, 175, 317, 324, 325; Sásánian rock sculptures at, 361
Persepolis, Persian man-of-war, 291
Persia, provision of water and re-afforestation required for regeneration of, 34; from Greek *Persis*, 321
Persian, language, 8; wit and proverbs, 203; character, 204, 457; dress, etc., 204
Persian Baluchistán, tribes of, 122
Persian and English horses, relative swiftness of, 147
Persian Gulf, 82-88
Persian Question, the, 453
Persian Telegraphs, 276
Persian Gulf Trading Co., 314
Perso-Afghán Boundary Commission, 396
Perso-Baluch Boundary Commission, 106, 107, 132, 224-231, 258, 357, 371
Perso-Russian frontier, 163
Peshdádian dynasty, 396
Peter the Great, 165
Petrovsk, 164
Peukestas, Governor of Persia, 175
Phoenicians, 83, 166
Piáz, Dasht-i-, 408, 409
Piffard, Captain, 244, 257
Pigeon, H.M.S., 275, 291
Pilo, boiled rice, 7
Pioneer, The, newspaper, 290
Pip, capital of Lashár, 119
Piper, M., Russian Consul at Astrabád, 11
Pír Dád, chief of the Hotukzái clan, 278
Pír Ghurík, or Grassy Defile, valley, 112
Pír Mohamed (formerly *Beglerbegi* of Herát), 103, 104
Pír Shámil, a holy inhabitant of Sind, 112
Píra-Zan, Kotal-i-, Old Women's Pass, 318
Pír-i-Bázár, 163
Pír-i-Jásus, or the Old Spy, a shrine, nea, Máshiz, 73
Pish Mant, or Place of the Dwarf Palm, 112
Pistachio nuts, Kermán province, 46
Plant, Captain, 251
Plato, 197
Plato Epiphanes, 363
Pliny, *Natural History*, 102
Polo, Maffeo, 261
Polo, Marco (the Father of Modern Geography), 34, 44, 57, 59, 61, 62, 101, 102, 145, 153, 155, 173, 206, 260-272, 287, 301, 420, 426, 439, 445
Polo, Nicolo, 261
Polo, or *pulu*, Tibet for ball made from willow-root, 334
Polo (*Gu-u-Chogán*), the game of, 326, 334-344
Polvár river (ancient Medus), 80, 327
Pomponius Mela, 48

Poona, 163
Portuguese, and Hormuz, 85, 207; defeated by English off Jásk, 86; capture Fort Gombrun, 299
Possmann, Mr, Director of the Persian Gulf Telegraphs, etc., 89
Pothán, on the Sirhá river, 310
Pottinger, Sir Henry, *Travels and Memoirs*, 95, 102, 104, 122, 138, 139, 141, 221, 228, 236
Poura (now Fahraj), capital of Gedrosia, 172, 173
Preece, J. R., Consul-General at Isfahán, 176
Prester John, 29
Price, Lieutenant C. V., 225
Ptolemy, *Geogr.*, 48
Pul-i- Imárat, 256
Puráli (Arabios) river, 170
Purchas, *Pilgrims*, 290
Purdil Khán, Sarbandi chief, 377, 381

Quarterly Review, 453, 456
Quetta, 20, 93, 131, 174, 232, 237, 359, 419

Rafsinján, 77, 185, 300
Ráhbur, 208, 301
Ráhnish, 401
Railways, in Persia, 448
Ráin, 144, 146, 211, 214, 268
Ráis, nomad tribe, 59, 373
Rakovzky, M. de, Austrian traveller, 149 203
Rakshán river, 93, 234
Rám Hormuz, battle of, 49
Rám Shahristán, 382
Rámishk, 305, 306, 309
Ramrud, ruins of, 372
Ran of Kach, 91
Rapsh, or Fánoch, river, 92, 114-116, 274, 275, 291
Rasmi, cultivated pea, 439
Ras, Arabic for cape, 90
Ráwár, 38, 199, 271
Rawlinson, Sir Henry, and Professor George (*Herodotus*), 48, 90, 386, 457; on the derivation of Baluch, 95
Rawul Pindi, 89
Raymond, Count of Tripoli, 162
Razi-u-Din, of Khiva, 59
Read, C. Hercules, of the British Museum, 443
Rei (the Rhages of Parthia, Rages of the Apocrypha, etc.), ruins of, 49, 177
Reki tribe, 131, 135, 356
Reshire, 313, 314
Resht, 5, 159, 163
Resht-Tehrán road, 164, 449, 450
Retreat of the Ten Thousand, 168
Rezá, *Imám*, 24, 158, 192, 412, 425, 427, 434
Rezá, *Mírza*, assassinates the Sháh, 240
Richter, Madame, Hôtel de Londres, Tiflis, 4
Rig Matti, in Rudbár, 143
Rigabád, 425
Rigán, 70, 215, 220, 350, 356
Rinds of Mand, 90, 233, 294, 303
Rion (ancient Phasis) river, 3
Riza Kuli Beg, 191
Roads in Persia, 449
Robát, 78, 185
Robát Kala, 360, 370
Rodgers & Sons (Karkhána Rájers), the cutlers, 309
Roe, Sir Thomas, *Diary*, 85, 86
Roggewein, Commodore, 103
Romance of Coeur de Lion, 213
R.A.S. Journal, 83, 84, 267, 339
R.G.S. Journal, 91, 379
Rubá, Tal-i-, or Fox's Hill, 352
Rubandi, silk embroidery, 423
Rudán, a sub-district of Fárs, 303
Rudbár (Marco Polo's Reobarles), 105, 142, 269, 304, 365
Rudbár, tribes of, 143
Rudkhána Duzdi, or the River of Theft, 303
Rúkh, Sháh (son of Tímúr), 64, 102, 149, 364, 366, 388, 399, 422
Rukn-u-Din, 61, 421
Ruknábád stream, 323
Rumbold, Horace, 343
Russia, and the Mongol invasion, 60; Jenkinson opens up trade with, 160; and Persia, 448, 451, 452; and Germany, 455
Rustam Beg, 65
Rustam, 214, 218, 220, 338, 361, 362, 379, 404, 414, 415
Rustam, Band-i- (afterwards Band-i-Akva or the Afghán's Dam), 364
Rustam, Kuh-i- (or Zor or Khoja), 378, 379
Rusticiano, 270
Ruy Gonzalez di Clavigo, 25, 178

Saad-ul-Mulk of Shuster, the, 252
Sábar, Sháh, ruins of, 395
Sábari, Dariá-i-, 395
Sabz, Kuba-i-, or Green Dome, in Kermán city, 194
Sabzabád, 312
Sabzawár, copper mines at, 413
Sad-bin-Zangi, Atábeg, 59
Sádi, 59, 148, 238, 316, 322; on polo, 340, 341
Sadr Azam, Prime Minister of Persia, 159, 253, 305-307
Sadr-u-Din Khán, Governor of Kermán, 66
Saffár dynasty, 55, 99, 103, 143, 229, 363
Safi, Sháh, 66

Safid Kuh, 93
Sagh, the blackberry, 145
Saghdár, valley of the, 145
Saghir, small, 209
Sahám-u-Dola of Bujnurd, 21
Sáhib Diván, Governor-General of Kermán, 71, 202, 211
Sáhib Zamán, or Lord of Time, 192
Sahroni tribe, 389
Saiáds, tribe of fowlers, 386
Saiíd, *Mírza*, 433
Saiidabád, 431, 433
St John, Sir Oliver, *Eastern Persia*, 106, 110, 112, 122, 126, 368, 417, 435
St Petersburg, 165
Sakastani or the Land of the Sakas (Sistán), 362
Saladin, 340
Sálih bin Musá Kázim, Mohamed, 183
Salmous in Rudbár, 173, 174, 269, 270
Sám, Kala-i-, 380
Sámán dynasty, 52, 99, 188, 340
Sámán-Sháhi, Gudár-i-, 409
Samangán, 433
Samarkand, 148, 164, 364
Sambur river, 16
Sammi tribe (Bazmán), 138
Samsor, 352
Samur (a name of the R. Atrek), 22
Samuri, the, 64, 102
Sandeman, Sir Robert, 233
Sang hamlet, 152, 211
Sang, Kala-i-, or Stone Fort (also known as Kala-i-Beiza or White Fort), 175, 430, 431, 433
Sang-i-Farsh, or Stone Carpet, 9
Sangun, 354, 355
Sanjar, Sultán, 13, 57
Santa Lucia, ruined chapel of, near Hormuz, 289
Sar Asiáb village, 61; range, 150
Sarakhs, 58
Sarangians, the, 362, 417
Sarawán, 128
Sarbandi tribe, 367, 373, 380
Sarbáz, "men who risk their heads," 128, 279
Sarbistán (Sablistán, Sarvistán), or the Place of Cypresses, 146
Sarbizan, 57, 210, 441; pass, 210 268; river, 211
Sárdu (the uplands of Kermán), 43, 50, 144, 209, 268, 301, 441; river, 146, 211, 214; nomads of, 210
Sargon I. of Chaldaea, 80
Sarhad, 92, 93, 107, 129-137, 352-354; resemblance between Palestine and, 373
Sariáb, 238
Sar-i-Cháh, village and pass, 401
Sar-i-Pahra, 128
Sar-i-Yezd, 182, 347
Sarjáz, 267
Sartáb, or cold water, 117
Sáru, Kuh-i-, 345
Sásánian, dynasty, 49, 50, 78, 99, 248, 253, 317, 336, 363; rock sculptures at the *Naksh-i-Rustam*, 326
Sataspes, 167
Satghar, 102
Satibarzanes, 362, 407
Sáva (now Saba), 264
Schindler, General Houtum, 31, 159, 267, 269, 271, 272, 332, 364
Scott, Dr, 247, 257
Scully, Dr, 81, 313
Scylax of Caryanda, Greek admiral of Darius, 91, 167, 169
Sealy, Mr, Director, Persian Gulf Telegraphs, 276, 279
Sefavi dynasty, 65, 103, 154, 180, 331, 332, 366
Seh Gudári pass, 435
Sehdeh, 409
Sehkuhá, capital of Sistán, 366, 367
Seiid Khán, *Sardár*, 376, 381
Seiid, meaning, 24; of Sirján, 434, 435
Seiláb, a flood, 171
Sela Khána, 5
Selby, Lieut., 246
Seljuk, Sháh, 184
Seljuks, the, 55, 58, 146, 154, 162, 183, 216, 267, 268
Semalgán (the Samangán of the *Sháh Náma*), 19
Semiramis (the Hindu Sami Rama), 170
Sennacherib, 84
Serv, 181
Sevastopol, 2
Seychelles, 446, 457
Shabankára (Soncara) or Ik tribe, 59
Shagharán, Tibetan, for polo-ground, 334
Sháh, *Malik*, 56, 57
Sháh, Ádil, in Kermán city, 193
Sháh, Kuh-i- (S. of Kermán), 413
Sháh, Kuh-i- (near Gulashkird), 445
Sháh-Kutb-u-Din-Haider, Kuh-i-, or the Mountain of the Saint, the Polar Star of the Faith, Haider, 207, 208
Sháh Náma (or *History of the Kings*), 19, 94, 98, 215, 216, 326, 335, 337, 361, 433
Sháh Sowarán range, 174, 218
Sháh Tímorz peak, 189
Shahabád village, 144
Shahdád, *Mír*, 233, 307
Shahdillu Kurds, 21
Sháhkin village, 405, 406
Sháhozáí (Karwáni tribe), 278
Shahr, quarter of Kermán city, 193
Shah Biumídi or the City of Despair, 433
Shahr-i-Bábek (Marco Polo's Shebavek), 54, 63, 69, 70, 78, 265
Shahr-i-Lut, or City of Lot, 32
Shahreki tribe, 367

Shahriár-bin-Táfil, Governor of Omán, 56
Shahristán village, 365
Shahristán (The City), ruins of, 382
Shahrukh Khán, Afshár, 67, 68
Sháhzáda, son of a Sháh, either temporal or spiritual, 425
Shái Mohamed, chief of the Sháhozái clan Karwán, 278, 310
Shakespeare, *Twelfth Night*, 151; *Tempest*, 298; *Henry IV.*, 386
Shál, shawl, 200
Shamál or North wind, 313
Shámi, cultivated pea, 439
Shams-u-Din, *Malik*, 103, 234
Shápur, 49, 253, 317, 318, 337; river, 315
Shápur II., 337
Sharifabád, 27
Shat-el-Arab river, 96, 242, 246, 452
Shátir Báshi (or Chief Runner of the Sháh), Governor of the Gypsies in Persia, 438
Shavey, Author's fox-terrier, 389, 392, 396, 417
Sheibáni Khán, chief of the Uzbegs, 66
Sheikhi sect, 195, 196
Sheiwáni tribes, list of, 330
Shekevand, 396
Shéla, a water-course (Sistán), 365; river, 372
Shelley, P. B., *Alastor*, 43
Shemákha or Shimakhi, 66, 160
Sherif Khán, *Sardár*, 376
Sherley, Sir Anthony, 341
Shia Mohamedans, number in Kermán city, 195, 196, 251
Shiblí, Sháh, 63
Shif, 314
Shikan, Khar-i-, or Donkey Destroying defile, 41
Shilália, 245, 248, 252
Shims, 69, 183
Shír Afkan, or Lion Slaying, an epithet of opium, 403
Shir Ali, of Afghánistán, 368
Shir Khán, *Malik*, 103
Shiráz, capital of Fárs, 54, 63, 80, 87, 148, 322; the Kawám-ul-Mulk of, 81
Shirázis, the, 348
Shirin, wife of Khusru Parvíz, 337
Shirinak hamlet, 439
Shirpurla, priest king of Lagash, 83
Shirwán, 22
Shujá, Sháh, 63
Shujá-u-Din of Zuzan, *Malik*, 60, 101
Shulgistán, 331
Shúr river, 145, 406, 408
Shur Serai, hamlet of, 28
Shuráf, or Salt Water wells, 136
Shurgaz, 106, 418; one of the salt *hámun*, 352
Shusp, 396
Shuster, 245, 252, 253, 317
Shuteit, Ab-i-, 245, 251, 253
Siá Band, 353
Siá Jangal, 355
Siadak, 390
Siawush, 335
Sib, 108, 222
Sibcháh, 412
Siláij, 99
Simla, 89, 240
Simpson, Captain, 311
Sinai desert, Pierre Loti's account of, 32
Sinán Ibn Seláma, second Arab Governor of Makrán, 98
Sinbad the Sailor, 85
Sinclair, Albert T., the "Romany Rye" of Boston, 437
Sind, 93, 99, 101, 104
Sinjeráni tribe, 390
Sinsin, 158
Siráf (modern Táhiri), 84
Sirhá river, 113, 114, 117, 118, 310
Siríz village, 152
Sirján (city and district), 53, 64, 101, 188, 270, 300, 430-433; the Kala-i-Sang of, 63; nomads of, 430
Sisab, 22
Sistán (Sagistán), 37, 56, 67, 70, 174, 359, 361-368, 392-395, 402, 414; Mission, the, 368, 408, 415, 418; the Consulate at, 370-385; resemblance between Egypt and, 373; Rud-i-, 381; Band-i-, 382
Sistánis, the, 67, 217, 406
Sivand village, 327,
Sivás, 262
Skárdu, 342
Skobeleff, General, 13, 21
Skrine and Ross' *Heart of Asia*, 14, 52
Smith, Sir Charles Euan, *Eastern Persia*, 183
Sofia, 259
Soghun, 175
Soghurk, Gudár-i-, 427, 429
Sonár Dágh watershed, 16, 19
Soncara (Shabankára), 59
Sophocles, 84
Során, 126, 142
Sorghin hamlet, 79
Sorhin stream, 114
Southey, *St Romuald*, 434
Spain, Embassy to Court of Tímúr, 25
Spenser, *Faerie Queene*, 447
Sphinx, H.M.S., 86
Spodium, 272
Stack, *Six Months in Persia*, 198, 272
Steel, Mrs, *On the Face of the Waters*, 149
Stewart, Colonel C. E., Consul-General at Odessa, 2, 12
Stiffe, Captain, *Ancient Trading Centres of the Persian Gulf*, 87
Strabo, 48, 145, 289
Strick & Co., 452

Stroeff, M. de, Russian dragoman at Meshed, 401
Subh Kuh, or Morning Hill (S.E. Taftán peak), 133
Sufi sect, Kermán city, 195, 197
Sufidak or Safidak, Little White Hill, 391
Sukhru, Sultán, Lance Daffadár 3rd Panjáb Cavalry, 127, 136, 165, 248, 254, 291, 300, 303, 306, 310
Sukhta Chál hamlet, 434
Suliáni village, 409
Suliman Khán, in charge of Goldsmid's Escort, 219
Suliman, *Mirza*, 227, 314, 315
Sulimáni (Suliáni) pass, 408, 409
Sultán Mohamed, the last Khwárizm Sháh, 60
Sultán Sháh, 56, 58
Sultánia, 62, 263
Sunni Mohamedan sect, 195, 196, 251, 275, 397, 404
Surán, 222
Surkátmush Jalál-u-Din, Governor of Kermán, 61, 62, 265
Surkh Gazi route, 414
Surkhdak, or Little Red Hill, 391
Surkwak, Gudár-i-, 417
Susa, 96, 175
Sykes, Miss E. C. (*Through Persia on a Side Saddle*), 176, 178, 185, 203, 206, 212, 213, 231, 251, 257

Tabari, 337
Tabarku, Hauz-i-, 154
Tabas, 31, 35, 57, 236
Tabas Sunnikhána, 397
Tabríz, 63, 85, 197, 263
Tacháp, Kuh-i-, 353
Táft (Taste of Barbaro), 182
Taftán, Kuh-i-, or Chehel Tan, in Sarhad, 92, 93, 129, 131-134, 139, 140, 353, 355
Tághur, Baluchi for a lagoon, 135
Táhir, the Ambidexter, ruler of the Khuzái tribe, 99, 399
Táhiri (ancient Siráf), 84
Tahmásp, *Sháh*, 160, 161
Tahmásp Kuli Khán, Governor of Kermán, 66, 70
Tahrud or River-bottom district, 214
Táj Mohamed, 367
Tajabád, 74, 79
Táj-u-Din, Sháh-in-sháh, *Amir* of Hormuz, 101
Takht-i-Pul or Platform of the Bridge, 390
Takí, *Mirza*, British Agent at Astrabád, 9
Takí Derráni, 68
Takí Khán, *Mirza*, 179
Takí Khán, Afghán chief, 42
Takí-u-Din, Dádá Mohamed, 422
Takkia, 435
Talbot, Sir Adelbert, Resident at Bushire, 87
Tal-i-Kháki at Dehbíd, the, 331
Tal-i-Rubá, 352
Tal-i-Samsor, 352
Talik Khán, *Mirza*, 66
Tamil, a Dravidian language, 94
Tanbur, Takht-i-, 434
Tandarustán, group of mud-brick buildings in Kermán, 192
Tanfield, Mr, Lynch Brothers' Agent at Shuster, 247, 252-254
Tang-i-Murdán or Myrtle Defile, 175
Tang-i-Turkán or Turk's Defile, 316
Tang-i-Zindán or Prison Defile, 301
Tangistánis, the, 278, 281, 283, 291, 306, 313, 314
Tangru, headquarters of the Karái tribe, 435
Tapa-i-Tiláí, or Golden Mound, 390
Tárikh-i-Guzida, 50
Tárikh-i-Rashidi, 55, 404
Tárum, 68
Tate, G. P., Indian Survey, 371, 378, 379
Taylor cylinder, the, 84
Taylor, Mr, of Basra, 245, 252
Tehrán, 27, 33, 44, 105, 159, 177, 178, 240, 256, 258, 450
Tejen hamlet, 40
Tekish, 58
Tekke Turkoman, the, 14
Tengli, 15
Tennyson, *Geraint and Enid*, 125; *Recollections of the Arabian Nights*, 232
Tent-pegging, invented by the Baluchis, 236
Thabas Induna, near Buluwayo, 378
Thang dynasty, China, 84
Thirty Years' War, 60
Tighe, Captain, Indian Political Service, 294
Tiflis, 4
Tigris river, 83, 263
Timorz, Sháh, peak, 189
Tímúr, "The Lame," 25, 64, 102, 148, 178, 340, 363, 364, 366, 388, 420, 433
Tíz, a city of Kermán, 100, 101, 104, 110, 299, 310
Tobit, Book of, 177
Todleben, coat of, in the Sevastopol museum, 2
Toghrul Beg, 53
Toghrul Sháh, 57, 100, 101
Toktámash tribe, 18, 19
Tomaniens, Russian firm of, 185
Tonocain, 273
Topus, a mace, 326
Townsend, Mr, of the cable ss., 279
Tozer, H. F., *History of Ancient Geography*, 167
Trade in Persia, British, 451
Transcaspia, 448

Transcaspian railway, 5, 11
Transvaal war, 259, 455, 457
Travels and Adventures of the Three Sherleys, 342
Trebizond, 3, 65, 261
Tripoli, Raymond Count of, 162
Tul, Kala-i-, 248
Tun, 377
Tun-u-Tabas district, 273
Turán Sháh, 48, 57, 58, 194
Turbat, 29, 93, 293
Turkán Khátun, 61, 265
Turkán Sháh, 57
Turkey, 448
Turkoman, the, 10-26, 408
Turkomanchai, Treaty of, 248
Turkun village, 79
Turnbull, I. M. S., Lieut., 225
Turner, Captain, 294
Turquoise mines at Gaud Ahmar, 74; of Kermán, 265
Tursháb, 415
Tutak hamlet, 441
Tutia, 272
Tyre (Tylos), 83

Udu Dass, Hindu *názim* in the Kej valley, 293
Unsuru 'l-Ma'áli' Kei Ká'us ibn Iskandar ibn Kábus, 339
Upper Kárun river, 250
Uráf, Rafsinján, 76
Urdigán hamlet, 440
Urzu, 445
Ushk, 181
Ussun Cassano, 65
Ustád, a master craftsman, 194
Uzbegs, the, 65, 366, 405
Uzbegs' Fort, near Kermán, 192
Uzún Ada, or Long Island, 5
Uzún Hassan (Hassan Beg), 65

Vakilábád, 219, 419
Valerian, Emperor, 253, 317
Vali Khán river, 66
Vambéry, Professor, 14, 259, 325
Vargun (now Aravirjun), 331
Várizk, Kuh-i-, 406
Varmál village, 373, 378, 415
Varthema, Ludovico, di, 241, 327
Vártun, 180
Veillon, M., 313, 315, 319
Venice, 261
Verámin, 106
Verdi Beg, Imám, 67
Vienna, 2, 259
Virgil, *Aen*, 141, 412
Vlassof, M., Russian Consul-General at Meshed, 26
Volga river, 261, 262
Vukt-i-Sáat, in Yezd, 421

Wahab, Lieut.-Colonel R., 225, 227, 228, 232
Wáis, 245, 246
Waller, Lieut,, 292
Wáráj, hamlet, 132, 135
Ware, Captain Webb, Assist. Pol. Agent, Chágai district, 356, 357, 360, 369, 378, 419
Wazirábád, 169
Weber, *Metrical Romance*, 153, 336
Welíd, 99
Western Asia, 456
Western Baluchistán, chief tribes of, 96
White, Dr, Church Missionary Society, 347, 424
White, Mrs, 347
White Sea, discovered by Richard Chancellor, 160
Whiteway, *Rise of the Portuguese Power in India*, 258
Whyte, Captain, 244, 257
Wilson, Colonel, Resident at Bushshire, 242
Wilson, Mrs, 242
Wilson, Mr, Clerk-in-charge, Chahbár Telegraph Office, 310
Windmills at Tabas, 397
Wolff, Dr, 27
Wood, Mr O., of the Imperial Bank of Persia, 279
Wood, King, Superintendent of Telegraphs, 319, 332, 333, 345, 346, 350, 351, 354-356, 370, 371, 378
Worm, fable of the, 215, 216
Wyatt, Captain, 38, 405

Xenophon, Retreat of the Ten Thousand, 168
Xerxes, 324, 325

Yádulla Khán, chief of the Koti tribe, 330
Yagli Olum, a fort on the Atrek, 16
Yáhyá, *Mírza*, (Subh-i-Ezel, or Dawn of Eternity), 196
Yáhyá, Mohamed, 58
Yákub-bin-Lais (known as Saffár, or Coppersmith), 52, 53, 56, 99
Yákut, 177
Yalta, 3
Yar Mohamed Sultán, Baluch chief, 351
Yár Mohamed, the Vizier of Sháh Kamrán, 399
Yarahmadzái tribe, 107, 131, 230
Yási, son of Abu Ali, 53
Yate, Colonel, *Khorasán and Sistán*, 20, 23, 364, 368
Yazdanabád village, 152
Yezd (Marco Polo's Yasdi) *Dár-ul-Ibáda*, or Abode of Devotion, city and territory, 37, 69, 77, 154, 155, 182, 263, 264, 300, 327, 347, 420; the Vukt-i-Sáat in, 74; silk looms at, 423

* 9 7 8 1 3 3 1 9 2 3 5 0 3 *
WS - #0089 - 310325 - C0 - 229/152/34 - PB - 9781331923503 - Gloss Lamination